Social Work
in Contemporary
Society

Social Work in Contemporary Society

CHARLES D. GARVIN
JOHN E. TROPMAN
University of Michigan at Ann Arbor

PRENTICE HALL, *Englewood Cliffs, New Jersey 07632*

Library of Congress Cataloging-in-Publication Data

Garvin, Charles D.
    Social work in contemporary society / Charles D. Garvin, John E.
Tropman
        p. cm.
    Includes bibliographical references and index.
    ISBN 0–13–816224–7 (casebound)
    1. Social service.   2. Social service—United States.
I. Tropman, John E.   II. Title.
HV40.G37   1992
361.3'2—dc20   91-20467
                                           CIP

Acquisitions editor: Nancy Roberts
Copy editor: William O. Thomas
Cover designer: Patricia Kelly
Prepress buyer: Kelly Behr
Manufacturing buyer: Mary Ann Gloriande
Supplements editor: Sharon Chambliss
Editorial assistant: Pat Naturale

© 1992 by Prentice-Hall, Inc.
A Simon & Schuster Company
Englewood Cliffs, New Jersey 07632

Printed in the United States of America
10 9 8 7 6 5 4 3 2 1

Credits for chapter-opening photos: Museum of the City of New York, 1; Ken Karp, 38,
84, 106, 304, 412; American Airlines, 65; National Institutes of Health, 130; American
Red Cross, 151; Earl Dotter/AFL-CIO News, 181; Irene Springer and S. M. Wakefield,
202; HUD, 224; Paul Conklin/Monkmeyer Press, 241; Rhoda Sidney, 328; Sony, 375;
United Nations photo/M. Guthrie, 394; Mary Hill for World Bank, 436; National Association of Social Workers, 456

0-13-816224-7

Prentice-Hall International (UK) Limited, *London*
Prentice-Hall of Australia Pty. Limited, *Sydney*
Prentice-Hall of Canada Inc., *Toronto*
Prentice-Hall Hispanoamericana, S.A., *Mexico*
Prentice-Hall of India Private Limited, *New Delhi*
Prentice-Hall of Japan, Inc., *Tokyo*
Simon & Schuster Asia Ptd. Ltd., *Singapore*
Editora Prentice-Hall do Brasil, Ltda., *Rio de Janeiro*

*We dedicate this volume to the intellectual spirit
and practice wisdom of the University of Chicago
and the University of Michigan, both pioneering schools,
both innovators in social work concern and knowledge.*

*We also dedicate this book to special people
at the University of Michigan:*

the memory of Fedele F. Fauri,

*a transformational leader
who
inspired the Joint Doctoral Program in Social Work
and Social Science;*

and Henry J. Meyer,

the transformational leader who made it all happen.

Contents

PART THREE: SOCIAL SERVICE INSTITUTIONS: THE LOCATIONS OF SOCIAL WELFARE ACTIVITIES

CHAPTER 10
The Structure of Social Service Systems   224

CHAPTER 11
Service Delivery for Enhancing Criminal Justice   241

CHAPTER 12
Service Delivery for Promoting Health and Meeting the Needs of the Elderly   268

CHAPTER 13

Service Delivery for Enhancing Education   304

CHAPTER 14

Service Delivery for Enhancing the Welfare of Families and Children   328

CHAPTER 15

Social Work in the Workplace 375

CHAPTER 16

Service Delivery for Enhancing the Environment and Housing   394

PART FOUR: PROFESSIONAL RESPONSIBILITIES, PRIORITIES, AND VALUES

CHAPTER 17

Knowledge Development, Data Collection, and Research   412

CHAPTER 18

Social Work and the Elimination of Social Exploitation   436

CHAPTER 19

The Profession of Social Work   456

APPENDIX
Code of Ethics of the National Association of Social Workers 479

Bibliography 484

Name Index 499

Subject Index 505

Preface

This text is intended as an introduction to social work methods and policies, as well as to social services. In an ideal world we could introduce all of these topics at the same time. And, indeed, to separate social work methods from the service systems and policies through which they are delivered is to do them a disservice. Analogously, to separate a discussion of policies and systems from the day-to-day interactions of social workers with individuals, families, groups, communities, organizations, and societies is to ignore the fact that these interactions are the dynamic and living aspects of the policies and systems.

Nevertheless, we have had to divide into separate topics a large entity (the society) composed of all sorts of people (social workers, citizens, policy makers, and so on) who interact in a variety of institutions (schools, prisons, counseling agencies, hospitals, and many more besides), in order to accomplish our goal of introducing the major types of knowledge that exist within social work. We are also committed to presenting these topics from an *ecological perspective* that emphasizes the transactions between people and environments, and we shall explain more about this perspective later in this preface.

Social Work Knowledge

Although we have developed our own conception of social work knowledge, one significantly guided by an ecological perspective, this book includes the following kinds of information in common with other introductory texts:

☐ It introduces the purposes and functions of social work as a profession and social welfare as an institution.

☐ It describes the evolution of social work and social welfare in Western societies.

☐ It presents an image of the community and society as an array of systems in which individuals, families, groups, and complex organizations, with their various ways of functioning, interact with service units devoted to such arenas as justice, education, health, and welfare.

☐ It places these individuals, groups, and organizations in a political context.

☐ It describes the way that change takes place in systems.

☐ It indicates the kinds of interventions engaged in by social workers who seek to bring about changes in individuals, families, groups, organizations, communities, and societies.

☐ It analyzes the nature of service-delivery systems related to social work and social welfare.

☐ It describes how social workers use research and data collection to accomplish their tasks.

☐ It presents the ways in which the social work profession utilizes professional and educational institutions to socialize individuals for the field and discusses the issues currently facing the profession in this context.

☐ It recognizes that social welfare institutions and social work as a profession have special commitments to oppressed and disadvantaged people, and therefore keeps the needs of members of oppressed ethnic groups, of women, of poor people, of the handicapped—to name a few categories—in mind throughout.

An important part of learning about social work activities is to understand how these are based on knowledge of human behavior and the social environment. While our book cannot replace a text on human behavior, we believe that this knowledge is necessary for an understanding of social work. We have consequently made frequent reference to information from the behavioral and social sciences, and we have referred the reader to more extensive discussions of related content.

An Ecological Framework

Since we have endeavored to place this entire text within an ecological (sometimes referred to as ecosystems) framework, it is appropriate at this point to clarify this framework. The ecological view originated in the life sciences as biologists sought to explain the complex interdependencies between living organisms and their environments. This view includes other living species, both animal and vegetable, and the inanimate as well—the terrain, the weather, the seasons, and so forth.

Several approaches to analyzing these environmental interdependencies have been drawn on by social work theorists whom we shall cite throughout this book. One is the field known as *ethology*. Ethologists study both the relationships between behaviors and contexts and the functions of a particular behavior in its context. An important function is that of survival, and social work has drawn on ethology to study the processes of client behavior aimed at survival.

Another approach is that of *ecological psychology*, which seeks to discover how the conditions of the person and the conditions of the ecological environment interact. An important view that stems from this approach is that of *need-press*. This view sees behavior as determined by the interaction between a person's needs and the press of the environment.

The third approach is that of *ethnology*, a discipline within anthropology that examines individuals in the process of the social interactions that are typical in specified social situations. Ethnologists believe that investigators should examine the processes that occur among people as they define and sustain their social realities. An example is how ethnologists might look at a social work staff meeting. They would note the values that the workers drew on in deciding what they wanted to accomplish, the assumptions they made about people, the knowledge they thought was relevant, and the tools they used. Tools in social work include sources of information, locations where social work activities take place, and even the computers used.

A last approach that has been drawn on in developing ecological theory in social work is *social systems theory*. This theory concentrates on the ways in which the immediate system (e.g., the individual) interacts with other systems (e.g., the group or the community) in social situations. Important aspects of systems theory are the way that energy is created and maintained within the system, the way that parts within the system become separate from each other and yet interact to form a whole, and the changing yet balanced way that the system maintains its overall structure and purpose.

Thus, a systems theorist looking at a staff meeting would note how the staff interacts with the administration and the clients. This theorist would also examine the different roles of the staff members and how these members coordinated their activities in their roles. Finally, the theorist would examine how the staff handled the threat of not being able to continue to accomplish its purposes in the face of internal conflict and external challenges.

As social workers have utilized these ideas to develop principles of practice, a large number of notions have emerged. One is that causality should be viewed in a circular rather than a linear way. This is a more complicated idea than it may at first appear, for it implies that in any change effort the human being trying to change another is likely to be changed in the process. Thus, from an ecological approach, a social worker seeking to help a client stop drinking is likely to be changed in the process of helping, and this change will have effects on the client that will create changes in the worker, and so on. This is to say nothing about the changes taking place in such systems as the client's family and the worker's agency as the process between worker and client unfolds.

Another important idea is that the problems clients bring to social workers are not seen as a result alone of client personality but as a result of exchanges between people and their environments. These exchanges take place within many types of systems, such as organizations, communities, and political and economic structures, and in various physical settings. Some of these exchanges are conducive to development and well-being, while others are maladaptive. Under the latter circumstance, the feelings and thinking of people may be injured. Their social development and functioning may be impaired. Even their environments may be hurt.

The task of the social worker from an ecological perspective, consequently, is to help to bring about changes in environment-individual transactions. This task requires the social worker to look at problems in a different way than had previously been the case. Social workers had been likely to use what has been called a *disease metaphor* in which they sought a cure. The ecological approach is appropriate for a *life model* that provides practice guidelines related to processes of living rather than to processes defined in terms of disease, disorder, and deviance.

A compelling way of looking at environment-individual transactions is through the concept of *goodness of fit*. This concept is based on a recognition that people and their environments mutually shape and influence each other. Organisms survive and develop satisfactorily, it posits, when there is a match between an individual's adaptive needs and the qualities of the environment.

Life stress, the effect on individuals of their person-environment relationships, is an important concept in ecological thinking in social work. Some stresses are experienced as challenges that the individuals or systems can meet, and these are likely to be growth-producing. Others are perceived by individuals and systems as jeopardizing their well-being. The way that individuals respond to stress is referred to as *coping*, and it involves the utilization of personal and/or environmental resources. When coping is inadequate because of a lack of these resources, emotional, behavioral, and cognitive disabilities can result.

Another important ecological concept that has been given a place in this book is *habitat*. This term refers to the physical and social settings as related to the culture in which they are found. Issues regarding the habitat, such as quality of housing and the effects on client health of such environmental problems as air pollution, have not traditionally been in the forefront of social workers' attention, and from an ecological point of view this is a serious omission that we address in this book.

Practice principles that stem from an ecological perspective can be identified as follows:

1. An ecosystem assessment requires that data be collected about each of the ecosystems that affect the situation that has come to the attention of the social worker (for example, workplace, home, and community).
2. Assessment should include data from the person and from significant others, as well as direct observation of the person in the situation.
3. Assessment should gather data on all the variables that describe the person *and* the situation that appear to have a bearing on the problem.
4. The assessment data should be combined into a comprehensive picture. This typically requires the use of diagrams rather than word descriptions in order to portray complex interrelationships.
5. The ecosystem assessment should be linked to a range of intervention strategies that are likely to seek changes in both the person and the environment. Thus social work practice may take many forms as long as it seeks to assist people to attain skills for effective coping with their environment and strengthens the fit between people and their environment. As readers of this book will see, this encompasses a very large array of strategies and techniques. Particularly important, however, are those that create social support. Since laypeople in the client's environment can often provide this support, lay helping is highly valued. A form this frequently takes is the self-help group.

The Ecological Perspective in This Book

Part One of this book presents an overview of the systems within which social work and social welfare function and how they evolved. Part Two deals with the various ways that social workers act to create change and how this relates to ecological ideas. Part Three offers an understanding of the ecology of specific settings for social work and social welfare activity, such as those serving people in their family, student, employee, and health roles. Part Four highlights three themes that pervade the book: the use of research, an understanding of culture, and the nature of social work as a profession.

PART ONE: THE HISTORICAL, POLITICAL, AND INTELLECTUAL CONTEXTS FOR SOCIAL WORK ACTIVITIES

Chapter 1 presents an overview of the evolution of social welfare and social work in Western societies, with particular reference to the evolution of an ecological perspective. The impact of ideologies such as social Darwinism on social work's changing views is portrayed. Two themes are emphasized: an environmental one—the role of the city in the development of social welfare; and an ideological one—social exploitation and how it arose, especially in urban environments. The chapter describes the emergence of social workers who specialized in various aspects of the individual-environment configuration and what impact that had on the shape of social work and social welfare.

Chapter 2 deals with the important linkages between social work ideas and the social sciences. A major issue for us is how various ideas from the social sciences are or are not conducive to the ecological perspective. Social work has benefited as well as been handicapped by the way the turf is divided among the social sciences (sociology, anthropology, psychology, political science, economics), and Chapter 2 portrays developments in these disciplines as they affect social work.

All of the systems of concern to us in this book operate within a societal structure that has been referred to as the *welfare state*. Chapter 3 undertakes an analysis of this kind of state, defining it as "a nation-state in which a substantial fraction of government resources and activity is used to provide for the needs of citizens, whether those needs are ordinary or extraordinary." From an ecological perspective, the concept of the welfare state becomes important as we consider the kinds of exchanges that are promoted among various subsystems, including those referred to as the private and public sectors.

PART TWO: HOW SOCIAL WORKERS ACT TO BRING ABOUT CHANGE

Chapter 4 begins our discussion of these various subsystems, notably as they interface with different social work activities and roles. Here we introduce systemic concepts such as *input, throughput, output,* and *open system.* The important idea of *system levels* is introduced, and the reader is helped to see how each level (individual, family, organization) can be a cause or a consequence of events at other levels. This leads to a discussion of direct and indirect intervention as a way of defining strategies.

Chapters 5 through 9 expand the general ideas presented in Chapter 4 as to how social workers intervene at various levels to facilitate change at the same or at different levels. At each level the reader is introduced to the methods that are used to accomplish change, how these emerged historically, and how change strategies are affected by the phase (beginning, middle, and ending) of the change process. Chapter 5 focuses on individuals; Chapter 6 on families and groups; Chapter 7 on organizations; Chapter 8 on communities; and Chapter 9 on whole societies.

PART THREE: SOCIAL SERVICE INSTITUTIONS— THE LOCATIONS OF SOCIAL WELFARE ACTIVITIES

The social welfare institutions that have been established to respond to people's problems have been organized along substantive lines. To the degree that the larger ecosystem affecting the problems is taken into consideration, this can be a problem for as well as a strength of these institutions. Chapter 10 introduces the reader to an overall view of welfare institutions. Different kinds of welfare systems have been created on the basis of different perspectives—levels of intervention, sectors of service, life-cycle events, and categories of social problems—and these are all influenced by such social strata as minority and gender populations. We explain the likelihood of social conflict growing out of clashes among these perspectives. We also point out that from an ecological perspective the apparent untidiness of the welfare system results from the many forces that influence it.

Chapters 11 through 16 use standard categories to describe various social welfare systems: those related to criminal justice (Chapter 11); health, mental health, and aging (Chapter 12); education (Chapter 13); families and children (Chapter 14); industry and the workplace (Chapter 15); and the environment and housing (Chapter 16). The last chapter in the part is especially important from an ecological perspective that recognizes the importance of the habitat for human functioning.

PART FOUR: PROFESSIONAL RESPONSIBILITIES, PRIORITIES, AND VALUES

The last three chapters of this book amplify several themes that we have incorporated in all the others. These are so important to our conception of social work and social welfare that we felt they needed separate chapters. Chapter 17 deals with the use social workers make of data collection and research. Chapter 18 deals with how the culture and status of many people lead to their social exploitation, one of the major themes of this book. And Chapter 19 draws much of the content of the book together in a discussion of the present and the future of the social work profession.

This book introduces many concepts, including some that are not typical of social work texts. We believe that all of this is necessary, for the task of helping people to mold the kinds of institutions that are conducive to human welfare—and for them (and us) to grow in the process—is a difficult, lifelong, demanding, yet so often exhilarating process.

Acknowledgments

We would like to acknowledge our families, colleagues, and helpers who made this book a reality. As in all large efforts, a book, especially a large book like this, depends on many people. Penny Tropman, ACSW, helped throughout and was especially involved in the teacher's manual. Elmer Tropman provided inspiration and guidance; Sarah, Jessica, and Matthew Tropman and David and Amy Garvin are looking forward to applying many of the concepts and skills to their respective fields.

We are grateful to the following reviewers of the final draft of the manuscript: Therese J. Dent, Washington University; David A. Hardcastle, University of Maryland, Baltimore; Mary Ann Jimenez, California State University, Long Beach; Thomas D. Oellerich, Ohio University; and Albert Roberts, Rutgers University.

We also want to thank our colleagues at the University of Michigan, and throughout the country, who have contributed to this volume through suggestions and ideas. Specifically, Professor Sharon Jablonski helped with the chapters on history, the profession, the welfare state, and macro change. Her assistance and counsel were invaluable. David Pollio helped with updating the social indicator data because of the time that elapsed between the original and final drafts of the chapters. Becky Bahlibi assisted with many of the final tasks of formatting and printing the manuscript.

Social Work
in Contemporary
Society

CHAPTER 1

A History of Social Welfare and Social Work

Introduction

The goal of social work, social policy, and social welfare is to improve the quality of life for persons individually and in organizations, communities, and societies through social intervention. History can provide us with some sense of the pattern of these interventions over time. While the effect of an intervention may not be clear in any given instance, a pattern of instances, using history, provides perspective and sweep that closeness to the situation may lack.

History is a prism. It illuminates certain aspects and constancies in the social welfare structure and allows examination of them to see both the limitations and enhancements to understanding that they create. Hence, beginning this book with a history of the field is more than just professional socialization, or a filling in of the gaps in our knowledge, although it seeks to serve that purpose. In addition, history helps to answer questions about what has worked in the helping area, what has not, and why. It provides us with patterns of ideas and action that we could not possibly see as an individual practitioner located in a particular time and place. History enlarges perspective and gives a more solid basis for judgment and assessment. When evidence in a particular case is lacking, or moot, when judgments become difficult and complex, we can draw on historical lessons and answers as guides. History thus exerts its own force on a profession, much as family history exerts its force on new members. As with families, this force can be positive or negative.

But the past is not only a guide and mentor; it is also a jailer. In U.S. society we have done much to obliterate history.[1] Immigrants take more conventional or Americanized names. Bland nicknames are quickly selected that conceal a person's origin and identity. And counselors help clients deal with issues of their own personal history. Although freedom from the past is not one of the freedoms people talk about, it certainly underlies much of social work's effort and intervention.

Whether the past we refer to is an individual's, a family's, or a nation's, it is helpful in changing the present to know about the constraints and bonds of the past. Hence, it is necessary to know history in order to free ourselves and our clients from it.

History, then, is both guide and constraint. It needs to be known, both in factual terms and in terms of its meaning to those affected. Social work and social welfare must both use and go beyond their history. The mere fact of social work's having done certain things in the past does not mean it should continue to do them. Similarly, that particular modes of practice have not characterized social work in the past does not mean they should not now be used.

Social Welfare, Social Policy, and Social Work

The attempts of society to provide humanitarian care and concern for human problems far antedate the profession of social work; indeed, these elements helped to give rise to the profession. Thus, our history will focus on social welfare generally, touch on important social policy issues, and then, when we reach the twentieth century, discuss social work itself.

Social welfare is the pattern of ways that society organizes to provide for its members' basic needs: food, clothing, shelter, and personal care.[2] It also concerns itself with the distribution of goods and with the rules and laws that govern these distributions. It is intimately involved with the normative and legal conditions of eligibility or ineligibility for various goods and services. *These rules or policies, at whatever social level, can be considered as social welfare policy. The larger pattern of meeting social welfare needs, which includes the basic structure of society itself, can be considered as the social welfare structure. Social welfare culture includes norms, conventions, myths, patterns, and practices about how needs are met.*

In general, social welfare policies seek to both change and enhance the social welfare structure. Social welfare policy decisions are controversial because, like all decisions, they allocate goods and values within the system.

What is the role and nature of social work within the realm of social policy? Social work is one mechanism that society has developed to help meet social needs. It is a profession of people who have special skills in providing help. The formal development of social work took place just before 1900. As industrialization and urbanization advanced, societies developed special individuals—social workers—to meet the needs generated by an increasingly specialized and differentiated social order. The development of social work is part of that general specialization and differentiation and occupies an important and prominent place. Social work helps at all levels of the social system and is increasingly differentiated within itself. Let us now turn to an overview of social welfare history, which will lead to a history of social work itself.

Social Welfare History

The history of social work is divided into several major parts. English social welfare history is important because its concerns and decisions served as models for U.S. welfare. The Poor Laws, the Poor Law Reform of 1834, and the Royal Commission of 1909 are landmarks because they represented important programmatic and ideological watersheds in welfare history. The needs they met and the concepts they used continue to be relevant.

As a young country with intellectual ties to Great Britain, the United States drew heavily on the English social welfare system. But U.S social welfare history, like the nation's society itself, also took on a life of its own. However, in many respects it continues to parallel that of the English experience.

English Social Welfare History

A discussion of the government's role in relieving financial distress most often begins with a reference to the English Poor Law of 1601. Karl de Schweinitz comments:

With this Statute, the Poor Law takes the shape that is to characterize it for 300 years. The Act of 1601, the 43rd Elizabeth E., Ch. 2, [is usually] spoken of as the culminating Statute in the development of the Poor Law. . . . Not until 1662 was anything of substantial importance added, and that is specifically concerned with settlement [residence requirements].[3]

De Schweinitz continues:

The Poor Law has reached the form in which it is to influence thought and operation for the next three centuries and more. The 43rd Elizabeth is the parent of governmental relief in England and in the United States, the parent in relation to which our present system of social security expresses both development and revolt.[4]

In short, the 1500s in England was a period of development and transition. And many of their concerns and ideas (for example, who should pay, how much aid should be given, and do the recipients deserve it) still have force today.

Before the Poor Law came into effect, relief had come from essentially two sources. First, there was the social structure itself. As Eric Fromm has pointed out, medieval social structure was reciprocal in nature.[5] Those in the higher ranks of society were due the loyalty, devotion, and support of those in the lower ranks. In return those in the lower ranks were entitled, at least at some minimal level, to protection by and support of those above them. Society thus made provision, however inadequate, for some care to be made available, for some support to be present.

The relationship between wages and subsistence farming in those days was the reverse of what it is today. In modern U.S. society the wage is the central vehicle through which income is generated and, for the majority of Americans, whatever supplement can be generated through home farming and the raising of poultry and small livestock is a plus. The U.S. government recognizes this possibility by setting the rural poverty rate at 15% below the urban one. In the 1500s, however, farming was the central occupation and working for wages was the supplement. An individual's basic daily bread came from a plot of land and the "job" was subsistence itself. Village dwellers had not only the property they themselves might own or, under the medieval structure, the property of the duke, from which the produce was theirs, but they also had the *common*.[6] The common was a large area of public land that could be used for public purposes, such as grazing livestock. Thus, a wage supplement, which would come a bit later under the Speenhamland provisions, was not as important at this period.

For individuals who were not able to support themselves under this system or for whom a casualty or other personal disaster made it impossible, the church was the center of charitable activities. Monasteries, local churches, and clergy, generally, had the historical imperative of doing good works.

However, these structural provisions were not adequate, and because of their perceived inadequacy the English Poor Law of 1601 came into being. As de Schweinitz says, "The experience of the years between 1349 and 1601 had convinced the rulers of England of the presence of a destitution among the poor that punishment could not abolish, and it could be relieved only by the application of public resources to individual need."[7]

Basically, the process that culminated in the passage of the Poor Law transferred responsibility for the poor from ecclesiastical authorities to the government. This responsibility was seen more positively. In early England an attempt to punish the poor and force them to work had been tried. In the 1500s, as now, there was great fear that able-bodied persons would not work. Hence, the following punishment had been prescribed. The able-bodied beggar was to be brought to a town

> and there to be tied to the end of a cart naked and be beaten with whips throughout the same market town or other place till his body be bloodied by reason of such whipping; and after such punishment and whipping . . . [he] shall be enjoined upon his oath to return forthwith without delay in the next and straight way to the place where he was born. . . .[8]

Relief was locally financed and locally administered. An overseer of the poor was appointed to coordinate efforts toward the poor. The law of 1601 provided for direct grants and contained provisions for making those who were able-bodied go to work.

The English Poor Law contains the same kinds of competing approaches to poverty that we have become familiar with today. One the one hand, there was a positive, compassionate view that recognized difficulties and problems and sought to provide help for them. On the other side, a negative and hostile view prevailed, which, although absent from the act itself, was nonetheless present in society and surfaced later.

The next major point in English welfare history, the law of settlement, occurred in 1662. De Schweinitz says:

> The effect of this Statute was to empower the justices to return to his former residence any person coming to occupy a property renting for less than 10 pounds a year, who, in the opinion of the overseers, might at some time in the future become in need. It was not a matter of such a person's asking for relief—merely the judgment of the overseers that he might on some later occasion be obliged to apply for assistance.[9]

This idea that the individual's local area of residence should provide the fundamental resources for assistance should they be needed is a part of the period's negativism. In the ever constant effort to reduce government expenditures, those that had to be made on behalf of the poor were seen as the easiest and most legitimate to avoid, either by direct reduction or by passing them on to other government units.

In the United States, law of settlement issues are still powerful. Policies of residence requirements, that send needy persons back to states of origin have been common. Although there are no records to prove local officials said something like "they just come to our town to get higher relief grants," we can imagine that if the words were not present the sentiment certainly was. As wages became increasingly important in the economy, it became increasingly clear that in many instances the average wage would not meet average expenditures. This is the historical problem of what we now call the working poor.

SPEENHAMLAND

In 1795, the problem of the working poor crystallized for English welfare administrators, in terms of what a man could make and what a man needed for his family. It was possible to set a minimum wage. That certainly could have been a way to deal with this problem. But it was not the route that England chose. When a meeting

> of the sheriff and the magistrates of Berkshire was called at the Pelican Inn in Speenhamland on May 6, 1795 . . . [i]nstead of raising wages to a point where they would meet the cost of living, the justices of the Berks proposed to use relief to make up the difference between a man's earnings and the minimum upon which they felt his family could exist. The scale which they drew up provided that when the gallon loaf sold for one shilling enough relief would be added to the laborer's wage to bring his income to three shillings; if he had a wife, to four shillings, six pence; if a wife and one child, to six shillings, and so on according to the size of the household.
>
> This plan of supplementing wages became known as the Speenhamland Act because Speenhamland was the place where the meeting was held at which the scale was adopted. . . . [10]

There were negative effects of the Speenhamland system, of course. Wages began to fall, as might be expected when the employers realized that they were not obligated to pay a decent wage but rather just enough to make the employee eligible for supplement. The result of this system was unexpected because it tended to make what the justices doubtless thought was a minimum system into a maximum system. What had started out as a floor became a ceiling, trapping many individuals very near the poverty line that was supposed to be their minimal basis for living.

A second problem had to do with the Roundsman system. Without a job, it was very difficult to get assistance. Hence, it was necessary to have a job, even at extremely low rates. Men therefore began to "make the rounds" from potential employer to potential employer, at each point seeking some kind of minimal work. While he perhaps overstates the result, Polanyi concludes:

> In the long run the result was ghastly. Although it took some time till the self-respect of the common man sank to the low point where he preferred poor relief to wages, his wages which were subsidized from public funds were bound eventually to be bottomless and to force him upon the rates. Little by little the people from the countryside were pauperized; the adage "Once on the rates always on the rates" was a true saying. But for the protracted effects of the allowance system it would be impossible to explain the human and social degradation of early capitalism. [11]

Early capitalism had many horrors but they cannot be blamed on social policy. However, several important points are raised by Polanyi's criticism, and it is important to touch upon them.

First, in making social policy many factors interlink. The unintended consequences can be seen here, effects that appear not to have been taken into account at that time. For Speenhamland, they were the potential of falling wages, the Roundsman's system, and the development of a ceiling rather than a floor. Each of these factors, problematic alone, may well have accelerated the impact of the others. It is well to remember that, both then and now, a simple policy that seems to help people in some instances may, in other instances, do actually the reverse.

A second point that Polanyi alludes to is a negative attitude toward receiving public funds: welfare, the dole, the rates, whatever we call it. This aversion is certainly manifest in U.S. society today. For example, one U.S. program, Supplemental Security Income, is being used by only about half of those eligible.[12]

Another element worth looking at in some detail with respect to the Speenhamland experiment is the need to recognize that, even at this early stage, wages had two parts: an economic part and a social part. This conjoining of the purpose of wages has fundamentally confounded the wage system. There is nothing in economic theory to suggest that wages should or should not provide a living standard of any sort for any particular recipient. The conflict between economic and social bases is fundamental.[13] This potential gap between what an individual could get from a grant and what he could get from a wage has always been a source of contention, and it became an important issue in the next major reform of the Poor Law in 1832–1834.

THE POOR LAW REFORM OF 1834

The Speenhamland Experiment, known as the allowance in support of wages, is what we today might call a negative income tax. It was designed to help the poor and the near-poor and tended to eradicate distinctions among various groups of individuals receiving public aid. Increasingly, public opinion in England began to shift against this plan. For one thing, like most universal plans, it was very expensive. (A universal plan pays benefits to everyone in a class, to all mothers, for example, or all children.) For another, there was the widespread perception that this kind of relief, called outdoor relief because it was given outside the confines of an institution such as an alms house or workhouse, was contributing to the dependency of the population. It was reasoned that poverty was not the problem, but accepting aid on behalf of poverty was. As de Schweinitz says, "The evil was held to emanate from the relief rather than from the situation which was the occasion of relief."[14]

The reform of 1834 in effect canceled all outdoor relief. Workhouses were introduced and a sharp distinction was drawn between what we might today call the worthy poor and the unworthy poor. Acceptance of relief, instead of being a right or an entitlement, as it had become or was becoming under the Speenhamland Experiment, became a noxious indication of failure. The poor law reform of 1834, as Disraeli commented, "announces to the world that in England poverty is a crime."[15] A conservative tide was sweeping the country. On August 14, 1834, the recommendation of the Royal Commission for Inquiring into the Administration of the Practical Operation of the Poor Laws was enacted into law.[16]

Several significant ideas result from the Poor Law Reform of 1834. One has already been noted, the very negative and hostile attitude toward the disadvantaged. Poor financial status was transmuted into poor moral status.

A second theme is what we would today call blaming the victim, but in a double sense.[17] Not only was the individual blamed for being poor but, if he accepted relief, he was even lower than poor. The acceptance of help became an admission of defeat.

This legacy is present today. It surely must be in part for these historical reasons that victims of rape are fearful of seeking help, that victims of child abuse and other forms of domestic violence keep quiet, and that older adults fail to come forward and accept the financial assistance that is their right. It is indeed a poisonous bequest that has done incalculable harm to the well-being of both English and U.S. citizens.

A third principle is not well known by its original phrase—less eligibility—but has become very important. The great fear both then and now, was that individuals would enjoy receiving public aid in support of wages rather than going to work. Simply put, the principle of less eligibility meant that the condition of the poor should be *less eligible*, or below that of the condition of the lowest working man. As a practical matter, it meant that any grant should be below what we today call the minimum wage, or perhaps below the lowest prevailing wage in the community. This approach, it was thought, would ensure a positive motivation toward work, and individuals would accept public aid only when it was less attractive than work. This principle is still operative today, though we tend not to call it "less eligibility." In a study of public aid in American states, Tropman found that, using several definitions of less eligibility, grants still fell below each of those minima.[18] In short, the themes and emphases that characterized 1834 are in a variety of ways with us today.

The notion of social Darwinism stems in part from some of the ideas expressed in the English Poor Laws, especially the Reform of 1834.[19] Darwinist notions of survival of the fittest found a perfect social application in this concept of the social order. The poor were poor because they were least fit. The well-to-do were well off because they were most fit. It is a seductive argument that permits complete bypassing of the social and structural features in poverty for a relatively easy blame-the-victim approach. The social Darwinist perspective covers this view with scientific gloss.

Recent U.S. writings on the poor tend to fall into a similar category. Work by Gilder and Murray are cases in point.[20]

In sum, the legacy of 1834, with its concepts of less eligibility, its desire to make charity noxious to receive, and its suspicion of the poor developed the negative attributions toward poverty and the poor in English and U.S. society today.

TOWARD THE ROYAL COMMISSION OF 1909

In some sense the reform of 1834 pushed English society back to a pre-1602 period. Churches began to do more and what we would today call the private sector began to develop in England. It is in this context of negativism and public withdrawal that the profession of social work really got its beginnings. Most notable was the emergence of the Charity Organization Society.

While in the past there had been voluntary efforts to aid the poor, the Charity Organization Society under the leadership of Octavia Hill and Charles S. Loch changed the focus by hiring initially one and then later more paid individuals to help voluntary citizens in their good works. It was this idea that people should and could be paid to help in the administration of charity that gave social work its beginnings. These beginnings, however, were not of an exactly liberal source. Octavia Hill said:

> I believe our irregular alms to the occupant of the miserable room, to the shoeless flower-seller, are tending to keep a whole class on the very brink of pauperism who might be taught self-control and foresight if we would let them learn it.[21]

What took place during the period between 1834 and 1900 was important for one aspect of social welfare, the development of private charity. Its beginnings anticipated two aspects that would characterize social work later: volunteerism, on the one hand, and professional charity work (paid and trained workers, among other elements), on the other. However, it must also be recalled that during this time, in the 1840s and 1850s, Karl Marx was developing his monumental work on the exploitation of workers by capitalism (*Das Kapital,* 1867). It was as if two streams dealing with the human condition, a private stream and a public stream, had been separated by the work of 1834, with the private, volunteer stream developing because of the more limited public role that the events of 1834 created. Because of its effect on the work of Marx, the ideas contained in the welfare reform of 1834 may have had a much more powerful effect on the history of the world than anyone could have imagined.

What Marx saw was the industrialization of England and the attendant social dislocation and social problems that it produced. What he proposed was a theory that required and demanded a complete restructuring of the state. That did not come about in England, but to an important extent portions of his legacy were picked up by socialist thinkers everywhere.

These two streams, the public and the private, met once again in the Royal Commission of 1909. Representing the private and scientific charity interests was Charles S. Loch, head of the London Charity Organization Society. Squaring off against him, was the formidable Beatrice Webb, a socialist representing a group of individuals and a pattern of thought that argued for a great deal more public responsibility (Fabian socialism). The report came out in a majority and a minority section, with some important differences. It was not like 1834, when unanimous recommendations could be legislated immediately. The more conservative posture of Loch and his colleagues secured majority support, with Webb and her co-believers taking the minority position.

But, as de Schweinitz points out, there was a great deal more agreement than has been generally recognized. The two factions joined together in rejecting the Poor Law concept of 1834. There was also agreement on some administrative details and most importantly on the idea of prevention and social provision, that is, the taking by government of a more proactive role. These agreements were not trivial. But the sections differed in how far government should go.[22]

In general, the majority report substituted the idea of treatment of the poor and a system of help for a test of their intentions via the workhouse. It replaced the concept of less eligibility.

One of the Poor Law proponents, testifying at hearings held by the commission, summarized the 1834 view of less eligibility as involving "first the loss of personal reputation, [what is understood as the stigma of pauperism (ed.)]; secondly, the loss of personal freedom which is secured by detention in the workhouse; and thirdly, the loss of personal freedom by suffering disenfranchisement."[23] This negative tone was replaced with the notion of a system of help.

> The program of treatment was to be administered by private charity, supplemented by specialized public institutions for children, the aged, the sick; and industrial and agricultural institutions, labor colonies, and detention colonies for the various catego-

ries of the able-bodied. Paralleling a public assistance committee to be developed in every community would be a voluntary aid committee.[24]

The majority fused public and private charity together in that system of help.

The Webb minority report rejected that fusion and developed the notion that the government itself has important responsibilities. They wanted to delegitimize the Poor Law concept of government help and provide positive government assistance through government agencies.

The minority report built its concept of treatment around the use of the specialist in education, health pensions, and mental problems. There would be a committee in each field, capable of meeting every ill from which the person seeking assistance might be suffering.[25]

The minority report spoke of entitlements, but these were not entitlements without obligation. And this point remains contentious to this day, both in England and the United States.

In return for public aid, should the recipient be required to perform any act or do any service? The minority report seemed to feel that the answer to this question was yes. It comments, "We come now to what appears to us the worst feature of the Outdoor Relief of today. With insignificant exceptions, Boards of Guardians give these doles and allowances without requiring a return for them, even the most elementary conditions."[26]

The current U.S. controversy (which is also an historical controversy) over whether or not any specific work requirements for the receipt of relief should be imposed is a continuation of this question. It is generally thought that liberals do not wish to impose requirements, whereas conservatives do. However, as the quote from Webb indicates, we should not assume that a liberal position is requirement free.

The 1909 Royal Commission, in several senses, represented a parting of ways with respect to social thought in Great Britain. Private charity had finally come into its own and was fully and legitimately recognized as a part of the need-meeting system and was sponsored and encouraged by government. In addition, the extremely negative and hostile tone characteristic of 1834 had been softened, although the public sentiment to which 1834 gave expression was neither silent nor completely suppressed. Furthermore, there was greater recognition of the structural causes of poverty, although the minority report dealt with them much more explicitly and straightforwardly than did the majority report. The 1909 act thus occurred on the verge of the welfare state. (See Chapter 3 for a detailed discussion of the welfare state. Briefly, that concept refers to the development of a strong government role and responsibility for the physical and mental well-being of its citizens.) Although not until the Beveridge Report of 1941 did the welfare state reach full bloom, much of its thinking was anticipated and justified in the minority report of 1909.

The time between major revisions of the English public assistance system grew shorter up to the Beveridge Report. The 1603 document lasted for over 200 years, until 1834. The 1834 document lasted about 80 years, until 1909. The 1909 report lasted about 30 years, until 1941. To some extent the majority report in 1909 conceptualized the then current state in Great Britain, whereas the minority report laid the plan for the future. England began a number of insurance and assistance plans between 1909 and 1941, but there were the usual complaints of inadequate benefits, excessive decentralization of control, and the consequent desire for coordination of service.

The wish to improve the system of help was strengthened by the fears of what would happen to the British population if war came. As de Schweinitz said,

> It was a desire strong enough throughout Britain to bring the announcement of the appointment of the Interdepartmental Committee while the country was in the darkest period of the war, facing imminent threat of invasion, and on the same day on which the Prime Minister reported to the House on the details of the loss of Crete.[27]

The resulting report introduced the concept of social insurance. This concept of using the collective power of the state to insure against known and devastating hazards had already begun to be developed, first in Germany and then in Britain. However, the Beveridge Report, which is largely taken to be the beginning point of the welfare state, extends and concretizes the insurance scheme through the provision of a national minimum and includes health and children's allowances as part of the package. These are programs that we have not yet secured within the American system. Specifically, the document:

> concentrates on one remedy: the national minimum. The effect of mass unemployment in interrupting income and the essential importance of putting an end to this threat are recognized. The whole Report, indeed, is based upon the assumption that this problem can and will be solved, but the particular goal of the Beveridge plan for social security was the abolition of want by providing that every individual in Britain shall have a basic income which will supply his (her) essential needs no matter what vicissitudes of life he (she) experiences. This aim is to be achieved through the use of the existing pattern of social insurance, supplemented by private insurance and assistance, and accompanied by a system of allowances for every child after the first child irrespective of the income of the family and including the first child where there is an interruption of earnings. Health is held to be so important, both to the family and the nation, that it is not left to individual arrangement. Instead, the Report makes a fundamental recommendation, stated as an assumption, that a comprehensive national health service be developed.[28]

The concept that the minority report of 1909 endorsed—fundamental governmental provision for all citizens—had by now been established. The universality of the program proposed by Beveridge fundamentally changed the previous character of poverty relief. It had been the central idea of poverty planners to identify certain categories of individuals or problems and provide aid for those individuals. Under the Beveridge Report, everyone would now be eligible. The line between the worthy and the unworthy poor had been erased. In fact, the very concept of pauperism (guilt through receiving public aid) had now been removed. The universality of these programs, at a single stroke, made the concept of poverty obsolete, or so it seemed. Eligibility for benefits cut across all classes and categories of people.

We cannot divorce the extensiveness and universality of the proposals contained in the Beveridge Report from the wartime conditions of England. It is appropriate to consider this report as an extension of the Minority Report of 1909 as well as an extension of organizational development of agencies of social care in the 30 intervening years. However, England was facing a period of potentially great devastation. Every citizen needed to do her or his part. When a nation is under an attack and threatened with such dire consequences as was England during the early 1940s, with German troops poised to cross the English Channel for an invasion, it may well wish to set aside social distinctions. The potential commonness of the fate for all emphasizes the commonness of responsibility and response. It might be said that the Beveridge Report represented a promise to the people of Britain. In effect, it said, "if we survive and if you do all you can to make us survive, we the country will reward you in the future." The beginnings of the welfare state thus can be thought of, in part, as a deal to both mobilize and reward a population who needed assurances that their sacrifices would be recognized. And should any individual make the supreme sacrifice, her or his loved ones would not be left without care.

THE WELFARE STATE: ISSUES SINCE 1943

With the Beveridge Report, our history of English social welfare policy largely comes to an end. England has continued to develop welfare state activities. Income and health supports have been expanded. Personal social services that involve counseling and other kinds of assistance that social workers have come to be known for are now available. Many services are now offered in a coordinated way within each English community. The problems of poverty are not and perhaps never have been exclusively those of financial deprivation, and the attempt to develop an umbrella of local services is an attempt to recognize the interdependence of problems.

   The need for money is the most public and most easily remediable difficulty that individuals face. It may be either the cause or the consequence of other difficulties, including psychological and health problems, relationship difficulties, and developmental disabilities. The cost of programs to deal with these problems is extensive, and the current government in England is very much like governments everywhere in seeking ways to reduce social welfare expenditures. Somehow social costs (rather than other potential candidates such as national defense expenditures) have been identified as major causes of the burgeoning public budgets. Hence, programs to cut them flourish. But the history of England reveals, as does the history of the United States, that conflicting attitudes about poverty, its causes, and mechanisms for its relief tend to be cyclical. The path from the Poor Laws through the Reform of 1834 to the Royal Commission of 1909, with its majority and minority reports, to the Beveridge Report all show conflicting values at work.

   More liberal and then less liberal proposals follow one upon the other. The only certainty is that the program currently in place will soon disappoint a majority of supporters, and a new program will be advocated with enthusiasm and vigor. But once in place, the new program will soon become old hat, and will be replaced by a program similar to the one it replaced. Conflict over these matters is continual; it is a situation of almost constant crisis, because the values on which the programs are based conflict.[29]

   It is important to understand the development of poverty relief in England, because the influence that the major acts of 1602, 1834, 1909, and 1941 had on U.S. society and social thinking was immense. Furthermore, such study reveals almost all the issues, concerns, perspectives about how to help those who are disadvantaged, what role the cause of the disadvantage should play, and the like, that we find today. And it is somewhat easier to discuss them in the British context because of the focal documents and clear-cut changes. In the U.S. federal system, with state and national government taking a part, and with the tasks of nation-building and expansion already beginning to take large fractions of our institutional energy, the history of attitudes toward and programs for the poor is much more diffuse, less focal, and less easy to comprehend. However, through the prism of the English system we can better understand why the United States did what it did and what the differences were.

United States Social Welfare History

United States social welfare history was similar to, but in important ways diverged from, the English experience. For one thing, the United States did not produce focal documents, the major studies that were so significant in British history. For another thing, the United States was a developing society, whereas European society was well developed and acting within a context of established social structure. The U.S. social structure was just developing, and the people who came here had left the European social structure because of its oppressive aspects. The United States, as Slater points out, was founded by runaways, although no one may have thought of the pilgrims as runaways until he suggested it.[30]

What immigrants ran away from were big institutions that limited their freedom— big government and big church, especially. This history has left us with a legacy of problem avoidance by government rather than problem confrontation. Planners in the social welfare field are well aware of the unwillingness of U.S. society to look ahead and plan ahead. The short-range, more episodic focus on problems characteristic of the United States has been much discussed. But Naisbitt suggests that there is a move toward a long-range view.[31]

A second point deals with the issue of aristocratic background. United States society is the only major industrialized society that does not contain a previously aristocratic social structure. It has thus been freed of the residual social oppression that such a society entails, but it also has been exempt from the community of interactions and support that such structure brings. Freedom from central government and its problems (at least in the early part of U.S. history) meant a freedom also from the responsibilities that such a government assumes. Among these is freedom from social welfare responsibilities.

The United States was also multicentric, conceived as a federalist republic. It became an embodiment of the founding fathers' idea of checks and balances. These checks were not only within the federal level of government (executive, legislative, and judicial), but also at state and local levels. Thus, there are at least nine centers (three times three) of formal governmental authority at a minimum. To this we might add the civil service, a fourth level of government at each level, making a total of twelve units of government. To this, we could add the development of special government districts, which number literally hundreds of governments, from educational districts and mental health catchment areas to park districts and waste disposal councils. It would have been difficult to have a focal document like those the royal commission groups in England produce, because the kind of agreement needed to make such documents central was simply not present in the United States.[32]

Uniquely, U.S. society provided a home for the free market. The absence of feudal structures made it the ideal capitalist society of the kind Adam Smith had in mind. Girvetz comments:

> However, rationalizations were promptly devised that condoned unemployment and poverty and argued against intervention by government. The unemployed were held to be lazy and shiftless, traits considered inborn and to be overcome only by the spur of need or the bribe of generous profits. The poor were improvident and unenterprising; poverty was a punishment for sloth and incompetence. Tampering with the verdict of the free market on the compensation that individuals receive by providing them with income when they are ill, or old, or unemployed would sabotage the only mechanism available for proportioning reward to merit.[33]

Because of the welter of actors and the multicentric nature of U.S. society, different social welfare and social work initiatives were taking place at different times. Thus, the periodization (or phasing) of U.S. social welfare efforts suggested in this section is more one of convenience than anything else. It divides the social welfare experience into six major periods. However, these should be viewed merely as a skeleton on which to hang a range of activities that were going on within the periods, rather than as definitive turning points. The first period, the English Period, spans 200 years from 1620 to 1820; the second period, the pre-Civil War Period, runs from about 1820 to 1860; the third segment, the Beginning of Social Consciousness, goes from the Civil War of 1860 to approximately 1900; the fourth period, the Growth of Social Work, from the turn of the century to the passage of the Social Security Act in 1935; and the fifth period, the Era of Public Development, from 1935 to approximately 1970. From 1970 to the present might be termed the period of retraditionalization, since the emphasis seems to be on reduction, retrenchment, and reemphasis on traditional values.[34]

THE ENGLISH PERIOD, 1620–1820

During this era the influence of England and the Poor Law of 1601 was strong. There were local poor relief allocations to individuals, and towns reported the provision of money to those who were found to be needy. The climate was harsh, and there was a scarcity of resources for the development of extensive social welfare provisions.

The system of indenture by which individuals were bound (contracted) to work for another more well-to-do individual in exchange for support was a common practice. Additionally, child welfare needs were handled through apprenticeship, by assigning a child to a particular craftsman or journeyman who cared for the child while teaching the child his trade. These systems seem woefully inadequate and thoughtless in the light of today's knowledge, and the suffering people endured was very substantial.

Yet a negative judgment must be tempered by an appreciation of the extremely difficult conditions under which early and subsequent settlers found themselves. These conditions were harsh not only in the conventional sense of opening up a new land, but in the more extensive sense that involves new social relationships, lack of traditional supports and understandings, and pervasive uncertainty about life itself. Under these conditions, early and later colonists did as they thought best.

THE PRE-CIVIL WAR PERIOD, 1820–1860

The pre-Civil War period saw the beginnings of large-scale immigration of Catholic and Jewish populations from Europe. This immigration differed from those that previously characterized American development, not only in the religion and region of the immigrants, but of the different belief systems they brought, which were often at odds with the prevailing white, Anglo-Saxon, Protestant "native" orientations. This period was also the beginning of mechanization and industrialization, and accidents associated with large pieces of equipment were becoming more common. Government did not develop systematic welfare plans, and private organizations arose to do this job. In 1825 the New York Society for the Prevention of Pauperism opened a children's institution. By 1852, Charles Loring Brace had founded the Children's Aid Society, which led ultimately to the development of foster care. Alms houses and workhouses were developed. The New England Home for Little Wanderers and Sheltering Arms Children's Agencies were established to aid children in need. Many of these organizations were in direct and indirect ways a response to the waves of immigration stimulated largely by political turmoil in Europe.

The federal government still refused to undertake much activity. Dorothea Dix, a woman very concerned about the conditions in mental hospitals and especially of the indigent insane, through intense activity caused many state governments to make improvements in the care of the mentally ill. And, in a singular piece of social action, she convinced the Congress of the United States to pass legislation allocating federal land to the care of the indigent insane, a kind of land grant mental hospital. This bill was vetoed by President Franklin Pierce in 1854, who outlined a policy that was to have force until after the Civil War:

> [I]f Congress has the power to make provision for the indigent insane without the limits of this District, it has the same power to provide for the indigent who are not insane and thus to transfer to the federal government the charge of all the poor in all the states. . . . [T]he whole field of public beneficence is thrown open to the care and culture of the federal government. Generous impulses no longer encounter the limitations and control of our imperious fundamental law.[35]

This opinion became federal policy. It held, essentially, until the passage of the Social Security Act in 1935, although there were some adjustments made in the form of the Freedman's Bureau and Civil War pensions.

The increasing recognition of the oppressiveness of slavery and the development of the abolitionist movement provided an outlet for a beginning stream of social protest. Churches and ministers played an important role by default as much as by design, in the sense that the large-scale units of government (the federal government and the state governments) were not really doing a great deal.

The development of independence from the homeland had a number of important sequels as well. Fischer[36] believes that this political liberation also released people from some sense of obligation to their own parents. Rorabaugh feels that the post-independence freedom from control encouraged people to overindulge in alcoholic spirits, a manifestation that in turn led to the development of the prohibition movement.[37]

This reference to alcohol is more than an aside. For much of the nineteenth century, overindulgence in alcohol was assumed to be a major cause of poverty. The history of the nineteenth-century prohibition movement[38] can be seen as a history of trying to control poverty by eliminating its cause. The drinking man and his victimized and unsupported family were often the image of the poor throughout this period.

But U.S. society had important social problems that were unique and accentuated its difference with England. First was slavery and the terrible tensions that it caused. Second were the twin concerns of immigration and urbanization.

A third factor unique to the United States was the frontier. These vast reaches of land were an attractive feature to potential immigrants. Whatever other effects the frontier may or may not have had with respect to U.S. history, it permitted it to hide problems. Poverty is one example. Hundreds of poor people living in one place are different from a poor but isolated farm family. Thus, the very size of the country and its resources fragmented our consciousness with respect to social problems, although they were present and growing.

Space cannot solve all of a nation's difficulties though, and reaction to the inequalities of slavery had to come to a head. They did in the Civil War.

THE CIVIL WAR PERIOD AND THE BEGINNINGS OF SOCIAL CONSCIENCE, 1860–1900

The Civil War was probably the most cataclysmic event in U.S. history. It certainly was the most costly in terms of lives. Countless explanations and interpretations of it have been offered. Some believe that the war was to preserve the Union, and it was at least that.

Others assert that it represented conflict between the forces of industrialization as represented by the North and forces of rural agrarianism as represented by the South. It was probably some of that as well.

A Marxist might say that the landed class as represented in the South had to be destroyed for the fuller development of industrialization and capitalism. Still others argue that the war was about freeing the slaves and making good on that part of the U.S. promise which said that all men are created equal. Surely it was a mix of these factors and others.

What is important for our purposes is that the Civil War was the true beginning of welfare activities on the part of the federal government and represents a shift from the Pierce veto of 1854. Two items of social need emerging from the Civil War illustrate the changed federal government attitude and hence its social policy. One was the provision for Civil War veterans and the second, for the newly freed slaves.

After the Civil War the federal government provided pensions for Civil War veterans of the North. This was the first large-scale government pension program and amounted to a public grant to older citizens, because by 1900 simply being a Civil War veteran and over 65 was the de facto criterion for eligibility.[39] The amounts were not trivial. Orloff and Skocpol suggest that it was the largest single expenditure in the federal budget exclusive of interest on the national debt. The point is important because it defines the time period when federal government activity in the provision of grants began.

A second and more well-known effort was the Freedman's Bureau established in 1865 by Congress to aid slaves. Coll comments:

> The former slaves were destitute and the South had no money to assist them. This situation led the Federal government for the first time in its history to provide direct assistance to needy persons. The Freedman's Bureau established by Congress in 1865 and administered by the War Department distributed food, clothing and medicine and assisted homeless blacks with settlement, housing and employment. . . . Attacked as radical and as encouraging idleness and pauperism, it was allowed to die for lack of funds in 1872.[40]

The influence of Civil War pensions and the Freedman's Bureau merit more explicit recognition in social welfare history than they have had. However, their influence should not be overstated. On balance, the period after the Civil War was still heavily oriented toward the development of private charity, and indeed many of the beginnings of social work can be traced to this period. Social settlements were developed in the 1880s, such as Lillian Wald's famous New York Henry Street Settlement and Jane Addams's Chicago Hull House. At the same time, Charity Organization Societies and family and children services were developing in major U.S. cities.

Jane Addams at work. (Photo courtesy of the Chicago Historical Society.)

The philosophies and origins of these two historical roots of social work were rather different. The Charity Organization Societies tended to be ameliorative in nature and had their origins in the English charity organization movement. Their focus was on scientific philanthropy. They generally presumed (though the presumptions were often unacknowledged) characterological, or later psychological, flaws within the individual person. A friendly visitor provided counsel, directly and by way of example, and this orientation was quite different from the social settlement. There prevention was the goal, and the deficiencies were seen in educational rather than psychological or characterological terms. Jane Addams, like other settlement workers, lived in the settlement, and the location of the facility in the area of need was an important component of social settlement philosophy. Settlements offered courses and facilitated, especially for immigrants, the acquisition of skills for success in the United States. These tensions between moral example and counseling and education and training remain in social work and are not yet resolved.

In 1873 the American Social Science Association was formed, which later became the National Conference of Charity and Corrections, which in turn became the National Conference of Social Work, which in its turn became the National Conference of Social Welfare. As a national organization that helped to coordinate other national coordinating agencies, the NCSW has enjoyed a distinguished past as a place where social welfare professionals have gathered. It is now largely out of existence, having lost its influence in competition with other organizations that have developed at the national level over time.

As positive ideas developed, there were also some that were more negative. One of the most powerful of these negative ideas is social Darwinism. The evolutionary theories of Darwin provide a basis in nature for the sorting of individual members of any species. The survival of the fittest idea tended to be thought of as a neutral social process that permitted those who were best to survive.[41] Tax and Krucoff comment that "Social Darwinism will be understood . . . as the convergence of social scientific facts with the corpus of 'conservative' values." They quote Herbert Spencer as saying "the men who have not done their duty in this world can never be equal to those who have done their duty."[42]

As Lieby has indicated, the late nineteenth century was a paradox.

> On the one hand, the Protestant ethic suggested that the needy were more likely afflicted by a lack of personal discipline. Social Darwinism went further to suggest that they were biologically unfit possibly because of their heredity or race. On the other hand the main religious tradition, forcefully upheld not only by Protestant evangelists but also by Catholics and Jews who were crowding into the big cities, held that one mission of the church was to help the forlorn and defeated, never mind the Godless Darwinists or liberal economics. Quite apart from formal religion the democratic ethos was solicitous about humble people. As Amos Warner said in *American Charities* (1894), which remained throughout several editions the leading work on the subject until 1930, there was a dialectic between the "philanthropists" who believed that something must be done to help the needy and the "economists" who believe that policy must follow the best scientific understanding of human affairs.[43]

In sum, the late nineteenth century represented conflicting perspectives. On the one hand, there was a great deal of negativism and hostility toward the poor specifically and those in need generally, a perspective that has almost become a U.S. tradition. On the other hand, the beginnings of a nascent welfare state can be discerned in the Civil War pensions, in the Freedman's Bureau, and in the development of some aspects of social activism in the Charity Organization Societies. Social work got its start in the United States during this period, but it was in the next era, the first part of the twentieth century, that it began to flower.

THE GROWTH OF SOCIAL WORK, 1900–1935

During the first 35 years or so of the twentieth century, social work as a profession came into its own. The beginnings are found in the private welfare activities of the previous period, both in England and in the United States: in the growth of Charity Organization Societies, the development of friendly visitors, and the rise of scientific philanthropy (the application of scientific principles to charity).

The turn of the century proved to be the turning point for social work's development. Important in this was the development of professional education. For example, two institutions of education joined together in Chicago, and this development signaled the beginnings of social concern, but in rather different ways. The University of Chicago had been created and had taken a social point of view as its hallmark, paying special attention to the importance of social conditions and hosting the new discipline of sociology. For many years, Chicago sociology would be the hallmark of American social analysis.

Into that developing fold of social concern and social science came the School of Civics and Philanthropy. Originally chartered as a training program for people in social agencies, it quickly developed its own focus, and when it joined the university it became the School of Social Service Administration.

The School of Social Service Administration was heavily female in orientation and remained so until the middle 1950s. It had a series of distinguished deans, including Edith Abbott and Helen Russell Wright. In 1956, Alton Linford became the first male dean of the school. Social work became and still is to some extent a place where women could develop professionally and secure professional degrees. Arthur Schlesinger comments on the importance of the role of women in the development of the social work profession.

> This middle class mission to the poor coincided with the release of energy which came from the new emancipation of women. Hull House and Henry Street, in particular, produced an extraordinary group of women whose vitality and compassion reshaped American liberalism. From Hull House came Florence Kelly who became the driving force in the National Consumer's League. The idea of the United States Children's Bureau was Lillian Walds' and its first two chiefs, Julia Lathrop and Grace Abbott, were from Hull House. The same hopes and ideals fired many younger women, Josephine Goldmark, Frances Perkins, Mary Doson, Mary Anderson, Edith Abbott. These were "the dedicated old maids." Social work not only relieved their middle class conscience, it also provided an outlet for their energy in a field which women could make their own.[44]

In a similar vein Leiby comments:

> One might say that social work spread and developed in the United States not just because there was a need for its concerns and services (and there certainly was), but also because there were many young ladies who were determined to serve and who wanted not a patronizing and undemocratic role as a charity visitor, which Jane Addams explicitly rejected, but a dignified and paid career.[45]

The New York School of Philanthropy was also formed about this time and later became affiliated with Columbia University as their School of Social Work (first the New York School of Social Work and later the Columbia University School of Social Work). In New York City, the Henry Street Settlement became a focal place for the development of aspects of the field of social work.[46]

The first juvenile court was created in Cook County, Illinois, in 1899. The U.S. Children's Bureau was founded in 1912 and located in the Department of Labor because of the issue of child labor. Children were an economic asset. At the turn of the century, children's income was an important family asset, and their economic utility doubtless prevented the vigorous development of child protective laws. As is so often the case, mixed motives stalled action.

While concern for child welfare and child abuse seems commonplace today, we must remember that only 80 years ago the situation was much different. In fact, one of the earliest child abuse cases in New York City could not be handled by a child protective agency because there was none. The case was handled by the Society for the Prevention of Cruelty to Animals under the idea that a child was an animal and thus should be treated with the same respect. This episode led to the development in many cities of Societies for the Prevention of Cruelty to Children. These were voluntary organizations operating out of a sense of scientific philanthropy. Only in very recent years did strict legal requirements with respect to child abuse arise.

Early programs were holistic in nature. As time went on, social work education became more differentiated and divided into a focus on individuals and groups, on the one hand, and larger systems of organizations, community, and society on the other.

Today the differentiation of social work into clinical (micro) and community–administrative–policy–research (macro) sections is well accepted. Such separation was not always the case, especially at the beginning of the profession's development. Charity Organization Societies had both an interpersonal and a social change focus. Although the social change focus was not as strong, in a number of developments around 1900 in U.S. society, social change was heavily emphasized. Lincoln Steffens's book *The Shame of Our Cities* pointed to municipal evils and stimulated urban reform.[47] Upton Sinclair's work on the packing house industry and other evils made him a sort of American Charles Dickens.[48] The social gospel movement was another social action effort, a way in which Christian motives could be translated into social improvement as opposed to the development of individual sanctity. Schlesinger comments:

> Both the Social Gospel and social work had arisen in the late 19th century as nonpolitical responses to the miseries and injustices of the industrial order. Socially minded ministers began to remind their parishioners that Christians had duties toward

their fellowmen, that Christian morality was relevant to slums and sweatshops, and that the Christian task would not be completed until the social order itself had been Christianized. . . . When society was transformed by Christian faith "rotten politics and grinding monopolies would shrivel and disappear; under its banner light and beauty, peace and plenty, joy and gladness would be led in."

This goal, the advocates of the Social Gospel reckoned, could be achieved within history. The Kingdom of God would in due time realize itself on earth, but it could not be achieved by the churches alone. . . . [W]hat was faith for the apostles of the Social Gospel became works for the men and women of the settlement houses.[49]

It was fair to say, however, that the movement for social reform and social change was never as strong in the development of U.S. social work as the move for personal improvement. While Mary Richmond's *Social Diagnosis,* a book for those interested in social analysis and social work, focused on the broad range of social context within which an individual client found himself, it still tended to place more stress on the individual person rather than on changing the social structure.[50]

In a sense, then, social work developed in two streams, though as time went on these streams became uneven. One focus was clinical, stressing the individual, albeit in a family or community context; and this was an extension of the early religious ministrations and charity visitations. It articulated well with the individualistic focus of U.S. society and with themes that emphasized the development and preparation of the individual for competition and achievement. It also tended to articulate well with more traditional care-oriented roles of women, albeit now offered in a new context. The case worker would listen to and help the client, but the focus was individualistic and somewhat more passive with respect to the social structure.

The other stream involved social change. Administration, and community organization, somewhat oriented to social change, was, after its initial development, always a secondary emphasis in the field, although it is as old as the emphasis on individuals and continues to attract an interested and committed group of students. It is also the case that social work education has sought to give emphasis to both aspects in the curriculum.

During this period, social work's identification as a profession concerned primarily with the disadvantaged became fixed. In retrospect, there is no reason why social problems of any sort should be thought of as the particular problems of the disadvantaged or poor. Clearly, lack of money exacerbates almost any problem, but the difficulties of substance abuse, the pain of divorce, separation, the travails of child rearing, the need for adoptive and foster care, the problems of child abuse and spouse and sexual abuse, the difficulties of self-esteem, and the like, are not the unique province of any class, race, or gender. The fact that much social change was concerned with restructuring society to make more advantages available to those at the bottom of the social ladder may have been one of the reasons for its unpopularity in U.S. society.[51]

The period thus saw the development of a more individualistic focus and treatment as hallmarks of social work. But this emphasis in social work was firmly based on a concern for the poor. It was only when, in a sense, the entire nation became poor that an adjustment had to be made that allowed for more policy-oriented developments and capitalized on the earlier social reform themes. The Great Depression was a cataclysmic event in U.S. society and ushered in the era of public development.

THE ERA OF PUBLIC DEVELOPMENT, 1935–1970

Until the time the Social Security Act was passed and finally signed August 14, 1935, national public responsibility for the care and well-being of individual U.S. citizens had been minimal. Stemming from the Pierce veto in 1854, the line of federal negativism had been broken only by the Civil War pensions and the Freedman's Bureau. Important as these precursors were, it is also important to reemphasize that both were allowed to die. They did not become programmatic forebears of welfare state activities. Rather, they became policy antecedents that signaled future directions but were not themselves direct progenitors of public programs. The hostility and negativism toward the disadvantaged had become so much a characteristic of U.S. society that an earthquake was needed to change it: the Great Depression.

The facts of the Depression are widely familiar to most readers: the failure of the banks, the plight of the farmers, the scourge of urban poverty. All these problems were significant singly and together added up to major disaster. It was clear something had to be done, and the programs developed by Franklin Delano Roosevelt provided the exoskeleton of response. America was, euphemistically at least, throwing in much of its old hand and calling for a New Deal, hoping that it could be made to work.

The centerpiece of social legislation that remains with us today is the Social Security Act. Other programs (the Works Progress Administration, the Public Works Administration, the Civilian Conservation Corps, and the Farm Security Administration among others) have passed into memory, but the Social Security Act, out of which the major portion of federal monies are funneled to individual people, remains vital. Today it has 20 titles and under its umbrella are such varied programs as public welfare (AFDC), the program we know popularly as Social Security, but that is technically called Old Age Survivors Disability and Health Insurance (OASDHI), which includes Medicare, medical payments to the poor (Medicaid), insurance paid to individuals when they are laid off from their jobs (unemployment compensation), and other programs to help children (the Child Welfare Titles).

Vastly expanded since its original passage, the Social Security Act is the U.S. welfare state. Its beginnings did not include disability insurance, nor did they include medical payments to older or to poor individuals, although some of those ideas were recommended in early drafts of the act. As minimal as it was, especially in comparison to some other countries, the Social Security Act represented a radical departure for the average American citizen; it involved reliance on and cooperation with government to ensure the individual's own financial well-being.

A second factor supporting the development of the Social Security Act is also worth noting. The Depression was the most significant. It was the kind of transcendent social event that, like war, makes people forget their previous positions and seek new solutions. However, the United States had had depressions before. Indeed, the United States had had social security programs at the federal level before, too, in the form of the Freedman's Bureau and the Civil War Pensions. But now, in the 1930s, the tide of Jewish and Catholic immigration becomes an important second factor. These immigrants had been coming since the middle of the nineteenth century, and now their influence and orientation helped make a difference in overall public attitude, both because of their numbers and because of their arguments. These immigrants came to the United States with what might be called a charity conscience, a sense of responsibility for their fellows that immediately manifested itself in the development of social welfare agencies such as Catholic Charities, St. Vincent de Paul, and Jewish Family and Children's Service, among others. While not overstressing this factor, it is reasonable to argue that there was an affinity among the more recent immigrants for undertaking a public responsibility for the needy, something which they themselves did within their own religious and ethnic confines. These supporting factors combined with the Depression ushered in the era of public involvement.

However, an experience subsequent to the Depression cemented our conviction that the federal government not only could act effectively and efficiently in the solving of problems and gave millions of Americans a chance to participate in the solution. That experience, World War II, provided millions of Americans with a firsthand chance to see the government in successful operation. Many were in the armed services. Those who were not experienced government controls (rationing and wage and price controls) at home and saw how the government could work.

The combination of Depression social policy initiatives plus the positive and involving experience of the World War II ushered in the era of public development. The antigovernment orientation, characteristic of U.S. society from its very beginnings, was basically changed by these experiences.

Based on these events, U.S. citizens saw their government engage in forceful, vigorous action, and came to believe the government could deal with other problems as well. It is not surprising, therefore, that the president of the United States used the armed forces as a vehicle for one of the first modern federal attempts at desegregation. When President Harry Truman ordered the armed forces desegregated in 1948, he was taking a social policy initiative within the military context.

It must have been a curiosity to Americans, both black and white, who had fought in two military theaters to preserve democracy, equality and freedom to find that those same benefits were absent for many individuals in the very country that touted them. It must have occurred to many Americans that, if the U.S. government could take important steps to reduce suffering brought out by the Depression and could be victorious in a world conflict, then that same strength of purpose could be used to eradicate some of the residual social injustices that plagued our society. It is not surprising, therefore, that the Supreme Court in 1954, continuing the initiative already begun in the armed services, ruled in *Brown* v. *Board of Education* that separate but equal in the educational system was unconstitutional and opened the way for a rising tide of social legislation on a broad range of fronts. This Supreme Court was the same institution that in 1899, in the famous *Plessey* v. *Ferguson* case, had ruled that separate but equal was constitutional.

Americans do not think of the 1950s as a period of high social activism. It was a time for the country to get back to work after 20 years of disruption caused by the Depression and World War II. However, those events generated a force for change that would burst open in the 1960s.

The profession of social work was itself developing and consolidating the individualistic and clinical focus that was preeminent in the 1920s and 1930s and had been cemented in 1939 in a classic book by Virginia P. Robinson, *The Changing Psychology in Social Casework.* As she comments, "This study, then, will limit itself in history to following this trend through the background of influences leading up to the psycholog-ical emphasis of the present day."[52] Such psychological emphasis would characterize social work up until the advent of the social action push of the 1960s.

The presidential election in 1960 signaled the release of latent energies empha-sizing social change. The leaders of the 1960s, women and men in their forties and fifties, had experienced as younger individuals the power and purpose of government during the New Deal and World War II era. Surely it must have occurred to them that similar U.S. energies focused on social problems could yield similar gains. The time was ripe for change also. The Eisenhower years had been relatively quiescent (although the *Brown* v. *Board of Education* decision made by the Supreme Court in 1954 might have foretold of changes to come), and a rededication to the public purposes of citizens' roles was called for.

The singular phrase of John F. Kennedy, "Ask not what your country can do for you, but rather what you can do for your country," found ready acceptance by many citizens. First among these were young people in their twenties who had grown up with the desperations of Depression and the worries of war behind them. The effort to mobilize community strength found a home with these individuals and others. The Peace Corps was one example. First proposed on the steps of the Michigan Union at the University of Michigan, the idea caught on and became a major force. Later a domestic counterpart, VISTA (Volunteers in Service to America), also became important. Ken-nedy consciously modeled his presidency on the Roosevelt example and sought dra-matic and innovative social programs. The community emphasis with respect to problem solving was also manifest in a less well known program, but one of great impact with respect to the social work profession, the President's Committee on Juvenile Delin-quency and Youth Crime. This initiative developed by President Kennedy was spear-headed by his brother Robert and piggybacked its own mission on one previously developed by the Ford Foundation called the Great Cities Program. It was designed to help improve the quality of urban life. The Great Cities Program represented a departure from what had come to be the traditional social work approach (if traditional is understood as being within the past 15 to 20 years). The individualistic focus that had held sway now began to give way to a more social action and community organization focus. Regrettably, the field of social work was somewhat excluded from these efforts. Some of the influential political and social science actors in Washington appear to have thought that social work had failed in its mission to deal with poverty, and now it was someone else's turn.[53]

The Great Cities Program first focused on schools and hoped to improve school community relations, and thereby improve the performance of individual students within the school. Its starting point was the notion, loosely conceived, of school–com-munity climate. The idea of community competence was advanced and generalized. Communities that did well could be called competent communities.[54] Alternatively, it was thought, communities with much delinquency or other kinds of social problems lacked community cohesion in some way, and thus the job of the social engineer, social helper, and social worker was to strengthen the structure of the community, rather than work with individual persons in trouble.

For the first time, via money granted to the President's Committee on Juvenile Delinquency and Youth Crime, the federal government was channeling funds directly into city and community organizations. (Hitherto, the federal system of government had virtually required that funds go to states to be distributed to cities).[55] Community organization began to develop and expand within schools of social work and to achieve a relatively vigorous enrollment. Social change efforts were now more popular.

The period from the election of John F. Kennedy to the election of Ronald Reagan was a period of great social policy development within U.S. society. As one example, the 1962 amendments to the Social Security Act vastly expanded the role of social workers in the public sector. While the social work profession was excluded from the poverty program to a large degree, it was making headway in public welfare. Congress believed that if there were sufficient trained social welfare staff, problems of poverty could be solved. Unfortunately for the profession of social work in the public sector, this strategy backfired. For a variety of reasons, including increasing marital separation and increasing willingness of desubordination (which means the development of social processes that legitimized or destigmatized the receipt of welfare for some persons and in some quarters) of the poor to apply for assistance, the welfare rolls increased. Between 1960 and 1970, welfare rolls grew by over 140 percent[56] and social workers were accused of promoting welfare.[57] Rather than being taken as a successful result, many in society took a dim view of this welfare gain. In a sense, it was true. Social work had used the rhetoric of getting people off welfare. We were, thus, as a profession trapped by our claims when the rates went up.[58] The rights revolution occurring in the 1960s, which emphasized the rights of people to their entitlements, included the right to social support through public welfare. As people exercised this right, society began to reconsider its commitments to it.

The public sector was expanding in another way. The President's Committee on Juvenile Delinquency and Youth Crime was still active. With the assassination of President Kennedy, President Johnson wanted a program with his own stamp that also honored his populist commitments and interests. The Juvenile Delinquency Program of Kennedy became the Antipoverty Program of Johnson. Hundreds of cities across the country had Community Action Agencies (CAAs) that engaged in social action, client advocacy, and in general combined the provision of social service with client advocacy. These efforts at community change and empowerment gave support to and received support from the civil rights movement. They also interacted with the antiwar movement. United States incursions into Vietnam were drawing local and violent opposition in an increasingly large-scale way. In spite of the initial exclusion of the social work community from the Juvenile Delinquency efforts and the Poverty Program efforts, social workers participated anyway. Many social workers became staff members of these organizations, and the profession was well represented in the civil rights and antiwar movements. One early university-level war protest at the University of Michigan, a teach-in mode that was widely copied, was organized with the help of the community organization faculty of the School of Social Work there and also involved local social workers.

In short, the 1960s could be characterized as the intersection of three related movements: social rights, civil rights, and participatory rights. It is difficult to know where one set of concerns begins and the other ends. It was a heyday for new social policy.

Certainly, the call for social rights demanded the establishment of basic entitlements of financial and other social supports to allow more effective functioning among a broad range of U.S. citizens. It would prove to be an important advance.

"Civil rights" refers primarily to claims by African Americans and other minorities of color, women, and people of different sexual preferences to be free to do the same kinds of things and have the same kinds of civil entitlements that everyone else in the society enjoyed.

"Participatory rights" is our term to link together opposition to the war in Vietnam with other demands for involvement in making decisions that affect us. Not since the 1930s had there been such an explosion of rights reform.

The gains were not exclusively limited to the area of public social policy, although they were most prominently observed there. Legislation against discrimination, movements for affirmative action, improvements in access for the handicapped and differently abled, and so on, make a long list of social policy gains.

Also, a realm of what might be called private social policy began to develop at an accelerated pace.[59] In essence, private social policy consists of fringe benefits, or entitlements that come through the workplace or job and a portion of which are usually paid by the employer. The concept of such private social policy began or was at least given a substantial boost by the Social Security Act in the retirement area. Cohen[60] has said that at the time of Social Security (1935) there were about 700 to 1500 private pension plans in the entire United States. The employee–employer sharing provisions of the Social Security Act (FICA or Federal Insurance Contribution Act) created an important precedent for this kind of collaboration between the worker and the employer in the workplace. However, the fraction of salary that was paid in fringe benefits grew rapidly during this period, partly because of the rights revolution and general public support for such increases, and partly because at that time such benefits were not subject to federal tax.[61]

This period of governmental growth also saw a tremendous acceleration in programs for the elderly.[62] Perhaps of all groups, they were biggest gainers during the period of 1955 to the late 1970s. One impressive development was the indexing of Social Security benefits in December 1978 so that the benefits would keep up with inflation. The provision in 1965 of Medicare or medical care for those over 65 (and others receiving Social Security benefits of various sorts) was a major step forward. The Older Americans Act of July 1965 made social services available to a wide range of people. The Age Discrimination Act of September 1978 prohibited discrimination in employment on the basis of age. The Internal Revenue Service continued the policy of allowing additional exemptions for individuals over 65. A new tax benefit for older Americans was added when it became possible to sell an owner-occupied home if the owner was over 55 without paying taxes on the gain (February 1964).

Social policy for the older American was a landmark development in the history of U.S. social policy. It had several unique characteristics. First, it was largely public. Some key federal programs have been mentioned, but we should not forget efforts by state and local governments expressed through taxes to provide public funds for the assistance of the elderly.

A second feature was its rapidity. While most social policy in the United States took years to develop, policy toward the elderly developed largely between 1955 and the late 1970s.

A third feature of policy toward the elderly is its universality. Policy toward the elderly is amazingly free of the categorization that characterizes other American social policy. We have not sought to identify particular groups of elderly as eligible for this, that, or the other program. While it is true that Supplemental Security Income is aimed at the poor elderly, that program is the exception rather than the rule.[63]

In general, programs to aid those over 65 are available on the basis of age alone, whether that program is Social Security eligibility, social services through the area Agency on Aging, or one of the many senior citizen discounts on drugs, groceries, meals, and the like.

A last feature of the development of social policy toward the elderly has been its good-heartedness. In general, social aid to individuals has been an uphill battle characterized by lots of suspicion. In the case of aid to older citizens, it has been more of a competition among public and private groups and state, local, and federal agencies to take a lead in providing various kinds of assistance.

This period of policy development and expansion came to an end with the election of Ronald Reagan to the presidency.

THE RETRADITIONALIZATION OF U.S. SOCIETY

The period after the election of President Reagan is certainly paradoxical, with conflicting streams and countervailing pressures. Nevertheless, it seems to be most typically characterized by a retraditionalization of U.S. society: a call to more traditional, private, and personal values, involving a declining interest in the public sphere and a refocus on individualism and individual achievement. An interest in traditional religion is on the increase, whether it be a return to orthodoxy among young Jews, the rise of the Catholic charismatic movement, or Protestant retraditionalization as manifest in the moral majority. Nowhere is this trend more clear than in the area of social policy. And negativism toward the poor and disadvantaged, reminiscent of the period of 1834 in England, began to surface again.

When he was running for president in 1964, Senator Barry Goldwater, Sr. (R., Arizona) mentioned the possibility of cutting Social Security. At that time, the suggestion was taken as evidence of his unfitness for the office. Anyone who could suggest such a bizarre tinkering with a hallowed U.S. institution should be viewed with utmost suspicion. By the time Reagan was elected to office, cuts in Social Security had been initiated, certain Social Security benefits were going to be taxed, and he was proposing even more cuts. This exemplifies a change in the tenor of social policy support within the U.S. polity. (Of course, as in any characterization of the political world, there was a great range of views by individuals in both major parties.)

What was once a growth industry has now become a vast wasteland of cutbacks. Social support has been replaced by social suspicion and social scarcity. Once again, we are on the downside of the welfare policy cycle in which programs are asserted not to have worked and to be too expensive, inappropriate, inconsistent with tradition, and so forth. The entire country seems to be disappointed with government activity and is seeking a return to traditional values. Trust in government is very low.[64]

But a new interest in voluntary agencies has sprung up. The Urban Institute did a major study of the voluntary sector and found it to be substantially greater than anyone had thought.[65] While there are many ways of counting nonprofits, the number was found to be up to 750,000, and the annual cash flow, including an estimate for volunteer contributions, was over $200 billion a year. It is so big that writers now call it the third sector, along with business and government.

This finding should come as no surprise. The growth of the entire society during the 1950–1980 period should have and did reflect growth within the nonprofit sector itself. If public and private social policy expanded, the third sector was not far behind. However, most attention was paid to the growth of the public sector in an anachronistic belief that the nonprofit sector was tiny and of minor significance. It was thus not until recently that the true size and scope of the nonprofit sector became clear.

The modern retraditionalization period has emphasized cutbacks across the total spectrum of human services. In addition to cuts in Social Security, reductions in or cancellations of other governmental programs were successful. Aid to housing, medical care for the poor, programs in education, and others have all been cut back at the federal level. Budgets of voluntary agencies have been cut both by the downplaying of federal contracting and grants, but also through increased pressure on and a decrease in private contributions to them.[66] Changes in tax policy have meant that less of the money taxpayers give to charity can be deducted from federal tax. And, to add to the woes of these agencies, both public and private demands on them have escalated sharply. Drug problems and AIDS, problems with children, and racial tensions are just a few of the many new and costly concerns facing the agency community.

Other social areas that have been supportive of social policy activity have also shown declines. Union membership, for example, is falling off and the potency of unions is decreasing. Interest in social change as manifest through the level of community organization and social policy enrollments in schools of social work has also been declining, along with the rate of increase in social work enrollments at the master's level.

These forces did not emerge overnight. Rather a rise in conservatism among the American people was manifested even during the period of increased government growth.[67] The election of Ronald Reagan was a crystalizing political event. It corrected a structural lag. The values of society had already shifted, but the political structures needed time to catch up.

The field of social work itself has not escaped these traditionalizing factors. A tremendous increase in the private practice of social work has been developing. The National Association of Social Workers Clinical Directory lists the names of more than 80,000 individuals, although not all are in private practice. In most schools of social work, a decline in interest in macro social work methods has been paralleled by a surge in interest in clinical training.

What will happen in the future? We believe that social welfare operates within a framework of competing values that we all share. It is the back and forth adjustment from one set of values to the other that causes the cyclical fluctuations in social policy as it seeks to adjust itself to those values.[68] Hence, it is logical from this perspective to expect an adjustment as we move from one set of values to another. Commitments to equity (essential fairness, or providing people with what they deserve based on the contributions they make) on the one hand compete with commitments to adequacy (providing people with the needed minimums) on the other. Interest in private sponsorship competes with interest in public auspices. Interests in personal achievement find themselves juxtaposed with family commitments. In short, there is a tide with respect to social policy. Indeed, Hirschman, suggests that this ebb and flow of preference exists in most areas.[69] From a social welfare point of view, it suggests a hopeful perspective. Times are more negative now but may well be more positive in the future.

The election of President Bush appears, at the moment, to continue these trends. In his famous phrase "a thousand points of light," Bush has called for more support for the voluntary sector. Yet he has also called for a "kinder, gentler" society, an idea that has been picked up by thousands of speakers across the country. Whether that means the country is seeking a return to community concern remains to be seen. Social workers are still in need of more support for agencies and programs.

Urbanism, Social Exploitation, and Social Welfare

The periodization of social welfare helps us to reflect on the march of events through time. Such a perspective focuses on change. There are however, some constancies in the social welfare arena. Two that are the most central are the rise of the cities and the ongoing process of social exploitation. Both represent social problems to which social work is a contemporary response, and they also represent a fundamental source of social work interest and concern.

THE CITY AND SOCIAL WORK

From many perspectives, the profession of social work is a creature of the city and of the process of urbanization to the extent that urbanization creates a large concentration of people, many with special needs. The city requires institutions to provide assistance to its citizens, although it is certainly true that many of the problems of concern to social work exist in rural and suburban areas as well.

The concentration of problems within the urban place makes it more difficult to ignore them and brings the needs into sharper focus. The city represents a freedom from more traditional value perspectives, which is the kind of openness that permits social work to develop in the first place. Not only is there freedom from traditional values, to some degree there is also freedom from traditional roles. Urbanization therefore represents a structural source of problems that must be met and a structural source of freedoms from conventional constraints so that new ways to meet these needs can be developed.

With respect to the history of social work, the kinds of problems presented by the city were legion. The presence of both medical and psychological disabilities within components of the population was clearly present. The city has also served as a magnet and transfer point for hundreds of thousands of individuals uprooted from more traditional homelands, who either voluntarily or involuntarily found the city the only source of potential support. The city has been a center for displaced persons.[70]

On the more macro level, the city has been a source of potential problems for political leaders, the resolution of which often required a type of social policy focus. The large number of individuals concentrated in the city made them a source of concern for rulers.[71] This concern with the urban masses continues up to the present day and was a central aspect of Piven and Cloward's argument in their book *Regulating the Poor.*[72] They felt that providing aid for cities and city populations was essential to develop political support for the presidencies of John Kennedy and Lyndon Johnson. Naturally, the urban riots in many U.S. cities during the 1960s drew attention to the role of the city in the political spectrum and made the city a target for both support and control.

The city has been a stimulus for social work efforts for another reason. Historically, in U.S. sociology the city was seen as a source of social disorganization. The freedom from traditional bonds could, when looked at in another context, be seen as the genesis of such disorganization. In many ways the city represented what Stein called the eclipse of community.[73] This apparent absence of community within the city was one of the energizing factors for the specialty of community organization. In recent years, however, more intensive study of African-American and ethnic communities (see, for example, Whyte and Stack[74]) has shown that subgroups in the urban place often retain a vigorous, well-developed form[75] of communal identification.

Not only has the city been a source of the kinds of problems that social work deals with, but it has also suffered from the absence of traditional helping networks. The community helping system (neighbors helping other neighbors and receiving help in return) of more rural areas was not present here and thus needs were less likely to be met and to be more prominent. Hence, social work developed in part to provide aid within an urban context.

Finally, the freedoms that generated problems for which help was required also freed individuals from traditional role and task limitations to be available as recruits to the new enterprise of professional helping. The role of women and of the link between evolving urban problems and the energy released by the emancipation of women is a case in point. But other individuals also wanted to help—out of religious motivation, social concern, or a willingness to help and an attraction to the problems presented in the city.

In sum, the urbanization process concretized and exacerbated the problems with which we deal. It was the locus of both the problems and of the energy to deal with them. Social work and the city are inextricably interrelated.

Today, in their complexity and interdependency, urban problems represent a continuing challenge, as in the founding days of the profession at the beginning of the century. One major mission of social work will be to find and fashion ways to be helpful to and within the urban context.

SOCIAL EXPLOITATION

A second idea that inspirits social work and provides it with energy and form is the concept of social exploitation.[76] Perhaps more than any other profession, social work reacts against and seeks to redress and correct social exploitation.

Social exploitation is a regular and pervasive feature of human society. In general, the sum total of needs and wants in any given society will at any given time exceed its resources. For this reason, all societies are plagued with a resource deficit and must find ways to make up the difference between the resources they have available to meet needs and wants and the demand for those resources. The structural solution to this problem is social exploitation. Social exploitation exists when society can force, induce, or otherwise convince individuals and organizations within the society to perform social tasks at less than market rates.

Over historical time, a range of mechanisms has been used to achieve this goal. Slavery is perhaps the most outstanding example of a mechanism society uses to secure free or cheap resources.[77] But discrimination of all sorts, including the exploitation of minorities, women, children, and other subgroups in various societies, is a form of social exploitation.

Sometimes force is not the mechanism used; rather, individuals are convinced to donate their services on a reduced fee basis. In this specific sense, voluntarism could be viewed as a form of social exploitation.[78] Thus, the general problem of how to get more resources to meet rising social needs and wants is a constant social problem.

Among the central tasks of social work are the prevention and amelioration of social exploitation. The achievement of social justice does not mean that there are not differences in the world, nor does it mean that some individuals are not healthier, wealthier, or wiser than others. It does mean that such health, wealth, and wisdom cannot be built on the forced, or perhaps even willing, sacrifices of other individuals. For this reason, the task of social work, with respect to social justice, is unending, because the pressure for social injustice is pervasive and continuing, and the other roles of social work with respect to achieving social justice are less systemic. Individual victims of particular aspects of injustice are assisted in finding a more comfortable and self-enhancing position for themselves within any given society.

To some extent, this mode of intervention continues to support directly and indirectly the more systemic forms of injustice. Hence, the role of the social worker is to balance micro change against macro change, the improvement of the condition of an individual against the improvement of the condition of many individuals. Macro change, especially with respect to social exploitation and social injustice, is the change that helps a broad range of individuals and meets a systemic need. On the other hand, changes of such magnitude and scope are usually slow, and we do not wish to put any particular individual on hold until appropriate adjustments in the social condition can be effected. Hence, there is also an appeal to the micro, more focused work with individuals and groups.

It should also be stressed that there is some independence between micro change and macro change. All individual distress is certainly not the result of systemic exploitation and the perils of urbanization. For example, particular psychoses may have biological and intrapsychic elements as their cause. Such problems need to be addressed at those levels. Conversely, even if we were able to effect macro social structural change sufficient to "make the world safe for democracy" or some other large-scale social goal, individual problems of substance abuse, health-related concerns, self-esteem, sexual preference, and so on, would continue to arise. The perspective stressed here is to avoid the reduction of problems from one level of social analysis to another. We reject the arguments of those who see all individual problems as manifestations of illness at the social system level and hence curable by interventions at that level. Similarly, we seek to avoid seeing the social system as merely an aggregation of individual difficulties and discontent.

Conclusion

In this initial chapter we have portrayed U.S. social welfare history in a broad way by slicing that history into comprehensible periods. The attempt to show the continuities and connections over time has been an important goal. Thus, time was spent on English history as a starting point for considering U.S. history. For example, the concern raised in the Poor Law reform of 1834 surfaced again in the work of Charles Murray and George Gilder in the Reagan presidency.[79]

A second effort was to emphasize two key themes that have been of great importance with respect to the history of social welfare and social work. One of these is the issue of urbanization and the concerns, problems, and opportunities that the city has brought forth. The other is social exploitation, the apparently unalterable propensity of societies to generate a set of needs and wants greater than any given supply of resources. The pressure here to exploit certain individuals or classes of individuals is strong and pervasive across societies and over time. For this reason, social injustice is always present and a target for social work and intervention.

Part of the history of social work involves a consciousness or commitment that is not so tied to material acquisition as is perhaps true of other occupational realms. Hence, social work in the business community is being met with ambivalence and uncertainty. We will discuss these issues in more detail in later chapters.

Notes

1. Lipset called America "the first new nation." See Seymour M. Lipset, *The First New Nation* (New York: Basic Books, 1963).
2. Coll defines it like this: "Social welfare is an organized effort to insure a basic standard of decency in relation to the physical and mental well-being of the citizenry." Blanche Coll, "Social Welfare: History," in John Turner, ed., *Encyclopedia of Social Work,* 17th ed. (New York: National Association of Social Workers, 1977), Vol. 2, p. 1503.
3. Karl de Schweinitz, *England's Road to Social Security* (New York: A.S. Barnes [Perpetua], 1961), p. 28. Copyright 1943 by the University of Pennsylvania Press.
4. Ibid.
5. Eric Fromm, *Escape from Freedom* (New York: Holt, Rinehart and Winston, 1941).
6. One remnant of that today in Boston is the Boston Common.
7. De Schweinitz, *England's Road to Social Security,* p. 29.
8. Ibid., p. 21.
9. Ibid., p. 40.
10. Ibid., p. 72; see also Karl Polanyi, *The Great Transformation*(Boston: Beacon Press, 1957) and Marc Blaug, "The Myth of the Old Poor Law and the Making of the New," *Journal of Economic History,* 23, 2 (June 1963). Interestingly, according to de Schweinitz, there were also systems of work relief administered through the local parish and other systems through which available work could be spread around.
11. Polanyi, *The Great Transformation,* p. 88, and Blaug, "The Myth of the Old Poor Law," feel that the results were due more to high unemployment in the Speenhamland parishes.
12. On supplemental security income, see W. C. Birdsall, *Does the Generosity of Welfare Encourage Participation?* (Ann Arbor: University of Michigan, 1987). The specific programs will be discussed later in the chapter.
13. By and large, we have resolved this conflict in favor of what Ehrenreich calls "the family wage system." She argues that the fundamental deal that has been made by society with

respect to wages (in Western society, at least) is that the wage of males is designed to take into account the fact that the male typically has a wife and family to feed. Thus, for women, wages would be regarded as supplemental, erroneous as that view is in fact. The feminization of poverty in modern America is a result of these supplemental wages becoming family income for the single woman and her family. Barbara Ehrenreich, *The Hearts of Men* (Garden City, New York: Doubleday & Co., 1983), pp. 2–13. See also Lenore J. Weitzman, *The Divorce Revolution* (New York: The Free Press, 1985). Hence, the idea of the market was and is a part of a negotiation process. When we think about the macroeconomic determinants of the wage system itself, there is no particular reason for minimum wages unless a social rather than an economic purpose is to be served by them. While we personally agree with this social purpose, it does exercise a confounding effect. We might wish, for example, to propose an alternative system in which social needs (basic health care coverage, insurance, disability coverage, and so on) are met through a collective source, thus freeing the marketplace to deal with more directly economic issues. While it seems we are a long way in the United States from having an economic wage and a social wage, it is a perspective worth serious consideration. Part of the reason that such an approach could make some sense is because of the overlap in bases for calculating wages and/or benefits, particularly at the lower end. While Ehrenreich asserts that we have made a family wage agreement in the society, this agreement is hidden and generally unclear. With the exception of medical care benefits as part of the fringe benefit package, wages do not take account of family needs in any explicit sense. This problem is particularly acute at the lower end of the wage scale. Here it is possible, if we take the lowest wage at any given point in a country's history and divide it by family size, to have a per capita family income that is simply inadequate. It is at this point, the explicit taking account of family size, that public programs tend to be more adequate since they always (or almost always) do take explicit account of family size. Hence, if a person gets a grant from the Aid to Families with Dependent Children program, to take one example, the basis of the grant is specifically pegged to the number of people receiving it. Thus, because of the different bases for the calculation of wage versus benefit, it is possible for an individual at the lower end of the scale to make more on welfare than in the marketplace (and in making this statement we are not taking into account fringe benefit differences of the wage package or fringe benefit analogues such as Medicaid and food stamps in the grants package).

14. De Schweinitz, *England's Road to Social Security,* p. 119.
15. Ibid., p. 124.
16. Ibid., p. 127. It is curious that on August 14, 1935, 101 years later, President Franklin D. Roosevelt signed the Social Security Act into law in the United States.
17. For the development of this idea, see William Ryan, *Equality* (New York: Pantheon Books, 1981).
18. See John E. Tropman, "Public Welfare," *Sociology and Social Welfare* 3, 3 (January 1976). One criticism of this study was that it did not account for the special benefits that welfare recipients received. While this criticism is correct, it is important to look then at the fringe benefits that nonrecipients received, so that the ratio of fringe benefits for the non-disadvantaged can be compared to those for the disadvantaged.
19. For a full discussion, see Sol Tax and Larry Krucoff, "Social Darwinism," in David Sills, ed. *International Encyclopedia of the Social Sciences,* Vol. 14 (New York: Free Press, 1968).
20. De Schweinitz, *England's Road to Social Security,* p. 146; George Gilder, *Wealth and Poverty* (New York: Basic Books, 1981); and Charles Murray, *Losing Ground—American Social Policy, 1950–1980* (New York: Basic Books, 1984).
21. De Schweinitz, *England's Road to Social Security,* p. 146.
22. Ibid., pp. 197–198.
23. Ibid., p. 188.
24. Ibid., p. 191.
25. Ibid., p. 197.
26. Ibid., p. 195.

27. Ibid., p. 229.

28. Ibid., pp.230–231.

29. Based on John E. Tropman, "The Constant Crisis," *California Sociologist,* 1, 1 (Winter 1978).

30. Philip Slater, *The Pursuit of Loneliness* (Boston: Beacon Press, 1970).

31. See John Naisbett, *Megatrends* (New York: Warner Books, 1982).

32. Perhaps that is one reason, too, why planning is so difficult; the checks make action difficult, as indeed they were supposed to.

33. Harry Girivitz, "Social Welfare," in Sills, ed., *International Encyclopedia,* Vol. 16, p. 513.

34. This periodization is similar, especially in the early segments, to those used by Joan Axin and Herman Levin, *Social Welfare* (New York: Dodd, Mead & Co., 1975), and the reader is referred to the excellent outline of significant dates in U.S. welfare history in C. Alexander and D. N. Weber, "Social Welfare: Historical Dates," in Turner, ed., *Encyclopedia of Social Work,* 17th ed., pp. 1497–1503.

35. Ralph and Muriel Pumphrey, eds., *The Heritage of American Social Work* (New York: Columbia University Press, 1961), p. 132.

36. David Fischer, *Growing Old in America* (New York: Oxford University Press, 1977).

37. W. J. Rorabaugh, *The Alcoholic Republic: An American Tradition* (New York: Oxford University Press, 1979). There is justice to this claim. Rorabaugh points out that the per capita consumption of alcohol in the 1820s was the highest it has ever been in the country. If there were any roaring 20s in our society, it was certainly the 1820s.

38. For further discussion, see Joseph Gusfield, *Symbolic Crusade* (Urbana: University of Illinois Press, 1963).

39. See A. Orloff and T. Skocpol, "Explaining the Politics of Public Spending," *American Sociological Review,* 49, 6 (December 1984).

40. Blanche D. Coll, "Social Welfare: History," in Turner, ed., *Encyclopedia of Social Work,* Vol. 2, p. 1507.

41. We wish to enter an important caveat to this discussion. In most discussions of social Darwinism, and actual Darwinism, the concept of fittest is never defined or it is defined in a way that is tautological, that is, those who survive must be the fittest; hence those characteristics associated with those that survive are in fact the ones we need to be fit. We are not convinced on a priori theoretical grounds that the fittest necessarily means anything in particular. It could be the survival of the strongest, the survival of the smartest, the survival of the wealthiest, and so forth. It may be, for example, that one definition of the fittest is aggressiveness. If this were so, then the theory could be rewritten as the survival of the most aggressive. The implicit assumption, however, that those characteristics that survive are most functional (or best) for the society should be examined very carefully. In our judgment, there is no a priori reason for linking the two (that is, survival characteristics and social functionality). An alternative and popular formulation, "nice guys finish last," suggests that individuals with very desirable characteristics in the social world might well not survive. Our point is to indicate that the discussion concerning the survival of the fittest concept has been much too loose, because fittest has no inherent meaning, and the statement becomes a tautology and could be read, "survival of those who survive."

42. Sol Tax and Larry S. Krucoff, "Social Darwinism," in Sills, ed., *International Encyclopedia,* Vol. 14, pp. 403,404.

43. James Leiby, "Social Welfare: History of Basic Ideas," in Turner, ed., *Encyclopedia of Social Work,* p. 1517.

44. Arthur Schlesinger, Jr., *The Crisis of the Old Order* (Boston: Houghton Mifflin, 1957), p. 24. It is perhaps no coincidence then that the two nascent developing fields, sociology and social work, did not develop more conjointly. Perhaps the new professors of the new discipline of sociology at the new University of Chicago were anxious about their status and felt that they could not advance it by aligning with women from social work. The women from social work, as Schlesinger indicated, were powerful, persuasive forces in their own right and surely had no wish to subordinate themselves to males in academia.

See Mary Jo Deegan, *Jane Adams and the Men of the Chicago School: 1892–1918.* (New Brunswick, NJ: Transaction Books, 1988).

45. Leiby, "Social Welfare," p. 1521.

46. The Chicago and Columbia Schools of Social Work are mentioned here because they were the first.

47. Lincoln Steffens, *The Shame of the Cities* (New York: P. Smith, 1948), originally published in 1904.

48. Upton Sinclair, *The Jungle* (New York: Doubleday, Page & Co., 1906).

49. Schlesinger, *The Crisis of the Old Order,* p. 24.

50. Mary Richmond, *Social Diagnosis* (New York: Russell Sage, 1917). This emphasis may itself have had something to do with gender. The development of the lady bountiful image in social work, with the worker as a counselor and understanding person, fit more closely with some aspects of the traditional role of women. Florence Nightingale seemed more appropriate than Joan of Arc.

51. Sometimes though, a different view was taken. As Leiby comments, "At our present stage of historical understanding it appears that the peculiar character of American social work, in contrast with that in England and even more with analogous functions in other industrialized nations of Europe, is largely the consequence of its affinities with American movements for social reform . . . changes aimed at the protection of the vulnerable or assistance to the disadvantaged. Whereas the Protestant ethic emphasized individual responsibility, discipline, and achievement in a vocation, the various reforms associated, often loosely or vaguely, with 'social welfare' sought in many ways to insure that the individual was not denied certain essential rights or a fair chance to become responsible, disciplined, and achieving." Leiby, "Social Welfare," p. 1520.

52. Virginia Robinson, *A Changing Psychology of Social Casework* (Chapel Hill: University of North Carolina Press, 1934), p. xv.

53. The range of theories of juvenile delinquency (personal fault, problematic parents, bad neighborhood, and so on) were brilliantly captured by Stephen Sondheim in his words to the song "Officer Krupke" in Leonard Bernstein's famous musical *West Side Story.* But one of the causes of delinquency, "I've got a social disease," brought the chorus out singing "So take him to a social worker," and thus makes fun of social work, and embodies the disaffection that society felt for social work at the time.

54. This idea came from Leonard Cottrell and his book *Interpersonal Competence and Divorce* (Chicago: University of Chicago Press, 1955). Cottrell believed that certain individuals coped better than others. This idea became generalized. Certain communities, organizations, and schools seemed to cope better than others. Today we might speak of this as organizational culture or community culture and ask about the set of norms and beliefs that characterize outstanding performers. In fact, a number of important variables need to be taken into account. At that time, however, it seemed that through mobilizing and organizing the community, the organization, or the neighborhood, the goal would be accomplished.

55. The anomaly of U.S. cities will be mentioned in the next section. They are creatures of the state and have no true independent status. They exist largely at the sufferance of state legislatures, frequently, and especially at that time, were dominated by rural individuals with little sympathy for "citified ways." Richard Cloward at a talk in Ann Arbor in 1969 has argued that it was imperative for the Kennedy administration to find some way to channel funds directly into the cities and to do so in a way that would only minimally irritate governors and other state officials. The President's Committee on Juvenile Delinquency and Youth Crime provided one such vehicle.

56. Cases (in thousands) were: in 1960, 5,715.9; in 1970, 13,379. *Encyclopedia of Social Work,* 1977, Table 30, p. 1649.

57. Desubordination is a juxtaposition of the phrase Joe Fegin used in the title of his book, *Subordinating the Poor* (Englewood Cliffs, NJ: Prentice Hall, 1975). For a variety of reasons, many Americans who would have been entitled to receive welfare were not enrolling, because, in part, they apparently believed that it was not right to accept money

from this source. Social workers did, of course, encourage people to use what they were entitled to have. Perhaps more important, though, was the general explosion of rights in the 1960s period.

58. As a result of some of the negative comments during this period, a cap was placed on the amount of federally reimbursable money states could spend for social services (states, of course, could spend as much beyond this cap as they chose).

59. For a discussion, see Lawrence Root, "Employee Benefits and Income Security," and S. Quattrociocchi, "Fringe Benefits as Private Social Policy," in John E. Tropman, Milan Dluhy, and Roger Lind, eds., *New Strategic Perspectives on Social Policy* (Elmsford, NY: Pergamon Press, 1981).

60. Wilbur J. Cohen, personal conversation, 1980.

61. In the early 1990s, the fraction of salary that is provided in this way is around 28 percent.

62. For further discussion, see W. Lammers, *Public Policy and the Aging* (Washington, DC: CQ Press, 1983).

63. Supplemental Security Income (SSI) became a part of the Social Security Act in 1974. It consolidated three previous welfare programs (Old Age Assistance [OAA], Aid to the Blind [AB], and Aid to the Permanently and Totally Disabled [APTD]) which had been administered by the old welfare administration through local departments of social services into a supplemental program administered through Social Security Administration offices.

64. See John E. Tropman, *Public Policy Opinion and the Elderly* (Westport, CT: Greenwood Press, 1987).

65. See Elmer J. Tropman and John E. Tropman, "Voluntary Agencies," in Ann Minahan, ed., *Encyclopedia of Social Work,* 18th ed. (Silver Spring MD: National Association of Social Workers, 1987).

66. It is no surprise that, at the same time the voluntary sector is being asked to pick up the slack, government contributions to the sector are declining. Such inconsistencies are part of an overall inconsistency, as Murray Edelman has pointed out in his book *Political Language: Words That Succeed and Policies That Fail* (New York: Academic Press, 1977). In this particular case, the government is responding to a nationally expressed desire to cut social services. Its frequent statements to the voluntary sector to pick up the slack are merely that, statements that are not really designed to be matched by actions.

67. Seymour M. Lipset and William Schneider, *The Confidence Gap* (New York: The Free Press, 1983), and Tropman, *Public Policy Opinion and the Elderly.*

68. For further discussion, see John E. Tropman, *American Values and Social Welfare* (Englewood Cliffs, NJ: Prentice Hall, 1989).

69. Albert O. Hirshman, *Shifting Involvements* (Princeton, NJ: Princeton University Press, 1982).

70. This concern goes back as far as ancient Rome and the cultural role continues to the present day. In medieval times, individuals who were able to spend a year and a day in the city were free of their feudal obligations (but also lost their feudal entitlements).

71. This problem again goes back as far as ancient Rome, where individuals detached from traditional mores, especially males, and often unemployed could be potential sources of civil unrest. The Roman games represented a sort of early "urban assistance program," providing bread and circuses to such individuals in order to keep them entertained and out of trouble.

72. Frances F. Piven and Richard Cloward, *Regulating the Poor* (New York: Pantheon Books, 1971).

73. Maurice Stein, *The Eclipse of Community* (Princeton, NJ: Princeton University Press, 1960).

74. William F. Whyte, *Street Corner Society* (Chicago: University of Chicago Press, 1943); Carol Stack, *All Our Kin* (New York: Harper & Row, 1974).

75. In a classic and still unrecognized paper, C. Wright Mills looked into "The Professional Ideology of Social Pathologists" (1941). Mills showed that the assertion of urban disorganization was largely the product of people who had themselves been characterized by a farm to city migration. He argues that people from this kind of rural background would

naturally see the city as disorganized in part because its forms of community were unfamiliar to them within the context of their own experience. C. Wright Mills, "The Professional Ideology of Social Pathologists," in Irving Lewis Horowitz, ed., *Power, Politics, and People* (New York: Ballantine Books, 1963.)

76. This section is based on John E. Tropman "Social Exploitation," unpublished manuscript (Ann Arbor: University of Michigan, 1990).

77. Karl Marx identified many historical modes of exploitation. But we should not become fixed on the exploitation of workers by capitalists as the only form of securing efforts of citizens inexpensively. At other historical times, other forms of exploitation may be prominent.

78. Obviously, the motivation and the function may differ. An individual may volunteer for social or religious reasons. However, the act of volunteering for free may allow others to get much more than their share of societal resources.

79. For elaboration, refer to Gilder, *Wealth and Poverty,* and Murray, *Losing Ground.*

CHAPTER 2
Social Work, Social Science, and Social Problems

Introduction

Social work, like all professions, prefers to think of itself as theory based. (In brief, theory is a statement of the relationships among ideas, usually involving cause and effect.) The social sciences are the obvious place for such theoretical development to occur, and social science may serve social work the way the biological sciences serve medicine. Especially in recent years, social work has drawn heavily from the social sciences in areas such as individual development theory, group theory, family theory, organizational theory, theory of state action, and theory of society. However general, all schools of social work have requirements in social science and usually offer some social-science-related content to Bachelor of Social Work and Masters of Social Work degree candidates. And social work courses in research rely on the methods of scientific research.

But there is also tension between the enterprise of science and its application through social work as a result of different orientations. This chapter explores the occasionally contentious relationships in these two areas and reflects and highlights some of the key contributions and contributors.

Social work and social science, in spite of differences, are each concerned with social problems. Each of these three areas (social work, social science, and social problems) deals with the same essential subject matter, the behavior and interactions of people. But their realms of concern, although intersecting, are also different.

SOCIAL WORK AND SOCIAL SCIENCE

The relationship of the social work profession to the various social sciences has been one of ambivalence. On the one hand, the profession not only needs the theory of science, but it also needs the methods of science. And social work has a long history of relationships with several social science disciplines, sociology and psychology especially.

On the other hand, there is tension: social workers *do,* social scientists *reflect;* social workers want to *change* the world, social scientists want to *understand* the world; social workers are *engaged in the world,* social scientists are *removed from the world;* social work wants *practical solutions to pressing and troubling human problems,* social scientists want *to fit the pieces together to solve the human puzzle.*

In spite of these differences, each needs the other, albeit at arm's length. Social work needs social science for ideas and tools. This relationship is obvious. It is perhaps a little less obvious why social science needs social work. But there are at least three reasons:

1. Anomalies (individual aberrant cases) are found in social work practice that social science cannot explain, and which thus provide a challenge to social science.

2.   Social work practice provides a locus for testing the ideas of social science.
3.   Complex problems (collective occurrences) are presented that stretch the limits of the science.

Despite these obvious interlinks, these tensions have often led to separation, with the discipline and the profession each working in its own corner. Let us consider the relationships a little more specifically.

SOCIAL SCIENCE AND SOCIAL PROBLEMS

Social problems are those fields or areas or realms that are commonly identified as of concern to individuals and society, such as alcoholism, racism, spouse abuse, mental illness, and the like. Social science has tried to both understand them and be helpful with respect to them.

Social scientists have had many different kinds of relationships with the social problems fields and with specific social problems. One common theme was an attempt to use the methods and results of science to assist in the solution to such problems. In social science there was an attempt to model the natural science impact. Thus, much as natural science helped in the solution to natural problems (disease is a very good example here), it seemed that social science could help in the solution to social problems. Early in the development of social science, the scientific philanthropy movement reflected this interest.[1]

The goals of any science are four, each of which has an implication for social problems. First is methods of measurement: how to observe, how to record observations, how to report, and, throughout, how to measure what we are supposed to measure. Accurate description is certainly a goal in all science. The early social statisticians were important here. For example, Henry Mayhew's *London Labor and London Poor* is a detailed description that most likely aided the Charity Organization Society of London in developing its programs.[2]

Analysis (probing for underlying uniformities and relationships) and explanation (probing for causes) are a second goal. Such activities are, ultimately, theory development.

Third, science is also interested in what are the antecedent (previous), subsequent (coming after), and corelative (happening at the same time) conditions of a particular social event. For example, we might understand something about divorce. There could even be a theory of divorce. But social scientists and social workers are interested as well in questions like "What leads up to divorce?" and "What are the subsequent impacts of divorce?" And they are concerned with what happens in life's other spheres while divorce is proceeding. For instance, "How is work life affected by divorce?"

Fourth, science has a goal of predicting what will happen. Forecasting events is a universal human desire. Examples like forecasting the weather are familiar to us. As complex as that activity is, forecasting more complex issues, such as levels of illness and the differential likelihood of certain specific populations being affected, is an important goal of science. And we would hope in the future to be able to predict such things as which marriages are headed for trouble or which children might become victims of child abuse.

SOCIAL PROBLEMS

Social problems are groups of behavior that a particular society finds objectionable, troubling, or in need of change. In this context, "social" can have several different connotations, although each with the same result—concern.[3]

One meaning of "social" is "collective" as in "social change." It emphasizes the problems brought by social change. A second meaning of "social" refers to the difficulties that arise from interactions among people, as in social disease. Here, interconnections are stressed. A third meaning of "social" refers to problems of those at the bottom of the economic and/or cultural ladder, as in "social deprivation." In this usage, social class meanings are brought to the forefront.

Each of these meanings can and tends to imply one or more of the others, especially as used in common conversation about social problems. Nonetheless, societal concern and social work intervention are appropriate in all three instances.

Social work seeks to use scientific information to control difficult social problems. Social work has not been unique in this desire. As Malinowski has pointed out, society has always sought to control life forces through the use of explanations.[4] At different times and in different cultures, human events have been explained in magical terms,[5] as the work of evil spirits, as religious in nature, such as through manifestations of God's will, or most recently in human history as a scientific phenomenon, like sibling rivalry (in this case, psychological science is used).

As Malinowski suggested, magic, science, and religion are functional substitutes for each other. For this reason, practitioners of each are often in conflict with practitioners of the others. For example, a physical illness may be treated by scientific medicine; but other individuals may use prayer or magical potions.

Historical Perspective on Social Thought

To introduce the specific theories and theorists that have helped inform social work practice, we will begin with four classic scientific thinkers who have informed social science itself, and, because of their importance to Western thought, social work itself. Plato, Aristotle, Adam Smith, and Auguste Comte occupy an honored position in the history of social thought and their influence is omnipresent.

As social scientific explanation developed, it was adopted by the existing order. The Enlightenment and the rise of science in the seventeenth and eighteenth centuries essentially replaced heavily religious explanations of events with emerging and ever more encompassing scientific explanations. (Plato and Aristotle, in the fifth century B.C., were a bit before the Enlightenment!) Astronomy and mathematics were among the first to experience scientific intrusions, and it was not long before social science began to develop theoretical perspectives on the human condition.

PLATO AND ARISTOTLE, FIFTH CENTURY B.C.

Plato and Aristotle in many ways remain the source of contemporary ideas and controversy about what is real.[6] Plato took the position that reality was one, and that the forms we see in daily life were simply imperfect manifestations of underlying structures. He spoke of our vision of reality as similar to someone who lives in a cave, outside of which grows a tree. The sun, shining on the tree, casts a shadow on the wall of the cave. The reality we see is, in Plato's view, the shadow and has as much substance. In essence, science is based on Platonic concepts, operating with the conviction that there are underlying regularities (scientific laws) that explain the seemingly random and disparate world of people and events that we see.

Aristotle, on the other hand, turned Plato on his head, as it were. He took the reverse view, that reality is what we see—this chair, this tree—and that generalizations are built up from empirical comparisons of forms in the world. We get the general idea of chair from all the specific chairs we have seen. The theoretical approach suggested by him is now used in social science. It is called grounded theory, grounded in the here and now and the day to day.[7] In essence, modern social science uses the commitments of Plato (that there is a reality out there) and the methods of Aristotle (that we need to measure carefully to find that reality).

Aristotle also suggested something else very familiar in social work today: the concept of precipitating and predisposing cause. He argued that events had these two sets of causes and that we need to pay attention to both. The predisposing causes are events that set up the problem; precipitating causes are events that immediately precede the problem. For example, a precipitating cause of a situation of wife abuse may be the use of alcohol. However, a predisposing cause might be the personality problems of the individual and or normative legitimation of violence in a particular culture.

ADAM SMITH, 1723–1790

An early work in social science, in this case economics, was Adam Smith's *Wealth of Nations*.[8] In this book, Smith talked about a large economic system adjusting itself, and he paid relatively little attention to the individuals and smaller social units who were ground up as the system shifted gears. Smith argued that social problems were individual failures to adjust quickly enough to the market. Some essential features of this idea of large-scale forces of the system adjusting themselves were also used by Darwin in his evolutionary theory and then applied to social life in the theories of social Darwinism.

AUGUSTE COMTE, 1798–1857

Another influential figure in the social sciences was Auguste Comte, who was a founder of positivism, of sociology, and of humanism. These were first dealt with in his two-volume treatise *Cours de Philosophie Positive*,[9] which presented a complete system of philosophy. Positivism became the basis for most social science thinking. It stressed the necessity of discovering the laws of human behavior through systematic investigation. His sociological thinking was further developed in his four-volume study *System of Positive Policy*.[10] One volume was devoted to social statics and dealt with the nature of society; another was on social dynamics and dealt with social change; the other volumes were devoted to the individual and the individual's morality and moral progress through history. Today, social workers use these concepts, though often it is not understood that they come from historical sources.

The Contributions of Social Science Theory

Social science theory has made many contributions to the ways social workers think about social problems and has set the stage for how workers approach intervention.

LEVEL AND CAUSAL MECHANISM

Once we pass from the Enlightenment to the modern day, the string of great social scientific thinkers becomes difficult to organize and present. The scheme here, detailed more fully in Chapter 4, is based on level of social analysis. Conventional levels are those that social work finds most comfortable and that, indeed, we have used to organize our own intervention strategies; change in the individual, group and family, organization, community, and society are the common levels that social workers use.

THE INDIVIDUAL LEVEL

Many thinkers argued that the cause and target of social difficulty was within the individual. Adam Smith, in effect, argued this position. Other important social scientists whose work is of this type are Freud, Skinner, and Piaget. The relevance to social work will immediately come to mind. Casework uses many Freudian concepts, and behavior modification draws from the work of Skinner. Child welfare work and developmental interests generally draw from Piaget.

SIGMUND FREUD, 1856–1939. Another great social scientist who influenced social work's perspectives was Sigmund Freud.[11] His discovery of the unconscious and his masterful analysis of clinical data transformed the field of social work more than perhaps any other social scientist. Some would question whether he was, in fact, a social scientist. Many influential thinkers were not social scientists in the strict sense of the term. Because he was systematic and theoretical, he is included here.

Just as Marx and Weber opened up whole areas of social inquiry that have been continued by thousands of others, Freud opened up areas of psychological inquiry that have been similarly used. His ideas on the interpretation of dreams and the importance of repression and suppression in human life force us to look at the human presentation of self as a carefully constructed symbolic act, the exact meanings of which often escape the actor herself or himself and friends and family as well. For Freud, psychological illness arose when the normal conflicts encountered in human development were not appropriately resolved. In social work, his influence was felt early, but it received its first full-scale treatment in the work of Bertha Reynolds.[12] Her work was very influential in presenting Freud to the social work community.

B. F. SKINNER, 1904–1990. Harvard University's B. F. Skinner developed behavior modification, which was quickly adopted by many social workers and other human service professionals and led to the development of an intervention methodology called behavior therapy.[13] Deriving essentially from a Pavlovian perspective on human action, behaviorism argues that human actions are the result of positive and negative reinforcements. The intentional, choosing aspects of the person were minimized or rejected.

Initially, behavioral perspectives and those with a psychodynamic orientation were frequently at odds in schools of social work. Three bases of difference developed. One, already noted, was the difference in orientation to the very basis of the human condition itself. A second was the methodology. In psychodynamic approaches, workers counseled and talked with clients; behaviorists developed schedules of reinforcement and extinction. And, finally, behaviorists developed a rigorous set of outcome measures.

Over time, the types of problems that seemed to be better handled by these two methodologies have become more clear, and the conflict is less marked. Behavioral therapy was expanded into behavioral modification, which allowed for elements of self-control, and counseling recognized some of the places where behavioral techniques were very helpful.

JEAN PIAGET, 1896–1980. Piaget's tremendous influence upon psychology and, consequently, upon social work stems from his investigations of human development, with particular reference to its cognitive (thinking) and affective (feeling) components.[14] He excelled in his ability to plan detailed observations of behavior and to fit these observations to developmental theory. His output was prolific (see note 14 for examples). One example of his theoretical contribution is his conclusion that the evolution of the thinking of children proceeds through four stages: the sensorimotor stage occupies the first 2 years of life, when the child possesses an empirical and largely nonverbal intelligence; the preoperational level occupies the next 5 years, in which objects come to be represented by words and are manipulated in an experimental manner; the next lasts for another 5 years, until the child is 12, when logical operations become strong; and the final stage, continues until adulthood, during which the individual experiments with formal logical operations and thought becomes a more flexible experimentation. Social workers have found his work very useful in helping to outline a life cycle approach to the human person, which outlines what workers should expect at different points in the development of the person.

GROUP AND FAMILY

After the individual-level social scientists come those interested in group phenomena. Group work has a well-accepted history in social work. Key theorists are Kurt Lewin, George Homans, and Alvin Zander. They are relatively recent and among the most influential. Early work by Le Bon and Simmel began the interest in group phenomena.[15] And Cooley developed "the primary group" as a key concept shortly after the turn of the century.[16] Each of these, as well as the Hawthorne studies discussed later, influenced the development of group work in social work. The thinkers discussed next were especially influential. While not a contribution of social science as such, it is important to note that in its own realm social work had recognized the importance of groups through the development of character-building agencies, like the Boy Scouts. The problem was that group work seemed to lack legitimacy, at least the theoretical legitimacy of casework. It was associated with recreation work, and for many years the census counted "group and recreation workers" as an occupational category.

KURT LEWIN, 1890–1947. While an interest in the individual has been a dominant theme in social work, definitions of social work have always stressed its social focus. Thus, there is a long history of interest in small groups in social work. Many, if not most, social workers recognize that virtually all individuals influence and are influenced by numerous groups, including the family and those found in the neighborhood, the school, and the workplace. The group is also a vehicle for offering services. Because of the power of groups to influence us, we can use that power for purposes of individual change. Lewin was one of the pioneers in the study of small groups (as well as of many other areas of interest to social workers), and thus he has had a considerable impact on social workers who seek to understand and have an effect on social psychological phenomena.[17]

Lewin and his colleagues created an approach to small group study, group dynamics, in which the group and its members were viewed as responding over time to a variety of forces that determined the nature and direction of change. These social scientists worked together in a group dynamics research center that was first located at the Massachusetts Institute of Technology and later at the University of Michigan. Among his influential books were *Principles of Topological Psychology* (1936), *Resolving Social Conflicts* (1948), and *Field Theory in Social Science* (1951).

GEORGE CASPAR HOMANS, 1910–1989. George Homans's 1950 volume, *The Human Group,*[18] was a landmark volume in the sociological treatment of the group, because it organized and rationalized much of the previous thinking about group influence. Social workers read his work as providing a source of legitimacy for group approaches.

ALVIN ZANDER, 1913– . Alvin Zander, like Lewin and others, was extremely influential in developing the whole area of group dynamics. Group dynamics emphasized the importance of group phenomena in personal life and in organizations. Early work in T-groups (training groups) attempted to improve the ability to work in groups in the workplace. Later, group dynamics became the basis for intervention of a therapeutic sort, with groups being used to provide for therapeutic intervention (Alcoholics Anonymous had used this technique for years). Zander's recent book, *Making Groups Effective,*[19] is an important synthesis of group research that focuses on how to make groups more efficient and effective.

THE ORGANIZATIONAL LEVEL

One development relatively recent in social work has been the recognition of the importance of the organizational level as a locus of social work practice. The emergence of administration as a specialization in social work was aimed at training those who will take administrative, management, and executive positions in human service organizations of the future. This development in social work is based the earlier and now continuing development of organizational science.

MARY PARKER FOLLETT, 1868–1933. Mary Parker Follett is an important thinker in the early development of organizational studies because of her contribution to scientific management (the application of scientific principles to the workplace, involving the study of how much light to have, how to divide tasks, and the like) and the fact that she was a woman writing in a field that was dominated by men at the time. Her work[20] is often used in courses in administration as an exemplar of early approaches.

PHILIP SELZNICK, 1919–   . Philip Selznick's book, *Leadership In Administration,*[21] is a classic work that is generally recognized as energizing a field. Selznick was one of the first to deal with the concept of organizational direction and development. He developed the concept of cooptation, which refers to the tactic elites often use in hiring or persuading those who object to a project, thus depriving opposition groups of direction and leadership. Social workers in community organization and administration have found Selznick's work especially useful.

ROBERT MERTON, 1910–   . Robert Merton was one of the first to consider the perils of organizations which begin as hierarchy (levels of authority) and turn into bureaucracy (levels of authority that have become stagnant). Merton used his theory of means and ends to explore what happens in organizations when means replace ends and the bureaucrat simply enforces the rules and policies of the organization, even though there may be no reasons for them any more. Social workers were sensitized to the actual operations of bureaucratic rationality that Max Weber has described.[22]

The ideas of Merton had more general application as well. As embodied in *Social Theory and Social Structure,*[23] he identified a dichotomy between the ends society decrees as appropriate for individuals and the means society provides individuals to achieve those ends. Alinsky has also developed this theme,[24] as has Rokeach in his study of instrumental terminal values.[25] Cloward and Ohlin[26] used Merton's idea to develop an opportunity theory of delinquency, which saw delinquent acts as the result of blocked channels of achievement due to resource denial while the traditional goals were still pursued.

MAYER ZALD, 1931–   . Mayer Zald's work on the political economy of organizations is a social science perspective that has been very useful in analyzing social agencies and the way that these agencies function in the world, organized around such questions as how to get staff, how to get resources, and so on.[27] Zald studied the YMCA as an organization, and this still represents one of the few intensive sociological studies of a human service organization.[28]

ERVING GOFFMAN, 1922–1982. Three works of Erving Goffman deserve comment here. First is the *Presentation of Self in Everyday Life,*[29] which took the idea of role very seriously and stimulated its use as a conceptual tool among social workers. His work on stigma reintroduced that concept into the contemporary social work lexicon. *Asylums* made the phrase "a total institution" a relatively common term within the profession. In the first work, he takes seriously the idea that "all the world's a play" and asks how we present ourselves to ourselves and others. In the second work, *Stigma,* Goffman asks how certain statuses, like the "handicapped" (now called differently abled) or "homosexuals" (now called gays or lesbians), come to be looked down upon, and explores what such a position does to the administrator and the recipient of stigma. The last book, *Asylums,* is perhaps the most used in social work. Goffman studied the effects of the total institution (where someone lives all of his or her life), and this book became the intellectual beginning of the movement toward deinstitutionalization.

ROSABETH KANTER, 1943–   . Rosabeth Kanter recently became the first woman editor of the *Harvard Business Review.* Her works, *Men and Women of the Corporation* and *The Change Masters,*[30] among others, have been important in introducing concepts of gender analysis and change analysis into organizational science. These works are much studied by social workers who seek to change social work agencies and understand the gender dynamics that seems to put men in disproportionate numbers of executive positions.

THE COMMUNITY LEVEL

While sociological and psychological perspectives have been heavily used by social workers, political science has had an important impact on social work as well, especially at the community and societal levels. Political science is the study of power, as a perspective on the world, in official settings, as in the operation of legislatures, and in ad hoc informal networks, as in the building of community coalitions. It has affected the social work field very heavily.

In a classic paper, Keith-Lucas talked about "the political theory implicit in casework theory."[31] He focused on the world view perspective on power. One element of the casework relationship is a power relationship, especially when there are differences between the worker and client that parallel society's wide power differences, as between a white male worker and a black female client.

Macro social workers, those involved in community organization and social policy, have always been interested in the operation of formal bodies of political power, such as city councils, state legislatures, and the federal Congress. These bodies must approve the policies that most social workers support, including better welfare benefits, social services, and the like.

Paying attention to, or lobbying, the formal structure is often not enough. Sometimes informal networks of influentials need to be brought together either to put pressure on the elected and appointed public officials or to work with them in a more informal way for the accomplishment of community purpose. Social workers build community and societal coalitions to achieve municipal reform, housing improvement, and all kinds of changes in social policy.

An early stimulus to the study of power came from Hunter in his work on community power structure.[32] Hunter worked for the United Way in Atlanta and studied the local community in which he lived; he argued that there was an interlocking group of individuals who were able to get things done. This argument, appearing in the middle 1950s, was similar on a community level to the larger national perspective offered by C. Wright Mills.[33]

The storm of controversy over community power structure that followed will perhaps never be resolved. The political science community, in general, took a pluralist as opposed to an elitist perspective, arguing that most communities were characterized by many circles of influence, depending on the interests they represented and were committed to. Others, like Hunter and Mills, espoused the view that a relatively few people from different sectors held the power to accomplish civic tasks, and that access to this power elite was essential for the accomplishment of these tasks.

From a practical point of view, both approaches need to be taken into account. Social advocates and community organizers have always tried to do so. Clearly, there are individuals who have transcendent influence, and we always hope to involve such individuals in community projects and, if that is not possible, to prevent their opposition. On the other hand, community organizers and other social advocates have recognized that to actually put a project across requires the cooperation of many individuals at both the policy deciding end and the policy implementation and program end. Hence, a full spectrum of effort is required.

The political science interest in power stimulated the social work community to take more seriously than it had for many years the advocacy role on a collective rather than a client-by-client approach and provided, as well, some of the intellectual framework that was needed to give that strategy bite and impact. Similarly, though, the elitist perspective was important as well. It is always well to consider mobilizing important people to help in your cause, even if their support is not all that you need.

GEORG SIMMEL, 1858–1918. Georg Simmel is an important influence on social work thinking, if indirectly, for two reasons. First, he was an early student of social conflict, and his work on the functions of social conflict[34] brought a fresh perspective to that topic. Second, he was one of the first to study group influence. There is a third less well known reason as well; Simmel was concerned about the increasing impersonality of the modern world, which worries many to this day and is often seen as the loss of community. He saw money as an exemplification of this impersonality and was one of the first thinkers who raised the question about the perils of industrialization.

THE CHICAGO SCHOOL. Formalization occurred of the developing discipline of sociology, centered heavily at the University of Chicago. The University of Chicago was a new university (just prior to 1900) and contained both an early school of social work plus a new Department of Sociology. Focus for both groups was on the city and its problems, and landmark works of urban social analysis emerged that combined important elements of social concern, including *The Hobo, The Gold Coast and the Slum,* and *The Jack-Roller,* to mention but a few.[35] The *American Journal of Sociology* was founded around 1900 and not too long thereafter *The Social Service Review,* the former affiliated with the Department of Sociology and the latter with the School of Social Service Administration. Early issues of each reveal a heavy mixing of social concern, social theory, and social intervention. Their basic view was that the city was a locus of social disorganization, which broke the bonds of the rural community and left people suffering from excessive individualism and lack of connection and cohesion.

ROBERT COOLEY ANGELL, 1899–1984. If the Chicago sociologists created a perspective of community disorganization with respect to the U.S. city, then the social work area of community organization was its antidote. One important supporter was Robert Cooley Angell. His 1950 work "The Moral Integration of American Cities"[36] was a turning point, for he turned what had been assumed (disorganization) into an empirical question (if so, then how much) and sought to answer it by a large-scale comparative study. Furthermore, of great and special interest to social work, one measure of integration that he used was the amount of giving to the United Way (then called the Community Chest in most cities.) Angell not only provided theoretical and methodological support for community organization, but also used social work indicators.

Angell also completed an earlier work, *The Family Encounters Depression.* He was referring to the Great Depression and was trying to see how families and communities had coped. It was a pathbreaking work because very few social scientists had actually looked at the effect of the Depression. It also was used by social workers to help understand clients from that period or influenced by that period. It remains one of the surprisingly few studies of the Depression experience and its impact on people, communities, and U.S. society.

LEONARD S. COTTRELL, 1899–1985. Leonard Cottrell's idea of interpersonal competence and divorce was generalized into an idea of community competence.[37] This concept was a generative force for the Mobilization for Youth program in New York City and for a broad range of attempts sponsored by the Ford Foundation across the United States to improve a community's ability to solve problems.

THE SOCIETAL LEVEL

Much of the activism through the years, which saw social conditions as crucial in determining the fate of individual persons, was supported by theorists of society. They looked at the structures of society and the relationships these structures engendered. But, in many ways, social science and social work followed parallel, if similar paths, now touching and now remaining apart. In the years before 1900, social science and social change were intermeshed. Karl Marx was a social scientist (or social theorist) who was equally involved in social theory and social change. To a great extent, his theorizing was stimulated by a concern for the disadvantaged worker. This pattern, of social concern stimulating social science, was followed by others for many years.

From the beginning, social work has been interested in the larger-scale manifestations of social problems and their causes. Elements of the social work community have been involved in social improvement and social change since Dorthea Dix sought support for what essentially would be land grant mental hospitals (recall that the idea lost in Congress in 1854) and since large numbers of women sought to end alcohol abuse through prohibition.

The Progressive Movement had its share of social work involvement, and Jane Addams won her Nobel Prize for working for world peace. The University of Chicago's School of Social Service Administration had a long tradition of being involved in social and political change. Certainly all those who worked for the Social Security Act represented a force for social improvement as well. And the activism of the 1960s represented a fresh stimulus to social work.

Many social-level thinkers had a concern for social improvement in mind. Marx, Weber, DuBois, Mead, and others represent this tradition of socially concerned social thinkers.

In recent years, anthropological perspectives have been among the newer ones to gain focus and ascendancy. First among these perhaps was the work of Oscar Lewis and his concept of the culture of poverty.[38] This controversial perspective involved the Protestant ethic idea and, in effect, stood it on its head. If certain norms and values help people to get ahead, might not another set keep them behind. The controversy pivoted around the tendency for this explanation to be used as a victim blaming technique in Ryan's[39] sense of the term. (Ryan talks about the tendency to blame the victim for her or his plight, thus making the more fortunate nonvictims feel better. Thus, the rape victim is blamed for being seductive, or the poor person is blamed for not getting a job.) A more balanced point of view would doubtless argue that there are, in some instances and in some areas, norms and values that hamper individual and collective achievement. On the other hand, it would be folly to deny that structural constraints, discrimination, and other systemic difficulties similarly act as achievement impediments. Rather than fighting about whether cultural or structural features are more important, a wise approach would be to recognize the possible importance of both and develop strategies to deal with them as appropriate.

KARL MARX, 1818–1883. Karl Marx is one of the most important societal-level thinkers in the modern era.[40] As one of the key developers of theories of social exploitation, Marx and his colleague, Frederick Engels, showed how the structure of the social system created the poor. They argued that the particular villain was the capitalist system itself (and prior to that the slave and feudal systems) in which the rich and well-to-do took advantage of their position to squeeze resources from the poor and those with no power. For them, the economic relationship was central.

It would be wrong to see Marx and Engels as only economic theorists, however. Theft of meaning was as important to them in some ways as theft of resources. The capitalist system not only stole money from the less advantaged, but it also caused the alienation of people from each other and finally of the individual from himself or herself.

It is a tribute to the power of their argument and the persuasiveness of their thinking that Marxism remains a vital intellectual force today. It is certainly true that some of their predictions, class revolutions for instance, have not come to pass in the way their theory predicted. It may be the essential class battle will be not within societies, but between richer and poorer societies. There are some who offer this argument today.[41]

A Marxian analysis has come to mean an approach to understanding social phenomena in which power and economic relationships are a basic part. This form of analysis is now used to help understand the essential features of a wide variety of relationships.

Another element of the Marxian approach makes it unique as well. There are many action elements in the theory. Marxism suggested ways to organize the exploited and provided the imperative to do just that. It is unusual for a social science theory to contain such specific action directions and implications, and perhaps that reason, as much as its theoretical cohesion, accounts for Marxism's continued popularity.

MAX WEBER, 1864–1920. Another important social theorist was Max Weber. Weber's classic work, *The Protestant Ethic and the Spirit of Capitalism,*[42] was a cultural argument about social life rather than a structural one. Whereas Marx and Engels looked at the patterns of organization to explain exploitation, Weber looked at the patterns of belief. (He also looked at other things, organizational and bureaucratic investigations among them.) In the case in question, Weber argued that the Protestant ethic made work sacred and holy and thus turned it from daily drudgery into God's activity. Furthermore, the Protestant ethic, as Weber interpreted it, saw worldly success as an indication of inner sacred status. Weber's suggestion unearthed a new and more blame-oriented approach to social caring, as Segalman suggested.[43] If wealth was a sign of goodness, then poverty must be a sign of badness. After the Protestant ethic, poverty became a symbol of moral disrepute. Weber's line of thinking has been used by many social scientists and emerged later in a concept called the culture of poverty.

W. E. B. DUBOIS, 1868–1963. Social work has had a long and deep commitment to meeting the needs of oppressed people. DuBois, who was an outstanding social scientist, is often cited by social workers. He was America's first African-American sociologist and was one of the most important leaders of social protest throughout his adult lifetime. He founded the Niagara Movement in 1905, which consisted of black intellectuals who dedicated themselves to advocating the rights of black people. He also helped found the National Association for the Advancement of Colored People (NAACP). His intellectual influence was begun with the completion of his doctoral dissertation at Harvard entitled *The Suppression of the African Slave-Trade to the United States of America, 1638–1870* (1896).[44] His book *The Souls of Black Folk* (1903) criticized the ideology of Booker T. Washington as one that, through its emphasis on accommodation, enslaved rather than freed blacks.

MARGARET MEAD, 1901–1978. The discipline of anthropology has had a considerable amount of influence on social work for several reasons. First, anthropology gave social work an understanding of the influence of culture on human behavior. Social workers interact with people from many different cultures, and they must strive to help people attain their goals through their own cultural norms and values rather than those of the social worker. Even when individuals adopt goals and means of attaining them that are a part of another culture than the one into which they were socialized, anthropological knowledge helps them to understand the processes involved in such acculturation. Through her examination of other cultures as well as her own, Margaret Mead made many important contributions to this understanding. The first of her many books, *Coming of Age in Samoa* (1928), demonstrated her strong observational abilities, and her works continue to be studied.[45]

RUTH BENEDICT, 1887–1948. Ruth Benedict was another anthropologist whose seminal work, *Patterns of Culture,*[46] was an important book in sensitizing the social work community to differences in culture. She also developed the general, but still important and used, differences between guilt and shame cultures, pointing out the different modes of social control societies use. While this application especially focused on differences between the East (shame) and the West (guilt), it has considerable general use. Social workers today regularly talk about shame and guilt orientations within many of the subcultures that exist in the United States, and culturally sensitive social work requires that one be aware of these differences in orientations.

From the left: Karl Marx; Sigmund Freud with his daughter, Anna; W. E. B. DuBois; Margaret Mead. (Credits: Marx and DuBois, Library of Congress; Freud, UPI/Bettmann Newsphotos; Mead, Courtesy of the American Museum of Natural History.)

HAROLD LASSWELL, 1902–1978. Harold Lasswell was a political scientist who made two important contributions to thinking about society. First, he was one of the first modern political scientists who advocated the study of political power, as opposed to the formal study of constitutions and political philosophy. Second, his book *Psychopathology and Politics*[47] sought to merge individual psychodynamics with the political actions of the larger system.

AMITAI ETZIONI, 1929– . The structure of social compliance has also been an area of important social science inquiry.[48] In general, there are three ways in which compliance can be achieved: through culture, economics, or politics, that is, through belief, bribe, or force.[49] These modalities are closely related to what Etzioni has called bases of power. For Etzioni, normative, economic, and political powers are representative of the ways in which social goals are accomplished. Etzioni did not carry his theory in a practical direction. However, Tropman and Erlich, in a discussion of community organization strategies, used this three-dimensional framework as a basis for a taxonomy of community organization intervention efforts.[50]

THE STUDY OF THE WELFARE STATE. Another area that we will cover is the study of the welfare state itself. In England, the work of Richard Titmuss[51] serves as an impressive case in point. In the United States, the works of Gilbert, Wilensky, and Zald

and Martin,[52] among others, have shed light on the major purposes, functions, and causes of the welfare state.

This area of study is interesting for several reasons. First, in the main, the contributions have run more from social science to social intervention than the reverse. The issues, problems, and concerns of the social work profession have not, as yet, come to be stimulating to social scientists in a general sense. The study of the welfare state is an exception. It is one of the few areas where there is an evolving mutual interest between those interested in social policy and those interested in social science. The mix of people involved is similarly heterogeneous. Sociologists, like Wilensky and Zald, have well-established reputations and connections to social welfare interests. Economics has made its most important contribution here, as well in the study of welfare economics, on how society should act to allocate goods when a mechanism of allocation should not be the market.

The questions raised by students of the welfare state are too broad to go into in any detail here. But they include issues that involve the relationship of demographic structure to the provision of social benefits, the value underpinnings of the welfare state, and why different nations have moved toward welfare state structures at different paces and in different styles. Generalizations as a result of these studies are not clear. Wilensky found that as the population grows older there is a greater inclination to provide more welfare state benefits. Such a generalization would certainly seem to apply to the United States. But whether it explains the growth of Social Security and other welfare state programs remains to be seen. Wilensky[53] also found, in an extensive study of European countries, that the presence of Catholic parties seems to correlate with increased welfare state activity, even when age is controlled.

POPULATION STUDIES. One final area of study should be mentioned: demography. Closely linked to sociology, it has also been one that has had great practical interest. Apart from its concern with the accurate counting of people, which has obvious policy implications, demography has often been in the forefront of population control studies because population control is one of the most important ways in which people–land pressure can be reduced and some aspects of poverty softened. This is an extremely practical social intervention result. Rainwater and Weinstein's work[54] details for the United States some of the important relationships between family size and poverty.

The Contribution of Social Science Methods

Thus far the impact of science has been described in terms of substantive impacts—the ideas and approaches of key social scientists that have influenced thinking about social problems or have defined the nature of important social problems themselves. However, the methods of science, such as the matter of measurement, has had its own impact. Indeed, so great has this impact been in terms of research on practice efforts that it often overshadows the substantive contributions, and the social scientist is thought of as someone who can only perform statistical tests. But the methods of science have entered social work in ways that are independent of substantive disciplines. The use of measurement has emerged as an important tool of social work practice, as a way of assessing practice and of charting progress or failure and as a method of intervention itself.

THE SOCIAL STATISTICIANS

Throughout the nineteenth and into the twentieth century, social concern and social analysis occurred together. Marx and Freud had social betterment in mind, and the social concern of the other social scientists was surely present.

The work of Émile Durkheim on social cohesion and suicide remains an important interpretation of these phenomena.[55] Durkheim tried to show, first, that there were different kinds of suicide: some as a result of social anomie and some as a result of social expectation. He pioneered in the use of data for the development of a social science argument, something that none of the other theorists were known for, with the possible exception of Marx. Other writers and thinkers belong in this group—Charles Booth and Henry Mayhew are two examples—who were not social scientists in the strict, contemporary sense of the term. They pioneered the analysis of social problems using factual data, however, and thus deserve mention here.

Charles Booth's *Life and Labour of the People of London*[56] is well known in social work. But even earlier, in 1861 in London, Henry Mayhew published his four-volume study *London Labour and the London Poor.*[57] This work is a detailed analysis of every type of poor person and poor person's occupation in London. It still is the most exhaustive study of the types of poor and their conditions that can be found to this day. One might think of him as a scientific Charles Dickens.

Works of Mayhew's type gave rise to the idea of scientific philanthropy. (The attempt to apply the rigorous methods of science to charity.) While the large-scale use of quantified methods in social science would not develop until after World War II (and developed into survey research), Mayhew began a trend that coalesced in the social survey movement and peaked in the United States in mid-1930s studies. These surveys were sponsored by the Hoover administration and entitled *Recent Social Trends*[58] (one famous one was the Pittsburgh Survey).

Another effort worth mentioning from the 1920s and 1930s represented a special variant of the community study emphasis, in that it looked in great detail at a single community. That study is the Middletown series by Robert and Helen Lynd.[59] These studies represented an early community study *(Middletown)* and then a follow-up *(Middletown in Transition)*. They have been recently followed up 40 years later by Howard Bahr[60] and his associates, who found a great deal of similarity in Middletown over the 40-year span.

These thinkers and commentators represented a different effort from that of the social theorists. They were less interested in formulating grand theories about the human condition and more interested in providing detailed quantitative descriptions of that condition. We might call them the social statisticians. (Of course, every generalization has its exceptions. Marx and Durkheim are such exceptions, fitting into both the social statistician and the social theorist category.)

After World War II, quantitative methods took a special hold and the methods of social science became, perhaps, more important than the ideas. Major research centers specializing in the collection of social science data sprang up. The Institute of Social Research at the University of Michigan and the National Opinion Research Center at the University of Chicago, two of the more prominent centers, began to tap public opinion. Gallup, Harris, and Roper became household words, and now each year thousands of surveys are undertaken to assess and document public view and public need.

QUANTITATIVE METHODS

These efforts continue to this day. Besides providing interesting information on their own, they have been a source of methodology for needs assessments, community studies, and so on, that serve as the basis for much social planning in the United States. Skills in developing the numerical representation of attitudes and feelings were important. (For example, "Do You Like this Section: a lot __ [5]; somewhat __ [4]; neutral __ [3]; somewhat dislike __ [2]; strongly dislike __ [1]; no opinion __ [0].") Survey research skills in developing questions, pretesting them, conducting the interview (or sending out the questionnaire), and coding and analyzing the data have been very helpful to social workers in providing a picture of the overall populations from which clients come, in doing studies of client populations, and so on. Statistical tests of causality and association are also helpful in developing an understanding of which variables are related and under what conditions.

It is important to stress that, in spite of the advances in social science methodology, social work remains somewhat skeptical about the utility of turning clients into numbers. Some of this concern is well founded. Other aspects of it probably come from the lack of comfort some social workers have with quantitative methods (the representation of elements of the human condition through numbers).

QUALITATIVE METHODS

Somewhat closer to social workers' preferred methodology are qualitative methods. These methods involve the social scientist in personally observing and recording aspects of the situation. Often, such personal observation involves being there and joining in, a method called participant observation. This methodology is most highly developed by anthropologists, specializing as they do in going to and living in other cultures as a means of understanding them. It is surprising, then, that more links between social work and anthropology have not been developed.

Several qualitative studies are noteworthy, among many that could be mentioned. One early effort is Whyte's *Street Corner Society,* an attempt to portray the lives of community people in their own context.[61] Later, *Tally's Corner*[62] and *All Our Kin*[63] portrayed the life of African-American men and women, respectively.

THE LOGIC OF DESIGN

A final area of social science method that has been helpful to social work is the area of logic of design, or research methods. Basic questions about the structure of knowledge, developed in social science, have been helpful to social work.

One set of key concepts involves the *validity and reliability of measurements.* Validity refers to the question of whether the investigator is measuring what she or he wants to measure; reliability refers to the accuracy of the measure chosen. To be a good indicator of a concept, a measurement must be both valid and reliable.

A second concept is that of *control groups.* This idea is especially important to social workers, who usually work with only affected populations. To that extent, it is often the case that clinicians draw conclusions based only on the affected group. A control group provides a point of comparison so that we can see what treatment does when compared to no treatment.

Finally, it is important to mention *randomization and random selection.* Randomization is a process that controls for bias in assigning people to treatment or control groups. For an example, hidden worker preferences may operate to assign clients more likely to succeed to treatment groups and those judged less likely to succeed to control groups. These judgments could well unintentionally influence the outcome of an experiment in intervention. Thus, assigning clients to treatment groups by chance prevents such bias from being a factor.

Similarly, when seeking to assess what the views of a particular population are, a random sample is necessary. This procedure assures the investigator that every candidate in the population has an equal probability of being chosen. With such a sample, statistical tests can be performed and have scientific meaning.

The Contribution of Social Work Research

So far, the emphasis has been on what social scientists have done for social work and how social scientific methods and theory have helped to define the nature of social problems by providing a language and concepts for discussing them and methods for assessing them. Social workers and socially concerned researchers have made contributions of their own, however, which need to be mentioned. In many of these cases, social work used the perspectives of social science and contributed to social science as well as to the field of social work.

Within social work itself there have been many efforts at research, which have been well reported by Tripodi, Fellin, and Meyer.[64] A few classic studies should be mentioned, however. Maas[65] divides them up into several groups or kinds of studies: effects of programs, studies of practice, and quantitative and qualitative research. Perhaps the best way, here, is to look at social work research contributions by the same level of perspective method that we have just used for the social sciences.

THE INDIVIDUAL LEVEL

There have been a number of classic studies within the social work field, including the Cambridge–Somerville Youth Study (on juvenile delinquency), the Hunt movement scale (attempting to assess how much clients had moved or progressed), and the studies at the University of Chicago on motivation, capacity, and opportunity (where clients were seen to progress based on these three variables and their combinations).[66] Meyer, Borgatta, and Jones provided a landmark study of the effectiveness of casework in *Girls at Vocational High.*[67]

THE GROUP AND FAMILY LEVEL

The development of group work by Garvin[68] and others was an important piece of social research that used social science approaches and concepts, yet applied them directly to social work interests. Vinter[69] developed the concept of treatment groups as well as recreational groups. Tropman, Johnson, and Tropman[70] introduced the task group into wider discussion in social work, including committees, boards of directors, and meeting settings.

More recently, the anthropological perspective has come to focus on myth and ritual. The work of Hartman and Laird is a case in point,[71] taking anthropological ideas from the analysis of other cultures and focusing them on the family. Thus, social workers may now ask questions about family myths and rituals and how they become established, what their meaning is, and how, when appropriate, they might be changed.

THE ORGANIZATIONAL LEVEL

Robert Vinter has made pioneering contributions in the area of organizational theory in his book (with Street and Perrow, two sociologists) *Organization for Treatment.*[72] His insight with respect to people-processing organizations and the importance they have might in some respects be derived from the work of Goffman, but his focus on the processes and procedures of the organization remains unique.

Other studies began looking at agency effectiveness and utilized an organizational level of analysis. It was not long before single case design emerged and available measures were used with individual cases to chart individual progress toward client goals. This furthered the development of empirically based practice. It should be noted that, when there is a lack of randomization and random selection, scientific, as opposed to clinical, advances cannot be easily attained. However, in spite of the limitations, the methods of science have made important contributions to social work.

THE COMMUNITY LEVEL

Community needs and service delivery across whole communities have been studied to assay the effectiveness and efficiency of social service systems in meeting community needs. The conditions of whole populations were considered and planning agencies constructed community profiles in order to provide better service. In the mid-1950 period, for example, a famous study by Buell looked at these issues in *Community Planning for Human Services*.[73] It has also been called the St. Paul Family Study, because it was conducted in St. Paul Minnesota. Buell found that, in November 1948, 6% of the families there were "absorbing well over half of the combined services of the community's dependency, health and adjustment agencies" (page 9).

THE SOCIETAL LEVEL

Large-scale studies by social workers have not been as typical as some of the smaller assessments. One, however, stands out as very illustrative. *Income and Welfare in the United States*[74] involved both social welfare professionals and social scientists and had a significant impact. Published just a little later than Galbraith's *The Affluent Society*,[75] it showed how great the income inequality was in the United States and was one of the stimulants for the poverty program.

What Social Work Needs from Social Science

The agenda of needed research in social science is certainly staggering, and it would be impossible here to detail all the areas of importance. Clearly, any advance in science has potential to assist social work in helping clients, communities, organizations, and others. However, work in a few areas would be especially helpful.

Certainly, a better understanding of cultural and structural systems is needed that will lead to an understanding of the interrelationship between culture and structure. More detailed analyses of the person in the environment are essential. Studies of human service organizations will continue to expand our limited knowledge in this area.

These and other substantive advances would not necessarily meet all the needs of social work, even if they were undertaken. While we certainly subscribe to the old adage that "there is nothing as useful as a good theory," it is not always clear how that utility might be maximized. Hence, research and practice procedure development must be combined. Thomas[76] and Rothman[77] have broken new ground here using social science methods and approaches to lay out the detailed steps required to translate a social finding into a social practice or social intervention.

Additional improvements are needed in the methods of science as well. The experimental method through the innovative application of single case design has led to the development of empirically based practice. Single case design uses social

Wilbur Cohen, author of the influential *Income and Welfare in the United States.* (Photo courtesy of Mrs. Wilbur Cohen.)

scientific measurement techniques to assess whether or not a particular intervention was associated with change in a particular client. Baseline measures are secured before treatment is initiated; then subsequent measures are taken to assess the trajectory of development. A number of types of single case design have been created so as to best ascertain whether an improvement is associated with the intervention.[78] Such clinical research is extremely useful for charting the course of particular clients or groups of clients within a practice or even within an agency. What has not happened, however, is the aggregation of these data in ways that permit scientific generalization. Hence, both the improvement of individual client measurements is needed, but also ways to aggregate these measurements so that they can have broader relevance and deeper meaning.

Conclusion

In this chapter we sought to illustrate the ways in which social science theory and methods have helped to provide paths toward the solutions to social problems. The initial and historical approach exemplified by people such as Adam Smith, Karl Marx, Max Weber, and Emile Durkheim were essentially of a theoretical problem discovery nature. Each outlined social problems that were to be considered and attended to, but only Marx provided a set of concrete suggestions for overcoming the problems he saw. His remedy—social revolution—was severe and certainly did not have the inexorability that he suggested. Sigmund Freud, on the other hand, was a theorist with an explicit interest in clinical practice, from which he drew most of his generalizations. All in all, we can view the nineteenth century as producing social theory, rather than social practice, as its contribution to social intervention.

In fact, of course, social work really did not begin to develop until the latter part of the nineteenth century, and this was surely stimulated by the scientific understanding of social problems that was beginning to develop. Attempts to chart the numbers of poor in London and the development at the University of Chicago of detailed studies of immigrant cultures were among the key influential areas here. It was really the methods of social science, rather than its theoretical insights and perspectives, that captured the imagination of the social work profession. Agencies wanted social scientists around, if at all, because they could help with research and data collection and were useful in social planning.

There remains a degree of suspicion between the social work community, however, and the social science community. The kind of harmonious working relationships that we would have hoped to develop have only emerged in isolated segments. Partly, there is a natural hostility between the world of action and the world of contemplation. Social work needs to *do,* and it needs to *do* on a day-in, day-out basis. It is not surprising that practitioners might be discouraged with the slower and perhaps more deliberate attempts to uncover relationships that characterize the scientists. Scientists, on the other hand, need perspective and controlled environments in which to test hypotheses. It is not surprising that they are suspicious of people regularly thrust into the maelstrom of human concern.

Yet a balanced view suggests that both are necessary.[79] In the medical field, for example, without the advances of the microbiologists and the biochemists, the practicing physician would have much less to work with than is now presently available. On the other hand, without the practitioners, the biological scientists would not have the kinds of problems and issues, the kinds of inexplicable conundrums that often generate scientific innovation. Similarly, social science and social work need to work together, each contributing its own expertise to the other and recognizing that the other does something special and different. Social workers should not seek to make social scientists into practitioners, nor should scientists seek to make theoreticians out of those in the action field. Through mutual respect and support, even more progress can be made than has been made.

Notes

1. For a discussion, see Robert H. Bremer, *American Philanthropy* (Chicago: University of Chicago Press, 1960), p. 54. Scientific philanthropy, like scientific management, was an attempt to apply the principles of science to help with social problems.
2. Henry Mayhew, *London Labor and the London Poor,* in four volumes (New York: Dover Publications, 1968).
3. For more information on these concepts, see John E. Tropman, "A Taxonomy of Social Services," in John E. Tropman and Harold R. Johnson, eds., *Social Work: A Knowledge Driven Approach* (Ann Arbor: University of Michigan School of Social Work, 1987).

4. See Bronislaw Malinowski, *Magic, Science and Religion* (Glencoe, IL: The Free Press, 1948).
5. Readers with experience in child welfare, particularly, will recognize the presence of magical thinking in children. Sometimes they inappropriately ascribe power to their very thoughts. Often unforeseen confluences of events (such as wishing for harm to come to someone and, by chance, harm actually comes to that someone) lead children to believe that they can control the material world directly with their thoughts. This experience is usually short lived. When it is not, the therapist has a job to do.
6. For a discussion of Plato and Aristotle, see Bertrand Russell, *A History of Western Philosophy* (New York: Simon & Schuster, 1945).
7. For a discussion of grounded theory, see Barney G. Glaser and Anslem Strauss, *The Discovery of Grounded Theory* (Chicago: Aldine Co., 1967).
8. Adam Smith, *The Wealth of Nations,* Great Books of the Western World, Vol. 39 (Chicago: *Encyclopedia Britannica,* 1952).
9. A. Comte, *The Positive Philosophy of A. Comte,* tr. H. Martineau, Jr. (London: G. Bell, 1896).
10. A. Comte, *System of Positive Policy,* R. Fletcher, ed. (London: Heinemann, 1974).
11. Sigmund Freud, *A General Selection of the Works of Sigmund Freud,* John Rickman, ed. (Hogarth Press & the Institute of Psychoanalysis, 1937).
12. See Bertha Reynolds, *Learning and Teaching in the Practice of Social Work* (New York: Farrar & Richart, 1942).
13. B. F. Skinner, *About Behaviorism* (New York: Alfred A. Knopf, 1974).
14. Jean Piaget, *Child's Conception of the World* (New York: Harcourt Brace & Co., 1929); *The Construction of Reality in the Child* (New York: Basic Books, 1954); *The Language and Thought of the Child* (New York: Harcourt Brace & Co., 1926).
15. Gustav Le Bon, *The Crowd* (London: T. F. Urwin, 1910); Georg Simmel, *The Web of Group Affiliations* (Glencoe, IL: The Free Press, 1955).
16. Charles H. Cooley, *Social Organization: A Study of the Larger Mind* (New York: Charles Scribner's Sons, 1909).
17. Kurt Lewin, *Principles of Topological Psychology* (New York: McGraw-Hill Book Co., 1936); *Twentieth Century Psychology* (New York: Philosophical Library, 1946).
18. George Caspar Homans, *The Human Group* (New York: John Wiley & Sons, 1950).
19. Alvin Zander, *Making Groups Effective* (San Francisco: Jossey-Bass, 1982).
20. Mary Parker Follett, *Dynamic Administration: Collected Papers of M. P. Follett,* V. Metcalf and V. Wick, eds. (New York: Harper, 1940).
21. Philip Selznick, *Leadership in Administration* (New York: Harper & Row, 1957).
22. For further discussion, see Hans Gerth and C. Wright Mills, *From Max Weber* (New York: Oxford University Press, 1958).
23. Robert K. Merton, "The Bureaucratic Personality," in R. K. Merton, ed., *Social Theory and Social Structure* (Glencoe, IL: The Free Press, 1957).
24. Saul David Alinski, "Of Means and Ends," in F. Cox and others, eds, *Strategies of Community Organization* (Itasca, IL: F. E. Peacock, 1979).
25. Milton Rokeach, *Understanding Human Values* (New York: The Free Press, 1979).
26. R. Cloward and L. Ohlin, *Delinquency and Opportunity* (Glencoe, IL.: The Free Press, 1960).
27. Mayer Zald and Gary L. Wamsley, *The Political Economy of Public Organizations* (Lexington, MA: Lexington Books, 1973).
28. Mayer Zald, *Organizational Change: The Political Economy of the Y.M.C.A.* (Chicago: University of Chicago Press, 1970).
29. Erving Goffman, *The Presentation of Self in Everyday Life* (Garden City, NY: Doubleday, 1959); *Stigma* (Englewood Cliffs, NJ: Prentice Hall, 1963); *Asylums* (Chicago: Aldine, 1961).
30. Rosabeth Kanter, *Men and Women of the Corporation* (New York: Basic Books, 1977); *The Change Masters* (New York: Simon & Schuster, 1983).

31. Alan Keith-Lucas "The Political Theory Implicit in Social Casework Theory," *American Political Science Review,* 57 (1953).

32. Floyd Hunter, *Community Power Structure* (Chapel Hill: University of North Carolina Press, 1953).

33. C. Wright Mills, *The Power Elite* (New York: Oxford University Press, 1956).

34. Georg Simmel, *The Functions of Social Conflict* (Glencoe, IL: The Free Press, 1955).

35. Nels Anderson, *The Hobo* (Chicago: University of Chicago Press, 1923); C. Shaw, *The Jack-Roller* (Chicago: University of Chicago Press, 1938); H. Zorbaugh, *The Gold Coast and the Slum* (Chicago: University of Chicago Press, 1929).

36. Robert Cooley Angell, "The Moral Integration of American Cities," in P. K. Hatt and H. J. Reiss, Jr., eds., *Cities and Society* (Glencoe, IL: The Free Press, 1957); *The Family Encounters Depression* (New York: Charles Scribner's Sons, 1936).

37. Leonard S. Cottrell and Nelson N. Foote, *Identity and Interpersonal Competence* (Chicago: University of Chicago Press, 1955).

38. Oscar Lewis, *Children of Sanchez* (New York: Random House, 1961); *La Vida: A Puerto Rican Family in the Culture of Poverty* (New York: Random House, 1966).

39. William Ryan, *Blaming the Victim* (New York: Random House, 1971).

40. Karl Marx, *Das Kapital* (Delhi: People's Publishing House, 1968 ed.). It is important to note that Marx and Engels said very little about the role of women. They recognized some kinds of exploitation, but not others (though one might want to look at Engel's *Origin of the Family, Private Property and the State*). Karl Marx and Fredrick Engels, *Collected Works,* translated by R. Dixon and others (London: Lawrence & Wishart, 1975).

41. According to Philip Hauser, the demographer from the University of Chicago, the world population by the year 2000 will be somewhere in the neighborhood of 7 billion individuals. Roughly, 5 billion of these will be in the less developed countries and will be relatively poor and relatively young. About 2 billion will be in the relatively more developed countries (North America, Europe, Russia, and Japan) and will be relatively richer and older. Given these demographic projections, we can easily see a conflict between the haves and the have nots arising, especially as questions about the disproportional use of world resources by the developed countries continues.

42. Max Weber, *The Protestant Ethic and the Spirit of Capitalism,* translated by Talcott Parsons (New York: Charles Scribner's Sons, 1958).

43. See, for more detail Ralph Segalman, *Poverty in America* (Westport, CT: Greenwood Press, 1981).

44. W. E. B. DuBois, *The Suppression of the African Slave-Trade to the United States of America, 1638–1870* (New York: Longmans, 1904). See also *The Souls of Black Folk* (Chicago: A. C. McClora, 1953); *Black Reconstruction; An Essay toward a History of the Part Which Black Folk Played in the Attempt to Reconstruct Democracy in America, 1860–1880* (New York: Harcourt Brace, 1935); and *Dusk of Dawn: An Essay toward an Autobiography of a Race Concept* (New York: Harcourt Brace, 1940).

45. Margaret Mead, *Coming of Age in Samoa* (New York: Blue Ribbon, 1928); *Growing Up in New Guinea* (London: Routledge, 1931); *Sex and Temperament in Three Primitive Societies* (London: Routledge, 1935); *Male and Female* (New York: Sparrow, 1949); and *Culture and Commitment* (New York: Columbia University Press, 1978).

46. Ruth Benedict, *Patterns of Culture* (Boston: Houghton-Mifflin, 1934).

47. Harold Lasswell, *Psychopathology and Politics* (Chicago: University of Chicago Press, 1930).

48. See Amitai Etzioni, *Societal Guidance* (New York: Crowell, 1969 ed.).

49. For a more thorough discussion, see John E. Tropman and John L. Erlich, "Strategy," in F. Cox and others, eds, *Strategies of Community Organization* (Itasca, IL: F. E. Peacock, 1984).

50. Ibid. It might be useful to explain what each of these dimensions represents. In the case of cultural, or normative, mechanisms, an attempt is made by individual or by society to secure the compliance of individuals in question through commitment, through convincing them that what they are supposed to do is right, appropriate, or proper, or, in some ways, showing

them that what they are doing is wrong or improper. In effect, socialization is the mechanism through which this goal is accomplished. We could view clinical intervention of a psychotherapeutic sort, for example, as instances of resocialization, perhaps followed first by instances of desocialization in which, through a process of relationship development and exchange within that relationship, clients decommit to various unacceptable patterns of behavior and recommit themselves to more acceptable ones. With respect to the economic or inducement form of compliance, individuals are simply rewarded for following certain desired paths. In the largest sense, the economy represents this structure. On a more micro level, often identified by the phrase "token economy," behavioral modifiers seek to use the mechanisms of reinforcement as ways to secure certain desired, behaviorally specific patterns. The last, of course, is force. Physical force has been an unfortunate and recurrent mechanism for achieving compliance over the history of our human species. If we take a step back from physical force, however, and think of political force as involving strong advocacy, the development of demonstrations, and the active and vigorous presentation of inequities and injustices to the general public, then this technique also has been characteristic of social work.

51. Richard Titmuss, *The Gift Relationship* (New York: Pantheon Books, 1971).
52. Neil Gilbert, *Capitalism and the Welfare State* (New Haven, CT: Yale University Press, 1983); Harold Wilensky, *The Welfare State and Equality* (Berkeley: University of California Press, 1975); Mayer Zald and G. Martin, eds., *Social Welfare in Society* (New York: Columbia University Press, 1981).
53. Harold Wilensky, "Leftism, Catholicism and Democratic Corporatism," in P. Lora and A. J. Heidenheimer, eds., *The Developments of Welfare States in Europe and America* (New Brunswick, NJ: Transaction Books, 1981).
54. Lee Rainwater and Karol Kane Weinstein, *And the Poor Get Children* (Chicago: Quadrangle Books, 1960).
55. Emile Durkheim, *Suicide, A Study in Sociology* (Glencoe, IL: The Free Press, 1951).
56. Charles Booth, *Life and Labor of the People of London* (New York: Macmillan, and Co., 1891–1897).
57. Henry Mayhew, *London Labour and the London Poor* (New York: Dover Publications, 1968).
58. President's Research Committee, *Recent Social Trends* (New York: McGraw-Hill, 1933). See also Phillip Klein, *A Social Study of Pittsburgh* (New York: Columbia University Press, 1938).
59. Robert Lynd and Helen Lynd, *Middletown* (New York: Harcourt, Brace, and World, 1959).
60. Howard Bahr, *All Faithful People: Change and Continuity in Middletown's Region* (Minneapolis: University of Minneapolis Press, 1983); P. Kellogg, *The Pittsburgh Survey* (New York: Charity Organization Society, 1909).
61. William Foote Whyte, *Street Corner Society* (Chicago: University of Chicago Press, 1943).
62. Eliot Liebow, *Tally's Corner* (Boston: Little, Brown, 1967).
63. Carol Stack, *All Our Kin* (New York: Harper & Row, 1974).
64. T. Tripodi, P. Fellin, and H. Meyer, *The Assessment of Social Research,* 2nd ed. (Itasca, IL: F. E. Peacock, 1983).
65. Henry Maas, *Social Service Research* (Silver Spring, MD: National Association of Social Workers, 1978).
66. Norman Polansky, *Social Work Research* (Chicago: University of Chicago Press, 1960).
67. Henry J. Meyer, E. Borgatta, and W. Jones, *Girls at Vocational High* (New York: Russell Sage Foundation, 1965).
68. Charles Garvin, *Contemporary Group Work* (Englewood Cliffs, NJ: Prentice Hall, 1981).
69. Robert Vinter, *Individual Change through Small Groups* (New York: The Free Press, 1974).
70. John E. Tropman, Harold R. Johnson, and Elmer J. Tropman, *The Essentials of Committee Management* (Chicago: Nelson-Hall, 1979).
71. Ann Hartman and Joan Laird, *Family-centered Social Work Practice* (New York: The Free Press, 1983).

72. Robert D. Vinter, David Street, and Charles Perrow, *Organization for Treatment* (New York: The Free Press, 1966).

73. Bradley Buell and others, *Community Planning for Human Services* (New York: Columbia University Press, 1952).

74. Wilbur Cohen, James Morgan, and Martin David, *Income and Welfare in the United States* (New York: McGraw-Hill Book Co., 1962).

75. John Kenneth Galbraith, *The Affluent Society* (New York: New American Library, 1958).

76. Edwin J. Thomas, *Utilization and Appraisal of Socio-Behavioral Techniques on Social Welfare* (Ann Arbor: University of Michigan, 1969).

77. Jack Rothman, *Social R & D* (Englewood Cliffs, NJ: Prentice Hall, 1980).

78. For further discussion, see M. Hersen and D. H. Barlow, *Single Case Experimental Design,* 2nd ed. (Elmsford, NY: Pergamon Press, 1984).

79. There were a number of parallel developments in other fields. Freud not only influenced the social work profession, but the profession of psychology as well. The development of clinical psychology on the one hand and behavioral intervention within psychology on the other has been an important part of that discipline's area of interest. And today it is generally considered to be true that with certain exceptions—the administration of drugs or the administration of specific psychological tests—psychologists, social workers, and psychiatrists working in clinical settings perform similar functions in similar ways.

CHAPTER 3
The Structure
of the Welfare State

Introduction

Any discussion of the profession and methods of social work and of contemporary society must contain some discussion of the nature of the welfare state itself. It is often unclear exactly what the concept "welfare state" means. To many, it indicates a government role in providing social assistance. But exactly what kind of assistance, how much, and under what conditions remains foggy. Then there are the moral and ideological attitudes. To some, the idea of the welfare state has a series of positive connotations, such as the acceptance by public policy makers of responsibility for the care of individuals who are unable to care for themselves. But for others the welfare state represents an unwarranted public intrusion on realms of the private. Still others view this intrusion as not only negative in and of itself but, additionally, destructive of the recipient of such aid.[1] One purpose of this chapter is to give a brief overview of the welfare state and the different perspectives that surround it.

The fact that government involvement is almost always a part of any approach to thinking about the welfare state provides a second purpose. We need to have some sense of the level of government expenditures involved in welfare state activity. It is also important to have a picture of the changes that have occurred in the last half of the twentieth century with respect to these government expenditures, as well as of the changes in the programmatic sectors that the government supports.

But government expenditures and efforts are not the only ones that characterize the modern welfare state in the United States. Important, too, is the voluntary sector, the typical social agency that social workers know well.[2]

The last sector of the welfare state is the business and corporate sector. Businesses and corporations contribute to welfare state activities through the fringe benefits they support and also directly through charitable contributions. This chapter explores these two additional topics.

Several other topics are considered as well. Questions need to be asked about why there is a welfare state at all. Different types of explanations for it are presented and considered. In particular, a perspective that suggests that U.S. society has positive and extensive welfare state programs at the same time as we have negative and hostile "poorfare state" attitudes is advanced. This discussion leads to a concluding consideration, which focuses on the value conflicts that currently swirl around the idea of the welfare state.

The Welfare State

From our point of view, the welfare state is a nation-state in which a substantial fraction of government resources and activity is used to provide for the needs of citizens, whether those needs are ordinary or extraordinary. In one sense, we might include all government expenditures under this category. However, our focus is on social welfare needs, which include health, food, shelter, clothing, and/or the resources to purchase these from the market. Hence, in most societies, social welfare programs such as pensions for older adults, income for individuals with physical and/or mental disabilities, income for individuals who are unable to locate work, support for mothers and children, the distribution of food, and so on, are among these kinds of expenditures. Additional expenditures for education and the needs of veterans are also included.

A further social welfare cost is the total amount of wages and salaries provided to the individuals who operate the system. In U.S. society this amount includes salaries for child welfare workers, Social Security personnel, public welfare workers, and so forth.

But the issue of what government expenditures actually fall into the welfare state count is far from clear-cut. Many countries classify schools and school expenditures under the social welfare umbrella, rather than in a category of their own. Also, substantial expenditures are made by the government through the military establishment, especially the Veteran's Administration, but also through military social work.[3]

Another complicating factor is whether the expenditures are direct, as in pensions, Social Security, and public welfare, or indirect, such as tax expenditures and expenditures for organizations like the Public Health Service and the Tennessee Valley Authority. Tax expenditures is a term given to the specific decision to give a taxpayer an income tax credit for some purpose. When these purposes are social in nature, they can be called social tax expenditures. This decision means that the government is not getting money it could or would have gotten otherwise. The value of the income lost is taken to be the amount of the expenditure.[4] Some examples are familiar to us. The tax exemption for children and other dependents, as a case in point, is a U.S. way of providing a children's allowance. The exemption for being over 65 and for being blind are two additional illustrations. But they are indirect, rather than direct.

There are, of course, other indirect expenditures, too. The TVA is a multimillion dollar operation designed to prevent flooding and generate electricity in the Tennessee Valley. Begun during the Depression, it continues today to operate in a vital way. Although it is a business in some respects, it began as a social movement with areawide improvement as its goal.[5] The expenditures of this organization are not included in U.S. social welfare accounts, nor are expenditures for public health, environmental cleanup, and occupational safety to mention others. We must be aware that social welfare expenditures is far from a clear category, and such expenditures do not benefit only the financially disadvantaged.[6]

Expenditures by government to meet basic human needs may and in most instances do stem from mixed motives. Charitable concern and a wish to alleviate human suffering in a planned way are undoubtedly part of the picture. Another part, which we in the social welfare field must never forget, is the political part, that aspect of government activity designed to provide benefits for citizens in exchange for commitments to the current elite in office.

Perspectives on the Welfare State

The question of how much the collectivity should do for individuals has been a historic controversy. Blau considers several perspectives on the welfare state.[7] In recent years, he suggests, there have been three dominant approaches to understanding the development of the welfare state. One explanation has come from the development of industrialization and the needs that industrial society presents. A second comes from a functionalist perspective on the need for balance in the society. And a third is ideological and comes from the concept of social rights as a development that should occur along with civil and political rights.[8] But welfare states developed differently, and with different histories and political processes. England began the development of substantial government responsibility long before anything of that sort occurred in the United States (in fact, given the Poor Law of 1603, even before the United States was settled.) As Ashford points out, the development of welfare states followed different courses. He suggests, for example, that France, as opposed to Britain, always had a sense of how welfare fit into the idea of a society; it was to help people be good citizens. Their view of welfare might be like our view of education (at least until recently):

> The development of social legislation in France was not so much to remove pressures from politics but to assert that each French citizen was entitled to the support needed for him or her to be a productive and active member of society.[9]

Ashford adds that "the harmonious interaction of state and society became an integral part of the French concept of the welfare state."[10]

However, the British never had this thoroughgoing approach. They were more like us. Ashford makes the point that "the welfare policies have become common in our lives even though fundamental philosophical issues remain unsettled."[11] As we shall see at the end of this chapter, these unsettled philosophical issues emerge as a conflict between the welfare state and the poorfare state, between the actual provision of help within the context of a hostile attitude.

For the present, Blau suggests that three perspectives on the welfare state are emerging: the conservative, the moderate, and the radical.[12] The conservative perspective criticizes the welfare state for its sheer size and argues for cutbacks. The moderates think that the limit of the welfare state expenditure has now been reached and suggest efficiencies and targeting, as opposed to cutbacks. The radicals agree that limits have been observed and wish to uncover their specific nature so they can be pushed back.[13]

The arguments about the current state of the welfare state tend to focus on three key perspectives as to what groups of people the government programs should target for help.

One perspective, for simplicity's sake, can be called the *"all-people"* perspective. It argues that whatever the government does should be done for all people. Children's allowances are an example of such a program.

The second perspective might be called the *"some-people"* perspective. Here the argument is that some people should be singled out for government help while others should not. Often those singled out have special needs—chronic illness, for example, or special problems in the workplace. However, they represent a subset of the total population.

A third perspective might be called the *"poor-people"* perspective, and it argues that, regardless of what other problems people may have, those who are financially disadvantaged should receive the highest priority for government help. Thus, if you have a chronic illness but come from a well-to-do family, it is your family's responsibility to take care of your illness, not the government's. If you have the same illness and are poor, the government should provide help.

United States society provides examples of each perspective. The Social Security program is, for most purposes, an all-people program, providing coverage to over 95% of the population in various categories and for various possible life conditions, including retirement and disability. While the United States does not have a children's allowance per se, the tax code does permit a tax deduction for the care of dependents, to which all taxpayers are entitled. In terms of some-people programs, many aimed at helping the elderly fall into this category, especially programs under the Older Americans Act, such as senior centers, Meals on Wheels, and other local programs funded by the state through federal dollars provided under this act. Finally, there are programs for those Americans who are financially impoverished, including financial assistance, food stamps, and the Medicaid program. Part of the contemporary fight over welfare state programs involves the costs of these programs.

An all-people program will be more costly than a some-people or poor-people program. On the other hand, though framed in terms of cost, debates should not be seen only in these terms. Important differences exist as well with respect to the perceived role of government. These differences should not be ignored as we consider different countries and different time periods within the United States.

The Scope of the Welfare State

There are many ways to analyze the scope of the welfare state. We could look at dollars expended, people served, employees hired, number and variety of programs, and concentration or density of programs, among other criteria. These possible variables illustrate the range we could use for such an assessment. The analysis here will stress the percent of government expenditures and their range and scope. Information will also be provided on voluntary and corporate expenditures.[14]

GOVERNMENT EXPENDITURES IN THE WELFARE STATE

The financial scope of the U.S. welfare state and its changes since 1960 in U.S. society can be seen in Table 3.1 (on page 70), which portrays the growth of the welfare state in just 27 years. The United States went from 10.3% of GNP for social welfare expenditures to 18.5% in 1980. Then a slight cutback was experienced, with the 1987 proportion down to 18.4%. Nonetheless, these changes represent a growth of 78.6%! In constant dollars (row 4), the rate of growth was 224.4%!

One specific program of great interest to social workers is public aid. How have outlays for public aid been affected? In 1970, public aid expenditures (including public assistance [PA], old age assistance, [OAA], aid to the permanently and totally disabled [APTD], aid to the blind [AB], and general assistance [GA]) were $8,443 million.[15] By 1988, that same number (by now, OAA, APTD, and AB had been converted to Supplemental Security Income [SSI]) had risen to $30,910 million, an increase of 266%. The average monthly payment (1988) under Aid to Families with Dependent Children

TABLE 3.1
Government Expenditures for the Welfare State, 1960-1987

Measure	1960	1970	1980	1987[a]
Percent of GNP	10.3%	14.7%	18.5%	18.4%
$, in millions	$52,293	$145,856	$492,528	$834,446
Per capita	$285	$701	$2,138	$3,364
Per capita, constant (1987) $	$1,037	$1,947	$2,948	$3,364

[a]Estimated.

Source: U.S. Bureau of the Census, *Statistical Abstract of the United States 1990* (Washington, DC: U.S. Government Printing Office, 1990), pp. 350, 352 (Tables 575 and 577).

(AFDC, also called public aid) was $374, with a range from $599 in Alaska to $114 in Alabama.[16]

In spite of the increases in dollars paid, the actual number of people supported declined somewhat between 1980 and 1988. In 1980, 6.5% of the population was receiving public aid. By 1988, that number had dropped to 6.1%, a drop of 6%.[17]

Another area of interest to social workers is Social Security, the all-people program that is a major governmental enterprise. In 1984, the Social Security Administration paid $283,238 million in benefits; in 1987 it paid $330,989, an increase of just under 17%.[18] In 1987, 37,973 thousand Americans received payments from retirement, disability, or survivor components of the Social Security program. Retirement was the largest component of this effort, involving 26,755 thousand citizens (70.4%).

It is clear that the welfare state involves massive government transfer payments to individuals. Some programs, like Social Security, are all-people programs that have vast impact. Others, like public aid, are poor-people programs that have more limited impact in terms of scope, but huge impact on the needy. For the public aid recipient, that income must represent (including additions for medical services and special payments) almost 100% of the family income. According to the Social Security Administration, social insurance benefits accounted for 8.8% of personal income for their beneficiaries.[19]

GOVERNMENT PROGRAMS IN THE WELFARE STATE

If we look at all the social welfare expenditures in different years, what were they and how did they change? Data are presented in Tables 3.2 and 3.3.

Changes in the overall programs and the support they receive are evident. The median amount of change from 1960 to 1987 was 52.5%. That represents a substantial reallocation of resources within the program categories. The index of dissimilarity, a figure that tells how different the columns are, is 29.6% This number indicates that 25.6% of the allocations in 1987 would have to be changed to make them the same as 1960. Both the median change and the index of dissimilarity suggest substantial change. Some of the proportions of change look very large because of the small initial base

TABLE 3.2
Government Programs in the Welfare State, 1960-1987

Program	1960	1970	1980	1987
Social insurance	36.9%	37.5%	46.6%	49.7%
Public aid	7.8%	11.3%	14.6%	13.3%
Health and medical[a]	8.5%	6.8%	5.6%	5.7%
Veterans	10.5%	6.2%	4.4%	3.4%
Education	33.7%	34.9%	24.6%	24.5%
Housing	0.3%	0.5%	1.5%	1.6%
Other social welfare	2.2%	2.8%	2.8%	1.8%
All health and medical	12.3%	17.4%	20.4%	24.4%
Total, %	100.0%	100.0%	100.0%	100.0%
Total $, in millions[b]	$51,923	$145,856	$492,528	$834,446

[a] "Health and medical" excludes program parts of social insurance, public aid (ED, Medicare, and Medicaid), veterans', and other social welfare programs. These items are included in "All health and medical."
[b] The dollar figures are the same as those in Table 3.1, row 2.

U.S. Bureau of the Census, *Statistical Abstract of the United States 1990* (Washington, DC: U.S. Government Printing Office, 1990), p. 350 (Table 575).

TABLE 3.3
Percent of Change in Government Programs in the Welfare State, 1960-1987

Program	1960	1987	±%	Absolute Difference
Social insurance	36.9	49.7	+35	10.8
Public aid	07.8	13.3	+70	5.5
Health and medical[a]	08.5	5.7	−33	2.8
Veterans	10.5	3.4	−67	7.1
Education	33.7	24.5	−27	9.2
Housing	0.3	1.6	+433	1.3
Other social welfare	2.2	1.8	−18	0.4
All health and medical	12.3	24.4	+98	12.1
Total	100.0	100.0		
Median change, disregarding sign			52.5	
Index of dissimilarity, 1960-1987 (absolute difference/2)				24.6

[a] "Health and medical" excludes program parts of social insurance, public aid (ED, Medicare, and Medicaid), veterans', and other social welfare programs. These items are included in "All health and medical."

Source: U.S. Bureau of the Census, *Statistical Abstract of the United States 1990* (Washington, DC: U.S. Government Printing Office, 1990), p. 350 (Table 375).

(housing, for example). Overall, the big increases are in Social Security, Public Aid, and All Health and Medical, which is essentially Medicare and Medicaid. Programs areas that have experienced substantial decreases are veterans and education programs. The national concern over education funding can be seen in these decreases, as well as the concerns about rising medical costs.

VOLUNTARY EXPENDITURES AND PROGRAMS IN THE WELFARE STATE

Any discussion of the welfare state in U.S. society would be incomplete without noting the tremendously large impact of the private sector. In fact, so significant is this area of expenditure that the phrase "third sector" is coming into common usage. In this framework, government represents one sector, business and industrial concerns the second sector, and private social welfare efforts the third sector. This sector contains not for profit organizations created to service civic purposes. Educational institutions and hospitals are involved, as well as organizations such as the Boy Scouts, Campfire Girls, family service societies, and so on. Substantial religious charitable activity is also represented. There is a mix of both charitable and fee-for-service components in this package.

The level of social welfare expenditures reported by the government at the end of 1987 was $834,446,000,000 (see Table 3.1). It may come as something of a surprise, then, to find out that the voluntary sector is still an extremely significant additional

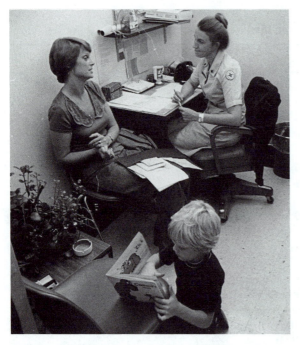

A serviceman's wife discusses her problems with a Red Cross caseworker—an example of social work in the voluntary sector. (Photo courtesy of the American Red Cross.)

TABLE 3.4
Revenue Sources of Voluntary Agencies in Twelve Communities, 1984, in Percent

Revenue Sources	All Sites
Government	38.4%
Service fees, charges, dues	29.6%
Direct individual giving	6.4%
United Way	5.4%
Religious organizations	1.3%
Other federated charities	1.5%
Corporate gifts	3.2%
Foundation gifts	3.5%
Endowment and investment income	4.6%
Other	5.7%
Unspecified	0.4%
Total	100.0%

Source: M. Gutowski, L. Salamon, and K. Pittman, *The Pittsburgh Nonprofit Sector* (Washington, DC: Urban Institute Press, 1984), p. 3.

financial contributor to the welfare state. Many in the social welfare field have tended to believe that the private sector is a small, financially insignificant part of the total picture. Because of these incorrect assumptions, its impact has for many years been significantly underestimated. In spite of the fact that U.S. society historically and currently has supported such efforts, it is only recently that good information on the size of the sector has developed.

Recent studies suggest that the actual cash flow of voluntary sector organizations in all fields amounted to about $160 billion in 1982! If we add an estimate for the value of voluntary service (that is, a cash estimate for the amount of money it would take to replace the effort people give freely to charitable agencies), the private sector social welfare component rises to over $200 billion.[20] This amount reflects the entire budget of the nonprofit sector, including income from fees, trusts, and so on. How much is donated to charity can be calculated from the annual tax forms and is reported by the Census Bureau. It reports $64.7 billion in 1983 (thus, of the $160 billion reported in 1982, 64.7 billion, or about 40%, comes from charitable donations. This fraction is not exactly the same as the 21.1% from all charity reported for 12 communities in Table 3.4).[21] Charitable giving rose to $104.4 billion in 1988.[22] In 1987, the average household donated $790 to charity.[23]

One example of the sources of funds for a 12-community sample is displayed in Table 3.4.

It is important to note that important sources of income from government, 38.4%, are included in these agencies' income. This amount would be duplicated in the government expenditure column, so we might wish to reduce the $160 billion voluntary agency budget by 38.4%. That brings the unduplicated dollar count for 1983–1984 down to $98.56 billion. Subtracting the amount for fees (29.6%) brings us to $69.38 billion.

TABLE 3.5
Distribution of Philanthropic Gifts, 1970 and 1988

| | 1970 | | 1988 | |
	$, billions	%	$, billions	%
Religion	$9.3	44%	$48.2	46%
Health	$2.4	11%	$9.5	09%
Education	$2.6	12%	$9.7	09%
Human service	$2.9	14%	$10.5	10%
Arts and humanities	$0.7	3%	$6.8	07%
Civic and public	$0.5	2%	$3.0	03%
Other	$2.6	12%	$16.5	15%
Total	$21.0	100%	$104.4	100%

Source: U.S. Bureau of the Census, *Statistical Abstract of the United States 1990* (Washington, DC: U.S. Government Printing Office, 1990), p. 372 (Table 620).

Finally, subtracting an amount for endowment, other, and miscellaneous income (10.7%) brings the new, lower total to $62 billion, or just a little lower than the $64.7 billion the government reported.

Where does all this money go? A distribution is displayed in Table 3.5. Unlike government allocations, those in the private sector have remained very stable over the 17-year period reflected in the table. The index of dissimilarity (absolute difference/2) is only 10%, as opposed to a 25% difference in government allocations. Religion continues to occupy a strong place, and human service and education have dropped slightly. Overall, though, the voluntary sector represents a stable and important part of the welfare state.

SOCIAL WELFARE EXPENDITURES IN THE BUSINESS SECTOR

The last component of welfare state expenditures to be addressed comes from the business sector. Increasingly, components of business are becoming involved in the provision of social welfare services. There are three principal areas to consider.

The first component is what we all know as the fringe benefits that come with our jobs.[24] Most fringe benefits, sometimes called private social welfare, focus on life insurance, medical care, and pensions. In many respects they mirror or are built to blend with coverages already available from Social Security. For established businesses and institutions, between 20% to 30% of an employee's compensation may come from these kinds of programs.[25] The fact that businesses have been under union pressure, as well as their own sense of need and appropriateness, to provide some of these benefits does not lessen their importance. Nor is the public and not for profit role thereby reduced. In fact, much of the public role in part arises because people do not have links with formal employment and, thus, not only lack income but access to these other social welfare benefits (such as medical care protection).[26] The contribution of fringe benefits to the gross national product is substantial, 7.7% in 1972 and 12.0% in 1987.[27]

The second area in which businesses are becoming involved in the social welfare system is through the provision of in-house social service activities. The most striking development along these lines is the widespread development of employee assistance programs within the larger organizations. Employee assistance programs are largely focused (and exclusively so in some instances) on dealing with problems of substance abuse within the organizational context. However, they are increasingly involved in providing other services that we also consider to be social services, including counseling troubled employees. How widespread this is cannot yet be determined since good data are not yet available. However, the important point is that not all personal help activities are provided through the family service agency. Some are available in the workplace.

The third kind of business involvement in the social welfare system is the for-profit human service organization. Many of these have been around for some time. In the health care field, for example, some hospitals have operated for profit for many years. The same is true for nursing homes. To these we now add for-profit counseling services and other kinds of personal help services. Included also are the large number of private counseling practitioners, including psychiatrists, psychologists, and, to an increasing degree, social workers, who are now hanging out their shingles and offering their services to the general public. The dilemmas and difficulties that some of these new developments have created will be discussed later. The important point here, however, is to think of them as an important component of the social welfare system.

In addition to these efforts, the corporation participates in many other ways in the welfare state. These are detailed in Chapter 15.

SHIFTING COMPONENTS OF THE WELFARE STATE

The social welfare state is made up of three basic components: government expenditures, a significant private sector, and a developing set of efforts within the profit-making business community (including fringe benefits, programs like employee assistance programs, and private practitioners of social work), all of whom are bound together in a loosely structured system that seeks to meet human needs.

All these changes have occurred within the past 50 years. It may be difficult for readers to imagine that U.S. society has gone from zero dollars at the federal level in 1935 to $800+ billion in 1988, an unbelievable shift. To this must be added voluntary and corporate care-giving efforts. Of the three sectors, perhaps the corporate is undergoing the most shift and change today, with fringe benefit packages changing, employee assistance programs developing, and so on. Within the governmental allocations packages, significant changes are occurring. Perhaps, because it is the oldest sector, the voluntary sector has been the most stable. However, it is coming under attack in the media and elsewhere as conservative and lacking innovation and a willingness to fund new agencies. Because the funding of the voluntary sector is limited and because it must also face the cutback of governmental funding, the voluntary sector may be in for a crisis.

The Reasons for a Welfare State

Given the tremendous level of expenditures and effort that has just been outlined, we might wonder how this development has all come about. How does one explain the welfare state? And, it should be noted, some of the previous perspectives can be thought of as explanations too.[28] There are several kinds of explanations, but we will summarize them under two categories: structural explanations (dealing with changes in technology, demography, and the like) and cultural explanations (dealing with changes in attitudes, beliefs, and values). Let us begin with the structural explanations.

SOCIAL STRUCTURE AND THE WELFARE STATE

When we think of the relationship between social structure and the welfare state, several factors come to mind. One is the age structure of the population itself. Directly and indirectly, the demographic weight of segments of the populations dictates, influences, and stimulates societies to develop programs in certain directions. The development of veterans' aid programs after the Civil War, for example, was noted in Chapter 1. That was a natural development because many veterans needed help. Similarly, the development of the Freedman's Bureau to help slaves who had been liberated was an equally logical development, given the presence and needs of a certain group of people at a certain time. Demographic weight does not always result in specific kinds of attention, but it is an important factor to be taken into account.

In U.S. social welfare history, for example, the development of child welfare programs began in part because around 1900 the fraction of children was greater than that of older adults. Programs for older adults did not really begin, to any significant degree, until after World War II.[29] In short, the age structure of a population has much to do with the kinds of social welfare assistance the society is likely to provide. Wilensky, for example, has shown with respect to European societies that the increase in the elderly fraction of a population is a very important factor in explaining the increase in social security type programs.[30]

Effects can be direct and indirect. The simple presence of needy segments creates an indirect pressure to take action on their behalf. This factor may be operative with children. Other groups, however, such as veterans, African Americans, and the elderly, may take much more direct political action on their own behalf. They make seek to influence political party platforms, become interest groups, press for their own cause, and in general seek through the use of the political process to provide benefits for themselves.[31]

A second factor is the level of resources available to a society. As one of the wealthiest societies in the world, the United States is in a position to provide resources through government activity. However, the role of wealth and the mere presence of resources should be further investigated, because they can have a prohibiting as well as a promoting effect in the following way. Although the presence of resources can lead to government expenditures, it can also be argued that the presence of resources permits individuals to meet their own needs. We could speculate, for example, that as per capita income increases in a society the way that social welfare needs are met changes. At a very low per capita income, these needs may simply remain unmet. At a moderate level of income, it may be efficient and effective for the government to organize and orchestrate a need-meeting system. At still higher levels of resources, however, individual idiosyncrasies may emerge, and we might come to prefer, for example, the private automobile over mass transit. Hence, more money does not mean that government uses it for, in this example, mass transit.

A third structural source of the welfare state lies in the development of technology, for two reasons: first, when basic needs, such as the need for food, can be met by a relatively minor portion of the population's work force, this frees a number of other workers to be involved in other kinds of activities. As Naisbett says, the shift from an agricultural to an industrial society was accomplished in part because we needed so few people, relatively speaking, to produce enough food for the rest of us.[32] He argues that we are now moving from an industrial society to an information society. In particular, he asserts that a transformation is now underway similar to that which characterized the agricultural to industrial transformation. In the future, he believes, a relatively small fraction of the working population will be involved in the production of manufactured goods. This transition will free large population segments to work in the social welfare system. From our perspective, this shift is already well underway.

However, this change leads to the second observation. We cannot offer large-scale services without the people to staff them. There also must be the technology to provide these services. The vast explosion in the provision of helping technologies is a case in point. Small schools of social work have become large ones, such as at the University of Michigan, the University of Washington, and Hunter College. Various programs in psychological and other kinds of counseling services have been growing. Training not only in individual intervention but in various kinds of advocacy, urban planning, and so forth, has been growing, too. Training programs in gerontology are among those with the most expansion. We are beginning to develop the technology of helping, as well as generating the administrators and managers needed to run the vast social welfare enterprise.

The development of this occupational group begins to exert its own force as large numbers of individuals obtain jobs and careers centered within the human service sector. They themselves become a demographic force worth considering. It is the occupational structure that now becomes important, along with the demographic structure. Significant changes in the social welfare system will cause people to lose jobs, and they will indirectly and directly oppose these changes to forestall that result.

Another structural element of importance is the increasing level of urbanization. As the number of people in cities increases, personal helping and farm-based self-sufficiency decline, leaving urbanites more vulnerable. And, to a certain extent, the urban place has made the problems of social exploitation more possible or at least more visible.

These factors are among the important structural ones that promote the development of a welfare state enterprise in modern nations generally and in the United States in particular. But social structure is not the only force at work. Culture is important as well.

THE SOCIAL CULTURE OF THE WELFARE STATE

The beliefs, attitudes, and values of a society are also important when considering why certain states move in the directions they do. The historical individualism and sense of personal responsibility for one's fate that has characterized U.S. society cannot be ignored as a factor in keeping us from moving as quickly as some other societies have toward the establishment of programs of human care. Coupled with this individualism, and a specific component of it, is a deep distrust of government. The people who established this country fled here because of government oppression. Many immigrants who have continued to come over the years have also been fleeing government oppression either directly or indirectly. For all its problems, the United States remains for most people in the world a desired place to be. Because of this governmental distrust, the United States America was perhaps slower than others to give the government the resources and the permission it needed to use them for programs of human care.

A second point has to do with the ethos of care itself. Different subgroups in society take different positions on the notion of helping the unfortunate. Within this context, the famous Protestant ethic cannot be seen as a charitable ethic. Rather, it supports the acquisition of funds, the importance of work, and the responsibility of each individual for getting ahead on his or her own. This was a basic ethic for U.S. society.

One other ethic, a point of view that competed importantly with the Protestant ethic, might be called the Catholic ethic.[33] Within Catholic tradition, there has always been the presence of a commitment to charity and help, something that has also characterized the Jewish tradition. But U.S. society did not have large numbers of Catholics and Jews until the middle of the nineteenth century, when waves of immigration from Poland, Ireland, and Italy began to arrive. These individuals not only came with a positive commitment to helping, but quickly set about forming organizations such as Catholic charities, St. Vincent de Paul, Jewish Welfare Services, and so on, to provide help to their own. While the specific presence and influence of this ethic as a competing view to the Protestant ethic remains to be examined, we believe that it is an important and overlooked component in supporting the growth of a welfare state.

Religious orientation might have been one factor, but its impact should not be overstated. Basic U.S. values of equality and fair play have also been mobilized, albeit recently, in support of a helping orientation. And the development of liberals from all walks of life into a sort of liberal coalition has provided a broad range of support for helping programs in government, voluntary, and corporate sectors.

Thus, in addition to the structural features, the increasing presence of a different point of view toward helping may have made helping easier. Most probably, when a full understanding of the welfare state emerges, cultural and structural factors will both play an important role.

United States Society: Welfare State, Poorfare Culture

The developments in social welfare, important as they are, do not come without struggle. Nowhere in the industrialized world has that struggle been more pronounced than within U.S. society. Attitudes that are suspicious of government, not very favorable to the poor, and in some instances even hostile toward the disadvantaged abound. At the structural level, the United States has moved into the ranks of welfare states, though not quickly. At the cultural level, though, the level of values, we have remained hostile and negative. Hence, the most accurate characterization of U.S. society at this point might be with the phrase "welfare state, poorfare culture," designed to communicate the dualism and difference found simultaneously in the society.

There has always had a moral tone to the discussion of welfare problems and social help in U.S. society. Perhaps it was picked up from England. Ashford comments:

> The intense moral tone of social reform is all the more graphic because of the ease of actually designing and implementing new social policies. To a greater degree than in other welfare states, [except the United States, which he does not write about here, ed.] the values of sobriety, thrift, self help and temperance dominated early British debates about the welfare state. . . . The severe moral judgements of the time are found in the records of the Salvation Army, The Charity Organization Society and the Christian Social Union.[34]

Even greater ambivalence seems to surround the provision of social welfare benefits in the United States. It seems unquestionably right for famous sport figures and popular music figures to have salaries totaling millions. It seems reasonable, apparently, that captains of industry can have salaries in six or even seven figures. If things don't work out, they can negotiate golden parachutes for themselves that allow them to live in a sort of derived luxury—derived not from current but from former employment. This same society, moreover, spends a significant portion of time railing against welfare chiselers and welfare dependency; it lets big stock companies who have misappropriated millions of dollars off with a slap on the wrist while vigorously pursuing welfare cheaters. United States society has progressed in the provision of social welfare benefits but has been uneasy about that progress. We are now in a position of beginning to cut back those benefits, at least those offered by government, and shifting to a system that we seem to prefer—private initiative. Social Security is being attacked while individual retirement accounts are being promoted. Although it is true that other societies are cutting back as well, that similarity should not obscure the fact that U.S. society is perhaps more negative and more hostile toward social welfare programs than any other large-scale country. Social work and social welfare must exist within this negative and often hostile context in which what we think of as doing good is considered by others as doing bad.

Value Dilemmas in the Welfare State

Part of the hostility toward welfare stems from the fact that our commitment to competing values sets us always at war within ourselves. The concept of value conflict has been mentioned before. It is now appropriate to give some specific examples, especially as they pertain to the welfare state.

Blau discusses the arguments over the social wage. Are citizens entitled to a basic wage no matter what they do?[35] Arguments about this point often revolve around different value emphases with respect to the *causes* versus the *consequences* of poverty. Those committed to looking at consequences argue that poverty could be prevented by providing a living wage. Those focusing on the consequences of poverty argue that providing a living wage will just encourage more people not to work.

Another conflict revolves around issues of equity and adequacy. Americans values conflict on commitments to social equity on the one hand and social adequacy on the other. Equity is a proportional concept, and it suggests that out of any situation you should draw rewards proportionate to what you contributed. Hence, if you work hard, you should get a good salary and that salary should somehow be seen as a reward for the investment. The more the investment, the more the reward. However, there is a conflict.

Problems of underequity are more troublesome than problems of overequity because they involve many more people and a competing value, adequacy. People ought to get enough to get by. If what they get from their workplace is too low, or inadequate, then some kind of supplement will be needed so that their resources can meet basic needs. Supplement is also needed if what a person receives from work, though equitable, is still inadequate, or if a person is not able to find a job at all. The crucial point is that, within the welfare state context, societies use competing principles to allocate resources in an appropriate manner.

A similar conflict within the context of U.S. society exists between private and public means. On the one hand, U.S. society is committed to doing things voluntarily and privately, whether by a business or a private social agency activity. On the other hand, we are also committed to the public weal, to the civic purpose, and to having a government that works for all. Perhaps more so than any other society, the United States has used private means (albeit with public stimulation) to meet large-scale social purposes. The Individual Retirement Account is simply a current manifestation of this tendency.

The important point here is to understand that over a range of values (only two possible conflicts out of many have been mentioned here) societies will experience tension around the welfare state enterprise.[36]

Conclusion

For a variety of demographic and other structural reasons, as well as an evolving and generally supported belief system, the welfare state seems here to stay. It involves a substantial portion of government resources and activity designed to provide for both the ordinary and extraordinary needs of citizens. However, important as the government base of these efforts is, we should not forget the fact that, for U.S. society at least, tremendously significant components of need-meeting activity are provided through the auspices of private business and through a very large nonprofit sector. This effort gives additional credibility to the activity portion of our definition, because much of the private and business expenses are supported through tax relief programs of government. For example, contributions to nonprofits are tax deductible, and nonprofits may pay no tax at all. (Compensation to employees, including fringe benefits, are also deductible from business income.) In sum, the welfare state, while based on government and supported by it, contains much private effort, too. But its shape in the future may increasingly be questioned. In U.S. society, the host of social problems we now face, such as female poverty, lack of literacy, drug abuse, and the decline in some urban centers, all occur within the framework of massive welfare state spending. The next iteration of the welfare state may well have to target its efforts better and defend itself for increasing skepticism and attack.

Notes

1. Recall from Chapter 1 that pauperization was the concept given to this idea that receipt of aid itself was destructive.
2. Sometimes voluntary agencies are called the private sector to differentiate them from the government sector. However, private has now become confused with corporate and business philanthropy, so it is becoming conventional to call the social agency part of the welfare state the voluntary sector. Because of government and corporate involvement, social agencies are also called the third sector. And, to add one more name to the list, Karger and Stoesz call it the hidden sector. H. J. Karger and D. Stoesz, *American Social Welfare Policy* (New York: Longman, 1990).
3. The Veteran's Administration runs a health care system bigger than that of many countries.
4. For some examples of tax expenditures, see S. M. Rosen, D. Fanshel, and M. Lutz, eds., *Face of the Nation 1987* (Silver Spring, MD: National Association of Social Workers, 1987). Tables 46 and 47.
5. An early history of the TVA by its first chair, David Lillienthal, was titled *T.V.A.: Democracy on the March* (New York: Harper, 1953).
6. Government expenditures for relief go back a long way. One early example is provided by the Coliseum in Rome. The Roman games were a sort of social welfare program sponsored by the Roman government to keep unemployed men occupied. It is hard to know what total fraction of the imperial budget those games consumed. Thus, expenditures to meet the needs of individuals on the part of government has a long tradition.
7. Joel Blau, "Theories of the Welfare State," *Social Service Review* (March 1989), pp. 27–38.
8. Douglas Ashford provides a series of other reasons. See Douglas Ashford, *The Emergence of The Welfare States* (New York: Blackwell, 1987), and footnote 32.
9. Ashford, p. 308.
10. Ibid. p. 310.
11. Ibid. p. 302.
12. Blau, "Theories of the Welfare State," pp. 29ff.
13. These three perspectives provide close parallels to three value orientations—neocapitalism, the administrated state, and welfare liberalism—discussed in R. Bellah and others, *Habits of the Heart* (New York: Harper & Row, 1986).
14. While using this particular indicator is far from the only way such an assessment could be made, three features recommend it. First, most readers have a subjective sense of what we are talking about when dollar amounts are given. While most of us do not deal in amounts of millions of dollars, we do have some sense of the relationship between 1 million and 10 million, 10 million and 100 million, and so on. This is not necessarily the case when we are talking about number of employees, number of programs, range of coverage, and so on. Hence, there is a built-in subjective basis for offering comparisons (using dollar amounts). Second, to a degree not possible with some other variables, it permits comparisons with other countries. Third, it provides us with the ability to compare over time. The tables in this section will provide some sense of the size, scope, and change in the welfare state in American society.

15. U.S. Bureau of the Census, *Statistical Abstract of the United States,* 110th ed. (Washington, DC: U.S. Government Printing Office, 1990), p. 367, Table 608.

16. Ibid., p. 368, Table 610.

17. Ibid., pp. 367, 368, Tables 609, 610.

18. Ibid., p. 354, Table 581.

19. Ibid.

20. E. J. Tropman and J. E. Tropman, "Voluntary Agencies," in Ann Minahan, ed., *Encyclopedia of Social Work* (Silver Spring MD: National Association of Social Workers, 1987).

21. U.S. Bureau of the Census, *Statistical Abstract,* p. 372, Table 620.

22. Ibid.

23. Ibid., p. 372, Table 618.

24. See also the discussion of fringe benefits in Chapters 7 and 15.

25. We must be careful to avoid double counting here. Part of what a business counts as its fringe benefit package frequently includes its contribution to the Social Security tax. Since those monies have already been counted under the government sector, they should not be counted here. However, even subtracting that fraction leaves a significant amount, which is part of the business expense.

26. The provision of social welfare benefits as a component of wages should not be confused with a point mentioned earlier about the family wage system. What we discussed there (Chapter 1) was the division of wages into an economic portion and a family support portion. To those two we now add a third portion, fringe benefits. This might be called the social welfare portion.

27. U.S. Bureau of the Census, *Statistical Abstract,* p. 349, Table 574.

28. Ashford, op cit., provides a review of explanations in his section "Welfare: Object or Subject of the State," pp. 20–29. He gives four kinds of studies (explanations) of the welfare state: (1) political studies seeing welfare as resulting from the changing demands of the polities, stemming in turn from industrialization, and other causes; (2) supply studies, seeing welfare as a result of imperfections in the marketplace; (3) quantitative and demographic studies (fractions of youth, the elderly, and so on); and (4) studies of the historical imperative of changes, like Marx. Jill Quadango's recent study, "Race, Class and Gender in the U.S. Welfare State," *American Sociological Review,* 55 (February 1990), pp. 11–28 can be seen in the light of these categories. She criticizes class conflict explanations of the welfare state (category 1) and advances the importance of race and gender (category 4).

29. A reader might wonder about the Social Security program since, as a pension program, it was heavily though not exclusively aimed at older adults. To this query, we would reply that, indeed, the generation of the Social Security program was, in part, a response to the perceived aging of the population (in the 1930s, for example, the baby boom was not anticipated, and demographers were predicting the rapid aging of the U.S. population) and to another structural feature, the Depression.

30. H. Wilensky, *The Welfare State and Equality* (Berkeley: University of California Press, 1975).

31. The operation of indirect effects requires that the unaffected portion of the population be aware of the difficulties experienced by the affected portions. The physical size and vastness of the United States permitted us to hide problems for longer than might have been true in Europe. Perhaps this is part of the reason why the United States is something of a welfare laggard in the provision of public benefits for those in need.

32. John Naisbett, *Megatrends* (New York: Warner Books, 1982).

33. For further discussion, see John E. Tropman, "The Catholic Ethic v. the Protestant Ethic," *Social Thought,* 12, 1 (Winter 1986).

34. Ashford, op. cit., p. 303.

35. Blau, "Theories of the Welfare State."

36. Competing values are not the only reason for such ambivalence, although they are a major source for it. As noted, additional reasons come from our historical context. For example,

the size of the country itself is a major factor, one that has often been commented upon. From our perspective, it is important because (1) it permitted problems to be hidden, to seem insignificant within the vast space, and (2) it permitted Americans the luxury of dumping problems in areas where they did not affect, right away at least, others. It was possible in U.S. society, as it was not in European society, to run people out of town and not run them into someone else's town. For this reason, the press of human problems was less visible here, although the level and scope may well have been similar to European countries.

CHAPTER 4

Choosing a System Level
for Change

The Concept of Levels and Systems in Social Work

Social work intervention typically has targets that range from the individual to the group, the community, the organization, or to society itself. On other occasions the world itself and its social relations are the target of social work intervention. Jane Addams, for example, one of the more illustrious women in our profession, won the Nobel prize in peace for her global efforts at creating peace. In special circumstances, the biological system may be the target of intervention.

The divisions we have just mentioned have a certain face validity. We intuitively understand that these system levels are appropriate targets of intervention. Anderson and Carter divide systems into culture and society, communities and organizations, groups, families, and the person.[1] However, they do not specifically use the word "level" to indicate those differences. Mehr[2] has chapters on micro environmental change and macro environmental change in his book, a two-level approach. Gilbert, Miller, and Specht[3] discuss intervention with individuals and groups in a section on direct services and in sections focusing on the context of social work practices and indirect services dealing with the organization and the community. Friedlander and Apte[4] focus on family, children, youth, and aging, among other topics in their work. Finally, Skidmore and Thackeray[5] focus on work with individuals, groups, community, and administration and related practices.

Perhaps the most common overall division is the one between micro, which focuses on the individual and perhaps the individual in a small group, and macro, which focuses on the larger-scale environment, often thought of as a context. We will use the word "context" in this chapter as well, but wish to emphasize at the outset that the concept of context as used here refers to the elements *outside* the target system in question. Hence, if the individual is the target, then the group and family, the community, the organization, and certainly society and the world become the context. However, if the community is the target in question and community change the goal to be achieved, then society and the world become the contexts in question. This use of context allows us to always remember that there are systems influencing our change target, which may at some point become targets themselves, as change in client context is sometimes needed to assist the client.

But we have now introduced the word "system." How does it relate to level? Levels and systems are interrelated concepts. System, however, is the more basic. "Level" refers to a relationship among systems and refers to the amount of complexity that a system contains. Therefore, a brief introductory discussion of systems as a way to introduce a more detailed discussion of levels is in order.

The idea of system has developed into a very general concept.[6] It is particularly useful in social work because it allows us to focus our diagnosis and intervention and produce a unit of action around which diagnosis and intervention can center, at the same time emphasizing the interrelatedness of the social elements that may affect a particular client. Sometimes the phrase "client system" is used to emphasize this connectedness.

SYSTEMS IN SOCIAL WORK

Anderson and Carter quote Hearn on the importance of the systems approach in social work.

> The general systems approach . . . is based upon the assumption that matter, in all its forms, living and non living, can be regarded as systems and that systems, as systems, have certain discrete properties that are capable of being studied. Individuals, small groups including families and organizations and other complex human organizations such as neighborhoods and communities in short, the entities with which social work is usually involved—can all be regarded as systems, with certain common properties. If the general systems approach could be used to order knowledge about the entities with which we work, perhaps it could also be used as a means of developing a fundamental conception of the social work process itself.[7]

The concept of systems, then, can be seen as fundamental to the social work enterprise because systems are fundamental units of the world in which we live.

DEFINING SYSTEMS

According to Anatole Rapoport, systems have the following properties:

1. Something consisting of a set . . . of entities.
2. Among which a set of relations is specified [for example, cell organization, human interaction, grammar, culture, etc.]
3. So that deductions are possible from some relations to others.[8]

To look at the definition in our terms, the entities could be cells, people, words, beliefs, and the relations could be cell organization, human interaction, grammar, social structure, or culture. As Anderson and Carter emphasize, quoting Buckley, a system is "a complex element of components directly or indirectly related in a causal network, such that each component is related to at least some others in a more or less stable way within a particular period of time."[9] Systems can be thought about as entities "some of which process matter or energy, some of which process information, and some of which process all three," as Miller suggests.[10] Seen in this light, systems could be families, individuals, organizations, communities, or societies, but one component of the definition is missing—history. The units with which we work in social work have a history, and what happens today or tomorrow depends in part on what has happened in the past.[11] Systems then are complex sets of interconnections and, at their own level, function as wholes. Rapoport suggests that "a whole which functions as a whole by virtue of the interdependence of its parts is called a system. . . ."[12] Levels are kinds of wholes that fit together to form larger and more complex entities but function as well in their own right. Within the system-level concept, a system is both a means and an end. It is a means to a larger system as individuals make up families, families in turn make up communities, and so on. But individuals and families, organizations and communities are systems in and of themselves as well.

KINDS OF SYSTEMS

Systems can be living and nonliving. Language is one kind of nonliving system. It has entities (words) and rules for assembling them (grammar). Computers represent another kind of nonliving system. Living systems are made up of animals, plants, cells, tissues, organs, either alone and in combination. Ecological systems are combinations of living and nonliving systems. The seashore is an example of a living and nonliving system combined. In social work, our primary focal interest is on human systems (the person, family, organization, community, or society), but we are also interested in the interaction between living and nonliving systems. The nonliving system of language, for example, may create certain problems for a particular client. Dyslexia could be thought of as a difficulty of exactly this sort. In another example from community organization, let's say a community development project, the village system may have a technological system that is inadequate for its needs; hence, the social work community organizer may seek to improve the technological system, say, food processing or food procuring, to help the village retain its balance with its environment.

ASPECTS OF HUMAN SYSTEMS

Just as human action can be divided into two major parts, thinking and doing, human social systems can be divided into two major parts, the cultural system and the social system. These distinctions have important implications for social work intervention. The social system is the interrelated pattern of actions, acts, and behaviors that is characteristic of a human entity. Anderson and Carter quote Olsen as follows:

> Very briefly, a social system is a model of social organization that possesses a distinctive total unit beyond its component parts, that is distinguished from its environment by a clearly defined boundary, and whose subunits are at least partially interrelated within relatively stable patterns of social order. Put even more simply, *a social system is a bounded set of interrelated activities that together constitute a single entity.*[13] [Emphasis in original.]

On the other hand, the cultural system is the interrelated set of beliefs, attitudes, norms, and thoughts that constitutes the distinctive set of mental activities of a system. These systems are called analytic systems because, while we separate them for purposes of discussion and examination, neither exists without the other. Actions and acts in human systems are guided by thoughts, values, beliefs, and so on, at least to some degree. Similarly, thoughts, values, beliefs, and attitudes are influenced by the actual patterns of behavior, the patterns of opportunities, and so on.

In fact, the articulation of these two systems is an important task for social work intervention. In a human system, when the pattern of ideas, thoughts, and beliefs does not develop as quickly as the pattern of actions and opportunities, it is called cultural lag. Cultural lag can occur when a new technological device is introduced into a village or tribe within a community development context. The tribe may not have the norms and values available to handle the increased production, wealth, and leisure that may result from the introduction of such a time-saving element.

Similarly, changes in culture, beliefs, values, and attitudes may not be mirrored at once by changes in the social structure or patterns of behavior. In this case, structural lag becomes the problem. A contemporary example of structural lag is the increasingly traditional orientation of U.S. public opinion over the past 15 years or so and the delayed manifestation of these traditional attitudes within the electorate.

President Ronald Reagan's election was produced by these changes. But we should not be misled by thinking that the current conservatism is a result of the incumbent. Rather, it is the reverse. The incumbent is the result of prior cultural changes within the U.S. electorate. A different example of this same problem occurs during adolescent development. As chronological age advances, parents frequently change expectations about the behavior of their children. This can be viewed as a change in family culture and in the set of norms and expectations surrounding the behavior of one of its members. But because of differential development trajectories, certain family individuals may not meet these average age expectations at any particular chronological age. Hence, the older adolescent may be accused of "acting like an infant," a common phrase that can now be redefined as an example of structural lag.

Similarly, when someone's attitude is referred to as rigid or hidebound, it is a case of cultural lag at the individual level. The individual's thoughts, ideas, and perspectives are trapped in prior social structures and are not evolving and developing appropriately for new situations.

SYSTEM DYSFUNCTION

Social workers are always concerned with the dysfunctioning of systems. One way to look at system dysfunction is to look at system function. Systems tend to have four major subsystems: (1) an input subsystem, (2) a throughput or processing subsystem, and (3) an output subsystem. These are the processing subsystems. Linking them and orchestrating their activity is the (4) executive system. Whether the system is processing units of energy, information, or materials, the unit must enter the system, and that is the input subsystem. Then it must be processed and moved out.

One example that social workers are familiar with is a residential treatment center. Intake is that subsystem through which clients are brought into the system. The throughput subsystem, or processing system, is the set of technologies that "works on" the clients in an attempt to achieve improvement and change. It is called treatment. Discharge is the output subsystem. The executive subsystem coordinates input, throughput, and output to assure a balanced and even flow. We are all familiar with operating difficulties that occur when these systems do not work well together.

For example, if intake is too great, the system becomes overloaded. If intake is deficient, the system begins to starve. If, on the other hand, output is too quick, the system also suffers and may starve. Similarly, if output is too slow, the system begins to swell. If throughput does not work well, the processing that occurs is either ineffective (does not work) or counterproductive (produces a result opposite from the one intended), as in the case of some prison systems.

The executive function of systems is designed to keep all the subsystems operating in synchrony and to make the requisite and appropriate adjustments. But systems do not exist by themselves. They have a context. Clients must come from somewhere, and it is important to understand where clients come from and the sources of influence that control, increase, or decrease client flow. Similarly, discharged clients must go somewhere. The discharge planners and hospitals face this specific problem. Without enough discharge facilities, hospital patients, especially the older patients, tend to back up into the hospital itself. Many medical care facilities, which design themselves theoretically as a revolving door system with people entering, being treated, and leaving, find that the revolving door becomes stuck because the rate of system exit (hospital discharge in this case) is simply too slow.

Executive systems, therefore, not only deal with intrasystem articulation of the subsystems among each other, but also seek to articulate the external environment with respect to input and output issues. In general, problems occur, then, in processing or in sequence or in the executive function itself. Paralyses in the executive subsystem may create problems in both the operation of the system and the direction and articulation of system components.

Social workers may thus seek in a particular organization to improve the intake process, to improve client processing, or to improve the discharge process, but they may also seek to improve the executive and decision-making process.

Analogous activities may occur at the level of the individual and the family as well. As Rapoport says:

The Nazi regime that produced the Holocaust can only be viewed as a pathological system. (Photo by UPI/Bettmann Newsphotos.)

> [H]uman social aggregates (families, institutions, communities, nations) exhibit all the features of organized systems. The degree of organization varies, of course, as does the robustness and "viability" of these systems. When a system or subsystem works poorly, it therefore makes sense to speak of the "pathology" of such systems.[14]

The notion of pathology has been well established at the level of the person, and we can even think of the pathological family.

It is perhaps a little stranger to think of the pathological organization, community, or society, but there are examples. The Holocaust, for example, certainly involves pathology of the social and cultural system, as do manifestations of racism and sexism within our own society.

Other examples of pathology are communities and organizations that are hostile and negative, depriving their members or clients of dignity, liberty, and meaning. Indeed, some major organization designed to provide assistance to individuals may be in a state of pathological crisis today. It is frequently asserted, for example, that none of these large organizational systems works well. The schools do not teach, mental hospitals do not heal, prisons do not reform, and so on. Indeed some even argue that pathology extends beyond the lack of goal accomplishment into a paradoxically inverse counterproductivity. For example, when an individual enters school, his or her IQ may drop. Or a person who enters a mental health facility may become more mentally ill. Or a person in prison may becomes more criminal. If true, these would clearly be system dysfunctions or system pathologies, and social workers can intervene in these systems to make them right.

The Concept of System Levels in Social Work

Social work typically refers to macro and micro as a way of distinguishing levels. We think of big levels and small ones. The society, the community, and perhaps the organization are big; individuals are small. This is what the terms micro and macro imply. But the reality is more complex. System levels refer to the way systems themselves are organized into packages. James G. Miller says:

> Complex structures which carry out living processes I believe can be identified at seven hierarchical levels—cell, organ, organism, group, organization, society, and supranational system. My central thesis is that systems at all of these levels are open systems composed of subsystems which process inputs, throughputs and outputs of various forms of matter, energy and information.[15]

For us, the organism is equivalent to the individual, and cell and organ are combined into the biological level. Miller goes on to say:

> The universe contains a hierarchy of systems, each more advanced or "higher" level made up of systems of lower levels. Atoms are composed of particles, molecules of atoms . . . organisms of organs, groups (e.g., herds, flocks, families, teams, tribes) of organisms, organizations of groups (and sometimes single individual organisms), societies of organizations, groups and individuals and supranational systems of societies and organizations. . . .

It would be convenient for theorists if the hierarchical levels of living systems fitted neatly into each other. . . . The facts are more complicated. . . . For example, one might conceivably separate tissue and organ into two separate levels, or one might, as Anderson and Carter have suggested, separate the organization and the community into two separate levels—local communities, urban and rural, are composed of multiple organizations just as societies are composed of multiple local communities, states, or provinces.[16]

Gerard looks at levels as "a species with interbreeding individuals" for which he uses the word "orgs." He goes on to say:

[T]he important levels are those whose orgs (entities) are relatively enduring and self-contained. . . . For us, individuals, families, groups, organizations and societies are "orgs." Thus, higher level orgs are likely to have a greater variety than lower level ones and they are likely to depend more on their particular past. They are more individual, but they are also less plentiful since several subordinate units contribute to each.[17]

Certainly this applies to human systems: the person, the family, the organization, the community, and society. All are systems in their own right and subsystems of other larger systems. Meyer and others refer to these as levels. They say,

[W]e use the term level to suggest broad distinctions that may be made in the objectives of social work practice—from helping individuals to changing features of the social system—as well as in the methods of achieving these objectives—from the use of interpersonal interaction to social legislation. The levels are, of course, interrelated.[18]

Each human system is involved as either a composing element in a larger system or a contextual element to a smaller system. This point has important practice implications, discussed later.

PARTS AND WHOLES

The concept of the composition and context of each system level brings the issue of parts and wholes into sharp focus. What is a whole system? What is a part of a system? These are important questions for intervention. What is the boundary of a level? When do we approach the next level? The human systems that social work addresses are open to some degree, but openness fuzzies the boundaries. Viewing the individual as a system is apparently relatively straightforward, at least in the physical sense. We can see the individual, she or he has a name and address, and so on. Yet we have often been surprised at how differently an individual behaves and thinks in different situations. Hence the individual in context may vary considerably.

The individual we see as a system might function very differently depending on context, and while the compositional subsystems (subsystems that make up the person) of the individual person may be relatively similar across persons (although there may be variation even here), the contexts may vary considerably and the individual may thus vary considerably in context. The family presents a set of different problems on the compositional side. Which members compose the family system? What if there is a blended family? Do we include the former partners as well as current partners? What are the relevant parts of the family system?

Similar questions can be asked of communities, organizations, and nations. Parts and wholes are in a constant process of development and change. It is for this reason that the *open system* concept is useful. It suggests that elements in a system are not necessarily fixed. Social work practice should be alert to the constant reconfiguration of parts and wholes within system levels. However, openness does not mean that any system level is less real than any other level. The fact that the organization, for example, changes clients, workers, directors, and location does not alone make the organization any less real. It has a history, a tradition, a location in space and time, which endure over the entry and exit of different workers, clients, and the like.

Similarly, the family system may change members but retain its identity (for positive or negative consequences) for its members. The fact, then, that a particular system level is a part of another system is an important contextual aspect of that system level, but it does not detract from the viability and importance of the system level in its own right. Thus, the concept of means and ends is useful when applied to parts and wholes. Each system level becomes a part of means for larger system levels.

EMERGENT PROPERTIES

Emergent properties distinguish system levels from each other. These characteristics of the system are unique to its level. In human systems, features emerge at the system level that are not present in the parts. Communities have a structure and character that continue despite changes in membership. Families have strengths and pathologies that seem to exist over historical time. Hence, history is one of the unique features that emerges at each system level. Family history is different from the organizational history, community history is different from individual history, and these histories shape and direct activities and acts, thoughts, and attitudes.

Other features to emerge at different system levels are variety, range, and diversity. At any time an individual may have a temperature, but an individual cannot have a standard deviation. As Gerard says, "thus higher level orgs (entities, units, parts) are likely to have a greater variety than lower order ones and they are more likely to depend on their particular past. They are more individual. But they are also less plentiful since several subordinate units contribute to each."[19] Gerard mentions history and variety, and he also introduces the notion of individuality and uniqueness.

For these reasons, social workers learn about each system level, because of the unique properties at each level. It is important to know how systems at each level function and the impact that they have on their members and environment.

REDUCTIONISM

There is always a tendency to reduce effects from one level to another, called reductionism. Because of emerging properties, each level is real in its own terms. Each is a part and a whole in its own right. This perspective is very important for social work practitioners because it means that analyses of the behavior of larger, more complex wholes cannot be explained away by reducing these wholes to their component parts and explaining the behavior of the parts. Societies, for example, cannot be explained in terms of the sociology of the communities and organizations that comprise them or by the psychology of the families and individuals who are their members, any more than an individual can be explained by looking at molecular functioning. Purcell speaks about this: "[W]e see how even [a] simple system works itself into great complexity when one tries to understand the essential problem of cooperative behavior. I suggest the astonishing stubbornness of [this] problem stands as a sober warning to anyone who attempts to carve a path of rigorous deduction from the part to the whole."[20] Rapoport deals with this problem, too, in an especially interesting way.

> [S]uppose a man quits his job. Examining the circumstances we find that he had quarreled with his supervisor, had no hope of promotion, and was offered another job at twice the pay. By any common sense criteria of "understanding" we understand why the man quit his job. Nor is this sort of understanding devoid of predictive power. We can state with some confidence that such an event will occur in most cases under similar circumstances. Nonetheless convinced as we may be that the whole situation is "ultimately" describable in terms of specific impulses and pinching on the nervous system of our man and on the transformation of these impulses into others leading to the activation of effectors, this outlook is all but useless for analyzing the event into its constituents which is what the analytic method requires. We understand the event directly by perceiving wholes rather than parts: the man, his circumstances, his preferences, etc.[21]

In short, it is important to see nations as nations, communities as communities, organizations as organizations, individuals and families as individuals and families—to perceive them as wholes and to understand their actions in the context of those wholes, rather than to seek fundamental understanding and explanation of the whole as the sum of the parts. An important caution is in order here, however. We do not mean to suggest that we will not gain important understanding from looking at the parts. As Rapoport says:

> Each of these wholes [the person, the nation, the culture, etc.] presents itself naturally because we perceive it as such. We *recognize* an organism, an individual, a nation, and we assume that in proper circumstances it *acts* as a whole. Still, if we confine our attention exclusively to the grossly observable patterns of these wholes, we would not make much progress toward understanding this behavior. We gain a deeper understanding of how an organism performs an act if we understand how the components of the act are integrated by its nervous system. We may gain a deeper understanding of why a nation reacts as it does to the "acts" of other nations if we understand how decisions are made within the body politic and how they are enforced.[22]

In short, we are taking the sensible middle course, which asserts that system levels need to be understood as systems levels, but the parts need to be understood as well. We should simply not make the mistake of assuming that all understanding comes from an understanding of the parts, which are compositional elements of the whole. To give practical examples from the social work field, we would object if someone said that organizational behavior is explainable simply in terms of the psychology of the individual members of the organization, or if a family pathology was explained solely in terms of the individual psychological states of family members. These pieces of information are certainly important and fit into an overall picture of why the organization or family acts as it does, but they do not constitute a total explanation.

A similar caution is due to those who might err on the other side and explain behaviors of particular wholes not in terms of parts, but rather in terms of the elements that form their context. In this case a social worker might assert that an individual's behavior was "determined by" his or her family, that a family's pathology is "completely the result of" the community in which it lives, that an organization's actions were "without doubt the result of" social policies in the nation at the time. This perspective deprives the individual unit of integrity. It relocates reality away from the individual into the family, away from the family into the community, and away from the organization into the society or whatever other contextual element is selected.

Clearly, knowledge of the context is important, but the context no more than the components explains fully what happens at the level of the person, family, organization, community, or the society. The essential reality of systems levels mitigates against that.

Hence, for any social worker there are always three aspects to an assessment. First, we must assess the functioning of the system level in question, the person as system, family as system, group as system, organization as system, community as system, and society as system. Then we must look at compositional elements. In the case of the person, for example, we would be foolish not to consider possible biological and pharmacological conditions that might affect particular behaviors. On the other hand, we also need to look at contextual elements in the case of the person, that is, the family, the community, and the organization. And we need to take care in making an assessment that we attend to all three aspects while not, at the same time, slipping either into compositionalism or contextualism.

These three perspectives are very important because they provide a way to conceptualize interventions. Sometimes, even though the problem occurs at an organizational level and we recognize this, intervention through the group level might prove to be most efficacious and sensible in the particular case. Similarly, even though a problem may occur at an individual level, intervention through a contextual element might be appropriate.

System Levels and Relationships

Social work involves the use of relationships, whether the relationship is in the clinical interpersonal interview with clients or lobbying with contacts for social policy on Capitol Hill. What is important is that the nature of the relationship between clients and contacts differs across levels.

As system levels become more complex, the intensity of relationships decreases. Generally, we can think of social work as being concerned with three modes of relationship intensity: primary, secondary, and tertiary. Primary relationships characterize our most intimate associations, including the association with ourselves, our family, and our dearest friends. They tend to be characterized by commitment, and these commitments exist over substantial time and space. Secondary relationships are communal in nature and involve memberships in territorial groups (geographic communities), religious and ethnic associations (functional communities), and communities of work (organizations), among others. Communal relationships involve commitment and identification. However, they vary from patterns of daily association, which are very close to primary associations, to those that are much more distant and resemble tertiary relationships.

A great deal of our daily life is spent in communal relationships, and they serve to balance the very intimate primary associations with the most distant and formalistic tertiary ones. Tertiary relationships involve civic roles and responsibilities. They tend to be formal and common rights, duties, and obligations. We are assured, for example, of free speech, not because we are nice people, but rather because we are a citizens of a particular nation or state in which free speech is emphasized.

Primary relationships occur for each individual with relatively few others and involve the small group and the family. Secondary relationships are much more numerous, but more limited in their emotional depth than within the family; they are still very powerful. Secondary relationships are among the more enduring ties and identifications that humans experience. Tertiary relationships may be very numerous; we are members of many civic associations and groups of that sort, but such relations are limited in emotional commitment.

In this sense, emotional commitment and number of relationships tend to be inversely related to each other. As we ascend the system levels, greater numbers of relationships occur but of a more limited emotional involvement. One difficulty that can occur among system levels is the malplacement of emotional identifications and attachments to the wrong levels. When, for example, communal relationships become a substitute for primary relationships, not only does that leave a vacuum in the life of the individual person, on the one hand, and something that social work may wish to attend to in terms of intervention, but it also overburdens the communal level, requiring it to provide gratifications that it is not prepared to provide and experience demands that it is not prepared to meet.

Another problem that can occur is inadequate functioning of a particular level. In some nations, for example, civic relations are so weak that communal relations tend to substitute for them. The state and other large-scale civic associations are thereby weakened. A converse situation can occur in which secondary associations become so weak that an entire society moves from primary to tertiary relationships. In this case, tertiary relationships take on a communal quality, and the individual becomes over-involved with the state as a source of meaning and identification.

In terms of intervention, the social work use of self during an intervention will be very different in primary, secondary, and tertiary types of relationships. Problems in primary relationships are best dealt with by clinical uses of self, and problems in secondary relationships with organizational uses of self. Problems in tertiary or civic-type relationships are perhaps dealt with by intellectual uses of self involving the creation of new patterns and new policies.

The whole idea of system levels, however, is that problems at any relationship level may involve or be the result of either composition or context. Problems at the communal level, in the organization, territorial community, or subculture, may in part be a result of difficulties at the primary relationship or tertiary relationship level. Hence, assessments there always have compositional or contextual elements to consider. This approach is discussed next.

System Levels and Social Intervention

For human systems, key levels are the individual, family and group, organization, community, and society. At each level, units can be considered wholes, as well as parts for the next level. Hence, families and groups are made up of individuals. Organizations are made up of individuals and groups. Communities are made up of individuals, families and groups, and organizations. Societies are made up of individuals, families and groups, organizations, and communities.

As Miller[23] suggested, however, the fit is not quite as neat as we would like, especially in the area of family and group and organization and community. The individual can be seen to fit as a part into other levels (as a family member, community member, employee, or citizen). Similarly, all the levels can be seen to fit into society, but in the middle things broaden out a bit. Families and groups are often thought of together because they are both small groups, but it might make better sense to separate them, especially when there are family groups, organizational groups, work groups, and indeed a whole range of groups that social workers deal with, that exist in a wide variety of settings.

In addition to this distinction, there are a number of purposes for such groups. The family group obviously has one set of purposes. A therapy group has a different set. A Boy Scout group presumably has yet another purpose, and so on. Hence, the family and group level may actually be a band with a lot of groups of various types and locations in it.

In addition, some groups may indeed be on the primary association level with highly committed relationships. Others, like a Boy Scout group, may fit more into a communal or quasi-communal level if we use relationships as a measure. Similarly, when we get to the level of organization and community, separation of these two becomes as much of a problem as integration did at the family and group level.

As social workers are well aware, community is an ambiguous concept. Indeed, many think of the community level as involving three elements: the organizational community, the territorial community, and the subcultural community.[24] Regarding geographical (territorial) areas as communities is perhaps the most common conception of community but functional (subcultural) communities of identification, such as the Catholic community, the Jewish community, the Greek community, and the African-American community, are also relatively common and may or may not have a specific geographic location for their members. Similarly, emphasis on the organization as a community has recently become more prominent with an emphasis on organizational culture.[25] Hence, for the purposes of this book, we have decided to divide communal relationships into two areas by taking the view that organizations are components of communities, but recognizing that organizations have communal aspects to them.

AN ILLUSTRATIVE GRID

One way to think about the problem and issues of levels and their compositional and contextual elements is to place them in a matrix format. This allows all the levels that we are discussing to be displayed simultaneously and points the way to potential interventions. The grid is displayed in Figure 4.1

Figure 4.1. System level as cause and target of intervention. On the diagonal (where system cause and system target intersect) is *direct* intervention; above the diagonal is *contextual* intervention; below the diagonal is *compositional* intervention. Source: Adapted from John E. Tropman, "The Loci of Social Change," in John E. Tropman and others, eds., *Strategic Perspectives on Social Policy* (Elmsford, NY: Pergamon Press, 1976).

		TARGET						
		BIOLOGICAL	INDIVIDUAL	FAMILY/ GROUP	ORGANIZA- TION	COMMUNITY	SOCIETY	WORLD
C A U S E	BIOLOGICAL	Medical tech- nology	Health Attitude Behavior	Quarantine	Medical care organization	Public health	Medical care policy	Education
	INDIVIDUAL	Drugs	Casework technologies	Family treat- ment	Workplace programs	Create self- help groups Develop facility	Create enabling policies	
	FAMILY/ GROUP		Individual counseling	Group tech- nology Quality circles Adult children of alcoholic group	Workplace programs Daycare Group health	Involve other communities Link programs (e.g., Blue Cross and retirement)		
	ORGANIZA- TION	Drug testing Environmental quality	Psychological testing	Daycare	Administration technology	Community pressure	Controlling policy Regulation of antitrust activities	World controls
	COMMUNITY	Renew water quality through treatment	Relocation	Family sup- port groups	Develop organiza- tional support	Community organization technology	Urban policy Tax policy for nonprofits	
	SOCIETY	Fluoridation	Education	Family devel- opment	Lobbying	Community advocates	Policy tech- nology Emancipation Proclamation	
	WORLD	Pesticide	Education of leaders	World family development	Regulation of multi- nationals	Community development	Develop supportive beliefs	All macro technology

Several features of the grid will now be discussed in some detail. The first of these is that we have included biological and world system levels to give a more complete picture of the total range of complex system levels that might be available. While social workers may not work much at the biological level in terms of intervention, clearly everything from illnesses to chronic conditions that require social work assistance exist there.

Similarly, some problems, such as chemical dependency, have biological manifestations, and social workers may need to link up with other professionals to deal with aspects of this issue. It is perhaps also true that social workers do not intervene much at the world level, although social work has a distinguished history in this area. But it is also clear that social work concerns, unlike politics, do not stop at the water's edge. Problems of world conflict and configuration are of concern not only because of their human cost but because of their potential for affecting the entire world. Some problems, like international drug trafficking, require global cooperation. While we will not focus much here on biological and world system levels, it is important for us to be aware that the levels we focus on are for the most part out of our own history rather than because of any logical requirement.

A second point to stress about the grid is that a level can be seen either as the source of a particular problem (one that occurs, for example, at the organizational level) or as a target of intervention, as Meyer and his colleagues suggest.[26] This perspective should help clarify social work diagnosis and intervention, because it more clearly outlines differences between problem locus and intervention locus and allows for a more variegated set of interventions.

Reading down the diagonal are boxes that we call direct intervention. Here the intervention occurs at the level where the problem exists. Hence, if a problem occurs at the individual level, individual level interventions are decided on and carried out. Similarly, if the problem occurs on a biological level, a biological intervention is conceived and carried out, and so on. But there remain a whole set of boxes off the diagonal. These we call indirect interventions and they are of two sorts. Above the diagonal are systems that form the context of the problem system. Hence, if there is a problem at the family and group level, we might wish to deal with it at the organizational, community, societal, or even, conceivably, world level. Contextual interventions are therefore available. On the left below the diagonal are the systems that compose the system in question. Compositional intervention is an indirect intervention that involves changing the composing elements of a system as a way of dealing with a particular problem at a system level. Hence, if a problem occurs at an organizational level, we may wish to change work groups or even individuals within the organization rather than attack the problem directly.

DIRECT INTERVENTION

The most typical and well-understood social work intervention is direct. We seek to intervene at the level where the problem exists. For the individual this is traditionally thought of as casework or interpersonal practice, and a variety of modes, such as counseling and behavioral modification, are used to help individuals deal with the problems confronting them.

Direct intervention: At a New York City neighborhood counseling center oriented to the Puerto Rican population, help is offered in the areas of health, housing, welfare, and employment. (O.E.O. photo by James Foote.)

Group work technology seems most appropriate for problems that emerge at the group level. Family interventions involving all members of an affected family are other examples. Gathering together various kinds of voluntary groups, such as the adult children of alcoholics or parents of murdered children, are further examples.

At the level of the organization, improving administrative technology (personnel, budgeting, policy management) is a way to approach organizational-level problems. At the level of the community, difficulties have been most often approached with the use of community organization technology. More specifically, social planning, community development or locality development, and social action have been useful strategies.

At the level of society, policy technologies have been the method of choice, including the proposing of laws and ordinances at all levels of government, the changing of executive regulations, and the use of judicial interventions. Each of these represents a different approach to policy change. In addition to proposing policy, policy implementation, policy review, and policy refurbishment have all been appropriate methods.

INDIRECT INTERVENTION: CONTEXTUAL STRATEGIES

Sometimes it is not possible to intervene at the level at which a problem occurs, either because intervention is impossible, unwise, politically prohibited, or for other reasons.

In that case, contextual interventions are an alternative. Thus, in the case of a particular medical problem, we might seek to modify individual health attitudes and behaviors as opposed to giving someone a particular drug. Also, changes in medical care organization and medical care policy might be used.

Similarly, at the individual level, in lieu of (or in support of) counseling with an individual person, family treatment might be used. Intervention in the workplace, self-help groups, or policy shifts might be possible. A number of other examples are suggested by Figure 4.1. We should add that it is not necessarily the case that contextual strategy be used in lieu of direct strategy. It may be used to supplement or to work on other aspects of the problem or to complete a treatment plan. For example, individual counseling with a particular person may be important, but without family treatment the same problems may repeat themselves.

INDIRECT INTERVENTION: COMPOSITIONAL STRATEGIES

Since systems fit together, another indirect strategy is also possible, and, for the same reasons mentioned in the use of contextual strategies, it may be necessary to supplement a particular direct strategy or a direct strategy may be ill advised or impossible for a variety of reasons. In that case, the systems that compose the particular level (or some of the systems) might be themselves targets of change. Consider the case of an individual person suffering from substance abuse. Apart from casework technology and individual counseling, drugs might also be needed to address the biological system, both to stabilize and enhance the results of individual casework.

Similarly, at the organizational level, drug testing, psychological testing, and the provision of daycare might be used. These biological, individual, and family group elements to supplement whatever administrative activity is going on could rectify a particular problem.

THE MIX OF STRATEGIES

The system-levels approach offers the social worker a mix of strategies. A direct, indirect, or both strategies may be used, either contextual and compositional, or all three may be used simultaneously. It is important for social workers to keep this grid in mind. Two other observations are important. First, with respect to direct strategies, the social work profession takes the view that all are valid. The problems of reduction or overcontextualization should be avoided. Individual problems cannot be argued away in terms of system responsibility or cause, nor can problems at the system level be reduced to and explained by the particular components. A full program of social welfare and social services addresses both context and composition as well as the direct cause or target system involved.

PREDISPOSING AND PRECIPITATING PERSPECTIVES

One other division is worth keeping in mind and has to do with the length of time that a cause is operative or an intervention may take effect. At the cause level, it is useful to think of predisposing and precipitating causes. Predisposing causes are those condi-

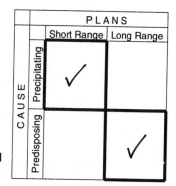

Figure 4.2. Time lines on causes of problems and trajectory of intervention.

tional and contextual elements that set the stage for a particular problem to manifest itself. Precipitating causes are those immediate precursors to an event. These causes often bring a client to a social worker (the presenting problem), although social workers are inclined to recognize the predisposing causes as well. Substance abuse involving alcohol provides a particularly useful illustration. An alcohol-related accident may require someone to come into counseling. The legal system may have made this assignment, yet workers recognize the deeper problems involved. Hence, there is a time line on intervention as well, which similarly consists of short- and long-range interventions. Short-range interventions deal with the specific here and now problem. Long-range interventions often deal with a broad range of solutions to problems. Typically, again, social workers will be involved with clients for both short- and long-range solutions. These possibilities are outlined in Figure 4.2.

Precipitating causes typically generate a focus on short-range interventions, and predisposing causes typically center on longer-range, more permanent solutions. It is important to note, however, that while these two sets of analyses and intervention strategies may go on at the same level, they may also go on at compositional and contextual levels. Hence, while the worker is seeking to improve family relationships through group counseling, there may also be a recognition that part of the family problem comes from the predisposing cause of high unemployment in the community and its associated stresses. Long-range solutions require the generation of jobs. It is our belief that intervention planning should always include analyses of system levels, both with respect to direct, contextual, and compositional interventions and to precipitating and predisposing causal analysis and short- and long-range considerations.

The Orchestration of System-Level Intervention

It should be clear from the forgoing discussion that social work work takes place on different system levels and around a particular client system. Hence, an individual may have a problem that requires work with that individual, particularly on precipitating causes and short-term solutions, but it may also require community- or policy-oriented work around longer-term solutions and predisposing causes. The fact that different system levels are involved becomes at times a problem for some social workers, since not only does their time not always permit multilevel work, but there are differences in the characters of system levels that may make the competence required for one system level different from that required for another.

Hence, it is often appropriate to have different workers involved with the same cases. This enhances the need for case management skills that, in effect, allows for intersystem as well as intrasystem coordination around a particular case. The issue of time is often administrative and related to the needs and foci of particular agencies. Therefore, we will examine the issue of differential character both between and within systems.

FAMILIARIZATION WITH ALL LEVELS

The first point to be made is that workers should familiarize themselves with the overall structure and functioning of all system levels. This perspective strengthens the intellectual rationale for generic training, at least in the beginning phase of social work practice. All workers should know something about the basic structures of the individual personality system, the biological system, groups, organizations, communities, and societies. Social workers should take it upon themselves to maintain ongoing responsibility for breadth as well as depth. Precipitating and predisposing elements of client system problems do not locate themselves neatly within the totality of one or another system level. Hence, a broader and deeper knowledge is required.

Current and historical propensities on the part of the social work profession to divide into level-related methods, such as case work, group work, community organization, and policy, do make a certain sense. What does not make sense, however, is that individuals become so specialized in one level or another that they have no knowledge of adjacent system levels. Furthermore, hostility among workers with different system levels can erupt. Such hostility is most likely to occur in cases of reductionism (for example, the belief that all problems can really be reduced to those within the bounds of the individual psyche) or contextualism (all problems are manifestations of large-scale social conditions and we must await change in these before intervening).

JUXTAPOSED CHARACTERISTICS

A second point of importance lies in the observation that system levels appear to contain contradictory tendencies within themselves. Workers who have had experience with individual counseling know how much individuals vary along dimensions of trust versus suspicion, open and revealing versus closed and unsharing, privately versus publicly oriented, ambitious versus lethargic, and so on. Indeed, single individuals vary within themselves. Hence, univariate or stereotypic characterizations of individuals or categories of individuals invariably select and articulate some subset, like color or gender, while remaining silent on other aspects of the person. The same point can be made for families, groups, organizations, communities, and societies. Each level contains contradictory tendencies among and within its members. Fellin points this out in his new book on communities.[27]

Societies, such as U.S society, can be both open and welcoming to immigrants, as we have generally been, or restrictive and hostile, as the experience of Japanese internment camps and Indian reservations also indicates.[28] Thus, social workers must be aware of the contradictory nature of systems and be prepared to work with and understand this. Reducing diagnoses to simplistic univariate statements does violence to the complexity, variety, and texture of system levels.

Conclusion

From a social work perspective, the system level concept is extremely important. First, it articulates the client system at a particular level, but in making that articulation it also locates the particular client system in its own structure and identifies the contextual and compositional elements that may also bear importantly on the potential problems and solutions of the particular client system. The concept of system levels not only lays out a course of study for social workers throughout their careers, but also provides a handy scheme for diagnosis and intervention—a set of checkpoints that we refer to as we think about particular client systems and their contexts and conditions. While it is recognized, of course, that any given worker may not be able to provide all the social work necessary to deal with the particular client system, the social work agency, through case management and cooperative relationships, can fill in these gaps.

Community organization agencies, for example, may not have the competence to do individual counseling, but they may be able to affect links with agencies possessing this competence. Hence, in their work at the community system level they will encounter, as we all do, people who are in need of this kind of individual assistance. Referrals can be affected through these interagency linkages. Similarly, family service agencies can call to the community organization agencies' attention items of community concern with which they are not prepared to deal.

However, we should not simply be satisfied with referrals. Small agencies are themselves systems that may lack sufficient differentiation to handle multiple tasks. As agencies become larger, however, it is indeed possible for them to assign particular workers to other system levels. Hence, the large family service agency, as a case in point, could have one community organizer, or a part of a person's assignment as community organization, so that some community-level problems will be dealt with in the agency.

Similarly, the dominant conception today is that a school social worker is some kind of counselor. However, many problems arising within the school structure come from the school system itself. Hence, an administrative or community organizer trained social worker will seek organizational adjustment and change. An ombudsman role might be assigned to such an individual. Alternatively, there may be community elements that should be mobilized in support of school efforts and policies around particular problematic areas; drug use, or bringing weapons into the school system are examples. Social workers with community organizing skills can perform a very useful function here.

The remaining chapters in this section will review and discuss social work activities and social change within each of the major contexts so far mentioned—the individual, family and small group, organization, community, and society. We will not focus on the biological system or the world system except to note that these two systems represent important compositional and contextual elements that should not be ignored in dealing with any specific case.

Some systems have a more clear-cut visibility than others. The individual and family certainly fall within this category. Yet as we mention family and group, a range of groups and family types immediately leaps to mind, giving violence to generalizations about where these might be located. Similarly, we have included chapters on the organization and on the community, while recognizing that organizations are one kind of community. Some geographic communities, for example, are smaller than many organizations, so the fit is not neat; but from our perspective it has at least face validity from the intervention perspective. As further theoretical advances are made in system-level analysis and structure, these systems may be reconceptualized and redivided, but for the purposes of current social work activity they make good sense.

Notes

1. Ralph E. Anderson and Irl Carter, *Human Behavior in the Social Environment* (Chicago: Aldine, 1974).
2. Joseph Mehr, *Human Services: Concepts and Intervention Strategies* (Boston: Allyn and Bacon, 1980).
3. Neil Gilbert, Henry Miller, and Harry Specht, *An Introduction to Social Work Practice* (Englewood Cliffs, NJ: Prentice Hall, 1980).
4. Walter A. Friedlander and Robert Z. Apte, *Introduction to Social Welfare*, 5th ed. (Englewood Cliffs, NJ: Prentice Hall, 1980).
5. Rex A. Skidmore and Milton G. Thackeray, *Introduction to Social Work* (Englewood Cliffs, NJ: Prentice Hall, 1982).
6. For further discussion, see James G. Miller, *Living Systems* (New York: McGraw-Hill Book Co., 1978). See also Anderson and Carter, *Human Behavior.*
7. Anderson and Carter, *Human Behavior,* p. 6. Originally published in Gordon Hearn, ed., *The General Systems Approach: Contributions toward an Holistic Conception of Social Work* (New York: Council on Social Work Education, 1969), p. 2.
8. Anatole Rapoport, "General Systems Theory," in David L. Sills, ed., *International Encyclopedia of the Social Sciences,* Vol. 15, (New York: Macmillan, Inc., 1968), p. 453.
9. Anderson and Carter, *Human Behavior,* p. 6. Originally published in Walter Buckley *Sociology in Modern Systems Theory* (Englewood Cliffs, NJ: Prentice Hall, 1967).
10. James G. Miller, *Living Systems,* p. 1.
11. See Anatole Rapoport "Forward" in Walter Buckley, ed., *Modern Systems Research for the Behavioral Scientist* (Chicago: Aldine, 1968). The Rapoport history of the system is called evolution.
12. Ibid., p. xvii.
13. Anderson and Carter, *Human Behavior,* p. 8. Originally published in Marvin Olsen, *The Process of Social Organization* (New York: Holt, Rinehart and Winston, 1968), pp. 228–229.
14. Rapoport, in Buckley, *Modern Systems Research,* p. xxi.
15. James G. Miller, *Living Systems,* p. 1.
16. Ibid., p. 25.
17. R. W. Gerard, "Units and Concepts of Biology," in Buckley, *Modern Systems Research,* p. 53.
18. Henry J. Meyer and others, "Social Work and Social Welfare," in Paul F. Lazarsfeld, William H. Sewell, and Harold L. Wilensky, eds., *The Uses of Sociology* (New York: Basic Books, 1967), p. 159.
19. Gerard, "Units and Concepts," in Buckley, *Modern Systems Research,* p. 53.

20. Purcell in Buckley, *Modern Systems Research,* p. 44.
21. Rapoport in Buckley, *Modern Systems Research,* p. xvii.
22. Rapoport in Buckley, *Modern Systems Research,* p. xvii.
23. Miller, *Living Systems.*
24. For elaboration, see John E. Tropman, John L. Erlich, and Fred M. Cox, "Introduction," in Fred M. Cox and others, eds., *Tactics and Techniques of Community Practice* (Itasca, IL: F. E. Peacock Publishers, 1977); and John E. Tropman and Harold Johnson, "Settings of Community Practice," in Fred M. Cox and others, eds., *Strategies of Community Organization,* 3rd ed. (Itasca, IL: F. E. Peacock Publishers, 1979), p. 214.
25. Edgar Schein, *Organizational Culture and Leadership* (San Francisco: Jossey-Bass, 1985).
26. Henry J. Meyer and others, "Social Work."
27. See Philip A. Fellin, *The Community and the Social Worker* (Itasca, IL: F. E. Peacock, 1987).
28. For a discussion of the whole matter of value contradictions, see John E. Tropman, "Value Conflicts and Decision Making: Analysis and Resolution," in F. M. Cox and others, eds., *Tactics of Community Organization* 2nd ed. (New York: The Free Press, 1984), pp. 89–98. See also John E. Tropman and Fred M. Cox, "Society: American Values as a Context for Community Organization and Macro-Practice," in F. M. Cox and others, eds., *Strategies of Community Organization,* 4th ed. (Itasca, IL: F. E. Peacock, 1987), and also John E. Tropman, *American Values and Social Welfare: Cultural Contradictions in the Welfare State* (Englewood Cliffs, NJ: Prentice Hall, 1989).

CHAPTER 5
Helping Individuals to Change

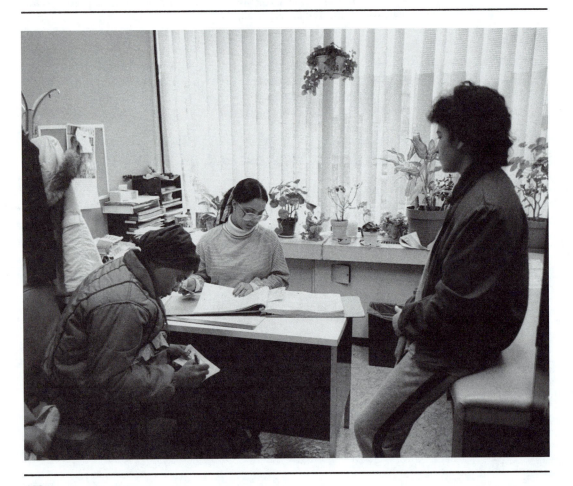

Introduction

Because of the large amount of information available regarding the kinds of problems faced by individuals, families, and groups and how social workers help with these, we shall focus on only individual problems in this chapter. We shall discuss how individuals may be helped to solve their problems by strategies at the individual level and at various system levels. Since we refer to the entry point as a *problem,* we shall begin with illustrations of the kinds of individual problems that often lead to the involvement of a social worker.

Individual Problems

One way of conceptualizing individual problems is to categorize them as relating to the normal processes of *socialization* or to a need for *remediation.* Table 5.1 shows how these problems can be related to stages of the life cycle. We wish to emphasize that we do not intend by the word "problem" to connote something negative or pathological. Rather, we use it, depending on the circumstances, to mean the same thing as "task" or even "opportunity." Thus, "problem" may refer to things like wishing to find a job, to pass a course, to adopt a child, to get out of prison, or to cease drinking alcohol.

By "normal processes of socialization," we mean that individuals take on new *roles* as they grow older and make choices about *positions* they wish to occupy, or these positions are imposed upon them. By "remediation," we refer to the fact that individuals sometimes develop a dysfunctional way of fulfilling a role and this requires that they must relinquish or unlearn this dysfunctional pattern and acquire or learn a functional one.

Since we utilize several terms that are important for an understanding of individual problems, we shall define them here:

Position: A socially recognized location in the system. Positions can be those that are formally created by systems, such as roles of mother and student, or they may emerge out of an interaction, such as "fool" or "clown" or "peacemaker."

Role: The behaviors associated with a position. Roles include acting as a mother, student, or supervisor.

Socialization: The processes through which a person learns how to fulfill the requirements of a position he or she has entered. These processes include formal education, opportunity to observe a model, and chances to try out a skill.

Social workers are not in the business of helping people with every type of problem. They do not pull teeth, build houses, or represent people in court (although they may help people cope with these occasions). Social workers help people with *problems in social functioning.* We define these as the problems people experience in fulfilling expectations of themselves related to their roles.

This brief definition takes into consideration the fact that, as people fulfill such expectations, they must regard their own motivations and capacities as well as the nature of their social situations. Thus, resolving problems in social functioning may be accomplished by changes in the way people cope with situations or in the situations themselves, or both. In this section, we shall indicate the need for both types of changes by enumerating problems in both the behavior of individuals and in the response of systems at various stages of the life cycle.

Examples of problems in social functioning are a parent who wishes to learn appropriate and effective ways of disciplining a child, or a parent who is disciplining a child in a way that constitutes child abuse (role is that of parent); and a student who wishes to learn more effective ways of studying, or a student who refuses to study and is about to be demoted (role is that of student). Let us now look at further examples of such problems as seen in the behavior of individuals at different periods of their lives.

SOCIALIZATION

We refer in Table 5.1 to a child developing eating and sleeping patterns in infancy. Parents may use the services of a social worker to help develop competency in responding to their child's sleep and food needs. They may seek out this service through a parent education program conducted by a social worker who is employed by a family agency, a school, a child guidance clinic, or a pediatrician. In fact, when people seek help to increase their competency to cope with these kinds of tasks, they are likely to come for this service on a *voluntary* basis. They are also likely to see themselves as *learners* seeking an *educational* experience.

Additional examples of problems in normal socialization that bring people to social workers are also provided in Table 5.1. We see in reference to school-age children that they are concerned with formal learning, developing their membership in peer groups, and improving their ability to function independently, by which we mean away from their families. They may receive help with these tasks from a social worker employed in a leisure time agency, such as a community center which conducts a friendship club for children. In this club, children discuss concerns about their school responsibilities while learning skills in peer relationships. An occasional camping trip supports the children's comfort in being away from parents. Another social worker employed by the school may also help these children through consulting with their teacher about ways of conducting classroom activities that are conducive to learning for these children, who may came from a different culture than that of the teacher.

In the cell that refers to socialization issues for young adults, we present items that relate to developing intimacy, preparing for a career, and initiating civic roles. An example of young adults who received the services of a social worker was a group of college students living in a college dormitory. A social worker from the college's counseling services conducted several discussions in the dormitory on ways of dealing with issues. In addition, the social worker consulted with the dormitory resident advisor on how to be supportive to several residents who were struggling to develop friendships. In one case, a student confided to the RA that she was a lesbian and didn't know where to make friends in an atmosphere in which she would be accepted. The social worker informed the RA about a support group for lesbians that was available at the counseling service.

TABLE 5.1
Types of Individual Problems

Stage of Life Cycle	Socialization	Remediation
Infancy (0–2)	Sleeping patterns Eating patterns Speech	Failure to develop healthy sleeping or eating patterns or adequate speech
Preschool (2–5)	Learn basic self-care; toilet training Relate to peers Initial separation from parents	Failure to develop self-care or peer contacts or separation
School age (5–12)	Formal learning Become member of peer group Increase independence	Failure to learn or relate to peers or separate from parents
Adolescence (13–18)	Develop satisfying same-sex and other-sex relationships Identity development Autonomy Career choice	Poor same/other-sex relations Confused identity Dependence Lack of career direction
Young adult (18–25?)[a]	Develop intimacy beyond family of origin Prepare for career Initiate civic roles Separate from family of origin	Failure of intimacy Failure of career preparation Failure to separate from family
Adulthood (25?–40?)[a]	Establish family[b] Establish career Establish roles in community Raise children[c]	Failure to establish family or career or community roles Deviancy
Middle years (40?–65?)[a]	Separate from children Progress in career Community leadership Plan for retirement	Severe family conflict Career failure Lack of community roles
Older years (65+)[a]	Adapt to retirement Develop satisfying role Cope with losses, including own mortality and vulnerability	Lack of satisfying roles Poor coping with loss and mortality

[a] These ages are arbitrary and are meant to be illustrative; they differ in terms of individual developmental patterns and culture.
[b] By "family," we mean intimate relationships and do not wish to limit our definition to traditional families.
[c] We also do not wish to imply that raising children should be expected of all families, but only of those who choose to do so.

Still another illustration of socialization activities relates to the middle years. One task to be accomplished during these years is to plan for retirement. A number of middle-aged people have met with social workers who are employed by businesses, universities, and community centers to develop such plans.

In the socialization examples provided so far, we have referred to individuals who are learning to cope with typical role issues. Some individuals, on the other hand, have not yet developed a need for remediation, but are highly likely to do so because of circumstances that make them very vulnerable. These circumstances might be internal, such as the state of their health or their mental abilities. They may also be external, such as lack of funds, decent housing, a good job, or a healthy community life. Such people are said to be at risk in the sense that, if something of a *preventive* nature is not done, serious problems might arise.

Such a preventive program must therefore either help people to find ways to offset personal limitations or create a better environmental situation, or both. An example of an agency that employs social workers whose mission is to engage in such prevention is the *Community Mental Health Center.* When workers in such a program are engaged in preventive work, they create support groups, educate people on how to manage stress, and meet with people in churches and other organizations to discuss everyday problems.

In a sense, all services that seek to fulfill a socialization function can also be described as operating in a preventive manner. The subject of prevention is important, because preventing the need for remediation is one of the most humane approaches a society can take to the needs of its citizens, and it is the least costly approach.

REMEDIATION

When infants fail to eat properly or are restless for a protracted period of time and unable to sleep, parents appropriately consult with their physician because of possible physiological reasons that can lead to these problems. If physiological causes are ruled out, a health professional (such as a doctor or nurse) might suspect that something was wrong in the parent–child relation. Often, he or she will then, refer the parents to a social worker. This worker might be employed in the pediatrician's office, or might work in a hospital, child guidance clinic, or family agency. In these circumstances, the social worker would work with the parents and would be unlikely to communicate directly with the child. An exception is when the worker models some way of interacting with the child for the parents.

A school age child might persist with difficulties in separating from parents. This might be manifested in a *school phobia* in which the child refuses to go to school or develops such physical symptoms as headaches or stomach pains whenever the time to leave for school approaches, or in a refusal to develop peer relationships or to be away from the parents except for a short time. The parents might contact a social worker employed by the school, a child guidance clinic, or a family agency to help them with this problem. Depending on her or his orientation, this worker might see the child and the parents together in *family treatment* or separately. All social workers would see this problem as embedded in the parent–child interaction (also sometimes involving other family members, such as grandparents, or institutions, such as the school) and would develop a course of action related to this view.

In young or later adulthood, an individual may have difficulty with intimate relationships. This may lead to an inability to create a family or the dissolution of a family through divorce. For help, the individual may consult a social worker in a family agency, mental health clinic, or outpatient psychiatric clinic. This worker may interact with the client on a one-to-one basis, but frequently the individual is invited to join a group in which members work with each other on relationship and intimacy issues and provide each other with feedback on how the individual is relating to the group.

As people become older, opportunities increase to use their previous experience to assume significant, often leadership roles, in the community. These roles may be in churches, political parties, community organizations, or on the boards of social agencies. Some individuals, because of limited opportunities previously and their own attributes, have not had and continue not to have community involvement, much less important community roles. This can lead to a sense of stagnation, impotence, and even of a wasted life. Increasingly, social workers are available in continuing education programs (such as the Center for the Continuing Education of Women of our own university), family agencies, older adult centers, and community mental health agencies who understand the importance of playing a role in community life and who work with individuals alone and in groups to promote and support such endeavors.

The preceding problems are often related to deficits in social resources, and these can also be described with reference to stages of the life cycle. Table 5.2 presents these social deficits.

A view that denies the validity of social deficits as a source of failure has been referred to as "blaming the victim."[1] Without denying our view of the harm caused by social deficits, it is true that, whenever possible, individuals should assume a responsibility to do the best they can for themselves despite social barriers and should work to change such barriers for the benefit of all who suffer from them.

The Evolution of Individual Helping in Social Work

We shall now describe ways in which social workers help individuals to reduce or remove their problems in social functioning. In order to provide a perspective on this for the reader, we shall begin with a brief summary of how social work approaches to helping individuals evolved. We shall then describe the stages of the process of helping as well as some of the major helping approaches used by social workers.

As we stated in the preceding chapter, throughout this book we shall maintain the idea that the worker may use different contextual and compositional strategies. In this chapter, we shall discuss family, group, and environmental, as well as individual strategies *for helping individuals reduce problems in social functioning.* In the next chapter, we shall discuss strategies to help families and groups improve their functioning *as families and groups.*

ONE TO ONE

One-to-one helping has historically been referred to as *social casework,* although some caseworkers refer to their work with groups and families as casework. This type of

TABLE 5.2
Social Deficits by Stage of the Life Cycle

Stage of Life Cycle	Type of Social Deficit
Infancy	Inadequate medical care
	Lack of financial resources required for food, shelter, etc.
Preschool	Lack of preschool resources
	Abuse from adults
	Neglect by parents
	Lack of adequate parenting alternatives when needed
School age	Poor educational resources as related to needs of child
	Racism, sexism directed at child
Adolescence	Racism and sexism, particularly as these affect identity
	Lack of educational resources related to individual aspirations
	Lack of appropriate job experience
Young adult	Sexism and racism as these affect:
	Lack of job opportunity
	Lack of educational opportunity
	Social stigma for identity choices
	Family sabotages independence
Adulthood	All listed for young adult
	Lack of resources needed for child rearing (income, housing, support, etc.)
	Lack of opportunity to develop roles in the community
Middle years	Lack of resources to care for adult children with special needs
	Barriers to career advancement, especially for women and members of oppressed groups
	Rejection from community leadership roles sought by individual
Older years	Lack of financial and other resources
	Forced retirement
	Rejection by others of individual's desired roles
	Lack of support for those who become frail

helping emerged out of the activities of a number of different kinds of practitioners, including many volunteers, who served in agencies to aid the poor toward the end of the nineteenth century. One of the most influential of these agencies were the Charity Organization Societies that were established in many cities (referred to hereafter as the COS).

The COS began in London in 1869 and in the United States in 1877. In the early 1900s, COS workers came to be known as social caseworkers as their work became more clearly specified and as they became employees rather than volunteers. Their methods were shared with other people who worked in hospitals, child welfare agencies, psychiatric programs, schools, and correctional facilities.

One pioneer in the development of the conceptual basis for social casework was

Mary Richmond.[2] Richmond was born in 1861 in Belleville, Illinois, and died in 1928. She began her work in charity organization in 1889 when she became the assistant treasurer of the Baltimore Charity Organization Society, and two years later she became its general secretary. She was concerned about the failure of people to respond to the service of the agency, and in 1897 she presented an influential address in which she called for a professional training school for social workers. Her books, which were also very influential, were *Friendly Visiting among the Poor* (1899), *The Good Neighbor in the Modern City* (1907), *Social Diagnosis* (1917), and *What is Social Casework* (1922). The last two were for many years major texts on the practice of social work. After her COS work in Baltimore and Philadelphia, she directed the Charity Organization Department of the Russell Sage Foundation and taught at the New York School of Philanthropy, as well as at an annual summer institute that she developed for secretaries of the COS.

In addition to such social workers as Mary Richmond, other writers outside the profession were heavily drawn on by early caseworkers to establish a conceptual base for their activities. During the 1920s and for several decades after, these tended to be psychoanalysts, primarily of a Freudian persuasion although several schools of social work adhered to the ideas of Otto Rank. The former caseworkers referred to themselves as "diagnostic" and the latter as "functional."[3]

An important person in the incorporation of psychoanalytic theory into social work and the development of a broad conceptual basis for practice that incorporated a wide range of knowledge was Gordon Hamilton.[4] Hamilton was born in 1892 and died in 1967. She was a graduate of Bryn Mawr College in 1914, and her first professional position was for the American Red Cross in Denver, where she met Mary Richmond, who encouraged her to take a position with the New York COS. In 1923 she joined the faculty of the New York School of Social Work (later the Columbia University School of Social Work). She published *Theory and Practice of Social Casework* in 1940, and this was to remain a classic text for many years, particularly for workers of a diagnostic orientation. She served as the Associate Dean of the Columbia School from 1952–1955 and was the editor of *Social Work* from 1956–1962. Her other books were *Social Case Recording* (1936), *Principles of Social Case Recording* (1946), and *Psychotherapy in Child Guidance* (1947).

By the 1950s, social science began to have a greater impact on social casework as social scientists took more interest in mental health services. Helen Perlman in her paper "Putting the 'Social' Back in Social Casework"[5] is an important example of this development.

The 1960s began a period in which there were many attacks on social casework related to its psychological perspectives, its alleged lack of effectiveness,[6] and its lack of responsiveness to the needs of the poor and oppressed. This led to the introduction of approaches that had more research support than earlier ones, such as behavior modification, more of an environmental focus, the introduction of systems concepts, and the use of such concepts in work with families and groups.

GROUP

At about the same time as some practitioners were developing casework in such organizations as the Charity Organization Societies, others were working with groups

"All journeys begin with a single step." (Photo by Ken Karp.)

in such places as settlement houses, YMCAs, YWCAs, Boys Clubs, and Jewish Community Centers. These institutions tended to be in city neighborhoods where residents were largely recent immigrants and industrial workers. The staff of these agencies, many of whom were volunteers, sought to help people through group experience to cope with their urban environments.

The settlement houses were among the most influential of these agencies. The first, the Neighborhood Guild was founded by Stanton Coit on the lower east side of New York City in 1886. Coit had visited a similar institution, Toynbee Hall, in London, and drew his inspiration from it. The settlement idea was to provide a place where social scientists and others concerned about the plight of people in poor and crowded sections of cities could live near and work with the residents of the neighborhood. The settlement idea spread, and by 1900 there were more than 400 in the United States.

Some of the agencies we mentioned preceded the settlements. The first YMCA in the United States was founded in 1851 and the first YWCA appeared 15 years later. A variety of agencies to serve the many East European Jews who immigrated to the United States came into existence about the same time as the settlements. The Boys Clubs of America emerged a little later in 1906.

Mary Richmond also encouraged social workers to focus on groups, as in her reference to "the new tendency to view our clients from the angle of what might be termed small group psychology."[7] The early group workers had different perspectives and drew from different sets of ideas than caseworkers, however. They did not view group members as requiring rehabilitation, but rather as demonstrating an important human capacity for mutual aid. They were influenced by such writings as those of Peter Kropotkin, particularly his book *Mutual Aid,* which was published in 1902.[8] In *Mutual Aid,* Kropotkin asserted that, despite Darwin's ideas of the survival of the fittest, cooperation rather than conflict accounted for human progress. He drew on many historical examples to support this contention, including the primitive tribe, peasant village, and medieval community, as well as contemporary ones such as trade unions and the Red Cross.

The group work pioneers also drew on political ideas, such as those of Follett and Lindeman.[9] These writers saw small group experiences as intimately related to the growth of democracy. John Dewey's idea of progressive education was also important to these workers.

By the late 1920s, group work training was offered by several schools of social work. In 1935, at the National Conference of Social Work, Grace Coyle and Wilbur Newstetter presented important papers that linked the methods of group work to those of social work.

Coyle was one of the earliest and most influential persons to conceptualize the practice of group work in social work. She was born in 1892 in North Adams, Massachusetts, and died in 1962.[10] She received her social work training at the New York School of Philanthropy and graduated in 1915. She subsequently received a master's degree in economics in 1928 and a doctorate in sociology in 1931 from Columbia University. Her doctoral dissertation, *Social Process in Organized Groups,* was published in 1930 and had an impact on both social work practitioners and academic social psychologists. Coyle worked in social settlements from 1915–1918 and in the YWCA from 1918–1934. She subsequently joined the faculty of the School of Applied Social Sciences at Western Reserve University in Cleveland where she taught for the rest of her life. Some of her other books were *Group Experience and Democratic Values* (1947), *Group Work with American Youth* (1948), and *Social Science in the Professional Education of Social Workers* (1952).

The theory and practice of social group work continued to develop throughout the following decades. An important aspect of this was the expansion of group work practice in the 1950s into all social work fields, such as mental and physical health, corrections, family and children's services, and school social work. This led to new approaches to social work with groups, such as that of Robert Vinter[11] and William Schwartz.[12]

Theory and practice changes in the 1960s related to efforts to integrate practice theory for work with individuals, families, and groups which many people began to call by such names as "social treatment," "micro practice," and "clinical social work." This led to a reduction in the attention given to the skills and knowledge base of social work with groups, as such. In the 1970s, however, social workers interested in groups sought to reverse this, to a degree, through their support of the journal *Social Work with Groups* and an organization, the Association for the Advancement of Social Work with Groups. A number of new texts and approaches emerged as part of this development.

FAMILY

Social work has been committed to enhancing family life since its origin. Mary Richmond, whom we have cited as a seminal person in social work, wrote:

> In some forms of social work, notably family rebuilding, a client's social relations are so likely to be all important that family caseworkers welcome the opportunity to see at the very beginning of intercourse several members of the family assembled in their own home environment acting and reacting upon one another, each taking a share in the development of the client's story, each revealing in ways other than words social facts of real significance.[13]

While the family was the emphasis of many social workers and Mary Richmond spoke of seeing several family members, this type of practice was not typical, and social workers primarily worked with people individually or in groups of unrelated members. This was because an understanding of family patterns was limited in all disciplines, and a set of techniques for working with several family members at a time had not yet been invented. Social workers worked with groups, but did not translate this into a methodology for working with families as groups.

In 1950s, professionals from a variety of disciplines, often working in an interdisciplinary way, began to discover that tremendous benefits might occur when families were worked with as entities. The people who are often cited as contributing initially to this new approach and their locations at the time are John Bell at Clark University; Nathan Ackerman at Jewish Family Services in New York City; Theodore Lidz at Yale; Lyman Wynn and Murray Bowen at the National Institute of Mental Health; Carl Whitaker in Atlanta; Gregory Bateson, Jay Haley, John Weakland, Don Jackson, and Virginia Satir in Palo Alto, California; and Ivan Boszormeny-Nagy and James Framo at the Eastern Pennsylvania Psychiatric Institute.

Most of these people are psychiatrists, although social workers were involved in almost all their work, and notable figures in the development of family therapy included such social work trained people as Virginia Satir, Lynn Hoffman, and Harry Aponte. All schools of social work offer courses in work with families, which has become a widespread practice in social work. A task for social workers, however, is to continue to develop those aspects of work with families that most relate to social work values and purposes. Hartman and Laird are examples of social workers who are in the forefront of this effort.[14] Judith Lang, in her review of their work, recognized this when she wrote, "Its broad view of social work's mission—the continuing attention to 'private troubles and public issues' . . .—are like a beacon of light that guides the reader from the family today, to social policy, to organizational context as it shapes practice, and finally to direct family practice itself."[15]

The Phases of Helping

Most social work writers find it useful to describe the methods social workers use to help individuals cope with problems by referring to phases of the helping process. All interactions have beginnings, middles, and endings, and there are activities typical of each stage, whether referring to a specific session or to all the sessions that occur from the first to the last. In this section, we shall discuss the latter.

In the beginning phase, the activities of the individual(s) to be helped and the social worker are directed at (1) becoming engaged with each other; (2) assessing the client's situation in order to select appropriate goals and means of attaining them; and (3) planning how to employ these means. The goals and means are incorporated in a contractual agreement between the client and the worker, which may be informal or may be incorporated in a written document.

In the middle phase, the worker and client implement the change plan. This often requires modification of the plan as new information about the client's situation emerges and/or as the situation changes. In the ending phase, the worker and client (1) evaluate the degree to which the client's goals have been attained; (2) cope with a series of issues related to the ending of the relationship; and (3) plan for subsequent steps the client may take relevant to the problem that do not involve the social worker.

In the beginning stage we referred to "the individual to be helped" and not the "client." This is because individuals who first contact (or are contacted by) a social worker usually have not yet decided to become clients, and the worker, also, has not decided whether this is appropriate. Some workers, following Perlman's lead, refer to the individual at a preclient stage as an *applicant,* whether or not the first contact was voluntary.[16] Another common term used when several people together (such as a family) contract with a social worker to help them as an entity is client system. An example is a family that asks a social worker to help them establish better lines of communication among family members.

THE BEGINNING PHASE

During the *engagement* period, the worker explores how the applicant came in contact with the agency.[17] An important consideration is whether this was on a voluntary or an involuntary basis and, if voluntary, whether others were involved in the decision. This information will explain many of the applicant's feelings at this time and will have a great deal of bearing on what, if any, goals the client will be willing to work on and how she or he will be willing to do this.

The worker will discuss relevant information about the agency with the client, particularly its policies (including fees). The worker will inquire about the problems with which the applicant wishes help, and the worker will describe the available kinds of help, at least in general terms. Client values, particularly those related to her or his gender and culture, will be discussed, as well as worker values in relationship to these.

Of particular importance in helping the applicant move beyond this stage is a consideration of her or his feelings about coming for help. If clients come voluntarily, they are likely to have many positive feelings. They hope that their difficulties will be overcome and that the social worker will be competent and friendly. This may lead to feelings of relief or even pleasure. They are also likely to have negative feelings associated with the ideas that their problems will not be solved, that the social worker will not be accepting and capable, and that their situations may even be made worse. In addition, there is often a degree of stigma related to seeking help. The person may be thought of by others in the environment as incompetent, bad, or even crazy, and she or he may even believe some of these things.

The worker, therefore, must elicit these thoughts and feelings and try to promote a resolution toward the positive. This is often necessary for the voluntary applicant to return. The involuntary client's feelings may be largely or even exclusively negative. He or she may be angry at being forced to participate in this experience and fearful of the outcome. The worker must be open to a discussion of these feelings, because very little in the client can be changed until negative feelings are reduced. If, however, the worker is an empathic person and does not join with other social forces to intimidate the client, it may be possible to find a common ground between what the applicant wishes and what the worker can legitimately do.

At this point, applicants may be ready and willing to discuss their problems in more detail. This will enable them and their workers to prioritize what they will work on together, based on such criteria as the areas of greatest discomfort, the levels of difficulty that will be encountered in trying to solve the problem, and what logically requires attention first. The first problem to be worked on will be specified in the greatest detail as the worker and client identify how long the problem has existed, what people are involved in the problem, and how the applicant has previously coped with the problem. This information will help the applicant and worker make decisions together on how they will try to resolve the problem and whom they will involve in this process, such as family members, friends, teachers, and employers.

As the process proceeds, the worker will try to promote a good professional relationship with the applicant. The components of this relationship are as follows: (1) The client experiences the worker as seeking to understand his or her communications and as being progressively more successful in this respect. This occurs as the worker provides information as to how she perceives the client's ideas and feelings and checks this out with her client. Such information about perceptions of client feelings is referred to as an empathic response. (2) The client experiences the worker as caring about the client in ways that do not inappropriately invade the client's privacy or that are not conditional upon what the client does. (3) The client trusts the worker to do what the worker promises to do and to be honest in what he or she says. When the worker and client are to engage in problem solving together, an aspect of their relationship is referred to as a *therapeutic alliance*. The client views himself or herself as an ally of the worker in seeking to modify that part of the client or that aspect of the environment that is troubling.

At about this stage in the process, the worker and the applicant are likely to determine whether the applicant should become a client, that is, whether to continue to work together to resolve the problem. If they agree either orally or in writing to continue, a contract is understood to have been created. The contract has terms that consist of the problem(s) to be worked on, the goals that are sought to reduce the problems, and the client's and the worker's roles in the process. Details such as the time, place, and frequency of meetings and what, if anything, the client will pay for the service are also specified.

Written contracts are increasingly being used in social work practice. The reason is that reviewing something in writing can help the parties to be clear as to what they do and do not agree to. In social work practice, nevertheless, the word "contract" is used only in analogy to law, and we are *not* referring to a legally binding entity. There may be legal implications, however, in some fields of service. An example is in child welfare when a parent's attainment of a goal specified in a contract with a social worker is a precondition to having a court return a child.

If the social worker and the client cannot agree on the terms of a contract, they may decide to continue meeting in an effort to resolve their differences. On the other hand, they may decide that this is not likely to occur. It is then the responsibility of the social worker to help the client to find a more appropriate service if the client wishes to avail himself or herself of that offer.

THE MIDDLE PHASE

During the middle phase, the worker and client carry out activities to help the client attain her or his goals. When doing this, however, the client and worker may determine that some goals and ways of working together are inappropriate and, consequently, they may repeat some of the tasks of the first phase and then resume with those of the middle phase.

When individuals seek to attain their goals, this may encompass changing themselves, their groups and families, or the systems in the larger environment. This choice of targets is an even more complex issue than first appears, because the process of changing one system may bring about changes in others. For example, a mother determined that she would spend more time with her children, and her husband, observing her doing this, resolved to do the same.

In another example, change worked the other way. A client decided that she would no longer settle for the inferior education her child was receiving and that she would pressure the school to provide better services. In the process of doing this, she learned ways that she could be assertive in other situations as well.

Because of this complexity, it is necessary to separate the different dimensions of the change process, even though in real life they are inseparable. Here we discuss attaining goals through changes in the clients themselves, and in subsequent chapters we will talk about changes in families, groups, and larger systems.

Furthermore, when individuals change, this undoubtedly occurs in a holistic manner, because the person acts, thinks, and feels differently. Change, however, can be *initiated* by focusing for a time on the individual's actions, thoughts, or feelings, and this is often what a social worker does. An example is an unemployed man seeing a social worker in a mental health agency. The man may be anxious about seeking employment (feeling), may have ideas about seeking employment that are dysfunctional (thoughts), and may lack the skills required for a particular job (actions). Depending on the circumstances, the social worker will work with this client at different times on the way he thinks, feels, or acts. It is possible that in even a few words several of these dimensions might be referred to, but the worker should be aware of how this happens.

For purposes of analysis, however, we shall break down the things workers do into those primarily directed at thoughts, feelings, and actions. An important advantage to this approach is that it moves us away from focusing on a particular theory and enables us to draw a number of theories, each of which can help us to be more effective in the ways we help people. Social workers have at times derived their actions from such theoretical systems as ego psychology, behaviorism, role theory, attribution theory, problem solving theory, and developmental psychology. We favor educating social workers in all these, while identifying specific procedures that can be employed for specific purposes.

We, therefore, think it is less important to be theoretically pure than to be aware of ways of being helpful that have been tested through research or through previous utilization whenever this is possible. Many times, however, workers must be creative if they are to do anything at all. We now present some of the procedures workers frequently use to help clients modify feelings, thoughts, and actions.[18]

MODIFYING FEELINGS. Workers can help clients *ventilate* their feelings. In doing this, they help the client to express, pent-up feelings, and many clients experience a sense of relief and support when this occurs in a social work relationship.

VENTILATION

Mrs. Jones, as she described her husband's declaration that he wished to divorce her, struggled to keep herself under control as she gazed imploringly at the social worker. The worker suggested that she might feel better if she let her feelings out. Mrs. Jones began to sob and, as she did so, she said she had tried so hard to be brave for the children. After crying for a while, she dried her tears and said she had better figure out now what she should do.

Workers also help clients to relax when the client is feeling anxious and tense. This may help the client to think better about an issue or to acquire information or a skill from the worker. Learning how to relax may also be useful when clients feel tense and are not with the social worker. One method that social workers use is referred to as *progressive muscle relaxation.* (A discussion of this technique is beyond the scope of this book but the reader can consult many excellent texts on the subject.[19]) An easier technique for workers to learn involves instructions to clients to focus on their breathing.

RELAXATION

Mr. Green came into the session panting. He said that he had just been told by his boss that he had to finish the big project that he was working on no later than the end of the week. He didn't know how he could do that and, if he failed to do so, they would never give him the time off that he had been promised. He would then have to cancel the long weekend trip that he had promised his wife that they would take, when they could spend enough time together to discuss their future plans.

The worker said that she might be able to help Mr. Green figure out some way to handle the situation, and it would be easier to do this if he was less tense. He agreed. She suggested that he breathe slowly and say the number "one" each time he exhaled. He did this for a few minutes and, as he did so, he visibly relaxed. The worker then told him to sit quietly for a few moments. When this was over, she asked Mr. Green what some of his alternatives might be.

MODIFYING THOUGHTS. A frequently used means for helping clients deal with problems by thinking differently is through altering the way they engage in problem solving. This involves helping them to learn to move progressively through stages in which they define the problem, determine goals, generate possible solutions, evaluate the solutions, choose an alternative, and then plan how to carry out the alternative.

PROBLEM SOLVING

Mr. Virtue said that he was likely to flunk several of his college subjects and this would threaten his continuing to get a scholarship. The worker asked him what was happening to get him into so much difficulty. He said that he was behind in turning in his written assignments. The worker asked why this was so. He said that he was working 25 hours a week and also had become the president of the film society. This left him little time to do the preparation needed to write the papers.

The worker suggested that he list the possible things he could do to free more time. He indicated that he could resign the job in the film society; he could ask the vice-president to take it over for the rest of the term; he could reduce his working hours from 25 to 15 and ask his father to lend him some money until his summer vacation began and he could work full time; he could also ask for a two-week leave of absence from his job and could, in that case, also ask his father for a loan.

The worker and Mr. Virtue then discussed each of the alternatives generated. In summary, the client concluded that he couldn't resign his job in the film group because he would appear very inconsistent. The group, however, would understand that his grades were important and that, if the vice-president took over, Mr. Virtue could still coach him on how the job was done. He didn't think he would be allowed to keep his job if he took a leave of absence, but he thought his employer might allow him to reduce his hours. He also generated the idea that if his father wouldn't help him, he could apply for a bank loan.

On the basis of this discussion, Mr. Virtue decided to temporarily relinquish his position in the film society and to reduce his hours at work. He planned to borrow money, from his father as a first choice, and from the bank as a second.

To help him carry out these decisions, the worker discussed with Mr. Virtue how he was going to approach his employer and his father.

Another way of helping clients think differently is to aid them to *elevate their self-concept.* Ellis and Harper describe a series of steps for a worker to use to help clients do this by improving the things they say to themselves about themselves.[20] The first step is to help the client understand the reasons for using this approach. The second is to educate the client in the kinds of self-defeating statements people make to themselves.

The third is to help the client analyze his or her own self-defeating internal statements. Finally, the client is helped to modify such statements.

ELEVATION OF SELF-CONCEPT

Ms. Low seemed very sad as she described her efforts to make friends in her new neighborhood. She had almost given up, she was so desperate. In fact, recently one of her neighbors told her to stop looking so sad or no one would want to be friendly with her. The worker said that one reason she might be looking this way and not making friends is that she was approaching people as if she expected them to reject her; this might cause her to act in ways that set up the rejection. A way to begin to change this is to change some of her thoughts.

The worker asked Ms. Low what some of her thoughts were when she started to talk with a potential friend. With the worker's help, Ms. Low listed the following: she thought that she was not as intelligent as the other person; the other person would not be interested in her; and if the other person rejected her, it would be proof that she was not desirable as a friend. The worker then helped Ms. Low to see that each of these ideas was irrational. Ms. Low was an intelligent person and, in addition, there were many things people value in each other besides intelligence. Ms. Low was also helped to see that she had many things about her that another person would find interesting. Finally, if another person turned her down, this was *not* a sign that she was not desirable as a friend. The time may not have been a good one for the other person, or there may be other reasons for this unrelated to Ms. Low.

Subsequently, the worker helped Ms. Low to replace the self-defeating statements with other positive ones. Ms. Low was able to do this. She was also helped to make friends through the use of relaxation as well as behavioral rehearsal techniques (the latter will be discussed later in this chapter).

Understanding the relationships among their thoughts and feelings and actions, relationships of which they were previously unaware, may help clients to think differently. The actions of the worker that promote this are *interpretations*. In psychoanalytic theory, interpretations help the client to become aware of phenomena of which he or she is not aware because of unconscious processes. We do not use the term "interpretation" in this restricted sense, but to apply to any association between events in the client's life that it would be useful for the client to understand. Within our meaning, then, a behaviorist provides an interpretation when he or she points out to a client that his child actually has more tantrums than previously when he reinforces this behavior by offering candy to the child to stop. Another example of an interpretation is a statement by a worker that an individual is acting in a manner that is similar to how the individual's parent acted.

It is important to recognize that an interpretation does not usually represent a single statement by a worker, but instead is a process that the worker and the client engage in over time, culminating in the client understanding the relationship between two or more sets of events. It begins with the worker's efforts to help the client identify each type of event and then to help the client see the connection between them.

Obviously, the next step involves determining what to do in the light of this understanding.

INTERPRETATION

Mr. Slow and the social worker were discussing his reluctance to apply for his disability benefits. The worker asked Mr. Slow how he felt about making out the application. He said that he felt very nervous. At the worker's encouragement, he went on to say that he was sure that they were going to turn him down. The worker asked Mr. Slow if this reminded him of any other events in his life. He said that when he had suffered his accident he had applied for workers' compensation. He had been turned down at first based on the report that had been turned in by his employer. He was afraid that his doctor would turn in a report now that would not be acceptable to the disability people. The worker pointed out to Mr. Slow that he was seeing the two situations as similar, but there was little likelihood of this. The employer had wanted to avoid getting a reputation of having an unsafe factory, whereas his doctor was on the "other side of the fence" and would want Mr. Slow to get the benefits to which he was entitled. Mr. Slow said that this conversation was a big help to him and he was sure now that he was ready to make out his application. In fact, he had brought the form with him today as he hoped the worker could help him to get over his block.

MODIFYING ACTIONS. Workers help clients to change their actions by using *reinforcement*. In technical terms, this occurs when a worker acts in such a way following the action of a client that the client's act is more likely to reoccur. In simpler terms, a worker's intervention frequently reinforces a client's behavior when the worker's behavior follows the client's and provides some pleasure to the client.

REINFORCEMENT

John had not been turning in his homework. The worker arranged for the teacher to keep a chart and each day indicate whether John had turned in his homework. At the end of the week, John would bring this chart to the worker. If there were at least four checks on the chart, the worker would take John out for a treat. Based on this system, after three weeks John was doing his homework every day. After this period, John continued to bring his chart to the worker for three more weeks and the worker, by previous agreement with John, praised him for his ability to maintain this progress. (It is likely that three responses functioned as reinforcement: the teacher's checks on the chart, the treat, and the later praise supplied by the worker.)

Another type of intervention, which we shall not discuss here, is *punishment*. This means that an action of the worker after that of the client *decreases* the likelihood that the client will act in that way. Obviously, social workers do not inflict physical pain on clients, but they may offer criticism, which can function as a type of punishment in a technical sense.[21]

Another way worker's help clients to act differently is to provide them with an example of behavior they can imitate. This is referred to as *modeling*. Modeling may occur when the client has an opportunity to observe the worker perform or when the worker encourages the client to observe the behavior of someone else. In addition, the client does not have to actually observe the actions of someone else but can be told about or read about them. A frequent approach that is used in social work to make modeling possible is *role playing*.

MODELING

Mr. Shy was being helped by the worker to be more assertive. The specific situation that was being discussed was Mr. Shy's interactions with his employer. The employer had been assigning Mr. Shy tasks that took more hours to complete than Mr. Shy was paid for. Mr. Shy had been working evenings to finish these tasks and had become very resentful, but was unable to say anything about this to the employer. He said that he didn't even know how to begin the conversation.

The worker suggested to Mr. Shy that he role play the employer while the worker played Mr. Shy. The worker then proceeded to demonstrate one way the employer might be approached. He looked Mr. Shy in the eye and said that, while he wished to be helpful to the firm, he also had other responsibilities and couldn't continue to work evenings. After this enactment, the worker asked Mr. Shy to change roles and be himself while the worker acted as the employer.

In this second role play, Mr. Shy was able to confront the worker as his "employer." He deviated from the model in that he looked down when he talked and apologized first for "bothering" the employer with "his" problem. The worker discussed this with him and suggested that he look up when he talked and that he not apologize. The scene was replayed and Mr. Shy was even more assertive. The worker complimented Mr. Shy on this and they subsequently discussed how Mr. Shy would feel doing this in real life.

Social workers also help clients to modify their actions by giving them *task assignments* or assisting them to make such assignments to themselves. These tasks are usually performed between sessions with the social worker, but they may also be enacted within the sessions themselves (This concept of tasks is similar to the concepts of homework assignments and behavioral assignments.)

TASK ASSIGNMENTS

Mr. Shy was now ready to approach his employer in a more assertive manner. The worker asked him when he thought he would do this, and Mr. Shy said he was ready to approach his employer the next day and ask for an appointment that week. The worker said he agreed with the idea of Mr. Shy doing this while he was "on the move," and at their next weekly session he would ask Mr. Shy how it went. The worker wondered if there was any additional help Mr. Shy needed to be able to carry out his task. Mr. Shy. indicated that he was sometimes nervous when he approached his boss. The worker reviewed with him relaxation techniques that the two of them had previously practiced. Mr. Shy also said that he often thought that his employer would think awful things of him for making requests. The worker then spent some time reviewing with Mr. Shy ways they had previously discussed to replace irrational thoughts with rational ones.

The following week the worker asked Mr. Shy "how it went" with being more assertive with his boss. Mr. Shy said that he had carried through on his approach to his employer and asked for an appointment. He and his boss had an interview in which he indicated he couldn't work evenings. When his boss told him how important it was, however, Mr. Shy said he would do the work when it was real. The worker and Mr. Shy then discussed this "giving in" and how Mr. Shy really wished he had not done this. Further discussions and a role play then took place on how Mr. Shy might handle the situation now.

INDIVIDUAL CHANGE THROUGH SYSTEM INTERVENTIONS. When workers interact with a family, group, or an even larger system, they may seek at times to change some aspect of that family, group, or system. At other times, the target of their activity is an *individual.* It is important, therefore, to recognize these added possibilities. In fact, the current position of many social workers is that they should work in the way that is most useful to the individual, rather than in the way preferred by the worker for reasons that are not relevant to the client, such as the approach in which the worker received her or his first training. This may require some workers to refer the client to another practitioner who was better trained to work with a particular type of system, such as the family or group.

The decision to help an individual on a one-to-one basis or in the context of a larger system must take into consideration the client's preferences and previous experiences, as well as the degree to which the client's problem is a response to forces within the larger system and whether change can be most readily attained by a change in the impact of that system on the individual.

So far, we have described how workers help clients to change their feelings, thoughts, and actions through one-to-one helping. We shall parallel this discussion by discussing these changes in the context of the group, family, or larger system.

The worker can enable a family or group to help a member with respect to *feelings.* One way this is done is for the other group or family members to provide feedback on the feelings they perceive the individual expressing. For example, a group member became aware of his feelings of affection for other members. The worker suggested that he turn to specific other members and tell them about his feelings of caring for them. The member addressed then gave feedback to the individual in question, such as "I liked the direct way you told me what you felt."

Members of a family or group can also help each other modify feelings. An example of this was a father in a family who was taught by a worker during a family session how to reinforce and monitor a relaxation program for his son. Workers do not usually seek to help members deal with feelings through interventions at an organizational level, but this is occasionally possible, as when a worker helped a school teacher to be more empathic when a student (who was the worker's client) was feeling frustrated while working on a classroom assignment.

Thoughts of individuals can also be modified through systemic interventions. This can also be accomplished through the process of feedback. That is, other members can describe their perceptions of events when these differ from the thoughts the individual has about the events, and this may lead to changes in the individual's thoughts. An example of this was a group member who thought that other group members believed he was stupid. The worker suggested that the other members tell the member in question what they thought. Several members stated that they sincerely thought the member was very intelligent. The member appeared startled by this and began to reflect on how long he had held to the notion that others thought he was stupid when this may have been a false idea.

Finally, *behaviors* may be modified through the actions of others in a system. They can alter the ways they reinforce an individual. An example of this occurred in a school setting in which the worker helped a teacher establish a reward system for a student who was having trouble turning in her work. Members may also provide models for each other. An example of this occurred in a group in which a member was getting ready to apply for a job. He was not sure how to handle the job interview. Another member who had successfully applied for a similar job volunteered to role play how she had done this, with the worker acting as the prospective employer. The member who needed the help observed this role play and then volunteered to be part of another role play in which he would practice how to would handle the interview. After the second role play, other members gave him further tips on how he might handle the actual interview.

Additional strategies are often used by workers to help individuals meet their needs in the environment. One of these is associated with the worker role of *broker,* in which the worker helps the client locate and make use of other resources in the community. The skillful worker will, at times, approach the resource to ensure that it will be receptive to the client's application for services.

Another strategy is associated with the worker's role as *advocate.* In this role, the worker seeks to secure a change in a system on behalf of the client. An example is a client who was denied benefits from a welfare department. The worker independently contacted the department to point out the department's own rule that made the client eligible for the service requested.

Still another strategy is associated with the worker's role as *mediator.* Here the worker helps the client and another individual or system to negotiate with each other so that each may attain their respective goals. An example is a worker who met with a student and his teacher. The student wanted the teacher to extend the deadline for an assignment. The teacher was concerned that complying with this request would be seen by other students as unfair. The worker helped each party to present her concerns. This led to a compromise in which the student was allowed to submit the assignment late but would receive a lower grade as a consequence.

TERMINATION

The way that workers help clients cope with ending the helping relationship also requires a great deal of skill. The specific techniques used by the worker may vary depending on such factors as whether the client is ending because her or his goals have been attained, because they have not been attained and the client is critical of the service, because the worker is leaving the agency, or whether a predetermined time period of service has expired.

In all these situations, a series of tasks must be accomplished by the worker to help the client to secure optimal benefits from the service that was offered. These tasks are to help the client (1) evaluate the experience, (2) cope with feelings about termination, (3) maintain beneficial changes, and (4) seek out new services if necessary.

The process of evaluation helps the client to identify the beneficial changes that may have occurred, as well as to recognize where change has not occurred or even ways in which he or she may now be worse off. Evaluation also helps the worker to learn ways in which he or she may be effective or ineffective and thus may lead to the worker offering better service in the future. This evaluation can be conducted in an unstructured manner or the worker and the client might employ charts, questionnaires, or psychological tests.[22]

The client (as well as the worker) will have feelings about termination. These feelings might be pleasant, such as pleasure that goals have been attained or that the client will not have to continue paying fees to the agency. Some may be uncomfortable, such as that the client will be sad to lose the worker, angry that the worker is deserting her or him or that goals have not been attained, or fearful that the client will not be able to make it on his or her own. The worker will help the client express these feelings and cope with them. This will help the client to retain what she or he has learned from the work done and may also help the client to deal with the other inevitable terminations that occur throughout life.

Workers help clients maintain changes in a number of ways. One is to clearly identify them. Another is to plan how to cope with challenges to progress that might be produced by people whom the client will encounter in the environment. The worker will also help the client to find ways of securing reinforcement for maintaining the changes. The worker may also produce some overlearning by encouraging the client to practice the change one more time before the service ends.

Finally, the client may have attained the maximum benefits from a helping process, but may require another service subsequently. The worker will help the client to identify this need and to secure the service. An example of this is a client who used a worker to help her decide whether or not she wished to place her unborn child for adoption. The result of this help was that she did decide in favor of adoption. Since the agency where this work was accomplished did not have an adoption service, the worker helped her to apply to a proper agency.

Conclusion

This chapter began with a discussion of the kinds of individual problems for which social workers provide help to individuals. These problems were classified into those related to socialization and remediation. Problems of socialization were defined as those encountered as individuals take on new roles. Remediation problems were defined as related to dysfunctional ways in which people attempt to fulfill roles. Examples were given of both socialization and remediation problems throughout the life cycle. We also described in detail how such problems may occur as a result of both the way the individual behaves and the opportunities present or absent in the environment.

We then described methods social workers have utilized to help individuals cope with problems and how these emerged historically. Major historical figures who played important roles in these developments in social work were introduced.

The bulk of this chapter described the processes of individual helping utilized by social workers. Beginning, middle, and ending phases were utilized to organize this presentation. In the beginning phase, workers act to promote an engagement between clients and themselves, to assess the clients in the context of their social situations, to plan the ways in which help will be offered, and to create a contractual agreement between themselves and their clients.

In the middle phase, the worker and the client seek to attain the client's goals through changes in the client, the client's environment, or both. With reference to changes in the clients, we referred to changes in feelings, thoughts, and actions. Techniques for producing changes in each of these were identified and illustrated. We also provided information on how such changes may be produced in the context of the family, group, or larger system. Larger system changes are often sought through the worker acting in the roles of advocate, broker, or mediator.

The final phase, usually referred to as termination, was also discussed. The tasks of termination, which consist of evaluation, coping with feelings, acting to maintain beneficial changes, and obtaining new services, were described.

The social deficits we have portrayed are frequently at least one of the causes, if not the main cause, of problems in social functioning. It is a serious mistake to assume that all such problems are a consequence of personal deficits or even of deficits in family life, although there is often a sequence of events in which social deficits lead to personal and family deficits that continue even when the social deficit is reduced or removed. The social worker, therefore, must act with and on behalf of the individual to reduce social deficits in general as well as their impact on her or him.

We now turn our attention to the interventions used by social workers to change groups, families, and larger systems.

Notes

1. See William Ryan, *Blaming the Victim* (New York: Pantheon Books, 1971).
2. The information on Mary Richmond is drawn from Dorothy G. Becker, "Mary Ellen Richmond," in *Encyclopedia of Social Work,* 17th ed., Vol. 2, John B. Turner, ed. (New York: National Association of Social Workers, 1977), p. 1224.
3. When these two schools represented the major split among caseworkers, an effort to clarify their differences was presented in Cora Kasius, ed., *A Comparison of Diagnostic and Functional Casework Concepts* (New York: Family Service Association of America, 1950).
4. This sketch of Gordon Hamilton draws from Shirly Hellenbrand, "Gordon Hamilton," in Turner, ed., *Encyclopedia of Social Work,* 17th ed., Vol. 2, pp. 517–519.
5. Helen Harris Perlman, "Putting the 'Social' Back in Social Casework," Helen Harris Perlman, ed., *Perspectives on Social Casework* (Philadelphia: Temple University Press, 1971), pp. 29–34.
6. See Joel Fischer, "Is Casework Effective? A Review," *Social Work,* 18 (1973), pp. 5–20.

7. Mary Richmond, "Some Next Steps in Social Treatment," in *Proceedings of the National Conference of Social Work, 1920* (New York: Columbia University Press, 1939), p. 256.
8. Peter Kropotkin, *Mutual Aid: A Factor of Evolution* (New York: Alfred Knopf, 1925).
9. Mary Parker Follett, *The New State* (New York: Longmans, Green, 1926), and Eduard C. Lindeman, *The Community* (New York: Association Press, 1921).
10. This discussion of Grace Coyle draws from Dorothy G. Becker, "Grace Longwell Coyle," in Turner, ed., *Encyclopedia of Social Work,* 17th ed., Vol. 1, pp. 197–198.
11. Robert D. Vinter, "The Essential Components of Social Group Work Practice," in *Individual Change through Small Groups,* Paul Glasser, Rosemary Sarri, and Robert Vinter, eds., (New York: The Free Press, 1974), pp. 9–33.
12. William Schwartz, "The Social Worker in the Group," in *New Perspectives on Service to Groups* (New York: Columbia University Press, 1961), pp. 7–29.
13. Mary Richmond, *Social Diagnosis* (New York: Russell Sage, 1917), p. 137.
14. Ann Hartman and Joan Laird, *Family-Centered Social Work Practice* (New York: Macmillan, 1983).
15. Judith Lang, Book Review, in *Social Work,* 30 (1985), p. 278.
16. See Helen H. Perlman, "Intake and Some Role Considerations," *Social Casework,* 41 (1960), pp. 171–177.
17. More detail on all these phases may be obtained from Charles Garvin and Brett Seabury, *Interpersonal Practice in Social Work* (Englewood Cliffs, N.J.: Prentice Hall, 1984).
18. This discussion draws from Garvin and Seabury, *Interpersonal Practice in Social Work,* pp. 243–256.
19. A detailed program for learning this technique is Douglas A. Bernstein and Thomas D. Borkovec, *Progressive Relaxation Training* (Champaign, Ill.: Research Press, 1973).
20. A. Ellis and R. A. Harper, *A New Guide to Rational Living* (North Hollywood, Calif.: Wilshire, 1975), pp. 202–230.
21. For more information on reinforcement and punishment according to the principles of conditioning, see Joel Fischer and Harvey Gochros, *Planned Behavior Change: Behavior Modification in Social Work* (New York: The Free Press, 1975).
22. Examples of these are provided in Garvin and Seabury, *Interpersonal Helping in Social Work,* pp. 217–235.

CHAPTER 6
Helping Groups and Families to Change

Introduction

In this chapter we are concerned with how to work with families and groups, rather than individuals, so that they become more capable of attaining their goals. Since the words "family" and "group" are used so frequently in casual as well as professional discussions, they may not appear to require definition. We have some ideas, however, about these systems that do not entirely conform to the popular view. We define the family in a broad fashion as a set of individuals who have economic and other commitments to each other, who are likely to meet each other's needs for intimacy, and who usually maintain a joint household. Thus communes, adult siblings living together, and gay male and lesbian couples are some of the many types of families, which include conventional families composed of two adults (one male and one female) living together with their children.

By "group," we mean a *small* group (usually composed of between three and twenty-five individuals). These groups are sufficiently small that their members are usually able engage in face-to-face interaction, and the behavior of any one member has effects on the other members. We must also understand larger groups, but they often develop structured and formal interactions to replace face-to-face ones, and to describe how they function[1] requires different concepts than we employ with small groups.

We consider families and groups to be small social systems and, therefore, to have many features in common. This allows us to use many of the same theories and concepts when we seek to understand their functioning. Groups and families develop leadership patterns, subdivide into cliques, assign their members to roles, generate a division of labor, and seek to maintain their structures and processes over time. At times these conditions are useful to the family or the group in attaining its goals and at times they are not. Social workers also use some of the same techniques to help families and groups to function better, but because of the separate development of group and family work, these similarities have not always been recognized.

There are differences in families and groups that require workers, at times, to work differently with each. These relate to the different functions fulfilled by the family and the group, as well as the fact that the family has a past and a future that the group usually does not have. But a distinction should be made between *natural* and *formed* groups. Formed groups have been created by the worker and/or the members for a specific purpose and usually terminate when the purpose has been achieved. Natural groups existed prior to the social work service and include such entities as gangs and residential groups in institutions. Natural groups have much in common with families.

Therefore, we shall discuss commonalities in work with families and groups, but we shall also identify the differences that arise because of the varying functions and histories of the two systems. We seek, moreover, to use a single set of terms to characterize group and family phenomena so as to enable the reader to better understand the similarities and differences that exist.

We shall also include consideration of two types of groups: those whose purpose is to enable individual members to change as a result of the experience (treatment groups) and those whose purpose is to attain some objective external to the group (task groups). The latter group includes committees that are created in organizations and communities to help those entities to accomplish their purposes.

We begin our discussion with a consideration of the situations that arise in groups and families that lead to a social worker offering a service to them. We then utilize a framework similar to the one employed in Chapter 5 to describe the role of the social worker with families and groups and illustrate these interventions with anecdotes.[2]

Group and Family Situations

In discussing individual change, we made a distinction between socialization and remediation. An analogous distinction, which we refer to as education or treatment and facilitation, can be made with regard to families and groups.

EDUCATION

Groups are often formed by social workers for educational purposes. These purposes include informing children how to avoid situations in which they might be molested, teaching adolescents about sexuality or the dangers of drugs, helping young adults to learn job search procedures, informing parents about parenting skills, helping adults to prepare for retirement, and helping retired people to develop new avocational interests.

An educational approach may also be taken with respect to task groups. Community workers may convene a leadership conference in which officers and members are trained in ways to improve the functioning of their groups. Such training may include information on parliamentary procedure, the creation of agendas, ways of publicizing group events, and means of fund raising. Similarly, a staff development person in an agency may offer training to agency committees on how to plan their efforts to achieve their goals within the required time frame or how to take responsibility for relating budgetary constraints to program requirements.

Educational approaches may also be taken with families. A single or several families may receive communication training in which they are taught ways of enhancing communication among family members or how to identify specific communication problems. Families such as those with a chronically mentally ill member, which some writers believe require treatment, are now seen by others as benefiting from education. An educational focus sees the chronically mentally ill member as suffering from an illness, and the other family members are not the causes of the illness, but rather are people who can function as therapeutic resources; however, they must *learn* how to cope with the difficult situation in which they find themselves in ways that protect their rights and enable them to meet their own needs.

TREATMENT AND GROUP FACILITATION

A social worker who possesses expertise in facilitating groups is also often called on to assist task groups that have encountered difficulties in carrying out their purposes. The worker may maintain a long-term relationship with the group or may become involved solely for the purpose of helping the group to resolve the difficulty. Under the long-term condition, the worker is usually seen as staffing the group. The group possesses its own officers and is autonomous, and the worker's role is to facilitate the work of the officers and members through consultation and support, while also performing tasks for the group, such as maintaining files, securing information for decision making, and handling communications.

Such groups include boards of directors, agency committees, and task forces in a community organization. The group worker in the case of the board of directors is likely to be the agency executive, and in the case of the community the worker may be employed by the community organization and is a community organizer. In the case of the agency committee, the worker may be the person designated or elected as chairperson. In all these examples, the worker must possess the knowledge of group phenomena and group facilitation described in this chapter.

Treatment and facilitation also occur with families at those times when the immediate purpose of the worker is to enable the family to become a better functioning family as such. Examples of families requiring this approach are the following:

1. Families in which the subgroups that exist interfere with family functioning. For example, a father has a closer relationship with a daughter than with his wife and the wife with another daughter rather than her husband.
2. Families that repeat a sequence of events that leads to negative consequences. For example, a child gets into trouble each time the parents have a fight; the parents join together to save the child; after this, the child does not get into trouble immediately, but does so when the parents begin to fight again.
3. Families that are too enmeshed, which is when members are overly involved with each other and overreact to each other. An example is a family that does not permit its teenage members to go out with friends, and the parents believe that family members must socialize almost exclusively with each other.

The Phases of Helping

We divided the phases of helping individuals into beginnings, middles, and endings, and we use the same cycle of events to describe ways of helping families and groups. An important issue to consider in reviewing such phases is the relationship between the phases of helping and the phases that occur in the life of the individual or system, from its creation to its ending. Different kinds of help may be offered in relationship to the different stages of the individual's life cycle. The same kind of analysis may be offered in relationship to family treatment and, in fact, many typologies of the stages of family life relate these to the ages of children: families who have *not yet* had children, families with infants, and so forth. One problem with this, of course, is that not all families raise children.

The issue with *formed* groups is different in that the phases of helping coincide with the life of the system. The group is created by the worker and typically ends when the worker says so. The worker, therefore, must consider both the group's need to evolve as a group as well as the phases of treatment. It is possible and even desirable for many groups to continue on their own after the worker leaves them, but this does not happen very often. Many social workers and social scientists have studied the stages of group life, referred to as group development. Hartford, after reviewing much of this literature, identified these as follows:

1. Pregroup phases
    1.1   Private pregroup phase
    1.2   Public pregroup phase
    1.3   Convening phase
2. Group formation phase
    2.1   Integration, disintegration, and conflict
    2.2   Reintegration or reorganization synthesis phase
    2.3   Group functioning and maintenance phase
3. Termination phases
    2.1   Pretermination phase
    3.2   Termination
4. Posttermination phase[3]

The issue of phases of change in relationship to phases of system development is relevant to many of the differences in the way social workers work with families and formed groups. The reader should bear this in mind as we consider the phases of helping.

THE BEGINNING PHASE

Because in formed groups the phases of helping coincide with the phases of system change, the worker must create the group before she or he can work with it. This usually begins with a decision as to the purpose of the group. Examples are to help abused women cope with that event and protect themselves, to help children of divorced parents, or to raise funds for a community organization. If the purpose of the group is treatment, the worker will recruit members and compose the group so that it is likely that members will be compatible with and able to help one another. Compositional decisions involve such things as the size of the group and the ways workers seek to have members who are similar to one another. Similarities with regard to age, gender, ethnicity, ways of interacting with others, and experiences relevant to the purposes of the group are most often considered.[4]

Work with families and groups begins with an engagement phase. When the system to be served is a formed group, the worker will help the members to tell each other their purposes for attending, and this will hold true for both task and treatment groups. The difference between these two types of groups is that the purposes members describe in the former relate to what they hope the group will accomplish in the larger environment; in the latter, the purposes will relate to what the member hopes to get out of the group for herself or himself. Workers also describe the roles they will fulfill with respect to the group.

In the engagement phase, the members have usually discussed with each other why they are seeing a social worker. Typically, when the worker asks the family this question, the spokesperson for the family will state that they are there because of the problems of a specified family member. Examples are a child who is failing in school or is in trouble with the law, an adult member who has been diagnosed to be mentally ill, or any member who is not living up to the expectations of the others. This person is referred to by family therapists as the *identified patient*. It is seldom that a family member will tell the worker that the family is there because something is a problem with the *entire* family!

In work with families and with treatment groups, the worker will usually ask for more information about the presenting problems. In treatment groups, this discussion will be similar to the analogous one with an individual, except the worker is aware that the members are listening to each other. They may wish to ask each other questions as they seek out similarities, and this is encouraged as long as it does not prevent each member from having her or his say. In the family situation, the worker may encourage each person present to give his or her view of the problem, and in this way the worker seeks to make contact with each family member.

In work with both families and groups, the worker will also assess the nature of the family or group as a system. In the family situation, this is a highly important process from the very beginning as the worker seeks to understand how the nature of the family system relates to its presenting problems. In the group situation, the nature of the group in its beginning stage will be considerably different from its nature as it evolves over time; the worker, nevertheless, will watch the group's evolution to learn whether this is happening in ways conducive to accomplishing its purposes.

We shall now present and describe a set of terms to describe the conditions that exist in groups and families.[5]

GOALS AND PURPOSES. Families and groups can be characterized by the presence or absence of goals and the degree to which they are shared among the members. For example, a group may have the goal of securing a daycare center in the community. A family may have a goal of saving enough money together so that all may go on a vacation. In the latter case, one family member may disagree with that goal and would rather see the family save money for a new television set.

CULTURE. Families and groups develop traditions, norms, rules, beliefs, and a shared sense of their own history. These views affect their goals and the actions they take to reach their goals. For example, a group began each meeting with a prayer. A family had the tradition that all members would celebrate holidays together.

STRUCTURE. The members of families and groups develop patterns in the way they interact with each other. These patterns have been categorized, and the term used to describe the pattern is noted in parentheses.

1. Certain members may associate more with some members than others (sociometric or affectional).
2. Certain members may communicate more or on different topics with some members than others (communications).
3. Some members may be most able to influence other members (power).
4. The members may each perform a different task for the group (division of labor).
5. Members may develop different roles in the group. This includes formal ones such as chairperson or secretary and informal ones such as clown or mediator (roles).

PROCESS. Families and groups develop sequences of events and some of these may repeat themselves. For example, in one family the grandmother would criticize the mother for the way she was raising her children. The mother would then turn some of the child-rearing tasks over to the grandmother. The grandmother would then stop criticizing, after which the mother would reassume control. The process would then repeat itself.

RESOURCES. Families and groups require resources in order to function. These include money, housing, equipment, and help from outsiders.

INTERACTION WITH OTHER SYSTEMS. Families and groups interact with individuals and systems in the environment. These interactions may be helpful, such as when a family got support from another family when they experienced the death of a family member, or harmful, such as when a group of teenagers was challenged to a fight by a group of aggressive youth.

BOUNDARIES. Some families and groups may have open boundaries and allow outsiders to enter and members to leave with little issue made of this. Others may have closed boundaries that isolate them from the outside world. An example of the latter was a family that physically abused its children; this behavior was not known to people in the community who might have interfered because the family kept all contacts with such outsiders to an absolute minimum.

CLIMATE. A "feeling tone" might be present in the family or group in a way that spreads to most or all of its members. Thus some groups present themselves as elated and of high energy, while others present themselves as depressed and unproductive.

In formed groups as opposed to families, workers help members to develop initial relationships with each other and to deal with the mixed feelings they may have about joining the group. The former can be accomplished by encouraging members to tell each other about themselves, by pointing out similarities among members, by introducing activities such as games that encourage members to enjoy each other's company, or by subdividing the group into small subgroups of two to four members who are asked to engage in a task that helps them to become better acquainted with one another.

Members frequently have mixed feelings about being in the group. Positive feelings are aroused by the hope that members' will accomplish their purposes for joining the group and that other pleasurable things will occur as a result of their participation. Negative feelings stem from the possibility that their goals may not be accomplished and that unpleasant things may happen, such as rejection by or ridicule from other members, as well as the social worker. The worker, particularly in treatment groups, will help the members discuss some of their feelings about the group so as to find ways of reinforcing the positive and alleviating the negative feelings.

In family situations, the worker must find some way of joining the system, that is, crossing the family's boundaries so as to be in a position of influence with regard to the family. She or he will do this in one of several ways: by pointing out similarities between himself or herself and some family members, by behaving in ways that the

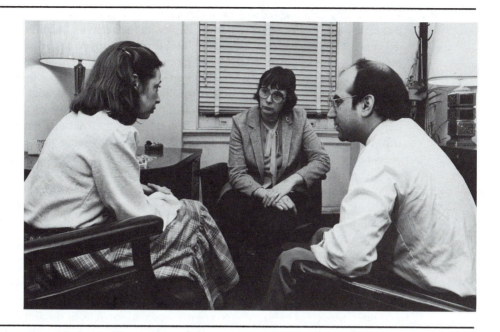

It's "All in the Family." (Photo by Ken Karp.)

family sees as consistent with its own patterns, or by temporarily joining in some family process, rather than challenging it (such as laughing with the family at its jokes or expressing pleasure or displeasure in the same way as the family does).

When the family or group members have clarified their purposes and goals for this service, resolved some of their ambivalence about participation, developed an initial structure that will enable them to function, and developed relationships among members (the last two in formed groups), they will be ready to move ahead with activities to carry out their purposes. They will then enter the middle phases of service.

MIDDLE PHASES

One way of indicating how the worker helps the family or group to change in order to attain its purposes is to describe how this change process may be initiated by the worker's interactions with various subsystems or systems. Thus, the worker may initiate change by interacting with an individual member, with several but not all members (a subsystem), with all the members, or with a system outside the group or family. We shall discuss and illustrate each of these separately.

INTERACTIONS WITH INDIVIDUALS. The worker will often seek to attain change in the family or group by working with an individual member. In task groups, this can be achieved by training and coaching the member to fulfill a role, such as chairperson of the group. The worker may educate this person in how to create an agenda, delegate responsibility, or conduct a meeting. A similar intervention occurs in a family when the worker meets with one individual, such as a parent in a one-parent family, and helps that person to organize household tasks, cope with the behavior of children, and secure resources. The concept of coaching implies providing support to the individual while offering advice on how to act and feedback on how well she or he is performing.

In these examples, the worker interacted with the executive or formal leader of the system. At other times, the worker may interact with an influential person who is not in a leadership role. In one group a member frequently disrupted the meeting by opposing the actions of the officers. The worker hypothesized that this member was frustrated because he had leadership potential that was not being utilized. The worker encouraged this member to volunteer to chair a subcommittee. This gave him a gratifying role to play and he was, subsequently, much less disruptive. A similar intervention was used in a family situation in which an adolescent disrupted the various projects initiated by his older sister. The worker suggested that he volunteer to plan a birthday party for his younger brother; he was attracted to this idea and received much praise for the way he carried it out. Afterward, he and his sister joined together on a number of projects.

INTERACTIONS WITH SUBGROUPS. Groups, particularly as they grow in size, tend to develop subgroups composed of a few other members in which members carry out tasks and meet needs for intimacy in ways that are not possible in the full group. These subgroups may be part of the formal structure of the group, such as the parental subgroup in a family or the subcommittee members of a task group. They may also represent informal groupings, such as a few members of a committee who regularly go out for coffee after meetings or the daughters in a family who play house with their dolls and exclude their brothers from this activity. At times, such subgroups can even hinder the way the group accomplishes its purposes, as when several bullies in a school age boy's group teased the other members.

Workers can intervene with subgroups, as they do with individuals, to affect the entire group or family. One typical example is when the worker interacts directly with the parents and not the children. Family workers tend to think of the parental subgroup as the foundation of the family and will help the parents to reconcile differences with each other in the way they raise their children; at times, also, the worker will see family problems as generated by marital conflicts and will engage in marital work as a means of reducing such problems.

The worker may also work with subgroups in formed groups. In committees, the worker may assist subcommittees in performing tasks for the full group; in treatment groups, the worker may focus on a subgroup by prescribing a group exercise for which the group is subdivided into smaller entities of two, three, or four members. The subgroups can be assigned tasks that will help them to examine and change their impact on the larger group. At times this process can be enhanced by using a "fishbowl" in which a subgroup interacts while the rest of the group observe and give feedback at the end of the interaction.

INTERACTIONS WITH THE GROUP OR FAMILY AS A WHOLE. We have described such group and family conditions as goals, resources, culture, structure, and process. When the worker decides with or on behalf of the members to seek a change in one or more

"Out of the mouths of babes. . . ." (Photo by Shirley Zeiberg.)

of these conditions, the worker and/or the members will assess the condition and select an approach to have the desired effect. Thus, the members of one family agreed that the worker should help them alter a process that repeatedly led to destructive behavior by one member; the members of another family agreed that they wished help in developing a consensus about their goals. The members of one group wished to change a structural pattern in which some members "did all the talking"; the members of another group thought that they had many problems in making decisions and wished to rectify this.

The preceding paragraph may sound as if workers and members consistently act as if they were a team of researchers in a laboratory who experiment with group (or family) conditions. Actually, many group and family conditions are in a constant process of modification with very little conscious attention from workers (much less members). It may only be after the fact, if at all, that anyone attempts to conceptualize these. We argue, however, that the knowledgeable worker will at least periodically review group conditions and quickly formulate hypotheses about those that are linked to problems in the ways the group is functioning.

Change strategies can then be initiated with full recognition, nevertheless, that there are likely to be consequences that have not been anticipated and that may, themselves, require further interventions. Actual practice, therefore, is a mixture of intervention plans based on careful analyses of social-psychological phenomena, plans based only on what the worker predicts will produce some very immediate response, and interventions that are inadvertent and are identified after the action, if at all.

The worker will also consider how to involve the members in identifying and changing their group or family conditions. But some workers fear that when members study their patterns they may be more likely to defend them than to change them. Other workers believe that when members become knowledgeable about how to study their group and family life, they may become empowered to function as their own change agents. We do not know of any research that illuminates this issue; consequently, decisions on this matter should be made in the light of an assessment of how a given family or group is likely to react, its goals, and the amount of time and energy it has to engage in such self-study. There are many instruments, moreover, that can be easily employed by group and family members who wish to secure information on how their group or family is functioning.[6]

The worker who seeks to alter or help members to alter a group or family condition, can employ procedures that are directed at members' cognitions, action patterns, activities, norms, and emotional states. Most procedures affect several, if not all, of these.

(1) Cognitions.   One important way of affecting the members' views is to help them to engage in a process of problem solving. The process of group problem solving closely parallels the phases of individual problem solving: defining the problem, determining goals, generating possible solutions, evaluating the solutions, choosing an alternative, and planning how to carry out the chosen alternative. The difference is that the worker helps the group to secure as much participation of members as possible in this process. Thus, members with knowledge and expertise relevant to the problem may have to be encouraged to contribute these to the group. Members sometimes hold back for a variety of reasons, including fear that their ideas will be rejected or even ridiculed by others. They may also be apprehensive about criticism of their ideas, even when this is legitimate.

Workers with groups have created a number of techniques to enhance group problem solving. One of these is brainstorming; members agree to generate as large a number of ideas as is possible within a specified time period before any evaluation of the ideas is permitted. Another is nominal group technique; members list their ideas in writing and contribute them orally in round-robin sequence, one idea at a time. A final phase of this process involves ranking the importance of these ideas.[7]

GROUP PROBLEM SOLVING

The executive committee of a community organization was charged with developing a fund-raising activity. Because the members thought that they must come up with a new idea to capture the interest of the members, they agreed with the staff member assigned to the committee to use a brainstorming technique. They were also aware of the fact that they needed to raise about $3,000. During the brainstorming period they generated over 20 ideas. An examination of these led to narrowing the choices down to a Gay 90's Casino Night, a theater party, a theatrical review starring local talent, a campaign in which local businesses would be asked to turn over a portion of their proceeds on specified days when people from the larger community would be urged to patronize these businesses, and the creation of a resale shop in the community.

The staff member then suggested that the members list the pros and cons of each of these ideas. Some of the pros they listed for the Casino night were that it would be fun for the members of the group to put it on and that the community would enjoy it. Some of the negatives were that it would require a great deal of work; they could also invest a lot of money in it and, if it were not successful, they would not only have to forsake any profits but would have to make up a deficit. The other ideas were discussed in a similar manner. For the theater party, they thought that they would not have to invest any money up front, but they would make less than from the Casino. For the idea of asking local merchants to turn over a portion of their proceeds on a given day, they thought that this had the disadvantage of not providing much fun to the committee or the community, but might raise a reasonable amount of money with little risk to the committee.

One issue the committee had to face during this discussion was the strong pressure from one of the members to sponsor the theater party. He said that he had a relative who owned a movie house. Other members indicated that they thought this was unduly influencing his opinion. The staff member said she hoped that, when the time came to make a choice, members would try very hard to focus on the positives and negatives that they had mentioned and that she had listed on the blackboard.

After considerable discussion of the pros and cons that were listed, the group members decided to take a vote. The voting procedure they used was that each member could vote for three ideas but would rank them 3–2–1. The idea with the largest total would be the one chosen. The staff member recommended this procedure because she thought it would allow for the selection of the idea that had the most interest on the part of the committee members.

The idea that won was to secure commitments from local merchants to turn over 2% of their proceeds on a given day. The committee would publicize the names of cooperating merchants for what they now called "Community Day" and they would mount this campaign not only in the community but in the city at large. After this was decided, the group turned to a discussion of the subcommittees that were needed to carry out this project.

Another way that workers seek to help group or family members change their cognitions is through *reframing*. Individuals sometimes define their reality in a way that maintains a group level (as well as an individual) problem. The worker can redefine this reality so as to open up possibilities for beneficial changes to occur.

REFRAMING

The Clint family had been referred for family therapy because of Jimmy Clint's withdrawn behavior in school. The teacher also saw him as a fearful and anxious child. It soon became apparent to the therapist that Mrs. Clint was highly overprotective; she insisted on knowing where Jimmy was at all times even though he was 11 years old. She accused others, including her husband, of being unaware of the many dangers that were the consequence of living in the city. Rather than insisting that Mrs. Clint was too anxious about her son, the worker said that it was apparent that she was a very caring mother. Mrs. Clint immediately smiled at the worker and said that this was the first time anyone had ever appreciated her efforts. The worker then suggested that an important topic for them all to consider was how Jimmy was now going to learn to take care of himself.

Still another way of viewing the worker's role with respect to cognitions has been referred to as *realities,*[8] defined as "a set of cognitive schemas that legitimate or validate the family organization."[9] The intent of the worker with respect to realities is not necessarily to modify but to understand them as a way of becoming a meaningful part of the family or group system and, thereby, selecting interventions that will be appropriate to the system. Laird, for example, has written on how a worker can elicit family stories as a way of understanding how the family has created roles with relationship to gender.[10]

REALITIES

The worker was discussing with her family Jill Flame's frequent running away. Jill was 14 years old. As part of this discussion, the worker asked the family to tell her some of the stories they were likely to tell about Jill when the family got together with relatives for holidays and other occasions. Mrs. Flame said she usually tells about how adventurous Jill was when she was a little girl. She liked to explore almost any house they visited and she was always excited when they went on trips. She always liked to keep her suitcase in her room and would keep a few of her clothing articles packed in it all the time. The worker asked what kinds of stories they would tell about Mrs. Flame. Mr. Flame recalled that Mrs. Flame's sisters would reminisce about how she hid in the family car once when their parents went on a vacation and left the children with an aunt. Mrs. Flame had hidden in the back seat and the parents had traveled almost two hours before they discovered her. Recalling these stories led the family into a discussion of how the girls in the family had resented the travels of others and had seen themselves as wishing to be the ones who went places, rather than the ones who were left behind.

(2) Action Patterns. The way family or group members behave can be modified by altering the contingencies related to their behavior. By this we mean that the worker can have an effect on the events that follow members' behaviors, and this effect may increase or decrease such behaviors.

CONTINGENCIES

This example occurred in a group of nine-year-old boys. The worker wished to increase the likelihood in group discussions that each boy would make comments that were relevant to the discussion topic. He brought a bag of peanuts to the meeting and, before a discussion of the boy's problems in school, he explained that each time a boy made comments that were relevant to the discussion the boy would receive a peanut. The boys thought that this would be fun. The worker noticed that the group had a much more focused and animated discussion than it usually had. As the discussion progressed, also, the rate at which the peanuts were dispensed increased dramatically.

Another way that behavior during sessions can be changed is by the worker directly requesting the change that he or she wishes to occur. The worker can ask that a member address his or her remarks to a specific person, can alter seating arrangements, or can make behavioral assignments. The latter, if required to occur outside of sessions, is often referred to as homework.

BEHAVIORAL ASSIGNMENTS

In the Blue family, a pattern developed in which Mrs. Blue's mother, Mrs. Green, frequently criticized the way Mrs. Blue was raising her daughter Sally. This led to tensions between Mrs. Green and her mother as well as between her and Sally. Mrs. Blue responded to this by leaving her daughter with her mother, saying, "you can handle her better than I can." After a short period of time, Mrs. Green would refuse to do this and would tell Mrs. Blue that Sally was her responsibility. A short time later, the pattern would repeat itself. The worker instructed Mrs. Green to take care of Sally for a full week (the two families were neighbors). At the end of the week, Mrs. Green said that she could see that Sally was a "handful" and that Mrs. Blue had "her job cut out for her." The cycle of events described did not repeat itself.

Another technique that the student should understand, but only use after considerable training, is *paradoxical instruction*. The worker either directs the client to perform a behavior that appears contrary to what the client expects or the worker requests seemingly contradictory responses. An example of the former was a worker who stated that a group member who wished to lose weight try to gain a pound during the following week. An example of the latter was a worker who indicated that a client should not reveal a piece of confidential information to the other group members until she felt comfortable, but when that happened, she was expected to do so.

When the timing is right and the worker's style of delivery supports seemingly incongruous statements, paradoxical interventions have been effective. We think that they work with clients who consciously or otherwise oppose both change and the worker as an instrument of change. The way such clients can be negative is turned about so that being negative means changing. The contradictory statement (sometimes referred to as the therapeutic double bind) also removes opposition, because whatever the client does (in the example, reveal or not reveal the information) is in some sense in conformity with the worker's demand.

The danger with this technique is that if it is badly executed the worker will lose credibility. The client may also see it as sarcasm on the part of the worker. There are also ethical issues with a practice that is not straightforward. Finally, the sophisticated client will simply charge the worker with using negative psychology. The last named is the easiest to counter by the worker who answers, "Yes, but that's not all!"

(3) Activities.   Social workers, particularly in their work with groups, have been pioneers in helping people to use program activities to attain their goals. Workers have participated with members in games, arts and crafts, dramatics, music, dance, food preparation, trips, and camping. Through these activities, members communicate with each other in ways that go beyond the limitations of group discussion, discover aspects of themselves and others that are likely to be developed through creative endeavors, and add new and important dimensions to their group and family life.

The role of the worker is not to be a recreation specialist, but to help people to draw on their own resources and those of others to have the social experiences that they need. The worker understands the meaning of nonverbal activities and the different kinds of experience that each activity supplies, whether in terms of physical movement, human interaction, clarification of values, new roles, opportunity for gratification, or skill development.

ACTIVITIES

The Social Club was one of the groups sponsored by the Community Mental Health Program for people who had been suffering for a long time with a disabling mental illness. At this meeting, the worker was strumming on her guitar as members arrived. The members joined the worker around a table and some began to hum in harmony with the worker's playing. After a short period, other members began to make requests of the worker and the group sang a few of these songs together.

The worker then stated it was time to begin their meeting. He asked Sam to "take the chair" as it was his month to lead the group. Sam did so (the worker had previously worked out an agenda with him). Sam said that their main topic was to plan a trip to take that month. Several of the members said that they wished they could have another picnic because the last one had been so much fun. Another member said that she heard that another club had gone on a treasure hunt and this had been the best activity they had had. The member asked the worker if he knew how to set up a treasure hunt and he said he did. Another member asked what a treasure hunt was. Several people explained that you received a clue to start, and it gave you a hint where the next clue was. When you found the next clue, it directed you to still another one, and so on. The worker said that if he made up the clues he would want to send the group to places that it would be good for them to visit.

After the treasure hunt was planned, several group members went to the kitchen to get the refreshments while others put place settings of paper plates and plastic dinnerware and cups around the meeting table. While the group was eating, the worker told about some films he had seen lately and he encouraged other members to do the same. He did this because he was aware that many group members stayed at home a lot and didn't go out very often to movies or other types of entertainment.

At the end of the session, the group members spontaneously formed their friendship circle. Several spoke of things they liked about the meeting. One said that she liked the idea that they had something planned for the future because she had so little to look forward to. Another member said that he liked the meeting because it was so peaceful and there were no arguments—he hated those. The members then said goodbye to each other and filtered out.

---

(4) Norms.   A major method that workers use to modify group norms is value clarification exercises. According to Simon, Howe, and Kirschenbaum, value clarification consists of individuals coming to terms with the following questions:

1. Are you *proud* of (do you prize or cherish) your position?
2. Have you *publicly affirmed* your position?
3. Have you chosen your position from *alternatives?*
4. Have you chosen your position after *thoughtful consideration* of the pros and cons and consequences?
5. Have you chosen your position *freely?*[11]

Value clarification exercises consist of the introduction of an activity that requires group or family members to determine their answers to one or more of these questions. The activity can be a discussion, game, dramatic device, or any other type of program.

VALUES CLARIFICATION

The Jelly family was discussing whether or not the parents should write a note to school saying Albert, their teenage son, should be excused from school when actually he had played hookey and gone fishing with his friends. The worker said that this involved a consideration of whether or not and under what circumstances it was O.K. not to tell the truth. He suggested an experiment. He would ask the family a series of questions. If the answer was "always yes" the family member should stand near the door; if "sometimes yes," near the window; if "sometimes no" near the desk; and if "always no," near the table.

The first question he asked was whether it was all right for a family member to inflict physical harm on another. All the family members stood near the table. The worker asked the family to discuss why they stood where they did. Mr. Jelly said he had always been against violence; he had seen what it could do when he had been a police officer. Albert asked how he could have that position and still spank his children. Mr. Jelly replied that he did not view that as inflicting physical harm.

Albert disagreed and said that when he was younger it had hurt him a lot. Mr. Jelly appeared disconcerted and said that he had always felt bad afterward but it was the best thing he knew to do. Mrs. Jelly said that she had tried to discuss this with Mr. Jelly at the time, but it was hard for him to talk about it.

The worker then asked if it was all right for family members to lie to each other. Mr. and Mrs. Jelly stood near the table but Albert stood near the window. The worker again asked the family to discuss where they stood. Mrs. Jelly said that if you couldn't trust your own family, who could you trust. Mr. Jelly said he agreed with her. Albert said that when family members weren't allowed to have any privacy, what else could they do. This then led into a discussion of how each family member felt about privacy.

The worker next asked if family members should lie *for* each other to outsiders. All the family members stood near the window. Again, they were asked to discuss this. Mrs. Jelly gave an example of telling whoever answered the phone to say that she wasn't home if she felt like not talking. Albert said that he had heard his parents talking about not telling the Internal Revenue Service about the extra money Mr. Jelly received helping neighbors to fix their cars. This led to a discussion on lies that did and did not hurt someone or did or did not break a law, and Mr. Jelly said that he had felt bad about not being honest on his tax returns and that he was going to amend his return to rectify this.

This led to a discussion of lying to the school about why Albert was absent. Albert said that he now felt the same way that his father did about the income tax, and that he should "face the music" about why he had been absent.

---

(5) Emotional States. Group and family members often experience similar emotions during a session. This occurs for several reasons. One is that they may be reacting to a similar event, such as when members are happy because the system has attained its goal or sad because a member has left. Another is due to the process of *emotional contagion:* observations of a member's emotional state elicit a similar response in the observers. Thus, a worker may notice during the course of a meeting with the group or family that the people present seem depressed, listless, elated, fearful, or angry.

The worker has several roles to choose from under such circumstances (aside from immediately feeling the same emotion, which does happen!). He or she can draw the member's attention to their feelings in order to start a discussion of the issues that have provoked the feeling. If the feeling is dysfunctional, such as one of strong anxiety, the worker can employ a group relaxation technique, such as asking members to fantasize a peaceful scene, or can even train the group in progressive relaxation.[12]

DEALING WITH EMOTIONS

This incident occurred at a meeting of the Senior's Club just after news was received that Mrs. Stone had died while visiting her son and daughter-in-law. The members entered in a solemn manner and sat quietly. Mrs. Morton asked what the agenda was for the meeting. The worker suggested that, before they have their regular meeting, they might talk about Mrs. Stone. Mr. Allen said that she seemed so well the last time he saw her; he couldn't believe what had happened. Mrs. Morton said that it seemed futile to make plans when you could "go" at any time. Mr. Appel commented that you never knew what would come next and you had to continue to lead your life. The worker reflected that they were all sad and even a little angry that things like this could happen. Mr. Allen said this was true; he and Mrs. Stone were supposed to have had lunch together and he had been looking forward to that.

The worker asked if they wanted to plan a little memorial for Mrs. Stone. Several members thought that was a good idea, and Mr. Appel said they could even invite Mrs. Stone's children. Mrs. Morton suggested that they might appoint a committee to set up the memorial, and everyone thought that was a good idea. They would have a good chance then to continue to talk about how bad they felt about losing Mrs. Stone. Mr. Allen said that it was good to know that when you died people didn't just forget about you.

INTERACTIONS WITH THE ENVIRONMENT. A final way that workers seek to help families and groups to change is through intervening with some system in the environment of the family or group. One of the most obvious ways that workers do this is through a change in the service agency itself. The agency can be asked, for example, to provide a resource to the family or group such as financial assistance, technical assistance (such as from a physician, lawyer, or budgeting expert), or a more appropriate physical facility for the group or family sessions in the agency. In the case of a group, the agency can be asked to recruit the additional members that the group requires to accomplish its purposes.

In family treatment, many agencies are structured so that the worker is a member of a family treatment team, and team members observe family sessions through a one-way mirror or by viewing videotapes of sessions. The team members make suggestions for family interventions, and the worker may convey these as coming from the team. When this procedure is employed, we view such actions as changes induced by inputs from the environment.

Another environmental input, which relates more to group than family work, is worker intervention with the families of group members. Examples are a worker who arranged for a group of abusing husbands to ultimately have a joint session with the group composed of their wives, and another worker with children of divorced parents who arranged for the parents to be present at a group meeting because the children wished to explain their feelings to their parents.

The worker may also intervene with other organizations to help the group attain its objectives. In one instance, the worker invited members of the police department to attend a meeting of youngsters who were beginning to get into trouble in the community. The group members wanted to explain to the officers the ways in which they thought they were harassed because they were all black and the majority of the officers were white.

This example should remind us that many environmental effects are due to the relationship of the group or family to the ethnic (or other cultural) group of which they are part and to their interaction with other groups who do not share their ethnicity or culture. A Puerto Rican group, for example, was strongly criticized by other Puerto Ricans in the community for taking a political stand that differed from a local council of Puerto Rican organizations. The worker, who was a community organizer, was required to mediate a series of meetings involving the group and the representatives of the other organizations to resolve the tensions created by this situation.

THE ENDING PHASE

In formed groups, two termination issues can arise: (1) one or more members leave while the others continue, and (2) the entire group ends. In the former situation, it is important for the entire group to participate in a termination process with the individual(s) concerned. Thus, it is desirable for these individuals to attend at least one meeting after they have decided to terminate. The termination process helps these members to make any necessary plans, helps other members to deal with their feelings, and helps to convince all members that others are invested in their presence. This is also true when the member who is leaving is the target of negative feelings, because this is also a form of investment and, if possible, should be dealt with to avoid the aftereffects of unresolved anger and guilt.

In treatment groups, when an individual leaves, the issues that are responded to are the same as when someone leaves individual treatment. These are an evaluation of the experience, the feelings about leaving, ways of maintaining beneficial changes, generalizing changes, and choosing new services when necessary. In contrast to individual treatment, however, the worker helps the members to help the one who is leaving with these termination issues. This is often a very powerful process as members build on each other's comments. The one who is leaving may have different responses, also, to each of the remaining members. Even those who are not ending will gain from this because issues that are similar to their own are uncovered.

It has not been as customary to deal with the termination of an individual member in task groups as in treatment groups. We believe that this is a mistake, even if the process is less intense and appropriately so. Nevertheless, task groups will sometimes have a party for or a vote of recognition for a departing member. When that individual is leaving because of dissatisfaction with the group, it will frequently be useful to the members to hear this. Members in task groups should also be convinced through the termination process that each person's membership is recognized and valued.

When the entire group ends, the same termination issues are dealt with, but more time must be set aside for such discussions and these may run over several meetings. The members of treatment groups will in turn evaluate changes they have experienced. The members will not only deal with feelings about leaving the group, but also about the fact that the group will no longer continue as an entity. Attention will be paid to how the group and the worker functioned: what was helpful and what was not.

When members discuss issues of stabilizing and generalizing individual change, they may be able to help each other in ways that the worker cannot. This is because, when they come from similar backgrounds and/or have similar problems, they may use this familiarity to anticipate both opportunities and barriers related to these purposes.

Task groups should also discuss many of these issues when they end. They will customarily not evaluate individual members or seek to stabilize individual change, but they will evaluate the group's success in attaining its goals; they may also make plans for efforts that may go on after the group ends through the actions of individual members and charges to other groups.

Groups often engage in a ceremony as part of termination. This may be a party, a graduation ceremony for members, or a ritual created for the occasion.

The termination of family treatment will have different components because, unless the end sought was divorce or the departure of young adult members, the family will continue, but without the participation of the worker. The focus of evaluation is usually on ways in which the family is now functioning better as a unit, although this does not preclude assessing the ways that individuals may be acting differently, particularly the individual whose behavior precipitated the treatment. The family members will have feelings about losing their connection to the worker and these should be expressed. Ways in which changes can be reinforced and generalized will also be discussed.

At times, the worker has engaged in interventions that have promoted family change when the strategy the worker employed precluded drawing attention to these maneuvers. A continuation of this strategy, particularly when the family is satisfied with its functioning, is to exit from the family without engaging in much of a termination process.

Another strategy that is sometimes employed by family practitioners is to continue work with an individual or a family subsystem after terminating with the entire family. Such workers may have been working to help create a family that is less enmeshed so that individuals are freer to pursue their own ends with the support of other family members. This may also be true when the worker continues with the marital pair, but discontinues work that involves the children.

Conclusion

This chapter described the ways that social workers intervene in task groups, treatment groups, and families to help them to bring about changes desired by their members. We began by discussing some of the similarities and differences among these kinds of systems that led us to considering them together in one chapter. We then considered the purposes that workers have when seeking to help groups and families, These were classified under the headings of education and treatment and facilitation. We proceeded to describe worker activities during the beginning, middle, and ending phases of work. The tasks of the worker with formed groups begin, however, before the group is actually convened as purposes are clarified, members are recruited, and resources that will be required by the group are obtained. The worker will also take principles of group composition into consideration when recruiting members.

The activities of the worker during the engagement phase include promoting relationships among the members and between the members and the worker, clarifying the purposes for the service, and assessing the group or family as a system. We provided a set of categories that may be used in conducting such an assessment at any phase of the work.

We discussed worker interventions during the middle phases of work in terms involving individuals, subgroups, the group as a whole, and the environment. Such interventions were discussed as they are directed at member cognitions, action patterns, activities, norms, and emotional states. Examples of each type of intervention were presented. The chapter concluded with a discussion of termination issues.

Notes

1. For a comprehensive discussion of the issues in defining groups, see Marvin E. Shaw, *Group Dynamics: The Psychology of Small Group Behavior,* 3rd ed. (New York: McGraw-Hill, 1981), pp. 4–8.
2. This discussion draws on our earlier work in Charles Garvin and Brett Seabury, *Interpersonal Practice in Social Work* (Englewood Cliffs, N.J.: Prentice Hall, 1984), pp. 273–289.
3. Margaret Hartford, *Groups in Social Work* (New York: Columbia University Press, 1972), p. 67.
4. A detailed discussion of group composition, while important, is beyond the scope of this text. Such information is included in Charles Garvin, *Contemporary Group Work,* 2nd ed. (Englewood Cliffs, N.J.: Prentice Hall, 1987), Chapter 3.
5. Garvin and Seabury, *Interpersonal Practice in Social Work,* pp. 144–162.
6. For examples, see Charles D. Garvin, *Contemporary Group Work.*
7. For complete details of these and other techniques to facilitate group problem solving, see Garvin, *Contemporary Group Work,* Chapter 15.
8. Salvador Minuchin and H. Charles Fishman, *Family Therapy Techniques* (Cambridge, Mass.: Harvard University Press, 1981), pp. 207–213.
9. Ibid., p. 207.
10. Joan Laird, "Women and Stories: Restoring Women's Self-constructions," in Monica McGoldrick, Carol M. Anderson, and Froma Walsh (eds.) *Women in Families: A Framework for Family Therapy* (New York: W.W. Norton & Co., 1989), pp. 427–450.
11. Sydney B. Simon, Leland W. Howe, and Howard Kirschenbaum, *Values Clarification: A Handbook of Practical Strategies for Students and Teachers* (New York: Hart Publishing Co., 1972), p. 35.
12. Sheldon Rose, *Group Therapy: A Behavioral Approach* (Englewood Cliffs, N.J.: Prentice Hall, 1977), pp. 120–123.

CHAPTER 7
Helping Organizations to Change

Introduction

Organizations, as units in the social system, often need help in their functioning just as individuals, families, and groups do at their own levels, and as communities and societies also do. In other words, any unit at any level in the social system may at times need assistance in functioning at its full potential. Because of the heavy involvement of social workers in organizations, it is important to us and society that these organizations function efficiently and effectively. This crucial role has both direct and indirect aspects.

In a direct manner, organizational functioning is important because we work in them. For most of us in professional social work practice, organizational activity of one sort or another makes up the bulk of our daily work life. For the rest of society, the work of the nation is carried out within an organizational context, whether a steel mill, an office complex, a department of social services, or a United Way.

Naturally, we hope that the places in which we work will have a positive culture and will be the kind of environment where we enjoy spending time. We also hope that the organization will be productive enough to meet our needs for salary, supplies, and equipment and will have the resources to put on the kinds of programs that we think are important or offer the goods and services at an appropriate level of quality that helps the larger system, the society, to function.

One of the most important indirect effects of organizational functioning occurs in the productivity area. If organizations do not function well, productivity lags. Although we usually think of productivity in terms of business, it applies to nonprofits as well. Whether in the public sector (government), profit sector, nonprofit sector, or some combination of these three large systems, when output declines the problems of human service workers on a personal level are increased. Larger numbers of unemployed men and women are one example of the result of poor organizational performance. Also, as organizational performance flags, resources begin to dry up as well, whether they are voluntary contributions made directly to a human service organization or tax dollars generated through the government and then reallocated to human service activities. Hence, at the very time problems are on the upswing, funds are on the downswing.

Many U.S. organizations today do not operate at an optimal level. Many speak of the organizational failures of U.S. business as a principal cause of productivity decline.[1] While problems in the business sector are relatively well known, we are also familiar with productivity problems in the governmental sector—red tape and bureaucratization slowing operations to a creep. In the human service field, we can also think of examples of human service organizations that do not seem to be working at their full potential.

Three general types of organizational clients, or client systems, may require the social worker to intervene. The first of these client systems is the human service agency itself. Often, it is the place where we work. Being especially aware of improvements that can be made close to home, workers often engage in an organizational change effort to improve their own working environment, not only for their own benefit but also for that of the client and the community.

A second client system is the human service network made up of the other human service agencies and human service organizations with which we regularly interact. We also know these agencies reasonably well. They are often the agencies from which we receive clients and other referrals and to which we make referrals. Problems in their functioning create problems for us. If we are working in a hospital social service department, doing discharge planning, and find that the agencies that take discharged clients cannot now or will not do so, we are thrown into difficulty, too. Or if a colleague agency suddenly begins to make an overwhelming number of referrals to our agency, we may not be able to handle the overload. Hence, change efforts may seek to improve relations, facilitate exchange of information and client flow, and so on, but the focus of effort is to change the other agencies in our network and the relationships between them and us or among them. That agency can be either public or private, a government organization at any level, or a voluntary human service organization.

The third target of organizational change is other organizations in our environment. These tend to be in the private profit-making sector. They may become the target of organizational change because of their actions or inactions. For example, a substance abuse agency received a large number of referrals from a particular organization. After three or four referrals had been processed, the director thought that something about the organization was aggravating substance abuse problems and may even have been creating them. He learned that the firm had a practice of having alcoholic beverages around at all times and freely available. While this firm's policy may have been to create friendly working conditions, it was also creating problems. There could be other explanations as well for the high level of problems. Perhaps the firm has an extremely negative and hostile climate in which human needs are not being met. Or perhaps the business is a stressful one, and stress reduction activities are not taking place. An outreach worker at the substance abuse center may make organizational change in that particular case a goal. The worker may begin by trying to get the organization to recognize its role in the whole process and to work with the organization to change.

In sum, any organizational unit may become a legitimate target for organizational change efforts. While the unit is often our own place of work, it is frequently other organizations in our network and other organizations as well.

In this change effort the social worker may play at least one of four roles and may actually play them all simultaneously. One role is that of the *employee,* an individual working in the agency or organization who is interested in his or her welfare and well-being and is willing to devote some of his or her time toward that end. The employee may have no particular expertise in organizational change, but may serve more as a catalyst and initiator of a change process that could result in trainers, consultants, and change agents becoming involved.

The *trainer* is a second role the human service worker might play in the organizational change process. A trainer is essentially a system educator, an individual with special knowledge and competence who presents material to organizational clients. Many trainers do not have any particular human service goal in their work. For example, when a new computer system is installed, a trainer is sent by the manufacturer to teach the staff how to use it. In the human service field, trainers tend to focus on topics that yield human and social rewards, such as reducing sexism and racism in the organization, achieving higher-quality interpersonal relations, and improving group decision making.[2]

A third role that a human service professional may play is that of *organizational consultant.* The consultant focuses more on working with the organization to analyze its particular problems and develop strategies for change and improvement. This focus is opposed to that of the trainer, who mainly shares prepackaged material, which may be essentially similar from organization to organization. The consultant's input is very different for each organization.

The first three roles, employee, trainer, and consultant, imply some degree of organizational desire to undertake a change process. Such desire is not always present, and then a fourth role, *the change agent,* role may be assumed. A change agent's mission is to be a stimulus for change in the organization, and also in communities and societies as a whole. In instances where there is active opposition to change, the development of a political base to support the change effort may be necessary. In others, opposition is less an issue than simple ignorance on the part of the organization about what is needed. In the latter case, securing commitments to change is easier because resistance is less.

Major Methods of Organizational Change

Again, we suggest two main thrusts or types of organizational change effort: education and intervention and facilitation. When a social worker is involved in organizational change efforts, we shall call them organization workers.

EDUCATION

In the organizational context, education is what trainers and, to a certain extent, consultants do. It involves teaching employees, workers, and clients substantive and procedural knowledge and skills to help the organization function better. Orientation seminars may be developed for new employees or clients. Instructional approaches of an in-service nature on the latest techniques in therapy or executive leadership might be offered. Education might be undertaken with boards of directors or with particular groups of individuals within the organization based on their special needs.

Alternatively, whole-organization training sessions that involve issues like racism or sexism that cut across any particular department or division might be scheduled. Education and training involve particular bodies of content that are transmitted. Educational formats range from the more formal lecture-type presentations to heavily participatory sessions in which content is not only presented, but organizational members are also assisted in working out the details and implications of the new material.[3] "Working out" here implies dealing with many of the feelings that accompany organizational change.

Sometimes the worker actually provides the education or training. For example, a worker in a substance abuse unit of a large business may have as part of her or his job assignment the presentation of substance abuse information to other employees in training settings. Alternatively, the workers may bring in outside experts to provide training.

It may also be part of the worker's assignment to pull together advisory groups of technical experts to assist in the education activity. Technical advisory groups that agree to serve as a backup resource for the organization fall into this category.

Ongoing education of the organization's members should be a part of regular agency life. Without it the organization is likely to become too routinized, over-bureaucratized, and out of date.

INTERVENTION AND FACILITATION

Sometimes education is not enough. For example, education can be provided to a substance abuser, and the substance abuser may, in some instances, recognize the truth of the material presented, but this may not be sufficient to create a change motivation. In short, education seems most successful where resistance is low and willingness to change is already present. In such instances the change problem becomes more or less a technical issue. Clients may say, "We're ready to proceed . . . what we need to know are the steps to take, the issues to be considered, the problems to be resolved. . . ."

In other instances, difficulty is being experienced in an organization, but there is a lack of willingness to deal with the issue in a concrete and direct manner. If resistance is mild, facilitation may be an appropriate technique. Consultants have a role here. They explore the nature of the problems in question with agency members. The facilitator assists staff to present their views about the various problems for discussion, examination, and eventual change and improvement. If resistance is high, a change agent may be needed to mobilize internal and external elements to place political pressure on the organization to consider change, to revise a policy, to adjust a practice, to undertake or discontinue a particular kind of activity, and so on.

KINDS OF PROBLEMS TARGETED FOR CHANGE

Social workers in their role as employee, trainer, consultant, or change agent are particularly concerned with the human problems that organizations experience, such as agency sexism and racism, tension among groups in the agency, worker–management conflict, and lack of attention to disadvantaged groups in the community, among others. Another set involves issues about organizational mission, role, goal, and focus. We shall discuss these problems more specifically in the next section.

Two Elements of the Change Process

The change process for organizations, communities, and societies especially (perhaps all change processes) can be broken down into two central elements that are always operative, though one may be emphasized more than the other depending on the nature of the method. One element is an intellectual method, and the other is an interpersonal method.[4]

Intellectual elements refer to the need for thoughts and ideas and their combination and synthesis to become an essential part of the change process. Change requires thinking. Several different kinds of thinking are usual. The first deals with simple knowledge of change techniques. The second deals with knowledge about the factual areas of change under consideration. For example, if you work in the area of changing attitudes toward sexism and racism, you need to know something about both the issues of sexism and racism and something about change as an area of study. Helping organizations to change is not any different.

A third area of knowledge deals with the organizations themselves, about which much has been written and studied in recent years. Thus, the worker who wishes to help organizations change needs to know something about the change processes, the substantive area for which change is desired, and the unit to be changed.

A fourth area is important as well: synthesis and selection. Intellectual elements become important in selecting from the previous three bodies of knowledge the one that might be useful for a particular case so as to be able to have a specific body of knowledge to draw on.

Fifth, action steps are needed. Intellectual elements are required in terms of having ideas about what to *do* in the particular case. Many of us know individuals who have a wide range of factual information but seem unable to convert that knowledge into practical use on specific issues. Often, such individuals are called theorists or eggheads. It is imperative that the knowledge be translated into knowledge in action.[5]

The other major skill element is interpersonal. Interpersonal skill involves not only a knowledge of self and how one relates with others, but also a knowledge of others and how to be persuasive with respect to change-oriented goals. Achieving organizational change (in community and societal change as well) is a multiperson effort. It certainly involves groups, and some elements of group-focused change have already been discussed in Chapter 6.[6]

But it is rare in the organizational change area to work with a single formed group, except in the unusual instance of working with a board of directors or a particular department staff group over a long period of time. Rather, there are many larger aggregates of individuals who hold a range of positions with respect to the client organization. Some may be employees, but others may be clients, ex-clients, alumni, parents, regulatory agencies involved with the services or some subset of services of the agency, official government agencies that provide part of the funding for the agency, relatives of previous donors to the agency, and so on.

These individuals can often do more harm than good in the sense that they are often able to stop a process from going forward, but are rarely able by themselves to push such a process through. Hence, a veto as negative power seems to be stronger than supportive and positive power. Part of the role of the worker who wishes to help organizations change is involved with building up positive relationships with the organizational network so that the worker can draw on that network for resources (including support) when needed. In the end, of course, it is the client system, just as it is the client, individual, group, organization, or community, that will have to continue with the change process, and then follow along in the new, changed way.

Overall, change of larger systems, or macro change, involves the mobilization of ideas and people. Thus, intellectual and interpersonal elements are needed.

Phases of Helping

The phases of helping discussed here involve, again, the beginning, middle, and ending phase, but help proceeds through some specific steps within each phase. The beginning phase is characterized by need assessment. This social diagnosis effort characterizes the start of almost all intervention activities. It is an important counter to those who practice the "ready, fire, aim" strategy of intervention, exemplified by the phrase "don't just stand there, do something." As appealing as action often is, understanding the situation diagnostically first is an absolute imperative if effort is not to be wasted. Clear as this is at the individual and group level, it is similarly important at the organizational, community, and societal level. The worker must have an understanding of the issues before proceeding to intervene.

The middle phase contains two specific steps: option generation and decision. Option generation refers to the development of a set of ideas about how to proceed. We cannot overemphasize the importance of this particular step and urge organizational social workers not to move through it too quickly. Frequently, when diagnosis occurs, it leads immediately to action. In such a situation there is no full and thoughtful consideration of the variety of ways that problems may be handled, goals achieved, and the potential perils and costs of any particular method avoided. Option generation also allows client decision making to flourish. All too frequently, professionals in effect say, "Here's the problem [needs assessment or diagnosis] and here's what I think 'we' should do about it" [*saying* the client and I, but *meaning* the client] [decision]." This behavior occurs even though it is not good practice. A confounding problem is that, at the organizational level, client decision making is not as clear a path, in the actual setting, as it is in the one-to-one worker–client situation. In such a situation it becomes very difficult for the client to really make an informed decision. To raise questions about the recommendation, given the scenario we just suggested, implies questioning the integrity, reliability, and knowledgeability of the professional; yet the professional here is, as always, a servant of the client's decision-making process. So clarification of options is crucial.

The second part of the middle phase is the client decision process. This too is often circumvented, perhaps more so in the macro area of organization, community, and society than in the more focused and identifiable areas of individual and group. After options have been presented and worked through, it is imperative that the system in question come to a decision. The decision process may involve a number of days, weeks, or months. Nonetheless, for the client system to proceed, decisions such as the following must be made: We are undertaking this new direction; we are stopping the offering of this service; we are reorganizing in these ways. Such decisions are absolutely imperative if the organization is to develop and advance. So prevalent is the lack of decision in our society that a poster exemplifying the implications of such resistance has achieved wide circulation. "Not to decide is to decide" has become a recognizable phrase to us all. Deferral of decision is indeed a decision, and the organization change social worker has a role in helping to crystallize the decision process.

The last or ending phase of the intervention process includes planning and implementation as the next step and, as a final step, evaluation and recycle. Planning and implementation refer to two interrelated processes that are subsequent to decision. After a decision has been made, the process of planning for the implementation and the actual implementation of the new product or service, the new program, or treatment begins. From our point of view, it is important to note that planning comes after policy. All too often, organizations begin planning before policy has really been made. Then the demands and imperatives of the implementation process work backward to drive the policy decision process. ("Since we have already begun implementation of a program, perhaps you as the board of directors would be so kind as to approve this direction.")

Evaluation and recycle represent the final phase of the intervention process. After the organizational change has been implemented, some kinds of evaluations are important to undertake. No new change, procedure, product, or service is without flaw, problem, and difficulty. Therefore, it is important to identify these at an early stage and begin the process of remediation. Some of these problems are problems *in* the product or service and thus can be fixed with relative ease. Some, though, are problems *of* the product or service. They require system redesign and readjustment.

These cases involving problems of the system initiate the recycle phase. The portion of the subsystem that is in trouble is recycled into the needs assessment phase, and the cycle is begun all over again: identifying problems, selecting options, making decisions, reimplementation, and so on.

We shall now discuss in more detail each phase and its particular parts, focusing on the kinds of activities that the organization worker might engage in during the various phases and the kinds of skills needed.

THE BEGINNING PHASE

Sometimes the presenting problem is clear-cut. There is some kind of performance or resource problem within an organization. For example, the neighborhood in which the organization lives has changed, and there is poor articulation between the organization's historical and current role and the people in its environment. From an economic point of view, this kind of problem is thought of as a market problem. Other types of problems might include a decrease in client flow, a decrease in grant and other support, and negative production from workers and staff.

Sometimes the problem is more implicit. One example would be the "satisfied organization." Everything seems to be going along reasonably well, but there appears to be a discernable lack of innovation and proactivity. Some in the organization might be worried not about its current position, but about its future role. In other cases, the organizational employees are satisfied, but others related to the organization (clients, funders, boards of directors) are not.

NEEDS ASSESSMENT. In all cases, an assessment of the problems should be undertaken, even though the problem appears clear-cut. Experienced organizational workers know that it is hard, on the surface, to distinguish between actual problems and symptoms of other problems. Hence, even where it appears that the problems are well defined, needs assessments are undertaken. Several mechanisms for ascertaining organizations' needs are available, which organization workers use in cooperation with agency staff.

One is the survey or questionnaire. In the survey, a number of predefined questions, often with fixed answer categories (agree, somewhat agree, neutral, don't agree, strongly disagree), are used to create a forced choice situation among the respondents. The questions are designed to pick out potential problems based both on what the organizational worker has found with respect to the organization in question and what the organizational worker knows to be common types of problems. These data may then be fed back to organizational change committees within the organization. (for more detailed discussion, see Chapter 17).

Another approach is the in-depth data analysis approach in which common organizational facts and figures are looked at in considerable depth and from an analytical rather than operational point of view. Such analysis often reveals patterns of organizational behavior that were previously hidden.

In connection with in-depth data analysis, the analysis of comparative information is often useful. For example, in-depth analyses can be compared over the years. A human service organization might find, for example, that the number of clients per worker seen per day has slowly declined over a number of years. Alternatively, comparisons with what other organizations are doing in terms of workload, pay, facilities, and so on, often yields important insights. If an organization has an information system, the source of these items may be relatively easy to get.

ETHICAL ANALYSIS. Organizational activities can be analyzed, too, according to ethical standards. The National Association of Social Workers has a code of ethics (reprinted in the appendix of this book) which prescribes certain kinds of permissible and not permissible behavior. Agencies occasionally engage in practices where ethical issues present themselves, and such practices need to be revealed and changed.

ENVIRONMENT SCANNING. Organizational change social workers may work with members of the agency and others to scan their local and national environments for changes that might affect agency practice. The United Way of America, for example, has made such a national environmental scan and it is of great use to local organizations, whether they are United Way members or not. Family Service of America has made an in-depth analysis of the American family and the changes affecting it. That document is useful. John Naisbett has outlined a number of national directions that he believes are here or will be here soon, several of which have important implications for social work practice.[7] The organizational social worker will review materials such as these and, with help from organizational members, develop an environmental change statement.

COMMITMENT TO CHANGE. Involved in the process of needs assessment is the building of commitment to change. The results from any method are not only collected in ways that provide information (task goals), but also to build involvement as well (process goal). In several instances we have mentioned that other members of the organization are involved or a committee of the organization is involved. This is standard procedure. The needs assessment done by an organizational social worker is not simply a tactical research job. It is the undertaking of an information gathering task that begins to build interest in and commitment to change within the organization via the process of collection, discussion, and analysis of the data, thus showing that the views of employees and others are valued. A needs group lays the groundwork for future change commitments in a larger organization. Organizational change workers should give much thought to the formation of an assisting committee or group, being sure, if at all possible, that all relevant stake holders in the organization's future are included. Thus, the committee becomes a sort of organizational microcosm. And in the process of working through issues with the committee, the organizational change worker is in a way working them through, at arm's length, with the organization as a whole.

THE MIDDLE PHASE

The middle phase of helping involves two large elements: (1) option generation and (2) decision.

OPTION GENERATION. Option generation involves further analysis of the data developed in needs assessment to provide alternative sets of directions that the client system (in this case, the organization) might wish to consider for future directions. Care should be taken to avoid premature fixation on a particular alternative before an array of them has been explored. How is such an exploration accomplished? There are a number of techniques, but we will mention three here: scenario building, brainstorming, and the use of consultants and experts.

(1) Scenario Building.   Scenario building involves playing out a hypothetical course of events to some point in the future with assistance from the organization worker. In the process of playing out the "what if, and then what if and then," a series of steps and options is often undercovered. Scenario building allows individuals to see more clearly the hidden implications of a particular course of action. It is good at generating alternatives and at testing any particular alternative, since the scenario building process requires the kind of specification that often gets glossed over, especially in the excitement of a new idea.

(2) Brainstorming.   Brainstorming can be used to develop options and alternatives. In a brainstorming session, the organization worker will often work with a committee, asking each person for ideas and listing them on a blackboard or sheet of paper. The rule in a brainstorming session is that there can be no criticism of an idea. Any idea, however bizarre or unusual, must be written down. In our experience, one or two committee members always try to test this rule with something truly bizarre (let's hire the Goodyear blimp to advertise our agency); the worker should write it down just like any other idea. Even if a particular idea is not a good one, it may suggest other ideas. As group interaction begins to build, a process of synergism begins to develop and ideas come quickly from one and then the next.

(3) Involving Consultants and Experts.   A third way that alternatives can be generated is through the use of experts and consultants. Indeed, depending on how the process got started, the organization worker may be such a consultant; but experts and consultants often have been through the kind of problem that one is struggling with

before. They can suggest a range of alternatives for consideration based on the experience of other organizations.

DECISION. Once a range of alternatives has been developed and discussed, option selection needs to occur. The decision point is a fulcrum event, a transforming event. At this point the task goal and process goal meet. Not only does such a decision represent a selection among options for a future direction of the organization, but it also represents and underscores some level of the organization's commitment to proceed. We have seen a number of situations in which the option generation phase was completed in an extremely high quality fashion and a number of very good ideas were generated, but the organization did not act because it did not wish to move ahead. The commitment building part was simply not present.

We have also seen the alternative situation; the commitment was there, but the ideas were not. Decisions were made, but they were of poor quality and really did not help the organization. Hence, the organization worker must be alert to the problems of decision making without quality alternatives and decision postponement due to lack of commitment.

A second set of problems is the wrong rejection and wrong acceptance problems. Wrong rejection involves turning down an option that would have been a very positive one for the organization. In research, this problem is illustrated by the drug company that rejects a drug that in fact would have helped. False acceptance is the reverse problem, or accepting an alternative that really will not help and may even be harmful for the organization. In research, the drug company accepts a drug that is improper for the illness under consideration and may even cause it to get worse. There is no magic way in which these problems can be prevented. A thorough study of options is one way to protect against the problems of wrong rejection and wrong acceptance.

There is normally hesitancy at the decision point in almost all systems. Therefore, the organization worker may need some techniques to help move the decision along. In effect, this decision development process has used the motivational and commitment enhancing processes we have already mentioned. But there are some other techniques to consider. One of them is gaming.

(1) Gaming. Gaming involves the creation of a theatrical display that actually puts people in roles and lets them work out the dynamics of their positions in an interactive format. A public welfare type of game, for example, might assign workers to roles as public welfare clients and give them a simulated experience with assigned client characteristics. An executive decision-making game might allow workers to play the role of decision-making executives for a while, facing them with the need for making choices the results of which they often criticize. The worker here can help with the gaming management.

(2) The Retreat. The use of a retreat is another good technique. A retreat involves taking individuals from the organization to a special place often physically distance from the work site for a day or two of analyses and decision making. The question of who should go on the retreat is often difficult. In smaller organizations the entire organization sometimes reviews the new ideas and all staff can process it together.

Sometimes, if the organization is larger, it involves the board of directors, executive staff, and representatives from the organization. Thought needs to be given to the exact composition of the retreat. However, the central point is that individuals who will approve the change and those who are needed to implement the change get together in an uninterrupted type of setting and talk through the issues involved and examine some of their own feelings concerning these issues. Frequently, the organization worker acts as a facilitator in sessions of this sort, and the skills of group work mentioned in Chapter 6 come especially into play.

THE ENDING PHASE

The ending phase has two major parts as well: (1) planning and implementation, and (2) evaluation and recycle.

PLANNING AND IMPLEMENTATION. Once a decision has been made, planning and implementation represent the next phase, which should not begin in any depth until a decision has in fact been made. The reason for this sequence was mentioned before. If planning begins, it in effect selects one alternative out of others and then may skew the decision process. Planning involves laying out the specifics and the step by step requirements for the organizational change in question. Decisions about new directions, or possible approaches are often somewhat general. It is not that they are completely devoid of detail, but rather than the entire detail requires too much organizational energy to work out, especially if there are three or four options among which choices are made.

Two types of planning need to be done: substantive planning and procedural planning. Procedural planning involves laying out the specific time lines, milestone points, decision points, and fail-safe points (a fail-safe point is that point beyond which one cannot return to a previous state) that are required for implementation. Substantive planning involves specifying the key skills and competencies required on the part of the organization to effect the change. If, for example, a human service agency decides to undertake the addition of behavioral modification to the services that it offers, then one substantive aspect to be considered involves the extent to which workers already have such skills or need to learn them. Perhaps education and training will have to be provided. Frequently, in the planning and implementation area, an organizational task force is useful. A group of individuals is assembled (involving members of the earlier group and some new ones as well) who have the technical and organizational knowledge to reconfigure the organization along the new lines now indicated by the policy change. In a school, for example, once a new curriculum design has been decided on, groups need to get together and actually put the course hours, sequence, lunch breaks, class size, room requirements, and the like, into place. The organization worker takes on a more technical role by assisting the planning and implementation group in their tasks.

EVALUATION AND RECYCLE. The last stage is evaluation. It is linked to planning and implementation because during the planning and implementation stage the organization worker suggests (if others do not) the building in of evaluation elements so that they do not have to be added later or perhaps are forgotten. Evaluation involves reviewing the ongoing operations of the change, making mid-course corrections, and making a final decision about how well the change is working. Many of the same tools used in the needs assessment phase can be used in the evaluation phase; in fact, this particular phase is called evaluation and recycle because evaluation is a kind of needs assessment. Needs assessment is a kind of evaluation. Evaluation involves review and correction if the problems are minor; review and recycle are required if the problems are major.

What would a major problem look like? The specifics can vary. But it would be that occasion where the organizational change process failed to address organizational needs. Suppose, for example, that an agency decided to offer a new service, announced it, and marketed it, but no one was particularly interested in using it. In this case, the organizational change effort is not successful and a new one will have to be undertaken.

Organizational Phases and Differing Techniques

Organizations, whether they are human service agencies, business firms, or government bureaus and departments, go through phases of development that are relatively well set off from each other. Workers should be aware of these phases, because the problems that organizations typically experience are different at each phase (as is the case with individuals and groups), and the techniques for helping that the worker might use are different depending on the phase. Although there is discussion about the exact number and duration of the phases, a set of five seems to have received general acceptance: the innovation stage, the implementation stage, the growth stage, the stabilization stage, and the renewal or decline stage. An overall summary of the phases is displayed in Table 7.1.

INNOVATION

The innovation stage occurs when the organization has just begun. An example might be a newly created information and referral service set up by a county. The law was passed, certain monies were allocated, and three people were hired and told to "go ahead and set the thing up." At that point the organization has no history, rules, or policy; it barely has staff to operate.[8] This stage is innovation.

Another example might come from the development of a domestic violence center. Suppose that two or three women in a particular community become very interested in and distressed by domestic violence. They agree, on their own, to set up a hotline so that women who are concerned about this kind of problem will have some place to call 24 hours a day. They agree to share responsibility for answering the phones.

Or consider a third example. A social worker works for a family service agency. She and her colleagues have noticed over recent years that there has been an increasing number of older clients and an increasing number of problems involving older children for people in their middle forties, and still older parents who are in their sixties or seventies. But the agency has no particular program to deal with this problem, nor any kind of special office or function that could be of assistance. After discussing it with the director, the worker is invited to make a proposal for reorganization that would establish an additional emphasis in the agency on gerontological social work.

All these new ventures are at their very first stages. In one sense, the examples

TABLE 7.1
Organizational Phases, Problems, and Differing Techniques[a]

Stage	Problems	Intervention/ Education	Facilitation
Innovation	Free creative blocks	Learn needs assessment	Eliminate rigid views
	Getting the idea	Technology	Explore service blocks
		Learn new approaches	Networking
Implementation	Start-up issues	Learn start techniques	Assist in securing financing
		Learn administration	
		Teach staff on board	
Growth	Manage growth	Learn growth-manage- ment techniques	Secure longer-range funding
		Teach or train new staff	
Stabilization	Respond to regularity	Learn efficiency and effec- tiveness	Develop policy and plans
			Develop routinization procedures
Renewal	Repurposing and rejuve- nating	Learn evaluation	Develop political pressure
		Learn repurposing and re- juvenation techniques	Develop dissatisfaction
			Facilitate change
			Conference
			Develop new strategic plan

[a] These stages are highly general and the problems are similarly general. Examples have tended to focus on human service organizations, whether public or private. Readers should know, however, that all organizations, sometimes slower, sometimes faster, go through stages approximating the ones described here.

given solve the problem already, because the main problem at the innovation stage is getting the idea in the first place. In a sense, workers are involved in program, service, or organizational creation more than change. Gaps and omissions in service are a special focus of attention. Areas where programs are needed are pointed out. Workers help organizations already in existence to consider additional services they might provide. Workers respond to people with ideas about possible service by talking the issue through and by helping organizational participants network with others who have similar ideas.

IT DOESN'T COMPUTE

The United Way in a local town has been going over its needs with a big computer manufacturer for information processing, information and referral services, client record keeping, and so on. The firm has made an attractive proposal to the United Way for a system that will allow everyone to use the same kinds of machines, all linked together. "But it will never sell," said Bill Smith, United Way president. "Mention the word computers around here and everyone goes bonkers."

Here, organizational workers can assist the United Way by bringing its constituencies together and seeking to develop an educational program that will allow member agencies (and some who are nonmembers, too) to see the benefits of a new computer-based system linking them all together.

IMPLEMENTATION

After a new idea for a service or program has been developed, we move to the implementation stage. As everyone is aware, a large number of good ideas never go anywhere. The reason for such stagnation, in part, is that the individuals who have the idea do not know what to do with it, and the organization does not help much.[9] Workers can here help in the implementation process. The central issue in this process is the starting up and running of a small agency or department. All the problems associated with new beginnings will occur here: securing financing, securing real estate, securing a place to work, and securing the requisite equipment. One way organization workers can assist organizations in the implementation stage is by referring those beginning new programs to courses on how to start and administer small agencies. A certain amount of education can be very helpful to the new agency director and staff. While the worker may not personally know these facts, the worker makes the link that helps the information to become available.

Then, too, the organization worker seeks to link up people with an idea with those who have already implemented, so that whatever lessons are available may be learned. Perhaps someone has started a domestic violence center or perhaps an agency has already developed a gerontological focus. Many services or parts of services have already been tried by somebody else, and workers can help during the implementation phase by trying to avoid "reinventing the wheel."

From an intervention point of view, organization workers help develop financial and interpersonal support for the new organization and can be instrumental in assisting in the development of early funding. The worker can also aid in the design of the organization and provide expediter help. For the domestic violence center, perhaps a large corner of a basement would be a good place to start and workers can help with its establishment. Alternatively, a corporation may be willing to donate some corporate space for such a worthy venture, and workers can help the innovators explore that possibility.

CRISIS AT THE CRISIS CENTER

Juanita Brown had donated all her time to the Women's Crisis Center. She got the organization up and running after the initial idea had been suggested by Sandra Daly. The two of them were really the mainstay of the organization. Now, they had been given a grant of $98,000 from a local community foundation to put themselves on a regular organizational footing. Juanita had interviewed 13 possible executives and rejected them all. She was feeling very blue.

In this case, organization workers can explore with Juanita and Sandra the organizational needs pressing on them at this transition point. There is a class at the local community college on starting your own organization, and it might be a useful class for both of these individuals to take. It would give them a sense of the kinds of things they are facing, things which they have never faced before in any of their activities. The worker may also seek to develop links to a temporary executive program run by the senior center so that a very experienced, but very temporary, executive could come in to help with start-up activities.

THE GROWTH STAGE

After the agency has begun, even in a very small way, growth occurs. Sometimes it is negative growth. The idea seemed like a good one at the time, but no one is really interested in the service or program offered. Frequently, under these conditions, the program dies after a while. It is unable to find clients or support, and an apparently good idea has to be set aside until it is improved on or until the timing is right. Often, though, the agency grows rapidly, and it is a fairly frequent occurrence for the initial founding members to find themselves completely overwhelmed with the number of tasks that must be done to keep the agency afloat.

It may be that the women involved in starting the crisis hotline had only a partial knowledge of the great demand for this kind of service. Thus, once the hotline was in place and the number posted, the phone began ringing off the hook night and day. Suddenly, the founders are confronted with an overwhelming demand for their service. Quarters need to be expanded, staff needs to be added, money needs to be found. Perhaps, at this stage, specific time-limited grants are provided, perhaps by a local community foundation, to help the agency weather this transition. However, more than money is needed, although that is certainly a key aspect. The whole problem here is managing the growth, directing, focusing, and channeling it, so that it is serving the program and service, rather than the other way around. From an educational point of view, workers can assist growing organizations in learning growth management techniques, and in taking time out to sort through what they actually want to do and what is superfluous, what will aid their mission and role, and what will not.

Frequently, agencies are founded with short-term funding, and the worker has to use intervention and facilitation to secure longer-range funding. Too many agencies spend much of their time just keeping themselves alive, rather than providing a service.

A danger point exists as the growth period evolves. Frequently, at this juncture the agency is successful in getting new funding for its service when before there was none at all. This stage becomes a transition from volunteer management, which had been handling the day-to-day activities of the agency, to one for which a director is hired, who in turn hires staff to be paid for out of the successful grant application.[10] It would seem that this is a state highly to be wished for. The early pioneers are probably tired. They can take a little bit of rest. Their hectic schedules can now become more balanced and even.

Unfortunately, this happy picture is a rarity. Individuals found new programs and services because they enjoy the challenge and love to have that kind of impact. Most do not take kindly to being replaced by more professional social work managers. Frequently, conflicts between the newly hired executive and the founding members surface. Almost always in the nonprofit world there is a board of directors, and they are not infrequently drawn into this conflict. Indeed, many members of the board of directors are likely to be founding members and have a view that things should pretty much stay as they are. "After all, didn't we do well with what we had." In terms of intervention, workers often need to help with this transition. Conflict management and mediation skills are especially useful here.

OVERABUNDANCE OF PUBLIC WELFARE

A local public welfare director is wringing his hands. A big business nearby closed and his case load has jumped, not only with requests for financial help, but also with child protective calls and other child welfare problems. He has received extra money from the state and his county office's budget has quadrupled within the past six months. But it seems to him the place is completely chaotic. He fears that he is losing control over the whole operation.

Organization workers in this case might assist the entire organization to take an inventory of its activities and pressures and chart a growth management course that will assist the entire shop to deal with this crisis in a more systematic way. Resources from the state department of social services are contacted, and their experience in assisting local units facing these kinds of crises is translated into written memos, which are then circulated to the agency to help caseworkers to focus their efforts.

STABILIZATION

The fourth stage is stabilization. Here the central problem is responding to regularity, in doing what was once innovative again and again and again, and doing so with high quality and efficiency. Workers help the organization change from a rapidly growing, and perhaps very exciting, human service center into one that is somewhat more sedate and regular.

The kinds of issues that characterize the growth stage and the energy and skills needed for that stage of an agency are not necessarily those required for the stabilization phase. In fact, it would probably be fair to say that they are not the same at all. Thinking of an organization as a single entity is probably not the appropriate way to approach the problem. Rather, we need to think about the needs of the organization at each stage. In the stabilization stage, education for efficiency and effectiveness is needed. Workers can help organizations review and study their procedures and learn techniques that will help them meet client needs better at lower cost. Because some of the original staff may now have lost interest or moved on to other enterprises, there should be a socialization program for replacement staff, just as there was a socialization program for new staff during the growth phase. In terms of intervention and facilitation, workers can assist organizations and agencies to develop routinized procedures and the policies, practices, and sets of rules that are essential to a well-run, well-regulated organization.

RENEWAL

The renewal phase is perhaps more the hoped for result than the actual result in terms of organizational growth and change. Of course, it is possible at any stage that the agency program will not continue. At the initiation or innovation stage, problems can occur that cause the idea to die, and it will never be carried to implementation. Either problems in implementation or faulty implementation can lead to program death at that point. The growth phase is one of the most traumatic. Changes are occurring in high-growth agencies almost daily. It is very difficult to keep up with what is going on. Sometimes executives and core staff actually lose control of the process, and the agency simply continues until some external event either sets it on a correct course or kills it.

Stabilization may seem like a fairly benign phase. After all, what could happen here? In fact, that is exactly one of the key problems. Nothing might happen, and therein lies the difficulty. Most organizational analysts assume that over time the environment changes. It may change reasonably slowly, but it changes nonetheless.

Thus, whatever the organization was set up to do regularly, and we hope does well, will, as time passes, become out of date. Thus stabilization changes to renewal. The renewal phase is a phase of challenge. The agency has to refocus itself. Agencies that have always dealt with children may see the need to deal now with children and seniors. Agencies that have focused on traditional families may now find families to be a very heterogeneous group indeed, with many different forms and problems within each group.

The educational component of organizational change has to do with learning and developing evaluation techniques. Environments are never silent. More often than not, we simply misread the cues or fail to take appropriate account of changes that are pressing in. Evaluation techniques bring home some of the problems, at least with respect to the agencies' services being offered. Environmental scanning techniques can also be learned, and these can be used to check the environment and to ask about the relationship between the agency's environment on the one hand and the agency's and program's activities on the other. Organizational techniques to reconsider purposes can also be learned, and these will help the organization consider what it wants to do and make decisions about how to get there.

In terms of intervention and facilitation, the worker may be very active at this particular point in many organizations because many organizations are perfectly happy being just where they are. This self-satisfaction is no less common in human service organizations than in other kinds of governmental and profit making organizations. A quick glance at the auto industry indicates that self-satisfaction can be monumental and disastrous. The things one misses do not have to be tiny, caught only by a few. In fact, they can be so pervasive that we might not even recognize that things have changed. The worker may need to bring pressure on the agency to reconsider its mission and purpose. A change conference can be organized in which new directions are specifically considered. Alternatively, political pressure through funders (the United Way might be one example) or through accrediting agencies, grant renewal hearings, and the like, may be needed.

Most organizations in the human service area receive funds from public and quasi-public sources. Thus, they often attend hearings and other budget negotiating sessions where individuals can raise questions about what they are doing. Often, the alert worker will take advantage of these opportunities to press her or his case. This procedure can raise the level of dissatisfaction and stimulate change.

The happiest outcome of renewal, however, is the recycle, going back to the innovation stage with a new program or service that one has discovered as a result of renewal activity, and beginning the cycle again. But it is rare that the whole organization goes though the recycle at once. Often one part is in one stage, while another part is in another stage.

THE INFIRM FIRM

A business firm recently called a local family service agency and asked for help in setting up an employment assistance department within the firm. It is the town's largest employer and the agency is eager to help, but it is not quite sure what to do.

In this particular case, organization social workers can find out from other cities the patterns for establishing such departments. They will then bring this information back and arrange meetings with the firm, and with the family service agency. The task is not difficult. The initial problem is in getting the requisite information. Then working the issues through with those involved can begin.

TRANSITIONS

Transitions are not actually a stage in the usual sense. They are in between periods, but they occupy a very important place in the organizational development arc, and workers should be prepared to assist organizations in dealing specifically with problems of and in transition. Two specific problem areas of a transitional nature require special mention.

One problem is the ambivalence, anxiety, or uncertainty about new directions that characterize transitional periods. It is the rare human service organization that goes through this cycle without a certain amount of conflict, confrontation, and cacophony. Organizational change workers can help minimize the drawbacks of the transition eras by developing and facilitating programs that deal with worker concerns and client questions.

The second feature about transitions that often requires help is beginning and ending them. Organization workers can assist organizations in beginning the transition process. This problem is especially acute, for example, in the stabilization phase, when work is needed to begin renewal. Ending the transition period is the other part of the problem. Indeed, without special attention to transition management as well as phase management, workers may find that an agency wanders aimlessly in transition, having left implementation but never able to firmly settle on an area in which it can grow or wants to grow.

THE AGING CHILDREN'S AGENCY

Children's Helpers, an agency established at the turn of the century, was for many years a national leader in the provision of child welfare services. Its office and headquarters located in a major American city was experiencing fewer and fewer referrals each year. All the kids seem to have gone to the suburbs. "The only thing we have left around here," the executive said, "is a bunch of old folks who want to come and use our gym."

In this case, workers may seek to work with the agency to achieve new levels of understanding about the nature of the changes in its environment, and explore whether the agency wishes to move to a location closer to its main clientele, children, or whether it wishes to change its program to deal more with those older individuals who are within its vicinity.

Organizational Features and Problems

It is clear now that organizational problems are associated with each stage of the organizational growth cycle. These might be thought of as archetypal problems. However, a number of organizational features have problems of their own, independent of the particular phase the organization is in. To use a medical example, medical problems are typically associated with each stage of the human cycle of growth and development. But some problems, such as an inflamed appendix or broken bone, can occur at any stage of the life cycle.

GOALS AND PURPOSES

At any age or stage, organizations can have a lack of goals, purposes, or sense of mission. Most organizations have a set of goals that they can dig out if anyone asks. These are typically too broad to be helpful and lack operational focus and bite. Thus, when competing action opportunities present themselves to the organization, it is difficult to know how to choose. Suppose that an agency has, as one of its goals, the improvement of the living conditions of the poor. This goal has so many possible operational interpretations that it ceases to provide guidance. Agencies with goals of this type tend to drift, being driven by whatever happens to be current at the moment. Thus, they are reactive to and responding to their environment, rather than seeking to shape it and be ahead of it.

The organization worker here will seek to assist the agency in goal specification and environmental scanning. The worker's objectives are to work with the organization to help it specify its goals and purposes and make them more relevant, to explore its values and to develop goals and purposes that align with its values, proactively and strategically, rather than in reactive and lackluster fashion.

SUBCULTURE

The subculture of the organization is the set of norms, values, and beliefs that characterize a particular agency. While there is a great range of organizational subcultures within the human service field, it is probably accurate to say that an emphasis on equality and support for the disadvantaged of our society are two hallmark values characterizing human service and social service organization subculture.

However, human service agencies and social service agencies, like other organizations, can have problematic subcultures as well, such as a value orientation that is either difficult in and of itself or causes subsequent problems within the agency operation. Human service organizations can have cultures that, for example, support unethical practices and do not supply the requisite support for whistle blowers, individuals who call such practices to the attention of relevant authorities. Other possible negative subcultural aspects include disregard for clients and staff or a devaluation of the worker and of the client. Some agencies, in our experience, have tolerated denigrating stereotypic discussion of clients. The support (often covert) of racist or sexist policies and actions is a subcultural aspect that has characterized some agencies.

Working to change these particular subcultural practices is a task that an organization worker might undertake. But subcultural problems such as the ones we have mentioned may exist in the whole range of nonsocial service agencies and businesses as well. Workers may well be involved in organization change efforts there, too. Examples of subcultural problems might be when machines and technology are valued over people or when a harsh and negative climate creates difficulties for employees. Similarly, an organization might have an orientation that disregards the environment; here increased cultural sensitivity to environmental matters should become a part of the ongoing organizational matrix.

In such cases, workers will assist in values exploration and values assessment. Thus, a process of feeding back the information received from such assessments to people in the organization, as a first step in the change process, is developed.

STRUCTURE

Organizations sometimes have a problem with organizational structure. Perhaps the division of labor is problematic, and certain individuals are required to do more unpleasant tasks than other individuals. Frequently, sex-linked division of labor in organizations is of this sort. Some individuals may be forced or encouraged to work for less pay than is appropriate. Hierarchies in the organization can be too large, impeding communication. There can be too much bureaucracy and red tape. These problems are common to all organizations and are found in human service organizations as well.

In such cases the worker might use an organizational assay technique (a questionnaire or open-ended interview schedule) to find out what people identify as the structural problems within the organization. These problems can then be brought out in the open and solutions can be considered.

SYSTEMS

Like organizational structure, organizational systems can be a problem as well. For the human body, a structural problem would be a broken leg, while a circulatory problem or some kind of neural damage problem would be a system problem. Organizations frequently have system problems. Information does not flow rapidly enough or accurately enough or it is blocked or changed somehow in the processes of transmission so that decisions made by the organization are inaccurate and of poor quality. The systems of power and resource allocation may also have problems. Power can be maldistributed in the organization. Frequently, individuals at the top of a hierarchy have a great deal of power and little knowledge about what is actually going on within the agency or bureau. Individuals at the lower levels who could benefit from greater delegation of power frequently do not have it. Restructuring the power balance in an organization is one of the most difficult organizational change tasks, but it is something that an organizational change social worker might work on.

Similarly, resource development and allocation systems may be problematic. Organization workers are frequently involved with human service agencies in assisting them to develop a more adequate resource base and to enrich and enlarge the resources that they now enjoy. Money is one crucial resource, but far from the only one. Clients, information, and staff are other resources that the organizational change social worker may help obtain.

STAFF

Organizations frequently have staff problems. They fall into typical groupings. The wrong staff are hired in terms of needed skills and knowledge. Staff are inappropriately promoted and rewarded, and staff are inappropriately let go. In addition, there are problems somewhat analogous to "failure to thrive" problems among babies. The staff comes, is used up, and resigns so that high turnover, though not from firing, is an issue of concern. Burnout is a staff problem that is now more likely to be recognized.

Once again, organization social workers would go through a problem identification process, seek to pinpoint certain specific difficulties, and begin a process of discussion and remediation.

ORGANIZATIONAL SKILLS

Depending on the goals and purposes of the agency, certain organizational skills are needed. Sometimes organizations change their goals and purposes without simultaneously helping the staff to acquire the needed skills for the new set of missions. Hence, there is a great discrepancy between what the agency says it is willing to do and wants to do and what it has the capability and competence to do.

Organizational workers help agencies identify the repertoire of skills needed for the goals they have chosen and plan steps to move the agency staff to the point where they will be possessors of the requisite skills and techniques. The ability of the staff to develop and improve is becoming an accepted part of agency needs. When staff are blocked from this developmental trajectory, problems can arise.

Stepping into a manager's role is hard work. (Photo by Irene Springer.)

STYLE

Sometimes organizations have a style that is inimical to the development and achievement of staff and the accomplishment and improvement of clients and client systems. In many ways, the style issue overlaps and intersects with culture, because style, being the way tasks are carried out, is often influenced by what workers believe. The difference is that style refers to what people in the organization actually do or do not do, whereas culture refers to what people in the organization think or do not think, believe or do not believe. Styles, for example, can be formal or informal, or liberal or conservative, low energy or high energy.

The organizational change worker does not simply try to change one style to another, because there is no particular style, either at the organizational or personal level, that is manifestly more effective than any other. The point here is to focus on the humanity and fairness of a particular organizational style more than anything else. Styles that are peremptory or episodic and do not treat people, clients, or staff with dignity and respect should be changed. Styles that embody racism or sexism should be changed.

Sometimes an organization wishes to change its style. It might like to be less command oriented and more consensus oriented. In such cases, the organization worker can provide assistance. Exploring and concretizing the desire for change is the first step, followed by working with the agency or organization to find examples of new and acceptable styles and to begin the development of procedures and practices that will implement the new style. As with culture change (the area of new ideas and thoughts), in style change (the area of new behaviors and actions) practice is needed. Individuals must try out the new style, and the organization worker may devise games, scenarios, or exercises to help the organization move from one style to another.

HE TREATS UNHAPPY COMPANIES

When Herb Martin works with a company that has a problem, he concentrates on what people feel as much as what they think. A clinical social worker in private practice for 15 years, he often uses humanistic principles in his capacity as a consultant to unhappy companies. "The key items in work systems are people and relationships," he says. "The systems don't just work by themselves."

He works on getting managers and employees to see how they become "stuck" in their work system. "We may take them for a 24-hour session, first working with employers and employees separately, then together. We look at human needs, at ways both can get what they want."

"The payoff," he said, "is in good feelings, less stress, and more effectiveness at work."

Pamela Edelman, "He Treats Unhappy Companies," *Detroit Free Press,* September 16, 1987, p. B1.

INTERACTION WITH OTHER SYSTEMS

The organization links with other systems, both the compositional ones of family, groups, and individuals and the contextual ones of community and society (contextual and compositional links are discussed in Chapter 4). As a subsystem within the total social system, the organization cannot ignore these other systems, and part of what the organization can do in carrying out its daily activities is to develop links with them.

On the family and individual level, beyond salary, organizations increasingly provide resources to assist in family functioning and prevent family problems. The whole area of fringe benefits—what some call private social policy—is a way to assist families in meeting a range of needs when problems occur.[11] For example, medical insurance, workers' compensation insurance, travel insurance, and life insurance help to protect a family when certain kinds of difficulties strike workers. Organization workers often seek to expand and increase the coverage available to workers through fringe benefit programs. Similarly, employee assistance programs frequently hire social workers as employees of the organization. Although employee assistance programs began with a focus on substance abuse in the workplace, and for many that is still an important and stressed objective, they have broadened to deal with other kinds of individual and family problems that may affect the worker and make him or her less productive.

One might, of course, raise a question about the organization's motivation for these programs. Is it ethical to provide services to get somebody to work harder for you? Perhaps not. However, perhaps the motivation does not matter; any kind of professional service offered, such as social work service, medical service, or legal service, by professionals through the organization stands on its own as a service, regardless of the reason for providing it.

Another question has to do with the matter of using the power component of employment as a way to force people to accept certain kinds of treatment, especially involving substance abuse. Although there is support for the use of authoritative intervention, questions have been raised as to whether this kind of force, which reduces the voluntary aspect of client status, is a good idea (similar questions are raised about the use of social workers in probation and parole departments, schools, and other institutions where legal authority is used to produce some aspect of client compliance). Doubtless these controversies will continue, as will the services.

On the contextual side, the organization needs community and society workers who can assist in developing and facilitating contextual links, or in some instances, like the Detroit example given next, oppose them. Organizations, as actors in the community and the society, perform positive or negative social roles extending from the kinds of products they produce and the purposes they pursue. Communities and societies have an overall interest in the way organizations perform and in the practices that organizations engage in, because of the importance of the organization's product and its employment and economic contribution. Hence, a variety of programs linking organizations and communities and societies exist to enhance organizational functioning and, on occasion, to change organizational functioning. An example of organizational enhancement is the provision of tax breaks to organizations locating in particular areas. A mixed case occurred in Detroit where the city purchased and destroyed an entire Polish community (Poletown) in order to make room for a General Motors plant. The city decided (wisely or not) that the community-wide benefit from additional plant expansion overrode the negative result of community destruction. Community social workers were active in seeking to prevent this action from occurring. The city ultimately was victorious. (Now the plant is not producing up to expectations.)

As another example of organization–community links, communities sometimes work with organizations to develop work–study or work-training programs linked with schools. Again the idea is to use the on-site ability of the organization to train people for special tasks as a more generalized job training method. School social workers might be involved with organizations to develop such programs.

Organizations, especially corporations of substantial size, are frequently large contributors to United Way campaigns and provide other kinds of separate charitable gifts. The cooperation of corporate officers for such campaigns is necessary if the charity or fund-raising effort is to reach workers through workplace soliciting methods. Thus, corporations provide an important social and public service, not only through their corporate gifts, but also through arranging access to employees to simplify the solicitation process. Community workers and organization workers are often involved in securing financial support from organizations for various kinds of community and societal projects.

The emphasis in this section has been on organizations in general by way of example. However, human service organizations face all the same problems and play the same roles. Human service organizations have fringe benefits that often are in need of improvement. Just because an agency offers counseling to others does not necessarily mean that the agency is sensitive to these same needs with respect to their staff. Organization change workers can seek to improve their own agency's links to workers and their families and to the needs and concerns of these groups and individuals.

BOUNDARIES

One troublesome issue for organizations is the particular problem of exactly where the boundary of the organization lies. Frequently, we tend to think that an organization is made up of employees. Perhaps a better way is to think of it as an open system. If it is such a system, then the clients who flow through the organization (like the students who flow through a school or university system) have an interest in it as well and may indeed be more interested than the employees. Yet, we do not often or certainly always think of clients as central to the organization's domain. Similarly, the spouses and families of organizational members are deeply affected by what happens within the organization. Yet few organizations would consider them a group that would have much to say about organizational activities.

Then too, especially for human service organizations, there is a set of funders who are frequently different from the users of the service. In a commercial organization, those who pay for the service and those who use the service are usually the same. In a not-for-profit organization, this distinction is a key point of difference. The clients may pay nothing or something on an ability to pay scale. Sometimes fees are paid by a third party, the state, or an insurance company. These individuals have an interest in the organizational activity and program as well.

But in all cases the question is who are the relevant members of the organization? Who are the relevant stake holders? How much of a stake do they hold? How much should they determine the organization's course, purpose, mission, and role? The organization worker helps the organization to sort out these multiple pressures and arrive at accommodations.

VALUE CONFLICT IN ORGANIZATIONS

Whether an organization has a very clear set of goals or its missions and purposes are somewhat ambiguous, it is sure to be the case that there are conflicts among them. Most of us grow up learning competing values. For example, most social workers believe in the value of equality, but most social workers also believe in the value of achievement.[12] The problem occurs when the value of achievement conflicts with the value of equality. Organizations are similarly beset with conflicting values and similarly have to find ways to accommodate these differences.

Let us give two specific examples of desirable competing goals within human service organizations. One is the conflict in public assistance between service and payments. This conflict is manifest in a number of ways. Sometimes the organizational structure of a department of public assistance emphasizes the social services aspect and is called a department of social services. In these cases the service aspect is likely to receive additional support, and those who do assistance payment work are likely to feel less central and less vital to the organization's mission. On the other hand, there are organizations that emphasize the money payment aspect, called departments of public welfare.[13] In these cases, service workers are likely to feel the same way as their assistance counterparts did in the other structure. A third structure has the same worker handling both service and assistance payments. Here conflict within the worker as to how much of each function to emphasize in a given case is continuous. It is doubtful if there will be a complete resolution of these conflicts. The two functions both support and conflict each with the other. Attention to both is needed. Joining and separating are likely to be popular solutions at any given moment, but may become disappointing as time goes on, creating countervailing pressures for the other "form," whatever that is.

Another well-known conflict is that between emphasis on the family and emphasis on the children as a unit of service in child and family service agencies. Social workers are well aware that emphasis on "the best interest of the child" may not simultaneously be in the best interest of the family. Similarly, attempts to keep the family unit together might require subordinating work with and attention to the interest of particular children. Since there are not enough resources to go around, there is continual strain between these two worthy goals.

At a more general level, there is the consistent conflict in all social agencies and human service organizations between attention to social change goals and attention to social amelioration goals. On the one hand, human problems press into the agency on a daily basis. Regardless of what social forces may cause a particular problem, let us say unemployment, workers have before them an unemployed individual who is in need of help in securing appropriate benefits and refocusing efforts toward securing a job. The pressing and urgent nature of this problem creates its own demand for attention and amelioration. On the other hand, if a clinical worker spends several weeks or several years with the same type of problem, the worker may conclude that the task of helping individuals is Sisyphian (readers will recall that Sisyphus is the man who kept rolling a stone up a hill only to have it roll back down again); it may seem that a change in the social structure that creates unemployment in the first place is what is really needed.

On the other hand, a social change social worker, focusing on the larger macroscopic picture, may develop a need for more concrete, more palpable results of work and thus may say seek direct practice as a way of fulfilling these needs. Of course, both emphases are needed. In all the cases discussed here, the tension is constant and ongoing. It is part of our life in organizations.

Organization workers, however, may provide several kinds of help with this problem. First, they may engage in value clarification and help organizations to better understand the conflicts they are facing. Clearly, without such understanding, steps to deal effectively with them is very difficult.

Second, the organization worker may help the organization find ways to choose between competing goals or to accommodate both of them. An organization may decide, for example, that "our focus is going to be families." Were an organization to make that decision it would have in a sense solved the conflict by its own rule. Individuals who became clients of that organizations would be apprised of the fact that there was a family focus, that the maintenance of the family and its enhancement were the overall goals. Individual needs would be subordinated to the achievement of that goal. If potential clients felt that this focus was improper for them, they might seek help somewhere else. Alternatively, of course, an agency might decide to have a child-based focus. "We are going to focus on the child and that person's best interest. If it conflicts with the family, so be it," the agency might say. Again, the choice is legitimate. It is not better than any other type of priority choice, but it may reflect the ability of the organization at that moment to delivery effective, high-quality services. The organizational change social worker can help in this process.

THE CLOGGED INTAKE

Jim Smith was a clinical worker at Family and Children's Service of Euphoria. He had been disturbed by one particular element in the agency's practice. Over time, the waiting list had grown quite long. Today it took about three to four weeks to be seen at his agency. He also knew that a number of his colleagues had extended the number of sessions that they had with some of their clients—particularly, he felt, their favorite clients—and this was part of the backup problem. Another part of the problem he felt lay in the large number of informal meetings that were held all the time in the organization. The way he counted, only about ten hours a week for most workers was actually used in client contact. People saw two or perhaps three clients a day. The rest of the day was devoted to various kinds of other activities, the nature of which seemed somewhat absurd. Jim wasn't sure what to do. On his own he put together a few figures giving the rough case loads as he knew them. He then checked informally with some of his colleagues in social work agencies elsewhere to find out the practices at those agencies. He found that his agency was universally low in client hour contact and was the highest in length of waiting lists.

Even though he hadn't had any particular training in organizational change efforts, he was beginning the process of needs assessment. He requested a special meeting with his supervisor and reviewed these figures with her. He tried to take a positive attitude and not give the appearance of being critical or negative. Rather, he shared his concern in a straightforward manner. His supervisor was interested and suggested that they might talk about some of these matters in a small group meeting. If the concerns were shared, they could set up a meeting with the executive. It seemed things were on their way.

CONFUSION ABOUT PURPOSE

Sheila Brown, M.S.W., worked for Organizational Research Associates, a consulting firm that helped organizations do strategic planning. The particular case that she was reviewing had to do with a mental health agency of about 20 staff. The agency had grown over the years from one that had only had a few employees to one that was, though still small, considerably larger. The difficulty was that many other mental health and family service agencies had developed, and this particular agency was not sure of what its mission and role should be or where its focus should lie. It got some funding from the United Way, from local church groups, and from client fees. The agency had sought to pursue grants, but, as she recognized, this was more an attempt to go where money was than to develop money where program interests lay.

Later today she was going to meet with the board of directors to lay out a suggested set of procedures for a strategic planning effort. It involved the appointment of a small committee from the board and professional and support staff working with her to interview other agencies in town about their view of this agency's role. She was also going to use the resources of her firm to collect general data about the position of similar agencies around the country and the ideas and programs that they were offering. She would act as a staff person pulling together these data and writing up a report to outline options that would be considered at a staff retreat.

She proposed two retreats. The first would involve the agency in discussion only. It was her experience that when discussion was separated from decision the discussion was much more interesting and fruitful, and, in point of fact, making the decision was much easier. After some time to digest the discussion, a second mini retreat was proposed. At this time decisions about new agency directions would be made. The period between the first and second retreat would allow modifications in the proposal if they were necessary and would allow checking with other community agencies to get a sense of their view of the options this particular agency was thinking about.

As she was reflecting on her proposal to the board, she also reflected on how much she had enjoyed her work. When she entered social work, consulting with organizations was not exactly what she had in mind, but it had turned out to be very satisfying. There were agencies all over town that she had helped, and she felt that social work service had very much improved in town because of her efforts in particular.

Organizational change social workers perform a range of tasks at the organizational level, with the organization as a client system. Change of the organization can come through education, or more specific interventions aimed at reorganization and repurposing, or a combination. The problems that the worker identifies can be worked on directly (at the organizational level), through changes in composition (working with units like the individual and the family that make up the organization), or through changes in context (through levels that influence the organization, such as the community and the society).

Within the organization, workers focus on specific areas that might need change. Staff composition or organizational structure and systems are loci for change efforts. The development and refurbishment of organizational strategy represent important arenas for intervention. The organizational subculture, too, often needs change. Beliefs and attitudes, especially those that are racist and sexist, rob the organization of humanness and limit its effectiveness.

Conclusion

Organization workers help organizations to deal with development in their environment and to make adjustments on ongoing bases. All organizations, human service organizations, government organizations, and other organizations, face this need. Without constant and ongoing adaptation and adjustment, the organization may find itself anachronistic, bureaucratized, repetitive, and not really meeting the needs of its community or clients. This process, which we call organizational rigidification, occurs slowly. For this reason, it is unlikely that people will notice changes in the organization or environment that cause organizational problems. Usually there is some dramatic crisis, a cash flow problem, a personnel exit, or something that causes attention to be riveted on the current manifestation of a problem in the organization that has been existing for some time. What is sometimes difficult to see is that organizations (and communities and societies, too, as we shall see) are clients, just like the individual in the chair across the room. These clients have decisions to make, actions to take, and conflicts to resolve, just as individuals do. Social workers—organization workers—help these clients process and decide, just as interpersonal workers aid individuals.[14]

Notes

1. See *Business Week,* June 30, 1980, pp. 3 ff.
2. OD professionals (organizational development) provide a wide range of ongoing continuing education activities to government, private, and voluntary organizations. A number of social workers are represented in this field, but individuals from other areas have joined as well.
3. Lecture discussion of one sort or another is not the only kit in the educational toolbox. Videotapes, games, and audiotapes are also used.
4. John E. Tropman, "Policy Analysis," in A. Minahan (ed.), *Encyclopedia of Social Work,* Vol. 2, 18th ed. (Silver Spring, Md.: National Association of Social Workers, NASW, 1986).
5. Howard Gardner deals with this issue in his book *Frames of the Mind* (New York: Basic Books, 1983).
6. Since much of social work training involves "people skills," a good reference is R. Bolton, *People Skills* (Englewood Cliffs, N.J.: Prentice Hall, 1979).
7. John Naisbett, *Megatrends* (New York: Warner Books, 1982). United Way of America, *Environmental Scan* (Alexandria, V.: United Way of America, 1985).
8. While it may have no history as an organization, there is a history of the development process that needs to be taken into account.
9. For this reason it is a good idea to appoint someone as an idea manager. See John E. Tropman, *Policy Management in the Human Services* (New York: Columbia University Press, 1984).
10. Eric Flamholtz calls this the transition from entrepreneurial to professional management. *How to Make the Transition from an Entrepreneurship to a Professionally Managed Firm* (San Francisco: Jossey-Bass, 1986).
11. For further discussion, see Larry Root, "Employee Benefits and Income Security" in J. Tropman, M. Dluhy, and R. Lind (eds.), *New Strategic Perspectives on Social Policy* (Elmsford, N.Y.: Pergamon Press, 1981).
12. See John E. Tropman, "Value Conflicts and Policy Decision Making," *Human Systems Management,* 4 (1984), pp. 214–219.
13. The names of actual departments do not, of course, always reflect their functions as in this example.
14. For further reference in the organizational change area, consider the following resources: Jon Alston, *American Samurai* (New York: de Gruyter, 1986); W. Bennis and Burt Nanus, *Leaders* (New York: Harper & Row, 1985); Burton Gummer, *The Politics of Social Administration* (Englewood Cliffs, N.J.: Prentice Hall, 1990); Y. Hasenfeld, *Administrative Leadership in the Social Services* (New York: Haworth Press, 1989); Y. Hasenfeld, *Human Service Organizations* (Englewood Cliffs, N.J.: Prentice Hall, 1983); Ann Minahan, *Encyclopedia of Social Work,* 18th ed. (Silver Spring, Md.: National Association of Social Workers, 1987), see articles on administration and organizations; Robert J. Myers and Peter Ufford, *On-Site Analysis: A Practical Approach to Organizational Change* (Etibicoke, Ontario: OSCH, 1989); H.J. Reitz, *Behavior in Organizations* (Homewood, Ill.: Richard D. Irwin, 1987); H. Resnick and Rino Patti, *Change from Within* (Philadelphia: Temple University Press, 1980); Robert Weinbach, *The Social Worker as Manager* (New York: Longman, 1990); M. Weiner, *Human Services Management,* 2nd ed. (Belmont, Calif.: Wadsworth Publishing Co., 1990).

CHAPTER 8
Helping Communities to Change

Introduction

Helping communities to change, improve, and be more viable has a history as old as social work. From the early days of the American Social Science Association in the 1870s through the National Conference of Charities and Corrections and the National Conference of Social Welfare, community problems have been a part of the annual discussions of these bodies.[1] There was a strong feeling among community leaders, academic professionals, and citizens at large that the developing urbanization and industrialization, which characterized the United States after the Civil War, was profoundly disorganizing to the old yet somewhat idealized rural community.[2] In the city, ties that bind were either broken or failed to take root. One approach, then, to understanding social problems—juvenile delinquency, urban crime, dependence on the dole, unemployment—was to see them as failures of community, a result of "community disorganization."[3] What better solution, then, to problems of community disorganization than attempts to provide community organization to rebuild the connections that bound individuals interdependently to each other.[4]

For all its historic presence in social work, however, community organization was subordinate to more individualistic views about the solutions to problems. It is for this reason, perhaps, that studying casework, and to some extent group work, has always been more popular in schools of social work than community organization and, later, administration, planning, and policy specializations. The reasons for these preferences are too manifold and complex to consider now and are in any event not completely clear. Suffice it to say here that Americans' penchant for individualism in sports and business and for rewarding good deeds and punishing wrongdoers appears as well in the helping professions. Individual counseling and other interventions in the micro area are more popular than those in the macro areas. In the medical field, individual physical care given by physicians is preferred over system-wide prevention offered by public health.

The difference between remediation and prevention provides one more clue to our preference. Americans' emphasis on freedom and lack of intervention tends to mean that we don't like to intervene until something has happened, until some problem has presented itself.[5] This view emphasizes, then, remediation over prevention, and to a certain extent the social work specializations in the macro area focus a bit more on the preventive aspect.

Thus, at least two reasons—emphasis on individualism, and emphasis on remediation—explain why social work tends to be dominated by interests in casework and counseling. Nonetheless, there is a long history of community focus as well. It is to this area that we now turn our attention.

It will be helpful to begin by asking what communities are. The word "community" has different meanings for different people. Breaking up the word into its parts helps us to understand its source: common-unity. Community refers to the uniting forces that stem from what individuals hold or have in common. What "things" are held in common? They can of course vary, but they can be an interest, a location, a belief, an identification, or an activity.[6] They could also be a personal feature or experience. Let's consider some examples.

People can have an interest in common; this interest can be in sports, helping others, great books, travel, or whatever. Individuals with these kinds of common interests might, within each interest sector, form a kind of community. Bonds of appreciation and connection can build up between them. Commonness of knowledge about the activity creates familiarity with each other. They may engage in common activities as a result of this common interest, such as attending certain sporting events or meetings together. The phrase "community of interest" refers to this kind of communal bond.

Alternatively, individual people may share a common location. Typically, this kind of community is referred to as a geographic community. It may begin with a block or neighborhood and extend to a several-block area of a large city (the south side of Chicago, the north end of Boston, a barrio, or a ghetto). Common residence often leads to or is linked with common interests and common interactions, which reinforce the bonds of common location.

A third kind of community comes from common belief or identification. Often religious communities are of this nature, and the phrase "community of believers" is meant to refer to this collection of communal identifications. Beliefs are often linked to common identifications, especially ethnic ones (the African-American community, the Italian community, the Jewish community. When an individual recognizes herself or himself as of Italian or Jewish or black ancestry and holds ideas, beliefs, interests, and locations very different from other people, an ethnic subcommunity exists (or a racial one, or a gender one). The concept of subculture or subcommunity refers to these ideas or identifications, when beliefs are present and identifications and behavior patterns (foods, holidays, and the like) are a defining characteristic.

Similarly, the presence of a common identifying feature or quality can create communal identification. Red-haired individuals have a common identifying feature that on occasion causes them to get together with each other and at least promotes a certain common identification. Other individuals with racial and ethnic features may similarly find themselves commonly identified, even if they themselves may initially not feel such a common identification. Individuals who have an affliction or a disease may also form a type of community.

Finally, communities may come from common activities. The organizational community or the community of the workplace is an example of this. Individuals who hold the same kind of job or work in the same place may form social roots or may press for better working conditions and more pay in the form of unions. These individuals may have little else in common but the time that they spend with each other, day in and day out over a series of years. The bond created by this kind of interaction can be very strong and becomes a kind of community.[7]

All these individual elements or features are each related to particular kinds of communities. The more powerful communities that hold claims on us may occur when several exist together. Hence, people with common beliefs often live near each other, thus creating a subcultural and geographic bond. Similarly, areas of a city are sometimes identified by race, class, or other common characteristics such that specific community identifications tend to reinforce each other.

Three Major Approaches to Community Change

How does one help communities to change?[8] In part, the answer to this question stems from the problem that the community is facing. Sometimes common features are present, but individuals do not perceive them as common or do not recognize the bonds that could arise as a result of these common features. Community development is called for here to help citizens develop and gain strength from their commonality, for its own sake and to accomplish other goals, too.

A second problem can occur when common features and common fates are recognized, but the community seems unable to crystallize its latent energy into purposeful steps to advance its own interests. In that case, community action is called for.

A third kind of problem occurs when there is a recognition of multiple community pulls and identifications. Such multiplicity of communal involvements can lead to community conflicts (for example, between the black community and the white community, between the Jewish community and the Catholic community, between the community of work and the community of geography). It may actually forestall the potential for action. Such a case is a good reason to call on community planning.

COMMUNITY DEVELOPMENT

Community development activities are actions engaged in by the community that promote the recognition of commonly held features and that lead to interaction based on those features.[9] Community development typically involves the worker taking the initiative by talking with a number of potential individuals members of such a community and assessing the extent to which they might have a beginning recognition of possible links with others and their willingness to talk with others in the same situation. For example, a community change worker might talk with several individuals on a particular block to assess their sense of common faith and their willingness to get together with other people in the block to talk about issues of common concern. A community change worker might talk with a number of women who have been victims of assault to see whether they would have any interest in getting together with other victims to explore common interests and concerns. In a remote village, a community change worker might begin working with local chiefs and opinion leaders to get village members together to focus on some common task.

In the women's movement, a phrase called "consciousness raising" is used to refer to this process, and it is a good general term for us to know. Consciousness raising is that process through which the common features, qualities, or fates that bind individuals together but have hitherto been unrecognized or acted on are brought to the surface. One fairly dramatic communal development, and a new one, is the emergence of the ACOA group (Adult Children of Alcoholics).[10] Children who grew up in a home where a parent was an alcoholic or otherwise emotionally impaired share common experiences with thousands of others. While this commonality was present, it was latent and unrecognized until the late 1970s and early 1980s. Now, there are ACOA groups around the country, there is a national conference, they get together and share common experiences, and they are making plans for common action. This emergence of a common unity is a perfect example of community development.

COMMUNITY ACTION

Sometimes there is a recognition of common identification or fate, but the community is not able to mobilize itself in ways that allow it to press its demands.[11] Here the community worker may seek to assist a group in undertaking community (or social) action. Community or social action is that set of activities involved in bringing political pressure on decision makers to prevent exploitation, to improve social conditions, or to increase benefits, among other results. It can involve mass mobilization or a lead influence or both. It can be based on geographic features, common interest, common fate, or common beliefs.

For example the union movement is a good case of community action. The community in question is the community of workers. Their needs involve better working conditions, better wages, greater job stability, and the development of an effective organized force that can act in parallel with the organized force of management and the organization. There was great resistance to formal union organization in its initial stages, as is often the case with community action efforts. Dominant forces seek to delegitimatize, deemphasize, and destabilize community action efforts in order to retain the advantages they have come to enjoy. But with assistance and persistence, community action can also be successful.[12]

Other examples, in which the community of older citizens is involved, are the

"If we don't hang together, we'll hang separately." (Photo by AFL–CIO News.)

Gray Panthers and the work of the AARP (American Association of Retired Persons). As older adults become a larger proportion of the society, because of their concentration in certain areas and their propensity to vote, they have become an increasingly political force and they can take effective community action. Community change agents working at senior citizens' centers around the country seek to bring together older adults and assist them in talking with each other about matters of common concern, such as the cost of health care, Medicare benefits, and Social Security benefits. Out of these discussions come letter-writing campaigns, political influence campaigns, and senior days in state capitols.[13]

A third example of social action comes from victims' rights activities. These individuals, concerned that more attention has been spent on the perpetrator than the victim, have sought to develop community action and attention to victims' rights by bringing victims together to allow them to develop common perspectives. Victim action activities have included pressing for and successfully passing legislation for victim compensation and victim testimony during sentencing and parole hearings and achieving victim advocate officers within local jurisdictions.

Sometimes community action involves mass demonstrations. The March on Washington for civil rights, spearheaded by Dr. Martin Luther King, Jr., is one such example. Activities of the well-known community activist Saul David Alinsky were often of this sort.[14] He would try to highlight the incongruities and conflicting commitments of individuals by picketing slum landlords as they left church, for example, or inviting all residents of a particular neighborhood to capture and kill a rat and deposit it on the steps of city hall. But elite connections are also used, as when community influentials seek through small meetings and informal interaction to influence key decision makers on a one-on-one basis. Sit-ins have also become a popular form of mass activity.

Community action involves the development of force and pressure to bring about needed improvements in a community. It is often used where the community and its members are victims of crime, social injustice, and exploitation.

COMMUNITY PLANNING

Because communities differ, it is sometimes the case that the demands of one community are opposed to the demands of another.[15] Thus, community conflict may result, or a situation may occur in which action cannot be taken because each demand cancels out the imperatives of the other. Particular communities frequently have particular interests stemming from the one or two features that they hold in common. There may be no overall view that takes into account the fuller range of interests that may characterize, let's say, a large city or county area. Community planning is a technique used in this kind of situation; community workers seek to use knowledge, research, and information, as well as the involvement of the several different groups concerned with the future of a particular issue or area, to develop and implement ideas beneficial to all concerned.[16]

While community development and community action tend to be participative, involving as many community members as possible directly, community planning tends to be representative and proceeds through the use of delegates. It is not possible to have all members of a Jewish community, the African-American community, the gay community, the various geographic communities, and so on, together, so the use of representatives is a logical choice. The community plan seeks to get influential representatives from various communities working together on some larger community committee or task force. Thus, the decisions made or views arrived at by the group of relative elite (or opinion leaders) will have a greater chance of acceptance by the specific component communities.[17]

Community planning is heavily based on the use of information and interaction around information. Environmental scans and needs assessments are used to provide information about impending pressures and problems. Social analyses provide a picture of the distribution of current difficulties and problems.[18] Technique exchange and program sharing among community planners provide one source of ideas about how to approach problems. The particular multicommunity group brought together for the issues in question is a second source. These issues of fact and value are then dealt with in the committee or group meeting, and over time the community planner seeks to achieve an agreement among representatives of different interests and communities for a course of action. By processing information through representative groups, the ideas and feelings of the broader groups should be taken into account. Criticisms of this approach, however, center on the extent of representation and the possibility of cooptation—getting the study group in question to forget the interests of their groups of origin.

Two Major Elements in Community Change

Two elements are involved in a community change effort, regardless of the model used: intellectual and interpersonal. Intellectual and interpersonal elements are both goals of community change efforts and means to goal achievement. At times, one or the other becomes the goal, and the other becomes the means. Let's look at each in turn.

INTELLECTUAL SKILLS

Intellectual skills[19] refer to the knowledge and competence of the worker. Several kinds of knowledge are needed. The worker should be informed about the social science of communities and the forces that shape and change them in general and within specific social and cultural contexts. Minority communities will be different from majority ones, urban neighborhoods from rural villages. Workers need to know what forces affect them in common and which are unique. And workers need to know where to get this information.

Community workers also need to know about the steps in the community change processes and the kinds of problems that might be likely to occur at any specific stage. (These stages are discussed later.)

Community workers need diagnostic skills and the ability to analyze the community situation and understand which of the many elements are important and crucial and which are less central. Synthesis, too, is crucial. It is the ability to pull together diverse views and positions and see what commonalities might lie beneath the surface.

INTERPERSONAL SKILLS

The community worker must be sensitive of the way she or he presents herself or himself in social interaction. Community members need to establish a relationship with the worker to develop open communication. Just as in more interpersonal modes of practice, community change workers must have a level of self-knowledge that allows them to examine the ways they are interacting with community members such that good relationships can be developed. Different presentations of self may be required as communities differ.

For example, in community planning efforts, the more technical aspects of worker skills may be involved than would be true in community development or community action episodes. Working with elite members of a community may require different presentations of self than working with other members of these same communities. Working with affluent members of a community may require approaches and interactions different from those appropriate when working with the very disadvantaged. Dress, language, and style of interaction may all change depending on the nature of the community. The important point is that the community change worker be aware of the need for differential presentation of self, assess the nature of self-presentation in a particular interaction, and decide on what presentation to offer.

Types of Communities

Types of communities differ depending on the basis of the common-unity that creates the bond. Interest, location, belief, identification, and activity are among the most common bases for community.

Interest refers to a common goal or fate. A class in high school or college is an example of a community of interest (although other bases such as activity might enter as well). A class in high school and college builds such strong bonds that reunions often bring people together years after the bases of community have left. Common fate means that people are commonly subject to the same external forces (although their specific fates may be different). Students are all subject to the procedures of the education system, like grading. Individuals living in the shadow of a volcano share a common danger.

But interests can also be things that one desires to secure. Older adults have a common interest in the continuation and improvement of the Medicare program and may form a community of interest to pursue those goals. However, this example reveals an element of community only hinted at before, an emotional, affective element. Just having a common wish to get some government benefit does not transform a collection of individuals into a community. It makes an interest group, to be sure, but interest groups are the client of the policy practitioner. Common values and behaviors, as well as common goals, are needed for community. A community has an emotional component, an element of feeling and involvement, a commitment.

Stages of Community Growth

Social units such as people, organizations, and societies exist in different stages or phases of growth, maturity, decline, and renewal. Different problems are generally associated with each phase. The community social worker should be aware of these phases as part of an overall awareness of community issues and difficulties.

Entire communities cannot be easily typed in this way. Some have growing and declining sections within them. Others have conflicting components, for example, a young population in a very old geographic area, and doubtless still other combinations will present themselves.

YOUNG COMMUNITIES

New communities tend to have the problems associated with youth everywhere: lack of control and of resources. Young communities often grow in a random fashion. There is often lack of regulation and structure focusing on what kind of facility goes where, and so on. Community development workers may need to help in the development of these kinds of structures.

Resource problems are another typical difficulty for young communities. Being new, they have not had the time to develop the networks of information and referral centers where individuals can get together and exchange information and help. They may not have had the time to discover community leaders and influentials.

Community development workers in young communities try to assist in the creation of community leadership, which in turn can identify needed resources with the worker and begin the process of resource development. New communities are typically communities of strangers, and community workers may assist in the development of legitimate mechanisms for interaction and interpersonal contact.

A young community, for example, may be a community of the newly separated and the newly divorced. Community workers may seek to assist in the development of parents without partners groups and other places where newly single individuals can meet others, talk with them, and develop patterns of mutually satisfying interaction. Young communities tend to be characterized overall by the need for community development, followed by community action and community planning. While planning can have great useful impact here, the motivation to plan may be low.

MIDDLE-AGED COMMUNITIES

Middle-aged communities are those that have existed for some time and function reasonably well. In fact, it is this "reasonably well" aspect that creates the problem. Middle-aged communities are often beset by community conflicts. A number of vigorous identifications may preclude or cancel out effective action. Community planning might be called for here. What kinds of conflicts might be present? Multiple community identifications to geographic locations, communities of work or business and profession, communities of religious belief and political interest might be among those competing for the identifications of the individual community members.

Community development is useful here to blend different identifications and seeks to create common purpose. Community action to improve civic facilities is helpful, while planning can help point the direction.

A second major issue in middle-aged communities is failure to change. The young community is changing all the time; it needs stability and organization. The middle-aged community needs to adjust and improve its houses, local facilities, social structure, and orientation to take account of the changing world around it. Community workers can help middle-aged communities chart the forces acting on them and prepare for action by planning for positive change.

OLD COMMUNITIES

Older communities are often in need of renewal. Geographic communities are not infrequently characterized by older industries and an actually older populace, although the older age of the populace is not always associated with the older community by any means. Younger individuals may well have left to follow job opportunities in new industry. Small rural towns and big cities fall into this category. Not infrequently a sense of depression and inadequacy pervades the older community. There may be community ties, but community conflicts may exist such that action cannot be taken. Therefore, community action to begin the process of community renewal is a good first step. Community planning cannot proceed without the development of a sense of efficacy.

There has frequently been a decline in the upkeep of facilities and the maintenance of preexisting outmoded patterns and forms. The community action worker may seek to revivify and reinstitute some of these elements with the cooperation of local leaders. And crime and decay are frequently features associated with the older geographic community particularly. They provide a good basis for community action. Neighborhood watch programs and other activities crystallize community energy around social activities that are helpful to the community as a whole, and present a good place to begin.

Communities other than those geographically based also have problems of renewal and recruitment.[20] The commitments, feelings, and emotions need to be passed on to newer members and recruits. Sometimes reorganization of the community, with different goals, purposes, and emphases is needed as well. The community worker can help in this renewal process.

Specific Community Features and Problems: Three Issues

Disorganization seems to be the overriding problem to which community organization addresses itself. But community disorganization is a vague diagnosis and lacks specificity. Three more focused kinds of difficulties can serve as an organizing basis for efforts in community change and development.

The first of these is lack of community cohesion. The second is lack of community capability. The third is lack of community competence. Cohesion refers to the basic

Community problems: where community organization often begins. (Photo by The New York Times.)

mutuality of identification that serves as the undergirding feature of communities. Capabilities refer to the ability to translate those mutual identifications into actions. Community competence refers to the scope, integration, and overall success of these efforts. Each, in a sense, builds on the other. Without cohesion, neither capability nor competence is possible. Without cohesion and capability, competence is not possible. Let us consider each in turn.

LACK OF COMMUNITY COHESION

One of the most basic problems for the community change worker is the development and building of community cohesion. A community that lacks cohesion is in some sense not a community yet. There may be normlessness or anomie (anomie is a lack of common values in a group of people) and a lack of mutuality and mutual identification. The community change worker seeks to select and propose projects that will increase community cohesion, projects that promote commonness and in which the goal is the development of a perception of common faith and involvement.

A typical project in the geographic community is a paint-up, fix-up campaign. The manifest goal is to get things looking sharper, crisper, and cleaner. However, the latent goal of such a campaign is to involve individuals in common activities, an experience they might not have had in this context for quite some time. As individuals work together on the paint-up, fix-up area designated, they have a chance to talk and interact with each other, and it is hoped they will begin to perceive some of the commonalities so clear to others but as yet hidden from themselves. Building on these kinds of perceptions can result in the development of community cohesion.

Workers involving local leaders may use other techniques as well. Community meetings where common problems are discussed are often a good technique. Frequently, here the critical incident method is used. The worker may have begun a process of informal one-on-one meetings with members of the community. A meeting is not, however, proposed as a first step; rather, the worker waits until some incident occurs that stimulates community interest and activity. It may be something like a crime or victimization. Community members may be willing to get together around a fairly simple issue of what to do about this particular incident. That is good in and of itself and begins the process of identification that might lead to community development activities of other sorts.

Workers here endeavor to "start where the client is" and involve the client around those issues and concerns that represent presenting community problems. As interaction with other community members develops, problems of a broader scope might be undertaken.

A typical beginning place is a block club. Community change workers may get people together who live on the same block (for our purposes, a block involves those houses facing each other on either side of a single street). It is frequently the experience of community change workers that individuals on such blocks do not know much about each other; or if they do know each other; they lack a sense of empowerment and ability to deal with common concerns.

Sometimes the worker seeks to build community cohesion by developing citizens' advisory groups, which are based on local neighborhood institutions. The community nursing home council is one example. Nursing homes are organizations that are often cut off from the local area in which they live. The development of a citizens' advisory group that can provide volunteer services to the nursing home, involve community individuals going in and out of the nursing home, and facilitate interaction between a nursing home and a local community represents the kind of community development activity that builds community cohesion.

In this sense, the nursing home council (or school community council or any other kind of organization–community link) serves a double purpose at least. One purpose is to assist the local organization and to aid in linking the local organization to the local community. As well, though, there is a reciprocal purpose: to influence the local organization to take certain actions and behave in certain ways that are helpful to the local community and reflect local community preferences and interests. However, the fact that members of the community get together to talk with organizational representatives and work through various exchanges of view builds community cohesion. The advisory council or community council might also be stimulated by an organizational change social worker working for the organization, in cooperation with a community change worker working for the local community or those interested in helping the local community.

There are always two goals in the development of community capability: a task goal and a process goal. The task goal represents the specific change effort under consideration and its achievement represents a task achievement. A process goal represents the increase in community confidence brought about by successful community change and improvement efforts. Thus, at one level we seek to develop a string of specific achievements by working with the community members. At another level, we seek to strengthen the community's capacity for capable action, which can arise from this series of specific successes.

LACK OF COMMUNITY CAPABILITY

The capability problem exists when cohesion is present, but there is no vehicle or organization through which action can occur. For example, in our block club the individuals may know each other, but it has not occurred to them that they could band together in organized form to influence the events that affect them. Here the community change worker might seek to build a block club federation based on representatives from different block clubs scattered throughout the particular community.

Alternatively, the community change worker might seek to build a neighborhood association or neighborhood service center. In this case, individuals interested in improving the local neighborhood might join together in an improvement association that is not specifically linked to block club organization. The community change worker might link up with other community change workers and organizational change social workers involved with various organizations serving the community and seek to develop a local settlement house operation that will serve as a focal point for the activities of the community.

Whatever the particular instrument developed by the community change worker, the goal remains the same: to build on the already existing common bonds in ways that give community members the experience of influencing their environment. This influence may occur through meeting with local organizations and seeking to persuade them to change their practices. It may mean meeting with city-wide organizations and seeking greater representation of neighborhood individuals in subunits that serve the neighborhood. For example, African-American communities like to have a high representation of African-American policemen and firemen in their neighborhoods. Actions to pressure for this kind of change from the city-wide administration will build community capability. Community social work seeks to develop the capacity of the community to carry out its wishes and desires.

LACK OF COMMUNITY COMPETENCE

If cohesion and capability are present, then the problem may be lack of community competence. Community competence is the ability of a local community area to act effectively over a period of time. Some communities are able, for a specific situation and for a relatively short time, to take capable action, to actually exercise influence in directions that benefit the community. But not infrequently the motivation or spirit making this effort possible fades, and the community is no longer characterized by capability.

Or, in an alternative situation, the community seeks to act but fails to "get together," or does act but fails in securing results. In both cases, competence becomes a problem, and a goal of the community change social worker might be to increase community competence. Competent activity involves the development of local community institutions that exist over a period of time. The longer time focus requires worker attention to the development of leadership in the local community. While leadership development has certainly been a goal throughout the cohesion and capability change effort, the worker inevitably performs more of an initiator and starter role, and performs a larger number of tasks than she or he will later. These tasks are taken on behalf of the community, but the worker always seeks to work with community members in the development of these particular tasks.

As communities develop, however, local leadership is needed, and a worker may link up local community members with city-wide or state-wide leadership development programs. Sometimes local schools run leadership development and social change programs as an outgrowth of public school or community or junior college activities. Sometimes the worker will link up with other workers around the community to develop their own leadership development program. However, without the development of community leadership, community continuity is unlikely to remain viable, and community competence is likely to decrease over time. For most community workers, there are a large number of communities with serious needs. Thus, the goal of the community worker is to work with and involve members of a particular client system so that they can carry on community activities on their own.

Community leadership development, then, assists specific community members, but there may also be programs that assist community groups and community organizations as part of the overall community competence development project. It is necessary for the component organizations within a local community to be reasonably viable as well.[21] Hence, leadership is developed that may both serve neighborhood-wide or community-wide organizations and take over leadership roles in specific local organizations that serve the community. As this process develops, the community change worker may seek to develop a community leadership council in which different leaders from different organizations meet to coordinate efforts and for the exchange of information and perspective.[22]

THE PROBLEMS EXIST TOGETHER

These three problems exist to a great degree simultaneously.[23] The difficulty for the community change worker is making an accurate diagnosis about where the community client system is so that beginning efforts can be made. And, in some sense, there will be a simultaneous effort to work on cohesion, capability, and competence.

Efforts in community cohesion tend to draw on community development skills; efforts in community capability tend to draw on community action skills; work in community competence involves community planning. Most community change workers find that, while these distinctions can be made for the sake of discussion, in the actual work of community change, development, action, and planning are often simultaneously involved.

The Phases of Helping

As in most helping and intervention efforts, the worker proceeds through phases as the process of help develops. There is a beginning phase, a middle phase, and an ending phase. In the real world of community development, action, and planning, things do not always proceed as neatly as this description implies, but it does represent a perspective that the worker seeks to implement, and it does alert the worker to things that might be missing in a quickly developing client system activity.

Our three-stage model allows us to use a common phase model for different kinds of helping. But a more detailed model may be helpful to consider. Cox and his colleagues use a five-stage model: (1) assessment, (2) option section, (3) mobilization and implementation, (4) administrative leadership and management, and (5) evaluation.[24]

THE BEGINNING PHASE

The beginning phase involves problem recognition, problem definition, and the assessment of information pertaining to a problem. These elements do not always follow the tidy order implied. Most desirable, of course, would be for the community change worker to work with individuals in a particular community area to recognize that a problem exists.

Problem recognition can occur on many levels. The problem of community cohesion is a theoretical definition and phrasing of a community problem. It is unlikely that community members would identify a problem as lack of community cohesion (or lack of community capability or competence, for that matter). But they might say something like, "Nobody knows each other around here," or "We seem to be a lot of strangers," or "With people moving in and out so much, it's hard to find out what's going on." Phrases like this indicate a problem of cohesion, and the worker can begin to think through with community members the kinds of things that might make life a bit easier with respect to these particular recognized problems.

However, problem recognition does not necessarily imply problem definition, and as intervention develops, increasing effort will need to be spent on problem recognition. For example, the fact that "Nobody around here knows anyone very much" is a statement of a result condition, but the contributing factors to that condition are unclear. It could be an area of high geographic mobility, or it could be an area of multicultural or multiethnic nature, and individuals from the subethnic groups are hesitant to cross ethnic or perhaps racial boundaries. It could be that the work schedules of individuals involved in a local community are staggered, and hence only a few people may be available at any particular time. Problem definition seeks to focus and identify the causes of particular community problems.

Information gathering seeks to put factual information together based on the problem definition. Sometimes these facts do not bear out the causal assumptions implicit in the problem definition, and it needs to be changed. Other times it provides firm and rich evidence to support community beliefs.

Problems of capability and competence are also involved. For example, the community change worker may be told, "The city is messing with us," or "The landlords aren't painting and fixing up their buildings, and are gouging people." Such problems suggest community action activities. Or members of the community might complain that there is a lack of coordination among the agencies and services offered to the community, and more work needs to be done here. Such a problem could suggest difficulties in community competence.

As a practical matter, workers may start at any point in the recognition, definition, and needs assessment area. Sometimes needs assessment is done first in order to provide the basis for problem recognition. At other times, some community members will assert that they have "recognized" a particular problem (just as someone might say to a doctor, "I have disease X"). A worker may withhold judgment on this diagnosis until the views of others have been explored and until needs assessment has been completed. However, even if the initial definition is wrong, it still provides the basis for working with and connecting with community members and can become a jumping off place for other efforts.

Needs assessments can range from very simple to very complicated activities. At the simplest level, the worker may assemble information drawn from informal discussions with community members and test out the overall conclusions from these discussions in community meetings. Often, though, more detailed and factual needs assessments are needed. In such cases, the worker might use published statistics about crime, infant mortality, and unemployment in the neighborhood, or about the behavior pattern of landlords, the number of rat bites, and so on, to provide a set of specific and empirical bases for community discussion.

At a still more complicated level, the worker may link up with local university researchers or others to approach an actual sample of the community with a detailed community questionnaire. These data may also be linked with published data based on the community in question, and they may serve to present a fairly detailed and scientific picture of community needs.

As in most areas of community development work, the needs assessment activity in the beginning phase serves a dual purpose. Part of it is to generate facts But the community change worker would make a mistake if she or he believed that was its sole purpose, and that its concerns were only technical.

The development of community information is an excellent opportunity to involve community members in activities that concern the community. Hence, efforts should always be made to bring in local community members as part of the needs assessment process.

In the more simple version, not only the worker must talk with community members, but other community members should do so as well, volunteering their time to fill out the information picture by interviewing their neighbors and friends. As community statistics are needed from city and other commercial sources, volunteer community members can share in the development of these statistics.

If the project becomes extremely technical and requires university and other professionals, community members can serve in an advisory capacity and can be trained as interviewers to follow the specific scientific needs of the particular survey. But the community change worker is always sensitive to the process needs of any activity as well as the task needs. Many needs assessment efforts have gone awry because they have been technically wonderful, but since they were done by people outside the community and involved no one in the community, their impact was very limited; sometimes they have even generated hostility, thus becoming counterproductive.[25]

THE MIDDLE PHASE

In the middle phase of community change work, emphasis is placed on goal selection, prioritization, and goal achievement. Toward the end of the beginning phase and at the beginning of the middle phase, a number of possible action steps will have been suggested by various members of the community. This moment is now the one for goal selection. In some instances, goal selection will have already occurred. Frequently, the very process of discussion of goal alternatives results in an almost automatic way in the clear selection or desirability of one particular goal over others.

On the other hand, there may well be competing interests and competing perspectives with regard to which goal should be selected. The worker needs to continue a process of interaction and encouragement with community members around the process of selecting a goal and prioritizing the efforts needed to get to that goal. For some communities, the goal of goal selection itself represents the achievement of a major process goal.[26]

Some communities are unable to crystallize their efforts around any particular goal, leaving their effort forever diffuse. (Social workers will recognize that individuals have this same problem. In individual work with a particular affected client, we may seek to help the individual outline possible alternatives, specify the consequences, and work through the problems of picking one for initial focus.)

In the process of goal selection and review, the worker will attend a large number of community meetings. Some of these meetings are with large groups of community members, some of them may be on specific blocks, and some of them are with an individual community leader or a small group of community leaders. In all cases, the issues involved are considered, the feelings and perspectives of the group are brought out, and as many community members as possible are involved in the review process.[27]

At times the worker should become involved with community leaders to set up a community decision instrument. It is frequently unclear what person or what group should make a decision for the community. Sometimes it is possible to get everyone together in a sort of "old New England town meeting." At other times, coalitions of existing community groups and agencies need to be assembled. The process of community decision making is often vague not only with respect to who should be involved, but with respect to the mechanism by which in the final analysis the decision is made.[28]

As a community moves toward a decision, the worker plays both an encouraging and supporting role, helping a decision to occur, but also raising questions and concerns about particular courses of action to be sure that all implications have been taken into consideration. For example, a community may quickly select a particular landlord to pressure for repairs on his buildings. The worker may diplomatically raise with the community decision makers the fact that the landlord lives in another state, and putting pressure on that particular landlord as a first step may be problematic. "Perhaps," the worker may suggest, "selection of a couple of local landlords as a first step might make more sense." The worker would never attempt to force her or his views on the community. But community change workers, like all social workers, must continually work with clients and client systems to help them understand the impact of the particular actions they are contemplating.

At this discussion stage, too, the worker raises questions about the particular specific steps that will be needed to move toward implementation. If a paint-up, fix-up campaign is to be undertaken, is there to be a community committee in overall charge of it, and, if so, who will be on that committee and what kinds of resources will they need? If resources are needed, how will these resources be procured? The worker always stands ready to assist the community in carrying out goals decided on by the community, but also takes care not to become a fallback decision maker ("Well," said a community member, "why don't you tell us what we should do?") or become overinvolved with respect to goal operationalization in lieu of the volunteer efforts of community members. The community change worker must always remember that the community's goal is being discussed, and therefore community members must take primary responsibility in carrying it out.

THE ENDING PHASE

The ending phase contains two subparts: (1) operation, and (2) termination, evaluation, and recycle.

Operation involves the implementation of the actual activities decided on in goal selection. If a community planning effort is to be undertaken, then it is here that the technical aspects of community planning occur (the whole process of goal development and selection is a part of community planning as well). The worker assists the community in the actual carrying out of the plan and may even become part of, for example, a paint-up, fix-up day, a needs assessment, and so on, provided that the worker does not become the implementor in lieu of community involvement. The change activity worker joins with but does not replace community effort.

Achieving the point of program or goal implementation always represents a high point for the community and to a certain extent for the worker and is frequently the result of months or even years of community change effort. The actual and successful completion of a particular community change process is gratifying to everyone. However, gratification in itself presents a problem since the process is not really over. During the operations phase, the worker makes suggestions about ways in which the particular change effort might be evaluated and asks about ways the momentum and enthusiasm developed by a particular project can be later turned to other goals and other projects, perhaps some of those on a goal priority list. Obviously, a client system focusing on a particular goal is not going to be very interested in issues of evaluation. Still, it is the worker's professional responsibility to initiate beginning concerns about these next steps, just as a physician who, in working with a patient, not only pays attention to the critical phase of an illness, but also talks with the patient about other issues, such as nutrition and life-style, that deal with next steps after the critical phase has been successfully completed.

Evaluations may range from simple debriefings of those involved in a particular meeting or change effort to reasonably complex numerical and statistical presentations about impact, percent of change, and so on. The reason it is important for the worker to initiate thinking about these issues during the implementation stage is that certain activities of an evaluation sort need to go on simultaneously with implementation. Although evaluation occurs after implementation, we should begin thinking about the evaluation design early in the interaction process.

The working through of an evaluation phase or process is a good way to initiate recycling. Recycling focuses on channeling the energy developed by one successful community intervention to the next community interventions that are needed. All too frequently, the feelings and community energy generated by such an intervention dissipate, and the worker needs to begin all over again.

It is at this point too that termination sometimes occurs. Community change workers are in short supply; community needs are high. Such workers cannot spend all their time with one particular community. It is hoped, as with an individual or organizational client, that once a successful cycle has been completed the community will be able, using its own leadership now developed, to continue the kinds of things that they have just been through. Frequently, workers will discuss with community members the worker's need to move to other communities where needs are present. Termination will frequently depend on factors other than the specific cycle. For example, worker funding frequently plays an important role. If the worker is a student, school year may also exert its own influence. But whenever termination occurs, the worker seeks to engage with the client system, and works to help that system set up mechanisms for its own continued involvement and development.

Conclusion

Community change involves enhancing, developing, and strengthening the commonly held bonds that people have with each other. So much that is possible through community effort is not possible by individual effort alone. So much of what happens to individuals depends on the community in which they live and the strength and vigor of that community. Yet it also true that individuals not infrequently fail to recognize the common unity that they share; or, if they recognize it, they fail to act on it or fail to act effectively and efficiently. Community change workers help in all these areas. Community development helps people understand the commonness that we all share. Community action seeks to enable individual communities to take specific steps to advance their own interests. Community planning seeks to regularize and institutionalize community influence efforts involving longer-range goals and a broader representation of community participants. In all these efforts, the community change worker plays a vital role.

Notes

1. Charles D. Garvin and F. M. Cox, "A History of Community Organizing Since the Civil War with Special Reference to Oppressed Communities," in F. M. Cox and others, eds., *Strategies of Community Organization*, 4th ed. (Itasca, Ill.: F. E. Peacock, 1987), pp. 26–63. Influential books included M. G. Ross, *Community Organization* (New York: Harper Bros., 1955); M. G. Ross, *Case Histories in Community Organization* (New York: Harper Bros., 1958); and R. Lippitt, H. J. Watson, and B. Westley, *The Dynamics of Planned Change* (New York: Harcourt, Brace, World, 1958).

2. M. Schwartz, "Community Organization" in H. L. Lurie, ed. *Encyclopedia of Social Work,* 17th ed. (New York: National Association of Social Workers, 1965).

3. J. Bernard, "Community Disorganization" in D. L. Sills, ed., *International Encyclopedia of the Social Sciences,* Vol. 3, (New York: The Free Press, 1968), pp. 163–169. See also Harold L. Wilensky and C. Lebeaux, *Industrial Society and Social Welfare* (New York: Russell Sage, 1958).

4. For a current discussion of community, see C. H. Reynolds and R. V. Norman, eds., *Community in America* (Berkeley: University of California Press, 1987).

5. For elaboration of this idea, see E. Burke, "The Search for Authority in Planning," *Social Service Review,* 39, 4, (September, 1965) pp. 261–270.

6. For further discussion, see J. Rothman, "Community Theory and Research," in A. Minahan, ed., *Encyclopedia of Social Work,* 18th ed. (Silver Spring, Md.: National Association of Social Workers, 1987), pp. 308–315; and H. R. Johnson and J. E. Tropman, "The Settings of Community Organization Practice," in F. M. Cox and others, eds., *Strategies of Community Organization* (Itasca, Ill.: F. E. Peacock, 1979), pp. 213–223.

7. While the term "community" is not typically applied to the work setting, there is a lot of discussion about "corporate culture." See S. M. David, *Managing Corporate Culture* (Cambridge, Mass.: Ballinger Publishing Co., 1984).

8. For a different approach, see Jack Rothman with John E. Tropman, "Models of Community Organization and Macro Perspectives: Their Mixing and Phasing," in F. M. Cox and others, eds., *Strategies of Community Organization,* 4th ed. (Itasca, Ill.: F. E. Peacock, 1987), pp. 3–26.

9. For more detail, see I. A. Spergel, "Community Development," in A. Minahan ed., *Encyclopedia of Social Work* Vol. 1, 18th ed. (Silver Spring, Md.: National Association of Social Workers, 1987), pp. 299–308. See also the section on "locality development" in F. M. Cox and others, eds., *Strategies of Community Organization,* 4th ed. (Itasca, Ill.: F. E. Peacock, 1987).

10. C. Black, *It Will Never Happen to Me* (New York: Ballantine Books, 1981).

11. For more information, refer to S. Burghardt, "Community Based Social Action," in A. Minahan, ed., *Encyclopedia of Social Work,* Vol. 1, 18th ed. (Silver Spring, Md.: National Association of Social Workers, 1987). See also the section on social action in F. M. Cox eds., *Strategies of Community Organization,* 4th ed. (Itasca, Ill.: F. E. Peacock, 1987).

12. R. B. Hudson and J. Strate, "Aging and Political Systems" in R. H. Binstock and E. Shanas, *Handbook of Aging and Social Services,* 2nd ed. (New York: Van Nostrand Rinehold, 1985), p. 554ff.

13. In some states, on Senior Day at the state capitol, the elderly and their supporters make their concerns known to the state legislature.

14. See Saul D. Alinsky, *Reveille for Radicals* (Chicago: University of Chicago Press, 1946), and *Rules for Radicals* (New York: Random House, 1971).

15. For more detail, see Robert M. Moroney, "Social Planning and Community Organization," in A. Minahan, ed., *Encyclopedia of Social Work,* Vol. 2, 18th ed. (Silver Spring, Md.: National Association of Social Workers, 1987); A. Lauffer, *Social Planning at the Community Level* (Englewood Cliffs, N.J.: Prentice Hall, 1977); see the section on social planning in F. M. Cox and others, eds., *Strategies of Community Organization,* 4th ed. (Itasca, Ill.: F. E. Peacock, 1987).

16. But of course there are "political" elements as well. See R. D. Vinter and John E. Tropman, "The Causes and Consequences of Community Studies," in F. M. Cox and others, eds., *Strategies of Community Organization,* 1st ed. (Itasca, Ill.: F. E. Peacock, 1971), pp. 315–322.

17. For further discussion, E. J. Tropman, "Staffing Committees and Studies," in F. M. Cox and others, eds., *Tactics and Techniques of Community Practice,* 1st ed. (Itasca, Ill.: F. E. Peacock, 1977), pp. 105–111.

18. For example, see United Way of America, "What Lies Ahead?" (Alexandria, Va.: United Way of America, 1989).

19. For a range of specific skills, see F. M. Cox and others, eds., *Strategies of Community*

Organization, and F. M. Cox and others, eds., *Tactics and Techniques of Community Practice,* 2nd ed. (Itasca, Ill.: F. E. Peacock, 1984).

20. A good example of the renewal and reorganization process in a worldwide community is Vatican II. For renewal in a local Catholic community, see D. Crumm and W. K. Knecht, "Parishes Go on the Line: Catholics Await Fate of Churches," *Detroit Free Press,* September 25, 1988, p. 10.

21. See the section on locality development in F. M. Cox and others, *Strategies of Community Organization* (Itasca, Ill.: F. E. Peacock, 1987).

22. W. Bennis and B. Nanus, *Leaders* (New York: Harper & Row, 1985). See also the section on administrative leadership and management in F. M. Cox eds., *Tactics and Techniques of Community Practice* (Itasca, Ill.: F. E. Peacock, 1984).

23. See Jack Rothman and John E. Tropman, "Models of Community Organization and Macro Practice: Their Mixing and Phasing," in F. M. Cox and others, eds., *Strategies of Community Organization,* 4th ed. (Itasca, Ill.: F. E. Peacock, 1987), pp. 3-26.

24. F. M. Cox, and others, eds., *Tactics and Techniques of Community Practice.*

25. Ibid.

26. Ibid.

27. For a discussion of different kinds of meetings, see John Tropman, Harold Johnson, and Elmer Tropman, *The Essentials of Committee Management* (Chicago: Nelson-Hall, 1979).

28. Different bases or decision rules may compete as well. One approach—the one person, one vote rule—assumes everyone's interest is the same. Another approach is to give more weight to those who are most affected..

CHAPTER 9
Helping Societies to Change

Introduction

What does it mean to help societies to change? The task is certainly a tall order for any social worker. Several areas come readily to mind, though. The first is any analysis or intervention that has national scope and impact, a result that is not limited to a particular person, group, organization, or community.[1] Events of this type are relatively rare and are often associated with well-known leaders: the civil rights movement, the feminist movement, auto safety developments, and ecology are some examples.[2] Social workers have been involved heavily in all these movements. Working toward world peace and disarmament is another example of a change effort of national, and indeed international, scope and impact that has involved social workers.

The popular and well-known national change efforts just mentioned, however, are not the only ones in which social workers engage in what could be called societal change. A second type of such change would include any effort that the worker undertakes that focuses on or links to the national government. Workers assigned to national agencies represent one example. Social workers who assist the legislative arm of our national government are another. Some social workers even run for elective office and serve in a national capacity. The National Association of Social Workers has a group within it that seeks to influence national elections and national legislation. All these involve societal change. Thus, societal change workers can be in government or outside, working for private auspices, but they share a common wish to influence the course of national life.

Within the United States, there is a third arena where national (or seminational) societal change efforts can occur. Societal change workers who work on behalf of specific groups that crosscut a wide variety of local, organizational, and communal boundaries would qualify. For example, individuals who are interested in developing beneficial social policy for the elderly would be involved in societal change. In the United States in the 1990s, there are approximately as many elderly as the population of Canada; hence, on the basis of scope and extensiveness, working for this particular subgroup would indeed qualify.[3] Jane Addams won a Nobel Prize working for peace. Similarly, working on behalf of the African-American community (there are also about as many blacks as there are either older Americans or Canadians) has national impact, not only because of the importance of these groups to the national purpose, but also because of their size and impact.[4] Work on behalf of the nation's children is another example.

A fourth area for societal change workers is at the state level. Here, scope is somewhat reduced, but still very substantial. But state level social change efforts always have the potential to become national models. And many states are as large as other countries.

A fifth area of societal change is aimed at the large, formal, national and multinational, organizations—which have great influence if they take certain actions or espouse certain policies. Convincing General Motors, or Ford, or IBM to undertake a certain policy direction helpful to social justice (disinvesting in South Africa, for example) or a policy that enhances workers' life quality (supporting an employee assistance program, for example) can have society-wide results.

Finally, societal change social workers may seek to change public opinion at large, which in turn may spark a change in policy. In the cases already mentioned, the goal of the societal change worker was to influence, directly, some group, policy, or practice. While change in behavior almost always goes on, workers, at the same time, may try to influence the beliefs, attitudes, and values of a populace. Workers use public relation campaigns, posters, advertisements in the media, and articles in newspapers. But opinion, values, and beliefs are never completely independent. Changing one usually creates pressure for change in another. In spite of this interrelationship, there are two targets, and societal change workers may aim at one, or the other, or both.

The two general goals that societal change social workers pursue are repair and enhancement. Perhaps most important is that societal change workers seek to repair by removing or changing oppressive ideas and values, policies, practices, and conditions. Societal change workers, for example, may seek to reduce or end discrimination. Discrimination exists in many forms, informally sanctioned if not legally permissible. Institutional racism and sexism are good targets.

On the more proactive end, societal change workers seek to improve and enhance the care and consideration that a society gives to its members. Improving the environment, working for peace, and improving educational opportunity are all examples.

The popular and well-known examples of societal change mentioned before have a particular feature that differentiates them from social change. *Societal* change, as the term is used here, is a kind of social change uniquely identified as *the product of individual and collective change efforts*. The civil rights movement has well-known leaders, but many less-well-known individuals worked for that particular goal. The same can be said for the feminist movement, auto safety, ecology, and world peace. It is true that societies are always changing, but they are not always changing as a result of concerted, focused change efforts, organized and targeted to achieve specific change goals. Often, change occurs because the society itself is developing new patterns and new norms.[5] Societal change workers aim their efforts at developing the individuals' and groups' interest in societal change, orchestrating groups already aiming at change in a certain area, and seeking to take advantage of change processes already going on. Although changing whole societies may seem to be a difficult task, there are examples of important successes. Indeed, success has occurred in each of the areas mentioned already. Certainly, those involved in each area would point to tremendous needs yet to be met. Nonetheless, the presence of future goals does not eliminate past triumphs.

Societal change workers focus on broad targets: changing policy, changing practice, and changing values and beliefs. Policies are a set of formal laws and rules, passed by law and rule-making bodies, that direct our life on a daily basis. Changes in policies can result in increased grants for the poor and elderly. Changes in policies can prohibit discrimination in public places. Changes in policies can require equal pay for the equal work of men and women. Sometimes benefits flow directly from changes in policy, and sometimes changes in policies only form a context within which other groups need to take affirmative and implementing action. Nonetheless, societal change workers understand that policy change is an important target and component of societal change.

Alternately, societal change workers also seek to improve the actual practice of particular societies. Often in spite of changes in policy, actual practice continues to be oppressive, discriminatory, and otherwise problematic. For example, in spite of laws governing pollution, illegal pollution continues. Despite the availability of resources for the clean-up of toxic waste, these resources have yet to be fully applied. Despite laws prohibiting discrimination, it continues. Constant work is required on the part of societal change agents to uncover and expose incidents of societal malpractice.

Societal change workers also understand that policy and practice are mutually influential and supportive. Sometimes practice can be changed by changing policy, but sometimes without a change in practice, policy change is not possible. Hence, change in policy and practice represents a continually interactive field in which laws and regulations are sometimes the target and actual practices follow; at other times, practices are the target, and laws and regulations follow.

The legislative, judicial, and executive branches of most governments within our government framework provide three locations for policy change. There is also the civil service core at each level of government, as well as hundreds of legal districts, school districts, sewer districts, and so on, that can be targets for change.

The legislative branch makes changes in the specific laws, rules, and ordinances that govern our lives. If these actions present unsatisfactory resolutions of current problems, societal change workers may turn to the judicial branch and initiate legal proceedings in courts of law at the local, state, and national levels, seeking to overrule or change legislation. If legal rulings are oppressive, the legislatures may again become the target. The executive department and executive rulings and administrative regulations also provide a locus for change. After having been passed, laws are then developed and implemented in detail by the executive branch. These administrative regulations can be favorable or unfavorable to societal change goals. Societal change workers will not be satisfied with simply the passage of a law, but will follow through its implementation to see that the actual intent of the passed law is carried out in practice.

Changes in laws or practices are often the public manifestations of societal change. Societal change workers, however, also seek to prepare a belief and attitude system within society to be ready for such change. Often the social work of coalition building, establishing networks, developing data bases, and engaging in various kinds of public relations and societal information activities set the stage for societal change and become an important component of it. Jane Addams not only provided national leadership in community work through her development of Hull House, but became an advocate for peace. Harry Hopkins, a social worker from the Roosevelt administration, was very influential in the development of the New Deal programs, and later, during World War II, became an important aide and assistant to President Roosevelt. These are two well-known examples that stand for thousands of other societal change workers who play national roles on a national stage, helping to improve our society for all its members. Currently, Congressman Ronald Dellums, a Democrat from California, is a social worker playing an important role in the national government.

Changes in beliefs, values, and attitudes are harder to document and measure than a specific change in a policy or procedure. And it is also true that, in spite of changes in values and beliefs, action and behavior sometimes lag behind.[6] For example, health consciousness and concern (values and beliefs) appear to be higher in the United

States of the 1990s than is reflected by health laws, such as not completely banning smoking.

On the other hand, changes in values may be slower than changes in what people are actually doing. Our attitudes about sexuality, as a case in point, may be more conservative than actual practice, and this lag may prevent needed public and open discussion about sexual matters.

Societal change workers stimulate and generate individual and collective interest in social change and orchestrate and focus the many change efforts already going on in a particular area. For example, social workers might call for and organize a national conference on homelessness to help all those interested in and working in this area to meet each other and focus their several efforts. These considerations can be summarized in the target box shown in Figure 9.1.

One half of the box, the values and beliefs portion, contains soft goals that societal change social workers may pursue. These goals do not have the specific, measurable results that are often desirable. Yet they represent an important component for social work intervention, because support in the values and beliefs realm is essential for the overall success of changes in policy and practice, the hard goals displayed in the bottom of the target box.

Two Major Approaches

Two basic approaches characterize the societal change area.[7] Policy management and analysis are one and political action the other. These strategies can be used at all macro levels (organizational, communal, as well as societal), but there is even some use of them at the micro level. Certainly, political activities are characteristic of some families and groups, and there is a certain amount of policy analysis that goes on in the family and group as well.[8] For example, the preparation of a will could be considered a personal policy document based on an analysis of one's income and expressing a set of desires for its distribution. Policy analysis and management stresses the conceptual, the idea aspect of societal change work. Without new ideas about what might be done and without thoughtful consideration of the problems and potentials of previous policy, little societal change can result.

However, emphasis on the idea is one thing. Implementation of the idea, putting new approaches into practice, is quite another. Others need to be convinced and involved, because new policies may not appeal to them. Sometimes societal change workers need to create strategies that politically defeat opponents of societal change. Political action involves the skills and strategies of mobilizing support for social change, supporting proponents of desirable new policies, and seeking to defeat those who oppose them.

POLICY INITIATION, ANALYSIS, AND MANAGEMENT

Policy initiation, analysis, and management emphasize the development of policy ideas, the research needed to demonstrate their validity, and the detailed follow-through needed to see them to implementation.[9] Idea generation, the synthesis of several

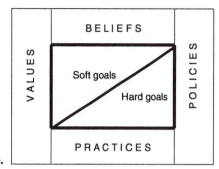

Figure 9.1. A target box for societal change.

different types of ideas, and their introduction into the ongoing political dialogue is a first step. Sometimes the ideas are old, such as "all men are created equal," but need fresh application, such as "all men and women are created equal," or "all men and women are created equal, but our actual practice does not reflect this historic commitment to equality." Refurbishing, reinventing and rearguing historic ideas are as important as introducing new ones. At other times, the ideas may be relatively new, such as ecological integrity and the ideas that sponsored child labor laws.

Societal change workers contribute to societal change by developing and bringing together ideas. These may be either their own, stemming from personal commitments and beliefs, or they may involve the ideas of others. Usually, policy ideas are a combination of the personal and the social. Whichever route is followed, ideas represent an important component of the policy process.

Policy analysis, however, is more than just thinking up or synthesizing new ideas. It involves the detailed research and analysis that can provide support for particular points of view.[10] For example, it is not enough to simply assert that there is gender inequality, even though everyone may know that this is generally true. The policy analyst will need to provide hard evidence and examples through the use of national statistics on jobs, income, and so on, of the extent, nature, and impact of gender discrimination. It is not enough to say that children are being abused, even though this may be publicly accepted as true. Specific facts and figures about where abuse is occurring, by whom, and to whom are needed. Numbers, trends, locations, and demographic outlines serve to buttress the point.[11] It is not enough to say that toxic dumping continues in violation of federal laws and regulations; specific laws and regulations must be cited, and specific incidents of waste disposal that violate these laws and regulations must be provided. In policy analysis, this process is called "doing one's homework," and it involves nailing down with facts and figures the assertions made, the ideas offered, or the policies proposed.

Sometimes other kinds of research work are required. For example, detailed studies of the impact of particular proposals on sectors of society are needed. One study reviews a wide range of proposed legislation with an eye toward the effect that particular legislation may have on family life.[12] Environmental impact groups study the impact of particular legislation on the environment. Legislators are not always aware of the effects that particular legislation might have in these and other areas; therefore, societal change workers not only should propose and support, but monitor, again with facts and figures, what might happen as a result of a particular policy change.

The policy management aspect of societal change refers to the ongoing attention needed to move ideas through the policy process. Simply suggesting an idea for a new law or social invention is not enough. Ideas for new programs and services require follow-up and follow-through. Ideas do not implement themselves.

Societal change workers do not perform these tasks alone; indeed, they cannot perform them alone. As in the case of community workers, they are constantly working with and through representatives to achieve societal change. Frequently, the instrument of change is a national organization. A national organization can be a permanent body, such as the National Association of Social Workers, or it can be more temporary, like a presidential commission or a legislative commission involved in exploring a particular area. Workers with the national organizations have a chance to facilitate the interaction of individuals from all over the country at periodic national meetings, conferences, and conclaves. The national organizations also monitor areas of specific interest: legislation, executive activity, and judicial activity. Because of the vast amount of national action going on at any one time, specific areas of interest must be followed by organizations that are especially committed to, for example, civil rights, ecological action, gender equity, the interests of the elderly, or the interests of children. Hence, policy change workers often read various reports put together by professionals who follow the legislative, executive, and judicial branches in their many activities and report on actions in specific areas of interest at national and state levels.

POLITICAL ACTION

Political action involves getting the support of national influentials and local influentials for substantive areas where societal change is needed. Just having ideas about ecological action or gender equity is not sufficient, nor is it sufficient to simply follow through on the ideas as they proceed through the policy process. In addition, coalitions of support must be built, involving individuals on a representative basis from around the entire country.[13]

This process often involves marketing and selling ideas and convincing individuals about the validity of new approaches and techniques, new laws and rules. It involves bringing individuals together at national meetings and network development and coalition establishment, which depend heavily on interactive, interpersonal elements. The development of national coalitions and networks can in turn lend support to particular political candidates or bureaucratic and judicial appointments that will favor the interests advocated by the national coalition. In addition, national networks and coalitions can bring pressure to bear on officials already in office, and call to their attention the information developed by policy analysts.

Network and coalition building require the involvement of citizens in causes that affect them and are of interest to them. Several aspects of political action might be involved. Public education is one such aspect. Often individuals are not aware of how current practices and policies or values and beliefs affect them. Political action, often involving societal change workers, can bring these effects to the attention of the populace. For example, the fact that the public schools are falling short of their

"The people shall judge." (Photo by Jack Kightlinger, The White House)

educational task may not be seen as having wide impact. Through media and public education campaigns, the message can be conveyed that such problems not only represent difficulties for the individuals involved but affect the working world through the undereducation of the work force as a whole. Similar campaigns have been run with respect to ecological awareness, AIDS education, and racial and gender inequality.

Public demonstrations are another technique of societal change workers. They are designed to dramatize key problems or issues, involve citizens in doing something proactive about the problem, and publicize both the issue and the degree of public interest.

Issue conferences are a third way that the societal change worker goes about her or his work. Often, these forums are locations where political candidates appear and discuss their views with each other and the general public.

Other techniques are used as well. These are but a few. The key point is to mobilize the commitments and interests of citizens around issues and bring that support to bear in the political system.

THE NATIONAL COMMUNITY

It is possible and appropriate under certain conditions to regard the nation as a community. In that event, helping societies to change is the same as helping communities to change. The same techniques discussed in terms of community change—development, action, and planning—can be used at the national community level. Specific communities, such as the national community of the elderly or national minority communities, may require development, social action, and planning, both within the community and as a way to link that community to others. Although we tend to think of communities as small, that is not necessarily the case, and particularly community change but also organizational change techniques may be used here, too.

The reverse is also true. Political action and policy analysis are usually associated with the societal level, but they are in fact used across the board, in communities and organizations as well as at the societal level.

INTERACTION OF APPROACHES

Each method of societal change, policy analysis and political action, interacts with the other. Political action techniques help policy analysis, and vice versa. Separating the two works better in theory than in practice. The societal change worker is continually sensitive to the political needs involved in information gathering and the policy requirements of political action.

Sometimes societal change workers need to perform both functions. In smaller organizations and groups, such a combination of roles is more likely to occur. On the other hand, in the more sizable national organizations, role specificity is more likely to be the norm.

All workers should be familiar with both approaches. Some will like both and feel comfortable using either, depending on what is required. Others, will prefer one. In those cases, a societal change worker may want to team up with another worker who has the opposite preference. Thus, all bases will be covered.

Two Major Elements in Societal Change: Intellectual and Interpersonal

As in the community change skill area, intellectual and interpersonal skills continue to be important and distinctive. Intellectual skills involve knowledge of the subject matter area in question (racism, ecology, world peace, and so on) and the ability to synthesize ideas and concepts. In addition, analytic capacities are part of intellectual skills, involving applied research, knowledge-generating skills, and presentation skills. In general, the intellectual elements involve working with ideas as a central motif.

Interpersonal skills involve working with people. While policy analysis might be more idea oriented, political action might be more people oriented. One needs the capacity to arouse and inspirit for political action, to generate enthusiasm, to create a sense of the possible. Social problems have been around a long time, and it would be easy for citizens to take a blasé attitude toward yet another new or revised approach to an issue. The societal change worker must have the skill to orchestrate and blend interested volunteers so that a fresh sense of excitement and commitment is generated. Furthermore, societal change, like all change, is a frustrating task, with many roadblocks and much opposition. Societal change workers need to have the internal motivation to continue so that they can help themselves and other workers avoid discouragement and provide support for volunteers.

Societal Features and Problems

Societal change workers trained in social work focus their interest in repair and enhancement on three general types of societal problems or issues. The first of these is promoting social justice. The second is facilitating social environments. And the third is expanding social opportunity. These societal problems, or issue areas, have the broadest possible relevance to all citizens. It may be that a particular oppressed group, for example, those suffering from gender inequity, is a subgroup of the society. However, the problems of inequity are societal problems that affect the beneficiaries as well as the victims of inequity. Slavery was corrosive for owner and slave alike. While societal change workers may labor in other areas, these three represent the largest areas of interest.

PROMOTING SOCIAL JUSTICE

Historically, the commitments of social work involve concerns with reducing social injustice and promoting social justice. Social justice involves the establishment and maintenance of social rights, which occur naturally to a person as a human being and which in some instances are guaranteed by our political system. The fact that individuals as humans are entitled to humane treatment by society's institutions is a principle everywhere agreed on and everywhere violated. Individuals are treated unjustly when they are treated inhumanely. However, humane treatment derivable from the phrase "all men are created equal" is a general injunction. The details of what such treatment would be are not always spelled out. Thus, societal change social workers may work to specify and nail down these implications, as in the proposed Equal Rights Amendment to the Constitution.

Societal change workers also labor to put an end to social exploitation.[14] Social exploitation occurs when members of society are, through personal pressure or societal pressure, forced to give up their labor for free or cheaply. The payment of women at wages below standard market rates for men doing equal work is a form of social exploitation, as is true for any group that does not receive market value for market contribution. Child labor represented a form of social exploitation. Discrimination and other forms of oppression are also exploitative in nature. Because of their historic interest in these areas and concern with the disadvantaged, societal change social workers seek not only to help the individually oppressed, but to change the policies and practices that both reflect and stimulate this oppression.

FACILITATING SOCIAL ENVIRONMENTS

Societal change social workers seek to develop facilitating social environments. Certain features of our society retard the individual's potential and limit the possibilities for achievement. Three examples will prove illustrative.

The first is nuclear war and waste. The threat of nuclear war as a Draconian solution to intercountry conflict hangs heavy over the head of all citizens in the world, regardless of race, creed, color, age, or location. It is clear that no one would be free of the devastating effects of nuclear exchange. Even areas that were not damaged by the immediate or secondary effects of an atomic attack would be devastated by the later effects of nuclear winter. Societal change workers, following in the path of Jane Addams, argue that development under such fearful conditions is stunted. Attempts to develop peaceful means of resolving international conflicts can only be for the benefit of everyone.

Nuclear waste and other pollution destroys our physical and social environments and cries out for imaginative and innovative solutions. Some of these solutions will be very technical and scientific, but without interest and support for the research and technological development required to come up with the scientific solutions, the problems of nuclear waste will continue to besmirch our developmental possibilities.

Issues of national productivity may also concern societal change workers because of the recognition that it is much easier to create adequate environments based on shares of an expanding pie than shares of a stable or constricting one. Issues of resource allocation will always be among the most hard-fought political issues in any society. Economic growth can mitigate the seriousness of this conflict and provide resources from the increased portion of national productivity that might otherwise never be garnered if they had to be taken away from those already in possession of them. This is not to say that the current distribution of resources should in any way be supported, but political reality also says that individuals do not willingly reduce their share of the pie. Thus, while working for redistribution on the one hand, societal change workers may also consider strategies of increasing growth and increasing the resource base from which they can perhaps more easily produce the needed resources for the disadvantaged.

A third example is prejudice and discrimination. A social environment that devalues and demeans is one that must necessarily stunt the development of the citizens.

The natural and social environments provide the social context for individual development, family health and well-being, and community prosperity. In a society characterized by oppression and the threat of war, development is truncated and skewed. Societal change workers seek to improve these contexts.

EXPANDING SOCIAL OPPORTUNITY

United States society is based on ideas of equality, and in particular equality of opportunity. Yet we are painfully aware of how equality of opportunity cannot exist if people are hungry, if people cannot read, if jobs do not exist. Therefore, societal change workers endeavor to improve those areas where equality of opportunity is limited. A key example is literacy. Especially as we move into the information society, with complex technology requiring mastery, literacy becomes an absolute essential. More, not less, school appears to be required. Yet groups who do not have access to schools or who attend school in a nonsupportive context, are experiencing a disadvantage of lifelong implications. Societal change workers may focus on this problem and propose programs of remediation for adult illiteracy and programs of support and encouragement for children who are currently in school but not performing well.

Another area that may require national attention is adolescent pregnancy. As young women in their teens become mothers, their own development becomes, in many instances, sharply curtailed. As they turn their attention to child care, they become less able to pursue their own development (but are less likely to have the economic, social, and other resources necessary for parenting). Through the efforts of societal and community change social workers, local school systems now have classes for pregnant high school students and some have nurseries so that the young women can continue to go to school. But more of these programs are needed, and more educational programs about the impact of teenage pregnancy on the mother are needed. And the impact of teenage pregnancy on and the responsibilities of the teenage father are only now coming to be discussed. It is exploitative for one partner to be left with the complete responsibility of a child that two created. Societal change workers are now beginning to explore the rights and responsibilities of teenage fathers. But this area of investigation lags behind that already underway for the teenage mother. Additional effort is required in both areas, which are key areas for societal change workers. Societal change workers must be continually interested in removing barriers and enhancing the opportunities available to individual citizens.

The Phases of Helping

The phases of helping have a three-step structure: a beginning, middle, and end. In the beginning phase, needs assessment is again the characteristic method, which may be approached with the policy management method or the methods of political action.

In the second, middle phase, building coalitions and networks, developing options, and managing the decision point are crucial elements. The ending phase consists, again, of implementation and evaluation. As a final portion of the ending phase, a fresh look at needs assessment is completed.

THE BEGINNING PHASE

The beginning phase involves assessment. Assessment focuses on what the problem is, what people think the problem is, how the problem might be defined, and what different definitions of the problem might imply. This phase is extremely crucial, because decisions made here about the problem definition may cause entirely different paths of analysis and action to be taken. If, for example, we define the problem of juvenile delinquency as a lack of work for youth, then options and policy changes in the area of work program development would likely follow. If, on the other hand, we decide that a cause of juvenile delinquency is due to inadequate police protection, then proposals and programs for beefing up the police are likely to follow. Knowledge of both the social facts and political facts are crucial. Societal change workers make assessments of both policy analysis and political modes, seeking to get the fullest possible picture of how problems are seen and to understand the differences in problem definition and discussion.

ASSESSMENT IN POLICY ANALYSIS. For policy analysis and management, analysis is just a first step. It begins with a review of the current legal situation with respect to the problem in hand. Relevant laws, legislation rulings, and administrative regulations are put together as they affect the particular group, problem, or issue in question.[15] In addition, national surveys, reports, and accounts are used so that hard data with respect to the concerns under review can be presented.[16]

Sometimes elite interviews are used as well that seek to present the particular views of local, state, and national influentials on particular issues. In the process of information development around particular policy concerns, national advisory committees are often formed with an eye toward both obtaining advice through the national data collection process, therefore involving national experts in these areas, and also trying to develop support.[17]

This approach is a perfect example of the interpenetration of intellectual and interpersonal techniques. Thus, individuals of influence who are both knowledgeable about or affected by a particular problem in question may well become members of a national advisory group on a particular problem, even though they may not have specific competence in data collection and analysis. Their contribution is in another area: hands-on knowledge about the problem's impact and what might be done about it.

Frequently, the results of these kinds of activities surface in the form of a national report or national action plan issued under the aegis of a national agency legislative body, congressional committee, or presidential commission. Not infrequently, the action plan not only reflects activities that might be undertaken by the national group that issued the plan, but also challenges other groups across the country to take action in their sphere of interest or in their locale. Often, before the issuing of the final plan, national groups will visit various sections of the country and listen to and take testimony from local leaders. This task is important not only because of the specific factual information that might be otherwise missed, but also because it generates, however imperfectly, the kind of national involvement that is a necessary precursor to national action.

It is to be expected in all change processes, but perhaps especially macro change processes, that options for action contain an overlay of self-interest. Individuals who make particular suggestions for change in many instances tend to favor their own systems or points of view. For example, in dealing with illiteracy, school systems are likely to propose additional funding for themselves. While such funding may in fact be sensible and helpful, there may be other nonschool ways to deal with the problems of illiteracy that should be considered. The broad involvement of citizens and others affected (including, at the societal level, communities, states, national organizations, local organizations, and so on) allows a range of ideas to surface and, because of wide representation, different and competing ideas may surface. Frequently, this process of policy competition allows potential problems and ideas for societal change to be tested before being put into practice.

From a detailed analysis of the problem and the suggestions of those involved, the societal change social worker prepares a set of options for decision making by the worker's sponsor.[18] It is important to distinguish the concept of sponsor from the client system. The sponsor is the group, organization, or community that has undertaken to spearhead a societal change effort and that employs the societal change social worker. Often sponsors are groups of citizens who are concerned about the nature of a particular social area—problems of juvenile justice, gun control, domestic violence, and the like—and seek to organize on a national basis to have society-wide influence, through change in public opinion, national laws, and national practice. While this distinction may have use at other levels, it is particularly important at the societal level because usually an organization sponsors the specific work of the societal change worker. A worker may be employed by a national agency in environmental improvement, disarmament, age-related concerns, or many other fields. Alternatively, the societal change worker may work for the national government in some capacity. The organization that pays the salary of the worker is the sponsor and sometimes the sponsor is the client system. The client system may be the body politic, the citizenry, or large groups of individuals. (Lawyers sometimes refer to suits with this kind of goal as class action suits.) A worker involved for example, on the national staff of the NAACP (National Association for the Advancement of Colored People) has citizens of the United States as a client system in general, although there would doubtless be more specific client systems involved in specific change efforts.

In preparing options and culling and synthesizing the variety of suggestions made in the initial phase of the change process, the societal change social worker must keep the sponsor in mind. Certain policy preferences are characteristic of sponsors, and the societal change worker must bear these sponsor policy preferences in mind when presenting societal change alternatives. These points often represent crisis points for societal change workers (as for any other worker). Sometimes a worker may feel that a more radical approach is needed or one that takes a different tack from those historically approved and pursued by particular sponsors. Societal change workers have the right and the obligation to make their case within the decision-making system of the sponsor. However, the sponsor makes the final decision. Client action depends on client decision. The only exception, which runs across all social work, involves ethics, as when laws have or may be broken or illegal or inhuman acts are being contemplated. Individual social workers, for example, are obligated under law in many jurisdictions to report instances of child abuse, whether a perpetrator client wants them to be reported or not. Social workers generally have an ethical, as well as legal, responsibility to report on past illegal actions and to prevent illegal actions from occurring in the future through cooperating with appropriate authorities. At the societal level, ethical constraints are of the utmost importance. Social workers cannot be involved in questionable ethical activities on behalf of a sponsor, which can be a serious problem when it is not clear which activities are questionable. But there is ample evidence from Watergate to contemporary administrations that even in the highest offices of our land the questions of ethics are not academic, but exist in a very real way and on a day to day basis.

ASSESSMENT IN POLITICAL ACTION. In terms of political action, early assessment involves understanding the points of view of both the man and woman on the street and the relevant elites. Care is taken by the societal change social worker to differentiate between the public and private roles that individuals sometimes need to assume. Some individuals may be willing to support certain change efforts, but because of their particular political position are not able to do so publicly. Societal change social workers recognize the value of private as well as public support, and encourage support of both kinds from interested parties across the nation.

In addition, financial support is frequently sought for the national organizations, publicity efforts, and other needs of societal change efforts.[19] Foundation grants and corporate gifts sometimes make important inroads in meeting financial needs. But many donors are hesitant about becoming involved financially with change efforts. Societal change workers should seek, as far as possible, to change this perspective. However, workers should also be aware that individuals can contribute in ways other than financial. Some have resources in the form of ideas and proposals about what should be done. In this case, workers can collect a variety of perspectives; this allows the development of a range of ideas and suggestions, from which options for action can be developed.

Assessment in the realm of political action involves finding out how citizens (as opposed to experts) see their own involvement in the issue at hand and assessing their degree of willingness to participate. If no one is interested in a particular problem, then the first job of the societal change social worker is consciousness raising, rather than presenting policy initiatives. Here, as in other areas of social work, we must "start where the system is."

THE MIDDLE PHASE

In the middle phase, the societal change worker seeks to refine and focus the options and prepare for a decision. There is frequently a great deal of interaction between the worker in a number of systems, including elements of the client system or the sponsoring system, as the decision point approaches. At this point, many back room deals are frequently made. Hence, a final proposal may come before a legislative body or board and be approved unanimously. On the surface it may look as if everything has gone very smoothly. Those who know the behind the scenes picture, however, may be well aware of how tenuous the decision was at many points and how many compromises had to be reached to get a draft that was satisfactory (while perhaps not pleasing) to the various stake holders involved.

A frequent question that workers must confront here is called the half-a-loaf question. The compromises frequently required to move societal change forward may be unsatisfactory. Individuals very unwillingly give up power and privilege, and societal change efforts frequently move in this direction. Small steps are therefore more likely to be successful than larger ones. However, this perspective may be opposed by those who argue that a stand should be taken even if the results are no progress at all. (Ivan Morris has dealt with this theme in a Japanese context.)[20]

DEVELOPMENT OF COALITIONS AND NETWORKS. During the assessment phase, the societal change worker has identified individuals, other than the sponsor and/or the client, who are interested in or opposed to social change in the target area. These are the change forces and the resistance forces with which the societal change agent interested in political action must deal. Coalitions and networks are built up of these change forces. What are coalitions and networks? Network is the more general term and refers to a loose system of individuals and organizations that have common themes of interest and mutual obligation. From any individual member's point of view, a network represents those individuals with whom one has ongoing relationships, to whom one provides assistance, and from whom one receives assistance, pretty much on an as-needed basis. Organizations, through key contact people in them, fit into the network as well. A network is a relationship system based on exchange and mutual help, without regard to an overall goal or target. Societal change workers invest in network development and maintenance because they are never sure what kind of resource they might need. Their network represents a trusted group of people and organizations that they can call on for assistance and to whom they provide assistance.

Given the substantive interests developed in the needs assessment phase, networks may be augmented by special individuals and organizations with the special knowledge and skills needed as identified by the needs assessment. The societal change worker may then activate her or his network by alerting regular and new members to the developing political action episode.

At this point, the societal change worker may form, or join, a coalition. A coalition is similar to a network, except that it has a focus or target to which all agree. Usually, we think of a coalition "for something," such as a coalition for peace or a coalition to end racial discrimination. Something like the hunger coalition is a coalition to end hunger.

Individuals and organizations join coalitions not for reasons of mutual help, as in the case of networks, but because they see that, through cooperation, some commonly held goal can be achieved. Thus, coalitions are the stuff from which the famous phrase "Politicians make strange bedfellows" was coined. Coalition membership is united by commitment to a common, external goal. Thus, a societal change worker might join a coalition of national actors with whom she or he has little in common, except for the fact that both are against hunger or seek some common congressional action on racism. Coalitions that already exist are discovered during the needs assessment process; if they do not exist, they are often created by the societal change worker to bring together interested parties for concerted political action.

Networks are very useful in helping the societal change worker understand and act on the needs assessments. Often, needs assessments provide a large amount of contradictory information, which needs to be thought through and processed, so that the societal change worker has an idea of how to build coalitions and around which issues coalitions are likely to form.

DEVELOPING OPTIONS. Workers interested in either policy management or political action use the middle phase to develop a set of options for next steps. For the political action emphasis, coalition building is key. For the policy manager, decision management is important. In either case, a reasonable set of alternative perspectives is needed so that the coalition can consider various options, and the sponsors and client system can have ideas to compare.

MANAGING THE DECISION POINT. While the societal change worker interested in political action is developing networks and coalitions, the worker involved in policy analysis is developing a strategy for managing the decision process. (It should be stressed here, again, that most workers are involved in both political action and policy analysis and management.) In the beginning phase, the needs assessment process provided a range of options to be reviewed by the sponsor and the client system.

The development of options allows the sponsor, the societal change worker, and appropriate elements of the client system to move toward decision. For some reason, at the decision point individuals and organizations often draw back. We have all had the experience in a small group when, at the moment of actual decision, there is silence in the group.[21] Somehow, even if the decision is relatively trivial, there is hesitation. This hesitation is compounded when the decision is extremely important, involving large-scale strategic commitments of personnel and resources to particular lines of action, which is likely to be the case in the societal change effort. Therefore, the societal change social worker cannot stop with the organization and presentation of action options, but must continue her or his work within the sponsor system to stimulate an actual decision. Several techniques are useful.

First, the presentation of options is itself a stimulus. An organized, well-researched set of options helps sponsors and clients to see the alternatives before them and to weigh the consequences.

Second, the development of a process of involvement of sponsors and client system interests during the needs assessment phase develops commitment and momentum for action. This involvement is one of the ways that policy research differs from academic research. In policy research, the sponsor or client is involved and interacting with the researcher on an ongoing basis. While this process has perils, such as attempts to inappropriately influence the outcome, it has great benefits as well—the development of momentum and the more accurate targeting of the research.

Third, the societal change worker's own expectation that action will be taken adds to the momentum. After all, the worker is involved in the societal change process, and sponsors and clients hope, at some level at least, that positive action can be taken. Worker expectations therefore guide this process.

Care, however, needs to be taken that in managing the decision process we do not manage the *outcome*. Policy management does not mean having the worker's preferences, specifically, be the outcome. This caution is familiar for social workers. We support client decision making, whether or not that decision is one we like or not. (The exception again is illegal action decided on by the client.)

It is thus important to distinguish between stimulating the decision process and lobbying for particular decisions. Social workers must recognize that, despite their particular preferences, it is the client or sponsor system that must make the final decision. In a variety of ways, we can let our preferences be known, but pressing for closure on the decision process does not mean pressing for a our point of view. Rather, it means stimulating the system to work through the options and to come to an agreed upon action.

THE ENDING PHASE

After a decision has been reached, the societal change effort moves into the ending phase. There are two parts to it: implementation and evaluation.

IMPLEMENTATION. After a decision has been reached on one of the options, the societal change social worker begins the process of implementation. In some sense, the process of implementation may in part already have been underway. To the extent that the processes of needs assessment, option generation, and decision making mobilize commitment for action, as indeed they are supposed to do, energy is available in the sponsor–client system to begin to put the new ideas, now decisions, into practice. But the specific targets of this energy are not clear until a decision is made.

The specifics of the implementation process occur now and fall into two general parts: planning and programming. Planning involves laying out the specific implementation steps. Planning occurs after decision making has set the major course. Planning involves the tactical development of specific ways in which the societal change effort will be undertaken and provides specific focus for the energy mobilized. Specific tactics might include the development of press releases for newspapers, and announcement spots for television and radio, a public speaking tour of nationally prominent individuals in the area, or a political support campaign involving the contacting of specific members of the legislative and executive branches of government. The decision will require elaboration and that specific steps be outlined. The development of these steps occupies the planning part of the implementation phase.

The programming part involves carrying out the plan. It involves establishing and actually operating or running the set of activities, the writing and distribution of press releases, the filming and showing of television clips, the recording and playing of audio advertisements for radio, and so on. The societal change worker continues to be involved in the planning and programming effort, partly because the worker's job, as assigned by the sponsor, is to continue efforts on through the actual implementing process. But societal change workers are also aware that how particular efforts are implemented has a great deal to do with their success and the extent to which they serve the originally intended goals. Great policy decisions made in Washington often falter when local implementation efforts get underway. It is therefore important that the implementation efforts be the sort that continue in the letter and spirit of the earlier decision.

EVALUATION. Once the operations part of the societal change effort is underway, evaluation begins. Evaluation may sound like another stage: it occurs after we have finished with a particular program and represents a judgment about how well the program performed. Unfortunately, if thought of in those terms, evaluation almost always occurs too late to help. The product is already on the market, and no one is buying it. Hence, a several-step conception of the evaluation process that involves both ongoing and arm's-length methods will permit both post hoc review and ongoing program adjustments on an as-needed basis.

In thinking about the evaluation process, it is helpful to divide it into the following sections: monitoring, oversight, assessment, and appraisal. The times at which these activities occur varies. Monitoring can occur on a daily or weekly basis. Oversight can occur on a monthly or a bimonthly basis. Assessment usually occurs about every six months, and appraisal is probably a yearly activity. In very fast moving societal change efforts, however, the cycle may be speeded up considerably.

Monitoring involves simply the regular (daily, weekly) observation of activities and recording of activity levels. In a social agency this might involve how many client hours today, how many canceled appointments, and things like that. It is the building of a numerical record base on which oversight can build.

Oversight is the beginning of judgment in the evaluation process. Using the activity flow reports from the monitoring stage, an attempt is made to see whether the goals outlined in the decision are being accomplished. Oversight is important because the ability to bring a particular programming effort back into focus is much easier when variation is small. A program that under political or other pressures begins to vary from the original intent can, if that variation is not great, be refocused rather quickly and easily. If, on the other hand, we wait until the program has been completed and then evaluate it, it is either too late to bring the program back to its original goals or the program is finished and is judged to have failed.

Assessment can occur on a six-month basis; it allows judgment to be made as to the substantial direction of accomplishment and whether or not mid-course correction of an appropriate nature should be taken. Assessment uses information from both monitoring and oversight efforts to make these judgments.

The final phase of the evaluation process is often what people refer to as "evaluation." Appraisal uses information from monitoring, oversight, and assessment phases to come to a continue or not continue, pass or fail judgment concerning the societal change intervention. If an intervention is judged to be successful, it can continue; if it is judged to fail, then the cycle of problem definition options, and so on, will begin again. It represents a final summary and substantive judgment on the societal change effort.

Students will recognize the stepwise nature of this system from their own experience. Monitoring is roughly similar to taking daily attendance in class. Oversight is equivalent to the frequent quizzes that provide information of a short-term nature on the position of the student. Assessment represents the midterm and final exams; they occur every so often and are major periods where work is thought to come together. Appraisal represents the final grade, in which all the information from monitoring, oversight, and assessment is taken into consideration, as well as other factors of judgment, and a final grade assigned.

The societal change worker is particularly alert to the evaluation process and seeks to introduce evaluation concerns and criteria early in the process.

Special Issues: Writing, Leadership, Gender

In societal change, three interrelated special issues arise; they are special not because they are absent in other areas, but because they take on special meaning in this larger context, where the worker plays a bewildering array of roles and parts, and where her or his interests as a citizen and person are more likely to overlap with, if not to become confused with, her or his role as a professional. These have to do with writing, leadership, and gender.

Professionals in macro change areas (organizational, communal, and societal) must have excellent skills in writing. Memos, pamphlets, reports, newspaper articles, and the like are the stuff of all the activities. While interpersonal interaction is important and has been stressed here, the ability to communicate persuasively through writing is crucial. In macro practice, those who workers seek to influence are often not present and need to be persuaded through written messages. Drafts of documents are the responsibility of the staffer, as are the taking of minutes and the keeping of correspondence for the various groups or change coalitions that the worker is staffing. Special attention therefore needs to be paid to skill development in this area.[22]

The second area is leadership. All social work requires leadership. Leadership, however, is nothing one can be appointed to or, for that matter, wait for. Leadership is self-appointed, in the best sense of that term. It is an offering of the self and a risking of the self. Interpersonal workers assume leadership with clients and families by helping to surface troubling issues so that they can be processed. Communal, organizational, and societal change workers take leadership in a somewhat broader context, with client systems, sponsoring systems, and in situations that involve many people and require public presence, over time, and the ability to accept and process public criticism. While interpersonal work is often performed in private (except when the sessions are being videotaped or are otherwise on display) macro social work is almost always performed in public. While all workers thus need to consider taking leadership roles in their practice, macro workers have special responsibilities to do so. Workers need to pay special attention to knowledge about and preparation for leadership roles, both in terms of content and in their emotional readiness to undertake these responsibilities.[23]

Readiness takes on a particular meaning in a profession with many women. Sexism trains women to hang back from leadership and let men take charge. Often, through obnoxious phrases ("ball buster," for example), the culture punishes women for taking leadership and characterizes that taking of leadership as specifically antimale (as in the example phrase.) To these issues are added the other differences in gender styles. In executiveship and leadership, current thinking suggests that neither stereotypically male or female styles are most likely to be successful. Rather, a blend of masculine and feminine styles is perhaps better.[24] It will be helpful for women to read some of the material that takes the mystique out of leadership for women and makes the accomplishment of this part of the professional role less scary and more fun.[25]

Conclusion

The societal change worker uses policy analysis and political mobilization strategies and models to improve societal and national conditions. The targets are what one might call big systems. A potential difficulty here is that change is particularly slow, and personal satisfaction deriving from specific accomplishments is extremely rare. Although working with a particular client around particular concerns may not change the world, clinical workers can take gratification from the help they are able to provide in that relatively focused context. A dilemma for societal change workers is that this kind of gratification is largely absent. Hence, the societal change worker needs to establish within himself or herself process standards that provide benchmarks of accomplishment. And, in the overarching view, there is satisfaction in working on and seeking to improve society's views of and behavior toward the largest, most terrible problems besetting the human race and in the belief that one is making an important if small step.

Notes

1. For elaboration, see A. J. Kahn, "Social Problems and Issues," in A. Minahan, ed., *Encyclopedia of Social Work,* Vol. 2, 18th ed. (Silver Spring, Md.: National Association of Social Workers, 1987), pp. 632–644.
2. See J. G. Hopps, "Deja Vu or New View," *Social Work* 33, 4 (July–August 1988), pp. 291–292; J. Leavitt, "Feminist Advocacy Planning in the 1980's," in B. Checkoway, ed., *Strategic Perspectives in Planning Practice* (Lexington, Mass.: D. C. Health, 1986), pp. 181–194.
3. One issue that has national impact is long-term care. See J. Tropman, ed., "Quality of Long Term Care," *Danish Medical Bulletin,* Special Supplement Series #5 (1987), pp. 2–6.
4. For further discussion, see A. Nicols-Casebolt, "Black Families Headed by Single Mothers: Growing Numbers and Increasing Poverty," *Social Work* 33, 4 (July–August 1988), pp. 306–314.
5. For one assessment of social change patterns on a large scale, see J. Naisbett, *Megatrends* (New York: Warner Books, 1982). See also D. Yankelovich, *New Rules* (New York: Random House, 1981).
6. For a discussion of cultural lag, see K. Wolff, "Cultural Lag," in J. Gould and W. Kolb, eds., *A Dictionary of the Social Sciences* (Glencoe: Free Press, 1964), pp. 158–159.
7. The material in this section is based on John E. Tropman and others, eds., *New Strategic Perspectives on Social Policy* (Elmsford, N.Y.: Pergamon Press, 1981); John E. Tropman, *Policy Management in the Human Services* (New York: Columbia University Press, 1984); B. Jansson, *Social Welfare Policy* (Belmont, Calif.: Wadsworth Publishing Co., 1984); B. Checkoway, ed., *Strategic Perspectives on Planning Practice* (Lexington, Mass.: Lexington Books, 1986); John E. Tropman, "Policy Analysis: Methods and Techniques" in Minahan and others, eds., *Encyclopedia of Social Work,* Md: National Association of Social Workers, pp. 268–283.
8. Tropman, *Policy Management.*
9. Tropman, "Policy Analysis."
10. Sheldon Danziger and R. Plotnick, "Poverty and Policy: The Lessons of Two Decades," *Social Service Review* 60, 1 (March 1986), pp. 34–51.
11. Mayer Zald, "Trends in Policy Making and Implementation in the Welfare State," in Tropman, and others, eds., *New Strategic Perspectives on Social Policy.* See also, Tropman, "Policy Analysis."
12. A. S. Johnson, "Preliminary Conclusions of the Family Impact Seminar," in Tropman and others, *New Strategic Perspectives on Social Policy.*
13. For further discussion, see M. Dluhy, "Developing Coalitions in the Face of Power: Lessons from the Human Services," in Checkoway, ed., *Strategic Perspectives on Planning Practice.*
14. See John E. Tropman, "Social Exploitation and Social Amelioration," unpublished manuscript, University of Michigan, 1990.
15. For further information, see A. Beaubien, "Library Resources for the Community Organizer" in F. M. Cox and others, eds., *Tactics and Techniques of Community Practice,* 1st ed. (Itasca, Ill.: F. E. Peacock, 1977), pp. 56–66. M. Lewis, "Social Policy Research: A Guide to Legal and Government Documents," in Tropman and others eds., *New Strategic Perspectives on Social Policy.*
16. For, for instance, R. Douglass, "How to Use and Present Community Data," in F. M. Cox and others, eds., *Tactics and Techniques of Community Practice,* 2nd ed. (Itasca, Ill.: F. E. Peacock, 1984), pp. 383–395; J. Gottman and R. Clason, "Troubleshooting Guide for Research and Evaluation" in F. M. Cox and others, eds., *Tactics and Techniques of Community Practice,* 2nd ed.
17. Except, of course, when the support is from ethically questionable sources.
18. John E. Tropman, "The Relationship between the Staffer and Policy Committees," in Tropman and others, eds., *New Strategic Perspectives on Social Policy.*

19. Again, though, caution must be exercised with respect to the source of support.

20. I. Morris, *The Nobility of Failure* (New York: Holt, Rinehart and Winston, 1975).

21. Sometimes a group of people does, collectively, something none individually wants to. See J. Harvey, "The Abilene Paradox: The Management of Agreement," *Organizational Dynamics* (Summer, 1974), pp. 64–79. See also R. Bolton, *People Skills* (Englewood Cliffs, N.J.: Prentice Hall, 1979); R. Fischer and W. Ury, *Getting to Yes* (New York: Penguin Books, 1983); John E. Tropman, *Meetings: How to Make Them Work for You* (New York: Van Nostrand Reinhold Co., 1984).

22. For example, see John E. Tropman and Ann Alvarez "Writing for Effect," in Cox and others eds., *Tactics and Techniques of Community Practice, 1st ed.* See also, M. Holcomb and J. Stein, *Writing for Decision Makers* (Belmont, Calif.: Lifetime Learning, 1981); D. Booher, *Send Me a Memo* (New York: Facts on File, 1984); John E. Tropman, *Policy Management in the Human Services* (New York: Columbia University Press, 1984), Ch. 11, "Policy Writing."

23. A good source is R. Portnoy, *What Every Leader Should Know About People* (Englewood Cliffs, N.J.: Prentice Hall, 1986). See, also, Bernard M. Bass, *Bass and Stodgill's Handbook of Leadership,* 3rd ed. (New York: The Free Press, 1990).

24. See Alice Sargent, *The Androgynous Manager* (New York: American Management Association, 1983).

25. B. Harrigan, *Games Mother Never Taught You* (New York: Warner Books, 1977).

CHAPTER 10
The Structure
of Social Service Systems

Introduction

The practicing social worker is concerned not only with methods of social work and with the particular arenas in which social work might be practiced, but also with social services and social service systems. As workers well know, services to clients are frequently hampered by a lack of coordination among social service systems. Arguments over turf and disagreements about who will pay for a particular service that a client needs frequently take as much or more time to work out as working with the client directly. Social services and social service systems represent a bewildering array of need-meeting activities, from adoption services to young adult services. Students might find it interesting to look in the yellow pages of the local telephone book under "Social Services." Most large cities have several pages of listings that reveal the wide range and complexity of the social services offered in any given community. (The Washington, D.C., yellow pages for 1988–1989 lists 14 columns of agencies and has another section for social workers.)

However, it is often difficult to know exactly what is offered by an adoption service, counseling service, or daycare or youth service. Hence, further time must be spent investigating a particular service to find out whether it actually offers a desired program. Confusion is often the order of the day.

The purpose of this chapter is to give students a general introduction to social services and the structure of the social service system. We first answer the question, "What are social services?" and then present a frame of reference, the 4C's, to help students organize the bewildering array of offerings.

THE 4C's PERSPECTIVE ON SOCIAL SERVICES

The first C stands for the characteristics of the client, and some services are aimed at helping the client deal with issues based on her or his *characteristics* ("dealing with" includes changing the world in which clients find themselves, not simply accepting it). A second area is *competencies.* Some services are aimed at teaching the client certain competencies or skills to better assist a client in dealing with his or her environment. In both cases, changing the public view toward the characteristics and competencies may also be involved.

The third C refers to the *conditions* of the client. The family system, work system, and community system are all small systems in which the client interacts on a daily basis. There is often a need to change a system. Workers assist individual clients by working on the system and working with the system directly. The last C is *context.* Context refers to the larger environment in which the client interacts; the nation, the gender group, and the racial or ethnic group, are client systems and targets. Often changes in client conditions and context need to be made to help the client. And contextual change can become a target of intervention in its own right.

STRATEGIC PERSPECTIVES ON SOCIAL SERVICES

We shall introduce a variety of strategic perspectives on the social services and examine different ways to look at social services that the field of social welfare has used. We do not argue that any one of these ways is superior to another. For various reasons, an individual student may find one way preferable to another. But, for an overall understanding of the system it is important to understand the different strategic perspectives that have been used to organize and present the social services to the field itself, to outsiders, and to students. We shall also deal with cultural and structural conflicts within the social service system.

What Are Social Service Systems?

Social service systems are organized ways that societies, communities, agencies, and other groups meet human needs. In the broadest sense, all forms of need-meeting activities are social service systems. These could include formally organized systems like religion and the economy, as well as departments of social services and Catholic charities. Informal systems could be considered as well, from the personals columns in local newspapers to the group that gets together at the local saloon. This whole area might be what Helen Witmer called social welfare. She said that social welfare strives "to fill up gaps in the usual institutional arrangements of our society."[1] She argues that social work gives "assistance to individuals in regard to the difficulties they encounter in the use of an organized group's services or in their own performance as a member of an organized group."[2]

Social services and social service systems, like legal services, medical services, and plumbing services, refer first to the availability of trained professionals in an art, science, or craft. Social services therefore involve social workers, but not exclusively, in the same way that lawyers, doctors, and plumbers are involved in their services. In each case, a range of professionals is involved in providing services.

But there is a second aspect to social services. As with medical, legal, or plumbing services, a problem with typical, usual, or expected functioning is involved. The expected aspect needs to be stressed, because social service, like the others, can come into play when the social system is not functioning as it could or might.

Social services, then, bring professionally expert skills to bear on difficulties in functioning. Social service systems are the interdependent, interacting, interpenetrating aspects of social services.

These ideas have been used by at least one operating agency. The United Way of America, the national organization of all United Ways in the world with special emphasis on North America, has a motto that describes social service systems. Their motto is "To increase the organized capacity of communities to help one another." That definition is very much like the 1939 Lane report definition of community organization: "to organize community resources to meet community needs."[3] Thus, social services and social service systems are indeed ways of organizing resources to meet needs. Being charitable or altruistic, being interested in doing good or helping others is always commendable but never sufficient. Unless the service is organized, standardized, and targeted to particular needy groups, its impact is likely to be occasional and episodic. Also, without organization, the potential of the community and society to help may never be realized.

Understanding the organization of social services and social service systems is a complex task. Not only is the system of organization itself difficult to comprehend, but it is also unclear what may be included in any particular service or agency. Part of the reason for this confusion is that the social work–social service profession has, as yet, not developed an accepted taxonomy of services. If we could all, as a profession, agree that a service such as daycare included the same set of agreed upon professional offerings wherever it was instituted, there would be a much better overall idea of what social services are actually offered in the United States. Until such a taxonomy is developed, our field will have to live with some of the difficulties of not knowing exactly what anyone means by a particular service designation.

A second problem is that the concept of services, positive as it is, sometimes strikes an insincere note, especially when applied to services over which the client has no choice; hence, a discussion of criminal justice services may ring a bit hollow to practitioners, perpetrators, and victims. In the context of force, the volunteeristic elements suggested by the word service seem out of place. This sour note highlights a crucial, if unstated, aspect of social services and social service systems. Participation in them is thought to be voluntary. The client or client system makes its own determination of need. When services are not voluntary, questions about their appropriateness arise. However, there is increased acceptance in some quarters of modest coercion, such as using the authority of the workplace to get employees the treatment they need.

Social services and their organization as discussed in this chapter focus on those offered by professionals (B.S.W.'s, M.S.W.'s), as well as those offered under the guidance of professionals, such as volunteer services. However, many other professionals, such as psychiatrists, psychologists, and guidance counselors, are also involved, as well as many nonprofessionals.

Typically, when we speak of the social work system of services, we mean those services in agencies that are staffed and run by individuals with the M.S.W. or B.S.W. degree and who have some individuals with the A.C.S.W. (Academy of Certified Social Worker) qualification and/or the diplomate (like the A.C.S.W., the diplomate is a form of certification of competence provided by the American Board of Examiners in Clinical Social Work).

The social welfare system, on the other hand, includes the social work system but goes beyond it to include all of those services offered by nonprofessionals. These individuals have trained themselves through experience or have been trained through some other profession to offer helping services in the community at large as well.

A Social Service Template

Given the difficulties and confusions about social services and the social service system, understanding it in some comprehensive way presents a challenging task. The *Encyclopedia of Social Work* handles this job in dictionary fashion, using the alphabet as an organizing principle.[4] Thus, it begins with adoption services and ends with youth services. But this approach does not provide any integrated or theoretical basis on which to base an understanding of social services and their interrelations. A scheme is needed that fits both a person and the environment and that allows workers to see the environment as an element that affects a particular client and that is a target for change in itself. The 4C's system presents such an integrated picture. It invites us to think about services in terms of four categories: helping the client with problematic *characteristics;* helping the client with problematic or nonexistent *competencies,* helping the client deal with difficult *conditions,* and helping the client deal with difficult *contexts.*

CLIENT CHARACTERISTICS

Individual clients are sometimes born with or acquire certain characteristics that become problematic to them over time. Physical disabilities, brain damage, and various other limiting conditions represent one kind of characteristic. Both acute and chronic illnesses are another. Sometimes personality development proceeds in such a way as to create problems within the realm of characteristics (as in character disorders or disorders of attachment). Social services help individuals assess the situations in which they find themselves and make plans about how to deal with the problems these characteristics present. Such plans may include, among other approaches, changing the characteristic in question, adding competencies, changing conditions or context, or some combination of these. Psychological testing services, medical assessment services, and school performance assessment provided by trained individuals are examples of the assessment of client characteristics and plan making. Individual change social workers fit in this service category.

CLIENT COMPETENCIES

Social services that assist individuals in developing specific skills to control or change their behavior or the behavior of those around them represent a competency developing service. Services that focus on techniques to stop smoking or lose weight might fall within this category. Educational services involving the acquiring of certain educational skills, such as reading or writing, would as well. Therapeutic services producing the skill of insight and self-knowledge are other example. Assisting an individual to increase interpersonal skills by providing specific techniques for meeting others and handling conflict is yet another example. Sometimes these services are remedial and develop skills that the individual missed acquiring in usual socialization. Sometimes they are replacement skills that assist the individual client to develop new skills to replace old and unproductive techniques. Sometimes the services are enhancing ones and assist the individual to increase his or her pleasure in life. Either individual or group settings can become a treatment mode, so both individual- and group-oriented workers can locate their efforts in this category.

CLIENT CONDITIONS

"Conditions" refer to the system in which a particular client finds himself or herself on a daily basis. It is the nearby, regularized arena of family, work, and neighborhood that creates the daily substance of a client's life. Services that assist in changing this environment, either on behalf of a particular client or for clients in general, fit into this category. Racist practices within a school system, for example, might become the target of change for a particular social agency on behalf of a specific client with whom it is working. The agency may also recognize, through having had several clients who experienced racism in this particular school, that a change in conditions is absolutely necessary if further problems are to be prevented. Similarly, change in the family system, rather than (or along with) change in an individual family member, is often required if a particular family member is to be helped. Indeed, some writers suggest that change in individual members cannot be accomplished without change in the conditions.[5] Because individual behavior is, in effect, a product of those conditions, changing the psychological environment of a client is one method to use.

Another way includes changing physical structures. Changing the layout of organizations is getting much attention now.[6] Working to provide ramps for handicapped people at fishing sites, for example, makes changes in conditions that mean a great deal to the handicapped. Almost all social workers place some of their effort here. Family systems workers, organizational change workers, and community change workers are especially interested in this kind of intervention.

CONTEXT

The context in which clients live consists of the larger institutional entities, such as cities and nations, racial and ethnic groups, gender groups, groups of sexual preference, and so on, that affect daily life on a regular basis. Context may not necessarily be changed. But it always needs to be taken into account on an ongoing basis as client change proceeds. Context also refers to the laws, policies, and other regulations that may prevent clients from achieving fulfillment or that may be unjust or inequitable. Social services that work to improve or adjust them would fall under this category. Community and social change workers fit here. Contextual elements may be approached directly, as when workers seek to change laws or work against institutionalized racism or sexism in society. Context may be hard to change or change very slowly. So working with clients to develop competencies in dealing with an oppressive context (without accepting the legitimacy of that context) may be appropriate as well. Sometimes it is important to assist clients to see the context in a new light. Consciousness raising groups may serve this purpose. Social workers need to be continually sensitive to contextual elements.

PREFERENCE TOWARD THE INDIVIDUAL

In discussing social services it may sound as if individual clients are the main focus. When we speak of services, we tend to have an individual client in mind. Thus, we can work to change laws on behalf of a client or work to change laws for the general good. Somehow condition and context changes seem less of a social service to some, but we do not agree with this view. We invite readers and students to think of social services not only as organized around doing specific things with specific client systems, but as doing general things with specific clients, even those individuals who are clients at risk or clients to be. Thus, a family service agency may sponsor a program on sex education in a high school not only to help particular clients (for some it may already be too late), but because without such a program, sexual ignorance is likely to contribute to instances of unwanted pregnancies and sexually transmitted diseases.

Eight Strategic Perspectives on Social Services

A strategic perspective identifies as its organizing principle a practical dimension or variable that is of preeminent importance. It is important for students of social work to understand the variety, or at least the key elements, of the perspectives that currently abound. We shall discuss here the most popular perspectives, such as the methods perspective, the levels perspective, the developmental perspective, and the problems perspective.

LEVELS AND METHODS PERSPECTIVE

One way to think about social services and the structure of social service systems, is by the level of intervention that they target or by the method that they use to accomplish the intervention. These are somewhat related, and students will recognize that the levels perspective has already been discussed in considerable detail in Chapter 4 and is to some extent implicit in the 4C's perspective. Services to the individual, family and group, organization, community, and society (with an understanding that services as a concept may tend to lose some of its meaning at the more complex, higher levels) show one way to think about services and their organization.

This volume has also organized its own presentation around methods: casework or individual change and group, organizational, community, and societal change. Because of the emphasis on levels already presented, we shall not say much more about levels here, except to emphasize one point. Cross-level, cross-method work is always an important component of social service and should be kept continually in mind. Casework, for example, may require other methods to support the goals that the worker and the client have selected. Societal change may require a specific focus on particular individuals. Cross-level work should always be kept as an option. Figure 4.1 reflected the compositional and contextual strategies that might on certain occasions be useful not only as an alternative to direct strategies, but even in preference to them.

SECTOR PERSPECTIVE

A second important perspective is the sector in which social services are being offered. Historical progression is involved in the relevant social welfare sectors. The private or voluntary sector began around the turn of the century. During the early years of this century, neither business nor government did much in the way of social services activity. Therefore, social services were thought of as private agencies, such as the New England Home for Little Wanderers, the Family and Children's Service, the Child Guidance Clinic, and the Boy Scouts, existing in an important third sector different for business or government and funded largely by charitable contributions and the contributions of volunteer time. It is from these contributions of volunteer time that the commonly used term "voluntary sector" has come to be used. (The term "independent sector" is, however, coming into use as well.)

With the passage of the Social Security Act of 1935, the development of a government welfare bureaucracy at both the federal and state levels began. It now employs tens of thousands of people in a wide variety of programs, including welfare programs, Social Security, Unemployment Compensation, Child Welfare, programs in the Veterans Administration, and programs funded under the Older Americans Act.

Passage of the Social Security Act, requiring the development of public social services, also stimulated the development of what have come to be called private social services. These services are offered through the commercial sector. Many of these programs parallel those offered by the Social Security system, including disabilities programs, insurance programs, and health programs. Many in the social work community do not regard these private social welfare programs as social welfare programs even now. The concept and the phrase are relatively new. Nonetheless, because they were stimulated by the Social Security Act (and required employer participation in some instances, such as contributions to Social Security payments), many analysts now include them in discussions of private social services.[7]

Recently, new programs have been added to these more institutionalized and publicly linked programs. As employers realize the value of the training invested in a worker and the very high cost of replacing skilled workers, they are offering social services within the workplace as a way to prevent employee loss. The Employee Assistance Program (EAP) began this trend, with the focus on substance abuse control in the workplace setting. However, EAPs have rapidly expanded to include various kinds of counseling referrals.

The last aspect of this sector is to some extent an extension of the commercial sector, and it refers to the private practice of social work. Private practice comes in several forms. Two main ones should be mentioned here. The first refers to the establishment of a private business by a social worker who has met state requirements. There are no professional requirements as yet that the M.S.W. must meet to open a private practice. However, at the moment conventional wisdom dictates an M.S.W. degree, followed by five years of experience with an agency context, and an A.C.S.W. certification as a minimum, before an individual establishes a private practice.

The question of whether this is a profit-making enterprise or not remains open. Many private practitioners make no more income from their private practice than they would make in salary from a local agency. For reasons of schedule, flexibility, freedom from bureaucratic procedures, and the like, they prefer to work on their own or in small clinical groups. The private practitioner of social work pays for supplies normally provided free by the agency, such as office space, heat, light, record-keeping facilities, secretarial assistance, and so on. These represent costs of service delivery that must be subtracted, along with the cost of salary, from total revenue to ascertain whether or not the private practitioner of social work is making a profit. More research is needed on the nature, difficulties, problems, and rewards of private practice.[8]

The other motive for private practice is the private profit-making business set up to deliver social services. A number of such organizations exist within the employee assistance field, contracting with large corporations to provide employee assistance programs. The avowed purpose of these organizations or agencies is to provide high-quality service under conditions that make a profit, thus having money left over for the investor/entrepreneur after all expenses including her or his own salary have been met. While this practice mode is not as yet a popular form of practice, we will probably see more of these organizations in the future.[9]

These last two modes of practice are as yet somewhat controversial forms of offering social work service. There is no question one of the oldest traditions in the field has social workers working in social agencies. Another tradition of social work has been to work within the public sector. The development of the field in its historical form thus never began with the independent practitioner. The private practitioner does not have any specific legitimacy in our field as yet, although it does in almost every other professional area (law, medicine, pharmacy, and the like). Today, though, thousands of members of the National Association of Social Workers are listed in the NASW Register of Clinical Social Workers.[10] Coming to some accommodation with the private practice movement and setting and developing reasonable and enforceable professional standards for entering into private practice are important tasks for the profession in the coming decade.

LIFE CYCLE OR DEVELOPMENTAL SERVICES

A third way that one might think of services is to see them as a link to the development of the life cycle of the human person. There are many ways to divide up the life cycle, but typically we think of such stages as newborn, infancy, preschool, school age, and adolescence, as primary areas. The life cycle literature does not do much with the middle years. From about 20 to 65, very little is written on the specific roles and developmental tasks that occur during these years. Some authors have tried to look in more detail at the middle years, but as yet this development remains relatively new.[11]

A range of well-known services fit into each of the well-known age or life cycle areas, however. Services for pregnant mothers and newborn infants have a long and honorable tradition; well-baby clinics and other medical services for the infant are well established. Medical services are taking on a particularly important role in recent years due to the rising number of infants born addicted to some substance. In particular, attention is being paid to the care of children born with AIDS.

Other kinds of services given to the young child often link to services for the mother. Sometimes, though a little less frequently, they also link to the father. These services are particularly aimed at adolescent parents.[12]

Preschool programs are familiar to many of us. They include daycare services, nursery school services, and child abuse prevention services (though abuse prevention services can be present at any age). The central theme of preschool services focuses on the health and wellness of the child and attempts to assess, to the extent possible, whether the child is moving along usual developmental tracks. Furthermore, children born with chronic illnesses or disabilities will need to receive help at this time.

The lack of a taxonomy deserves stress again at this point. When we mention nursery school services or daycare services, it is rather unclear exactly what is included in these particular services. Some are minimal child-minding types of programs and others involve education and developmental stimulation of a high order. Hence, it is not possible to know exactly what services are being offered in terms of the specifics of the

Entering the system. (USDA Photo.)

service itself within this age group. Youth and school age services refer to programs offered to children from about the time they begin regular school (at the age of five or six) until they begin high school.

At the high school level, adolescent services begin; however, there is no clear line here, and services in the youths' school area continue on through the early and even into the late teenage years. Social workers perform school social work services, working with children and families on problems of discipline within the school, adjusting to school, school phobia, and so on. They also work with school personnel to help them become more understanding and sympathetic about the problems of the students with whom they are dealing.

Other out of school services also begin at this point: Girl Scouts, Boy Scouts, Boys and Girls clubs, and others of the character-building services. These are offered to provide similar kinds of interesting and exciting activities for age mates, assistance in skill development, and aid in the acquisition of interpersonal skills. Religious organizations offer programs that are heavily involved at this point. The Jewish Community Center programs often focus on developing groups for youth within the Jewish community.

These services are followed by adolescent services, though the focus of adolescent services changes somewhat. Social workers are now dealing with individuals who are fully into the young adult category. Issues of sexuality and substance abuse leap to the forefront here, and issues of relationships with the other sex become a very important focus of attention. The organization of cross-sex groups (as opposed to single-sex groups in the latency age period) is often a focus of social work activity in the group work arena. The profound biological changes that characterize adolescence stimulate a range of needs for counseling and therapeutic intervention.

The adult life produces its own set of problems. Issues of employment and career development, issues of forming intimate relationships and having them break up, issues of health and parenthood are among those for which service is offered in the middle years. Personal and marital counseling, assistance in overcoming sexual dysfunction, employment counseling, and programs to reduce stress and weight and eliminate smoking all fall into services offered to the adult citizen. The social services system seeks to deal with this very broad range of problems. It also works in the area of income through Aid to Families with Dependent Children (AFDC) and General Assistance (GA), as well as on programs providing disability support for handicapped adults.

At the end of the life cycle a special group of services called geriatric services is beginning to develop into a full package of programs and activities. The older adult was generally ignored in U.S. society until about the mid-1950s, and a concentrated effort by researchers and policy makers has developed a number of policies and programs to assist the older adult. This emphasis is consistent with the rising population of senior citizens in our country and can doubtless be expected, in one form or another, to continue.[13] The social services system deals with income support through Social Security and through the development of pension programs. Medical programs are developed through the Medicare system and other health insurance programs to provide help for seniors. Nursing home care is one of great interest. Housing programs, Meals on Wheels, and nursing home programs are among those that the social service system offers.

PRODUCT PERSPECTIVE

A fourth way that services might be thought of is to look at them in terms of the products they seek to deliver to clients. In this particular case, a goal or end result is specified in advance, and clients select a particular product, program or service because they seek that particular result. Usually, we can be behaviorally specific about the outcomes of these programs and services and the outcomes can be measured. One example is a stop smoking program. Behavioral guide lines and protocols are developed and individuals are processed through this program with the goal of helping them to stop using cigarettes. Similarly, weight loss programs have an equally specific role. A goal of losing a certain number of pounds in a certain period of time following a specific behavioral schedule is established. Programs for substance abuse also fall into this category.[14] The goal is straightforward: to enable or to empower the individual to stop abusing a particular drug. In the case of substance abusers, the goal is abstinence. Alcoholics Anonymous has a very successful program that falls into this category.[15] The theme is 12 steps and was developed by Alcoholics Anonymous founder Bill W. (anonymity is a precept of AA). His prescriptions are followed in Alcoholics Anonymous meetings.

Some products, however, are less specific than the ones we have just mentioned, but nonetheless have a sense of concrete outcomes about them. Programs to speak better, overcome shyness, enhance self–esteem, or improve family or sexual relations do not have the same kind of measurability that stopping smoking or drinking or losing weight does. But they do focus on a particular outcome desired by the individual. Whatever processes the individual goes through, they are aimed at achieving a particular goal.

Many programs of a product nature focus on the large-scale environment as opposed to the specific individuals. Programs to clean up toxic waste in a river or reduce the number of abandoned homes in a particular neighborhood fall within this category. There is a specific goal that is measurable, at least to some degree, and can be behaviorally specified.

Other programs may seem to fall into this area, but actually do not because of the absence of a specific goal. A program to reduce poverty, for example, would not be a product-related service unless a specific goal, such as by 4% or 8%, were outlined. The specification of at least a semimeasurable goal is crucial to the product perspective on social service delivery and systems.

This particular perspective emphasizes the importance of a product or result as the outcome of social service intervention. Individuals taking this perspective often feel that social services are too vague or unspecific and believe that behavioral focus and goal specification are absolute requirements for effective intervention, regardless of whether it is a social service or any other kind of venture. Critics reply that all social services cannot be so specifically measured and that flexibility is needed.

PROBLEM PERSPECTIVE

A fifth strategic perspective on social services is the problem perspective. Here a particular problem is taken as the point of departure. Often social services are thought of as organized by problems across macro and micro lines. The value of this perspective is that we can amass knowledge about the problem in question in its many manifestations. If, for example, we are interested in problems of alcohol and other drug abuse, then the problem perspective allows us to encompass all manifestations of this problem.

Sometimes the problems are of large scale, such as difficulties with the environment or problems of juvenile delinquency or poverty. Indeed, vast social service systems have been developed to deal with these problems. Sometimes, the problem is on a specific level, such as the problem of low self-esteem or depression. Social systems have been developed to provide mental health services to individuals in these categories.

The problem perspective is similar to the product perspective. The difference is where the emphasis lies. In a product perspective, the emphasis lies on specifying some measurable output; everything else comes second to that. In the problem perspective, the emphasis lies on the finding of the problem in a particular sector to begin with. Everything else comes second to that.

IMPACT OR POSITIONAL PERSPECTIVES

Often in the social service field we hear about differences between direct and indirect services and between residual and institutional services. These perspectives are common and need to be understood.

Some thinkers divide services between direct and indirect.[16] The direct services attack a problem specifically, often using techniques at the same level (see Figure 4.1). Direct techniques involve treating problems at a particular level with techniques at the same level. Individual problems demand individual treatment. Problems at the community level demand community-level intervention.

On the other hand, indirect services approach problems from another level in a compositional or contextual way (see Figure 3.). Hence, problems of adolescent pregnancy may not be handled directly with the pregnant adolescent, but rather a program may be developed to provide sex education through the schools, thus dealing indirectly with the problem in question.

However, if the problem in question is defined as a lack of sex education, from which adolescent pregnancy is an unfortunate result, then it is possible to view a sex education program as a direct service at the community level dealing with a community problem. Much needless argument has occurred over the direct versus indirect division, because direct services are believed to be better than indirect services. The truth is that both are needed and each depends on the other.

The distinction between residual and institutional services has a similar flavor to it and so is included here.[17] Residual services fill in the gaps where the societal social system, that is, the regular need-meeting mechanisms of our society, have somehow failed. Thus, it is expected that normally people will be able to find jobs, earn money, and support themselves. Some individuals however fall between the cracks, and this needy group becomes the target of social services. Under the residual view, social services would only be provided for those individuals who had not somehow managed to meet their needs (however adequately) using regular social routes and routines.

An institutional perspective, however, argues that social services are part of an ongoing set of activities that any society should undertake. Indeed, the reason why individuals fall through the cracks in the institutional view is that enough services are not provided; furthermore, the institutional view argues that it is inefficient and inhumane to wait for someone to experience a problem before moving to help. Rather, the institutional view argues, "Lets see if we can't prevent the problem before it begins." Once again, neither attitude is right, solely. Both are needed.

CULTURAL, ETHNIC, AND GENDER PERSPECTIVES

The cultural, ethnic, gender perspective argues that the particular culture or belief system in which the individual has been brought up or is involved is the most important aspect for the provision of services to those individuals. In years past this argument manifested itself mostly in the development of sectarian or religious-based social services.[18] The argument was that being a Catholic or a Jew, for example, was a fundamental aspect of the individual's identity. It thus made sense that services be offered by a Catholic agency or a Jewish agency by Catholic or Jewish staff. The religious identifications of staff were required to give individual clients the benefit of the fullest possible understanding of the particular problems that they were experiencing and to increase the clients' confidence by working with individuals who were deeply aware of what was going on with them. Today, similar arguments are made with respect to gender, race, sexual preference, and ethnicity, to mention a few. The essential arguments are still the same: that it requires a minority agency to counsel a minority client and the client will only open up to someone who speaks their language.

There is much argument now, as there was earlier, about whether this perspective is valid. Our view is twofold: First, if a client believes that she or he needs an individual of similar identification to work with, then the perspective is certainly valid since the individual will not be willing to discuss the problem with anyone else. Furthermore, in many of these histories there are unique aspects that affect a particular culture and worker competence can be enhanced. On the other hand, there is also a case to be made for issues and successes that cut across cultures. Key here is the issue of client and worker choice about how to receive and offer services.[19]

A PROBLEM-SOLVING PERSPECTIVE

Yet another perspective focuses on the process of help. While these processes differ with each level (individual versus societal services, for example,) there is a common problem-solving process idea that crosscuts all the methods in social work, and hence can be regarded as a service perspective.[20] The problem-solving process can be approached in many ways. Almost anyone's definition, however, sees the service as being offered through a series that includes the following steps: (1) needs assessment and diagnosis; (2) development and consideration of options; (3) selection of one option for work; (4) development of plans of action required by the option selected; and (5) putting the plan into action. A last phase is (6) ongoing evaluation of the activity and dynamic modification of the needs assessment and diagnosis and subsequent steps if evaluation reveals that the plan is not working.

Some services, like diagnostic services or needs assessment consultation, work only with one phase of the process and locate their services in that specific sector. Other social services seek to work with clients through the whole process.

Conflicts in a Social System

As can be seen from the wide range of perspectives discussed, the social service system is alive with conflicts about how services are to be offered, thought about, and organized and coordinated. Basically, these conflicts fall within two general realms: conflicts of culture, or beliefs about social services, and conflicts about structure, or how social services are to be delivered.

Cultural conflicts within the social services have been dealt with extensively elsewhere,[21] so only brief attention is required here. Our beliefs about social services conflict with one another to a certain degree. One tension is that between residual perspectives and institutional ones. To some extent, it is possible to have both. But it is important to recognize that residual and institutional perspectives do conflict with each other and that emphasis on one will in time diminish focus on the other. This juxtaposition may also cause additional tension within the structure of social services.

Let us give one other example. Most of us believe that financial grants to individuals who need cash should be *adequate* to meet their needs. On the other hand, readers may also believe that such grants should be *fair* (or equitable). Fairness may be based on past or future societal contributions and linked with what others receive. These two bases, meeting individual's needs versus rewarding or prerewarding them for contributions to this society, are values that are both deeply ingrained within U.S. culture and within the social service system itself. Yet they conflict with each other, and emphasis on adequacy will in time erode emphasis on fairness and equity, and vice versa.

Perhaps no other area within U.S. society (and this may be what makes the social service system unique) is as full of conflicting and competing points of view.

There are a variety of ways of working out these conflicts: compromise, adjustments over time, and so on. But none is very long lasting simply because, at bedrock, some conflicts cannot be compromised. This is not to say that either is right or wrong; it is just that each conflicts with the other. The matter is made even worse when the conflict is not between us and them, but rather within us. Thus, from a cultural point of view, we can expect the social service system to be in constant crisis. These crises should not be surprising; they are simply part of the problem of dealing with competing bases for providing help to individuals.

The structural elements of society also cause conflicts. While cultural conflicts occur within the norms, values, and ideas that we hold, structural conflicts occur within the specific institutional arrangements that we provide. These arrangements are well known to all of us. We have already mentioned three sectors: the public sector, commercial sector, and voluntary, not for profit sector. Social services exist within each of these, and we can expect conflict because of the differences in their structural arrangements. For example, some not for profits are going into nonrelated business, hoping to make money to sustain their budgets, but they are doing so while retaining their tax-exempt status granted to them as a not for profit. Commercial organizations are complaining. In the nursing home field, a similar development is occurring. Some nursing homes are run on a charitable or not for profit basis, while others are run on a proprietary or for profit basis. The tax treatment of these two organizations is very different, and the proprietary organizations complain that the not for profit ones are getting special breaks. This conflict is inherent in the structure of our society itself.

Additional structural conflicts occur within the government arena because of the different levels and branches of government. There are local, county, state, and federal governments—four levels at least, to take into consideration. Each level can and does offer some social services, sometimes in concert and sometimes not with those offered by the other levels. The higher levels (federal and state) often make rules that irritate or are inappropriate for the lower levels (state and county). Hence, conflict is to be expected.

Also, each level of government has three and we would argue actually four branches. There are three historical branches, the legislative, judicial, and executive. Each has something to say about what social services are to be offered where and under what conditions. A fourth branch linked to the executive branch is the cadre of civil servants attached to the federal, state, county, and city or municipality bureaucracies. These individuals are different from the politically appointed executives and often have yet a fourth view. If we have four branches and four levels, that means that the average social service system in the government area alone has 16 potential centers that can influence, change, adjust, and in general busy themselves with the social service system. It is clear that there will be conflicts among these various branches and centers for structural reasons alone. When one adds to this the cultural conflicts already mentioned, we can see why the social service system is often so troubled and seemingly in disarray.

Conclusion

This chapter provides an outline of the social service system and gives examples of the variety of social services within it. A number of strategic perspectives or points of view popularly current as ways of looking at the social service system were described, including levels of intervention and methods of service, sectors of service, and seeing services as divided up over the life cycle, as products, as responsive to problems, as direct or indirect or residual or institutional, and as differentiated by cultural, ethnic, and gender identification. These different perspectives are all ways of organizing essentially the same set of services, but the perspectives identify different elements as having central or possibly explanatory or causal value.

Those who take a methods perspective, for example, think that methods should be central, and services should be organized along the lines of the methods used to deliver the services. Others think the particular position in the life cycle should be the crucial factor. Still others think that behaviorally specific outcomes should be the way services are organized. As a way of helping the reader understand this welter of perspectives, we provided one of our own. The 4C's perspective sees services as aimed at the characteristics of the client, the competencies of the client, the conditions in which the client lives, and the context, which considers the problem from a state, regional, or national perspective. However, because of the structural and cultural conflicts within the system, it is not likely that any perspective will provide a completely integrated point of view.

Conflicts were also identified as occurring within cultural and belief systems, in which problems occur because we are committed to a competing basis for providing services, and within structural systems because we are in different positions within the commercial, public, or not for profit sector. It is important to understand that different interests have different points of view.

At one level, the social services system must seem untidy and in disarray. It would be so much nicer and easier if we could put up a chart and say, "Here is the social service system." However, from another point of view, this untidiness and disarray can be reinterpreted as openness and responsiveness to a wide range of viewpoints and problems in a country that cherishes freedom and independence, and which has a diverse population. It is not to be expected, for example, that everyone will agree that the residual or institutional perspective is better; hence, we do some of both. Probably for some individuals, their cultural identification, gender, or race is not as central an identification as it is for some others. Hence, services are available for those who wish to have culturally specific services, and other services can be used by anyone. We suspect that this is going to be what the future looks like. It is not well organized and tidy, but rather differential and responsive, representing an open system with a wide range of viewpoints to be considered and accommodated.

Notes

1. H. Witmer, *Social Work: An Analysis of a Social Institution* (New York: Rinehart and Co., 1942). Quoted in A. J. Kahn, ed., *Issues in American Social Work* (New York: Columbia University Press, 1959), p. 3.
2. Ibid.
3. Robert P. Lane, "The Field of Community Organization," in *Procedures of the National Conference of Social Work, 1939* (New York: Columbia University Press, 1939).
4. A. Minahan (ed.), *Encyclopedia of Social Work,* 18th ed. (Silver Springs, Md.: National Association of Social Workers, 1987).
5. For further discussion, see R. Middleman and G. Goldberg, *Social Service Delivery: A Structural Approach* (New York: Columbia University Press, 1974).
6. John Kotter, Lenard Schlesinger, and Vijay Sathe, *Organization* (Homewood, Ill.: Richard D. Irwin, 1986).
7. Larry Root, *Fringe Benefits: Social Insurance in the Steel Industry* (Beverly Hills, Sage Calif.: Publications, 1982).
8. For further discussion, see E. Margenaw and others, *Encyclopedia of Private Practice* (New York: Gardner Press, 1990).
9. Another profit-making service being offered is in the nursing home field.
10. National Association of Social Workers, *1991 Register of Clinical Social Workers* (Silver Spring, Md.: The Association, 1991).
11. See Daniel Levinson, *The Seasons of a Man's Life* (New York: Knopf, 1978); Erik Erikson, *Childhood and Society* (New York: W.W. Norton, 1950); S. Hunter and M. Sundel, *Mid Life Myths* (Newbury Park, Calif.: Sage Publications, 1989).
12. The father's role in child development has been only recently studied. Sir Michael Lamb, *The Role of the Father in Child Development* (New York: John Wiley & Sons, Inc., 1976). See also M. Bloom, *Life Span Development,* 3rd ed. (New York: Macmillan, 1985).
13. For further detail, see Elizabeth D. Huttman, *Social Services for the Elderly* (New York: The Free Press, 1985).
14. E. Kurtz, *AA: The Story* (New York: Harper & Row, 1988. See also G.T. Rogers, "12 Steps," a videorecording. Skokie, Ill.: G.T. Rogers, 1986).
15. Bill W., *Alcoholics Anonymous* (New York: Alcoholics Anonymous, 1955).
16. For example, see H. L. Wilensky and C. Lebeaux, *Industrial Society and Social Welfare,* (New York: Russell Sage, 1958).
17. Wilensky and Lebeaux, *Industrial Society.*
18. See W. J. Reid, "Sectarian Agencies" in J. B. Turner and others, eds., *Encyclopedia of Social Work,* Vol. 2, 17th ed. (Washington, D.C.: National Association of Social Workers, 1977), pp. 1244–1254.
19. For a further discussion, see K. Kozaitis, "Culture and Social Work: An Anthropological Perspective," unpublished manuscript, University of Michigan, 1990.
20. See John E. Tropman, *Policy Management in the Human Services* (New York: Columbia University Press, 1984).
21. See, for example, John E. Tropman, *American Values and Social Welfare* (Englewood Cliffs, N.J.: Prentice Hall, 1989).

CHAPTER 11
Service Delivery for Enhancing Criminal Justice

The Function of the Criminal Justice System

In this chapter we shall examine the various institutions that society has established to deal with illegal behavior and the role that social work has been assigned or has assumed within such institutions. A major concern for social work, and for society as well, is that the rights of individuals be protected when societies respond to deviant behavior. These individuals include both the perpetrators and the victims of illegal behavior. Social work has a major stake in the maintenance of social justice. But a major value issue is to determine how far society should go in limiting behavior that threatens social stability and what threats to such stability should be tolerated, or even encouraged, in the interests of social change and individual rights.

There are many institutions in society devoted to ensuring justice for its citizens. Agencies such as welfare departments have provision for fair hearings in which clients can contest decisions regarding their access to material resources and services. Physical and mental health services such as hospitals are required to appoint patient–client rights officers who investigate and seek to rectify wrongs perpetrated by these systems. These exist alongside all the systems established to deal with crime and criminal behavior. While we should consider this whole range of institutions, space limitations force us to consider primarily the latter. The reader should remember, however, that social control and the ways that justice should be protected in its application are much broader than the issue of crime.

All societies create policies and institutions to deal with individuals who violate social norms, whether in formal legislation or in the values shared by large numbers of people in the society. These policies and institutions are established to secure conformity to social norms.

From a social science perspective, the policies and institutions that seek to reduce what social scientists refer to as *social deviance* (defined as behavior that is in violation of major social norms) operate in a variety of ways. They may restrain individuals who have not violated norms from doing so. An individual tempted, for example, to engage in shoplifting may not do so because of an awareness that he or she may be caught, arrested, and punished. At times, societies will also seek to identify people who are likely to act in deviant ways and prevent the emergence of such behavior. Thus, children who live in communities with high crime rates and poverty may be offered social programs in an effort to promote their access to socially acceptable opportunities. This relates to the concept of primary prevention described in a preceding chapter.

Second, societies respond to deviant acts once they have occurred. A wide range of possibilities exists and these may be viewed along a time line from the moment the act is detected by someone to final acts of punishment, rehabilitation, restitution, and so forth. Thus, when Sam Jones discovers Bob Smith in the act of robbing his house, he may or may not be entitled to take the law into his own hands to protect his property. He may, instead, secure the help of the police to seek for Bob Smith and apprehend him.

Once Smith has been apprehended, the police have a variety of options. Particularly if he is a juvenile and has not been known to have been in trouble before, they may refer him to some form of treatment rather than to a court (this is referred to as *diversion*). Or Smith might be brought before a court. Even in that event, the court staff (who are often social workers) may defer bringing Smith before a judge and, instead, seek both to help him and protect society by providing a variety of court services. Then or later they may decide or be required by law and/or policy to expose Smith to formal courtroom procedures, including an appearance before a judge and usually a trial.

As a result of courtroom procedures such as a trial, Bob Smith may be placed on probation, in which case he will be required to maintain contact with a probation officer (who is often a social worker) for a specified time, and he will usually be required to reappear in court for a report on his behavior. After a period of time and appropriately positive reports, he will be discharged from probation and his court case will be closed.

Alternatively, Smith may be sentenced by the court to some sort of confinement, or fine, or restitution to the court for its trouble and/or to Sam Jones for his loss. He may be released from confinement at some time prior to the end of his sentence (referred to as *parole*) and be required to remain under the supervision of a parole officer (also often a social worker). At the end of his parole or other form of release from the correctional system, Smith may receive other services from the community to make it more likely that he will be able to maintain law abiding behavior. Later we shall discuss many of these societal institutions that compose the correctional system.

The Function of Social Work in the Criminal Justice System

Social work has a role to play in all the types of events that befell Bob Smith, and we therefore turn to a consideration of the functions fulfilled by social work in the correctional system. Social work's focus is on helping people by altering the interaction of the individual and the environment. This has been well stated by Studt, who wrote:

> Specifically the problem (to be addressed by social work) concerns an offender's inability to conform in his behavior to the community's moral demands as they are enforced on the population segment to which he belongs together with a rejection by the community of its responsibilities toward that person. This is a problem in social relationships that requires as much change on the part of the community as on the part of the offender for adequate resolution.[1]

Thus, it is apparent that the correctional system requires the utilization of all the social work methods described in the preceding chapters. The way the individual is viewed, however, has been shifting in social work with offenders, and we emphasize that this is appropriately so and long overdue. This shift is away from seeing the offender as a sick person. Again, as Studt points out, "to label the vast majority of institutional inmates as 'ill' does violence to reality while it socially handicaps the offender by introducing into his life still another stigma."[2] In line with the function of social work, we see social workers working with the offender to enhance his or her ability to conform to moral demands while also working to enhance the way the community fulfills its responsibility to that person. This can be by creating opportunities for the offender to participate in an empowered way in the community, while meeting his or her needs for employment, housing, and education through socially acceptable actions.

Thus, social workers help offenders to find alternatives to illegal acts to meet their needs. For some, this might involve helping them to solve problems that contribute to their acting illegally, such as those involving the family or addictions. For others, help with overcoming behaviors caused by mental illness or developmental disabilities (for example, mental retardation) might be required. Because of differences in definitions, the estimates of the size of this population varies. Studt estimates it to be about 10% to 15% of the population. Santamour and West, in their review of the literature on incarcerated individuals, find numbers that range from 4% to 27%, with most studies averaging around 10%. By including individuals with learning disabilities and personality disorders, Mays and Rogers came up with a figure around 25%.[3]

Social workers will also help offenders to act in more empowered ways, both for humane reasons and through a recognition that this might help them learn to satisfy their wants in a socially acceptable manner. Within the institution, this can mean questioning policies by utilizing the machinery that has been established for this purpose. Within the community, this means acting assertively to secure one's rights. An example of the latter was an ex-offender who filed a grievance against her workplace for discriminating against her when an opportunity for promotion was denied and she had reason to believe her status as an ex-offender was the reason. As Studt again so wisely states, "Most of all the inmate in a correctional institution needs the experience of belonging as a responsible member to a community that fulfills its responsibilities towards him."[4]

Social workers will also interact with inmates on a group level.[5] Within an institution, such groups usually consist of therapy groups and occasionally of some type of inmate government program. Several decades ago, Studt and her colleagues demonstrated the rehabilitation value of creating a community in a prison largely through the device of establishing a large array of groups for treatment, educational, and governing purposes.[6] Such a vision has still not been widely replicated within the nation's prisons.

Correctional program administration is another area in which social workers will be found; all social workers in such programs should be aware of their responsibility to influence the administration of these programs to be more responsive to the needs of offenders. Studt makes these points very strongly when she states:

> Social workers must be prepared to share in the management of the correctional institution if the inmates present life is to become a realistic preparation for the future and if the institution itself is to become an organizational setting in which social work methods can be effective. The great need of correctional institutions at the present is for managers who can turn bureaucracies into "pools of human resources for flexible use" in which the relationships among inmates and all kinds of staff actually support human growth and creativity. Social workers need both more technical knowledge about how to run institutions and more skill in managing organizational relationships. The development of such organizational sophistication is essential if social work in the correctional institution is not to remain a program appendage used by administration primarily to process records and "keep the lid on".[7]

Social workers may be found in the ranks of those who administer components

"You'll soon be on your own." (Photo by Federal Bureau of Prisons.)

of correctional programs, such as treatment units, and also among those who direct programs, such as training schools for delinquents. Less frequent but not unusual is the employment of a social worker as a prison warden, and recently the director of the State of Michigan Department of Corrections was a social worker. Probation and parole agencies, halfway houses, and other community-based programs are also frequently directed by social workers.

The kinds of objectives we have portrayed for social workers can only be attained if social workers find ways of influencing correctional policy. This can be accomplished in part through research, and the examples of the work of Sarri and of Vinter are good ones in this respect.[8] In addition, social workers must find ways through occupying policy-making positions to influence the entire system. Again, as Studt so well puts it:

> This is not to repeat the old clichés that social workers should avoid positions of authority in corrections or should refuse to be concerned with the control of behavior. Rather it emphatically asserts that social workers must achieve positions of authority if they are to gain power in institutions to raise inmates to the position of dignity and responsibility necessary for sound social learning. Of all the disciplines concerned with correctional reform, social work appears to be the one with the appropriate knowledge and skills to guide such a basic reform in correctional institutions.[9]

In the preceding paragraphs, we have raised a number of heavily value-laden issues, such as the role of social workers with respect to social control and the desirability of raising inmates "to the position of dignity and responsibility." These issues relate to the very different value and ideological positions that divide people in the field of corrections, which go well beyond the views of social workers to include policy makers, correctional theorists, and all the professions employed in the correctional field. An understanding of these views is essential to any planning by social workers as to how they will affect correctional institutions.

Values and Ideologies in Corrections

Clemens Bartollas, who has written several of the major corrections texts,[10] divides ideologies regarding corrections into three categories: rehabilitative, justice, and utiliitarian punishment. We shall summarize his conception of these views.

REHABILITATIVE

The goal that this philosophy proposes for correctional programs is that they "help offenders cope more effectively with their environments".[11] The means to accomplish this goal are not limited to what is customarily referred to as treatment, but include any (intervention) used by the facility, such as the restrictions placed on an offender by a parole plan. Coping more effectively does not only mean the elimination of illegal behavior, but also positive outcomes that improve the quality of life of the individual.

A rehabilitative philosophy is embedded in three models that have influenced ideas about corrections: the medical, adjustment, and reintegration schools of thought. The medical model views the offender to be suffering from an illness. The implication is that the function of the correctional system should be to diagnose and treat this illness. Punishment, therefore, has no more place in responding to the offender than it would have for any other sick person. It clearly follows that the program of any correctional facility should be guided by mental health practitioners.

Proponents of the adjustment model agree with those of the medical model that offenders need treatment, but they more strongly emphasize that offenders should also be held responsible for their actions. As Bartollas states in summarizing this position, "while offenders cannot change the facts of their emotional and social deprivations of the past, they can demonstrate responsible behavior in the present and can avoid using their past problems as an excuse for delinquent or criminal behavior."[12] This approach, places less emphasis on pathology than the medical model and more on helping offenders make an adjustment to society.

Experts who follow a reintegration model focus less on individual attributes and more on community circumstances. They focus on the opportunities in the community that support lawful behavior and the use the offender makes of them. Such opportunities are seen as related to the social roles of the offender, such as employee, parent, or spouse. A major thrust of this approach is to locate correctional services *in the community,* where they can best have an impact on community resources and how the offender uses them.

Many activities in the correctional field can be seen as stemming from a rehabilitation model. These include the following:

1. *Indeterminate sentencing and parole:* Since the purpose is to rehabilitate the offender, he or she should be released when such rehabilitation has been accomplished.

2. *Diagnosis and classification of offenders:* Rehabilitation should be related to the specific needs and circumstances of the individual.
3. *Activities to improve the skills of the offender:* Unlawful behavior is seen as at least in part a consequence of a lack of such skills.
4. *Psychotherapy:* assumed to be the basic component of at least the medical model.

In recent years, much controversy has centered around rehabilitation philosophy. A highly influential book by Lipton, Martinson, and Wilks examined all the available research evidence regarding the effectiveness of treatment programs in corrections and presented largely pessimistic conclusions.[13] As Martinson stated in another publication, "With few and isolated exceptions, the rehabilitative efforts that have been reported so far have had no appreciable effect on recidivism."[14] This was seen as the equivalent of saying that "nothing works."

Other writers who reviewed the same studies examined by Lipton, Martinson, and Wilks were more optimistic. Palmer, for example, found support for at least selective utilization of individual counseling, group work, community-based therapeutic programs, intensive probation and parole, and milieu approaches for rehabilitation of male adolescent offenders.[15] Roberts presents an interesting explanation for the findings of Lipton and others. He suggests that a factor that may interfere with the programs is the perception by the clients that rehabilitation is simply another kind of punishment.[16]

The controversies around rehabilitation philosophy are also a response to whether or not one believes that offenders, as part of their civil rights, are entitled to humane treatment whether or not this rehabilitates them. Those who oppose rehabilitation programs may see them as coddling offenders and may be quick to look for evidence that they are ineffective to boot. There is also the humanistic argument against rehabilitation: it may force an offender to change in ways that she or he has not agreed to. Some forms of rehabilitation may even disguise what some would see as a form of punishment, such as shock therapy and drug therapies.

Supporters of a rehabilitation philosophy, in contrast, argue that rehabilitation programs are often so few and so poorly supported in almost all ways that, in a sense, they have not really been tried, at least for the majority of offenders. Even when an individual in an institution receives some form of rehabilitation, he or she may not receive the follow-up that is needed to maintain any progress on return to the community.

A final point is the basic question as to whether any form of therapy used to rehabilitate offenders can be beneficial when conducted in a custodial and often punitive institution by people who usually are employees of the institution. Both proponents and antagonists of rehabilitation programs provide arguments and evidence on either side of this issue.

Social workers have been heavily invested in many of the programs that are associated with rehabilitation. Forms of counseling and psychotherapy as part of community-based and institutional programs are often offered by professional social workers. Their professional titles are often those of probation officers and prison or training school counselors or social workers. The philosophy of rehabilitation of offenders and of viewing offenders as suffering from a personality disorder rather than as morally defective is compatible with the ideology of social work, which emphasizes the interaction of people and environments and the worth of all individuals.

JUSTICE

The justice approach arose in response to many acts perpetrated on offenders under the guise of rehabilitation that were in fact ineffective at best and repressive at worst. Because correctional programs were described as therapeutic, they were presumed to be exempt from safeguards for offender's rights. An example was the indeterminate sentence under which the actual amount of years to be served was to be decided by such agents as a parole board. This type of sentencing gave offenders, who were already under the stress of incarceration, the added stress of uncertainty as to when it would end. This might be justified if such boards could really predict recidivism. Proponents of the justice model, however, saw this process as replete with deception and misjudgment on both sides. As one of the major writers on this model stated:

> The indeterminate sentence had turned out to be a tool for lengthening terms or punishing people who did not conform to prison programs. I saw the system as a degradation of justice by those who were charged to be the agents of justice.[17]

The principles underlying the justice model are that society is entitled to promulgate laws and ways of enforcing them, punishment is a legitimate part of law enforcement, punishment should be proportionate to the crime, and people have the capacity to make choices in the face of known consequences. These consequences are sometimes referred to in simple terms as receiving one's "just desserts."

Consistent with these ideas, probation is not seen as a form of treatment but as another consequence of engaging in prohibited behavior. Treatment of any sort should be voluntary and not related to punitive consequences imposed on the offender. In total, all the events that befall an offender should be determined through the most scrupulous legal processes. Thus, offenders are to be treated with respect and dignity.

A number of changes have occurred in the correctional system as a result of the work of advocates of the justice model. One has been tighter practices in prisons for guaranteeing due process for inmates. The imposition of such disciplinary measures as solitary confinement (usually referred to as segregation) must usually be preceded by an appropriately conducted hearing, rather than made by the arbitrary decision of a prison official. Most important, a number of jurisdictions have abolished indeterminate sentencing. Advocates of this model are continuing to press for an overall limit on prison sentences for all offenses with the exception of premeditated murder.[18] It has been suggested that determinate sentencing will continue to become more popular until massive prison populations and increasing costs force legislators to reassess their positions.[19]

One issue raised in discussions of the justice model is whether society will accept a criminal justice system based primarily on the principle of retribution, even if it is conceived and administered in terms of well thought out principles of justice and respect for offenders. A broadly accepted means of relating sentences to the seriousness of offenses does not exist. Another is whether the legal, executive, and judicial systems can be expected to operate in a fully just manner in terms of political realities, as this may be a utopian expectation. Finally, it is argued that the justice model could lead to an excessively rigid system that, in itself, contained much injustice. Thus, the broadest criticism of the model is that it leads to a "movement that assumes the values they have opposed."[20]

The basic idea that all offenders should receive justice is highly compatible with social work values. Fogel, whom we cited earlier as a major proponent of this approach, for a number of years worked as a social worker and was identified as such. The idea, also, that therapy should be undertaken voluntarily is also compatible with the views of many social workers, although others work with involuntary clients and seek to develop a therapeutic relationship with them.

The idea that wrongful behavior should have consequences is not likely to be rejected by any social worker. On the other hand, limitations on the opportunity to individualize offenders by considering individual and social circumstances would be difficult for many social workers to support. We suspect, therefore, that a justice philosophy is acceptable in its broad outlines by social workers who, nevertheless, debate its policy implications with each other.

UTILITARIAN PUNISHMENT

This set of views is the traditional one: crime will be deterred and society protected by punishing criminals. Thus, this approach shares the value placed on punishment with the justice model but for a different set of reasons. This approach supports its views by drawing on evidence; it therefore, does not reject the idea of rehabilitation programs, but only if they demonstrate effectiveness. A negative view is taken of much rehabilitation because of a lack of such evidence.

The concept of utilitarianism is drawn on in the assumption that humans can function in a rational manner and their behavior will be affected by its consequences. Another basic premise is that the rights of the law-abiding citizen must be protected as a primary consideration. The idea of justice does enter in that the amount of punishment should be determined by the severity of the crime. Deinstitutionalization is not favored because it is viewed as too soft to deter crime.

Those identified with utilitarian punishment views support a number of policies. According to Bartollas these include:

> An increased use of incapacitation, a hard-line policy toward serious juvenile offenders, a greater use of determinate and mandatory sentences, more effective court systems, a get-tough policy with drug offenders, and the return of the death penalty. . . .[21]

The net effect of these policies is that more offenders will be sentenced to institutions and judges will have less discretion regarding sentences. At least one class of offenders, those who commit drug-related crimes, would be treated more harshly.

These views appear to be popular in the current climate. Many people in our cities have grown fearful for their safety. Experts have simultaneously asserted the ineffectiveness of rehabilitation and community treatment methods.

Critics of utilitarian punishment assert, in contrast, that repression does not work. They question that criminal behavior, and therefore its deterrence, is based on rational decision making. They point to the evidence that crime is committed by the poor, the addicted, and the mentally unstable. They see imprisonment as often nothing more than revenge. Furthermore, no emphasis is placed on the social conditions that lead to crime.

Thus, it is easy to see why few social workers espouse these ideas. While they understand that harmful behavior should have consequences, they are more likely to desire to combine punitive consequences with opportunities for rehabilitation, humane treatment, and the elimination of social conditions that lead to frustration, social inequality, and acts that are often taken in desperation.

An Overview of the Criminal Justice System

HISTORY

A brief review of the history of correctional programs in the United States will help the reader to better comprehend the issues facing the correctional field today.[22] During the colonial period, the major societal response to law breakers was to severely punish them with fines and lashings and in more severe cases the stocks and the gallows. The colonists did not typically create institutions because they did not believe that these would lead to rehabilitation; the lack of resources required for this was also likely to be a factor.

The idea of prison was, surprisingly, a consequence of the Enlightenment and its ideas of the possibility of changing humans and their societies. An historic event occurred in the United States when Dr. Benjamin Rush presented a paper to a group at the home of Benjamin Franklin on the idea of a prison. Rush recommended that institutions supported by prison labor be created for criminals.[23] Rush's ideas led to the creation of the first prison in Philadelphia.

The next stage in the development of corrections occurred during the Jacksonian period when the penitentiary emerged. The idea behind this development was to compensate for the bad environments that were seen as the causes of crime. The idea emerged from the work of the Philadelphia Society for the Alleviation of the Miseries of Public Prisons. The penitentiary was to provide solitude along with opportunities for labor and recreation. A Bible was provided for moral guidance. The term and even the idea of the penitentiary came from the Middle Ages, when analogous institutions were developed by the Catholic Church in which wrongdoers could experience penitence.

The Pennsylvania plan was enacted by the Pennsylvania legislature when it created the Western Penitentiary in Pittsburgh in 1826 and the Eastern Penitentiary in Philadelphia three years later. Another type of approach was tried in New York at the Auburn State Prison, erected in 1819, in which prisoners were prevented from communicating with one another. The latter prison also emphasized severe forms of punishment and humiliation, including beatings.

After the Civil War, the country sought to reform its penal institutions and thus created the reformatory. The idea for this was developed at the National Congress of Penitentiary and Reformatory Discipline in 1870. The ideas created at this meeting included an emphasis on rewards, such as the opportunity to reduce one's sentence, earn money, and obtain privileges. These ideas had already been employed successfully in Australia. The first attempt to employ them in the United States occurred in 1876 at the

Elmira Reformatory in New York State, and similar programs were started in 12 states over the next 20 years. Nevertheless, such institutions basically remained violent in atmosphere and prisonlike in appearance.

The Progressive era in the United States saw yet another phase of correctional reforms. These included the individualized treatment of offenders, inmate self-government, and an increase in indeterminate sentencing. The ideology that supported these developments was emerging in the social sciences, that social problems could be understood and solved. The Progressive idea was that the state could play a role in these developments. In the forefront of these developments were sociologists, social workers, and psychiatrists (for example, the meeting ground of social workers was then known as the National Conference of Charities and Corrections).

An emphasis on the psychological causes of crime was also embodied during the Progressive period in the creation of the Juvenile Court in Cook County, Illinois, in 1899. This court was seen then and for many years later as essentially a treatment institution. The language of the 1905 *Commonwealth* v. *Fisher* decision is often cited: the court "is not for the punishment of offenders but for the salvation of children . . . whose salvation may become the duty of the state."[24]

At about the same time, the idea of probation for juveniles emerged. According to Bartollas, several decades elapsed before social workers adapted their casework ideas to adult probation.[25] The same kinds of psychological ideas were also used in the development of parole in the beginning of the twentieth century.

The idea of democratizing the prison began with the Mutual Welfare League at Sing Sing Prison in New York State. This innovation included the election of representative bodies for making prison rules, raising money to offer amenities, and determining penalties for violating the rules.

The influence of psychiatry during this period was utilized to create diagnostic centers in prisons, although it was often not clear how diagnosing prisoners would affect their subsequent treatment during incarceration. The idea that this was more humane than what had proceeded helped to further the hold of the medical model on prisons. By the 1970s, however, many of these ideas had been rejected because of studies of recidivism.

At about this time, the idea of moving away from institutions in all fields of welfare took hold. This affected the correctional system as well and led to the many experiments we now see in place to maintain offenders within the community. The pendulum has swung again, however, and a harder line for criminals is again being advocated.

CURRENT SITUATION

A few statistics will help the reader to comprehend the immense size of the correctional system in the United States today. The entire criminal justice system includes law enforcement, the courts, and the correctional component. The following statistics for 1986 show how many people were employed in each component:

Law enforcement	662,117
Courts	271,000
Corrections	402,780[26]

During 1984, it was estimated that there were 8.9 million arrests for crimes. The costs of the criminal justice system in the United States were $26 billion. The direct economic costs to victims was $10.9 billion.[27] Other costs to victims, such as psychological ones, are impossible to estimate.

The number of people in prison in 1990 was 755,425, and the number of prisoners in the United States was at an all-time high. This represented a 6% increase over the preceding six-month period, which was only slightly less than the record 46,000 rise in the first half of 1989. Stephen D. Dillingham, the director of the Bureau of Justice Statistics, called the increase "the largest growth in 65 years in prison population statistics."[28]

The number of people in prisons has also been higher than in other countries. For example, the highest state incarceration rate in the United States in 1977–1978 was 416 per 100,000 population, and the average for the country was 245;[29] the comparable figure for Holland was 27; for Spain, 28; and for Switzerland, 59. No Western European country had a rate even one-half that of the U.S. average.[30]

Netherland, in the review article from which we have secured the above statistics, presents some startling information about offenders. This includes the fact that their rates for consuming alcohol and drugs were much higher than the rates found in the general population. The drug consumption of inmates and their number of convictions were also correlated. Despite this, little drug treatment takes place within correctional institutions. Netherland also points out that African Americans and certain other minority groups are overrepresented in arrests, convictions, and prison populations, even though studies indicate that there is little relationship between race and crime.[31] This means that law breakers are more likely to be treated aversively when they are members of minority groups.

The statistics related to juvenile offenders in the United States are also alarming. Roberts, citing the Federal Bureau of Investigation's *Uniform Crime Reports of 1985,* states that the total number of arrests for youths under eighteen is over 2 million. Eighty-eight percent of the crimes involved property (defined as including burglary, larceny, theft, motor vehicle theft, and arson), and 12 percent were violent crimes (murder, forcible rape, robbery, aggravated assault). He also notes:

> While the official statistics may be appropriate in examining the extent of the labeling process, law enforcement and juvenile courts statistics are of limited usefulness in measuring the full extent and volume of delinquent behavior. Since not all delinquent behavior is detected (and therefore cannot be officially recorded), true acts which are recorded do not represent a random sample of all delinquent acts. In other words, official statistics provide only a limited index of the total volume of delinquency.[32]

The data regarding placement in detention and training school facilities demonstrate some trends with regard to their utilization.[33] These data, expressed as rates within the larger juvenile population (specifically, the rate per 100,000 youth aged 10 to upper age of juvenile court jurisdiction), show that between 1979 and 1989 the rate of male admissions to detention increased 24.5%, while for females it increased 6.0%. The actual number of youths admitted to detention during these two years went from 344,633 in 1979 to 382,528 in 1989. In addition, the average length of stay for these individuals increased from 11 days to 15 days.

Based on a one-day count, the number of males in detention that day increased during this period from 7,964 to 15,765 and this reflected a rate increase of 79.7% (from 59 to 106 per 100,000). The statistics for females went from 1,614 in 1979 to 2,531 in 1989 (from 12 to 18 per 100,000), and this represented a rate increase of 50%.

Training school admissions for males went from 55,457 in 1979 to 55,793 in 1989 (from 378 to 427 per 100,000), a rate increase of 13.0%; for females, the admissions went from 8,444 in 1979 to 7,031 in 1989 (from 60 to 56 per 100,000), and this represented a rate decrease of 6.6%. A one-day count showed that on that day in 1979 there were 19,471 males in training schools and in 1989 there were 25,087 (from 138 to 192 per 100,000); this represented a rate increase of 39.1%. On that day in 1979 there were 2,857 females in training schools and in 1989 there were 2,736 (from 21 to 22 per 100,000), and this represented a rate increase of 4.7%.

These data reflect the trend away from institutions and long-term institutionalization, but they also reflect the continued high rate of delinquency and the use of detention for delinquents. The fact remains, also, that boys are far more likely than girls to break the law.

Despite this, the drop in female rates in training school admissions is clearly significant in terms of social policy. This is undoubtedly due to a shift in judicial and institutional practices, that is, the deinstitutionalization of status offenders (youths who commit offenses that are not crimes when committed by adults). Females are more likely than males to be charged with such offenses. The lower female rate, therefore, reflects the success of national policies favoring the deinstitutionalization of status offenders.

Because the law creates separate systems for children and adults, we shall discuss these separately. Nevertheless, we utilize a common framework that subdivides these systems into three types of programs: (1) those that are utilized prior to adjudication or that divert offenders from the judicial system; (2) those to which individuals are sentenced as a result of a judicial determination such as prison or probation; and (3) those to which offenders are referred after the terms of their sentence have been completed.

When speaking of child offenders, we primarily refer to adolescents, because behavior that brings the child to the attention of the justice system is more likely to occur in the teenage years than in earlier childhood. Specifically, the age of arrest accelerates at age 13 and peaks at about age 17.[35] The age at which a youth is handled by the adult system differs in different states and is often decided in the individual case depending on the seriousness of the crime. The maximum age in which jurisdiction can fall to the juvenile court is 18, although some believe that anyone over 16 can understand and take responsibility for the nature of his or her acts and, consequently, should be handled in an adult court.

Prevention can be attempted prior to arrest or adjudication. This prevention may take one of the following forms:

1. Programs to meet the needs of youth in prosocial ways, such as recreational, vocational, and educational activities for those believed to be at risk of becoming delinquents.
2. Family, individual, or group therapy involving at risk youth.
3. Substitute family arrangements, such as foster care.

Another issue related to the development of many social programs is that the youth may behave in ways that are deemed to be illegal for minors but not for adults—the so-called status offenses. Two major types of such offenses are violations of parental authority, such as running away from home, and truanting from school. Consequently, agencies to work with runaway youths and their families and alternative school programs to meet the needs of youths who cannot respond to typical schools have been developed. Current thinking is to divert as many status offenders as possible out of the correctional system and into social agencies established to help them.

Even if a youth has been arrested by the police because they believe she or he has committed a crime, the police have a good deal of discretion as to whether to bring the youth before a court. The youth may be reprimanded by the police or may be referred to an agency for help. This is referred to as *diversion*. The court staff also may choose to use diversion prior to an appearance before a judge. An example of a major resource for diversion is an agency such as a Youth Service Bureau established to provide a range of services for youths to prevent a reoccurrence of delinquent acts.

If the youth is referred to a court and if she or he has committed a serious offense that requires that the community be protected until a court hearing is held, she or he may be placed in a court detention facility. This may also happen if the youth requires protection from parents or others in the community. In any case, an initial screening of the youth will take place, and this is usually done by a social worker. As a result, the complaint may be dismissed, the youth may be diverted to another agency, the court may maintain informal supervision of the youth, or a petition may be filed to bring the youth before the court.

As a result of the court hearing and if the charges against the youth are not dismissed, the court will decide on one of the following alternatives: a fine, therapy, probation, placement in a foster home or other facility, or commitment to a public training school (which in many senses is similar to the decision of an adult court to imprison an offender). The hard core older youth can be sent to an adult prison.

After the youth who has been placed by the court in a training school is released, she or he will usually be assigned for aftercare to a state department of public welfare, youth correction agency, or other state department charged with this function. A parole or aftercare officer, who is often a social worker, will be responsible for helping the youth reintegrate with the community. The youth may be placed at that time with his or her own family, in foster care, in a residential or day treatment program, or even in an independent living status.

Youths who are ordered to receive some service by the court, at the time the order is terminated, may also continue to receive services to prevent future problems. These services are often prevention-oriented.

Programs specifically aimed at preventing adult crime do not exist in the same way as those for preventing juvenile crime. Certainly, any program whose purpose is to improve the economic and social well-being of the community may reduce adult crime, although its intent is usually far broader than that. Nevertheless, reform has been taking place in the correctional field with the aim of diverting many offenders from imprisonment. Such diversion takes place through releasing some offenders, who are required, as a consequence, to participate in supervision and some form of counseling. Other approaches include helping citizens to resolve disputes outside the courts and referring drug offenders to treatment programs, such as therapeutic communities.

Many offenders are required to appear before a court. The court may be part of a city, state, or federal system. Which court the offender faces depends on which system's laws she or he has broken. As a result of the court hearing and if the charges are not dismissed, the court will similarly decide on one of the following alternatives: a fine, therapy, probation, or commitment to a prison. A death sentence is also a possibility in a number of states.

If the offender is sentenced to serve time, depending on the level of government whose laws have been violated, he or she will be confined in a city, county, state, or federal facility. Based on an assessment of how much control must be maintained over the individual, he or she will be assigned to a minimum, medium, or maximum security facility. The minimum and medium categories include prison farms and forestry camps, as well as many city and county jails. Younger offenders, such as those in the 18 to 25 or 30 year old category may be separated from the older ones in institutions often referred to as reformatories.

Again, as with juveniles, the adult with an indeterminate sentence might be released on parole. Increasingly, other programs are employed for early release, such as halfway houses in which the offender resides, thus enabling him or her to work or continue an education in the community.

After the offender is released from prison or from the jurisdiction of the court, as in probation, too few programs exist to prevent future crime. This is unfortunate, because the individual with an adult criminal record suffers from a stigma that can prevent his or her securing employment. Consequently, ex-offenders can suffer the stresses that make recidivism likely. Organizations do exist, such as the John Howard Association, to help them with such problems, but clearly not enough services are available for people who have adult criminal records.

We shall now present the major components of the criminal justice system in more detail so that the reader will understand the issues that confront practitioners and policy makers in this field.

Selected Components in Detail

COMMUNITY-BASED PROGRAMS: JUVENILE

Community-based programs include parole and probation, community residential facilities, therapeutic activities, and day treatment. These programs serve several functions: to prevent delinquency, to divert youth from the consequences of court appearances, to serve as a substitute for incarceration, or to help youth to readapt to the community after having been institutionalized.

Any discussion of such programs would be remiss not to mention the *Mobilization for Youth* (MFY) experience. This agency grew out of a meeting among several agencies on New York's lower east side and the School of Social Work at Columbia University to deal with concerns over city-wide rates of juvenile delinquency. Planning for this new agency was completed in September 1962, and support was obtained from the National Institute of Mental Health, the President's Committee on Juvenile Delinquency and Youth Crime, the Ford Foundation, and the city of New York. The guiding philosophy of the MFY involved militant community action and full participation of community residents in all aspects of its work. During its decade of operation, the MFY conducted a vast number of youth and family programs, as well as programs geared to improving community conditions. Its militancy undoubtedly contributed to the severe political attacks that it suffered and that ultimately led to fundamental changes in its mode of operation.[35]

The contemporary development of community-based programs for delinquent youth in the United States is largely a consequence of *The Juvenile Justice and Delinquency Prevention Act* of 1974 (42 USC section 5601) and its subsequent amendment in 1977. This act requires that status offenders not be placed in juvenile detention or correctional facilities. Instead, the state is to provide the least restrictive alternative, which is primarily understood to mean community-based programs. This federal mandate is enforced by the requirement that a state's eligibility for funding under the act be terminated if full compliance is not reached within the specified time.

According to many authorities in the field, the limitation of this act is that it does not prevent status offenders from being brought before juvenile courts. Such a requirement is technically referred to as *diversion*. Diversion is seen by them as an essential component of a system that wishes not to subject many young people to the trauma, stigma, and punishment that can ensue from court appearances.[36]

While some states (such as Maine and Alaska) have engaged in diversion, other states have, by their failure to do so, placed the burden on the courts of finding other ways of responding to the needs of such youth in sufficient quantity and quality. The 1974 act gave support to therapeutic programs, but it also included youth advocacy as a means of seeking to improve community conditions that lead to status offenses, as well as other types of delinquency.

In the 34 states, probation activities are conducted by the juvenile court; in the rest of the states this activity is conducted by other agencies, such as the department of corrections. The probation officer often also handles court intake. This process involves making decisions as to whether to bring the case into the courtroom and whether to place the youth in detention.[37]

Typically, the intake worker sees youths who are either brought in by their own parents or by the police. The parents will frequently complain that the youth is out of their control. In many cases, the officer may seek to develop a contract between the youth and his or her parents; alternatively, the officer may refer the family to a family counseling agency or to such organizations as Big Brothers and Big Sisters. Particularly if the officer intends to bring the family before a judge, he or she will conduct an investigation of the family and of the youth and will prepare a report for the judge on the findings.

After the court hearing, the judge (or a referee who is empowered to act for the judge for lesser offenses) may sentence the youth to probation. Conditions for such probation often include restitution to victims, community service, school attendance, conformity to specific parental requirements, and obeying a curfew. The probation officer monitors compliance with these requirements and may force the youth to return to court at an earlier time than the one set at the initial trial if they are violated. The judge may then impose other penalties.

In addition to this surveillance, the probation officer may also seek to provide psychosocial treatment to the youth and his or her family. This may include individual and family sessions. The officer may in some situations form a group composed of several youths or even several families for treatment.

Another form of community-based programs for juveniles is parole, which is often referred to for youths as *aftercare*. This comes about because in almost all states the youth's term in a training school is not limited except by the youth reaching the age of majority. The institution, therefore, will release the youth to the community when the youth is seen as ready to cope appropriately with community living. This decision may be made by the staff or by other agencies and boards on the recommendation of staff.

In most states, such aftercare is provided by the Department of Public Welfare. The aftercare worker may visit the youth in the institution prior to release and will be involved in arrangements for placement, such as in foster care, if the youth cannot return home. The ways aftercare workers seek to help youths are very similar to those used by probation officers. The consequence of violation of the rules of aftercare, however, may be a return to the institution. To protect the youth from the negative effects of conflict with the aftercare worker inappropriately affecting this process, the worker must typically secure a final decision from another authority.

A variety of residential and day treatment programs may be used to help youths who require more help than that provided by probation and parole to remain in the community. One frequently used type of residential arrangement is *foster care*. This can often be a very constructive arrangement for the youth but a scarce one. It is not easy to find foster parents who are willing to accept adolescents, much less adolescents who are often hostile and disruptive. In a variant of the typical foster home arrangement, the agency provides the physical facility (often an apartment) and hires the foster parents as employees.

A frequently used community residential placement is the *group home*. This often consists of a home housing about 13 to 25 youths. It is located in a residential community so that youths can attend the neighborhood school, which may also be the one they went to previously. The parents may even live nearby, thus making contact with them very easy if this is desirable. Instead of a single set of parents, group homes are likely to have a supervisor and a set of staff members who are scheduled to be on duty on a rotational basis; they do not reside in the facility except when they are on overnight duty. A variety of treatment approaches can be found among group homes, such as guided group interaction and behavior modification.

With guided group interaction, the staff works to create a highly cohesive group in which the predominant norms are prosocial. This is done through confrontation and some ambiguity regarding the youths' future in the program so that they cannot easily fool the system. Rewards, instead, accrue when individuals are open with one another, manifest a good deal of caring for each other, and work on individual problems.[38]

Behavior modification approaches involve establishing a system of rewards for each individual based on attaining agreed on goals, such as school attendance, avoiding fights, personal hygiene, and participation in activities. This is closely related to an arrangement whereby youths who maintain improved levels of behavior for specified periods are granted a variety of privileges, such as later curfew time, permission to be on their own away from the home for longer spans of time, and more desirable living space, such as a private room.

Day treatment programs have been considerably expanded in the last decade; this is a consequence of their conformity to the community-based concept while still providing a structured and therapeutic environment for a large part of the day. The cost of such programs is well beneath that of residential ones. In addition to providing basic education, such programs may also offer vocational opportunities not provided by the standard schools. An example is a program conducted by the Associated Marine Institutes in Florida. The participants are referred by the courts or the Division of Youth Services and receive training in seamanship, diving, and other nautical skills in addition to basic education classes.[39]

We should not leave the topic of community programs without mention of a few others that have reported a considerable degree of success. One is *Outward Bound,* which is a wilderness survival program. Youths who participate learn the survival skills required in a strenuous environment, such as rock climbing, rappelling, high altitude camping, and survival, which depend both on interdependence and being able to take care of oneself. They apply these skills on field trips often lasting several weeks. This experience has a strong impact on the youth's sense of self-worth and positive identity. Another survival program, *VisionQuest,* combines an alternative school and group home resource with such experiences as wilderness training, a sea survival experience, or a cross-country mule or horse wagon trip.[40] The little research on the effectiveness of these programs suggests that they are as effective, and in some cases more effective, than traditional institutional treatment.[41]

Finally, another development is that of runaway programs. These received federal support from the Runaway and Homeless Youth Act, Title III of the 1974 Juvenile Justice and Delinquency Prevention Act. Such programs operate in most communities and provide shelters for runaways, combined with individual and family counseling to create a long-term and stable plan for the youths.

COMMUNITY-BASED PROGRAMS: ADULT

Much impetus for community-based programs for both youths and adults was provided by the *Law Enforcement Assistance Administration,* which was created by the Omnibus Crime Control and Safe Streets Act of 1968. This program was phased out by the early 1980s as a result of a more conservative and austere government climate.

Community-based programs, particularly for adults, have now fallen on rough times. As Bartollas states, nevertheless, "the more than one million offenders involved in adult community-based programs each year still outnumber those incarcerated in jails and in federal and state correctional institutions."[42] Bartollas goes on to point out that evaluation studies show that they are "at least as effective as, and far less expensive than, institutional confinement."

A number of states have passed community-based corrections legislation. In Minnesota, for example, counties with approved programs receive a state subsidy for community-based programs. They are subsequently charged a specified amount from their subsidies for any adult sentenced to a state institution for less than five years. County programs in that state include halfway houses, substance abuse facilities, therapeutic communities, work and study release centers, and psychiatric care.

In his 1985 publication, Bartollas noted that there were 400 pretrial release programs in the United States.[43] These included release on recognizance and supervised release programs. Another option sometimes permitted is to allow a defendant to deposit a percentage of the bail with the court and to receive most of it back at the time of court appearance. These programs allow the individual to remain as a functioning member of the community while awaiting trial.

Diversion programs are also used with adults, which prevent many from ever having a trial at all. One type is a resolution of citizen disputes program in which the court offers to mediate in minor conflicts. Some issues that have been dealt with in this way include bad check complaints, disorderly conduct, and criminal damages.

Another type of diversion program is referred to as *deferred prosecution.* This parallels the approach used with some juveniles in that the offender's appearance before a court is canceled if he or she successfully participates in a prescribed diversionary activity.

In the case of drug offenders, a variety of programs, including *therapeutic communities,* is used to divert them. These communities, such as Synanon in California and Phoenix House in New York, seek to attain change in the offender through structured programs, group meetings that are highly confrontational, and interactions that produce a degree of humiliation to break through the facades presented. Constructive activities are reinstituted through hard work both in the maintenance of the community and in economic activities that may be sponsored. The applicability of these communities is limited by the number of offenders who are willing to undergo their regimen. Abuses of the rights of residents have also led to criticisms of the programs, which further discourage applicants.

A variety of other residential programs also serve, as with youths, to maintain offenders in the community. People who are assigned to them require more structure than if living independently in the community; they may also be parolees who enter as a condition of parole. In a typical facility, such as a halfway house, residents leave in the morning to go to work or school. The facility may also provide support in finding and keeping a job or remaining in school. Other services include group, individual, or family counseling; referral to other community services; and training in social and work skills.

INSTITUTIONAL PROGRAMS: JUVENILE

Despite the trend to deinstitutionalization, the states typically still have an array of public and private institutions for delinquents. A few states, however, such as Massachusetts, have closed all their public trainings schools. In most states, these have been for one sex or the other, but states are now experimenting with coeducational programs.

The institution typically offers a full educational and vocational program. The better programs seek to maintain small classes staffed by teachers specially trained to deal with youth with learning difficulties. Vocational training may include such classes as automotive design and printing for boys and beauty culture and sewing for girls. Recreational and athletic activities are also conducted.

Great variability exists as to the type of therapeutic programs found in such institutions. One predominant type is either guided group interaction or a variation of this approach, *positive peer culture*.[44] The latter version clearly specifies the format of group meetings wherein the group focuses on selected individuals and their behavior; problematic behavior is categorized through the use of labels that the group members learn. The youths are required as part of their learning to care for one another, to monitor each other's behavior throughout the day, and to bring this information into group sessions, which are held almost every day.

Another common treatment used in both community and institutional settings, is behavior modification. The institutional setting, however, as with positive peer culture, affords a much larger arena for the inmates' lives as the context for monitoring and planning behavior change. Transactional analysis has also been used in juvenile institutions. This is a therapeutic system in which the youths learn to analyze their own behaviors and those of others in terms of the ego states of the parent, the child, and the adult and to examine sequences of behaviors as they constitute "games."[45]

The preceding statements about treatment programs in public institutions may imply that they are equivalent to the better psychiatric facilities. This is often far from the case as, despite the efforts to humanize and modernize them, they can still be the breeding ground of brutality and inhumanity. As Bartollas states:

> The training school receives the worst of the labelled—the losers, the unwanted, the outsiders. These young men consider themselves to be among the toughest, most masculine and virile of their counterparts and they have the social credentials to prove it. Yet in much the same way as they are processed, they create, import, and maintain a system which is as brutalizing as the one through which they passed. If anything, the internal environment and the organization and interaction at TICO [the training school in Columbus, Ohio being described] are less fair, less just, less humane, and less decent than the worst aspects of the criminal justice system on the outside. Brute force, manipulation, institutional sophistication carry the day, and set the standards which ultimately prevail. Remove the staff, and a feudal structure will emerge which will make the dark ages seem very enlightened.[46]

The system of institutions also includes a variety of privately run programs that utilize the full range of treatment and program modalities. These institutions, however, at their best do not have to deal with the bureaucratic pressures of the state political apparatus and can control the number of youths they receive (at least insofar as their budgets will allow).

An example of this is *Boysville* of Michigan, which is continuing to open group homes in many Michigan communities and which conducts a large campus program in Clinton, Michigan. Supported by an order of Catholic Brothers, Boysville was an early pioneer in the use of positive peer culture and is now seeking to develop a family therapy model that is appropriate to delinquents and their families. Such institutions do receive referrals from the juvenile courts and are funded, at least in part, by payments for these youths. In this sense, therefore, they have a public character.

INSTITUTIONAL PROGRAMS: ADULTS

Typically, when adults enter prison, they are first placed in a reception center and remain isolated from prisoners not in the center. At this time, they usually take psychological tests, and this and other information available to the staff are used to classify the prisoners and assign them to a prison component and a level of security. This assessment process has been heavily criticized because it is often performed by unqualified personnel, results are unreliable, and the system may be unable to relate assignments to assessments anyway.

While the individual is in prison, various types of therapy may be made available, although many corrections officials question the appropriateness and effectiveness of therapy in a prison setting. Nevertheless, a range of treatment approaches is used, including psychodynamically oriented therapy, behavior modification, and group therapy.

There have been a few attempts to turn prisons into therapeutic communities, despite the fact that prison authorities are reluctant to modify the prison environment to this degree or to give a great deal of authority to mental health professionals. Programs in these settings usually involve prisoners in self-government and make available a variety of types of therapy. Prisoners are also given the opportunity to have input into decisions regarding individuals. The reader who is interested in up to date thinking on this modality can consult Toch's excellent volume.[47]

Group modalities, while often used, must overcome a number of conditions that limit group effectiveness. Many of these relate to the norms that exist in the inmate subculture, such as that inmates should "do their own time." This prohibits prisoners from probing too deeply into each other's lives and certainly from doing so in the presence of a staff member (even if this person is a psychologist, psychiatrist, or social worker).

In addition to therapeutic activities, prisons usually offer educational and vocational programs, religious activities, and even employment opportunities for inmates. Academic instruction is made available through basic education programs, and inmates who do not have a high school diploma are helped to acquire a general education diploma (usually referred to as a GED). Many prisons either offer college-level courses on the premises or allow selected inmates to take courses at nearby colleges. Correspondence course enrollment may also be facilitated.

As with juvenile institutions, adult prisons also are very likely to provide vocational training. Bartollas's listing of such training consists of printing, barbering, welding, meat cutting, machine shop work, electronics, baking, plumbing, television and radio repair, air conditioning maintenance, automotive body and fender repair, sheet metal work, painting, blueprint reading, and furniture repair and upholstering; he notes, however, that fewer types of training are made available to women, who are likely to be offered beauty culture, secretarial training, business machine operation, data processing, baking and food preparation, and key punch operation.[48]

Despite this impressive list of alternatives, at least one expert does not believe that the overall quality of such training is very good. Criticism is leveled at the quality of instruction, the equipment, and even at the marketability of the specific skills taught.

Ready for rehabilitation. (Photo by Laimute E. Druskis.)

Inmates may also have trouble gaining membership in the trade unions when this is a condition of employment.[49]

The prison may offer inmates employment in a variety of ways. These include leasing prisoners to private firms, allowing such firms to establish factories within the prison, taking contracts for work from state agencies, and utilizing prisoners for public works projects. Most states, however, have laws prohibiting prisons from selling their products through regular markets to prevent competition, because inmates are paid very low wages. Conditions in this respect are better in the federal than the state prisons.

One of the oldest forms of rehabilitation offered in prisons is religious programs. Nevertheless, only a small proportion of prisoners participate in religious activities although the federal prison system has 62 full-time chaplains and the state system another 600 to 1,000.[50]

Prisons offer many other programs, including recreation and self-help. An example of the latter is the application of Erhard Seminar Training (EST) to prison settings. Werner Erhard, the founder of this approach, conducted the first prison group at the Federal Correctional Institution at Lompoc in 1971. The intent of this experience is to help members examine their basic attitudes toward life so that they can act in their own best interests, rather than in their habitual ways. The goal is to help prisoners become active agents in their own behalf.[51]

Issues and Directions

In spite of the many constructive programs that exist in one or another setting, we agree with Netherland who wrote:

> At present, the criminal justice system in the United States is an incomprehensible, inefficient, unproductive, multilevel, administrative maze. The prison environment is violent, depressing, regimented, boring, and dehumanizing. Most prisons are located miles away from needed resources and the population they serve. Prisons are outdated, overcrowded, and far too large. Activities are duplicated, programs fragmented, and resources wasted.[52]

To move away from the overall dismal picture just portrayed, there are a number of issues we must consider and problems we must solve. The first concerns the attitudes that exist in society and the societal conditions that promote either crime or the way society responds to crime. A pendulum frequently swings from a stance that favors programs to advance the welfare of those in need, including offenders, to one that favors individual rather than social responsibility. A period that emphasizes individual responsibility is also one when punishment rather than rehabilitation is favored.

We believe that society can advance so that the most destructive ideas do not reoccur. This is demonstrated by the increased protection of the rights of offenders both before and after they have been judged, as well as the development of community corrections. Social workers and others with similar values must continue to work for an understanding on the part of the public, in general, as well as the representatives in legislatures of the reasons to sustain and advance this development.

A closely related issue is the connection between crime and other conditions, such as racial discrimination, poverty, unemployment, and lack of educational and vocational opportunity. It is consistent with the values of many policy makers to punish offenders and lock them away from society rather than to work to create a just society, even though the former course may be more costly than the latter. Table 11.1 offers a good indication of these kinds of relationships.

As noted earlier, for example, the proportion of members of minority groups in prison is greater than their proportion in the society, even though there is good evidence that the proportion of crimes they commit is not greater. It is hard to resist the conclusion that in many ways the correctional system functions to control the wrath of the nonwhite groups caused by their disadvantaged status in the society.

In the process of dealing with these basic issues, the monumental question still remains as to how we should try to mold the correctional system so that it is just and humane and benefits the offender and, we believe, consequently the society as a whole. It is clear that it is almost impossible for large institutions to operate in these ways for either adults or juveniles. The move from large institutions to small and community-based ones must continue.

When individuals are exposed to all the conditions of the correctional system, there are likely to be negative consequences, even if there are positive ones. The negative consequences are due to labeling and stigma, to the influences of other offenders, and

TABLE 11.1
Marital and Educational Distribution of the U.S. Male and Prison Populations, and Index of Dissimilarity

	Males, 1987	Inmates, 1986	Difference, Disregarding Sign
Marital Status			
Married	65.5	20.3	45.2
Never married	25.3	53.7	28.4
Divorced	6.7	18.1	11.4
Other (separated/widowed)	2.5	7.9	5.4
Total	100.0	100.0	90.4
Index of dissimilarity (difference/2)			45.2
Education			
< 12 years	24.4	61.6	37.2
> 12 years	75.6	38.4	37.2
Total	100.0	100.0	74.4
Index of dissimilarity (difference/2)			37.2

Source: U.S. Bureau of the Census, *Statistical Abstract of the United States 1989* (Washington, DC: U.S. Government Printing Office, 1989), Tables 49, 213, 319.

to the poor conditions that often prevail. Therefore, we must find ways to divert individuals from the system if society does not require the degree of protection provided by incarceration. This is certainly true of adolescent status offenders and adults who have committed victimless crimes, such as substance abuse. This requires an expansion in the availability of all the diversionary programs we have described.

Even when an individual must be institutionalized, much further thought and research must be done to learn about the kinds of programs that will promote rehabilitation. We must learn to assess law breakers more adequately and to use this assessment in creating a good match between the individual and the program. In any case, since education and employment are the keys to success in the society, *quality* educational and vocational programs must be central to any correctional facility for either youth or adults. Individuals who are almost totally devoid of power are also unlikely to feel good about themselves or the society into which they must fit. Consequently, all correctional programs should encourage offenders to participate in the governance structure.

At all phases of the correctional process, a key question is how to reintegrate the individual into the community after the commission of a crime. This requires the creation of community linkages and support systems through the most effective of community organization activities.

Social workers have central roles to play in the molding of public opinion, the creation of public policies, the development of new programs, and the staffing of rehabilitative activities. A major problem for the profession of social work, however, is the current emphasis in the curricula of schools of social work upon psychotherapy with voluntary, more advantaged populations.

As we have stressed throughout this book, this is contrary to the historic mission of social work and the priorities that we believe should exist for publicly supported services within the society. Professional schools should make these priorities clear in their official and unofficial announcements and in the experiences they provide to all students. Only then can social work create the kind of expertise the field of corrections so desperately needs.

In addition, schools must place more emphasis on problematic populations. The expansion of the social work mission to all persons (the NASW motto is "We help people just like you") creates a tension of focus between the voluntary client and the involuntary, or those in various conditions judged difficult by society. Achieving a balance is one of the more important current tasks of the social work profession.

Conclusion

We began this chapter with a discussion of the function of the justice system within the larger society and the rationale for the role of social work within this system. To clarify the various directions the correctional system has taken in fulfilling its function, we described three ideologies in this field: rehabilitation, justice, and utilitarian punishment.

We presented an overview of the criminal justice system, both as it emerged historically and as it exists today. Following this, we provided more detail on each major component of the system: community-based corrections and institutional programs for both children and adults.

The chapter concluded with a review of the major issues facing the correctional field and a projection as to the direction that we believe should be taken in addressing them. The issues that stand out are those of societal values regarding offenders and how offenders should be treated; the social causes of crime; the use of the system with reference to oppressed minorities; the overall negative effects of large, isolated prisons; the inappropriate use of institutions for people who do not endanger the society; the importance of community resources; the role of rehabilitative activities and the match between the activity and the offender; and, finally, the considerable responsibility of social work to provide well-trained professionals motivated to work in this field.

Notes

1. Elliot Studt, "Crime and Delinquency: Institutions," *Encyclopedia of Social Work,* Vol. 1, 17th ed., J. B. Turner, ed. (Washington, D.C.: National Association of Social Workers, 1977), pp. 208–213.
2. Ibid., p. 211.
3. Ibid., p. 211; Miles B. Santamour and Bernadette West, "The Mentally Retarded Offender: Presentation of the Facts and a Discussion of Issues," in Miles B. Santamour and Bernadette West, eds., *The Retarded Offender* (New York: Praeger, 1982), pp. 7–37; Joseph W. Rogers

and G. Larry Mays, *Juvenile Delinquency and Juvenile Justice* (Englewood Cliffs: Prentice Hall, 1987), p. 10.

4. Studt, "Crime and Delinquency," p. 212.

5. For an extensive discussion of this, see Charles Garvin, "Resocialization: Group Work in Social Control and Correctional Settings," in *The Group Worker's Handbook: Varieties of Group Experience,* Robert Conyne, ed. (Springfield Ill.: Charles C. Thomas, 1985), pp. 113–134; Charles Garvin, *Contemporary Group Work,* 2nd ed. (Englewood Cliffs, N.J.: Prentice Hall, 1987), pp. 254–268.

6. Elliot Studt, Sheldon L. Messinger, and Thomas P. Wilson, C-*Unit: Search for Community in Prison* (New York: Russell Sage Foundation, 1968).

7. Ibid., p. 212.

8. For example, Rosemary C. Sarri and Robert D. Vinter, "Justice for Whom? Varieties of Juvenile Correctional Approaches," in *The Juvenile Justice System,* Malcolm W. Klein, ed. (Beverly Hills, Calif.: Sage Publications, 1976), pp. 161–200; and Robert D. Vinter, ed., *Time Out: A National Study of Juvenile Correctional Programs* (Ann Arbor: University of Michigan, 1976.)

9. Studt, "Crime and Delinquency," p. 212.

10. Clemens Bartollas, *Correctional Treatment: Theory and Practice* (Englewood Cliffs, N.J.: Prentice Hall, 1985); *Juvenile Delinquency,* 2nd ed. (New York: Macmillan, 1990).

11. Bartollas, *Correctional Treatment,* p. 25.

12. Ibid., p. 27.

13. Douglas Lipton, Robert Martinson, and Judith Wilks, *The Effectiveness of Correctional Treatment: A Survey of Treatment Evaluation Studies* (New York: Praeger Publications, 1975).

14. Robert Martinson, "What Works?—Questions and Answers about Prison Reform," *Public Interest* 35 (Spring, 1974): 22–54.

15. Ted Palmer, *Correctional Intervention and Research: Current Issues and Future Prospects* (Lexington, Mass.: D.C. Heath, 1978).

16. Albert R. Roberts, *Juvenile Justice: Policies, Programs, and Services* (Chicago: Dorsey Press, 1989), p. 159.

17. An interview with David Fogel cited in Roberts, *Juvenile Justice,* p. 42.

18. Ibid., p. 47.

19. Rogers and Mays, *Juvenile Delinquency and Juvenile Justice,* p. 480.

20. Francis T. Cullen and Karen E. Gilbert, *Reaffirming Rehabilitation* (Cincinnati: Anderson Publishing Co., 1982), p. 138.

21. Bartollas, *Correctional Treatment,* p. 67.

22. Much of this material has been drawn from Bartollas, *Correctional Treatment,* pp. 3–19.

23. Wayne Morris, "The Attorney General's Survey of Release Procedures," in *Penology: The Evolution of Corrections in America,* George C. Killinger and Paul F. Cromwell, Jr., eds. (St. Paul, Minn.: West Publishing Co., 1973), p. 23.

24. 213 Pa. 48, 62 A, pp. 198–200.

25. Bartollas, *Correctional Treatment,* p. 8.

26. U.S. Bureau of the Census, *Statistical Abstract of the United States: 1990* (Washington, D.C.: U.S. Government Printing Office, 1990), Tables 307 and 308.

27. Federal Bureau of Investigation, *Uniform Crime Reports for 1984* (Washington, D.C.: U.S. Department of Justice, 1985), pp. 172–176; U.S. Department of Justice, *Sourcebook of Criminal Justice Statistics, 1983* (Washington, D.C.: U.S. Department of Justice, 1985), pp. 15–17.

28. *New York Times,* October 8, 1990, p. A6.

29. By 1990 the U.S. average incarceration rate had increased to 289 (Netherland, "Correction System: Adult").

30. Ibid., pp. 351–352.

31. Ibid., pp. 352–353.

32. Albert R. Roberts, "An Introduction and Overview of Juvenile Justice," in *Juvenile Justice*

Policies, Programs, and Services, Albert R. Roberts, ed. (Chicago: Dorsey Press, 1989), pp. 3–15.

33. All the following data on detention and training schools are from D. A. Willis, J. Battle, I. M. Schwartz, A. Grasso, and A. Vestevich. *Juvenile Justice Trends: 1977–1989* (Ann Arbor: Center for the Study of Youth Policy, The University of Michigan School of Social Work, in press).

34. Clemens Bartollas, *Juvenile Delinquency* (New York: Wiley, 1985), p. 64.

35. For an extensive discussion of the MFY experience, see Joseph H. Helfgot, *Professional Reforming: Mobilization for Youth and the Failure of Social Science* (Lexington, Mass.: Lexington Books, 1981).

36. See Solomon Kobrin and Malcolm W. Klein, *Community Treatment of Juvenile Offenders: The DSO Experiments* (Beverly Hills, Calif.: Sage Publications, 1983), pp. 19–39.

37. Bartollas, *Juvenile Corrections,* p. 427.

38. Details on this approach may be found in LaMar T. Empey and Stephen Lubeck, *The Silverlake Experiment: Testing Delinquency Theory and Community Intervention* (Chicago: Aldine Publishing Co., 1971.)

39. Ronald H. Bailey, "Can Delinquents Be Saved by the Sea?" *Corrections Magazine* 1 (September, 1974), pp. 77–84.

40. Paul Sweeney, "VisionQuest's Rite of Passage, *Corrections Magazine* 8 (February 1982), pp 22–32.

41. Albert R. Roberts, "Wilderness Experiences: Camps and Outdoor Programs," in *Juvenile Justice Programs, Policies, and Services,* Albert R. Roberts, ed. (Chicago: Dorsey Press, 1989), pp. 194–218.

42. Bartollas, *Correctional Treatment,* p. 102.

43. Ibid.

44. Harry Vorrath and Larry Brendtro, *Positive Peer Culture* (Chicago: Aldine Publishing Co., 1974).

45. See a comprehensive description of how behavior modification and transactional analysis were used in youth correctional settings in California, as well as comparison of outcomes, in Carl F. Jesness and others, *The Youth Center Research Project* (Sacramento, Calif.: American Justice Institute, 1972).

46. Clemens Bartollas, Stuart J. Miller, and Simon Dinitz, *Juvenile Victimization: The Institutional Paradox* (New York: Halsted Press, A Sage Publication, 1976), p. 271.

47. Hans Toch, ed. *Therapeutic Communities in Corrections* (New York: Praeger Publications, 1980.)

48. Bartollas, *Correctional Treatment,* pp. 143–144.

49. Ibid.

50. Ibid., p. 146.

51. Ibid., pp. 152–153.

52. Netherland, "Corrections System: Adult," p. 358.

CHAPTER 12
Service Delivery for Promoting Health and Meeting the Needs of the Elderly

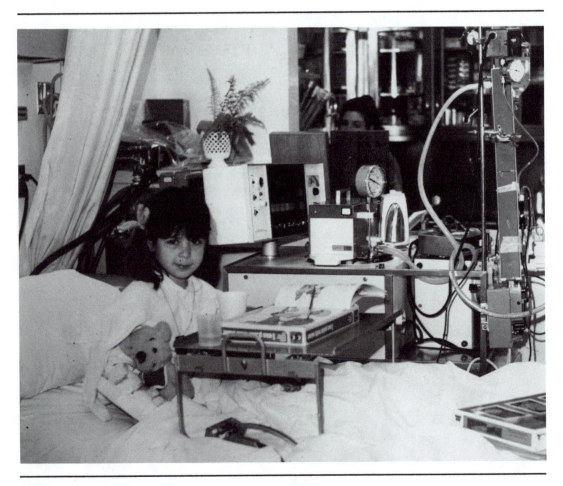

The Function of the Health System

This chapter presents a discussion of those institutions in society that promote the health of its members and work to reduce the frequency and negative effects of illness. Our special focus will be on the role of social work in such institutions.

We believe in a holistic view of the human being as a complete organism that is more than its parts and functions added together. Anything that has an impact on how the organism functions can affect and be affected by any of the organism's aspects, whether these are conceptualized as mental, physical, or social. Thus, while some institutions, such as a hospital or a mental health center, are classified as elements of the health system, all social workers, *wherever they are employed,* have an impact on the processes of health promotion and illness prevention for their clients.

Social workers in correctional, family welfare, income maintenance, and child welfare services, to name a few, should be able to examine how the health of people influences and is influenced by the issues that brought them to these agencies. As a consequence, all social workers must understand these processes. In addition they must be able, when necessary, to facilitate the way clients utilize health services, as well as to advocate the creation and availability of such services.

In some social work texts, separate chapters are devoted to mental and physical health services. Because of our holistic perspective and conviction that planning for these services should not isolate them from each other, we bring this content together here. Many concepts, such as those regarding levels of prevention, have been drawn from public health ideas that apply to both physical and mental problems, and this is another reason against separating this material. Nevertheless, institutions and policies are often directed at entitities classified as "mental" or "physical," and we shall recognize this also.

The functions of the health system are to promote the health and reduce the incidence and effects of disease among individuals. We use the terms "health," "illness," and "disease" almost daily and may fail to distinguish among them. In this chapter, we shall use "health" as defined by Terris: "Health is a state of physical, mental, and social well-being and ability to function, and not merely the absence of illness or infirmity."[1]

Banta cites a definition of disease as "a failure of the adaptive mechanism of an organism to counteract adequately the stimuli and stresses to which it is subject, resulting in a disturbance in function or structure of any part, organ, or system of the body."[2] The same author discusses the term "illness" as having "social and psychological as well as biomedical components".[3]

The health–disease issue is related to the broader topic considered in each of these chapters on service delivery systems: the function of the system to both prevent dysfunction and to rehabilitate individuals who have become dysfunctional. In fact, a major goal of most people who seek to mold our health care system is to strengthen its prevention aspects.

Health, then, involves all the things we do to enhance our growth and functioning, such as eating proper foods, engaging in exercise, or meditating, as well as specific medical acts like taking pills. Health institutions should and often do promote these behaviors. In fact, social workers together with a variety of other professionals have a clear mandate to facilitate health, whereas the treatment of disease is more clearly the legitimate province of a limited set of professions such as medicine and dentistry. There is less certainty about who treats mental as contrasted with physical illness. A recent report, for example, indicated that social workers offer a larger proportion of psychotherapy in the United States than is offered by other professions.[4]

The distinction between disease and illness is important, because a person may suffer from one and not the other in ways that affect the health care provider's activities. The former consists of specific pathological processes detected through medical procedures, whereas the latter is the individual's reactions to these processes. Individuals may, for example, suffer from heart disease but not treat themselves as ill (such as failing to consult a doctor) and, consequently, engage in behaviors that will exacerbate that disease. On the other hand, people without heart disease may, in contrast, treat themselves as having such a disease as a way of avoiding responsibilities, thus taking on the role of being ill. Social workers have sought to help these two types of individuals to behave in more appropriate ways.

It is also important to realize (as Figure 4.1 indicates) that services to enhance the health of individuals may be directed at the community or the environment as well. Activities in the first two categories are often essential to the health of the population and include such things as ensuring pure drinking water, waste disposal, and food inspection. Community activities also might affect individuals, such as requiring immunization. The scope of health care activities is underscored by the statistic that there are more than 16 health workers for every physician in the United States.[5]

Another, frequently used way of discussing the functions of the health care system is to subdivide them into curing and caring. The former includes all the activities directed at the disease itself. The latter recognizes that the disease occurs in a person, who has needs as well as thoughts and feelings about the illness. That person may or may not have trust in the concern of medical personnel for his or her welfare, comfort, and general well-being. As McKeown states, "Since most serious diseases and disabilities are likely to prove relatively intractable if they cannot be prevented, the role of therapeutic medicine should be modified to include as the major commitment the concept of care. Such a change would carry important implications for medical science and service and should affect the content and orientation of medical education."[6] The issue of providing care is central for social workers. They are often involved independently or are utilized by physicians to ensure that the patients' needs are met and their well-being maintained.

The Function of Social Work in the Health Care System

Social workers have always had a major interest in health care. A recent manifestation of this interest was the Health Policy Statement of the National Association of Social Workers.[7] As one writer stated in summarizing this document:

The NASW statement addresses the entire resident population, ensures uniform services for all groups, and provides equal access without separate categories, arrangements, and services. The primary emphasis is on preventing illness and dysfunction and promoting health. Health services must be seen in terms of medical, psychological, and social components. There must be allowance for decentralized community planning and management and consumer involvement and participation. Delivery systems should take into account local variations in need, continuity, and linkage in levels of care, opportunities for consumers to choose plans, input by professional providers (including qualified social workers) into planning and service delivery, and individual and family service needs. The federal government must establish organizational and fiscal standards and assure accountability at the national, state, and local levels. A national health care program must be publicly funded through progressive taxation for long term stability. There must be fair and equitable income payment for professional personnel based on cost-funding methods and standards. The payment mechanism should provide incentives for illness prevention programs, cost containment, negotiable rates of reimbursement and cost-saving health systems such as HMOs. . . . Emphasis should be on the development of primary care providers, the recruitment of minorities and women in health care professions, and uniform national licensure and certification standards.[8]

The NASW document also discusses standard setting for health care practice, the development of primary care providers, the recruitment of minorities and women as health care providers, health research, and health planning.[9] As this brief summary of topics demonstrates, the views of the social work profession regarding health care are comprehensive and touch on many aspects of the health care system.

Probably because of the variety of professions involved in health care, not to speak of the preeminent role of the physician, social workers have struggled to define a framework for their practice in this field. Although we believe that the view of social work as concerned with the interaction between the individual and the social worker can easily be applied to the health field, there are ways this concept must be further defined for our current discussion.

Schlesinger selects four frameworks to define social work practice related to health care: (1) a public health perspective, (2) the concept of person–environment fit, (3) the continuum from cure to care, and (4) the idea of "the careers of illness."[10] All these frameworks are related to social work's individual–environment transactional perspective.

THE PUBLIC HEALTH PERSPECTIVE

The public health perspective that social work draws on focuses on preventing disease and promoting health. The closeness of these two fields is increasingly being recognized by both sets of practitioners and is shown in the development of dual degree programs sponsored by schools of public health and social work.

Social workers now utilize a number of public health concepts in their work. One is epidemiology, which is "the study of why and how diseases are distributed within a community."[11] Epidemiology involves an examination of the interaction between the individual who may develop the problem (the host), the factors that produce the problem (the agent), and the environment that may promote or prevent the problem. Environmental factors may be material, such as poor sanitation, or social, such as unemployment and high crime rates. A major implication of this approach for social work practitioners is that a reduction in disease or an increase in health may be brought about by changes in any one of these three factors. As Schlesinger states:

> For example, people who have developed coping skills that serve them well in a crisis may be better able to withstand the threats posed by environmental stressors such as family disruption. Conversely environments conducive to good family functioning (adequate income and housing) may reduce the susceptibility to disease. This approach can clarify our thinking about those people particularly prone to health problems because of the situations in which they find themselves. It can also help to develop efforts to effect change.[12]

Another public health concept is the population at risk, which consists of all people in the community who may acquire a condition. In addition to its application to physical conditions, this concept has been utilized by social workers to examine a variety of social problems that have health implications, such as child abuse and other forms of family violence, suicide, teen pregnancy, and sexually transmitted diseases. All these problems involve interactions among people, their coping capacities, environmental conditions, and specific stressors. Prevention, therefore, can be accomplished by social workers and others who seek to have an impact on these dimensions.

Social workers deal with these issues at several levels. For example, a worker interested in preventing adolescent pregnancy might develop programs that provide young people with sexual information and guidance, opportunities in the community for career planning, employment, recreation, and support from their families. Such programs help youth to cope with sexuality while reducing the stresses that may promote impulsive sexual behavior.

The worker engaging in primary prevention of teenage pregnancy, will carry out the activities described in the preceding paragraph. The worker engaging in secondary prevention will work with young people who are about to become parents to make plans for the child and their own futures. This early intervention might help to prevent subsequent pregnancies, child abuse and neglect, and economic dependency. The worker engaging in tertiary prevention might be involved with young people who have been identified as abusive or neglectful, who are continuing to conceive children, or who have become financially dependent to find better ways of coping in more supportive and nurturing environments.

PERSON–ENVIRONMENT FIT

The person–environment fit perspective holds that the "fit between people and their environments can affect and is in turn affected by their health."[13] This perspective directs us to examine life changes, including those related to stages of the life cycle and the degree to which the environment meets the needs of individuals as these changes occur.

Among the issues that can be examined from this perspective are the needs of the disabled, the chronically ill, children, and the elderly. It is also a useful way to look at crises that occur. A *crisis* is defined as a hazardous event that places the individual in a vulnerable state during which the individual's customary ways of coping with stress are not adequate. The individual will often find some way of resolving the crisis within time, although the way chosen may not be very effective and, in fact, may lead to more serious problems.[14]

The crisis may be provoked by a health problem of one family member, such as when a parent has a heart attack. Other crises, such as a loss of employment or a divorce, may lead to health problems. Social workers understand how effective helping during crises enhances health and reduces illness.

These ideas about person–environment fit and crisis intervention are compatible with the public health perspective. They extend the perspective, however, through a close examination of how people in at risk situations can be helped to cope with and alter those situations.

THE CONTINUUM FROM CURE TO CARE

In her work on social work in health care, Schlesinger presents an extensive discussion of the relationship of curing to caring; she sees caring as those activities that develop from a recognition that it is people who have varying states of health and illness. Thus, people's needs, situations, and roles in relationship to their wellness must be considered in terms of both their health and the total quality of their lives. She, therefore, defines care as "the range of perspectives and practice technology thought to contribute to 'wellness,' to prevention of disease and illness and to the reduction of the economic, social and psychological burdens related to illness and disease."[15] Schlesinger uses this definition to create a typology of caring. Caring tasks include those directed at prevention, cure amelioration (in which she sees a greater role in social work for amelioration or "to make better"), and maintenance (which she sees as sustaining levels of functioning). Prevention involves health education, humanizing health care environments, and averting family disorganization during the illness of a member; amelioration includes helping people to cooperate with other health care providers such as physicians, coordinating the services of such providers, and helping people to make their needs for health care known; maintenance includes helping people to cope with illness when no improvement is likely, providing resources to ill people, and creating self-help systems.[16]

CAREERS OF ILLNESS

Health care-oriented social workers have also used the sociological concept of career to analyze their professional roles. A career involves a series of interdependent activities and tasks that an individual undertakes or experiences in some sphere of life. Thus, we can speak of a work career or an educational career. We can also speak of careers that are not desired by the individual or society or both such as a criminal career or an illness career.

As Schlesinger states, "When this concept is applied to illness and its social and psychological consequences, it focuses attention on the fact that these consequences vary with the nature of the disease or illness; the different stages that can be expected; and the medical, social, and psychological interventions that need to be used at different stages."[17] This career concept is broader than a medical concern with the course of a disease; it involves the full range of reactions and needs of the sick individual throughout the course of the illness and the responses of the environment to these reactions and needs.

An example of this analysis as applied to social work practice is a man who has suffered a stroke that left him with a slight paralysis. While in the hospital, he and his family wanted to know about this condition, what caused it, and how much recovery could be expected. There was also the issue of the financial needs of the family while he was recovering. His daughter, with whom he had been very close, was also more upset by his condition than other family members. The medical social worker, at this stage of his illness career, sought to provide information to the family and to interpret their information needs to their doctor. The worker also became involved with financial planning and family counseling in which one focus was the reactions of the daughter.

After the patient's release from the hospital, he was seen on an outpatient basis for physical therapy and the prescription of medications that would lessen the probability of future strokes. His wife reported to the social worker that he was failing to take his medication and the worker focused on this issue during family and individual sessions.

As time went on, it became apparent that the patient was unable to do his salesman's job, which required standing up for long periods of time. He was depressed about this, and his wife suggested that she increase her working hours so that he could stay at home. The worker recognized the many negative effects on all family members of this change in family roles and, instead, encouraged the patient to apply for another position with his firm. He was able to obtain this, even though his new job entailed a shift to a salary basis rather than a commission one. He had been a successful salesman and had earned high commissions, so this change entailed a reduction in income. Nevertheless, his knowledge of the field meant he will still be employed by his firm at a valued job. His compliance with medical advice improved also.

The worker was able to anticipate the family's needs in this case because of his knowledge of the disease itself at various stages of onset and recovery, as well as the likely responses of the patient and family. The worker also anticipated the effects on and reactions of other systems in which the patient was involved, such as his place of employment. In all these interventions, the worker was acting consistently with current ideas regarding the role of a medical social worker in a hospital setting.[18]

Thus, we see that the public health perspective focuses the worker's attention on environmental conditions that place groups of people at risk, an essential type of information for any program of prevention. The person–environment fit perspective helps the worker to examine individual capacities as these relate to environmental circumstances. The continuum from cure to care helps social workers to place themselves within the broad spectrum of health care services. And the concept of career helps social workers to examine their roles in the process of change that occurs as people experience and cope with stages of illness.

ROLES AT DIFFERENT SYSTEM LEVELS

As in all other fields of service, social workers concerned about health intervene at the individual, family, group, organizational, communal, and societal levels (see Figure 4.1). At the individual level the worker helps patients obtain medically recommended aids, cope with emotional and other reactions to illness, respond to the needs of others in the systems in which the patient is located, satisfy his or her own needs, learn facts about the illness, secure home supports, and acquire additional services that may be needed. The worker will also help the patient to find ways of modifying the responses of individuals and systems that stand in the way of meeting needs.

The health-oriented worker, like all other social workers, also considers family issues. These may require the worker to interact with other family members or with the family as a whole. At times this is required to maintain the health or alleviate the illness of the family member in question. At other times, family intervention serves to restore the functioning of other family members or the family as a unit.

Group skills are often utilized by these social workers. When the client is a resident of a medical setting, such as a hospital, the worker will examine how group interactions among patients affect their treatment, and the worker may intervene in these interactions, such as by holding ward meetings. The worker may form groups of clients so that they can help each other cope with health and illness issues. Workers in the health field understand the value of self-help groups, particularly for people with chronic conditions. Examples of such groups are those for women with mastectomies and people with ostomies, chronic mental illness, heart disease, Alzheimer's disease, and cancer. Many self-help groups have also been created for the families of people with health-related conditions to help the family to cope better with family stresses related to the condition.

Social workers in the health system must frequently employ organizational knowledge and interventions, even if they are not personally responsible for administering a social service department. Social workers should be highly sensitive to the impact of the organization providing the health service on its consumers. Thus, social workers should pay close attention to findings in such fields as medical sociology that bear on this impact.[19] The workers should have skills in bringing this information to the institution and in working for change.

Social workers often find these roles difficult because of the status accorded the physician. Like the nursing profession, social workers must identify their unique expertise in the health field and acquire the authority to utilize that expertise. This issue is compounded by the fact that the majority of physicians in medical settings are men and social workers, women. To status issues related to professional differences are added those related to gender.

Another major organizational topic is that the social worker in a health setting is typically a member of a team, which may consist of doctors, nurses, and occupational and recreational therapists, to name a few. An organizational challenge is for the social worker to contribute to the overall functioning of the team so that the needs of patients can best be met. The training of social workers for service in health settings should include helping them to understand the functioning of interprofessional teams and how to facilitate this collaborative activity.

Other administrative topics that involve social workers in these settings are the financing of social services, social work quality and quantity assurance considerations, the collection and utilization of data related to social services, and cost–benefit analyses of these services.

Community factors are heavily involved in placing people at risk, and community resources are involved in prevention and treatment. Social workers are involved, therefore, in identifying at risk populations and seeking to change community conditions. Typical activities include lobbying for the creation of community health facilities and for the eradication of unhealthy community conditions. Social workers fulfilling community organization roles will mobilize community residents to work for these types of changes.

This kind of community activity has an old and hallowed history in social work. Among people who heavily influenced social work were settlement house founders such as Jane Addams (Hull House, Chicago) and Lillian Wald (Henry Street Settlement, New York). Addams had herself appointed neighborhood sanitation inspector. She also engaged the first woman physician graduate of Johns Hopkins Medical School to come to Chicago in 1893 to open the country's initial well-baby and pediatric clinic. Wald was a pioneer in public health nursing, and Henry Street Settlement was first called The Nurses Settlement. At that Settlement, visiting nursing services were provided at little or no cost, as well as many other health-related activities. As Miller and Rehr state:

> In large measure their initiatives (Addams, Wald, and others in the settlement field) and zeal were responsible for the establishment and growth of neighborhood health centers, baby clinics, diagnostic centers, first-aid rooms, open-air camps, and sanitaria. Health reform during the era of the early days of the settlement movement is an exciting chapter in the history of social work, particularly medical social work.[20]

Social workers have also consistently been involved in influencing health policy. In addition to the NASW health policy statement, a major example was the role of social work in relationship to the Comprehensive Health Planning Act (CHP) of 1966. This act provided funds to states for establishing state health planning agencies. As one authority on this program states,

> At the peak of planning under CHP, social workers were very visible. They provided leadership not only as directors and deputy directors of CHP agencies but also in key staff roles. One study (Finney, Pessin, and Matheis, 1976) of health planning agencies under CHP demonstrated the wide range of activities in which social workers were involved. In the 196 agencies studied, social workers held 9% of the executive director positions and 7% of the deputy positions. Of the 165 social workers in the agencies under study . . . seventy-four per cent were working in the area of plan development and implementation and 26 per cent in project review. Also, 179 social workers were spread out among 50% of all the agency boards, and 25% of the 196 member agencies had two or more social work members.[21]

The CHP act was terminated with the passage of the Health Resources and Development Act of 1974. A similar role for social workers was anticipated in the latter program. Subsequently, the role of the federal government in health planning was diminished during the Reagan administration. Nevertheless, a large number of social workers continue to be ready to play important roles in policy development in the health field.

Values and Ideologies in Health Care

The ways social workers in health care fulfill their roles are heavily influenced by a number of value positions. One that is shared with many other health care professionals is that *health care is a right.* Banta, for example, cites Thomas Jefferson, who wrote

> Without health there is no happiness. And attention to health, then, should take the place of every other object. The time necessary to secure this by active exercises should be devoted to it in preference to every other pursuit. I know the difficulty with which a strenuous man tears himself from his studies at any given moment of the day; but his happiness, and that of his family depend on it. The most uninformed mind, with a healthy body is happier than the wisest valetundinarian.[22]

Health care in the United States is only a right for some parts of the population, such as workers with health insurance, the elderly who receive Medicare, and the poor who receive Medicaid.[23] In the mid-1980s approximately 39 million Americans (19% of the population) had no health insurance.[24]

Social work policy recommendations have consistently supported a universal health insurance plan. In contrast to many industrial nations, the United States has not enacted such a program because of opposition from major interest groups, particularly the American Medical Association. The AMA position has been presented in terms of opposition to any "compulsory" program which many Americans view as "socialist."[25]

Even if the United States adopts a universal plan, this will raise additional value issues. Perhaps foremost is that no society can afford to provide every health benefit its citizens could desire. As Banta states, "Some form of rationing of health care seems inevitable."[26] We strongly agree with his comment that "One would hope that denying access to underprivileged people would not become a mechanism for rationing."[27] One mechanism for dealing with this issue might be the degree to which the individual has contributed to the illness. Perhaps society will say that fewer medical resources should go to the individual who has acted in ways (smoking, for example) that have been instrumental in the development of the illness.

A related issue to whether health care is a right is the priority we place on health compared to other rights. People smoke, drink alcoholic beverages, and travel with seat belts unfastened. These behaviors are encouraged by advertising for liquor and cigarettes and by manufacturers who fail to install seat belts that fasten automatically. A broader issue relates to the values that support these behaviors. An important set of value questions is how far society ought to go in curtailing the behavior of individuals and institutions to increase the health of the population. Is it the responsibility of society to educate its citizens regarding health maintenance, to curtail their behavior, to make unhealthy substances unavailable, or even to reduce the stresses that may lead to unhealthy behavior?

Related to the basic social work emphasis on self-determination is the notion that consumers of health services should be involved in policy making and that the provider should be accountable to the consumer.[28] Social workers act in accord with this value when they form organizations of community residents to influence health policy, take positions as patient's rights officers in health delivery systems, and advocate on behalf of patients with other health care providers.

Another self-determination issue is whether the health care provider honors the client's value system. We do not have easy answers as to how to respond to conflicts between the client and health care providers when health care is refused because it violates a client's beliefs or wishes. Such circumstances may even result in the death of the client, such as the refusal of life supports by a terminally ill patient. We would like to trust the legal system and due process to mediate situations of this type with full regard given to the opposing sides to the question.

In less critical circumstances, many clients believe in health approaches other than those embodied in Western medical practices. Examples are the employment of *curanderos* by some Chicanos, of spiritualists by a number of other ethnic groups, and of medicine men and women by Native Americans. In many cases social workers have helped medical personnel to work cooperatively with these types of practitioners and with the client in ways that benefited the client and respected his or her beliefs.

A number of issues posed earlier in this chapter have strong ideological components. These include the emphasis on prevention and a view of health and illness as having psychological and social, as well as physiological, aspects. We urge the interested reader to consult some of the more extensive discussions of these and other value topics.[29]

An Overview of the Health Care System

HISTORY OF HEALTH CARE

HEALTH CARE OVERALL. Although our emphasis in this chapter is on social work in health care, we shall briefly review the broader historical picture. While health planning has existed in some form throughout most of the history of the United States "providers did their own planning in isolation from each other and outside influences. . . . Community leadership decided whether or not a hospital was needed."[30]

Furthermore, "citizens recognized that they had responsibility for those among them who were unable to work productively as a result of physical illness, lunacy, blindness, or other physical impairment."[31] The early colonists drew on their English experience, the Elizabethan Poor Law of 1601. Consequently, the needy group was not differentiated, although the more affluent were largely cared for within their families. The poor were ministered to in public institutions variously called almshouses, county homes, or hospitals.

These institutions throughout most of the nineteenth century were largely supported through philanthropy and "served as institutions of social control, isolating those individuals deemed less desirable by the community."[32] It was not until the twentieth century that institutions such as Brooklyn Jewish Hospital began to turn to the paying patient when they could not keep up with increased costs. Shortly, however, technological advances also led to the type of medical care that could only be provided in institutions. The hospital also became an appropriate place to train medical students.

Another development occurred during the Civil War period when governments began to seek solutions to community health problems. The increased urbanization of the United States led to such problems as polluted water, spoiled food, and garbage accumulation. Epidemic conditions threatened not only the poor, but the wealthy, who were powerful enough to press for public health measures.

These developments paralleled other events related to how the mentally ill should be treated. As Friedlander and Apte state,

> In Western Europe and the United States before the nineteenth century, the mentally disordered were quartered in madhouses where they were often chained to the walls. Kept in barren unsanitary rooms, the insane and the mentally retarded mixed freely. Children and adults were kept together. Harsh treatment and ridicule were heaped upon them, with no regard for their well-being. Local communities hired wardens to care for the mentally disordered in squalid, overcrowded buildings, paying for their care on a per capita basis at a predetermined rate.[33]

The end of the eighteenth century saw a number of changes in this situation. Among the influences for change were the publication in England of *Treatise on the Moral Treatment of the Insane* by William Tuke, who was a Quaker interested in the problems of the mentally ill. He advocated a more humane treatment of the insane as a way of curing them. Tuke founded an asylum called the Retreat at York based on his book. These ideas spread to the United States, where Benjamin Rush used them in his mental hospital in Philadelphia in the early 1800s. The first hospital, however, dedicated to providing moral treatment was built by the Quakers in 1817, and by 1847 there were 30 in the United States. At about the same time in France, Pinel removed the shackles from the insane and proclaimed that they were not criminals. The rest of the nineteenth century, however, did not witness events that were as dramatic as these.[34]

For example, the federal government did not assume any responsibility in this matter, but left it to the states. Mentally ill patients were admitted to Pennsylvania Hospital as early as 1756 and in 1773 a mental asylum was established in Williamsburg, Virginia.[35]

In the 1850s, Dorothea Dix, a prominent social reformer, proposed that the federal government support mental institutions through the transfer of federal lands to the states. A bill to accomplish this was passed by congress but vetoed by President Pierce in 1854. Dix was responsible, nevertheless, for many other projects, such as the creation of St. Elizabeth's Hospital in Washington, D.C.

In the 1930s, the President's Committee on Economic Security recommended a health insurance program. President Roosevelt thought this would jeopardize other programs and did not support this recommendation, although in many addresses he referred to the right to good medical care. One exception to this poor history of federal health activity was the Maternal and Infancy Act, which was passed in 1921 and continued under the Social Security Act.

Organized efforts on a nongovernment basis began when councils of social agencies formed in the 1920s began to plan for community health care and other services. An outgrowth of these were hospital planning councils; the first was established in 1937 in New York.[36] Other types of planning were related to specific diseases, such as the National Association for Tuberculosis founded in the early 1900s.

One of the first pieces of federal legislation for health planning was the Hospital Survey and Construction Act, better known as the Hill–Burton Act, of 1946. The purpose of this act is "to assist the several states in the carrying out of their programs for the construction and modernization of such public or other non-profit community hospitals . . . as may be necessary, in conjunction with exiting facilities, to furnish adequate hospital, clinic, or similar services to all their people."[37] Amendments passed in 1964 and 1970 significantly expanded this program to finance comprehensive health planning.[38]

Health planning was continued through the Public Health Service Act Amendments of 1966 (Public Law 89–749). Since the objectives of this program are consistent in some ways with the values we have discussed in this chapter, they merit quoting here:

> The Congress declares that fulfillment of our national purpose depends on promoting and assuring the highest level of health attainable for every person, in an environment which contributes positively to healthful individual and family living; that attainment of this goal depends on an effective partnership, involving close intergovernmental collaboration, official and voluntary efforts, and participation of individuals and organizations; that Federal financial assistance must be directed to support the marshalling of all health resources—national, state, and local—to assure comprehensive health services of high quality for every person, but without interference with existing patterns of private professional practice of medicine, dentistry, and related healing arts.[39]

Unfortunately, the emphasis on noninterference with private practice was a main impediment to changing the health system. In any case, experts in the field deem this program to have been a failure due to insufficient funds, poorly trained staff, unclear legislative mandate, and blurred lines of responsibility.[40]

Another step toward health planning was taken with passage of the Health Resources and Development Act in 1974. This legislation was intended to remove the weaknesses of the previous legislation. It provided for more direction from the secretary of health, education, and welfare, the establishment of the National Council on Health Planning and Development, a network of health planning agencies across the country, assistance to state governments for health planning, and procedures for implementation. The effects of this act were weakened, however, with the passage of the Omnibus Budget Reconciliation Act in 1981, which, among other things, gave governors the power to eliminate regional health planning within the state.[41]

Until World War II, the federal government did not actively support mental health services. The exceptions were a narcotics department and some veterans' psychiatric hospitals. The states supported mental hospitals for their citizens.[42] These were often poor in quality, despite the ideas of such people as Rush that were developed as early as the beginning of the nineteenth century. Miller's description is quite graphic regarding this:

> With few full-time psychiatrists on staff, patients were cared for primarily by untrained

attendants, while the back wards housed patients, who sometimes had been hospitalized 20 and 30 years. Some of these state facilities had been built in the late nineteenth and early twentieth century, institutions frequently situated in isolated locations, the more invisible to the community the better. In the post World War II era this author paid a first visit, as a social work student, to a state mental hospital. All wards were locked, access was gained by the insertion of a large key into a fortresslike door that provided entrance into a bare, square unfurnished room in which unkempt, ragged inmates either lay on the floor or crouched against the wall, arms crossed on their knees and heads bent against their chests. A series of small rooms lined one side of the corridor for patients requiring solitary confinement, each a small cubicle containing a mattress on the floor. Beyond was a large ward with iron cots lined up on either side of the room. The windows were covered with metal mesh; the walls were bare—not a poster nor a picture. In these deteriorated institutions, miserable, unhappy, forgotten people spent their undifferentiated days.[43]

Because of the experience in caring for mental casualties of World War II, a National Mental Health Act was passed in 1946 that created the National Institute of Mental Health (actually founded in 1949). This led to a considerable expansion of national investment in mental health training and research. Innovations in mental health services grew out of this endeavor, such as the creation of day treatment programs and halfway houses, and many institutions experimented with the creation of a therapeutic milieu. Another development was the passage of the Mental Health Study Act of 1955, which resulted in the Joint Commission on Mental Illness and Health. Major developments also took place in the use of therapeutic drugs. All these changes supported the idea of deinstitutionalization as a more humane and, it was hoped, more effective alternative to previous practice.

The campaign to remove the stigma from mental illness.

This trend was supported in 1963 by an important piece of legislation, the Mental Health Facilities and Community Mental Health Centers Construction Act. Grants for personnel to initiate the program were not provided, however, for another two years. The act sought to create Community Mental Health Centers in geographical areas throughout the country and envisioned that both prevention and treatment would be offered in these agencies.

Specifically, the centers were to offer inpatient, outpatient, emergency care, partial hospitalization, and consultation and educative programs to the community. Additional amendments were passed in 1967, 1972, 1975, and 1978. All except the last set expanded the program, such as creating services for substance abusers, children, and the elderly. The 1981 legislation, however, changed the program from one of categorical to block grants for the states, thus eliminating much of the federal initiative. Fortunately, the earlier effects of this legislation continue to be felt.

SOCIAL WORK IN HEALTH CARE. The role of social work in hospital care received its first major sanction in 1906 when Richard C. Cabot established social services at Massachusetts General Hospital and appointed Ida M. Cannon as its first director of social services. Social workers had been active in health promotion, particularly in the social settlements, but their movement into hospitals added greatly to legitimizing their role in the health field. This movement rapidly developed so that by the late 1970s "some 75 percent of the hospitals with more than 200 beds have social service departments."[44] This trend has continued into the 1980s. Taylor and Ford term the growth to be disproportionate to that of other professionals in hospitals.[45]

In any case, the activities of health-oriented social workers in these several fields were linked, as evidenced by Jane Addams's address to the American Hospital Association in 1908. Her topic was "The Layman's View of Hospital Work among the Poor" and she spoke of the failure of hospital staff to see the patient as a person. This was clearly quite advanced thinking for a social worker almost a century ago![46]

Psychiatric services early in their development also turned to social workers. In 1910, two years before its opening, Boston Psychopathic Hospital included social workers in its planning. Its first director of social services, Mary C. Jarrett, developed the first in-service program for special social work training and coined the term "psychiatric social work." This educational program led to the first course in psychiatric social work at Smith College in 1918.[47]

Another step in the development of medical social work was taken following World War I, when the surgeon general of the U.S. Public Health Service asked the Red Cross to organize social services in federal hospitals. During World War II, a psychiatric social work consultant service was established for the military, and today social work is an established part of military medical services.[48]

As this brief history implies, although medical social work and psychiatric social work have had separate histories, they share common ideologies. These relate to helping the client to negotiate the health care system, to cope with environmental stresses, to reduce interpersonal dysfunctions, and to be seen in an holistic manner by other health care providers. We agree with Miller and Rehr, who see this model as blurring "the strong demarcation between medical and psychiatric social work functions," thus leading to the concept of a "health social worker."[49] These authors conclude, "The sanction for the roles and functions social workers perform in health settings remains secure as long as we maintain our social orientation to patient care. No other health provider circumscribes practice from this perspective; it is our domain."[50]

CURRENT SITUATION

A large sum of money is spent in the United States on health services. In 1987, this expenditure was $500 billion annually. This amounted to over 11% of the gross national product; in 1965, such expenditures were $43 billion or 6.2% of the GNP.[51] The current amount is increasing annually at a faster rate than any other sector of the economy.[52]

McCarthy and Thorpe utilize two categories to analyze these expenditures: (1) research and medical facilities construction and (2) payments for health services and supplies. The largest part of all these expenditures was for personal health care expenses: $442.6 billion in 1987. Of this latter amount, five types account for over 80% of the total: 38.9% to hospitals, 20.5% to physicians, 8.1% for nursing home care, 6.8% for drugs, and 6.6% for dentists.[53]

Of these expenditures, 56.1% ($280.8 billion) was paid directly by consumers. The government allocation was 41.4% ($207.3 billion) and about three-fourths of that was from the federal government. Twenty-two percent ($139.1 billion) was paid through insurance companies.[54]

The way these resources are used is as follows: in 1987, there were approximately 5.5 visits to physicians per person, and at least 75% of the population made one visit. In general, females made more visits than males, and the visit rate increased with age. In 1986, the average number of dental visits was 2.1 and about half the population was involved. In 1987, about 34.4 million people were discharged from hospitals. The average hospital stay was 7.2 days, and this represented a continued downward trend since the early 1970s.[55]

Although it is obvious that people consult health professionals for many reasons other than prevention and treatment of serious and possibly terminal disorders, it is interesting to note the major causes of death in the United States. Heart disease is the leading cause, followed by cancer and stroke. There have been, however, decreases in death from these diseases since 1950 but with differences between whites, blacks, men, and women. As Schlesinger states,

> Between 1950 and 1982 mortality related to heart disease declined from 307.6 to 190.8 per 100,000. Furthermore, there has been a 25% decrease since 1970 in deaths attributable to heart disease.
> A more detailed analysis by race and sex shows the following: (1) the age adjusted death rate for white men declined from 381.1 per 100,000 in 1950 to 288.7 per 100,000 in 1978; (2) comparable figures for white women are 223.6 and 136.4 per 100,000, respectively; (3) rates for black men declined from 415.5 per 100,000 in 1950 to 321.0 per 100,000 in 1978; and (4) comparable figures for black women are 349.5 and 201.1 per 100,000, respectively.[56]

A similar set of statistics applies to strokes, in which a decline is apparant for both whites and blacks, but with blacks having higher rates of strokes. As Schlesinger states, "Clearly black men are at greatest risk, followed by black women." In contrast, there has been an increase in cancers of the respiratory system with blacks still having higher rates. Schlesinger attributes this to different smoking patterns and greater exposure to hazardous environments for African Americans.[57]

Schlesinger notes that there is considerable data on African-American health patterns because much of the data is coded and analyzed according to "white/nonwhite" characteristics. There is strong reason to believe that there are major differences between whites and other ethnic groups as well. For example, she describes the situation for Native Americans and notes that their life expectancy is well below that for whites. There has been improvement, however, in the health statistics for that group, which she believes is due to the efforts of the Indian Health Service, which represents another major governmental activity.[58]

These discrepancies between white and black health patterns show up in other ways as well. Schlesinger reports that "only 36% of blacks compared to 51% of whites or members of other races consider their health to be excellent. Twice as many blacks as whites perceive themselves to be in fair or poor health." Schlesinger notes similar findings with reference to income, with wealth correlated with health. Gender shows a similar association, with women reporting themselves as having worse health than men.[59]

An analogous set of issues is present with reference to mental health, but this is complicated by the unreliability of mental health assessment. As Schlesinger states,

> Recent data suggest more men and minority group members are admitted to specialized mental health facilities than women and nonminority group members. Men are more likely than women to be diagnosed as alcoholic and schizophrenic; women are more likely than men to be diagnosed depressive and schizophrenic. Whites were most frequently categorized depressive, and nonwhites were more likely than whites to be diagnosed schizophrenic.[60]

In discussing these data, Schlesinger indicates that additional studies show that the poor and minority group members "are more likely to be falsely diagnosed as suffering from the more severe disorders." The same appears to be likely for women. Nevertheless, there also is evidence of an association between the stresses experienced by minority group members and mental health problems.[61]

Because of deinstitutionalization, the number of state mental hospital inpatients declined from 558,922 in 1955 to 107,100 in 1987 and is still decreasing. This represents shorter patient stays in such hospitals, but does not represent a decline in admissions.[62]

In view of a decline in the number of seriously mentally ill people in hospitals without a decrease in mental illness, it is important to ask where these people are. One estimate is that between 1.7 million and 2.4 million people in the United States can be classified as seriously mentally ill. A seriously mentally ill person is defined as an individual who suffers from a major psychiatric disorder such as psychosis, who is so disabled as to have partial or total impairment of social functioning (such as vocational and homemaking activities), and who has had a long or a number of short stays in a mental hospital.

It is estimated that about 150,000 of the seriously mentally ill are in institutions,[63] about 750,000 are in nursing homes (including about 400,000 who suffer from forms of senility), and between 800,000 and 1.5 million are living in the community under the supervision of programs such as community mental health centers.[64]

In general, it is clear from available data that there are many problems in the United States with regard to the availability of good and consistent health care for poor people. A recent report of research conducted by the Survey Research Laboratory of the University of Illinois and the Wisconsin Survey Research Laboratory of the University of Wisconsin and issued by the Robert Wood Johnson Foundation concluded that the poor minorities and people without health insurance have less chance of getting medical care than they did four years ago.[65]

This report, based on a random sample of 10,130 people, demonstrated that 16% of Americans or an estimated 38.8 million people needed health care but had difficulty obtaining it during the 12 months preceding the survey. The reason given by half the respondents was financial, and the investigators estimated that 1 million people tried to get help but could not afford it. Eighteen percent (which would mean nearly 43 million people) said they had no regular source of health care, whereas only 10% were in that category in a similar survey four years earlier.

The statistics were even more alarming for poor people from particular ethnic groups. For example, the percentage of Hispanics who said they had no regular source of health care tripled from 10% to 30% in the four-year period between the two surveys. Nineteen percent of the sample said they had not visited a doctor during the year despite having a chronic or serious illness. On the basis of these kinds of data, in a statement accompanying the report the foundation stated that "a number of improvements in access to health care have been reversed since the last . . . survey in 1982. The result is that the gaps have widened in access to care for those who are uninsured, the poor, and minorities."

In 1983, almost 8 million people were employed in health care. The National Association of Social Workers reports that for 1981, out of a total membership of 85,000, 60% of the members practiced in health and/or mental health (about 10% in private practice).[66] The largest proportion of social workers in health care is employed in acute and long-term hospitals (about 22,000). A slightly earlier study indicated that social workers also account for 42% of the staff of all mental health facilities.[67] About three times as many social workers enter psychiatric as compared to other medical settings.[68]

In the next section of this chapter, we shall discuss the various components of the health system in detail so as to enable the reader to understand social work issues related to each component. A brief overview of the system is presented here so that each piece ma be seen in relationship to the whole.

The point of entry to the health system for many people is through some type of *primary care*. Primary care is described by Jonas and Rosenberg as follows:

> In ideal primary care, an appropriately trained health professional or team provides most of the preventive and curative care for an individual or family over a significant period of time, coordinates any services that must be sought from other health professionals, and integrates and explains the patient's or family's overall health

problems and care, giving adequate attention to their psychological and social dimensions.[69]

The individual with a health problem typically makes first contact with the health system through a primary care physician or, in some cases, through a nurse-practitioner or physician assistant. The individual may also draw on a group practice where several physicians share resources.

Typically some or all of health care cost in the United States is paid for through a private insurance arrangement because approximately 85% of the population is covered by some form of health insurance. The three major categories of private health insurance are Blue Cross and Blue Shield, commercial insurance companies, and prepaid and self-insured plans.[70]

Increasingly people are served by a Health Maintenance Organization (HMO). This type of service was encouraged in the United States by the Health Maintenance Organization Act of 1973 (P.L. 93–222). The individual usually becomes a member of the HMO as an employee benefit or through some other group arrangement. The monthly fee paid by or on behalf of the individual to the HMO entitles him or her to prepaid medical and hospital services. The individual's access to the services of the HMO is governed by his or her primary care physician, who is also a part of the HMO; this physician has both prevention and treatment functions and must determine what additional services are needed and then make appropriate referrals.

Although the United States has not enacted a comprehensive national health insurance program, it has sought to provide medical resources for two groups that are less likely to have private insurance coverage: the poor and the elderly. The program for the elderly is called Medicare and consists of hospital insurance financed by Social Security payroll taxes and a supplementary medical insurance, which is voluntary and paid for partially by the individual and partially by the federal government.

The program for the poor is Medicaid and it provides medical assistance to certain categories of low-income people, including the blind, aged, disabled, and members of families with dependent children. It is financed partially by the state and partially by the federal government, but is administered by the states. In 1986 the Medicaid budget consisted of $23.7 billion in federal and $19.3 billion in state funds. At that time, the administration was in the process of proposing limits on the growth of the program and changing the nature of the federal partnership in other ways as well.[71] A variety of other programs, such as hospital and community clinics, also provide primary care.

The individual who must receive hospital care may enter an institution that is publicly or privately owned. The former may be supported by the federal, state, or local government. The latter includes both nonprofit and investor-owned institutions. In 1983, there were 6,888 hospitals in the United States with 1.35 million beds. Almost 39 million patients were hospitalized during the year; another 273 million people were given outpatient care in hospitals.[72]

Hospitals serve a patient for a limited period of time while he or she undergoes surgery or other treatment. Some individuals require long-term care, because they no longer need the kind of medical care provided in hospitals yet will not be able to function independently for a long time. As Kane and Kane state:

Long-term care is a range of services that addresses the health, personal care, and social needs of individuals who lack some capacity for self-care. Services may be continuous or intermittent, but are delivered for a sustained period to individuals who have a demonstrated need, usually measured by some index of functional dependency.[73]

Long-term care is provided in institutions such as nursing homes, homes for the aged, and skilled nursing facilities; through such in-home services as home health care, homemaker, and chore services; and through agencies that monitor patient need and link the patient to a variety of services, such as community mental health centers. A great deal of development has taken place recently in hospice services. These services are offered to terminally ill patients and their families so that the patient can live as fully and comfortably as possible in ongoing contact with family members who are also supported during this period. A hospice program does not focus on curing the disease but on coping with the final stage of disease, that is, with dying and bereavement.

Selected Components in Detail

PRIMARY CARE

One major problem for health care consumers in the United States is that U.S. medical practice has become highly specialized. As of 1982, about 83% of all physicians in office practice classified themselves as practicing a specialty other than general or family practice. Thus, over 80% of all patient office visits were to specialists.[74]

For members of an HMO, these facts may be less of a problem as the HMO is expected to have a primary care physician who coordinates their use of medical services. For others, the process may be confusing because they will have to coordinate their own health care as they consult internists, gynecologists, orthopedists, psychiatrists, and so forth.

Many people with a medical problem do not go to a private physician but make use of the outpatient services of a hospital. Depending on the condition, the patient will go to the emergency room of the hospital or to an outpatient clinic of the hospital. About 95% of community hospitals in the United States have emergency units.

Outpatient clinics, on the other hand, are typically only found in hospitals in areas where people are unlikely to have their own physicians or in hospitals with teaching programs, and only about 46% of community hospitals have clinics.[75] Although we do not have supporting data, we believe that the picture is changing and that more hospitals are engaging in outreach. As Jonas and Rosenberg state, "It is probably not coincidental that emergency outpatient services, particularly for critically ill patients, are not among those services that private physicians can easily provide in their own offices; whereas the type of service provided in clinics can usually be given by the private physician, economic considerations aside."[76]

Clinics to serve poor people have existed in hospitals since the nineteenth century, although today they are less likely to provide free care. They may employ, however, a means test and a sliding scale for some patients. Hospitals often maintain such services as an educational function for medical students or as a way of securing patients for research. Because of these purposes, clinics parallel physician specialties. Some are organized by medical specialties, such as cardiology, neurology, or allergy; some by surgical specialties, such as orthopedics or urology; and some for pediatrics or obstetrics.

The hospital usually assigns its junior staff to such clinics, as well as its interns and residents. Staff who are being trained either complete their training or are rotated among specialties. Patients, therefore, who are having health problems monitored and treated over long periods of time may see a different physician on each visit.

The patients who make use of hospital clinics, consequently, face several types of problems according to Jonas and Rosenberg.[77] They may have an ordinary problem (such as a sore throat) for which no clinic exists. They may have an uncomplicated case of a disease that has less interest to a teaching and research-oriented staff and therefore receive less attention than people with more complex conditions. Or, worst of all, they may have several diseases and will have to attend different clinics on succeeding days, thus spending many hours in clinic waiting rooms. No one, under these circumstances, takes a holistic view of the patient.

In addition to the obvious function of the emergency room to care for critically ill or injured patients, it is often required to care for people who cannot reach their private physician or when their clinic is not open. In fact, a study conducted in the 1970s showed that half of the people using emergency services were classified by the staff as being there for "nonurgent" reasons.[78] These nonurgent people will often be kept waiting while true emergencies are treated. This is also a very costly form of service.

The use of emergency services by individuals without acute physical problems increasingly involves the issues of homelessness and the homeless mentally ill. The use of emergency rooms by these groups increasingly presents a challenge for the social worker. The homeless mentally ill often use hospital emergency rooms to seek psychiatric attention. For these and the previously mentioned reasons some hospitals are opening walk-in clinics with weekend and evening hours for nonurgent care.

An innovation to solve some of the problems of clinic and emergency care is the free-standing "emergi-center." Because the center is not located in a hospital, it is not used by those with severe emergencies. By 1984, there were about 1,000 to 2,500 of these facilities. Patients appear to like the service because they are not kept waiting while the staff responds to severe and time-consuming emergencies.[79]

Some communities also offer primary care services through health departments, and these historically have been provided at no cost. The medical profession has often opposed such services since they compete with those offered by private physicians. But it has been less likely to oppose them when private physicians are not as interested in providing service, as in routine well-baby examinations, the diagnosis of venereal disease or tuberculosis, family planning, and general home public health nursing.

Because of controversies surrounding health department service, less than 3% of ambulatory personal health services are presented in this way. Some experts, however, would like health departments to take a major responsibility for social and medical services for the poor.[80]

Still another primary care facility is the neighborhood community health center.

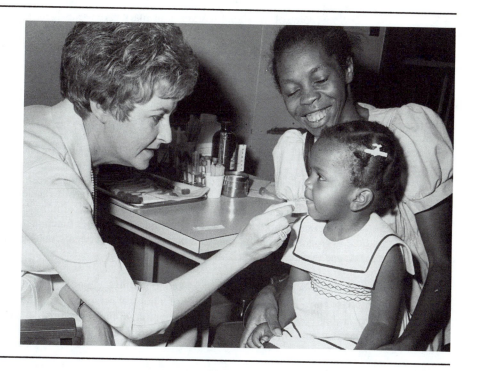

Recovery is complete. (Photo courtesy of Centers for Disease Control, Atlanta.)

This type of program expanded as part of a movement in the later 1960s and early 1970s to locate multidisciplinary health services, including social workers, in the community under community control. This development was part of the War on Poverty of Lyndon Johnson's administration.

In the early 1970s at the peak of the development of community health centers, as they were initially defined, it was estimated that there were about 200. In the mid 1970s the program, now called Community Health Centers (CHCs), was revised so as to concentrate on medical care and to de-emphasize other activities that had been adopted, such as employment of poor people as health providers, training, community economic and social development, and environmental health measures. By the early 1980s, there were 800 CHCs serving over 4.5 million people. By 1984, however, with declining federal support, the number of federally supported programs declined to 530.[81]

Primary care must pay attention to psychological and social dimensions and this is where social work most clearly enters in. One way of providing for this is for the primary care physician (or physician group) to employ a social worker. This may well be a growing trend even though the data do not provide grounds for high optimism. A 1978 report indicated that there were 1,000 social workers attached to 300 primary care clinics and medical groups.[82] In addition, hospitals often assign social workers to their primary care clinics, HMO teams often include social workers, and primary care physicians may either use social workers as consultants or refer some patients to them.

Some roles of the social worker in primary care are as follows:[83]

1. The patient may be referred to the social worker routinely as part of the initial screening process. The task of the social worker is to identify patients with psychosocial stress factors or psychiatric problems and help them with these.
2. Social workers in large practices may devise high-risk screening criteria that are used to identify patients who are likely to experience psychosocial stresses and psychiatric problems. They can then proceed to explore whether these conditions are actually present and then provide help. An alternative is to work with patients who are specifically referred by the other members of the primary care team. The consequence of this, according to Miller, is that it "is responsive to the total health needs or concerns of the patient, and it allows for good communication between one or more health providers and the patient, a procedure that contributes to patient compliance with medical regimens and effective psychosocial care."[84]
3. The social worker may also fulfill indirect social work functions such as participating in program planning, policy formation, needs assessments, outreach, health education, and the creation of self-help groups.

A number of forces have operated to inhibit the employment of social workers in primary care. These include the lack of a holistic perspective on the part of physicians, governing bodies of HMOs, and other community programs that reflect an upper-income bias that financially able clients do not need social work services and a lack of interest in prevention.

HOSPITAL CARE

Hospitals vary greatly in size: some have as few as a dozen beds and provide primarily outpatient services, obstetrics, and pediatric care; others have almost a thousand beds and provide a vast number of therapeutic services. Some hospitals specialize, such as for ear, nose, and throat conditions, or only serve women.

Another way of categorizing hospitals is whether they are teaching hospitals, part of multihospital systems, public or private, or profit or not for profit. Teaching hospitals are "larger, provide more specialized service, and give more unreimbursed care."[85] They offer a large percentage of highly complex services and care for a high proportion of the poor.

Hospitals are classified as being part of multihospital systems "when they are either leased under contract management or are legally incorporated by or under the direction of a board that determines the control of two or more hospitals."[86] An example of this is the Hospital Corporation of America, which owns or manages 390 hospitals and other medical facilities worldwide. National Medical Enterprises owns psychiatric hospitals, retirement centers, and hospices, as well as a number of other health-related businesses. We also classify Veteran's Administration hospitals as a multihospital system. A not-for-profit system of this sort is the 28 Kaiser hospitals and the 28 hospitals owned by the Sisters of Mercy Health Corporation in three midwestern states.

Public hospitals are owned by units of federal, state, and local government. The federal hospitals typically serve a restricted population such as Native Americans and military installations. State hospitals largely consist of psychiatric hospitals and facilities to care for patients with chronic diseases. Some local hospitals are located in small towns and are staffed by private attending physicians. Others are found in large metropolitan communities and are staffed by paid physicians and residents. The latter are likely to serve poor people, such as "the 'shopping bag lady,' the poor prostitute, the poor drug addict or alcoholic, the disruptive psychiatric patient, the destitute aged person, and the prisoner."[87]

According to Kovner, public hospitals may experience mismanagement due to the civil service or patronage system used to obtain staff. Such hospitals may also suffer from their status of serving the poor in terms of their surroundings, appearance, and amenities. When they function, however, as major teaching centers, their technical medical quality may be high.[88] In view of the function and character of local public hospitals, the same author concludes that "What we seem to be re-creating during the Reagan years is a reinstitutionalization of a two-class system of medical care—one system for those with adequate health benefits and another for those lacking such benefits."[89]

One major problem in contemporary hospital care is that of constantly increasing costs. The average 1983 per diem costs in a community hospital were $369.49 compared to $81.01 in 1970 and $32.23 in 1960. Efforts to combat this have included emphasizing outpatient care, prevention, the use of second opinions before surgery, and the creation of diagnosis-related groups (DRGs).

The idea of DRGs was developed in the 1983 amendments to the Social Security Act (PL 98–21), which dealt with payment for Medicare and Medicaid patients. This payment was set at a specific amount based on the type of case and the average cost for all Medicare patients. An elaborate typology was to be used based on diagnostic categories related to the systems of the body, as well as on the diagnosis and other clinical data. Payment variations were also allowed for urban as compared to rural hospitals and for other variables related to the hospital's overhead. Since the development of the DRG concept for Medicare payments, its use has been spreading to a variety of third-party payment plans.

The DRG idea has been criticized on a number of grounds. These include the fact that, despite the elaborate classification system, patient complexity and severity of illness are not considered. This may lead some hospitals to pass on potentially more costly patients to other facilities. A variety of other manipulations that are detrimental to the development of good medical care have emerged or are likely to as a way of increasing the profit margins of hospitals.[90]

To understand the role of social work in the hospital, it is also necessary to comprehend how hospitals are organized. Physicians have major control over the type and amount of services that may be offered patients. They fall into two administrative categories: attending physicians who are not salaried by the hospital and physicians who are employed and paid by the hospital. The hospital, however, is responsible for the services its staff provides on orders of the physician. It may also be held liable for the conduct of physicians.

Physicians are organized in the hospital according to their medical specialties. The typical hospital departments are internal medicine, surgery, pediatrics, obstetrics–gynecology, psychiatry–neurology, radiology–diagnostic imaging, pathology, and anesthesiology. Some hospitals may also have units for eye diseases, urology, orthopedics, and other specializations. (There are 23 medical specializations for which medical practitioners may be professionally certified).[91]

The physicians and dentists practicing in the hospital will have a medical and a dental staff organization with rules that are approved by the hospital's governing body. One major provision of such rules pertains to the medical officers of the hospital and how they are selected. A number of committees typically are created, such as an executive committee, credentials committee (for the evaluation of the credentials of applicants for staff positions), infections control committee, tissue committee (deals with quality control of surgery), and medical records committee (ensures documentation of the care given patients).

Along with this organization of the physicians, the hospital will also have a chain of administrators. These may include persons designated as vice-presidents for finance, ambulatory services, support services, and professional services. In addition, there are likely to be directors for other professional departments, such as nursing and social work.

As hospitals have become more complex, ambiguities have arisen as to the jurisdictions of its lines of command. For example, social workers and nurses are employees of the hospital and clearly subject to its rules (even if these at times may contradict professional norms), whereas most of the physicians are not employees and see themselves as more subject to the norms of their profession than the rules of the hospital. One way that some hospitals have sought to deal with this is to organize almost all services along medical division lines. For example, a surgical division, under the direction of a medical division leader might have full control of nursing, social work, and other services offered in the division.

There are many problems with regard to how social workers see their function as compared to how other professionals, such as doctors and nurses, see it. The latter often view social work as a processing role or as part of the caring activities of the hospital. In processing patients, the social worker is typically called on to make sure the patient has the resources he or she requires upon leaving the hospital. Caring activities include helping patients and their families cope with the stresses related to the illness. Power issues, particularly the authority of the physician, must often be dealt with by social workers who have a broader idea of their expertise.

This broader idea of the social worker's function in the hospital is strongly related to social work's emphasis on health and social strength and, consequently, on prevention as well as treatment of illness. It does not replace the processing and caring functions but supplements them. It involves helping patients to anticipate and cope with stress, supporting community resources that the patient can draw on in this regard, and improving the patient's access to health services. This last point is particularly relevant for members of oppressed groups.

Social workers, therefore, in hospital as well as community settings will be involved in high-risk screening. This includes identifying the characteristics of patients who are likely to require social work services and then determining in each individual case those who will be offered service.

Consequently, the skills the hospital social worker will utilize include consultation, advocacy, collaboration, education, and research.[92] In our experience, too many hospital social workers fulfill only the narrower functions, as prescribed for them by other professions in the hospital. To remedy this requires the profession to do a much better job of training social workers for health settings and of educating the entire health care field regarding the role social workers should play.

Social workers can only play appropriate roles when their presence in the hospital in sufficient numbers is maintained. This is difficult when social services are not supported either by patient fees or by third-party arrangements. It is the responsibility of social workers to demonstrate the cost savings of social work services in the hospital, and several studies are now available that do precisely that.[93]

Social workers in hospitals will typically acquire specialized knowledge with reference to the patients on the services to which they are assigned. Examples are social workers on oncology services who help patients and their families face the suffering and loss associated with cancer, on dialysis services who help patients and families cope with dependence on a machine in order to live, and on psychiatric services, who help families and patients learn how to adapt to a mental illness while seeking to maintain or achieve as high a quality of life as possible.

LONG-TERM AND HOSPICE CARE

An individual may require long-term care when the disease in its acute phase has been treated but the individual is still not able to return to full, independent living. A major reason that we have seen an increase in the need for long-term care is the increase in the number of older people in the population, particularly those over 75. This relates to the fact that the prevalence of chronic disease and impairment increases with age. As Wetle and Pearson state,

> For example, 14.8% of all visits to a physician in 1980 were made by persons aged 65 and over, and it is estimated this will increase to 18% by the year 2003; 43% of all hospital-care days in 2003 will be rendered to aged persons, compared to 39.3% in 1981; and there will be a dramatic increase in the number of nursing home residents— from the current 1.3 million to a projected 2.1 million in the year 2000, 2.9 million in 2020, and 5.4 million in 2050.[94]

Wetle and Pearson cite a number of social changes associated with a reliance on long-term care programs. These include the movement away from extended family living arrangements under which family members cared for each other, as well as the greater participation of women in the labor force, thus preventing them from caring for relatives.[95]

Long-term care can be divided into institutional and community-based programs. The former include nursing homes, homes for the aged, psychiatric institutions, facilities for children, homes for the handicapped, and chronic disease and extended-care facilities of hospitals. A decade ago, the U.S. Department of Commerce surveyed long-term care facilities. At that time, the United States had over 23,600 such programs and the majority (77%) were nursing homes; psychiatric institutions and those for the mentally handicapped each accounted for 7%, 6% were for children, and 3.5% were for people with chronic diseases and physical handicaps.[96]

Nursing homes, in addition to being the predominant category, also raise many issues for health professionals. Even defining them can be a subject of argument, although the National Nursing Home Survey defines a facility as a nursing home if

> nursing care is its primary and predominant function and it meets the following criteria: it employs one or more registered nurses or licensed practical nurses; and 50% or more of the residents are receiving nursing care, that is, one or more of the following: nasal feeding, catheterization, irrigation, oxygen therapy, full bed bath, enema, hypodermic injection, intravenous injection, temperature/pulse/respiration check, blood pressure reading, application of dressings and bandages, and bowel and bladder training.[97]

Nursing homes are further categorized according to the amount of services that must be provided residents. The specific designations are skilled nursing facility, intermediate-care facility, and facilities that combine the two functions.

One major problem in the nursing home sector is the placement of the patient in the appropriate facility. In addition, many nursing homes are of poor quality, and there are well-documented cases of patient abuse, dangerous physical conditions, and negligence.[98] Social workers considering facilities for the elderly and the disabled look for cost-effective care. One new idea in this area is that of self-care. Prevention is being actively looked at as one way toward reducing costs.[99] In addition, physicians are typically not readily available and are not well trained in meeting the needs of such patients. Even the better facilities are plagued with rising costs, heavy paper work, and confusing reimbursement requirements.[100]

While community-based programs are an important component of long-term care, the amount of resources they can draw on are much less than for residential services. In 1977, state and federal Medicaid expenditures for home health care benefits totaled only $241 million, while institutional care expenditures were 5.8 *billion*.[101] Some of the services that are supported in this way are discussed next.

IN-HOME HEALTH SERVICES. These include nursing, rehabilitation, and personal care services as offered by visiting nurses associations, privately owned agencies, public agencies, rehabilitation facilities, and private individuals. A number of public programs provide some financial resources for this. These services are supplied primarily by nurses, social workers, and home health aides. Some of these services are reimbursed by Medicare if the patient requires skilled nursing care or speech or physical therapy and if the services are supervised and reviewed by a physician who certifies their necessity every two months.

HOMEMAKER AND CHORE SERVICES. These provide house cleaning, meal preparation, shopping, laundry, and other services that the patient cannot do for himself or herself. In this way, the individual is able to maintain a considerable degree of independence and remain in his or her own home. A major source of funding for this is Title XX of the Social Security Act. While not classified in this way, services that deliver meals to people or that monitor their functioning fulfill some of the same purposes.

HOSPICE CARE. This service is offered to terminally ill patients and their families so that their quality of life can be maintained while the patient remains in his or her own home. The basic purpose is to enable patients to live their remaining days in as comfortable a manner as possible in the family context that is most meaningful to them. Some additional features of hospice care are its multidisciplinary nature and its efforts to keep the patient as pain free as possible through well-chosen medications. Services are typically available on a 24 hour a day, seven day a week on-call basis. The hospice also helps the family with the grieving process after the death of the patient. Hospice services may be paid by Medicare as provided by 1983 legislation.

ADULT DAYCARE. These programs provide such services to their clients as recreational and therapeutic groups, vocational training, counseling, and education. The clients therefore secure some of the services of hospitals while still living in the community.

COMMUNITY MENTAL HEALTH CLINICS. These facilities were established in 1963 to provide comprehensive mental health services to the community, but they have also played a major role in providing long-term care for the chronically mentally ill, particularly as deinstitutionalization has continued to be a major policy goal in the United States. Despite the fact that the 1981 Omnibus Budget Reconciliation Act consolidated all federal funds for mental health and alcohol and drug abuse services into a block grant for the states, this role has continued to be maintained albeit often at a reduced level of funding. Specifically, these agencies have provided case management services, medication and medication monitoring, employment and vocational education programs, day treatment, and crisis intervention.

People in need of long-term care are often neglected by the health care professions because their needs are chronic and they are not seen as being cured and then fully discharged from the service delivery system. Rather, they may go through phases in which they function well alternating with phases in which they do not.

This type of cycle requires the skill of professionals who can monitor and evaluate the patient's needs, see to it that they are met, and plan for help to be available when it is needed. Practitioners seek to expand the length of time when the individual and his or her family can function independently. Many social work experts in the health care field believe that social work should be the core profession for this by coordinating, planning, and delivering services for these patients. As Schlesinger states,

> That function derives from a social work perspective on social functioning and the emphasis on the person–situation interface. To this function social work brings a knowledge of person-in-situation, sensitivity to the unique dispositions of varying ethnic and cultural groups, and intimate acquaintance with the community and its available resource systems as well as analysis of additional resources. In addition, special attention must be paid to the assault on self-image of those affected and their families when confronted with severe disability. Given the expanding need for long-term care, for innovation, and for continued development of new models of delivery, an approach that focuses simultaneous attention on individual and systemic change needs is particularly crucial in long-term care.[102]

Specifically, when the need for long-term care has been established, social workers will have a major role in seeing that the psychosocial needs of the long-term patient are met. Since these needs will vary over time, the social worker, often in the role of case manager, will monitor the situation and work with the patients and their families to connect them to services. The task of helping these two entities to connect requires a high level of skill in assessing the situation, helping people make use of services, and making service systems more humane and responsive to the needs of consumers. These activities will require social workers involved in long-term care to work directly with individuals and families and to engage in program development, the creation of community resources, and the development of social policies.

These functions for social workers in long-term care are recognized in the relevant programs as social workers are well represented in each type. Kane, however, notes that "Despite the leadership of social workers as formulators and model builders, the reimbursement rules severely constrain the profession from achieving its full potential in LTC [long-term-care]."[103]

For example, nursing homes that are certified for reimbursement under Medicare and Medicaid must appoint a staff member as social service designee, but this person does not have to possess a professional degree (although MSW consultation must be available). This consultant, nevertheless, has the opportunity to train and advise the designee, the staff, and the administrator.

Issues and Directions

The major issue for social work in health care is the problem of the availability of quality services, particularly for poor people and those in need of long-term care. In recent years, cutbacks in health and social programs have moved us farther away from, rather than closer to, adopting a national health insurance plan. A major objective for social workers, consequently, must be to keep alive the goal of making good health care a right for all.

The crucial foundation for such health care is the primary care system, which is offered through a variety of providers ranging from the general or family practitioner to the often inappropriately used emergency room. Even under the best circumstances, the psychosocial needs of people that affect their health are often not recognized when primary care is provided. An objective of social workers must be to work toward the universal availability of good primary care and the identification of social services needs and access to them when primary care is provided. This might eventually save resources because of the prevention component of this approach.

Social work has an important role to play in planning for these and other necessary health services, especially if the federal block grant concept is maintained. Social workers must help local governments to make the health needs of their citizens known to the states so that resources to meet these needs are as competitive for funds as other types of programs. But competing for scarce funds is also as inefficient as it may be unjust. As Kane states, "Therefore, the reorganization and restructuring of health and human services are a first-level priority, for no social agency or clinic no matter how comprehensive its service can meet all the needs of a diverse population."[104]

Issues are also present as to how society wishes to meet the needs of long-term patients and how the ideology of deinstitutionalization fits with this. For example, we may not be maintaining psychiatric patients for long periods of time in large state mental hospitals, but we may be institutionalizing them instead in nursing homes and other community facilities, among which other sets of inhumane practices may also be found.

We also may refuse to face the fact that simply living in the community does not guarantee a high quality of life and that many services must be offered to prevent community living from being the exchange of one sordid set of circumstances for another.

We must also realize that all the good things we wish to offer escalate costs. A variety of approaches to containing such costs has been described, such as DRGs, cost sharing, and prioritizing needs. This area must be studied so that better and more effective solutions are found. Not the least of these will be ways to eliminate inefficiency and duplication and to determine the most efficient site for each type of service.

Health is a unitary phenomenon. As Miller puts it so well:

> As schools of social work continue to reorganize and change their curricula and as more health settings develop a comprehensive approach to health care, the profession of social work urgently needs to reconceptualize the historic division between the medical and psychiatric specialties. To more accurately characterize the functions of the worker, the role needs to be defined as a health (or health care) social worker who handles the psychosocial aspects of both physical and emotional illness, no matter what the practice setting.[105]

The Aged

Because of the special concerns the elderly group has with respect to health care needs, some focused attention is appropriate. The field of gerontology, the study of the elderly, is new. It really began only after the Korean War, in the middle 1950s. After all, the United States was a young country with a young population. Youth was celebrated. The elderly did not seem to require much attention, and very little was known about the needs, wishes, and concerns of the elderly group. Studies at the Institute of Gerontology at the University of Michigan, under the direction of Wilma Donahue pioneered the study of the actual condition of older Americans.

Attention of this sort might have begun earlier had not World War II developed. After all, the Social Security Act of 1935 provided partial pensions for individuals when they reached the age of 65 (and under certain other conditions as well.) Because of this act, the age of 65 became the standard for senior citizen. Because it defined, until recent legislation, the age of Social Security Retirement, it became the unofficial age of retirement, (unofficial because it was not the subject of federal law, but was adopted by many firms). In addition, the Social Security Act called attention to the older adult because of another title. If the senior citizen was not eligible for Social Security, she or he could get OAA, Old Age Assistance. This program no longer exists, having been folded into the program now called SSI, Supplemental Security Income. However, the attention drawn to the elderly in the 1930s did not begin to flower until the 1950s. After that, a great growth in programs for the elderly occurred.

Between 1955 and today, it is probably fair to say that the most social policy progress has been in the area of the senior citizen. Social Security benefits have been indexed to inflation. Coverage has been expanded. The Older Americans Act provided funding for a range of services to seniors through grants to states. Local senior centers, Meals on Wheels, and the like, are among the kinds of programs supported, in part, by this legislation. Discrimination by age is now prohibited, and people can work as long as they can do the job. The elderly have a national medical plan, Medicare, which is a benefit yet to be gained by other citizens. And not only the federal government has been involved in this policy support. States have been helpful as well, and even private firms, by offering discounts to seniors on drugs, movies, airplane flights, and meals in restaurants, among other items.

In many ways, the policy attention to the elderly group is an exemplar of how social policy can address the issues of a needy group. A host of issues remain, however, many, if not most, health related.

First is the lack of agreement on the age at which old age begins. Sixty-five remains a popular, but less powerful hallmark. Movements in both directions are occurring. Social Security eligibility will move to 67 in the early years of the next century. On the other hand, eligibility to join the powerful aging organization, the American Association of Retired Persons, is 50, long before most are retired. Not only is the minimal age of aging an issue, but the older age, too. There is much variation in the golden years; we can understand that the difference between 60 and 90 is substantial. Some gerontologists talk about young old, middle old, and old old groups, but there is not agreement that this approach is fruitful.

Whatever age is used (and let's use 65+ for the moment) the American population, like the populations of other industrialized countries, is aging. In the United States in 1990 12.4% were over 65, about as many seniors as there are Canadians. The proportions ranged from 3.8% in Alaska to 17.8% in Florida![106] This result comes not only from increased longevity, but also from decreased births. Society is aging, and the issues of health, long-term care, and housing, which have special meaning to an elderly population, are growing.

Key problems remain in services, too. While poverty has been reduced among older citizens overall, large pockets of needy elderly remain untouched by programs of assistance: African Americans, women, and other minorities. In general, those who were poor before they were elderly (using 65 as the yardstick) are poor later, because they are unable to build up the assets and equity from which support comes.[107]

Health issues are also of great importance. Childhood killers have been largely controlled; degenerative diseases associated with the process of aging have not. Cancer, Parkinson's disease, Alzheimer's Disease, bone problems, and others are all serious and prevalent within the elderly population. The higher medical costs for the elderly citizen (as compared with the younger citizen) are causing concern. And the issues of long-term care are serious. Not only is the question one about providing long-term care, but also about who should receive it, when, and for how long. Many seniors and others are concerned about the cost of long-term care and are taking out insurance policies to pay the bill should long-term care develop for them. And while only a small fraction of older adults are in long-term care (around 5%), the probability of experiencing long-term care, given that one is a senior, is much higher (20%+). Obviously, these issues are of great concern for everyone and of even greater concern for the poor.

Family relations are an issue, too. The popular novel (and movie) *Dad* underscores the troubling dynamics of older, middle, and younger generations.[108] Therapists are finding that not only do older citizens have issues to process, but these issues involve the history of family systems and surface unresolved historical concerns and grievances,

"If you don't use it, you'll lose it." (Photo by Ken Karp.)

such as incest, which may have happened 40 years ago, or family secrets finally coming out.

Social workers will have many areas of services through which they can provide assistance to the elderly and those related to the elderly. Illness-related services, such as hospital social work and case management services, are prominent. Services to families living in distant locations who need someone to be on site to provide help to their aging parents are important. Therapy for the older depressed adult and for adults concerned about the poor choices and problems of their adult children are also developing. One has of course heard about the adult child of the alcoholic. Perhaps of equal importance, in the future, will be the older parent of the adult alcoholic. Social workers may find a role here. As financial pressures squeeze generations together, intergenerational tensions are sure to erupt. And at the policy and community level, providing improved policies for the older adult and working to integrate them into the community and the organization more fully will be challenging tasks. One thing is certain. There is no reason to turn off social concern when folks reach 65. Social workers have taken and will take the lead in being of service to this group.

Conclusion

The first part of this chapter described the functions of the health system as both to promote health and to prevent and treat disease. These were described as being not simply opposites, because health relates to a state of physical, mental, and social well-being, and not only the absence of disease, which is a failure of the adaptive mechanism of an organism.

Another basic idea was that health is a holistic concept that relates to the integrated functioning of physical, emotional, intellectual, and interpersonal aspects of the individual. Another important proposition is that this function is fulfilled by seeking to have an impact on individuals so that their health may be maintained and their diseases treated, as well as on the environmental conditions that affect health and disease.

Social work in the health system has had a long history in which it has played a major role in the prevention and treatment of disease and the maintenance of health. Admittedly, the role of medicine in treatment is central, yet social work has been an active participant, particularly in what has been termed the caring process. Drawing from the writings of Schlesinger, we characterized social work activities as having (1) a public health, (2) a person–environment fit, and (3) a continuum from cure to care perspective. In fulfilling this perspective, social workers in health care have intervened with individuals, families, and groups, as well as in program planning, organizational processes, community development, and social planning and policy formation.

Philosophical issues faced by social workers in the health field were described as based on the concept of health care as a right. This leads social workers to have a strong concern for groups whose health needs are less likely to be met, such as the poor, ethnic minorities, and those in need of long-term care. Another important issue is how health care as a right relates to other rights, such as self-determination, even when the latter leads to threats to health.

The current situation regarding health care was discussed along with the historical circumstances that led to it. This included a description of public and private responses to health care needs. Detailed analyses were presented of the major components of the health care system: namely primary, hospital, and long-term care. These services include those offered in the community as well as those that are institutionally based. We then provided a summary of some of the major trends and issues facing all health care providers today. The chapter concluded with a discussion of the special problems facing the aged.

Notes

1. M. Terris, "Approaches to an Epidemiology of Health," *American Journal of Public Health,* 65, 10 (1965), p. 1038.
2. *Blakiston's New Gould Medical Dictionary,* 2nd ed. (New York: Blakiston Division, McGraw-Hill, 1956); as cited in H. David Banta, "What Is Health Care?" in Steven Jonas, ed. in *Health Care Delivery in the United States,* 3rd ed. (New York: Springer-Verlag, 1986), p. 13.
3. E. Cassell, *The Healer's Art* (Philadelphia: Lippincott, 1976), p. 48; as cited in Banta, "What Is Health Care?" p. 14.
4. Daniel Goleman, "Social Workers Vault into a Leading Role in Psychotherapy," *New York Times,* April 30, 1985, pp. 17 and 20.
5. H. Banta, "What Is Health Care?" p. 19.
6. T. McKeown, "A Historical Appraisal of the Medical Task," in G. McLaughlin and T. McKeown, eds., *Medical History and Medical Care* (New York: Oxford University Press, 1971), p. 48.
7. *NASW News,* "Health Policy Statement," 25 (1) (1980), 18–19.
8. Doman Lum, "Health Service System," in A. Minahan, ed., *Encyclopedia of Social Work,* Vol. I, 18th ed., (Silver Spring, Md: National Association of Social Workers, 1987), p. 729.

9. Ibid.
10. Elfriede G. Schlesinger, *Health Care Social Work Practice: Concepts and Strategies* (St. Louis: Times Mirror/Mosby, 1985), p. 127.
11. B. C. Smith, *Community Health: An Epidemiological Approach* (New York: Macmillan, 1979), p. 17.
12. Schlesinger, *Health Care Social Work Practice,* p. 129.
13. Claudia Coulton, "Person-Environment Fit as the Focus in Health Care," *Social Work* 26 (1) (1981), p. 20.
14. For a more detailed discussion of crisis theory, see Naomi Golan, *Treatment in Crisis Situations* (New York: The Free Press, 1978).
15. Schlesinger, *Health Care Social Work Practice,* p. 143.
16. These are only a few of the items that may be found in Schlesinger, *Health Care Social Work Practice,* pp. 147–149.
17. Ibid., p. 150.
18. Salie Rossen, "Hospital Social Work," in A. Minahan, ed., *Encyclopedia of Social Work,* Vol. I, 18th ed., (Silver Spring, Md.: National Association of Social Workers, 1987), pp. 816–821.
19. David Mechanic, *Medical Sociology,* 2nd ed. (New York: The Free Press, 1978).
20. Rosalind S. Miller and Helen Rehr, "Health Settings and Health Providers," in Rosalind S. Miller and Helen Rehr, eds. *Social Work Issues in Health Care,* (Englewood Cliffs, N.J.: Prentice Hall, 1983), p. 2.
21. Edward A. McKinney, "Health Planning" in Minahan, ed., *Encyclopedia of Social Work,* 18th ed., Vol. I, pp. 718–719; the citation within this quotation is R. Finney, R. Pessin, and L. Matheis, "Prospects for Social Workers in Health Planning," *Health and Social Work,* 1 (3), 8–25.
22. Banta, "What Is Health Care?" p. 20.
23. These programs will be described later in this chapter.
24. Banta, "What Is Health Care?" p. 20.
25. The history of proposals for national health insurance is important for an understanding of ideological concerns over the right to health care but is too lengthy for inclusion here. Such details can be found in Steven Jonas, "A Review of the Past; Visions of the Future," in Jonas, *Health Care Delivery,* pp. 504–509.
26. Ibid., p. 21.
27. Ibid.
28. Gary Rosenberg, "Practice Roles and Functions of the Health Social Worker," in Miller and Rehr, eds., *Social Work Issues in Health Care,* p. 123.
29. See Daniel Callahan, "Health and Societies: Some Ethical Imperatives," in John H. Knowles, ed. *Doing Better and Feeling Worse: Health in the United States,* (New York: W.W. Norton, 1977), pp. 23–34; Helen Rehr, *Ethical Dilemmas in Health Care: The Professional Search for Solutions* (New York: Prodist, 1978); Gavin Fairbairn and Susan Fairbairn, *Ethical Issues in Caring* (Brookfield, Vt.: Avebury, 1988).
30. Edward A. McKinney, "Health Planning," p. 715.
31. Rosalind S. Miller, "Legislation and Health Policies," in Miller and Rehr, eds., *Social Work Issues in Health Care,* p. 79.
32. Ibid.
33. Walter A. Friedlander and Robert Z. Apte, *Introduction to Social Welfare,* 5th ed. (Englewood Cliffs, N.J.: Prentice Hall, 1980), pp. 414–415.
34. Ibid.
35. Ibid., p. 81.
36. Ibid.
37. Page 1.42, section 291, U.S. Code 1958.
38. Steven Jonas, "Planning for Health Services" in Jonas, ed., *Health Care Delivery,* p. 392–393.
39. Section 314(a) of Public Law 89–749.
40. Jonas, "Planning for Health Services," in Jonas, ed., *Health Care Delivery,* p. 396.

41. McKinney, "Health Planning", p. 718.

42. Miller, "Legislation and Health Policies," p. 99.

43. Ibid.

44. *Encyclopedia of Social Work* (Washington, D.C.: National Association of Social Workers, 1977), p. 616.

45. R. Taylor and J. Ford, *Research Highlights in Social Work: Social Work and Health Care* (London: Kingsley Publishers, 1989), pp. 11–20.

46. Miller and Rehr, "Health Settings and Health Providers," p. 2.

47. Ibid., pp. 3–4.

48. Ibid.

49. Ibid.

50. Ibid., p. 5.

51. The 1965 data are from Carol M. McCarthy and Kenneth E. Thorpe, "Financing for Health Care," in Jonas, ed., *Health Care Delivery in the United States,* p. 303. The 1987 data are from U.S. Bureau of the Census, *Statistical Abstract of the United States: 1990* (Washington, D.C.: U.S. Government Printing Office, 1990), Table 134.

52. Doman Lum, "Health Service System," p. 726.

53. McCarthy and Thorpe, "Financing for Health Care," pp. 303–305. Their data have been updated to 1987. See *Statistical Abstract,* Tables 136 and 138.

54. Ibid., p. 305.

55. Steven Jonas, "Population Data for Health and Health Care," in Jonas, ed., *Health Care Delivery in the United States,* pp. 48–51. These data have been updated to 1987. See *Statistical Abstract,* Table 165.

56. Schlesinger, *Health Care Social Work Practice,* pp. 11–12.

57. Ibid.

58. Ibid., p. 13.

59. Ibid., p. 18.

60. Ibid., p. 28.

61. Ibid.

62. Steven P. Segal, "Deinstitutionalization," in A. Minahan, ed., *Encyclopedia of Social Work,* 18th ed., Vol. I, pp. 377–378. Updated to 1987. See *Statistical Abstract,* Table 181.

63. This is a larger number than cited in the previous paragraph because it includes people in veterans' facilities, private hospitals, and local facilities in addition to those in state hospitals.

64. Howard H. Goldman, "Epidemiology," in John A. Talbott, ed. *The Chronic Mental Patient: Five Years Later* (Orlando, Fla.: Grune and Stratton, 1984), p. 22; Charles Kiesler and Amy E. Sibulkin, *Mental Hospitalization: Myths and Facts about a National Crisis* (Newbury Park, Cal.: Sage Publications, 1987).

65. *Ann Arbor News,* April 30, 1987, sec. C, p. 3.

66. Miller and Rehr, "Health Settings and Health Providers," p. 1.

67. Neil Bracht, "The Scope and Historical Development of Social Work," in Neil Bracht, ed., *Social Work in Health Care* (New York: Haworth, 1978), pp. 3–18.

68. *Health Resources Statistics: Health Manpower and Health Facilities,* 1966–77 ed., (U.S. Department of Health, Education, and Welfare, Public Health Service, Office of Health Research, Statistics, and Technology, National Center for Health Statistics, Hyattsville, Md., 1979), p. 249.

69. Steven Jonas and Stephen N. Rosenberg, "Ambulatory Care," in Jonas, ed., *Health Care Delivery in the United States,* p. 153.

70. Leonard J. Marcus, "Health Care Financing," in Minahan, ed., *Encyclopedia of Social Work,* 18th ed., Vol. 1, p. 702.

71. Lum, "Health Service System," p. 722.

72. Anthony R. Kovner, "Hospitals," in Jonas, ed., *Health Care Delivery in the United States,* p. 187.

73. R. L. Kane and R. A. Kane, *Values and Long-term Care* (Lexington, Mass.: Lexington Books, 1982), p. 2.

74. Jonas and Rosenberg, "Ambulatory Care," p. 128.
75. Ibid., pp. 132–133.
76. Ibid.
77. Ibid., p. 136.
78. Steven Jonas and others, "Monitoring Utilization of a Municipal Hospital Emergency Department," *Hospital Topics,* 54 (1) (1976), 43–48.
79. C. A. Miller, "An Agenda for Public Health Departments," *Journal of Public Health Policy,* 6 (2), (1985), 158–172.
80. Ibid.
81. Jonas and Rosenberg, "Ambulatory Care," pp. 146–153.
82. P. Hookey, "Social Work in Primary Health Care Settings," in Bracht, ed., *Social Work in Health Care,* pp. 211–226.
83. This list draws from Rosalind S. Miller, "Primary Health Care," in Minahan, ed., *Encyclopedia of Social Work,* Vol. II, 18th ed. (Silver Spring, Md.: National Association of Social Workers, 1987), pp. 321–324.
84. Ibid., p. 322.
85. Anthony R. Kovner, "Hospitals," in Jonas, ed., *Health Care Delivery in the United States,* p. 189.
86. Ibid.
87. Ibid., p. 191.
88. Ibid.
89. Ibid., p. 192.
90. Ibid., pp. 321–322.
91. Ibid., p. 200.
92. Schlesinger, *Health Care Social Work Practice,* p. 256.
93. C. J. Coulton and N. Butler, "Measuring Social Work Productivity in Health Care," *Health and Social Work,* 6 (3) (1981), pp. 4–12. Gary Rosenberg, "Concepts in the Financial Management of Hospital Social Work Departments," *Social Work in Health Care,* 5 (3) (1980), pp. 287–296. Z. Butrym and J. Horder, *Health, Doctors, and Social Work* (London: Routledge and Kegan Paul, 1983), pp. 6–23.
94. Terrie T. Wetle and David A. Pearson, "Long-Term Care," in Jonas, ed., *Health Care Delivery in the United States,* p. 214.
95. Ibid., p. 217.
96. Ibid., p. 220.
97. Ibid., p. 221.
98. F. E. Moss and V. J. Halamandaris, *Too Old, Too Sick, Too Bad: Nursing Homes in America* (Germantown, Md.: Aspen Systems Corp.), 1977.
99. D. Haber, *Health Care for an Aging Society: Cost Conscious Community Care and Self-care Approaches* (New York: Hemisphere Publishing Corp., 1989).
100. Wetle and Pearson, "Long-Term Care," p. 225–226.
101. Ibid., p. 226.
102. Schlesinger, *Health Care Social Work Practice,* p. 292.
103. Rosalie A. Kane, "Long-Term Care," in Minahan, ed., *Encyclopedia of Social Work,* Vol. II, 18th ed., p. 68.
104. Miller, "Legislation and Health Policies," p. 111.
105. Ibid., p. 116.
106. U.S. Bureau of the Census, *Statistical Abstract of the United States* (Washington, D.C.: U.S. Government Printing Office, 1991), p. xii.
107. Lawrence S. Root and John E. Tropman, "Income Sources of the Elderly," *Social Service Review* 58 (3) (September 1984), pp. 383–403.
108. W. Wharton, *Dad* (New York: Alfred A. Knopf, 1981).

CHAPTER 13
Service Delivery for Enhancing Education

The Function of the Educational System

The focus of this chapter is on the institutions created by society to educate its citizens and the role that social work plays within such institutions. Although discussions of school social work typically focus on social work programs in schools for children and youth, we believe that the mission of social work in educational settings extends to serving adults as well.

Admittedly, there is a longer history, a clearer mandate, and a larger body of knowledge regarding social work in educational programs for children. Nevertheless, we believe that social workers have analogous roles in such educational programs as colleges, vocational training centers, and the lifelong learning programs for adults conducted by a variety of educational establishments. Thus, throughout the chapter we present information and ideas about social work in relationship to adult as well as child education.

The support that a democratic society gives its educational system is based on several convictions. A primary one is that a democracy requires educated citizens who are able to sufficiently understand the key issues confronting the society to participate in it in essential ways, such as by voting for its policy makers and supporting their decisions, by paying taxes and obeying laws for example. Another conviction is that every citizen is entitled to a sufficient amount of formal training to function in a productive manner, which means being able to support oneself and one's dependents.

A major source of controversy is how much education is essential for these purposes to be achieved and, therefore, how much should be (1) required of all citizens and (2) freely provided to all by the society. Some argue that the minimum should be a grade school education, although more typically the minimum is a high school education. Many jurisdictions take the position that even an advanced education should be made available to all who qualify without regard to their economic resources. In addition, governments at various levels (local, state, and federal) often provide educational programs for specific adult categories, such as the unemployed or the handicapped, to enable them to accomplish the objectives of the educational system.

Another question has been the responsibility of the society to provide an education for those who cannot fully benefit from the type of education offered to the majority. Increasingly, public policy has moved in the direction of insisting that all people, including those handicapped in various ways, must be offered suitable education so that they might function as citizens and self-sufficient individuals to the fullest degree possible. As Constable and Flynn state:

> By the end of the decade and the beginning of the 1980s there has gradually emerged a refined body of court decisions, laws, ensuing regulations, Office of Special Education policies, and Office of Civil Rights findings which have defined what is an irreversible direction toward the rights of handicapped people. . . . The overall direction of judicial decisions and regulations is toward the broadening of the traditional focus of the school in the process of providing and facilitating a free, appropriate,

public education for handicapped children. . . . The new concept of a right to an education was to encompass, as Weintraub and Abeson clarified, "equal access to differing resources for differing objectives."[1]

A number of problems exist in the ways that the U.S. educational system fulfills the purposes we have stated. Writing in the 1970s, Costin presented a list that is as timely now as it was then.

1. Inequality of educational opportunities stemming from continuing widespread racial and economic segregation.
2. Persistent stereotyped beliefs that low income and nonwhite children have limited capabilities, resulting in lowered expectations of them.
3. Faulty school practices related to control of pupils' behavior.
4. Placement of value on conformity to the detriment of individuality.
5. Lack of communication between the school and the community it serves and between the school and the home.
6. Irrelevance of much of the educational process for different population groups, which intensifies children's feelings of alienation from their school and from the larger society.
7. Learning experiences that fail to offer children and young persons the opportunity to feel involved—experiences that instead are too often inflexible, repetitious, or unrelated to their present and future.[2]

Many of these problems also apply to educational programs that serve adults. This is certainly true with regard to inequality of educational opportunities, beliefs about minorities, lack of relevance, and alienation of students and is manifested in the frequent occurrence of demonstrations by and on behalf of minority groups on college campuses. It is less true for those issues that apply mostly to minors, such as control of pupil behavior.

An issue of considerable controversy is whether the educational institution's function is exclusively to meet the educational needs of its students or whether it has functions with respect to the larger community. The way this issue is manifested in the primary and secondary school involves the proposition that the school is a community resource for all residents. This once was called the lighted schoolhouse concept through which such activities as continuing education, community organization, and recreation for all ages took place. The same proposition has been made regarding educational institutions serving adult constituencies.

Several authors have pointed out that a broad view of the functions of the educational system has had some negative effects.[3] For example, the educational system has been blamed for community disorders because of its failure to educate minority children.[4] In discussing this topic, Jencks, has pointed out "that Americans have always tended to assume that good schools can offset all the numerous shortcomings of the home, the church, and the employer."[5]

That the functions of the educational system have limits leads us to the question as to what we should expect from a successful system. We agree with Downs that there are four desirable outcomes for educational institutions serving children and youth: (1) all students should be helped to attain some basic minimum level of proficiency; (2) all students considered as a group should be helped to attain the best outcomes possible in terms of the overall resources of the system; (3) all students should acquire the same basic capabilities for the next portions of their lives (equal opportunity for all); and (4) each student should be helped to attain his or her maximum individual potential.[6]

The preceding discussion has presented the ideal functions of the educational system. Writers such as Sarri, however, point out that some functions fulfilled by the educational system are implicit rather than part of a formal mandate. For example, while the ideal is that the system provide equal access to statuses, in fact it "mediates the supply and demand of workers and the assignment of social statuses" and "has a mandate from the larger society to select students for adult roles by differential evaluation of their ability and performance."[7]

Consequently, Sarri calls on us "to understand the educational processes involved in career assignment and to determine if the school's mandate is being fulfilled as it was expected to be." In this respect she draws our attention to such facts as the lower status and fewer resources assigned to vocational as compared to college preparatory education.

Contrary to common sense, Sarri notes that "Some schools in the inner city have almost no vocational training programs, while schools in the suburbs have equipment that goes unused because their students are uninterested in such training."[8] Even then, she argues that such vocational instruction, wherever found, has not kept pace with technological changes and does not adequately prepare students for contemporary jobs. In addition, various devices are used to track students so that some are placed in noncollege-directed streams because of their social class or race rather than their individual talents and interests.

The Functions of Social Work in the Educational System

The discussion of social work in educational settings provides us with many opportunities to illustrate a basic thrust of this book: the utilization of ecological concepts to analyze and describe social work and social welfare activities. This is because the field of school social work has almost universally come to use an ecological framework as its main perspective. Within this framework, school social workers view problems found in the school as related to the ways students, parents, staff, and community members interact with each other. Solutions to problems must, consequently, be found in the altering of these interactions, rather than in seeking change in any one set of participants. As the writers of a recent text on school social work, aptly subtitled *An Ecological Perspective,* state:

> The school is an open living system whose members are engaged in ongoing transactions and interactions with each other and significant others in the community. Productive exchanges develop the competence and self-esteem necessary to promote the desired learning and growth of all persons in the school organization: pupils, parents, teachers, and administrators.[9]

This ecological approach is different from other models of school social work

Sometimes the social worker comes to class. (Photo by Laimute E. Druskis.)

described in the literature. Alderson identifies these as the traditional clinical model, the school change model, the social interaction model, and the community school model.[10]

The traditional clinical model sees the worker as focused on individual students with problems that interfere with their ability to learn. The school change model, in contrast, sees the worker as concentrating on identifying and changing school policies and practices that lead to pupil problems. The community school model sees the worker, particularly in disadvantaged communities, as helping the school to create linkages with and services for the community.

The social interaction model sees the worker as acting "to mediate the process through which the individual and his [sic] society reach out for each other through a mutual need for self-fulfillment."[11] The school social worker, therefore, mediates between the various constituencies of the school, such as between students and teachers or parents and administrators.

A worker employing an ecological model might engage in any of the activities described in these four approaches, but with an awareness of how the activity will subsequently affect the interactions among all the components of the school as a system. An ecological orientation should also help the worker to choose a change goal that, when achieved, will lead to an increased ability and opportunity for the various components of the school system to engage in effective transactions and negotiations.

In recent years, conceptualizations of school social work have clearly been within an ecological perspective. This was the thrust of a 1978 document of the National Association of Social Workers, which defined three categories of tasks performed by school social workers:[12] (1) crisis resolution, (2) the solution of identified problems, and (3) the development of personal and interpersonal coping skills among all groups in schools. Winters and Easton add a fourth category, which is mentioned in the NASW document but not as one of its categories: early identification and service delivery to populations at risk (essentially an approach to prevention).[13]

Within such an ecological perspective, crisis resolution might be needed by any subsystem of the school, such as pupils, parents, classes, administrators, or the school as a whole. A crisis is defined as any stressful event experienced by an individual or set of individuals that cannot be coped with in the usual ways. Obviously, the social worker will not be involved in all crises. Nevertheless, the social worker possesses skills to help people cope with stressful situations, and these skills can be drawn on in many school crises.

The social worker brings to any problem-solving situation, and certainly those directly involving students, a perspective that views problems as related to the interactions among several components of the school system. As Winters and Easton state:

> Findings suggest that pupils' learning varies directly with particular features of the school organization and pupil–school–community relations. Positive outcomes repeatedly correlate with such characteristics as high teacher expectations, the provision of incentives, the extent to which children are encouraged to take responsibility, the match between instructional strategies and pupils' learning styles, the extent to which curriculum responds to pupils' needs and the degree to which academic performance is rewarded by the system as a whole.[14]

Because of this ecological view, school social workers when working with pupils and families will also target the broader conditions affecting them. The workers will consequently engage in such activities as pointing out the effects of school conditions on student behavior and learning to school personnel. A strong element in this type of activity is that of prevention as school social workers anticipate the impact of school conditions on students, families, and staff.

A similar ecological perspective is utilized as social workers help the various constituencies of the school to increase their coping skills. They will be involved, for example, in training teachers in communication and other interpersonal skills; training parents in parenting skills, particularly as these relate to supporting their child's education; and helping children to make their needs known in responsible ways to their teachers.

Social workers also work with community members in helping them to make their wishes known to the school. This has been an important contribution when the schools have faced such serious challenges as those posed by desegregation. An example was when social workers in Milwaukee facilitated desegregation by helping community groups develop linkages between the schools, administration, and each other. This included sponsoring cultural and human relations activities and encouraging ethnic content in the curriculum.[15]

But can such a comprehensive array of tasks actually be performed by such workers? That this does occur was attested to in a study of a national sample of school social workers by Allen-Meares:[16]

Factor analysis of the data yielded seven factors. In rank order of importance, these are: clarifying the child's problem with others; tasks preliminary to the provision of social work services; assessing the child's problem; facilitating school–community–pupil relations; educational counseling with the child and parents; facilitating the utilization of community resources; and leadership and policy making.[17]

This finding supports the proposition that school social work has moved away from a predominantly clinical approach. It shows, however, that practice still falls short of the full utilization of the ecological approach, with its emphasis on identifying group at risk, changing adverse social conditions and responding to crises.

Analogous activities are engaged in by social workers in other settings such as those for higher education and vocational instruction. Social workers are often employed by colleges, where they are usually assigned to the counseling center. As with traditional school social work services, these workers may restrict themselves to strictly clinical activities, but many take a broad systemic view.

From this latter stance, social workers in colleges have identified and sought to change campus conditions that interfere with the education of some set of students, such as poor facilities for handicapped students. They have stepped into crisis situations, such as counseling with students in a dorm when a dorm resident has committed suicide. And they have worked with a variety of groups in the college setting to eliminate racist and sexist actions that broadly interfere with its ability to function as a sound environment for learning.

Social workers in schools may choose the individual student, groups of students, families, the entire school, the community, or the society as both the systems with which they interact and the targets of their efforts. When the school social worker works with the individual student or staff member, the emphasis is on helping that person cope with the requirements of the situation. Thus, the student might be assisted to secure a remedial service for an academic deficit or a means of interacting more effectively with teachers or peers. A teacher, on the other hand, might be helped to develop a better understanding of the needs of a student so as to better respond to them.

Many school social workers' efforts on behalf of individual students are in compliance with Public Law 94–142. This act relates to school services for handicapped children and requires an individualized educational plan (IEP) and that the social worker have an important role in specifying social work goals and means of reaching them as related to the larger objectives of the plan.

Social workers also work with groups of students in the school setting. Such groups might include students with similar problems with the educational situation. Social workers, in this situation, help to create a mutual aid system in which the members help each other to deal with these problems.[18] The potential for such groups to lead to stigmatization of its members is present, however, so workers must act judiciously when deciding to create them. Another possibility for working with groups is to interact with entire classrooms. An example of this was a worker who utilized a set of almost life size dolls that represented children with special needs (physical handicap, Down's syndrome, blindness, and so forth) to enact a series of skits to help children understand and deal with such differences.

Workers also interact with parents. This might help them to acquire ways of assisting their children to meet academic expectations and teach them parenting skills through parent education groups. Another possibility is to help groups of parents to identify needs the school might not be meeting in order to present this information to appropriate bodies.

The school as an entity is also targeted. The worker may see the need to change adverse school conditions, such as the absence of needed services, the existence of policies that are undesirable for some sets of students, an administrative arrangement such as how grievances are processed, or the many ways that the school responds or fails to respond to the ethnic backgrounds of students. The worker may then pursue these changes through meetings with parents, administrators, teachers, or even the school board. Often a social worker is the director of special education services for the school system and is then in an excellent position to seek system-wide changes.

We have presented a good example of the worker's role in the community, which involved school desegregation in Milwaukee. Another view of the school social worker's role in the community is offered by Deshler and Erlich.[19] In their approach, the worker is now called a "school–community agent." Agents are attached to the local school and are responsible to the principals. Nevertheless, they must not be seen as captives of the school system, while still being in close contact with teachers and administrators. Their role specifically is

> that of a professional trained to stimulate and guide the community development process, assist the school in fulfilling its educational goals, and help individuals and groups in the community to strengthen the attitudes, interests and skills required for full participation in seeking and implementing effective solutions to school–community problems.[20]

Deshler and Erlich give a number of examples of activities that school–community agents have engaged in, such as forming food-buying cooperatives based in schools, sponsoring summer recreation programs, and supporting community-generated housing rehabilitation programs.[21]

The school social worker is in a good position to see the needs of various groups of students and to use this information to influence policy makers. Such groups include ethnic minorities, handicapped students, and students with special learning needs. The worker can also see the effects on students of such policies as those related to discipline and compulsory school attendance and can offer testimony regarding alternative approaches to these issues.

A good example of the efforts of social workers to influence educational policy is the work in the 1960s of Rosemary Sarri, Robert Vinter, and others at the School of Social Work of the University of Michigan supported by funds from the federal government and five southeastern Michigan school systems. Vinter and Sarri summarize some aspects of this work as follows:

> This study, conducted during the 1960s, was one of the first to address new concerns about the effectiveness of public education, and the nature and causes of schools' handling of youth who were regarded as presenting difficulties or otherwise "mal-performing" with respect to educational goals. These were paramount concerns of the

funder, and the project's general results (beyond the 5 systems themselves) had considerable impact on national debate about these matters.[22]

Vinter and Sarri indicate that the impact of their work on policy was attained by reporting to personnel in the school systems (social workers, teachers, supervisors, principals, superintendants, and boards) and to a larger audience through publications. A major change target of the project, based on its research findings, was the practice of tracking as it affected lower-income and minority students. As Vinter and Sarri describe it:

> Because the funder supported a number of projects aimed at other facets of similar problems, including inner city and large school systems, it was able to incorporate these findings into broader and more comprehensive policy proposals and recommendations. By sheer coincidence, this project's findings comparing Ann Arbor's system to others was released early and received extraordinary attention in the national press, thus helping to stimulate greater recognition of problematic school practices and their effects on many youth.[23]

Vinter and Sarri conclude their discussion with a review of the dramatic events and confrontations that occurred in Ann Arbor following the release of the report as staff and board reacted to it. While efforts were made to counter its impact in the short run, over the longer run community, staff, and court actions led to important systemic changes.

Value and Ideological Issues in Education

Allen-Meares and her colleagues present a well-conceptualized discussion of the applications of social work values to social work in the schools. They translate the value of recognizing the worth and dignity of each person into valuing each pupil "regardless of any unique characteristic"; the value of the right to self-determination into believing that each pupil should be "allowed to share in the learning process and to learn"; the value of respect for individual potential into the idea that "individual differences should be recognized" and that "intervention should be aimed at supporting pupils' educational goals"; and the value on the right to be different into the belief that "each child, regardless of race and socioeconomic characteristics, has a right to equal treatment in the school."[24]

Allen-Meares and her colleagues add to the above beliefs the convictions that "children are entitled to equal educational opportunities and to learning experiences adapted to their individual needs" and that "the process of education should not only provide the child with tools for future learning and skills to use in earning a living, but be an essential ingredient to the child's mental health."[25] At times, however, the child's needs conflict with those of others. The principle often cited by school social workers in these instances is that of the best interests of the child. An effort is made to ascertain what such interests may be and to optimize these. A more complex issue is posed by value conflicts affecting adult learners; here the social worker is more likely to seek to mediate than to take sides.

Disciplinary issues pose difficult value questions for school social workers. The right of the school to control the behavior of children is derived from the legal principle of in loco parentis (in place of the parents), which permits the school to assume the same control over children that parents have at home. Thus schools not only prescribe courses of study, but also speech, dress, and a variety of other behaviors. It has also permitted a variety of penalties, such as expulsion, suspension, and corporal punishment. Largely as a consequence of the civil rights movements of the 1960s, however, schools have limited (or been forced to limit) the applications of in loco parentis, but much controversy regarding the extent of the school's control over behavior remains.[26]

The values of social workers have tended to place them in the forefront of groups seeking to find humane ways of maintaining order in schools that respect the dignity and rights of students. As Allen-Meares and her colleagues state regarding the roles of social workers,

> They can assist in the development of policies and procedures for securing and maintaining records; they can consult with school officials regarding basic human rights; they can provide firm, constructive counsel to pupils about their responsibilities and remind them to have respect for others; and they can take the leadership in developing and refining pupil codes of conduct.[27]

These authors suggest additional ways that school social workers can draw on their expertise and their values to enhance the operation of the educational setting, which include lobbying the school board for restrictions on corporal punishment, acting as advocates for students who have been unjustly punished, and providing teachers with training in ways of managing the classroom without corporal or other harsh punishments.

Another important way in which the rights of students and their families were expanded pertained to the student's school records. This occurred largely through the enactment of the Family Educational Rights and Privacy Act, which was a rider to the 1974 education amendments.[28] This act prohibited the disbursement of federal funds to schools that did not allow parents to have access to their child's school records or, if the student was over 18, to him or her.

After reviewing the record, the parent can challenge the validity of any information contained therein. The school is restricted from sharing any information with a third party. While many social workers favored these extensions of student rights, they did have an impact on their practices. They became more careful as to the kinds of information they placed in students' records. They also were more sure to secure the permission of parents before interviewing their children. In addition, social workers sought to help other school personnel in their use of student records. Finally, social workers often aided parents to make appropriate use of the information they found.

Thus, social workers have found many applications for their broad values in the educational setting. They have collaborated with their colleagues from the field of education to ensure that the school is a humane setting that teaches such values by example to its students.

Overview of the Educational System

HISTORY

During the early years of the United States, educational policy issues were whether children should receive a free public education, what that education should include, and whether (and which) children should be required to attend. The way those children's needs should be met, if not immediately related to classroom instruction, was rarely discussed. Slowly throughout the years before World War I, however, progress was made in resolving these issues: the first state to make attendance compulsory was Massachusetts (1852) and the last was Mississippi (1918).

Child labor was closely related to the issue of compulsory school attendance. Those who made profits off the work of children would not be well served if all children were required to attend school and, in addition, restricted from specified hours and types of employment. The early leaders in the child welfare field, consequently, saw the issues of compulsory school attendance and restrictions on child labor as complementary.

Once the principle was established that all children should be helped by the society to achieve their potential through education, the question became how to overcome barriers to accomplishing this. The field of school social work grew out of this concern and was initiated by agencies that were not part of the school system. This development occurred during 1906–1907 in three cities: New York, Boston, and Hartford. The New York effort was conducted by settlement house staff from Hartley House and Greenwich House. They believed it was necessary to interact with the teachers of children who came to the settlement to enhance understanding between staff, children, and schools.[29]

The Boston social work–school activity was conducted by the Women's Education Association, which assigned visiting teachers to the schools to enhance cooperation between the school and home. The term "visiting teacher" was also used by many of the schools that later adopted this type of activity. In Hartford, this type of service was initiated by its Psychological Clinic.

Rochester, New York's Board of Education was the first to sponsor a social work service. In 1913 it established a visiting teacher program to bring about an environment outside the school that was conducive to the child's education. In doing this, the board recognized the value of integrating school social work with other aspects of its program.

As school social work developed, its practitioners recognized a need to create a supportive organization, and they formed the National Association of Home and School Visitors and Visiting Teachers in 1916. The 1916 conference of this organization was held in conjunction with the National Education Association and the 1919 conference with the National Conference of Social Work, which demonstrates the dual relationships that exist for school social workers.[30] Social work pioneers also recognized the relevance of the school setting to the mission of social work as attested to by Sophonisba Breckinridge's address to the National Education Association in 1914 in which she spoke of the school's role in "testing social relationships" and in "improving social conditions." There was also Lillian Wald's position that the school fails when "it separates its work from all that makes up the child's life outside the classroom."[31]

The definitions of school social work that were developed in this early period have a very contemporary sound. As Jane Culbert stated in 1916:

Interpreting to the school the child's out-of-school life, supplementing the teacher's knowledge of the child . . . so that she may be able to teach the whole child . . . assisting the school to know the life of the neighborhood, in order that it may train the children for the life to which they look forward. Secondly, the visiting teacher interprets to the parents the demands of the school and explains the particular difficulties and needs of the child.[32]

These ideas were very influential and enabled the expansion of school social work throughout the country and from elementary into high schools. The development of school social work was also furthered through demonstrations under the auspices of the Commonwealth Fund. The fund gave the National Committee of Visiting Teachers support for a countrywide demonstration in which social workers were placed in 30 different communities. Through these types of projects, by 1930 there were about 244 school social workers in 31 states.

Like other human services, school social work was severely cut back during the Depression of the 1930s, and school social workers strove during this period to improve their methods rather than to expand their availability. Ironically, this led to a retreat from efforts to change school conditions and to provide family–school–community linkages; instead the focus was on individual work with children. There were, nevertheless, voices of resistance to this. An example was Bertha Reynolds, a social work educator, who saw the social implications of directions taken by the profession:

It is clear that the contribution of social casework is to supplement the basic public administrator, not to struggle to make up for mistakes of a poor one. If a faulty school curriculum is causing every year thousands of school failures, it would be stupid to engage visiting teachers to work individually with the unsuccessful children. Why not change the curriculum and do away with that particular problem at one stroke.[33]

Toward the end of World War II, the development of school social work services moved forward again, and by 1944, 266 cities throughout the United States had visiting teacher services.[34] Nevertheless, the focus on work with the students and their families continued, although some interest in utilizing group work methods began to surface.[35] This narrow focus began to change in the 1960s, largely because of the criticisms that schools were poorly serving low-income and minority group children. It was in this context that the previously described work of Vinter and Sarri and of the pioneer school–community agents was accomplished. Federal legislation was another factor in this development. Title II of the Economic Opportunity Act of 1964 created the Headstart programs, which employed many social workers.[36] Title I of the Elementary and Secondary Education Act expanded educational programs for disadvantaged students. The Education for All Handicapped Children Act of 1975 established the requirement of an individualized instructional program for each child, and social workers had a major role to play in the team efforts to create such plans.[37]

There was considerable interest during this period as to what was actually being done by school social workers and what various interests saw as the essential components of the role. Some studies supported the idea that the clinical function was predominant, while others demonstrated a commitment to expanding the worker's policy roles.[38]

Throughout the 1970s a number of events took place that helped to establish the current view of the school social worker as operating from social systems and ecological frameworks. One was a national workshop, "Social Change and School Social Work," held at the University of Pennsylvania in June 1969. The papers that grew out of this workshop were published in a book entitled *The School in the Community.*[39] We have utilized many of the papers from this volume throughout this chapter to describe innovations that developed in school social work.[40] The expansion of certification programs for school social workers, the first National Conference of School Social Workers in Denver in April 1978, and the adoption by the National Association of Social Workers on January 20, 1978 of a set of standards for school social work[41] all contributed to the efforts to conceptualize the mission of school social work in a contemporary manner.

CURRENT SITUATION

School social work is part of a very large enterprise today. In 1988–1989, expenditures for primary and secondary education amounted to $199 billion, with public schools accounting for $183 billion of this. More than 59 million pupils from kindergarten to grade 12 were enrolled, with 8 million in private schools.[42]

The typical employers of school social workers are the local school districts, and their salaries are comparable to those of teachers with similar amounts of training and experience. It is difficult to estimate the number of school social workers because of the lack of a central reporting system, but Costin believes there are between 8,000 and 12,000 in the United States.[43] The recession of the 1980s had serious effects on school budgets, and this may have caused some cutbacks of school social workers.

A factor that may have limited this cutback was the requirement that school districts implement Public Law 94–142. Because of the importance of this piece of legislation, entitled the *Education for Handicapped Children Act,* we shall summarize its provisions here.[44] The act guaranteed a "free, appropriate public education which emphasizes special education and related services" to meet the needs of all handicapped children between the ages of 3 and 21. Handicapped children were defined as "mentally retarded, hard of hearing, deaf, speech impaired, visually handicapped, seriously emotionally disturbed, orthopedically impaired, other health impaired, deaf-blind, multi-handicapped, or is having specific learning disabilities, who because of these impairments need special education, and related services."

The children identified in this way are provided with an individual educational program, which is revised annually. The program is typically devised by a team composed of the social worker, teacher, administrator, and other relevant school personnel. The parent and often the child also participate. The program includes statements of goals, means of attaining goals, and ways of evaluating this attainment. This conference can be handled by a systems-oriented social worker as a kind of network therapy in which a variety of individuals related to the family are enabled to interact with the family in a therapeutic manner.[45]

Furthermore, such children must be educated in the "least restrictive environment." Thus, the child should either spend part or all of his or her time in a regular classroom or in an environment that is as close to this as possible while still leading to the attainment of the educational goals. Implicit is the idea that schools should move away from labeling and stigmatizing handicapped children.

Finally, these services should be provided at no extra cost to the family. This is in recognition of the philosophical principle that society should assume responsibility for the education of *all* children. This also requires that the child be provided with related services such as, for example, speech therapy and counseling. Related services are defined as "services provided by qualified social workers, psychologists, guidance counselors, or other qualified personnel."

Public Law 94–142 had a major impact on the activities of school social workers, who have had a major role in the development of educational plans. They also have been case managers for the implementation of the plan. In this respect they "are responsible for coordinating the efforts of other school personnel—principals, teachers, specialized support personnel—and parents."[46]

Implementing this piece of legislation is not without its problems. One is inadequate funding. Another is the number of children who, despite this legislation, do not receive the mandated services. According to Allen-Meares and her colleagues,

> Hundreds of thousands of children are still denied federally mandated services. Many children remain on waiting lists for evaluation. Black children are misclassified and inappropriately placed in classes for the mentally retarded, at a rate three times that of white children. Handicapped children are illegally suspended or expelled from school, and school districts fail to inform parents of their rights. There is an apparent failure to develop effective monitoring procedures to implement the intent of the law.[47]

Finally, the act assumes that the school will be able to coordinate the various services needed by the child. Unfortunately, many political, jurisdictional, and funding issues stand in the way of attaining this objective.

Selected Components in Detail

Because the activities of the social worker do not differ as much from one institution to another as among the various functions fulfilled in *each* institution, we shall discuss these different functions in detail, rather than the settings. The functions that we shall treat relate to preventing school failure, disruptive behavior, nonattendance, and substance abuse and educating pregnant young women. Some of these functions differ with adults in postsecondary educational settings.

PREVENTING SCHOOL FAILURE

One type of program to prevent school failure serves the preschool child. The importance of such a program is that it seeks to counter the negative effects of early years of deprivation on later learning. Begun in 1965, Head Start programs are protypical of this effort. These were funded by the federal government throughout the United States. They provided educational, medical, dental, and nutritional programs and sought to link families with other community services.

"You're never going to believe this!" (Photo courtesy of National Education Association/Joe Di Dio.)

Unfortunately, an evaluation of the Head Start program in 1969 demonstrated that the gains that the children made during this experience were not maintained in later grades.[48] Although these findings remain controversial, they had a negative effect on support for preschool programs.

A more positive result of this evaluation was the creation of Follow Through to continue services to disadvantaged children through the third grade. Even then, however, an evaluation of this program showed considerable variance in outcomes.[49]

Social workers have important roles to play in enhancing the effectiveness of programs for preschool children, and they have frequently been directly employed by them on either a full- or part-time basis. Their activities have included encouraging families to enroll their children, securing supportive services (such as financial resources, health care, and transportation), and helping to resolve family problems that impede the child's participation. They have also consulted with teachers to help them cope with problematic child behavior or with problems with parents. They have also advised teachers on ways of dealing with various classroom conditions, particularly those that deal with interpersonal relationships and classroom climate.

Social workers provide many services to children throughout their school careers to prevent them from becoming school failures. They consult with teachers regarding ways of helping children who are in academic difficulty. The worker may seek out contacts with the family in order to identify family conditions that interfere with the child's learning, such as family conflicts and lack of adequate resources (housing, sleeping and study space, and food, to name a few). The worker may help the family directly with these problems or refer the family to appropriate community resources.

The worker consults with the teacher about group processes in the classroom relating to such conditions as scapegoating, interpersonal conflicts, ethnic tensions, the needs of members of ethnic groups for a classroom environment that is consistent with their own cultural values, and poor communication among students or between students and teachers. All these conditions may produce a classroom climate that is not conducive to learning. The social worker helps with these concerns by observing classroom processes and providing feedback on these to teachers, facilitating mutual support among teachers, or in some cases working on a temporary basis with the teacher in the classroom to deal with a difficult classroom dynamic.

Controversy surrounds whether the school social worker should work with individual students as contrasted with helping the student to utilize other resources. In many systems where there is only one social worker assigned to a school (or even several schools), the worker is not in a position to do ongoing individual work. Systems also often employ special education teachers and counselors who do individual work facilitated by the insight provided by the social worker.

Social workers are more likely to work with groups of students who have similar problems that interfere with their learning such as poor study habits or poor interpersonal relationships. Rooney, for example, developed a task-centered group work approach that was very effectively employed by school social workers in both an elementary and a high school in Chicago's south side.[50] School social workers have been concerned, however, with the potential destructive effects of forming groups of children who then may be negatively labeled by their peers and ostracized by them.

In their preventive role, school social workers are in a good position to identify conditions in the school that hinder students' school success. One example is the existence of school policies that determine courses of study based on cultural stereotypes rather than individual aptitudes. Many social workers have been in the forefront of actions to prevent this.

Another way in which social workers intervene in the school system is to promote the development of needed services, such as speech therapy, day treatment, special education, health promotion, and special educational activities for gifted children.

DISRUPTIVE BEHAVIOR

School social workers are frequently involved in developing plans for students who act in disruptive ways, such as violating school rules or verbally or physically attacking other students and even teachers. In these circumstances, schools have resorted at times to corporal punishment, and social workers have consistently pointed out that this approach is "counterproductive and damaging to the child."[51] Radin notes that this type of punishment is more often inflicted on black than white students, particularly black males.[52]

Similarly, Radin notes that suspension is more frequently imposed on blacks than whites and that this occurs in ways that are "arbitrary and capricious."[53] She asserts that:

As with corporal punishment, the technique is dysfunctional even if suspensions were administered fairly in completely nonbiased fashion and only for serious reasons. The Children's Defense Fund report on school suspensions aptly summarizes the problem by stating that the procedure jeopardizes the pupils' prospects of securing a decent education and pushes the children and their problems into the street, thereby causing more problems for them and for the rest of the community.[54]

Radin concludes that neither of these disciplinary measures deals with the underlying problems that lead to the disruptive behavior. This is frequently, as she states, "a mismatch between the middle-class expectations of the school and the cultural norms of subgroups of students; that many students, particularly those not college bound, find school tasks trivial and boring; and that schools are governed by the authoritarian imposition of rules against which many students rebel to assert some autonomy."[55] It is the job of the social worker to work with other school professionals so as to confront these underlying problems.

Alternative procedures to suspension and corporal punishment that social workers often cooperate in implementing include in-school suspension, timeout, assignment to an alternative school, behavior contracting, and social skills training. Each has its use in relationship to specific reasons for the disruptive behavior. For example, in-school suspension provides a special location in the school where the student can complete school assignments while removed from classroom stimuli that provoke acting out; social skills training helps the student to learn peaceful rather than disruptive ways of handling stressful situations.

The social worker's role in responding to the needs of disruptive students involves the following:

1. Enabling the school to develop a full array of alternatives, other school personnel to decide on the appropriate utilization of an alternative, and the student to make use of the opportunity provided.
2. Consulting with school personnel as to how to effectively use the alternative.
3. Collaborating with school personnel in implementing an alternative (for example, evaluating whether behavioral goals have been achieved).
4. Advocating for students who may be denied a constructive school response to their disruptive behaviors.

Radin notes that once an alternative program is in place there is still a danger that the school may try to abandon it. She recommends, consequently, that the social worker be prepared to act as an advocate for its continuance.

NONATTENDANCE

School social workers have been involved in the issue of nonattendance since the beginning of this field of service. They help in the assessment of children with this problem and the development of ways for children, parents, and other school personnel to work together to reduce it.

One major assessment issue is to differentiate between *school phobia* and truancy caused by other circumstances. The school phobic is a child who is either afraid to leave home or has exaggerated fears of the school situation. These fears are often expressed through complaints of physical illness, which disappear after the child is allowed to remain at home. If the child experiences pressure to attend school, he or she may enter into a panic state.

The school social worker may treat the milder forms of this disorder by working with the entire family to modify family patterns that tie the child to the home. The worker may also utilize behavioral approaches to help the child to reduce his or her anxiety about the school situation.[56] In more severe cases the worker will refer the family to agencies, such as child guidance clinics, that can work with the child and family over longer periods of time to reduce dysfunctional family patterns, as well as the child's debilitating anxiety about the school situation. The worker will work with that agency by enabling the school to cooperate in its treatment plans.

In contrast to the child with school phobia, other children who refuse to attend school regularly (typically referred to as truants) are likely to be disruptive and rebellious when in school and to have poor academic records and poor relationships with parents. The social worker will have conferences with the parents to help them reinforce school attendance. Work with the child will involve counseling her or him about career goals so as to increase motivation to attend school and helping the child to increase social and academic skills that will contribute to school success. A behavioral approach in which rewards are given for gradually increased school attendance is also sometimes used.

The school social worker must also work with the school, itself, so that it will be a better experience for this type of child. This includes establishing alternative schools and innovative school programs. The worker may seek to modify teacher attitudes toward particular groups of children, which may lead to the development of new learning materials. At times, offering interesting extracurricular activities also leads to changing the child's attitudes toward school. Another approach is to help the child through participation in committees to contribute to changes in the school that she or he would like to see.

SUBSTANCE ABUSE

Substance abuse has become a major problem in schools, particularly secondary schools, although it is even affecting younger children. According to Allen-Meares and her colleagues,

> Substance abuse is becoming an increasingly serious problem for adolescents. A study conducted in 1974 for the National Institute of Alcohol Abuse and Alcoholism indicated that 90 percent of high school seniors and more than 50 percent of seventh graders had experimented with alcohol. Another study conducted in 1975 by the same institute indicated that 1.3 million Americans between the ages of 12 and 17 have a serious drinking problem. A survey of high school youths is conducted annually by the National Institute of Drug Abuse. It indicated that 16.9 percent of the 1975 graduating class had used marijuana by the time they had completed ninth grade and 25.2 percent of the class of 1978 had done so.[57]

Many factors make schools a key place for the promotion of substances. Obviously, many young people are brought together in the school. Pushers who sell drugs therefore have a ready-made opportunity to reach large numbers of customers. Students also make arrangements at school to attend social events where various drugs are made available and their use encouraged. Some youths will also meet at school and truant together to use substances.

The immediate causes and the consequences of substance abuse also center in the school. Youths who are already doing poorly for other reasons may use substances to relieve the emotional stress of failure. A vicious cycle is then created in which failure leads to substance abuse, which leads to further failure. In addition, substances such as marijuana may have negative effects on the individual's motivation to succeed in school.

Because the school has access to virtually all young people, it is the logical setting in which to fight substance abuse. Unfortunately, drug education programs do not appear to have much impact.[58] Instead, authorities suggest approaches to help youths acquire alternative ways of coping, such as support groups and rap sessions that use peers and professional counselors. Drug education can be incorporated into this approach, rather than presented in an isolated manner by people with whom the youths do not have relationships. Work with parents is crucial so that they can identify drug problems in their youngsters and take steps to deal with them. All these types of activities fall well within the role and the competency of school social workers.

Social workers should work with other school personnel on this problem. This includes helping them to take constructive rather than punitive actions when drug problems in students are identified. The school social worker must also work with agencies outside the school system to help and encourage them to create adequate services for substance abusing youth.

EDUCATION OF SCHOOL AGE PARENTS

According to statistics compiled by Allen-Meares and her colleagues, more than 1 million teenagers become pregnant each year, 10% of young women will give birth before they reach 18, 85% of these women will keep their children, and almost 50% will be unmarried when their child is born. These figures should not be surprising in view of the fact that 60% of young people between the ages of 13 and 19 have had sexual intercourse.[59]

The birth of the child for the mother and often for the father, if he also assumes responsibility, has effects well beyond the assumption of the parental role. These include the loss of further schooling and thus of access to desirable occupations and to many of the social experiences that prepare young people for a variety of adult tasks.

In recent decades, the opinion has been strongly held by educators that "to be married or pregnant is not sufficient cause to deprive [the teen mother] of an education and the opportunity to become a contributing member of society."[60] In fact, Title IX of the Education Amendment of 1972 (PL 92–318) "prohibits schools that receive federal funds from excluding any student on the basis of pregnancy or a pregnancy-related condition."[61] This is an important right, as two-thirds of pregnant teenagers drop out of school. It has also been found that teen pregnancy will affect one-quarter of school age females.[62]

Because of social workers' knowledge of the needs of such young people and the community resources that can meet these needs, they are in a good position to give leadership to educational programs for pregnant students. Allen-Meares describes one such program directed by a team composed of school personnel and community social service providers. The coordinator of this team is the school social worker, who works directly with the young people on interpersonal and value issues. A nurse on the team deals with childbirth and child psychology and visits the student at home after the child is born. A guidance counselor coordinates the student's educational activities. A food service person consults on nutrition and budgeting. The team also involves the family in order to develop a support system for the young parent.[63]

A closely related issue that is clearly prevention oriented is sex education. While this is often provided by regular classroom teachers, such as in health classes, social workers have been active in promoting such programs, developing the content, and consulting with teachers on how the content may be best delivered. Social workers also meet with parents to secure their support for and understanding of sex education.

POSTSECONDARY EDUCATIONAL SETTINGS

The role of the social worker in colleges, lifelong learning programs, and vocational programs for adults will differ from the role of the worker in primary and secondary educational settings because of serving adult rather than minor students. Thus, such issues as reducing harsh discipline, disruptive behavior, and nonattendance are essentially absent because the law does not require adults to attend school or to conform to school regulations in the same way as it does for children. Educational programs for adults may, of course, discipline their students by expelling them from certain activities or ultimately from the institution itself.

In a more positive light, adult students may utilize social work services to derive the maximum benefits from their educational program. For this reason, many educational programs for adults employ social workers. They are typically assigned to the counseling services of the institution, but may also be employed to provide special services to minorities. At one university, for example, the Office of Student Services had staff members who were known, respectively, as advocates for Hispanic, African American, Native American, and Asian students. Several of these "advocates" had social work training. Their mission was to help members of these groups handle the cultural conflicts they experienced in the university, advocate for students who were exposed to racism, and confront racist practices.

Social workers and other mental health professionals in counseling services report a number of issues that are fairly typical of those brought to them by students. These include homesickness from students who are away from families for the first time and loneliness on the part of students who must make new friends.

Many students also have difficulty meeting academic expectations because of the greater responsibility they must take for their learning in college as compared to high school. Others have difficulties because of worry that education now is more serious and that certain professional opportunities may be lost if they fail. Even students working on doctoral dissertations may be handicapped by anxiety, and social workers have formed support groups for students at that final stage of their student careers.

In all these situations, social workers perform functions that are similar to those fulfilled at the public school level. Through individual and group counseling, they help individuals to deal with the interpersonal and academic issues that they face. They consult with teachers and administrators about individual situations, as well as policies and procedures. They engage in crisis intervention in classrooms and dormitories when a tragic event such as a suicide takes place. They work on behalf of groups experiencing some form of oppression in the setting, such as members of minorities, women, gay and lesbian students, and the handicapped.

Issues and Directions

A number of issues confront social work in education today. One of the first is the defensive posture that this field has been forced to take in view of budgetary cuts in recent years. Thus, while we believe in the principle of accountability on all occasions, this is certainly a time when school social workers must demonstrate the effectiveness of their practice. Thus, these workers must maintain data on services and outcomes. Evaluations must be conducted of work at all levels, whether it be on the individual, the group, or the community.

Second, training for school social work must be improved so that the ecological perspectives described in this chapter become part of the education of school social workers. In their educational programs, they must also have good supervised experiences in schools that have this perspective.

If ecological ideas are to be the concepts that guide practice, school social workers must be able to interpret and defend them to policy makers within the educational system. Intrinsic to this is the idea that the social worker provides linkages between the school, the family, and the community, and the importance of this should also be expressed. This approach diminishes, to a degree, the individual perspective that has dominated school social work, while clearly not eliminating it. But it increases the importance of the role the social worker has in educating other school personnel to understand the crucial roles the social contexts of the school, family, and community play in the ability of the child to maximally benefit from her or his education.

School systems must continue to develop more effective programs for children with special needs such as the handicapped. Social workers also have a contribution to make here because of their systemic perspectives, but they must enhance their knowledge of these special needs. With such knowledge, social workers can play a major part in the design of these programs.

If our view is accepted that social workers have roles to play in educational programs for adults that are analogous to those in programs for children and adolescents, then the issue is to provide better conceptualizations of this continuum of social work in education throughout the life cycle and particularly how an ecological perspective informs school social work for adults.

Finally, but probably of the greatest importance today, is the role that social work must play in the education of oppressed groups such as African Americans, Asian Americans, and Hispanics. Many social work schools are now emphasizing oppression as a topic of the highest priority. This kind of educational emphasis should help graduates who enter school social work to focus on such issues as the impact of tracking such students, being insensitive to their cultures, and ignoring social oppression as an educational topic. Education plays a major role in the social mobility of these students, and social workers must recognize their responsibility to contribute to the removal of educational barriers.

Conclusion

This chapter began with discussion of the function of the educational system in meeting the needs of individuals to fulfill their social roles and the need for the society to have competent citizens. The function of social work within the educational system was then portrayed within an ecological perspective as an institution that enhances the interactions among such systems as the school, the family, and the community so as to promote the education of the student. The ecological perspective contrasts in many ways with other views of the role of school social workers and these contrasts were also analyzed.

Since social workers interact with teachers, administrators, parents, and other community institutions, the nature of these interactions was portrayed. Several examples were provided. These activities are heavily value laden and, consequently, we examined values surrounding societal responsibilities for education and especially for the education of people with special needs. Additional value questions concern rights of the educational system to control specific behaviors and to discipline those who do not conform.

An overview of the history of social work services in the schools was then provided. The current situation in terms of social policies and school resources was also examined. Of special importance in this discussion was the impact of Public Law 92–142, which established educational opportunities for handicapped children.

Special components of the educational system as related to school social work were then discussed: preventing school failures, coping with disruptive behavior, reducing nonattendance, eliminating substance abuse, educating school age parents, and promoting social work in adult education. We concluded with a review of some of the major issues facing school social work today.

Notes

1. Robert T. Constable and John P. Flynn, *School Social Work: Practice and Research Perspectives* (Homewood, Ill.: Dorsey Press, 1982), pp. 93–94.
2. Lela B. Costin, "Social Work Contribution to Education in Transition," in Rosemary Sarri and Frank Maple, eds., *The School in the Community* (Washington D.C.: National Association of Social Workers, 1972), p. 31.
3. Paula Allen-Meares, Robert O. Washington, and Betty Welsh, *Social Work Services in Schools* (Englewood Cliffs, N.J.: Prentice Hall, 1986), pp. 58–59; Christopher Jencks, "Who Should Control Education?" *Dissent*, March–April 1966, pp. 145–163.
4. *Report of the National Advisory Commission on Civil Disorders* (New York: Bantam Books, 1968).
5. As quoted in Allen-Meares, Washington, and Welsh, *Social Work Services in Schools,* p. 59.
6. Paraphrased from Anthony Downs, *Urban Problems and Prospects* (Chicago: Markham Publishing, 1970), p. 276.

7. Sarri and Maple, eds. *The School in the Community,* p. 18.

8. *Ibid.* p. 19.

9. Wendy Glasgow Winters and Freda Easton, *The Practice of Social Work in Schools: An Ecological Perspective* (New York: The Free Press, 1983), p. xi.

10. John Alderson, "Models of School Social Work Practice," in Sarri and Maple, eds., *The School in the Community,* pp. 57–74.

11. William Schwartz, "The Social Worker in the Group," *Social Welfare Forum, 1961* (New York: Columbia University Press, 1961), as quoted in Sarri and Maple, eds., *The School in the Community,* p. 71.

12. *NASW Standards for Social Work Services in Schools* (Washington, D.C.: National Association of Social Workers 1978).

13. Winters and Easton, *The Practice of Social Work in Schools,* p. 16.

14. Ibid., pp. 17–18.

15. Lanette Brown, Irvan Corbett, and Linda Paricio, "Desegregating Public School System: A Community Human Relations Approach," in *Federal Legislation and the School Social Worker* (Washington: National Association of Social Workers, 1978), pp. 29–37.

16. Paula Allen-Meares, "Analysis of Tasks in School Social Work," *Social Work* 22, (3) (May 1977), pp. 196–201.

17. Allen-Meares, Washington, and Welsh, *Social Work Services in Schools,* p. 30.

18. D. J. Scrivner Blum, *Group Counseling for Secondary Schools* (Springfield, Ill.: Charles C Thomas, 1990).

19. Betty Deshler and John L. Erlich, "Changing School–Community Relations," in Sarri and Maple, eds., *The School in the Community,* pp. 233–244.

20. Ibid., p. 236–237.

21. Ibid.

22. Robert Vinter and Rosemary Sarri, "Exemplar Schools Project: A School of Social Work, Agency and Community Collaboration," in Rosemary C. Sarri with Robert Vinter and Martha Steketee, eds., *The Future of Social Work and Social Work Education: Final Report of the Interdisciplinary Seminar* (Ann Arbor: School of Social Work of the University of Michigan, 1988), p. 2.

23. Ibid., p. 3.

24. Allen-Meares, Washington, and Welsh, *Social Work Services in Schools,* p. 67.

25. Ibid.

26. An extensive discussion of these issues, as well as important legal cases related to them, may be found in Allen-Meares, Washington, and Welsh, *Social Work Services in Schools,* pp. 105–127

27. Ibid., p. 124.

28. Public Law 93–380, Title 20, section 1232g.

29. This discussion of the history of school social work draws extensively from Allen-Meares, Washington, and Walsh, *Social Work Services in Schools,* pp. 16–39.

30. Betsy L. Hancock, *School Social Work.* (Englewood Cliffs, N.J.: Prentice Hall, 1982), p. 7.

31. Sophonisba P. Breckinridge, "Some Aspects of the Public School From a Social Worker's Point of View," *Journal of the Proceedings and Addresses of the National Education Association,* July 4–11, 1914 (Ann Arbor, Mich.: National Education Association, 1914), p. 45; Lillian D. Wald, *The House on Henry Street* (New York: Henry Holt & Co., 1915), p. 106.

32. Jane Culbert, "Visiting Teachers and Their Activities," *Proceedings of the National Conference of Charities and Corrections* (Chicago: Hildman Printing Co., 1916), p. 395, as quoted in Allen-Meares, Washington, and Welsh, *Social Work Services in Schools,* pp. 18–19.

33. Bertha C. Reynolds, "Social Casework: What Is It? What Is Its Place in the World Today?" *The Family* (December 1935), p. 238.

34. Hancock, *School Social Work,* p. 10.

35. See Paul Simon, "Social Group Work in the Schools," *Bulletin of the National Association of School Social Workers,* 31 (1) (September 1955), pp. 3–12.
36. Public Law 88–452, section 2701.
37. Public Law 84–142, Title 20, sections 1232, 1401, 1405, 1406, 1411–1420, 1453.
38. See Allen-Meares, Washington, and Welsh, *Social Work Services in Schools,* pp. 24–26, for a summary of these studies.
39. Sarri and Maple, *The School in the Community.*
40. See, for example, footnotes 7, 8, and 18.
41. *NASW Standards for Social Work Services in Schools: Policy Statement No. 7* (Washington, D.C.: National Association of Social Workers, 1978).
42. U.S. Bureau of the Census, *Statistical Abstract of the United States: 1990* (Washington, D.C.: U.S. Government Printing Office, 1990), Tables 209 and 211.
43. Lela B. Costin, "School Social Work," in Minahan, ed., *Encyclopedia of Social Work,* Vol. 2, 18th ed. (Silver Spring, Md.: National Association of Social Workers, 1987), p. 538.
44. This summary of the act draws heavily from Hancock, *School Social Work,* pp. 33–35.
45. R. V. Speck and C. Attneave, *Family Networks* (New York: Random House, 1973.)
46. Costin, "School Social Work," p. 543.
47. Allen-Meares, Washington, and Welsh, *Social Work Services in Schools,* p. 148.
48. Westinghouse Learning Corp., *The Impact of Headstart: An Evaluation of the Effects of Headstart Experience on Children's Cognitive and Affective Development,* Executive Summary (Athens: Ohio State University, 1969).
49. Allen-Meares, Washington, and Welsh, *Social Work Services in Schools,* p. 157.
50. Ronald Rooney, "Adolescent Groups in Public Schools," in William J. Reid and Laura Epstein, eds., *Task-centered Practice* (New York: Columbia University Press, 1977), pp. 168–182).
51. Norma Radin, "Alternatives to Suspension and Corporal Punishment," *Urban Education,* 22 (4) (January 1988), pp. 476–495.
52. Ibid., p. 477.
53. Ibid., p. 478.
54. Ibid.
55. Ibid., p. 479.
56. For further discussion, see James E. McDonald and George Shepherd, "School Phobia: An Overview," *Journal of School Psychology,* 14 (4) (Winter 1976), p. 304.
57. Allen-Meares, Washington, and Welsh, *Social Work Services in Schools,* p. 169.
58. Hancock, *School Social Work,* p. 191.
59. Allen-Meares, Washington, and Welsh, *Social Work Services in Schools,* p. 160.
60. M. Howard and L. Eddinger, *School Age Parents* (Syracuse, N.Y.: National Alliance Concerned with School-Age Parents, 1973), p. 29.
61. Allen-Meares, Washington, and Welsh, *Social Work Services in Schools,* p. 161.
62. Evelyn Hunt Ogden and Vito Germinario. *The At-Risk Student* (Lancaster, Pa.: Technomic Publishing, 1988), pp. 149–155.
63. Paula Allen-Meares, "An In-school Program for Adolescent Parents: Implications for Social Work Practice and Multidisciplinary Teaming," *School Social Work,* 3 (2) (1979), pp. 66–77.

CHAPTER 14

Service Delivery for Enhancing the Welfare of Families and Children

The Functions of the Systems of Services
for Families and Children

Services related to families and children have a very broad framework since they encompass everyone. We all at one time have lived in a family (or at least in a situation that was meant to substitute for a family). Also, we all have been children; there is no exemption from that experience!

We have chosen to discuss services to children and families together because current social work thought militates against a definite separation when we engage in or plan for interventions with families and/or children. The idea behind this type of thinking is that a practitioner should not engage in any work with families without giving high priority to the needs of the children in the family, because they are often the most vulnerable and defenseless family members and the welfare of future generations is dependent on the care that young people receive. Similarly, when family policies are promulgated, the effect of such policies on children should be a prime consideration.

Child welfare practices and policies should also take into consideration family issues for several reasons in addition to those cited. First is the proposition that children are best served *when it is possible* for them to be cared for by their biological parents because of the role this plays in helping children to develop their identities through an awareness of the historical continuity of their families. Second, such care helps children avoid the trauma of separation.[1]

Another reason for a family focus in working with children is that the welfare of children is highly dependent on the quality of care they receive either from biological parents or from some substitute. It is sometimes necessary that the child be removed from biological parents either temporarily or permanently. The goal then becomes to help family substitutes meet as many of the child's' needs for family care as possible. The family orientation of service providers must be translated into helping family substitutes attain this objective.

In this chapter we use some concepts that can have different meanings. Because of their centrality to the material we are discussing, we shall define them here. In Chapter 6 we defined the concept of family as follows:

> a set of individuals who have economic and other commitments to each other, who are likely to meet each others' needs for intimacy, and who usually maintain a joint household. Thus, communes, adult siblings living together, and gay male and lesbian couples are some of the many types of families, which include conventional families composed of two adults (one male and one female) living together with their children.

The preceding definition was developed to accommodate our discussion of family treatment, which in most, but not all, cases involves people living within a single household. When we discuss family policy, however, we must consider the characteristics of families more generally than how families appear in treatment situations. We agree with Allen, therefore, that "the dominant family structure is not nuclear, but what has been called modified extended."[2] This concept refers to the idea that many people function in families that consist of a number of nuclear families that have a degree of dependence on one another while retaining a great deal of independence. As Allen indicates:

> Mounting evidence supports the idea that families may be housed in nuclear units, but actually function in extended networks. Citing two recent surveys, Moroney (1980) points out that in contrast to the picture of families as isolated and self-sufficient units, a high rate of intergenerational contact, mutual aid, and support is present in today's families.[3]

This idea of modified extended families should be borne in mind as we discuss policies in this chapter. It characterizes many families and, consequently, has many implications for policies.

Another important concept is that of *child welfare*. As with the concept of family, this at first appears to be a term with an apparent definition, and yet it is argued over by people with various vested interests. We favor Kadushin and Martin's conceptualization in which they state the following:

> Child welfare, broadly defined, has to do with the general well-being of all children and with any and all measures designed to promote the optimal development of the child's bio-psycho-social potential in harmony with the needs of the community. Child welfare services, as a field of social work practice, are more narrowly focussed. Such services are concerned with particular groups of children and their families. They are "specific services" provided to specific populations by specific types of agencies. In defining child welfare service as a field of social work practice, the Child Welfare League Of America notes that these "are specialized social welfare services which are primarily concerned with the child whose needs are unmet within the family and/or through other social institutions."[4]

But Kadushin and Martin are also not really satisfied with this definition because it represents what is characterized as a "residual orientation," which sees "social services as appropriate when the normal institutional arrangements for meeting crucial social needs break down." A contrasting "institutional or developmental orientation" would see child welfare services as available to all families to help them meet normal living needs because "every family might need such help" because "in a complex world no family is entirely self-sufficient."[5] Kadushin and Martin note that we must distinguish between realities and goals and a residual orientation to child welfare is what, in fact, exists although many groups have recommended such a developmental orientation.[6]

Family services may not have a great deal of controversy associated with their definition, but the definition is often very broad and still changing. This is in part due to the fact that all social work services have been characterized as having a major focus on understanding and strengthening family life.

At various times the Family Service Association of America (now called Family Service America) sought to define the functions of its member agencies. In 1953 these were "to contribute to harmonious family interrelationships, to strengthen the positive values in family life, and to promote healthy personality development and satisfactory social functioning of various family members."[7] This goal was to be accomplished through casework and participation in community planning as primary services and group education, professional education, and research as secondary services.

The definition of functions began to broaden with the advent of the War on Poverty in the middle and late 1960s. At that time, because of criticisms that their focus was narrow and middle-class oriented, family agencies moved in a number of new directions, which included *family advocacy* and efforts to influence family policy. According to one definition, "Family advocacy is a professional service designed to improve life conditions for people by harnessing direct and expert knowledge of family needs with the commitment to action and the application of skills to produce the necessary community change."[8]

It would be a mistake, however, to equate family services with the activities of member agencies of Family Service America. The federal government makes funds available to the states for a variety of family services. The states, in turn, provide some of these services directly through their own agencies, such as departments of social services, and purchase other services from private agencies.

THE PURPOSES OF FAMILY AND CHILDREN'S SERVICES

Ideally, the purposes of family and children's services should be congruent or at least complementary. For historical reasons, this congruence has frequently not been the case. Services in the former field were often intended for intact families and in the latter for children who had been removed from families. Separate national service organizations exist (Family Service America and Child Welfare League of America), and each organization publishes its own journal, *Families in Society* by Family Service America and *Child Welfare* by Child Welfare League Of America.

Despite this degree of separation, many private family and children's agencies have combined into *family and children's* agencies to provide an integrated focus on maintaining families and ensuring good child-rearing environments. Nevertheless, even within such an integrated agency, it is likely that separate administrative units will exist for family and for child placement services, with the consequent danger that the dual focus will not be maintained.

Meyer also points out another problem that relates to the boundary between the field of mental health, particularly child mental health, and family and children's services. Thus, in Chapter 12 we discussed such child mental health services as the Child Guidance Clinic, and these are certainly meant to enhance the welfare of both children and families. We concur with the following statement of Meyer's in which she moves us toward conceptualizing unity among these fields:

> Even though conceptually the welfare of children is inseparable from the welfare of their families and the welfare of both may involve issues and services in the mental health domain, institutional requirements suggest that the three fields of practice will remain separate from each other through the perpetuation of many kinds of boundaries. The field of social work itself, influenced by the public's desires and by governmental structure and funding, is seeking forms of specialization. It is unlikely that social work will adjust its structural boundaries, but no political or economic barrier interferes

with the melding of professional concerns when it comes to considering the mental health focus or the family as the center of Child Welfare practice itself. *In practice, families, children, and mental health have to be wielded into a single focus.*[9]

As a consequence of this idea of a single focus, we believe that all communities should seek to develop a system of services for families and/or children that can fulfill the following objectives:

1. The system should support family life and development and prevent family dysfunction. It should also provide for early identification of families in which such dysfunction may lead to the placement of a child and provide services that might lessen the probability of such a placement.
2. The system should identify and ameliorate sources of tension and conflict among family members so as to reduce the probability of family dissolution and increase the likelihood that each family member's needs will be met. These needs should be viewed in the light of an understanding of life tasks at various phases of human development, such as childhood, adulthood, middle adulthood, and old age. These needs may also be for services on a continuing basis, as well as when the family or child is experiencing a crisis.
3. The system should protect children from abuse and neglect from both family and nonfamily members, while preventing placement whenever possible. When it is determined by valid means that the child is likely to suffer serious and/or long lasting damage if not placed, and when such placement cannot be prevented by provision of suitable services, the system should provide for support to the family and child in coping with separation. The system should also make known the precise conditions that should be attained by the family for the child to return to her or his family or to secure a permanent alternative to that family. This alternative should be the one that can best meet the child's needs.
4. The system should provide help with the problems experienced by the child and the family during the period of substitute care.
5. The system should seek to create community and societal conditions that are conducive to healthy family life and child development, including the existence of such material resources for the family and/or child as income, employment, and housing; adequate schools; and community recreation. These and other resources must recognize the special needs of different people related to their gender and cultural background. A functional community for the child and family provides support from appropriate social networks.
6. The system should recognize that conflicts occur between the interests of children and parents. When these occur, the interests of the child, as the more vulnerable, should take precedence.

TYPES OF INSTITUTIONS

A number of different types of agencies exist that attempt to achieve the goals described. A major division is between public and private agencies. Public agencies are those created by law, funded by government, and responsible to the executive branch of a government unit. Several types of private agencies exist. One is the private nonprofit agency created by citizens and for which citizens constitute the policy-making body. Historically, these were funded by contributions, but today a mixture of funds is likely to come from government sources (such as the purchase of service contracts and outright grants), fees for services, and private fund raising. Second is the large public sector. Two other categories of agencies exist and offer family and children's services. These are private profit agencies and services offered by places of employment.

Although there is no clear distinction between the services offered by public and private agencies, in many cases the public agency serves the poorest and/or most oppressed children and families because it is required to serve specified categories of people. The private agency can refuse service for such reasons as the size of its caseloads, geographical distinctions, religious requirements, and so forth.

Public agencies may have either separate or unified child welfare and family service organizations. The child welfare organization, based on contemporary funding patterns, is likely to offer a range of substitute family services, such as foster care and adoptions. Because of the eclipse of government funding, family services are often less adequate and more fragmented. For example, in the earlier days of the Aid to Families of Dependent Children (AFDC) program, the workers who administered the financial grant offered a range of services to strengthen family functioning. In 1956 the financial assistance and service components were separated, and in 1980 such services were further reduced.

A potent force in the development of child welfare programs has been the U.S. Children's Bureau, which was established in 1912. It was given a very strong start in its initial mandate, which was to

> [i]nvestigate and report . . . upon all matters pertaining to the welfare of children and child life among all classes of our people and . . . investigate the questions of infant mortality, the birth rate, orphanage, juvenile courts, desertion, dangerous occupations, accidents and diseases of children, employment, legislation affecting children in the several states and territories.[10]

In contrast, there only existed for a brief time a Bureau of Family Services in the federal department that preceded Health and Human Services.

In portraying child welfare services, we find it useful to use the set of categories employed by Kadushin and Martin: supportive, supplemental, and substitutive services.[11]

Supportive services include those offered by both home-based and child protection agencies. These may be on an individual, group, or family basis and are intended to reduce stress on and increase the coping abilities of the family. Such services are intended to prevent family dissolution and breakdown and/or child placement.

The child protection agency is specifically mandated to eliminate child abuse and neglect. Child protection agencies that are under public auspices are required to investigate and take appropriate action in all reported cases of child abuse or neglect, and state laws now universally require specified categories of people (such as social workers and teachers) to report all cases of child abuse and neglect that they encounter.

Supplementary services differ from supportive inasmuch as some resource is supplied to the family and/or child in addition to psychological help, which is the main feature of supportive service. These include financial assistance, homemakers, and daycare. Homemaker services provide trained individuals who spend time in the home performing such tasks as cooking and child care. Daycare provides periods of time each day in which the child is cared for by professionals on a group basis, which provides both socialization and educational experiences.

Substitute services are used when the situation is so severe that the child must be placed either temporarily or permanently away from the home. Substitute services include foster care, adoptive homes, and institutions.

The Function of Social Work in Services for Families and Children

Social work as a profession is not likely to be the dominant one in many organizations: in health, it is likely to be a physician; in education, the teacher; and in corrections, the criminal justice professional. This is not the case in family and children's agencies in which social workers are apt to be the administrators, supervisors and line workers. The social worker, therefore, does not have to struggle as much to define her or his role because it is the central and guiding one.

This does not mean that social workers are the only professionals to be employed in family and children's agencies. Psychiatrists, psychologists, nurses, teachers, and home economists are utilized for purposes appropriate to their professions. Multidisciplinary teams may also be formed.

The central role that social workers play in these agencies does not imply that they have as much of an impact on social policy as one might expect. As McGowan and Walsh state:

> Despite this tradition and mandate, the influence of the professional Child Welfare community on social policy developments during the past fifty years has been relatively limited. Many different explanations have been offered for practitioners' failure to address social policy issues or to have any significant impact when they do become engaged in social change efforts. These explanations include: the professional's tendency to have limited goals and to become preoccupied with technical problems; the historic polarization between the segments of the profession involved in direct service and social reform activities and the traditional perspectives on social policy and client's rights held by many direct service practitioners; the organizational constraints imposed on the activities of agency-based workers; and lack of knowledge and technical skills necessary for effective political action.[12]

Social workers in the family and children's field, as in most of the fields we discuss in this book, are increasingly taking an ecological approach to their work. This is certainly true in work with families; we believe it is inevitable that ecological ideas will become increasingly important in any work that involves children as practitioners improve their understanding of how interactions among the child, family, and environment should be the change targets of their interventions.

Germain does an excellent job of pointing out the relevance of ecological concepts in work involving children.[13] One concept that is important to an ecological framework is *stress that ensues from exchanges between person and environment.* She reminds us that "Most parents and children enter the Child Welfare System because they are experiencing demands that exceed their personal and environmental resources, or because institutions or individuals in the environment have been stressed by the parents' or children's behavior or by indications that children's needs are unmet." She adds that "Stressors common to members of the Child Welfare population are: poverty, institutional oppression based on color, ethnicity, social class, gender, and age; and systems of work, no-work, or undervalued work (including child rearing)."[14]

Another concept is *coping,* which requires "both personal and environmental resources for effectiveness."[15] Among the resources that are of special concern to ecologically oriented family and children's practitioners is the presence of social networks composed of family, friends, self-help groups, and other mutual aid systems.

Germain presents an excellent synopsis of the intervention foci of these practitioners when she states:

> In summary, the paradigm of stress and coping suggests that the Child Welfare practitioner's interventions with children, biological, foster, and adoptive parents, and child care staff are oriented toward (1) removal, reduction, or amelioration of stress; (2) supporting the problem-solving function of coping by teaching such skills as parenting, negotiating environments, assertiveness, and interpersonal relationship development; (3) help in managing negative feelings and elevating self-esteem through empathy, supporting adaptive defenses, and easing maladaptive ones in the context of a trusting relationship; (4) providing information about child development, environmental resources, or other information a family may lack; (5) furnishing opportunities for decision-making and action within an adequate time frame; (6) helping to inhibit dangerous action through consideration of consequences, the development of alternatives, and where needed, by limit-setting; (7) restoring connections to relatives, friends, neighbors, church and other groups, if the person or family is interested; and (8) helping to obtain needed resources from the formal network of services.[16]

Finally, Germain points out that these activities may not be sufficient because the environment is detrimental. As she states, "efforts must be made to ensure that the community and the Child Welfare organization alleviate, rather than exacerbate, stress and support, rather than undermine coping efforts."[17]

Thus, all social workers concerned with the welfare of families and children are encouraged to use the ecological perspective proposed by Germain; we have also proposed the adoption of this framework in each of our other service chapters. But at any given time, workers may be interacting with or on behalf of specific individuals, families, groups, organizations, communities, or societies. They must be concerned with the interactions among these levels and, consequently, either shift the level of their own interventions to attain their objectives or cooperate with other practitioners to achieve the same effects.

To illustrate further, a practitioner might do any of the following with reference to a child not receiving a needed service:

1. Help the parent learn how to identify the needs of her child and secure necessary services (individual interaction).
2. Help the child and the parents together to communicate about the child's needs (family interaction).

3. Enroll the parent in a parent education group in which one topic will be understanding the child's needs (group interaction).
4. Seek to bring about agency changes so as to better meet the child's needs (organizational level).
5. Work with other agencies in the community so that they will be better able to meet the child's needs (community level).
6. Interpret to a legislative body the kinds of legislation that will provide needed services for children (societal level).

Values and Ideologies in Services to Families and Children

Many value and ideological conflicts confront the family and children's field of service and we shall try here to identify some of the major ones. Many of these issues relate to social definitions and such definitions are often in the process of change.

As Kadushin and Martin point out, "childhood" itself is a social construct.[18] In earlier historical periods, the dependency of the young was viewed as lasting for a much shorter period. This was a consequence of both a shorter life span and the nature of economic activity. Children began to earn a living at six or seven years and, according to one sixteenth-century statute, "Children under fourteen years of age, and above five, that live in idleness and be taken begging may be put to service by the government of cities, towns, etc., to husbandry; or other crafts of labor."[19] Consequently, many contemporary values regarding the responsibilities of the family and society for children and the rights of children were irrelevant until the nineteenth and twentieth centuries, which saw a shift in the social definition of childhood.

A related issue is the legal status of the child. In early European history, children were the property of the parents who had full control over them. In contemporary times, the power of the parents is more likely to be seen as "a trust to be employed in the best interests of the child."[20] This is exemplified in the United Nations Declaration of the Rights of the Child, which was adopted in 1954. Kadushin and Martin state in their summary of this document that it

> affirms the rights of the child to have special protection and to enjoy opportunities and facilities that will enable him or her to develop in a healthy and normal manner; to have a name and a nationality from his or her birth; to enjoy the benefit of social security, including adequate nutrition, housing, recreation, and medical services; to grow up in an atmosphere of affection and security, and wherever possible, in the care and under the responsibility of parents; to receive special treatment, education, and care if one is handicapped; to be among the first to receive protection and relief in times of disaster; to be protected against all forms of neglect, cruelty, and exploitation; and to be protected from practices that may foster any form of discrimination.[21]

Gil argues that many of these rights of children are not realizable in our society.[22] This is due, he believes, to unequal access to employment and income, social structural arrangements that stand in the way of caring human relationships, jobs and education that alienate and oppress people, and social arrangements that are unstable and insecure. He sums this up in the following statement:

When children grow up in environments in which their own and everyone else's fundamental human needs tend to be frustrated constantly, their innate capacities usually do not unfold freely and fully. *Their development is stunted, they do not fare well, they fail to thrive.* As a consequence of the prevailing social, economic and political structures, dynamics, and ideology, the United States appears to be such a growth inhibiting environment for children, irrespective of the social class position of families. This fact is usually acknowledged with respect to children in poor and low income homes. Paradoxically, it is also true for children in middle income and affluent homes; material adequacy and affluence do not lead directly to the realization of relational, developmental, security, and self-actualization needs, as they do not insulate children from the dehumanizing and alienating effects of inegalitarian, competitive, and exploitative patterns of everyday life.[23]

There are, of course, differences of opinion among experts as to the strong stand taken by Gil, although virtually all see major impediments in our society to creating optimal conditions for the welfare and growth of families and children. In addition to these broad social concerns, additional ideological and value issues stem from the evolution of child and family services. One issue results from the primary emphasis placed on the child in traditional child welfare agencies and the family in traditional family agencies.

While, on the surface, we can find little fault with these emphases, in practice they lead to an underestimation of the value of preserving families by the child welfare agencies and an underestimation of the long-term negative consequences to children when they live in dysfunctional (and even abusive) families by the family agencies. The issue of preserving families is not only a value issue but an empirical one in view of the demonstrated importance to the child's security and identity of continuity in living with his or her family.

Another value issue stems from decisions as to whether to create children at all. Specifically, we refer to contraception and abortion. In human history the issue has even been whether to allow children to continue to survive after they are born.[24] Kadushin and Martin, in fact, make the interesting point that when societies legislated against these types of solutions for the problem of unwanted children they then found it necessary to provide institutions for child welfare.[25] The religious, ethical, and practical issues surrounding contraception and abortion are complex and beyond the scope of this book.

Another issue that has both empirical and value implications centers on the debate as to whether families are to blame for such problems as delinquency and mental illness or whether the larger society has created problems that severely tax the ability of families to deal with them. The former proposition leads to the effort to create programs to meet the needs of families and youth; the latter focuses primarily on programs to treat families.

The issue of mental illness, in this respect, is somewhat more complex because of the introduction of a third factor, biology, into the causal equation. Families are often blamed for the existence of their severely mentally ill members, such as those who suffer from schizophrenia, whereas current thinking tends to see severe mental illness as a disease requiring medical as well as psychosocial treatment. When the idea of illness is accepted, the focus of the helping professions shifts to supporting the family's efforts to attain help for the mentally ill member, rather than treating the family's disorder.

Still another value issue related to services to families and children is when the family should be the final arbiter of decisions affecting members and when society may intrude on the family's decisions. Inroads have been made on what were once family prerogatives, such as requiring formal schooling for children or certain medical procedures such as inoculations. Child protection laws represent another such intrusion. Many projected policy changes affecting families and children raise this issue anew.

An Overview of the Systems of Services for Families and Children

HISTORY OF FAMILY SERVICES

The history of family services is in many ways the history of social work inasmuch as a major focus of social work has always been on meeting the needs of the family. Thus, in the early 1800s a number of agencies developed relief and aid societies. Through these, volunteers distributed relief to people in their homes. Because such assistance was sometimes duplicated or offered in a haphazard fashion, the Charity Organization Societies (COS) were created to handle this effort in a systematic manner.

The COS movement began in London, England, in 1869, and the first society in the United States was formed in Buffalo in 1877; within two years, 12 cities in the United States had such agencies. By 1892, the number had grown to 84. Riley describes their broad purposes:

> They considered large-scale relief giving to be injurious and aimed to eliminate poverty by discovering and removing its causes. They were convinced that there was a "science of charity," and that scientific methods would be used to cure the illness of poverty. Along with an emphasis on factual knowledge and methods based on theory was a strong sense of fairness and a belief that life should not be so bleak and barren for the working class and the poor. There was recognition of the needs for self-fulfillment, for human dignity, for recreation, and for planning for old age. . . . Emphasis on finding and removing causes of poverty and family troubles led to the accumulation and transmission of experience through agency training and eventually (in 1898) into the establishment of the first school of social work.[26]

The COS assisted families on a case by case basis, but also worked for social reform, such as "better working conditions and more adequate pay, better housing and health practices."[27] As these agencies moved from volunteer to paid staff and as more people were involved in decisions on services, training moved toward formal courses. This also led to the publication of articles and books, such as Richmond's *Friendly Visiting among the Poor: A Handbook for Charity Workers.*[28]

The COSs from various cities sought to interact with one another, and this led to the formation of a charity organization committee of the National Conference of Charities and Corrections. The next development was the creation in 1911 of the

National Association of Societies for Organizing Charity. The name of this organization has changed a number of times since then, such as when it became the American Association for Organizing Family Work in 1919. This was a particularly important change as it reemphasized the importance of the family in the work of the societies. By 1925 the organization included 220 member agencies. It is now known as Family Service America.

The role of the government in the provision of family services has been less consistent than that of the private sector. Its major development occurred as a result of the passage of the Social Security Act in 1935. Aspects of that act, such as the Aid to Families of Dependent Children program, provided financial and social services to families. When that act was amended in 1974, particularly through Title XX, major additions occurred in the provision for family services. Many Title XX provisions were modified in subsequent years, particularly during the Reagan administration.

HISTORY OF CHILD WELFARE SERVICES

There are a number of different roots of our current child welfare system. One comes from what has been termed *the child saving movement*. The basis of this idea was that children who were being reared in the homes of parents who were a burden to the community should be prevented from falling into the same way of life. This was accomplished historically through outdoor relief (as financial assistance was called), as well as through the use of the almshouse, indenture, and placement.

Relief was a fairly widespread remedy, but typically inadequate. This was because of the negative attitudes toward the poor, who were often regarded as responsible for their plight and therefore unworthy. An alternative to relief was the almshouse into which were placed a variety of needy people, including the mentally or physically ill and the elderly. Children in the almshouse were provided with some education and then put to work.

Indenture involved apprenticing children. The overseers of the poor in the locality were responsible for making this arrangement by binding out the child to a master workman, who was compensated by the child's labor. Costin believes that many indentured children were better off than those in almshouses despite some examples of cruel masters.[29]

During the early part of the U.S. history, a number of institutions were also created, such as orphanages and reform schools. Children tended to stay in these facilities for long periods of time. According to Costin, "These institutions tended to be an improvement over the mixed almshouses, but too frequently they provided inadequate sanitation and poor nutritional and medical care which encouraged epidemics of contagious disease from which many children died."[30]

Foster care was a later development than the other programs we have described. Its inception occurred in 1853 through the work of Charles Loring Brace, a minister, who founded and worked through the Children's Aid Society of New York. Brace was concerned about the large numbers of immigrant children to the United States, many of whom were homeless. He created a program to place large numbers of them into rural locales. They were first placed in the North Atlantic states and gradually shifted to the

West to the homes of farmers. All in all, 31,081 children were served in this way between 1853 and 1929.[31]

Brace's program was controversial. Some saw it as providing a better environment than that offered otherwise. Others criticized the fact that many children were unnecessarily separated from their parents. In addition, most were Catholic children and were placed in Protestant homes. This led to an increase in sectarian child welfare services. In addition, there was little quality control or follow-up.

Because of these developments in foster and institutional care, a debate ensued as to which was better. By the 1950s, this subsided in favor of the notion that both were part of a continuum of services that should be made available in relationship to the needs present in the specific situation. Another issue surfaced at that time, however. This related to the long period of time many children spent in foster care during which efforts to reunite them with their families did not occur. Solutions to this issue, discussed later, took several decades to emerge.

Another historical development was the *child rescue movement*. This came into existence somewhat later than child saving because of the doctrine that parents should be permitted to control their children as they saw fit. An example was a 1646 Massachusetts statute that "authorized putting to death any child older than sixteen years where sufficient evidence could be supplied that he was 'stubborn and rebellious and will not obey his [parents'] voice and chastisement.' "[32]

The right of parents to control their children, even if this involved cruelty, was gradually restricted. Costin cites as an example of this an Illinois case in 1969 in which the court labeled as "shocking inhumanity" the imprisonment of a "blind and helpless boy" in a "cold and damp cellar without fire, during several days of midwinter." The court concluded that parental authority "must be exercised within the bounds of reason and humanity."[33]

In view of these occasional court tests, an important development was the creation of the Societies for the Prevention of Cruelty to Children. The first such society in the United States came about in an unusual fashion. A church visitor in New York City learned in 1874 about a girl who was neglected as well as whipped in an abusive manner. This child had been placed with the abusing family when she was two years old by the Department of Charities. The visitor investigated the situation and brought it to the attention of public officials as well as child-saving agencies.

Neither of these offered any help, so she contacted the New York Society for the Prevention of Cruelty to Animals. Henry Bergh of that society brought the case to court as a private citizen. His attorney was Albridge T. Gerry, who as a result of this experience founded the first Society for the Prevention of Cruelty to Children in New York City.[34] The need for this kind of service is indicated by the fact that by 1900 more than 250 societies had been formed in the United States and additional ones in England and Europe. Nevertheless, in some municipalities the society served to protect both children and animals and, according to Costin's investigations, the latter sometimes took precedence.[35]

This development had both negative and positive aspects. While it led to a decrease in parent prerogatives, especially when these were clearly detrimental to the child, it also included the imposition of the reformer's values on many families. Thus, returning the children to their parents was not a high priority. This led to a split among the societies, as some, such as the Massachusetts society, under the influence of the growing profession of social work, moved toward rehabilitative and preventive work with parents. Gerry, of the New York society, resisted this. According to Costin:

> He was adamant about any intrusion from the new social work philosophy and Mary Richmond's principles of social casework. He refused to concede any overlapping areas of concern between destitute and dependent children and neglected and abused ones. He opposed legislation for a federal Children's Bureau, terming it an invasion of state rights, and a dangerous scheme to exercise jurisdiction over state and local agencies concerned with child welfare.[36]

Gerry's views, however, did not prevail. In 1921, when the Child Welfare League of America was founded, its first director was C. C. Carstens of the Massachusetts society who had pioneered in implementing a social work perspective. In succeeding years, the societies changed their approaches to incorporate constructive ideas about work with families, although conflicting views regarding child versus family rights are present today.

During the early part of the twentieth century, controversy existed regarding the nature of public responsibility for meeting the material needs of dependent children. This was largely a state responsibility and many states provided *mother's pensions;* there was considerable opposition to supporting fathers as they were expected to find work under all circumstances. Illinois was the first state to make such a provision (1911), and by 1921 forty states provided for children in this way.[37] This picture changed with the passage of the federal Social Security legislation in 1935.

The history of child welfare in the United States would be incomplete without a discussion of the Children's Bureau. The key figures in its creation, who brought their proposal to President Theodore Roosevelt, were Lillian Wald (founder of New York's Henry Street Settlement), Florence Kelley (a major advocate for government protection of women and children), and Edward T. Devine (editor of *Charities*). After several years of pressure from welfare organizations, Congress finally passed the necessary legislation in 1912.

Julia Lathrop was named the director of the Bureau (1913–1921), followed by Grace Abbott (1921–1934). These were important days for the bureau as its staff worked hard for federal child labor regulation (attained in 1938 but not approved by the Supreme Court until 1941) and the reduction of infant and child mortality (leading to the Sheppard–Towner Act of 1921 to enhance the health of mothers and children); many major studies were conducted on such topics as child nutrition, mother's pensions, unmarried mothers, delinquency, care of dependent and neglected children, and adoption.

These early years of Children's Bureau activities were not without opposition from many groups (including physicians and the Public Health Service) who were averse to involvement of the government in the health field. In fact, the Sheppard–Towner Act lapsed in 1929, although its provisions were later incorporated into the Social Security Act.

CURRENT SITUATION

According to Erickson, it is difficult to state how many family agencies exist because of a lack of a universally acceptable definition of such as an agency.[38] We can use as a measure the agency membership of Family Service America, even though not all agencies that could affiliate with it have done so. In 1984, it had 268 member agencies and 16 affiliate members. In addition, 110 were affiliated with the Association of Jewish Family and Children's Agencies. Moreover, there are family service divisions of the Salvation Army and the American Red Cross and family programs in church-related social agencies. It is estimated, in fact, that there are about 1,000 voluntary family service agencies.[39] In 1982, Family Service America reported that agencies offered service to 1.1 million families involving some 3 million people.[40]

The programs of these agencies vary with the nature of the community served and the political and social climate in the larger society. Thus, when the government developed financial assistance programs, family agencies moved heavily into counseling. As prevention approaches evolved, the agencies moved to early intervention with families at risk, as well as to family education activities. Because the climate of the 1960s favored the development of social action and family advocacy programs, many family agencies moved in these directions.

When the government cut back on the provision of material resources in the 1980s, family agencies sought to fill some of the gaps that were created. The identification of new problems such as AIDS, family violence, and child sexual abuse led to programs to provide services to affected groups.

A critical problem for family agencies in recent years is the adequacy of their funding. Both federal support for their programs and private funding through the United Way agencies have decreased. This has led to fee increases and efforts to qualify for third-party insurance payments. Many agencies have reduced services and staff.

A report published by Family Service America in 1985 indicated that "the major concerns of families are unemployment, single-parenthood, increased family violence, incest, blurred sex roles, depression and loneliness, and alcohol and drug abuse." The picture looked particularly bleak for the poorest families.[41]

As described earlier, the federal role in family services was largely fulfilled through Title XX of the Social Security Act. Federal policies changed, however, and many of these Title XX services were reduced or eliminated as a result of the Omnibus Budget Reconciliation Act of 1981. This act created a formal block grant, which eliminated the requirement that states match federal funds; it also merged separate federal grants for social services, staff training, and child care. According to Kimmich, this led to a net loss of over 13% between 1981 and 1983 for such child welfare services.[42]

Many contemporary child welfare services are provided through the Adoption Assistance and Child Welfare Act of 1980. These include limited federal assistance for foster care for AFDC eligible children and federal adoption assistance payments to promote the adoptions of children with special needs. The Reagan administration proposed a modification of this act in 1983 that would have reduced the role of the federal government in these programs, but such legislation was not enacted.

Child abuse and neglect prevention is supported through still another federal grant

Preparing a child for first grade. (Photo by Ken Karp.)

program. In 1982 the Reagan administration tried unsuccessfully to do away with this.[43] Child care programs are also provided for by federal block grants, and in fiscal 1982 approximately 20% of all such social service funds were distributed in this way. Even then, this was 14% below the 1981 Title XX level.[44] Still another federal program is Head Start, which consists of early childhood education programs for preschool children which is the only federal child welfare program that received increased federal support in 1982.

Other changes that occurred as a result of the Omnibus Budget Reconciliation Act of 1981 were a redefinition of the age of childhood as 18 and younger, rather than 21 and younger; a limit on AFDC assistance to pregnant women by allowing it to start only at the beginning of the third trimester of pregnancy; prohibiting AFDC to strikers and their families; and including a stepparent's income when determining eligibility for AFDC. Further modifications occurred in 1984 through the Deficit Reduction and Tax Reform Act, which made Medicaid available to first-time pregnant women who would be eligible for AFDC once the child was born and extended for 9 months Medicaid eligibility for AFDC recipients who lose AFDC because of the limit on earnings disregards (with an additional 6-month extension available at the option of the individual state).

Summing up these changes of the Reagan years, Kimmich writes:

As a whole, social service programs affecting children fared worse than the other broad groups of programs listed in table 3; a loss of 18 percent in inflation-adjusted dollars occurred between 1981 and 1982; modest increases in outlays the following two years raised this loss to 14 percent for the three year period. The reconciliation act directly affected only two of the eight social service programs listed in the table—the social services block grant and the community services block grant. However, because these block grants are two of the three largest sources of funds for children's social services and together account for 60 to 70 percent of the federal social services outlays, aggregate social services spending clearly reflects the block grant funding levels.[45]

Efforts have been made to estimate the number of children in the United States receiving child welfare services but, as Kadushin and Martin point out, this is a difficult task because "there is no central agency with responsibility for collecting the overall statistics."[46] They do cite data, however, from a special survey of public social services provided to children in 1977, which showed that "some 1.8 million children were receiving such service."[47] Because this survey was outdated, Kadushin turned to available data on specific services in the United States. From this he determined the following:

1. In 1982, 929,000 cases of abuse and neglect were reported to protective service agencies. (By 1987, the number had increased to 2,025,200.)
2. In 1981–1982, the estimate of the total number of children in substitute care provided by public agencies was 273,000.[48]

An update of Kadushin's information can be found in data supplied by the U.S. Department of Health and Human Services. These indicate that 275,756 children were in foster care in 1984 and that this represented a decline of 9% from 1980.[49]

These data, however, conceal the fact that nonwhite children are more poorly served by the system. Hogan and Siu, for example, point out that African-American children who are placed are much more likely than white to be in and stay longer in foster care rather than the more expensive services such as group homes and residential treatment. These authors conclude that "Even when other variables—such as economic status and family situation—are held constant, the differences persist, which suggests that racial bias was a key factor in the differential treatment."[50]

Another major issue is that African-American children are less likely to find adoptive homes. Hogan and Siu state that "Although the percentages of white and black children legally available for adoption closely matched their relative proportions in the child welfare population, homes were found for 54 percent of the white children and for only 37 percent of the blacks."[51]

Native American children have also suffered from the child welfare system, particularly through the fact that they have been separated from their parents at a disproportionate rate. Again, according to Hogan and Siu:

Surveys in 1969 and 1974 documented that between 25 and 35 percent of all American Indian children were placed in foster or adoptive homes or institutions. Transracial placements were overused, with more than 80 percent of the placements to white homes. In 1971, the Bureau of Indian Affairs boarding school census revealed 34,538 American Indian children in institutional facilities. The boarding school system had begun in 1879, and children from ages 5 to 20 had been placed in facilities that prohibited use of native language and observation of cultural customs.[52]

The child welfare policies that were imposed on Native American children were strongly protested for many years, and this ultimately led to the passage of the Indian Child Welfare Act (P.L. 95–608) in November 1978. While the intent of this act was to build Native American social services and to prevent racist practices, it has not been adequately funded and has continued to be a source of conflict between Native American tribes and state governments.

Many problems with the child welfare system also have special effects on Hispanic families. One of these relates to the increase in intercountry adoptions from Latin America. According to Hogan and Liu, "Problems with this practice include inadequate screening and selection processes and preadoption care being provided by unqualified institutions." The same authors note that many problems ensue from unfair use of protective services because of lack of cultural understanding. They point out issues that relate to the lack of services for Hispanic migrants and their children because of "language barriers, unfamiliarity with services, and cultural differences."[53]

Another report from 1984 showed that 1,024,178 families were officially reported for child abuse and neglect and these reports related to 1,726,649 children.[54] In addition, the estimate of the numbers of children who experienced sexual abuse in 1984 was 100,000.[55]

The six states that together accounted for more than 40% of these children were California, Florida, Michigan, New York, Ohio, and Texas. These data partially reflect the populations of these states, because the six states with the highest report rates in 1984 (reports per 1,000 children) were Missouri (55.13), Delaware (50.88), South Dakota (49.25), Maine (44.20), Alaska (43.53), and Nevada (37.59). The reader should remember, however, that these are report rates and may or may not reflect the actual amount of abuse and neglect.

Again, according to Hogan and Siu, we are likely to find racial differences:[56] The trend of overrepresentation of African-American child abuse and neglect reporting has been consistent over the years. African-American families are more prone to involvement in reported neglect situations; between 55% and 65% of reports between 1976 and 1982 were for neglect only. African-American parents involved in the reports are more likely to be single and receiving assistance, and the caretakers tend to be younger and female.

Selected Components in Detail

FAMILY SERVICES

In many ways, social workers have viewed family services as analogous to general practice in medicine, and it is more than a coincidence that such medical practice is often referred to now as family practice. In fact, it would be hard to find a problem situation with which social workers deal that is not encountered in a family agency, whether under public or voluntary auspices. This scope has broadened as family agencies either expanded their services to include those customarily defined as child welfare or as family and children's agencies merged into family and children services.

It is fitting that the family agency should fulfill such broad functions inasmuch as almost any problem can negatively affect family functioning. In addition, the family can often assist or hinder the attainment of solutions to the problems of its members. Individuals who do not appear to have any current contact with their families do, of course, present themselves to human service agencies. Even in these cases, good practice may require helping these people reestablish their family ties. When this is not possible, it may have ensued from a lack of good family services at an earlier time.

A good example of the points made in the preceding paragraph is provided by the consequences of the current policy and philosophy of deinstitutionalization, in which individuals previously committed to institutions are maintained in their communities. These individuals may be seriously mentally ill, elderly, handicapped, dependent children, or ex-offenders and are likely to need their families to do for them what institutions may have done. This poses severe problems for families who can only perform these functions if they are supported and educated and not stigmatized in the process. More recently, this kind of support and education has been emerging as an important family agency service.

Historically, the special province of the family agency has been problems that occur in the relations among parents and children, between spouses, and between adults and their aging parents. Even here, contemporary social conditions provide a new twist as families present themselves in new forms: living together unmarried couples, gay and lesbian pairs (often with children), communal living together groups, single individuals who adopt, and so forth. More traditional family forms are also affected by changes in social norms, such as those related to sexuality, the roles of men and women, and a host of generation gap issues. As Erickson states in summarizing some of the findings of a Family Service America report:

> The report stated that a 1983 FSA survey of 280 family service agencies in the United States and Canada found that the major concerns of families are unemployment, single-parenthood, increased family violence, incest, blurred sex roles, depression and loneliness, and alcohol and drug abuse. The report concluded that the current prospects are bleak for families near and at the bottom of the economic scale. Families in multiproblem situations often feel helpless. Family structures are besieged and weakened by unemployment, poor schools, loss of family support systems, family violence, drug and alcohol abuse, and depression, and new classes of the poor are emerging.[57]

While typically family agencies have been staffed by social workers, the new challenges require a variety of other staff inputs. Psychiatrists have almost always been employed to assist in the assessment and treatment planning, but they may be supplemented with vocational counselors, lawyers, sociologists, and psychologists. Direct services may also be offered by homemakers, home economists, nurses, and teachers.

Because of their focus, family agencies have had a theoretical orientation toward family. Until the last few decades, however, this was a largely undeveloped theoretical field. The evolution of family systems concepts and theory has strongly influenced family agencies and given them a stronger theoretical base.[58] Nevertheless, family agencies still have a long way to go to fully understand and carry out the implications of family systems theory in their services. For example, one public agency with which we are familiar requires all children's workers to create ecomaps and genograms[59] for all clients, but it is unclear how this information is utilized by the staff to offer better services.

Typically, clients of a family agency either apply directly for services (they may have seen agency public relations announcements) or they may be referred by other professionals (social workers, teachers, doctors, and so forth). They are likely to be interviewed by an intake social worker who may or may not continue to be assigned to them because in many situations the client is assigned to either a worker who specializes in the specific problem (for example, spouse abuse) or the next worker with an opening in his or her caseload. The individual may also be referred to other professionals in the agency for psychiatric or psychological evaluation and then for group work, homemaker services, and so forth.

Some agency services are preventive in nature, such as family life education. Workers visit local institutions such as schools and churches and present information on such topics as parenting and conflict resolution. They may also consult with others, such as teachers and ministers, to help them provide better services. Still other workers engage in advocacy and other interagency and agency–community activities. While the worker assigned to the case may advocate for specific clients, others will do *class advocacy* by representing the needs of groups of clients, such as the homeless, the unemployed, single parents, and minority group members.

Many family agencies have started new programs in response to the development of new social problems. For example, the current AIDS (acquired immune deficiency syndrome) epidemic has caused some family agencies to offer support group and other services to patients and their families. The growing awareness of the problems of adults who previously were the victims of incest or were children of alcoholics has led to services (typically groups) for these people. Family agencies have also provided services for abused spouses and abused elderly with the increased recognition of these problems. These services are provided to both victims and perpetrators.

The changing funding pattern and recognition of need have been the impetus for family agencies contracting with business and industry to provide employee assistance services. At times these have been in the nature of referral activities, but because of the generic nature of family agency services, these agencies have offered direct help with many problems that affect workplace functioning, such as substance abuse and family discord.

HOMEMAKER SERVICES

Homemaker services are often offered by family agencies, although a variety of other organizations also offer these services. These include child welfare and health agencies as well as those devoted exclusively to this function.

Homemaker services are those designed to supplement the nurturing role in families when the individual(s) who might perform this role is incapacitated. The role is broader than that of a housekeeper who shops, cooks, or even provides child care. The homemaker helps meet emotional needs. She also (homemakers have typically been women), as a member of a human service team, helps to restore the functioning of family members by, for example, coaching them in their responsibilities.

Homemaker service has been seen historically as a child welfare role and has been used in the past "to supplement the maternal role in families when the mother is temporarily incapacitated by illness or other crisis."[60] In the contemporary scene, however, a homemaker may be employed in families without children, such as those with a handicapped or elderly member. The function is the same: to help the family to meet the needs of members in their own household rather than in institutions.

The origin of homemaker service is often cited as having occurred in the 1890s in activities of the "Little Sisters of the Poor" who "went out during the day to clean the house and help out in the homes of children whose mothers were incapacitated."[61] A service that came closer to today's concept was initiated in 1923 by the Jewish Family Welfare Society of Philadelphia. Its function was to provide assistance to families when the mother was absent for a short time, usually for medical reasons or childbirth.

While there was a substantial growth in homemaker services in the ensuing years, it has still not fulfilled its promise. Robinson cites a 1978 survey of public social services to children and their families that "showed that only 7 percent of the cases reported received homemaker service. Care outside the home, however, was reported used four times as often."[62]

Despite this, homemaker services are widespread. They were enhanced through the home health aide services of Medicare as provided for in Title XVIII of the Social Security Act. This legislation was associated with a growth in such units from 303 in 1963 before Medicare to 759 in 1966 after it. By 1984, the number had grown to 8,000 in the United States and Canada including many for-profit agencies.[63] Unfortunately, the impact of this expansion on child welfare has not been as great as hoped as it has recently been estimated that 85% of these services are to the elderly; even the remaining 15% is divided between families with children and those with disabled members.[64]

Some of this expansion is due to the fact that homemaker services are often referred to as homemaker–home health services and money for health services, while inadequate, is more plentiful than money for social services for any age group.[65] This issue bears on the evolution of the National HomeCaring Council, which Anderson describes as follows:

> When national organizations and agencies of the federal government met in 1959 and 1961 to discuss homemaker services, the possibility of placing the representation for them in either the National League for Nursing or the Family Service Association of America was discussed. The consensus of the attendees was that either placement would result in fragmentation of a service which should be unified. A new national organization, therefore, was incorporated as the National Council for Homemaker Services, later Homemaker–Home Health Aide Services, now the National Home-Caring Council.[66]

Whether homemaker service is part of a comprehensive agency (such as a family agency) or is devoted only to this service, social workers typically are involved in the assignment and supervision of the homemaker or in providing consultation to her. They therefore participate in the assessment of the family's needs in this regard. Some of these assessment issues are the following:

1. Since the service is meant to maintain the family unit, is this a legitimate goal?
2. Will the service enable the family to function adequately at some time in the future?

3. How are the family members likely to react to and accept the service? What will be their level of cooperation with it?

As a result of the assessment, the social worker, other team members, and the homemaker plan for the nature of the actual service. One issue that must always be dealt with is how the homemaker will successfully gain entry to the family in a social-psychological sense and negotiate appropriate roles for herself. In this process, family members may either seek to burden the homemaker with too many tasks or, in contrast, trust her with too few. These issues may be discussed with the social worker and with the homemaker herself.

The social worker will continue to work closely with the homemaker and will typically operate with eight to ten homemakers. Social workers utilize their understanding of the needs of the family and family dynamics in this work. An important aspect is the worker's understanding of cultural differences in families so that the homemaker will take this into account in her work. The homemaker, in turn, keeps the worker informed about any changes in family conditions that affect how the social worker and other team members work with the family.

A very important part of this service is the use of homemakers in the prevention of child abuse. When the abuse is exacerbated by stress on the family, the homemaker can help to reduce this stress by the tasks she performs and by giving the parents respite from child care. Abuse can also ensue from the parents' lack of parenting skills, and the homemaker can help here, also, by modeling such skills and teaching the parents how to use them.

Kadushin and Martin report on a number of studies that sought to evaluate the effects of homemaker service.[67] These studies indicate that homemaker service allowed many children to remain in their own homes rather than experience placement; homemaker services are especially economical when there are a number of children in the family. Some parents who required hospitalization were more likely to accept it when they knew that homemaker service was available and were more likely to follow medical advice as to how soon they might resume family responsibilities when they returned home, and some mentally ill parents were enabled to continue to function within their families.

A number of problems exist that affect the future of homemaker services. One is whether this service should be tied most closely to health as compared to social service agencies. Another is how closely homemaker services should continue to be linked to social work activities. Still another is how priorities should be established for the scarce homemaker services that exist.

Despite the time that has elapsed since the inception of these services, there still is confusion as to how they should be defined to the community, who should be recruited, and how they should be trained. Standards for homemaker service continue to be a concern, especially with the expansion in the number of private individuals and proprietary agencies that are involved in offering it. As Kadushin and Martin state:

> The National HomeCaring Council has established standards and is acting to accredit agencies that meet the standards. This is a difficult task, however, so that by 1978, there were only 124 agencies that were accredited by the council. There is concern that homemaker service, like nursing-home service, may present opportunities for unscrupulous operators.[68]

DAYCARE SERVICES

Daycare services, which may be carried out inside or outside the home, substitute for the parents' care of the child. They may be offered for some of the same reasons as homemaker service such as to relieve a parent who is ill or experiencing stress from child care responsibilities. A more common reason, in view of the large and increasing number of working mothers in all social strata, is to provide care while parents work. It is estimated that women will constitute almost two-thirds of the new entrants into the work force between now and the year 2000 and that many will have small children.[69] Another important statistic is that in 1980 about half of the children under 6 were in some type of daycare outside their homes.[70]

A variety of daycare arrangements exists in addition to those in which a friend, relative, or paid person comes to the home. One is a *daycare center* that operates under a license and cares for groups of 12 or more children; a similar group service may be offered by someone in his or her own home, and this is referred to as a *daycare group home*. Finally, an individual or family may provide care for six children or less and this is termed a *family daycare home*. The daycare arrangement is called *day treatment* when it serves handicapped children. In viewing the alternatives available to families that seek daycare, it should be noted that parents tend to prefer in-home care by a relative or at least services close to home.[71]

A distinction exists between daycare centers and nursery schools although the latter may be employed for daycare purposes. Daycare centers provide care during times that the family requires the service. Nursery schools have a variety of time schedules. The emphasis in nursery schools is educational, also.

Historically, daycare developed out of the need to provide services to working mothers. An early example occurred in Switzerland in 1767 for mothers who worked in the fields.[72] However, daycare is much more a consequence of industrialization; an early U.S. example was a program set up in New York City in 1854. The working widows of Civil War soldiers provided another pressure for daycare services, and when the National Federation of Day Nurseries was founded in the United States there were 175 known day nurseries. Most of these services were provided under private rather than government auspices. The development of daycare took another spurt during the depression to support the employment of women, largely through Works Progress Administration nurseries.[73] By 1937 there were 40,000 children in 1,900 nurseries, and this was the first time federal and state funds supported this service.[74]

Although World War II created more need for this service, many centers were closed after the war, and daycare did not see additional growth until the 1960s with the passage of the Head Start Act in 1965. The 1961 Social Security Amendments provided federal grants-in-aid to state public welfare agencies, and some of these resources were used to enable states to establish daycare standards through licensing. The first federal regulations of this sort were in 1969, with the Federal Interagency Day Care Requirements.[75]

The support of daycare again took a downswing with the conservative trend of the 1970s and 1980s. An example of this was the failure of Congress to override President Nixon's veto of the Comprehensive Child Development Act of 1971, which sought to develop a nationwide plan for quality daycare services. Further efforts to create a comprehensive child care program were defeated in 1976 and 1979. Efforts to create national standards were also defeated. As Emlen states:

> A series of comparative studies of state licensing showed wide variation in adult–child ratios, little attention to group size, and practices that fell short of the revised FIDCR (Federal Interagency Day Care Requirements) standards, but with passage of the Omnibus Budget Reconciliation Act of 1980 (P.L. 96–499), federal regulation of day care was on its way out. By 1981, day care under the social services block grants would comply only with the standards set by state and local laws. In 1985, a model child care standards act (P.L. 98–473) was passed to assist states with guidance and training.[76]

Continuing a process that had already begun, President Reagan pushed for a shift toward the private sector in child care. This led to an increase in the number of employer-assisted programs and private, for-profit, centers. As of this writing, some reversal of this trend seems possible in the Bush administration through a compromise between the president and the Democratic Congress.

This should create more federal support for daycare and is a result of demands for this service from *both* middle- and low-income families. The differences that separated the president and Congress had to do with the amount of subsidy, eligibility of middle-income families, maximum benefits, whether school age children as well as preschoolers will be covered, and whether national quality standards will be set. Pressing for the more liberal program, called The Act for Better Child Care Services (ABC), is the Children's Defense Fund, a major child welfare advocacy group.

Two major approaches to financing child care are involved in these controversies. One directly covers the costs of child care. The other allows the parents an income tax credit for some proportion of these costs. The latter concept has been in operation since the Revenue Act of 1971 (P.L. 92–178.) It clearly benefits middle-income families, while it is of no use to people too poor to pay an income tax.

Daycare centers operate under several kinds of auspices. These include nonprofit organizations, church programs, and chains of large centers operated by for-profit companies. The largest chain is Kinder-Care; it has over 950 centers in 40 states and Canada and serves over 100,000 children. The second largest chain, La Petite Academy, has over 400 programs in 24 states.[77]

Social workers function in a number of different roles in daycare. They are sometimes directors of such programs, but more typically they do intake, consult with staff regarding the handling of child and family problems, and refer children and families to other services that they may require. Social workers operating in agencies outside the specific daycare setting may advocate for more and better daycare facilities.

Social workers are especially useful to mothers who experience stress in meeting the multiple demands of work and parenting or in making a transition from the home to the workplace. They help children to make the transition from home to the daycare setting, which may be their first significant separation from the family, and prepare the mother to deal with this issue. Despite the value of these services, only a small proportion of such centers employ social workers, and social services are least available in proprietary centers.[78]

A major problem in daycare programs is the training of the staff members, as many do not have appropriate education. Another is a lack of enforcement of good standards regarding other aspects of the service, even though states are likely to require licensing. These standards deal with such matters as ratio of staff to children, group size, physical facilities, safety standards, health standards, educational facilities, the age of the children to be enrolled, and the relationship of program to age. Controversy especially surrounds whether and how children under the age of 2 and 3 should be served. Still another issue is to what degree the goals of daycare ought to include education in addition to basic caring.

A major matter that continues to nag at policy makers is whether care outside the child's own home, whatever the source, is destructive to the child. Kadushin and Martin cite a number of studies that support the conclusion that daycare is not intrinsically harmful to children and in many cases is beneficial. They add that this refers to good daycare settings with children who are appropriately placed.[79] Similar qualifications are placed on the advantages and disadvantages to children of having working parents, although research suggests some advantages of maternal employment beyond the financial, such as father involvement, the mother as role model, and child independence.[80]

ADOPTION SERVICES

Adoption is a method of transfering the legal rights, responsibilities, and privileges from one set of parents (usually biological parents) to another. This may occur because the parents wish it or because their rights have been legally terminated against their will. It is a very old institution, as illustrated in the Old Testament when Moses was adopted by Pharaoh's daughter. Other ancient civilizations have used adoption for political, religious, and economic reasons. Despite this, adoption was not covered by English Common Law because of opposition in England to inheritance by other than blood relatives.

In the early years of U.S. history, adoption was not extensively used because of the practice of indenture by which dependent children were placed with families who benefited from their work. Nevertheless, some families who wanted to establish family ties wanted safeguards against the birth parents' reclaiming their children. At first, this required private bills because this matter was not covered by English Common Law.

Gradually, the states passed adoption legislation; one of the first was Massachusetts in 1851, and the legislation of that state became a model for others. As described by Kadushin and Martin, it provided for

1. The written consent of the child's biological parents.
2. Joint petition by both the adoptive mother and father.
3. A decree by a judge, who had to be satisfied that the adoption was "fit and proper."
4. Legal and complete severance of the relationship between the child and biological parents.[81]

As state laws evolved, they dealt with issues such as seeing that the rights of all parties were respected: biological parents, adoptive parents, and children, although the child's needs came to be regarded as primary. The laws also tended to shift the investigation of these matters from the courts to state welfare departments or child placing agencies.

A set of principles evolved to guide current adoption practice. One idea is that the child should remain with his or her biological family, if at all possible, and this family should be supported to make this achievable. When the child must be placed, this should be with a family that is of the same ethnicity, religion, and nationality as the child. These decisions should be made as promptly as possible so as to prevent the child from experiencing an unnecessary degree of uncertainty regarding his or her nurture and family stability.

Many authorities have also concluded that adoption is to be strongly preferred over foster and institutional care as a long-term arrangement. Adoption offers the child a guarantee of stability and continuity of parenting, as well as the benefits that come from having all the rights and privileges (including the family name) of biological children.

This is undoubtedly true when the adoptee is an infant. But many adoptees now are older children, and these include children who have been abused as infants. It is more difficult to find adoptive homes for older children, although recent approaches have focused successfully on achieving this goal. These difficulties have forced some children to spend long periods of time in foster care. Our experience is that such children may be harmed further if they are removed from a good foster care home and stressed yet another time because of the value placed on adoption.

A major development in adoption practice took place in the 1960s when it was recognized that many, particularly poor, minority, and handicapped, children were being badly served in long-term foster care because of the lack of continuity in a particular home; in fact, many children were frequently moved from one foster home to another and between foster homes and institutions. This situation led to the creation of new agencies to place these children in adoptive homes, modifications in the practices of established agencies, and eventually to the passage in 1980 of Public Law 96–272. It required states to establish adoption programs and provided federal support for state programs to subsidize parents who were willing but lacked resources to adopt children "with special needs." Specialized techniques for recruiting parents for these children and helping both parents and children cope with the issues that result from the child's special needs were developed. Nevertheless, much research and program development remain to be done regarding this type of adoption as a result of its relative newness in the child welfare field.

There are a number of overall trends in the field of adoptions. First is an increase in the number of older children and a decrease in the number of infants who have been adopted. This is undoubtedly a consequence of the number of unmarried mothers who choose to keep their children and of mothers who choose abortion. Kadushin and Martin summarize a study of the National Committee for Adoption[82] as follows:

> Surveys estimated that there were 50,720 unrelated adoptions in 1982—19,428 arranged by public agencies, 14,549 by private voluntary agencies and 16,743 independent adoptions arranged by private individuals. Some 14,000 of these were adoptions of special needs children and some 9,600 were adoptions by foster parents. The 50,720 unrelated adoptions in 1982 compares with the peak total of 89,200 such adoptions in 1970.[83]

An even later survey published in 1989 by the Child Welfare League indicated that there were at least 34,000 children, the majority (82%) with special needs, who wait an average of two years to be adopted. Minority children were 46% of this group.[84]

There are special issues relevant to the adoption of minority group children. For example, a major issue in the African-American community is that, while the same proportion of black families adopt children as white families, there is a large number of black children in substitute care awaiting adoption. As Kadushin and Martin state, "Although black children comprise 14 per cent of the child population, they are 25 per cent of the foster care population, 33 per cent of the children free for adoption, and 37 per cent of the children free for adoption who are not in adoptive placement."[85]

Another issue regarding black children is whether or not they should be adopted by white families. Some authorities argue that this represents a disservice to these black children, who must then struggle with identity issues and how to cope with racism without African-American role models. The National Association of Black Social Workers in 1972 stated strong opposition to transracial adoption as "a growing threat to the preservation of the black family."[86]

Other authorities point to successful adaptations of black children adopted by white parents and conclude that this was a better arrangement than the uncertainties of long-term foster care.[87] Although the number of transracial adoptions has been decreasing, it comprised between 20% and 35% of all nonrelative adoptions of African-American children between 1969 and 1976.[88] Kadushin and Martin reviewed a substantial number of research studies of black children who were adopted by white families. On the basis of this research, they conclude that

> In general, research on transracial adoptions and on adoption of foreign-born children suggests that these children can develop into well-adjusted individuals who feel good about themselves and their lives. However, the data also repeatedly point out that parents play a particularly important role in helping their children successfully adapt. Not all adoptive parents make the necessary effort to help their children interact with others who are culturally and racially like them, and not all parents attempt to help their children successfully identify with their racial group. In fact some actively ignore or deemphasize these issues. In these circumstances, their children will also be less likely to acknowledge their differences, and will be less well-adjusted than they would be in more supportive family environments.[89]

An issue related to that of the adoption of minority group children is that of foreign adoptions. Such adoptions, particularly from South American and Asian countries, have been a response to both the numbers of dependent children in those countries and the shortage in the United States of white babies for adoption. In addition to the issues noted regarding transracial adoptions, serious questions have been raised as to whether the rights of the children's parents have been safeguarded, as in the airlifting of babies from Vietnam after the war.

Current practices of international adoption agencies such as Traveler's Aid International Social Service with headquarters in Geneva, Switzerland, as well as state child welfare agencies, involve close scrutiny of the appropriateness of the adoption and the adequacy of the adoptive home. These criteria must be attested to before the U.S. Immigration and Naturalization Service will approve the child's immigration. Nevertheless, many still argue that these adoptions deprive the child's country of an important resource, its children, while subjecting older children to severe culture shock and denying younger ones any significant connection to their cultural heritage.

Social workers play a considerable role in all aspects of the adoption process, and this can best be described by briefly describing the stages of the process. First, a determination is made usually by a social worker, as to whether a particular family is appropriate for adopting a child and whether a child's needs are best met through being placed for adoption. Determining whether a family is appropriate begins by employing agency criteria. These typically relate to the age, physical and mental health, economic situation, marital stability, and parenting abilities of the parents (or sometimes single parent). A judgment is usually rendered as to whether the parents have suitable personality characteristics, and this can be highly subjective, especially where infants are involved because of the much greater demand than supply. Several studies cited by Kadushin and Martin indicate that social workers assessing adoptive applicants may vary widely in their judgments.[90]

Less stringent criteria may be used when the child is in a hard to place category, such as an older or handicapped child. Previously, considerable attention was paid as to whether the adoptive applicants were infertile, as it was assumed that fertile individuals could conceive their own children; this is not emphasized as much today, although there is not a clear consensus on this issue.

Little help has traditionally been offered to single individuals who wish to adopt children, but, again, the pressure with reference to the hard to place has led to more openness to these types of adoptions. Nevertheless, these individuals are likely to be very carefully evaluated with reference to their stability and social support networks. A very controversial issue is that of approving gay males and lesbians as adoptive parents, yet practitioners we have consulted believe that there has been a slight increase in acceptance of this type of adoption.

The next step is to effect a match between the child and parent. Social workers also tend to be involved in this process and, although efforts are made to consider child need and parent abilities, much individual worker judgment is involved. In some cases, parents are shown tapes of the child to avoid the traumatic experience involved in exposing the child to multiple families. In one case, when a match between a couple and an older child seemed a good one, the couple were allowed to observe the child while he was on a sight-seeing expedition to an airport with his social worker. The child was not aware of their presence.

An innovation in preparing adoptive applicants for the placement of the child is to use group meetings. The group members discuss a variety of issues related to the adoption experience. Typically, some parents who have already adopted a child are invited to participate and to share their experiences.

When an actual match has been determined, the worker has the task of helping the specific child and parents prepare for each other. This involves helping each to learn about the other and to deal with feelings about the process. For the child, this can involve dealing with such emotions as loss and confusion regarding her or his biological parents. Even though this process may continue for a long time, it is important to start dealing with it at this point. Another issue is the child's reaction to leaving the foster home. Social workers have developed and are continuing to develop many techniques to help children with these issues.

When the child's birth parents are still in the picture, they must also be helped by the social worker to deal with their feelings about relinquishing the child. When this situation is not well handled, the result may be a later fight to regain the child, with tremendous emotional costs to all concerned. This helping process should continue as long as the birth parent needs it; unfortunately, this principle is not as widely practiced as it should be.

In some circumstances, it helps in the placement process if the child and the adoptive parents visit with each other prior to the date of final placement. In one case in which a child moved from a foster to an adoptive home, the adoptive parents first visited him in his foster home and then in their own home. An overnight visit also preceded his actual move. A social worker can help to make these types of arrangements and can work with the child and adoptive parents to assist them with this process.

After the child is placed in the adoptive home, the social worker will help the child and parents in adapting to each other. This service usually lasts until the adoption is legally finalized (usually six months to a year later), but it may extend beyond that time. This is also a trial period, and in some cases the social worker and the parents decide to abort the adoption process and another plan is made for the child.

At the end of the probationary period, a petition is filed asking the court to finalize the adoption. If the biological parents have not yet relinquished or been deprived of their rights, they must do so at this time. If the child has reached a particular age, in some states as low as 10 or high as 14, she or he must also approve the adoption. The court orders an investigation of the situation, and this is usually satisfied by an adoption agency report. The court then holds a hearing and makes a decision that is usually not final for an additional period, typically between six months and a year.

A social worker may offer help to the family during the months and years following adoption, and this is particularly desirable when the child has special needs that cause stress for the family. The issues that come up then, in addition to those that may arise with any child, have to do with the meaning of adoption; how the family, including other children, and the adoptee adapt to each other; how the special needs of the adoptee are met; and how the family uses both formal and informal resources as supports.

The adoption field is still struggling with a number of issues. One of these is the search by adoptees for their biological families, typically when they have reached adulthood. The current consensus is that this is a healthy thing for some adoptees to do, while recognizing that it is equally appropriate for some not to.

However, many child welfare agencies are not helpful when adopted children return years later asking for help with a search; at least one agency has even told them that it is a sign of pathology. Admittedly, the search for birth parents is a complex matter involving legal procedures and the rights of many sets of people. The importance we now attach to this subject is attested to by the fact that "By 1985 some thirty-five states had adopted laws permitting adult adoptees to obtain identifying information regarding their birth parents."[91] National organizations have also been created to help adoptees with this process, such as the Adoptees Liberty Movement Association.

Because of this issue, much thought is being given to the idea of open adoptions. Baran, Pannor, and Sorosky define this as an adoption in which "the birth parents meet the adoptive parents, participate in the separation and placement process, relinquish all legal, moral and nurturing rights to the child, but retain the right to continuing contact and to knowledge of the child's whereabouts and welfare."[92] Much controversy surrounds open adoptions and, admittedly, these procedures create risks; nevertheless, the idea is becoming increasingly accepted and we believe that the benefits outweigh the dangers. Open adoption is not a new idea. It was the primary type of adoption in the United States through the beginning of the twentieth century. The first state to close adoptions was Minnesota in 1917, which passed a sealed record law. This idea did not catch on until 1938, when the Child Welfare League endorsed secrecy in adoption.[93]

Another issue is independent adoptions, those not made through the services of a child welfare agency. These may be brought about through direct arrangements between biological and adoptive parents; in other cases, a lawyer or other third party may make the plan. These adoptions may pose dangers to all concerned: the child may be placed in an unsuitable home, the natural parent may experience coercion, and the adoptive parents may find the biological parent acting in intrusive ways. Although studies indicate that many independent adoptions are satisfactory, we recommend that such adoptions be investigated by a social service agency because of the great harm that can occur.[94]

FOSTER CARE SERVICES

Foster care is defined by the Child Welfare League of America as "a Child Welfare Service which provides substitute family care for a planned period for a child when his own family cannot care for him for a temporary or extended period and when adoption is neither desirable nor possible."[95] As with adoption, examples of children being cared for by people other than their parents can be found throughout history. An early form of this was indenture. As provided for in the Elizabethan Poor Laws, the master accepted the child into his home and provided her or him with all the necessities and training in a means of earning a living. The master was compensated by the results of the child's work.

Contemporary foster care in the United States began with the work of Charles Loring Brace at the New York Children's Aid Society. Perhaps as a result of criticisms of that program, such as its removal of children far from their families, alternatives were created. One involved placing the children within their own areas, and this was done through what were called State Children's Home Societies.

The first of such societies was begun by Martin Van Buren Arsdale, a minister, in 1883 in Indiana and Illinois. By 1923, 34 states had such programs in addition to similar ones that were conducted under sectarian auspices. People involved in such work soon developed a conceptual framework for what they were doing. A pioneer in this respect was Charles Birtwell, who directed the Boston Children's Aid Society from 1886 to 1911 and sought to clarify the means whereby the child's needs could be assessed and met through a consideration of a variety of alternatives.

In the next decades, much attention was placed on the role of social workers in improving the quality of foster care services. This role included sensitive handling of the placement process and enhancing the adaptation of foster parents and children to each other. Another extensively discussed issue was the differential use of institutions and foster homes in meeting the needs of dependent children.

More recently, new issues have been raised regarding foster care. One concern is the instability of many foster home placements so that some children experience frequent moves from one setting to another. Another is that some children spend years in foster care when it would have been more appropriate to either have worked to return them to their biological parents or to have placed them for adoption (in some cases with the foster family being the adopting one).

Several changes have taken place in the child welfare system to deal with these issues. One is the requirement that each foster care situation be reviewed on a regular basis. This requirement is at times imposed by the agency itself, and it is required by legislation in many states. To receive reimbursement for AFDC-FC the federal government also requires the states to develop and review plans for each foster child. Public Law 96-272 (The Adoption Assistance and Child Welfare Act of 1980) requires this kind of monitoring for specified categories of foster care.

These changes have led to the creation of new approaches to monitor the child's situation and to help biological parents to change the family conditions that led to the removal of their children. These include instruments to enhance such monitoring and to promote behavioral contracts with parents.[96]

A 1987 report indicated that there were 276,000 children in foster care during 1984. As an indication of the high replacement rate, the report stated that about 180,000 children moved in and out of foster homes during the year. The median time the children were in such care was 17 months. This number, while large, represents a decline over other recent years, which may well be a result of the emphasis on permanency planning. Nevertheless, African-American, Native American, and Hispanic children are over-represented in foster care. In 1982, 34% were African American and 7% were Hispanic. The age of children in foster care has also been rising, and most are now 10 or older.[97]

Social workers play a role in the foster care system that is in many ways, analogous to the role described earlier for adoptions. They are responsible for initially assessing the child's need for placement and, although this is an important task, a high likelihood of agreement among workers has not been demonstrated.[98] The most frequent reason given for such placements (75% to 80% of cases) is parent-related problems such as abuse, neglect, illness, or imprisonment; this is followed by child-related problems (15% to 20%), such as the child's handicaps or behavior; least often cited is environmental stress and deprivation (3% to 5%).[99]

Another task is the recruitment and selection of foster parents. This may be done through advertisements, talks to civic groups, and referrals from people who already are foster parents. Much has been written on the evaluation of such families and how to determine the likelihood that they will be able to provide the care required and how they will respond to children with differing needs.[100]

Several issues affect this selection process, and a primary one is the fee to be paid. While undoubtedly many families perform this service for altruistic reasons, they take on a costly responsibility; limitations on agency fees may be one factor that limits some otherwise appropriate families from coming forth. Another issue is how the role of the foster parent is defined. Are they clients of the agency or its employees? The former definition may cause some families to feel depreciated; the latter may offer them the rewards of being treated as colleagues. Agencies demonstrate how they define the role, for example, through either offering therapy in the former case or educational and other collaborative opportunities in the latter.

Once the worker has determined that foster care is needed by the child and a suitable foster home has been selected, the parties are helped to prepare for each other. The placement experience is always traumatic for the children, and the worker will help them to deal with feelings of rejection, guilt, and worthlessness. Unlike adoption, however, they will frequently be returned to their biological parents and are also likely to have visits with them on a regular basis.

The placement process is similar to adoption in some respects, however. The actual move should be accomplished through a series of preplacement visits unless the situation is an emergency, in a case of severe abuse or the incarceration of a single parent.

After placement occurs, the worker will help the biological parents, foster parents, and foster child to make the experience as constructive as possible. Currently, many agencies conduct group sessions for each of these sets of people so that they may help and support each other through the processes of mutual aid. Frequently, the placement does not work out, although the child still requires foster care. This leads to replacement, which is emotionally costly. Each replacement adds to the likelihood that the child will have difficulty forming a relationship with the next set of foster parents; such children can also be difficult for the new foster parents to relate to, thus adding to the probability of further placements. This is another reason for either working for time-limited foster placements or adoptive ones.

Any one of several outcomes of the foster care experience requires additional activities by workers. If the child returns to her or his biological parents, the worker must be assured that the home is once again appropriate. Or if it becomes necessary to seek a termination of parental rights, an adoption process may be initiated. Increased attention is now being paid to emancipating older children and supporting them to live on their own. Finally, some children must remain in foster care for a long time, such as when the ties to the biological family are strong but that family cannot resolve its problems and fully reintegrate the child.

Much research has been conducted regarding the impact of foster care on children. Kadushin and Martin conclude the following from these studies:

> The general conclusions that might be drawn from these studies of the immediate outcome of foster family care is that this experience is not clearly injurious to the child's development; . . . However, the proportion of children displaying some type of cognitive, social, or emotional difficulty is fairly substantial, suggesting the need for widespread and sometimes intensive services to enhance the child's capacity to perform optimally.[101]

Kadushin and Martin also report on a series of studies of adults who had experienced foster care as children. They conclude that the responses are not too different from those secured shortly after placement had ended. Most young adults who have been foster children are functioning well; a significant number, nevertheless, were dissatisfied with the experience and continue to have relationship or other difficulties in living.[102]

One problem foster care experts seek to solve is that, despite the progress described earlier, many children remain too long in foster care. Adequate foster homes are also in short supply, and this is especially crucial for minority children.

Another minority issue is the placement of children in homes that do not reflect their cultural heritage, particularly Native American children. For this reason, Congress passed Public Law 95-608, the Indian Child Welfare Act of 1978, which seeks to prevent the unnecessary breaking up of Indian families and to reinforce the rights of tribal courts to make decisions on this issue.

PROTECTIVE SERVICES

Protective services are the activities of social agencies to prevent child maltreatment. These agencies may be public or private and may or may not be specifically established for this purpose. Maltreatment frequently occurs in the form of physical abuse, sexual abuse, or neglect. Neglect includes the failure to provide life's necessities, medical care, or education. Other kinds of maltreatment are economic exploitation of children and emotional abuse and neglect. Parents may be the perpetrators of all these undesirable events, but so may child caring institutions, schools, and even strangers.

Several societal factors complicate this definition of maltreatment. One is that historically children have been seen as the property of their parents, who have been free to treat them in any way they deem desirable. This right, however, has been limited by the ancient concept of parens patriae, which holds that the state has the obligation to be parent to all children and to defend their rights. In contemporary times, there has also been a shift toward the notion that children have rights and that children belong to themselves "in the trust of their parents."[103]

Beyond these general ideas, there are also cultural differences within the society as to how children are to be raised. Some cultural groups lean toward more strictness; others toward permissiveness. Other groups accept physical punishment and even encourage it (spare the rod and spoil the child), while others view it as immoral.[104] The way the larger society defines permissible child-rearing practices can run counter to these cultural variations.[105]

The progress begun with the creation of the New York County Society for the Prevention of Cruelty to Children in 1875 and the development of protective agencies in the early part of this century faded between the 1920s and 1960s. But progress returned on a more intensive level during the 1960s largely due to the activities of a number of pediatricians and psychiatrists.

An example was the work of Henry Kempe and his colleagues, who in 1962 published a study of children hospitalized because of abuse.[106] This study led to a number of federal and state initiatives, such as state legislation requiring the reporting of child abuse. A federal Child Abuse Prevention and Treatment Act was enacted in 1974 to provide assistance to the states to develop appropriate programs. Increased concern is also exemplified by the large number of books and articles that have appeared within just a few decades devoted to this subject.[107]

It is difficult to provide estimates regarding the incidence of child abuse and neglect due to the definitional issues and the obvious problems in reporting. Efforts have been made to overcome these problems such as a national study of child maltreatment conducted by the National Center on Child Abuse and Neglect in 1979–1980. This study

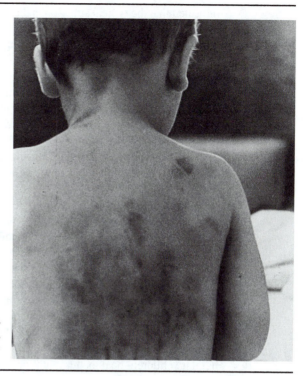

Social workers are required by law to report all cases of child abuse that they encounter. (UNICEF photo by Lazzopina.)

utilized a sample of 26 counties in 10 states. It concluded that "at least 652,000 children are abused and/or neglected annually in the U.S."[108] Many of these cases had not been officially reported.

Statistics on reported child maltreatment are also available on an ongoing basis from the American Association for Protecting Children, a unit of the American Humane Association.[109] By 1987, the number had reached 2,178,000 in 1,404,000 families. This number reflects duplicate reports in that, if a family is reported more than once, it is counted more than once in this statistic. The principal type of maltreatment in 1986 (the association did not provide this breakdown for 1987) was neglect, constituting some 54% of all reports recorded. Varying degrees of physical abuse, including sexual, constituted 38% of the children who were reported. In the same year, sexual abuse made up 14% of the reports. Emotional and other maltreatment accounted for 19%.

In recent years, it has been recognized that sexual abuse is a more frequent and serious problem than had been believed earlier, although estimates of its incidence vary widely. This is in part because of the embarrassing nature of such abuse for all concerned and the difficulty of securing information about sexual abuse from young children. In the plurality of these cases, the victim is a girl (77%) and the perpetrator is a male; the mother in a number of cases has denied the possibility of this type of abuse and has failed to protect the child.[110] A number of new techniques have been developed to obtain this information, such as interviews in which anatomically correct dolls are used as props.

Data are also available regarding families who maltreat children. One report indicated that the typical situation is that of a low-income family with between two and three children. The family also is likely to be a single-parent, female headed one. Nonwhite and Hispanic families are overrepresented among these families with regard to neglect, but not abuse, and this is seen as a result of the economic handicaps under which many members of these populations live.[111] This is not to deny the fact that child abuse and neglect occur in all types of families, social classes, and cultural groups.

Substance abuse is often cited as present in maltreating families. As one report states, "In 1988 crack use was identified in over 8,521 cases of child neglect in New York, over three times the number of such cases identified in 1986." Fatalities as a result of child abuse have also been increasing, and these rose 5% in 1988 to 1,225. For three straight years these deaths were in excess of 1,100 and since 1985 have increased over 36%.[112]

When responding to cases reported to them, child protective agencies may determine in many situations that the case is not severe enough to categorize it as abuse or neglect. Nevertheless, whether a family is actually abusing children or not, to be reported represents a stress on the family. This stress may lead to family responses that are detrimental to the children, especially if the protective service agency has staff who are too overworked to be of help to such families.

Social workers perform a large number of tasks when they are involved in protective services. An important one, primary prevention, provides services to families that are stressed well before abuse or neglect occurs through parent education for people who are already parents and those who will become parents, child education directed at helping children deal better with parents who are stressed, and public education regarding child maltreatment. Attention has been given to instruments to help social workers identify parents who are at high risk of maltreating their children so that this may be prevented.[113]

Social workers also try to make contact with those who might abuse their children. In some communities this is done through announcing services through the media and publicizing the existence of a hot line that people can contact at any time. Other types of announcements tell those who witness child maltreatment whom they can contact. State legislation usually *requires* such professionals as doctors, nurses, social workers, and teachers to report child maltreatment to the protective service agency.

When maltreatment is reported, a protective service worker must investigate if the report is at all credible. Although such an investigation might be a highly disturbing event, this is not necessarily the case. Protective service workers are likely to be trained to introduce themselves in a nonjudgmental way as seeking to benefit children by helping parents. The worker is also trained to respond helpfully to the expressions of anger and fear that may be evoked by the contact. Nevertheless, the investigation is an unwanted intrusion that is experienced negatively by almost all families.

As a result of this visit, the worker must determine whether further contacts are necessary. The facts that will be used is whether there is evidence of abuse or danger, how vulnerable the child is, such as being very young, how often maltreatment has occurred, how much responsibility the parents or other perpetrators take for the maltreatment, the mental status of the parents, the level of cooperation of the parents in correcting the problem, the amount of stress the family is under, and the supports available to them.

Based on this assessment, if workers believe they should remain active in the situation, several options are open to them. These include offering services, referring the family for other services, immediately securing the legal right to remove the children, or petitioning a court to hold a trial at which placing the children is a possible outcome. The decision the worker makes at this point is crucial and often difficult. This is underscored by the frequency of newspaper reports of serious or even fatal harm inflicted on a child *after* a report has been made to protective services.

There are many studies to help social workers deal with the question of which parents are likely to maltreat their children. The findings from such studies are at times inconsistent, which makes it difficult for workers to apply them in specific cases, because complex interactions between psychological and social factors are present, in addition to the factors in a specific situation when maltreatment occurs.

In examining this research, Kadushin and Martin find such factors as the parents' low self-esteem, poor impulse control, poor relationships, and unreal expectations of children. These parents often lack parenting skills and see the child as responsible for meeting their needs. They often experience a great deal of stress and do not receive much support from others in their networks. Some had been maltreated when they were children, but this was not the case with others. Certain children are also more likely than others to evoke maltreatment, such as those who are highly active, irritable, or aggressive or have greater needs because of illness or handicap. Studies have also shown that premature infants are at greater risk of maltreatment.[114]

A variety of services may be offered to maltreating parents, such as individual counseling, group work, parent education, and family therapy. To reduce stress, they may be offered a homemaker or respite through daycare for the children. In offering these services, the worker must be able to handle the resistance the family is likely to present.

If the worker believes the child should be removed from the home, she or he can suggest this to the parents. If they refuse, the worker has recourse to the court, which occurs in about 18% of the cases.[115] Legal proceedings are then instituted in which there are three sets of attorneys: one for the protective service agency, one for the parents, and one for the child, who is referred to as the guardian *ad litem* and whose job it is to protect the interests of the child. In some jurisdictions, social workers have been trained for this role, in which case they have legal counsel available to them.

When the court determines the disposition of the case, its options include returning the child to its home (often under court or agency supervision), placing the child in foster care, or terminating parental rights and making the child available for adoption. The parents may also be punished by fine or even imprisonment for severe physical or sexual abuse. In making a decision, the court will examine a report submitted by the protective service agency; social workers may also be called on to testify as expert witnesses for any of the parties involved.

Although more well-executed studies of the effectiveness of protective services should still be done, a number of such research reports are available. Kadushin and Martin summarize these and offer the following conclusion:

> In summary the evaluation studies suggest that agencies have achieved some modest measure of success. The amount of change one might reasonably expect the agencies

to effect must be assessed against the great social and personal deprivation character-istic of the client families. Even the modest success achieved may have been more than could have been expected initially.

The resources available to treat these families are limited. The technology available to the worker in trying to effect changes in such families is blunt and imprecise. The low level of confidence in the technology available to treat problems of child maltreatment is indicated by the fact that 39 percent of some one thousand seven hundred human service personnel interviewed by Nagi agreed that "we just don't know enough to deal effectively with problems of child maltreatment."

Scarce resources backed by a weak technology applied to a group of involuntary, disturbed clients resistive to change and living in seriously deprived circumstances would seem to guarantee the likelihood of limited success.[116]

A number of problems must be solved if better protective services are to be offered. Through its policy making processes, society must define more clearly what kinds of behavior of adults toward children are unacceptable. Current definitions of abuse and neglect provide deficient guidelines for social workers and legal authorities. Another major issue is that when clear-cut cases of maltreatment are reported adequate services may not be available because protective services are severely underfinanced. As reporting systems improve, the limited resources must be spread even thinner.

Those protective service workers who are available may be overworked and burned out. This causes high turnover rates, with the result that workers are often inexperienced and inadequately trained. Increasingly, therefore, agencies have been moving to the concept of treatment teams in which workers can support and substitute for each other in the more time-consuming and difficult cases. These teams may include psychiatrists, physicians, nurses, and lawyers.

RESIDENTIAL SERVICES: INSTITUTIONS AND GROUP HOMES

The reader's image of the children's institution may derive from classic stories of orphan asylums, but the contemporary institution, more often thought of as a residential facility, has come a long way and now provides many different forms for different purposes. The only generic definition, therefore, is "a twenty-four hour residential facility in which a group of unrelated children live together in the care of a group of unrelated adults."[117] This separates this type of program from specialized foster care facilities, which may serve only one or two children and in which the children are cared for by a family or related couple.

A distinction is made between *group homes* and *institutions,* although we believe there is a continuum among such services and some agencies conduct both activities so as to have flexibility in treatment planning. Standards have been set for each of these programs. The Child Welfare League of America suggests, for example, that the group home should have between 5 and 12 children, and groups of children under 12 years old should include both boys and girls.[118] The federal government has set a limit of 25 on the number of children that can be served in an institution for dependent children that receives federal support (P.L. 96–272, 94 Stat. 504).

Some of the kinds of children for whom different institutions exist are the following: (1) dependent and neglected children, (2) physically handicapped children, (3) severely retarded children, (4) delinquents, and (5) emotionally disturbed children.

Institutions for children have had a long history. Many of the earliest programs, however, placed children who needed care in institutions that also served adults. This was true of the *xenodocheion,* which was created in 325 in Nicaea to care for the sick and poor. An early program primarily for children was established in 787 in Milan. A number of centuries later, in 1633, St. Vincent de Paul established homes in France for abandoned children.

In the United States, the early pattern was to serve children together with adults in almshouses, although there were a few exceptions. One was in New Orleans and was created to care for children orphaned when their parents were killed by Indians. Another in Philadelphia served those orphaned through a yellow fever epidemic. While both types of institutions existed, there were many investigations of the condition of children living in almshouses; by the latter part of the nineteenth century, these investigations led to many states prohibiting the care of children in almshouses and to the building of orphan asylums instead.

The first state institution for children was established in Massachusetts in 1866, and by 1923 there were 1,558 orphan asylums.[119] But debate continued during this period regarding the relative merits of institutional and foster care. A strong force against the institution was set in motion in 1951 through a publication by John Bowlby that provided evidence of the negative impact on child development of institutional care.[120]

Institutions are used when it is decided that the child cannot effectively use the resources of either an adoptive home or a foster care facility. Children referred to institutional settings are more likely to have been removed because of an inability to succeed in home settings. Sometimes it is decided that a more protected environment is needed.[121]

The kinds of children who can best be served in an institution are typically those who have been removed from their homes because of their own serious problems rather than those of their parents. These children may have some combination of emotional problems, relationship difficulties, and cognitive handicaps. Their afflictions have made it impossible for their parents to respond helpfully to them, and this would also be true of substitute parents; they also may not be well tolerated in the community. The conclusion, consequently, is that they require a more structured and protected situation.

The problems these children experience are likely to have resulted from unhealthy family situations. Nevertheless, these situations are not clearly abusive or neglectful: if that were the case, the child who is removed might well benefit from foster care. It is possible, however, that in some cases children may be placed in institutions because their parents' behavior is too disruptive for foster families to handle, and institutions are in a better position to protect children from that.

For several reasons, many children placed in institutions are adolescents. First, the acting out that can occur in adolescence may be particularly hard on foster parents. Second, some adolescents with difficulties may be more responsive to help offered by the peer group than by parent substitutes.

A number of characteristics of residential settings make them valuable in the circumstances described. First is the staffing pattern, which provides the children with access to a variety of adults in their search for someone to whom to relate. When the children's behavior is stressful for adults, this burden can be borne better by a number of people than by one couple. The intensity of relationship that is demanded in a family is also diluted in an institutional setting. This strength can also be a limitation if staff turnover is too great, as it often is in institutions that provide poor pay and other working conditions.

The institution can also assemble a variety of elements to meet the individual needs of children. These include different therapies, recreational activities, and special education programs. Because of the presence of a number of children, group work services can and should be a major component.[122] The existence of the structure found in the institution may be valuable to children whose lives have been chaotic and unpredictable.

One advantage of a group situation is the way in which the group can support each member's individual development. In most institutional groups, the focus is primarily on peer groups. Although increments in change are small, a developmental approach can be effective.[123]

While group living is the essence of the institution, if its processes are not well understood, it can be destructive. Polsky, for example, has described the systemic elements that must be worked with by staff to ensure that the group provides support and nurture to its members, rather than another deviant culture.[124]

Kadushin and Martin present the following data regarding residential settings.[125] In 1980, about 232,000 children were living in institutions in the United States, and the largest number were in delinquency settings or those for the physically and mentally impaired. Only about 18,276 were in 368 facilities classified as residential treatment centers. In these centers, the average bed size was 54 to 55 and two-thirds had fewer than 50 beds. Only 9% to 10% had 100 beds or more. Most of these treatment centers were under private auspices. Current ideas about residential settings are operative inasmuch as the general length of stay in general child care institutions is nine months and in residential facilities, fifteen months.

Social workers and teachers represent the largest staff groups in residential settings. A 1983 report indicated that 2,419 social workers were employed in this way, mostly full time, compared to 654 psychiatrists, of whom only 7% worked full time.[126] Social workers are employed at all levels of the residential facility as directors, supervisors, and direct service workers.

The direct service workers function at each stage of the child's career in the institution. They are usually responsible for assessing the child's situation to determine whether an institutional placement is the best solution of the child's problems. If the decision is in the affirmative, they work with the children and their families to help them with the placement process; in this way they use skills that are analogous to those used in foster care and adoptive placements.

The work with the parents involves discussions of their feelings, as well as concrete arrangements regarding such matters as visits, vacations, obtaining reports, medical care, and fees. The parents and children learn about life in the institution and visit the facility. Some programs, however, limit parents from actual observations of children already living in the institution because of privacy issues.[127] The children, however, may have several visits during which they meet the group with which they will live and possibly eat a meal with them prior to actual placement.

This process continues after placement as the social worker helps the child to become oriented to the institution and to deal with separation issues. The worker both before and immediately after placement will also help the other children in the group and the relevant child care staff to adapt to the new child.

Once the children have passed the entry phase, the social worker usually has a good deal of responsibility for subsequent service and treatment planning for them. A number of different patterns exist, however, for the kinds of roles different staff members play in the institution, and this can create a certain amount of role conflict and ambiguity unless these issues are carefully thought through by administrators.

A typical arrangement has the child cared for by child care staff who are scheduled to be on duty throughout the day and night. The social workers will treat the children and their families individually and in groups and will consult with child care workers, teachers, recreation workers, health specialists (such as doctors and nurses), and others to coordinate the care and treatment of the child. Since the child care workers and teachers are, as Trieschman and his colleagues put it, responsible for "the other twenty-three hours" (the one hour is formal therapy) where a great deal of the actual therapy takes place, this can lead to conflicts between these two groups and an underestimation of the role of the child care professional.[128] The social worker must be mindful of her or his role as a team member who seeks to integrate a variety of services that are all potentially important to the child.

Finally, the social worker is typically responsible for determining when the child has received the maximum benefit the institution has to offer and is ready to return home, to a foster or adoptive home, or to an independent living arrangement. This must be carefully planned as it is often easy to continue the child in institutional placement well beyond the point where it is necessary, thereby risking the creation of a child who cannot adapt to anything but an institutional arrangement. The same amount of planning as was required to place a child in the institution is required to help him or her and significant others deal with the transition back to the community.

A number of studies have examined the effectiveness of institutional placements. The findings vary considerably because of the range of institutions, types of children, and role of the institution in a continuum of treatment that begins before placement and continues afterward. As Whittaker states:

> The most powerful determining factor of the child's postdischarge adjustment is the nature of the postdischarge environment. Central in this environment is, most generally, the family. Thus the extent of family support and the nature of familial relationships are crucial variables.
>
>   Further, in light of this powerful factor, other factors such as preadmission characteristics, characteristics measured while in residence, and specific treatment interventions are not strongly associated with postdischarge adjustment. These findings point to the importance of planning residential care within a continuum of services to families and children.[129]

A number of concerns confront the residential field in child welfare. Most have existed for a long time and still have not been solved. One of the most crucial relates to the staff group whose presence is essential to the institution, the child care staff. This group works long hours at low pay with little status: according to one survey, more than half make less than $8,000 a year.[130] The idea of further professionalization of this group through educating them to a greater degree, raising their status, and improving their pay and working conditions has often been recommended and seldom implemented.

Writers such as Bruno Bettelheim have written extensively about the need to coordinate and integrate the work of various people in the institution. Bettelheim sees this as avoiding fragmentation in the child's treatment milieu.[131] The child often comes from a fragmented family and can be said to have a psychic structure that is also fragmented. When this problem is experienced in the treatment milieu as well, the milieu can be said to be part of the problem, not the solution.

Indeed, child welfare services in the community are often fragmented and poorly coordinated. This can lead to some children's receiving residential care who do not need it and others not receiving it when they should. Some children may be sent long distances, often out of state, for services. This works against those children who need ongoing contact with their families.

Because of problems of staffing and funding, cases of abuse and neglect of children in institutions are still reported, particularly those that house delinquents. State legislation requires the reporting of these kinds of events, but some are concealed.

Institutions should work with families, especially when the child's plan includes return to the family. But many social workers in institutions are not trained in this modality. An interesting exception is Boysville in Clinton, Michigan, which involves structural family therapy and regular collection of data on its impact on the families and the children. Apartments are maintained on the campus of this institution to house families who may have to travel a long distance to participate. Every living unit is assigned a family worker who serves the families of the youth in that unit.

Finally, in the institutional field there are many deficits in service to minorities, and this is particularly true for institutions that are the most treatment oriented. These deficits also extend to the kind of programming available in the institution, which may not be sensitive to minority issues and needs.[132]

Issues and Directions

Because of the amount of information presented in this chapter on services to families and children, we shall highlight here some of the major directions this field is taking.

First is an emphasis on strengthening families as a value in itself and a way, whenever possible, of preventing the placement of children away from their families. This family work is accomplished through family life education programs, in-home services, and as activities that are more remedial in nature. While current social policy does not prevent all family breakdown by providing every family with adequate resources, this is certainly the objective of every professional in this field and every welfare reform proposal offered.

When placement of the child is absolutely necessary, social workers are being educated to select the option that best meets the need of the child and to work to create a suitable array of options in every community. Again, what we know is desirable frequently exceeds what is available. We also have well-tested ideas as to what intervention approaches should be used to meet the child's needs while in placement. Frequently, these ideas may not be employed because of staff shortages (particularly of well-trained staff), turnover, and overload.

Often services must be offered through more specialized agencies, such as those that deal with substance abuse, sexual abuse, youths who are single parents, and parents who need respite in crisis situations. This places the worker in the position of case manager who sees that each child and family receives what they need. Again, there are problems in the availability of all these services and in the training of workers to fulfill a case manager function in an effective manner.

Much more must be done to ensure that services for children in danger of abuse and neglect are sufficient. The persistent problems of training, staffing, and availability of an array of services occur in this part of the service field also.

All these problems are intensified when we review the situation of children and families from economically and socially oppressed minority groups, as well as older children with special needs. Although efforts are being made to recruit and educate staff members from minority groups who will be more sensitive to these issues, the need is great and the pool of such staff limited.

All this implies that child and family work can be stressful. The stress has been increased by an awareness on the part of child welfare workers of their liability to prosecution when a child in their caseload suffers harm that they presumably could have prevented. While we hold no brief for incompetent or even malicious workers, the situation may be one in which a competent and well-meaning worker is overloaded and does not have sufficient backup from the agency.

An already complex picture is being made more so by the privatization of many functions, such as through the creation of proprietary daycare centers, homemaker services, adoption agencies, group homes, and the like. Social workers are consequently hard pressed to understand and utilize available programs on behalf of their clients.

The overall funding pattern is also problematic. National standard setting has been replaced by state control as block grants became the way the federal government participated in financing child and family services. This has led to a tremendous diversity of programs; while some are undoubtedly good, others may be regressive. As Kadushin states in summarizing this picture,

> There is, however, some cause for optimism. Although federal support of social welfare programs has been eroding, there have also been repeated indications that Congress is concerned about children. The Adoption Assistance and Child Welfare Act passed in 1980 gives clear support for programs assuring greater permanence for children. In 1982, a special congressional committee, the Special Committee on Children, Youth, and Families, was created to give greater visibility to the special needs of children and youth; in addition, Congress supports the objectives of the Child Abuse Prevention and Treatment Act (P.L. 93–247) by continued approval and funding.
>
> Child welfare services are not declining, but the industry is growing more slowly than in the immediate past. Commitment to program objectives has been maintained. Consensual acknowledgment of the need for the programs—as of their legitimacy and social work's responsibility for them—is unquestioned.[133]

Conclusion

The chapter began with a discussion of the functions of services for families and children. We discussed the presumably separate fields of family and children's services together because a priority for any service to families should be the needs of its children and because a priority of child welfare services is to maintain the child's family relationships whenever possible. We defined family and child welfare. Various types of institutions and their purposes were also described, such as those that focus on family welfare, child placement, protective services, and supportive services like homemakers and daycare.

The functions of social work in the family and children's field were covered next. Social workers play a very central role in social welfare agencies serving families and children, although they are not as central in the policy-making process as it affects families and children. The conceptual approach utilized by social workers in this field is increasingly systemic and ecological, especially since these are also becoming the dominant ideas in work with families.

Value and ideological issues were then addressed. These relate to such issues as how childhood is construed in a society, what the rights of children are conceived to be, and what value is placed on maintaining the strength and integrity of the family.

The history of child and family services and their current status in the welfare structure of the United States provided a broad background for understanding them. Such historical events as the founding of the Charity Organization Societies, the replacement of many children from eastern urban homes to the rural west, and the beginning of a child rescue movement were described as antecedents to our current array of services.

In discussing our current situation we indicated the impact of the decline in federal funding on family and children's services. We then described how state, local, and private organizations have sought to maintain at least a minimum level of activity. Despite cuts, some services, particularly in the child welfare field, have continued to be supported by Congress. We also pointed out the special disadvantages experienced by minority children as services have been cut.

Family services, homemaker services, day care services, protective services, foster care, adoptions, and residential care were given detailed coverage. The chapter concluded with a summary of some of the major issues confronting the services offered today.

Notes

1. For an extensive discussion of a family perspective in child welfare, see Robert M. Rice, "The Well-Being of Families and Children: A Context for Child Welfare," in Ann Hartman and Joan Laird, eds., *A Handbook of Child Welfare: Context, Knowledge, and Practice* (New York: The Free Press, 1985), pp. 61–76.
2. Jo Ann Allen, "Understanding the Family," in Hartman and Laird, eds., *Handbook of Child Welfare*, p. 151.
3. Ibid.
4. Alfred Kadushin and Judith Martin, *Child Welfare Services*, 4th ed. (New York: Macmillan,

1988), pp. 6–7. Quotations from this work are reprinted with permission of Macmillan Publishing Company. Copyright © 1988 by Macmillan Publishing Company.

5. Ibid.

6. Robert M. Moroney, *The Family and the State: Considerations for Social Policy* (New York: Longman, 1976); Robert M. Rice, *American Family Policy—Content and Context* (New York: Family Service Association of America, 1977).

7. *Scope and Methods of the Family Service Agency,* Report of the Committee on Methods and Scope (New York: Family Service Association of America, 1953).

8. Ellen P. Manser, *Family Advocacy—A Manual for Action* (New York: Family Service Association of America, 1973).

9. Carol H. Meyer, "The Institutional Context of Child Welfare," in Hartman and Laird, eds., *Handbook of Child Welfare,* p. 111.

10. *U.S. Statutes at Large* 37, pt. 1 (1912), 79–80, cited in Brenda McGowan and William Meezan, *Child Welfare: Current Dilemmas. Future Directions* (Itaska, Ill.: F.E. Peacock, 1983), p. 60.

11. Kadushin and Martin, *Child Welfare Services,* 4th ed., pp. 26–31.

12. Brenda McGowan and Elaine Walsh, "Social Policy and Legislative Change," in Hartman and Laird, eds., *Handbook of Child Welfare,* p. 253.

13. Carel Germain, "Understanding and Changing Communities and Organizations in the Practice of Child Welfare," in Hartman and Laird, eds., *Handbook of Child Welfare,* pp. 122–148.

14. Ibid., p. 126.

15. Ibid., p. 127.

16. Ibid., p. 128.

17. Ibid.

18. Kadushin and Martin, *Child Welfare Services,* pp. 47–48.

19. Robert H. Bremner (ed.), *Children and Youth in America—A Documentary History,* Vol. 1 (Cambridge, Mass.: Harvard University Press, 1970), p. 64, quoted in Kadushin and Martin, *Child Welfare Services,* p. 47.

20. Ibid., p. 51.

21. Ibid., pp. 51–52.

22. David G. Gil, "The Ideological Context of Child Welfare," in Hartman and Laird, eds., *Handbook of Child Welfare,* pp. 11–33.

23. Ibid., p. 27.

24. See Kadushin and Martin, *Child Welfare Services,* pp. 35–43.

25. Ibid., p. 42.

26. Patrick V. Riley, "Family Services," in Neil Gilbert and Harry Specht, eds., *Handbook of the Social Services* (Englewood Cliffs, N.J.: Prentice Hall, 1981), p. 83.

27. Ibid.

28. Mary Richmond, *Family Visiting among the Poor: A Handbook for Charity Workers* (New York: Macmillan, 1899).

29. Lela B. Costin, "The Historical Context of Child Welfare," in Hartman and Laird, *Handbook of Child Welfare,* p. 37.

30. Ibid. p. 38.

31. Ibid., p. 39.

32. Bremner, *Children and Youth in America,* p. 101, cited in Hartman and Laird, *Handbook of Child Welfare,* p. 41.

33. *Fletcher et al.* v. *Illinois,* cited in Lela B. Costin, "The Historical Context of Child Welfare," p. 41.

34. Etta Angell Wheeler, "The Story of Mary Ellen Which Started the Child Saving Crusade Throughout the World," (Albany, N.Y.: American Humane Association, Publication No. 280, circa 1910).

35. Costin, "The Historical Context of Child Welfare," p. 42.

36. Ibid., p. 46.

37. Ibid., p. 56.

38. A. Gerald Erickson, "Family Services," in A. Minahan, ed., *Encyclopedia of Social Work,* Vol. 1, 18th ed. (Silver Spring, Md.: National Association of Social Workers, 1987), p. 589.

39. Ibid.

40. Alfred Kadushin, "Child Welfare Services," in Minahan, ed., *Encyclopedia of Social Work,* Vol. I, 18th ed., p. 270.

41. Family Service America, Minahan, ed., *Encyclopedia of Social Work,* 18th ed., *The State of Families: 1984–85* (New York: Family Service America, 1985), pp. 592–593.

42. Madeleine H. Kimmich, *America's Children Who Cares?: Growing Needs and Declining Assistance in the Reagan Era* (Washington, D.C.: Urban Institute Press, 1985), p. 12.

43. Ibid., p. 18.

44. Ibid.

45. Ibid., pp. 19–20.

46. Kadushin, "Child Welfare Services," p. 270.

47. Ibid.

48. Ibid. p. 244, The 1987 figure is from *Statistical Abstract of the United States: 1990,* Table 296.

49. Sumner M. Rosen, David Fanshel, and Mary E. Lutz, eds., *Face of the Nation 1987: Statistical Supplement to the 18th Edition of the Encyclopedia of Social Work* (Silver Spring, Md.: National Association of Social Workers, 1987), p. 97.

50. Patricia Turner Hogan and Sau-Fong Siu, "Minority Children and the Child Welfare System: An Historical Perspective," *Social Work* 33 (6) (November–December 1988), p. 494.

51. Ibid.

52. Ibid., p. 495.

53. Ibid.

54. Rosen, Fanshel, and Lutz, eds., *Face of the Nation 1987,* pp. 100–101.

55. Ibid. p. 102.

56. Hogan and Siu, "Minority Children and the Child Welfare System," p. 494.

57. Family Service America, *Family Service Profiles: Agency Staffing and Coverage* (New York: Family Service America, 1984), cited in Erickson, "Family Services," p. 593.

58. See Chapter 6 for a discussion of family systems concepts.

59. These are graphic devices for portraying the relevant systemic conditions of the family, either currently or historically.

60. Kadushin and Martin, *Child Welfare Services,* 4th ed., p. 419.

61. Nancy Day Robinson, "Supplemental Services for Families and Children," in Hartman and Laird, eds., *Handbook of Child Welfare,* p. 398.

62. Ibid.

63. Ibid., p. 399.

64. Ibid.

65. Ibid., p. 400.

66. Ibid., p. 406.

67. Kadushin and Martin, *Child Welfare Services,* 4th ed., pp. 163–165.

68. Ibid., p. 167.

69. Julie Johnson, "Child Care: No Shortage of Proposals," *New York Times,* (March 26, 1989), Sect. 4, p. 5.

70. Arthur C. Emlen, "Child Care Services," in Minahan, ed., *Encyclopedia of Social Work,* Vol. 1, 18th ed., p. 237.

71. Kadushin and Martin, *Child Welfare Services,* 4th ed., p. 202–203.

72. Robinson, "Supplemental Services for Families and Children," p. 410.

73. Ibid.

74. Emlen, "Child Care Services," p. 233.

75. Judith W. Seaver and Carol A. Cartwright, *Child Care Administration,* (Belmont, Calif.: Wadsworth, 1986, pp. 8–13).

76. Emlen, "Child Care Services," p. 235.

77. Ibid., p. 237.

78. Kadushin and Martin, *Child Welfare Services,* 4th ed., p. 200.
79. Ibid., p. 179.
80. Ibid.
81. Ibid., p. 535.
82. National Committee for Adoption, *Adoption Fact Book: United States Data Issues, Regulations, and Resources.* (Washington, D.C.: The Committee, 1985).
83. Kadushin and Martin, *Child Welfare Services,* 4th ed., p. 539.
84. *NASW News,* 34 (4) (April 1989), p. 16.
85. Kadushin and Martin, *Child Welfare Services,* 4th ed., p. 539.
86. *New York Times,* April 12, 1972.
87. Lucille Grow and Deborah Shapiro, *Black Children–White Parents: A Study of Transracial Adoption* (New York: Child Welfare League of America, 1974); E. D. Jones, "On Transracial Adoption of Black Children," *Child Welfare,* 51 (March 1972), pp. 156–164; Joyce A. Lardner, *Mixed Families: Adoption across Racial Boundaries* (Garden City, N.Y.: Doubleday & Co., 1978).
88. William Feigelman and Arnold R. Silverman, *Chosen Children: New Patterns of Adoptive Relationships* (New York: Praeger Publishers, 1983).
89. Kadushin and Martin, *Child Welfare Services,* 4th ed., p. 632.
90. Ibid., p. 552.
91. Ibid., p. 581.
92. Annette Baran, Reuben Pannor, and Arthur D. Sorosky, "Open Adoption," *Social Work,* 21 (2) (March 1976), p. 97.
93. Jean Warren Lindsay, *Open Adoption: A Caring Adoption* (Buena Park, Calif.: Morning Glory Press, 1987), pp. 60–67.
94. Kadushin and Martin, *Child Welfare Services,* 4th ed., pp. 610–613.
95. Child Welfare League of America, *Standards for Foster Family Care.* (New York, 1959), p. 5.
96. Theodore J. Stein, Eileen Gambrill, and Kermit T. Wiltse, *Children in Foster Homes: Achieving Continuity of Care* (New York: Praeger Publications, 1978).
97. Kadushin and Martin, *Child Welfare Services,* 4th ed., pp. 355–356.
98. Ibid., p. 362.
99. Ibid., pp. 358–359.
100. Rosemarie Carbino, *Foster Parenting: An Updated Review of the Literature* (New York: Child Welfare League of America, 1980).
101. Kadushin and Martin, *Child Welfare Services,* 4th ed., p. 427.
102. Ibid., p. 431.
103. Ibid., p. 219.
104. Joan Vondra, "Sociological and Ecological Factors," in Robert T. Ammerman and Michael Herson, eds., *Children at Risk: An Evaluation of Factors Contributing to Child Abuse and Neglect* (New York: Plenum Press, 1990), pp. 151–170.
105. For an extensive study of variations in the definition of child abuse, see Jeanne M. Giovannoni and Rosina M. Becerra, *Defining Child Abuse* (New York: The Free Press, 1979); Lawrence S. Wissow, *Child Advocacy for the Clinician: An Approach to Child Abuse and Neglect* (Baltimore: Williams and Wilkins, 1990).
106. C. Henry Kempe and others, "The Battered Child Syndrome," *Journal of the American Medical Association,* 181 (1) (1962), pp. 17–24.
107. See Elizabeth Kemmer, *Violence in the Family—An Annotated Bibliography* (New York: Garland Publishing Co., 1984).
108. U.S. Department of Health and Human Services, Children's Bureau, National Center on Child Abuse and Neglect, *National Study of the Incidence and Severity of Child Abuse and Neglect* (Washington, D.C.: U.S. Government Printing Office, 1981).
109. American Humane Association, *Highlights of Official Aggregate Child Abuse and Neglect Reporting 1987* (Denver, Colo.: American Humane Association, 1989).
110. Ibid.

111. Alene B. Russell and Cynthia M. Trainor, *Trends in Child Abuse and Neglect: A National Perspective* (Denver, Colo.: American Humane Association, Children Division, 1984).

112. Deborah Daro and Leslie Mitchel, *Child Abuse Fatalities Continue to Rise: The Results of the 1988 Annual Fifty State Survey,* Working Paper 808 (Chicago: National Committee for Prevention of Child Abuse, 1989).

113. William Altemeier and others, "Prediction of Child Abuse: A Prospective Study of Feasibility," *Child Abuse and Neglect,* 8 (1984), pp. 393–400.

114. Kadushin and Martin, *Child Welfare Services,* 4th ed., pp. 258–267.

115. Ibid., p. 278.

116. Ibid., p. 291.

117. Ibid., p. 669.

118. Child Welfare League of America, *Standards for Group Home Services for Children* (New York: Child Welfare League of America, 1978).

119. Henry Thurston, *The Dependent Child* (New York: Columbia University Press, 1930), p. 39.

120. John Bowlby, *Maternal Care and Mental Health* (Geneva: World Health Organization, 1951).

121. Kadushin and Martin, *Child Welfare Services,* 4th ed., p. 681.

122. Henry Maier, *Developmental Group Care of Children and Youth: Concepts and Practice* (New York: Haworth Press, 1987).

123. Ibid., pp. 9–33.

124. Howard Polsky, *Cottage Six—The Social System of Delinquent Boys in Residential Treatment* (New York: Russell Sage Foundation, 1962).

125. Kadushin and Martin, *Child Welfare Services,* 4th ed., pp. 688–689.

126. Richard Redick and Michael Witkin, "Residential Treatment Centers for Emotionally Disturbed Children, United States, 1977–1978 and 1979–1980," *Mental Health Statistical Note No. 162* (Washington, D.C.: Department of Health and Human Services, 1983).

127. A moving account of how some children are prepared for residential placement may be found in Bruno Bettelheim, *A Home for the Heart* (New York: Alfred A. Knopf, 1974).

128. Albert Trieschman, James Whittaker, and Lawrence Brendtro, *The Other Twenty-three Hours* (Chicago: Aldine Publishing Co., 1969).

129. James K. Whittaker, "Group and Institutional Care," in Hartman and Laird, eds., *Handbook of Child Welfare* p. 635.

130. John Myer, "An Exploratory Nationwide Survey of Child Care Workers," *Child Care Quarterly,* 9 (1) (Spring 1980), pp. 17–25.

131. Bettelheim, *A Home for the Heart.*

132. Ann Shyne and Anita Schroeder, *National Study of Social Services to Children and Their Families* (Washington, D.C.: Department of Health, Education, and Welfare, 1978), p. 153.

133. Alfred Kadushin, "Child Welfare Services," in Minahan, ed., *Encyclopedia of Social Work,* Vol. 1, 18th ed., p. 273.

CHAPTER 15
Social Work in the Workplace

Introduction

The idea of social work in a workplace setting is a relatively new development in social work. Although a few social workers have been employed by the commercial sector in a variety of roles, the development of the social work in the workplace field or occupational social work has come about since the 1970s.[1] Historically, social workers have mainly worked in the private, nonprofit social work agency, in schools, in mental hospitals, and in hospitals for the care of the physically ill. More recently, social workers have been employed in the public social services network, which had not been developed at the time that social work was born as a profession. In effect, social workers have been *agency* workers, plying their trade within the auspices of a formal entity.

Thus, it is perhaps surprising that social work did not develop more within the corporate mold. Indeed, we might have expected such activity since corporate bureaucracies were becoming a widespread phenomenon during the same period that social work was developing, and social workers were becoming a fixture in many public bureaucracies.

Perhaps their absence was because some activities of social work sought to undo the human damage caused by the often inhumane attitudes of corporations. Davis-Sacks and Hasenfeld quote one authority on corporate attitudes as follows:

> Scott and Hart assert that the work organization treats those below the managerial and professional levels as units—"functional, completely interchangeable, low priority components of the organizational machine."[2]

Not only was the treatment of the individual worker problematic. Corporate policy on layoffs and plant closings created much misery for workers and their families. When corporations moved their capital from problematic enterprise to ones more potentially profitable, it "had devastating effects on employment, with strong ripple effects on worker's families and communities."[3]

From a value point of view, working with the enemy was a bit hard to take. However deeply ingrained this attitude was, however, it has recently begun to change. One reason is that the accumulated resentment from decades of cavalier treatment began to take a toll on organizations. Workers retired on the job, unions became truculent, and public opinion began turning against the "business is business" mentality.

A second reason was the realization that productivity and quality required the participation and involvement of workers. It became clear that the machine model of employees was wrongheaded and self-destructive of the corporation's goals. While social workers had been making this point for years, it took the astonishing production of Japanese firms and the Japanese management techniques to drive the point home.[4]

A third reason is the development of corporate social welfare. Under union pressure and governmental encouragement and from their own sense of social responsibility, corporations have developed an impressive network of social and philanthropic activities.[5]

Hence, one result of the antipathies just mentioned was that social work was not included until recently as a profession that might have something to say about corporate social welfare activities, including programs of corporate philanthropy, corporate foundation efforts, and corporate in-kind contributions. But social work is now seen as having a role in the industrial, occupational, commercial sector. There is now a growing presence of social work within the workplace context. Social work in the workplace involves the development of an exciting new area for trained social workers. But much more needs to be known about both the problems and the opportunities.

History of Workplace Social Concern

Social work has always been concerned with, if not always involved in the workplace. Conditions of work and the problems they create have been a crucial focal point of social work effort. Upton Sinclair's book *The Jungle* detailed some of the difficulties that individuals in the meat-packing industry had to endure. While social workers have not been muckrakers, as such, they have always been supportive of ideas that espouse corporate social responsibility and corporate care for employees.[6]

Social work has also been interested in the plight of the worker and has historically been involved in programs to prevent worker exploitation by business and industry. Social work concerns and union concerns have always been close and to this day many United Ways retain a structure that has a labor representative sitting on the committees and on the board of directors.

Social work joined with union representatives, concerned citizens, public health advocates, and others outside business to promote social reform. Important too, from the turn of the century forward, were those business persons who were civic minded and had a sense of civic purpose (even though their gains might have resulted from social exploitation). The target was not only the reactive one of helping the individuals harmed by corporate decision making, but proactive as well. That is, ways to improve the quality of that decision making and the level of concern that informed it were examined. But because of mutual suspicion and criticism, the relationship between social work and business was at arm's length. Historically, this early phase was characteristic of the first quarter of the twentieth century.

The middle phase of social work's relationship with the corporate workplace occupies approximately the next 50 years, from 1925 to 1975. Basically, the relationship was occasional. Social workers in the workplace were definitely not the norm. Hudson's Department Store, for example (now Dayton-Hudson), had a social worker to assist employees with personal difficulties.[7] Doubtless, other firms had similar relationships, but, it was not common.

If anything, the company store idea acted as a limit on the role and responsibility that firms took with respect to their employees and created employee suspicion of any efforts that firms might undertake.[8]

This middle era of the twentieth century was essentially characterized by suspicion between workers and management. The great union movements were born and succeeded within this era, and the assumptions that lay behind the union movements, that management had to be forced to the table to make concessions, was a sort of theory X *of* the firm, shared, of course, by the theory X held *by* the firm.[9]

In theory X, management assumed workers did not want to work and had to be forced to work and constantly checked. Workers thought that management had narrow conceptions of corporate interests and had to be forced to the table. A companion theory, theory Y, suggests the reverse; here management felt workers wanted to work and the role of the manager was to free and motivate the worker. Workers' views here were that management was helpful, had their interests at heart, and would respond to collaborative problem solving. Part of the distance between social work and the corporate world hinged on just this matter. Theory X and theory Y represent two different assessments of the human condition. Social work, as a profession, espouses theory Y. We assume that people want to work, want to be good parents, and want to be good citizens, but that certain factors get in the way. Thus there was a clash of cultures between social work and business, which kept their interactions occasional. Obviously, not all firms were theory X. But with the recent rise of a more people-oriented management style, more theory Y firms are developing. This change will not only welcome the social work input, but will appreciate and welcome the social worker's contributions. This new situation has opened the way to the third era.

In the third era, the development of social work in the workplace has taken hold and indeed flowered. There are a variety of reasons for this development. However, as a beginning point it is important to review those things that management did do on its own in the social welfare area before social work became an actual part of the firm team. Changes in society, changes in the workplace, and changes in the profession have combined during the last quarter of this century to allow the profession of social work to build on the social welfare activities already developed by business and industry. Let us first look at corporate social welfare.

Corporate Social Welfare

For a variety of reasons during the course of this century, corporations have become more interested in social welfare and philanthropic activities. The reasons span a mixture of motives.

Clearly, the muckraking and charges of robber baron activities during the early part of the century had an effect. Some great foundations and philanthropies began then. The Rockefellers, the Carnegies, and the Guggenheims have left their philanthropic mark on the country. And while this money was personal in one sense, it was also clearly seen to have derived from the corporation. Bellah and others point to the sense of civic purpose that was represented here.[10] Public criticism did have some effect.

A second reason was government law. With the passage of the Social Security Act in 1935, corporations were required to contribute one-half of the social security tax (what we know as the FICA tax). This change in national policy brought corporations into the social welfare business. It began the idea of securing fringe benefits for workers, something that has expanded to a significant proportion (around 30% in big companies) of salaries and wages today.

The reasons for corporate social welfare are semiselfish, of course. In their wish to protectively transfer wealth to other members of the firm's family, firms have given it away to family foundations (rather than giving it to the government). This suggests that the tax system has been an important incentive for corporate philanthropy. And we should not forget the sense of *noblesse oblige* that often affects some members of a society's elite, probably extending to a feeling of guilt among the managers of big firms. Power may also be a factor. There is also an attempt to create a favorable public relations climate for the firm. These factors are all important in understanding why corporate philanthropy exists at all.

CORPORATE PHILANTHROPY

Corporate philanthropy is a potent force. It falls into a number of categories, which we will briefly discuss so that the extent of already existing corporate social welfare activities can be fully understood as a basis for the emergence of social work in the workplace.

FOUNDATIONS. Most well known to the average citizen are the great corporate foundations: Guggenheim, Ford, Carnegie Endowment, Rockefeller Foundation, Dow Foundation, and the Lilly Endowment. All these organizations represent substantial pools of money that are made available for civic purpose, usually upon the death of a principal in a corporation, although sometimes, as in the case of Andrew Carnegie and some of the Rockefeller money, before the death of the principal. While each foundation has its own purpose and these may change over the years, they are all committed to civic betterment in some way or other.

In spite of the family name linking them to major charitable foundations, many companies have their own company foundations. The Ford Motor Company Fund, for example, is a smaller pool of money available for civic betterment in a wide range of realms; it is funded by operating cash from the Ford Motor Company. Such company foundations are one way to handle the charitable demands made on them.

CORPORATE DONATIONS. Another way corporations contribute to the social welfare system is through direct corporate donations from operating corporate coffers. Sometimes these contributions are made as cash gifts to specific charities; the United Way is an example. Corporations make contributions to the United Way independent of those made by their individual employees. Sometimes, however, donations are in the form of civic programs. The Texaco Corporation, for example, has sponsored a Saturday afternoon opera performance for many years. While this example is from the arts rather than social service, it illustrates the point. It is important to remember that corporations, as citizens of the community, sometimes act well and sometimes not, just like other members of the community. (It is true, of course, that corporations may have a broader range of interests and resources than other citizens.) The census has tabulated corporate donations for a number of years. In 1975, corporations donated $436.8 million to philanthropic causes. In 1988 that number had risen to $1,643 million. By any standard, these are substantial monies.[11]

EQUIPMENT DONATIONS. Corporations also donate used and leftover equipment to charitable purposes. If sold, this equipment, which has already depreciated, would be an income item upon which corporations must pay tax. Corporations donate the equipment to charity instead. Securing equipment donations from corporations is a way some social agencies can secure initial supplies.

LOANED EXECUTIVES. Some charities have worked with certain industries to develop a loaned executives program. Under this program, as part of the ongoing job of a particular executive, an assignment is made to a not-for-profit enterprise. The executive receives the same pay he or she would have received while working at the corporation, but for a limited period of time works in the not-for-profit sector.

INDIRECT SUPPORT FOR VOLUNTEER CONTRIBUTIONS. Business executives and organizational personnel at all levels are frequently sought after to play volunteer roles in a variety of civic tasks. These tasks range from spending time answering a crisis hotline during business hours to being chairperson of a major fund raiser or annual charitable campaign. The very demanding volunteer roles cannot be undertaken strictly on the individual's own time, even if in adding up the specific hours we could argue that only the individual's time was being used. The flow of demands over the workday almost invariably means that, for the major roles at least, time has to be taken off during traditional working hours. Many corporations support and even encourage executives to undertake these kinds of activities. In effect, the corporation is making a personnel expenditure or donation of cash via time donated by the executive.

THE JOBS BANK. One interesting kind of contribution involves collaboration between the union and a firm, for instance, a cooperative arrangement between the Chrysler Corporation and the UAW. Funds are contributed to a jobs bank by both labor and management. Laid-off workers are then put into a jobs bank and are assigned from it to civic projects that need to be done, but for which specific funding is not available at that time. The plan has many positive aspects: workers continue to get paid, important projects get completed, and a certain amount of good feeling is shared by all.[12]

ROLES FOR SOCIAL WORKERS. Roles for social workers exist in each of these areas. Social workers can work for major foundations begun by companies. Social workers can assist in the philanthropic efforts of company foundations by helping to process their philanthropic requests and decisions and by developing relationships with the voluntary sector. Social workers can play a range of roles within the corporate sector beyond these specific ones, as well. Workers could assist corporate decision makers in not losing sight of the human impact of corporate action, which affects us all. The roles remain to be developed.

Kurtzman provides an impressive list or job description of tasks that social workers might undertake in business:

Social workers may undertake programs to reduce employee stress and eliminate smoking.

☐ Counseling or other activities with troubled employees in jeopardy of losing their jobs to assist them with their personal problems and to help them achieve and maintain a high level of performance;

☐ Advising on the use of community services to meet the needs of clients and establishing linkages with such programs;

☐ Training front-line personnel (union representatives, foreman, line supervisors) to enable them to determine when changes in an employee's job performance warrant referral to a social service unit and carrying out an appropriate approach to the employee that will result in a referral;

☐ Developing and overseeing the operation of a union or management information system which will record information on services and provide data for analyzing the unit's [human resources] program;

☐ Conceiving of a plan for the future direction of the [human resources] program that is based on the identification of unmet needs and current demographic trends;

☐ Offering consultation to labor or management decision makers concerning the development of a human resource policy;

☐ Helping to initiate welfare, community health, recreational or educational programs for active or retired employees or members;

☐ Assisting in the administration of the benefit and health care structure and helping plan for new initiatives;

☐ Consulting on the development and administration of an appropriate affirmative action plan for women, minorities and the disabled;

☐ Advising on corporate giving or labor coalition building and organizational positions in relation to pending social welfare legislation.[13]

These kinds of tasks could be carried out through a variety of positions. Kurtzman mentions, among others, the following jobs:

personnel services worker, educational program director, occupational safety and health officer, health and security plan manager, membership services coordinator, career training and upgrading advisor, preretirement services, workaday care consultant, legislative analyst, benefit plan administrator, community services coordinator, alcoholism program supervisor and director of retiree services.[14]

And we could add *social worker* to this list, as well.

PRIVATE SOCIAL WELFARE

There is an entirely different area of contribution that corporations make to the social welfare system which has lain unexplored for many years. This area of fringe benefits might be called private social welfare. Fringe benefits represent an important fraction of wages and salaries. To begin with, all employers who hire anybody and pay them more than $50 in a three-month period are required by law to pay one-half of their Social Security tax (FICA, or Federal Insurance Contributions Act), which amounts to about 7.5% on the first $52,000 of income.[15]

This contribution is legitimately called private social welfare because it is private in the sense that the employer does it; it is social in the sense that it is constrained by collective acts of will known as legislation; and it is welfare in that it is broadly distributed to everyone upon demonstration of their entitlement. While some of the programs were government initiated, as was Social Security, other private social welfare programs resulted from union–employee pressure and from the social sense of responsibility of the firm.

From this minimal beginning, private social welfare benefits extend to very substantial levels. The range is between 7.5% of salaries and wages to programs that may amount to as much as 35% of salaries and wages. For example, at the University of Michigan, people who fall in the high-middle bracket enjoy a fringe benefit package that is calculated at approximately 28% of salaries and wages.[16]

What is involved in these extended packages? Most of us are already familiar with the components; health care, life insurance, and disability insurance are among the most popular. Dental coverage and prescription drug coverage are somewhat less popular but still quite frequent. Despite the fact that private social welfare was, in effect, stimulated by the Social Security Act (August 14, 1935), the social work profession is only now beginning to be involved in the job possibilities in administering private social welfare programs within industry. Up till now, they have been largely left to personnel officers. Even in today's expanded social work–workplace relationship, this area has not yet been fully exploited.

Fringe benefits have been reviewed in detail elsewhere.[17] Rather, the point here is to indicate that there is an important private social welfare dimension that remains yet to be capitalized on by the social work profession as an employment opportunity and venue for service.

WHY SOCIAL WORK AVOIDED BUSINESS

In spite of the close relationship between some corporate social welfare activities and social work activities, social work has played a minor role in the corporate sphere. There have been a number of reasons for this avoidance.

First, the cultures of social work and business clash. Business is largely a culture of competition, whereas social work is a culture of concern (theory X versus theory Y). In each of these dominant cultures, concern and competition exist as subdominant themes. However, the overall perception of cultural difference creates a bridge that is difficult to cross. As anyone involved in work designed to bring different cultures together knows, the perceptions of differences are often greater than the actual differences. Still, what is perceived to be real, is real in its consequences, and this perception has undoubtedly had an important impact.

Second, the corporation is seen as concerned with privilege, while social work is seen as concerned with poverty. The corporation is seen as hard hearted; social work is seen as soft hearted. The corporation has been dominated by males; social work has been dominated by females. These differences singularly are significant, but taken together they can create a polarization that both contributes to and augments other differences in culture, such as general social orientation and different systems of evaluation and promotion.

Apart from specific cultural clashes between competition and concern, the internal cultural norms of each arena created further polarization. During the first 75 years of the twentieth century, business saw workers as essentially replaceable parts. The machine model of workers was dominant. Hence, concern for the worker and the expenditure of money on the worker's behalf were seen as foolish.

Similarly, within social work the dominant ideology was that social workers worked in social work agencies. Indeed, a rule for field training in social work was that one had to be supervised by an MSW. A narrow construction of this rule had the unfortunate effect of limiting social work placement to those locations which already had social workers. It naturally excluded places, unintentionally, that did not already have MSWs present.

However, a variety of changes in society, in the workplace, and in the profession itself has begun to overcome these juxtapositions and polarizations. Businesses are beginning to value the human resources of people more fully. And social workers are beginning to recognize that it might not only be necessary to start where the client is psychologically, but go where the client works occupationally.[18]

Social Change and Social Work in the Workplace

Changes in society, the workplace, and the profession are beginning to decrease the cultural distance between the social work profession and the professions of production and service. We will discuss each separately, although, obviously, social changes in one area affect the others.

CHANGES IN SOCIETY

Society in the United States has changed dramatically during the last half of the twentieth century and certainly during the last quarter. Perhaps the most significant change has been the rights revolution, the desubordination of individuals who were previously kept by cultural chains, mental shackles, laws, and institutional barriers in subordinate roles. African Americans and women number heavily among this group. But individuals of differing sexual preference, the handicapped, and the chronically ill and disabled are all taking their rightful position as ongoing members of an ongoing society. These were the same groups that, among others, have been identified as needing championing by the social work profession. As the groups gain legitimacy, so do their issues, concerns, and problems. A role for social work seems a logical extension of these developments, and to the extent that these individuals increase their representation in the work force, a role for social work in the workplace is thereby developed.[19]

There has also been a dramatic shift in Americans' willingness to discuss and deal with sexual problems and concerns. What this change both stimulates and reflects is an even more powerful change, an increase in Americans' willingness to discuss the undiscussable. Sexual problems and concerns are only one of a series of undiscussables that have been brought to public view and are now openly discussed; child sexual abuse, the sexual rights and practices of the handicapped, feelings of shame and worthlessness engendered by an alcoholic parent are examples. Mechanisms for dealing with the flood of emotions released by this openness thereby become necessary. Helping has moved from the back room to the front window. It is now OK to ask for help and to receive help. Naisbett talks about this as a shift from independence to interdependence.[20]

And the helping is not done solely by professionals. Self-help groups of every stripe are formed regularly. Groups of people who have experienced miscarriages, groups of people whose children have been murdered, groups of people whose spouses have left them, groups of people who have shared a wide range of experiences get together to share support and engage in mutual emotional sustenance. Mental wellness is as OK as physical wellness. And much of the responsibility for wellness, has moved into the workplace. These societal-wide changes stimulate, reflect, and articulate with changes in the workplace and profession.

CHANGES IN THE WORKPLACE

The role of the workplace and its position in U.S. society are changing. As our society becomes more information driven, the value of the individual worker and the workplace condition in which that worker finds himself or herself become of increasing importance. For example, your life may be saved by an unbelievably competent surgeon operating in the nick of time, only to lose it because a sanitation worker is unable to read certain instructions about protective clothing. This illustrates the crucial importance of all members of the work force team. Indeed, the very concept of team has become a buzzword in the workplace. But attention to team implies and requires

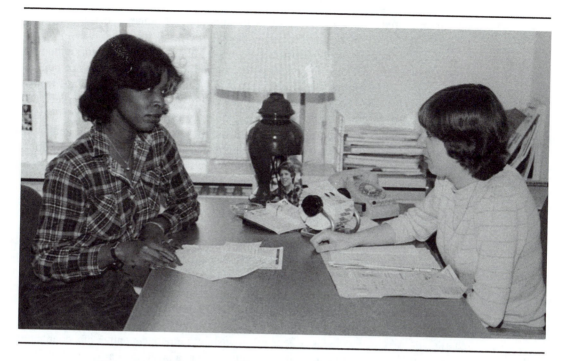

African Americans and women are two groups most affected by the rights revolution in the workplace. (Photo by Jane Latta.)

attention to the complex interactions, feelings, and passions that are let loose when individuals work together. If a member of a team cannot function or carry her or his weight because of alcohol abuse, substance abuse, or marriage or family problems, then these problems become, in effect, the team's problems. In years past, and perhaps to a great degree still today, such problems were ignored and not dealt with. When John came back from a three-martini lunch clearly unable to function, everyone worked around him and covered up for him. (Now it's called codependency.) But because of societal changes, it is now more legitimate to confront John with this issue and, because of the increased legitimacy of providing help, the offer to help is now considered part of the interdependence that makes the world work.

Alcohol advertising provides an example; early advertisements read in essence "if you drink, don't drive." The responsibility was on the drinking person. A greater recognition of interdependence characterizes the current ads, which emphasize the responsibility of those around the drinker not to let someone who has had too much to drink drive home. Intervention is legitimized by these advertisements. And while such intervention may occur at the cocktail party level, it may also occur through the help of a professional trained in alcohol abuse problems from the field of social work who has experience in dealing with issues of this kind and who can assist the organizational novice in the intervention process.

These kinds of interventions are based in part on human fellow feeling and concern for colleagues. But they are also motivated by a recognition that retraining a new worker to replace a fired worker is expensive. A small amount of money spent in assisting a worker to recover former capabilities may pay big dividends in productivity.

Teams emphasize the diversity of the worker population. Before, worker populations consisted heavily of white males with a sprinkling of others. Workplace populations are today heterogeneous, with African Americans and Asian Americans from a range of countries and backgrounds, men and women, older and younger workers, and so on.[21]

Diversity brings great strengths, but it also brings issues that cannot be dealt with by the old hierarchical method of ordering everyone to keep their nose to the grindstone. What are some of these issues? They run the range from pace and tempo of work, to preferred foods and recreations, to different attitudes toward time, discipline, cooperation versus competition, language, and family styles among others. Organizational development teams and human resources departments assist organizations in dealing with conflicts among cultures, with clashes of needs, and with the inevitable human frictions that result from the presence and the benefits of diversity. There are no magical solutions. Organizational development (OD) teams and professionals simply seek through discussions, group sessions, educational programs, and employee involvement to create a greater climate of understanding and acceptance.

The diverse work force has also brought a host of fresh issues that require processing: demands for on-site child care, for maternity and paternity leaves, for job sharing, of two career couples (where a firm wishes to hire one member of a couple but needs to assist the other member of the couple to find a position nearby), and of older workers. All present opportunities for social work in the workplace.

CHANGES IN THE PROFESSION

Societal and workplace changes may create opportunities, but whether a profession will seize them or not is a different question. The answer here is yes, although progress and change have been slower than one might have thought.

The most critical change perhaps from a professional context has been the development of psychotropic medication. Today, many individuals who would have been institutionalized and many who were institutionalized, are now in the community under medication, at work or applying for work. Workplaces realize that access to professional skill is important when working with employees who are being sustained by medication, but might need additional counseling.

The profession of social work was, in many ways, as institutionalized as the clients it served. Deinstitutionalizing them also deinstitutionalized the profession. Social work in the workplace became as natural as social work in the schools. After all, we have never had any particular problem in working in a school setting, that is, in a secondary setting, because it was a good place to work with children. Furthermore, some of the problems the children had concerned school-related issues specifically and being on site made a great deal of sense. The same could be said for medical or hospital social work. Fueled by the pressures of deinstitutionalization, help began to be extended to adults as well as children and to the workplace as well as the hospital and school.

A second issue has to do with pay. The social work profession is not overall very well paid. There are doubtless a variety of reasons for this situation. Among them has been social work's emphasis on the disadvantaged (and who wants to pay to help the poor), and the fact that pay discrimination within the social work profession is a version of pay discrimination among women in general. The profession has perhaps relied too much on the good will of its workers.

In any event, the liberation of women also liberated social work women. The opportunity for better pay for social work functions within the corporate setting was appealing to some social workers, though troubling to others, who felt that seeking better salaries was unseemly for social work.[22] Nonetheless, the opportunity was present and fueled by a sense of liberation. Women as well as men took up the corporate challenge.

A third change in the profession was an increased emphasis on outreach. It became increasingly clear to many professionals that sitting in one's office and waiting for the clients to come in was not sufficiently proactive. Even the staid managerial literature recognized the need for proactivity. The famous initials that Tom Peters invented, MBWA (management by walking around), stressed the need on the part of managers to get out of the office and mingle with the workers in the workplace. The same impetus toward outreach was stressed in the social work field. It had long been known, for example, that men as opposed to women were less cooperative clients. It finally occurred to professionals that the 9 to 5 office hours of many social workers created time frames at odds with the jobs of many potential male clients. Many could not get off for a social work interview during business hours. The idea of evening hours or Saturday hours began to develop, along with questions like "Why don't we have an office in the plant?" For the average adult member of the U.S. population, outreach means doing something in the workplace, since that is where these adults are during the day.[23]

These changes were both reflected and assisted by changes in the professional training of social work. After some opposition within many schools of social work, faculties accepted the development of and the implementation of joint programs with schools of business. (The opposition came from those who felt that the values of business and social work are too different.) The University of Michigan has such a program and there are similar programs at other universities. While large numbers of individuals are not gravitating to these programs, it still represents the endorsement of a direction and an alliance that has hitherto been seldom considered.

Other kinds of workplace-related programs are developing as well. For example, the University of Michigan has a social work in the workplace program. Even if the student does not join the joint MSW-MBA partnership, she or he can still get an emphasis on and a certificate in workplace-related concerns while studying within the MSW framework. Thus school preparation becomes a cutting edge activity signaling to the profession where new areas are developing, in this case, social work in the workplace. Courses in occupational social work and workplace social work are developing and research and scholarly work are being produced.[24] Thus, the schools reflect change as well as initiate it. The circle and cycle of change thus continue.

These three sets of changes—in society, in the workplace, and in the profession—mutually reinforce each other. They have together created a development in which social work activity in the workplace has increased substantially.

Social Work in the Workplace

In the last quarter of the twentieth century the role of social work in the workplace has begun to truly blossom.

RECENT DEVELOPMENTS

The movement began with the overall societal change, the increased recognition that employee well-being was essential to employee productivity. This insight may seem trivial today, and in some sense employee well-being has always been seen as necessary (or just assumed); but what happened when employee well-being was not present varied greatly. In the past the employee was simply fired and a new employee was ordered up from the vast pool of potential employee immigrants who were flowing to these shores from abroad. Employee well-being was, therefore, seen as solely the responsibility of the employee. The employer assumed little responsibility for employee well-being, even if the employee became ill or injured directly as a result of work activity. Claims of workplace-caused injuries were often vigorously fought by employers. Naturally the more subtle complaints against sexual harassment, racial discrimination, or negative and hostile cultures that reduced work life to a daily, anxiety-filled interval had even less credibility.[25]

Increased interest in employee well-being has increased the presence of social workers in the workplace. At the same time a range of social policy concerns has come to the fore for which social workers can be helpful. Affirmative action legislation involved social workers in designing and implementing programs. Legislative activity that made it more difficult to fire employees increased the value of employees already present and involved social workers in the process of helping those employees. New rules on occupational safety targeted employers as a causal factor in harming or potentially harming employees and pinpointed them as the responsible parties for correcting hazardous working conditions. Social workers as community relations officers helped work with affected communities. These forces, among others, set the stage for the entry of social workers into the workplace

ALCOHOL AND SUBSTANCE ABUSE

The abuse of alcohol provided the most substantial opening wedge for social workers in the workplace. Alcohol abuse is widespread in U.S. society, and it may be this fact that allowed it to play a major role in opening up corporate coffers to pay for employee assistance. After all, corporate executives were as likely to know about or have experienced the problems of alcohol as those to whom the program was offered. Alcohol abuse was initially thought of as essentially a blue-collar problem. Drinking on the job and then sick days off because of alcohol-related accidents became subjects of concern. What was new was a willingness to discuss the undiscussable. Pretense was stripped away. We needed to intervene for the benefit of the team and the workplace, as well as out of concern for the individual. These new legitimacies fueled a range of agencies and programs. Employee assistance programs (EAPs) provided substance abuse counseling and intervention to employees who were identified as having alcohol and substance abuse problems (EAPs started to develop about 1975).

In these programs, the leverage of the employer can be used to overcome the counterleverage of denial that many substance-abusing clients evince. However, the use of this leverage created as yet unresolved ethical problems within the profession. The same problems occur when social workers work in probation and parole. Personal change is thought to be truly effective only when voluntary.[26] The voluntaristic aspect of social work clienthood has always been a hallmark value. It is troubling to think that individuals can be forced into a change mode because of what an employer, judge, or probation officer says. The use of force is not part of our background.

Strong counterarguments exist, however. Is it appropriate, we might ask, to wait until somebody has reached bottom before intervening? While every alcohol problem may not be recognized, certainly many will.

And it is reasonable to ask whether the authority of the workplace ("Joe, if you want to keep on working here, you'd better get into treatment") is any less noxious than the authority of information ("Joe," his doctor said, "if you keep on drinking, you will die"), or the authority of persuasion (Joe's family gathered around, told him how much they cared for him, and sought to convince him that treatment was appropriate). In any event, these questions will continue to be asked, as they should be. But, while discussion goes on, programs go forward, and many organizations now have EAPs, and these programs have social workers as clinicians and managers. Still other social workers have formed their own organizations and contract employee assistance services to target firms.

FROM ALCOHOL ASSISTANCE TO EMPLOYEE ASSISTANCE

Although initial intervention occurred around alcohol and substance abuse concerns specifically, needs for other kinds of counseling rapidly emerged. After all, if we can counsel an alcohol or drug abuser, why not a wife or child abuser? If we can deal with an individual who drank to overcome the pain of a ruptured relationship or grief-stricken loss, why can't we deal with that pain or loss even though alcohol or another substance is not involved?

The answer is that we can, and employee assistance programs are now expanding rapidly to provide a wide range of counseling and help services to employees. Employers are not insensitive to the fact that providing some of these services themselves may save them fringe benefit dollars paid on behalf of individual clients to outside professionals. It may be cheaper to have your own counselors and psychiatrists than to pay market rates on an ad hoc basis. But, as always, self-interest is mixed with concern for others. And the correct analysis sees both factors as powerful and operative.

But Jim Francek, ACSW, who has developed an independent firm (Watershed Corporate Services, Inc.), comments as follows in the foreword to an NASW study of occupational social work:

> In many places the nature of work itself has changed. The rapid implementation of new information technology has redistributed the direction and flow of power within

organizations. Whole levels of organization have been deemed no longer necessary. The race for companies to be both high producers and low-cost competitors has left many individuals at a loss. Often, they experience troubling changes which may include loss of familiar work, experienced co-workers, job security, a sense of future career, loyalty to the company, and in many cases, even one's job.

As people experience these transitions, tremendous pressures act upon them. From my perspective, this set of circumstances creates critical points of growth for people involved. Insofar as we, as social workers, are experienced and see ourselves as agents for positive change for both individuals and groups, we come ready to address the complex experience of work as we know it today. The difference between companies that will remain healthy and those that will not, to a great extent, depends on how they treat their human resources. If they choose to over-burden, burn out and discard those resources, they will reap the eventual results of such policies. If, on the other hand, the leaders of the workforce create a context for positive and creative change, they will reap the benefits of that approach. "What goes around, comes around."[27]

It is this sentiment that inspires occupational social workers.

OTHER WORK AREAS IN BUSINESS

Employee assistance programs are not the only places where social workers work in the workplace. Considering some of the historical social welfare concerns that businesses have had, there is ample opportunity for social work professionals to fill positions in a range of other areas. Social workers work as members of human resources departments doing, in effect, community organization, organizational development, cultural change, and a whole range of organizational improvement activities which do not have much to do specifically with the clinical process of interpersonal helping. Social workers are also becoming influential in the area of corporate philanthropy, serving as the contact person for outside individuals who wish to involve the organization in charitable endeavors. And social workers are beginning to seek personnel positions.

Nonetheless, social workers have not yet begun to tap the range of positions available to them. Social workers do use specific social work skills in counseling, interpersonal practice, community organization, and elsewhere to good effect within the workplace. However, increasingly large numbers of social workers are beginning to do what lawyers have always done; they use social work training as a generic basic training for a wide range of corporate positions. Hence, we should not think that the role of social workers in the workplace is limited to specific social work jobs; rather, there are a wide range of other opportunities for which social work training is an appropriate preparation.

DEMOGRAPHY

It is hard to know how many social workers are working in the workplace/occupational arena. A study by NASW in 1985 identified 2,200 individuals from a variety of lists. Questionnaires were sent to these individuals and 1068 (47%) were returned. The numbers that follow are based on this survey.[28]

Most workplace/occupational social workers (79.2%) have the MSW degree, are white (90%), and work in the Northeast (45%). While males are in a minority in the

Northeast region (39.9%), males predominate in the other three regions (North Central, 52.7%; South, 58%; and West, 52.4%).[29]

The respondents held a variety of occupational titles. Among them were employee assistance, 28.5%; business function, 21.5%; and social work, 9%.[30]

The compensation picture (in 1985) is complex. The median income was $32,950 (compared to the 1982 NASW median of $21,303).[31] Within this group, 1.4% made less than $10,000; 3.6% made more than $65,000. Compensation differed greatly by the auspice of employment among other variables.

The study reports the following differences: employees of private profit-making organizations had a median salary of $38,268 (the high), while those working for the private, nonprofit sector (religious) organizations had a median income of $22,999.[32]

An interesting difference by race occurs. White males had a median income of $35,187; black males, $40,999; white females, $29,624; and black females, $31,249.

The following clusters of task were identified, with some showing close affinity to others: linkages; case planning and management; therapeutic intervention; quality assurance; group work; crisis evaluation; protective service; teaching daily living skills; providing tangible service; advocacy; interpersonal problem solving; mediation skill based instruction; classroom instruction; staffing; program management; fiscal management; data analysis; program development; community outreach.

This survey suggests that social work in the workplace is a broad area, with many tasks and jobs available. It seems to attract more men than other areas, and perhaps that is part of the reason that the pay is better. Hundreds of social workers are involved in a variety of ways in occupational/workplace social work, and the field promises to expand in the future.

Conclusion

This century has seen the beginning of an explosion with respect to social work roles in the workplace. Previous social welfare activities on the part of business and industry set the stage. The curtain was opened by societal changes that placed increased emphasis on the importance of worker well-being. Workplace changes and changes in the profession provided the lights. The play was authored by alcohol and to a lesser extent by general concern over substance abuse within the workplace context. Having begun, however, this play began to take on an extra life of its own. A focus on alcohol problems expanded into a concern with worker problems whether or not they were specifically related to alcohol. From these two jump points, social workers began to take positions in human resources departments, organizational development, personnel offices and executive suites. Some social workers have continued their specifically social work identification and activity. Other social workers, although continuing their social work identification, have undertaken a broader range of activities and view social work training as more general preparation for a wider range of workplace tasks.

In sum, we see the opportunity for explosive growth to be present and waiting. Whether or not the social work profession will be able to exploit this opportunity or not remains to be seen. Professions in general, and social work is no exception here, are not known for their willingness to embrace change. Many colleagues still feel that working for business and industry is somehow selling out. Still others feel that social work's historical mission was focused on and should remain focused on the disadvantaged. The employed are not considered in that group. Counterarguments, however, arise as rapidly as complaints. Problems are problems, people say, and the pain of an alcohol problem is not necessarily made better or worse by being black or white, male or female, rich or poor. The question is whether the dissension will continue while development continues or whether it will stifle forward development and become, instead of constructive discussion about different perspectives on helping in the helping profession, noxious name calling in which each party seeks to tar the other with the brush of some ideological lapse.

Notes

1. P. Kurtzman, "Industrial Social Work (Occupational Social Work)" and M. L. Davis-Sacks and Y. Hasenfeld, "Organizations: Impact on Employees and Community" in A. Minahan, ed., *Encyclopedia of Social Work,* 18th ed. (Silver Spring, Md.: National Association of Social Workers, 1987). Vol. I, pp. 899–910 and Vol. 2, pp. 217–228.
2. Ibid., Vol. 2, p. 221. They refer to W. Scott and D. Hart, *Organizational America* (Boston: Houghton Mifflin, 1979), p. 89.
3. Ibid., p. 218. The authors also review numerous studies of worker losses due to plant closings and organization reconfiguration.
4. The social work community had, for many years, been criticized as unbusinesslike because it took a more humane attitude toward employees. It is ironic that when advocated by the social work community this perspective was dismissed. These same orientations constitute what has come to be called Japanese management techniques and are now widely accepted.
5. In the early 1980s, the corporate social welfare system spent around $400 billion, about the same as the public welfare system. Kurtzman, "Industrial Social Work," p. 899.
6. Upton Sinclair, *The Jungle* (Champaign: University of Illinois Press, 1906). Muckrakers were writers and journalists who, shortly after the turn of the century, began to publicly expose, through press and book, the urban and industrial problems so long ignored.
7. Kurtzman, "Industrial Social Work," p. 902.
8. "The company store" is a term given to stores that were operated by companies (mining companies were one, but others as well) that the workers were encouraged or obliged to use and that in many instances exploited workers through enmeshing them in debt to the company through their store purchases. It was not seen by society in general as helpful, but rather as another way to exploit the workers.
9. Douglas MacGregor, *The Human Side of Enterprise* (New York: McGraw-Hill Book Co., 1960).
10. R. Bellah and others, *Habits of the Heart* (New York: Harper & Row, 1986).
11. U.S. Bureau of the Census, *Statistical Abstract of the United States, 1990* 110th ed. (Washington, D.C.: U.S. Government Printing Office, 1990), p. 373, Table 623.
12. James Ricci, "The Autoworkers and the Dumpster," *Detroit Free Press,* November 15, 1989, pp. 11a.
13. Kurtzman, "Industrial Social Work," pp. 900–901. He quotes from S. Akabas and P. Kurtzman, eds., *Work, Workers and Organizations: A View from Social Work* (Englewood Cliffs, N.J.: Prentice Hall, 1982), pp. 201–202.
14. Ibid., p. 900.
15. Of course, the employee makes a contribution as well.
16. See John E. Tropman and Carol Kinny, "Fringe Benefits," unpublished, the University of Michigan.
17. Larry Root, "Employee Benefits and Income Security: Private Social Policy and the Public Interest," and S. Quattrociocchi, "Fringe Benefits as Social Policy," in J. E. Tropman, M.

Dluhy and R. Lind, eds., *New Strategic Perspective on Social Policy* (Elmsford, N.Y.: Pergamon Press, 1981), pp. 97–109 and 422–433.

18. It is also important to note that pay in corporations often compares favorably with pay in social work agencies.

19. In some respects, the change is not so great. Certainly working class women and minority men and women have always worked. But now large numbers of women of all types are working, and there is a greater representation of minorities in key sports and in women's sports.

20. John Naisbett, *Megatrends* (New York: Warner Books, 1982).

21. Of course this case should not be overstated. Diversity in the workplace can still mean diverse groups of workers who are similar within the group—groups of whites, groups of African Americans, and so on.

22. We are referring here to social workers who work for companies as social workers. Some social workers, work for companies in corporate capacities that only indirectly use their professional training.

23. Of course, to be really effective, social work might take a leaf from the Televangelists, and develop "Telesocialwork Programming."

24. A recent title is S. Straussner, *Occupational Social Work Today* (Binghamton, N.Y.: Haworth Press, 1990) See also the bibliography of Kurtzman, "Industrial Social Work."

25. A negative or hostile culture is one in which the very atmosphere of work is tinged with trouble. For example, some cultures of men use profanity, make sexual jokes, show sexual photos, as an ongoing part of what they usually do. For a woman, entering such a culture may be exceptionally stressful. She may find herself the constant butt of sexual jokes, the constant recipient of sexual innuendoes, and so on.

26. As a California light bulb story goes; how many people does it take to change a light bulb in California? Only one, but the light bulb has to really want to change.

27. J. Francek, "Foreword," in R. Teare, ed., *National Survey of Occupational Social Workers* (Silver Spring, Md.: National Association of Social Workers, 1987), p. vii.

28. Ibid.

29. Ibid., p. 10.

30. Ibid., p. 18.

31. Ibid., p. 21. Recall that this sample is heavily male; NASW membership is heavily female.

32. Ibid., p. 22.

CHAPTER 16
Service Delivery for Enhancing the Environment and Housing

Introduction

How to study, modify, and protect the environment is typically the domain of biological and physical scientists and the professions that draw on these disciplines, such as engineering, public health, and medicine. Housing has often been the concern of architects and city planners. It is our contention, however, that environmental factors and housing affect many of the issues that social workers deal with; thus, it is a mistake for social workers to leave these fields entirely to other disciplines and professions. Consequently, in this chapter we discuss social work's role and concerns in the areas of environment and housing. The roles of social workers in these areas have not been well worked out; this chapter, therefore, seeks to open up perspectives and possibilities for social work.

The Functions of Systems
That Focus on the Environment and Housing

The idea that the quality of the environment can be a problem is of recent origin. Previously, when people engaged in their occupations and their activities, they seldom thought these had an impact on the health and welfare of humans and other living things. The air they breathed, the water they drank, the land that produced the food they ate, the raw materials for their houses, and the fuel that kept them warm seemed limitless and unaffected by human consumption.

Historically, people created problems by the way they treated their environments, but these were likely to be local and limited in nature. As R. F. Dasmann stated:

> For the most part, however, primitive man survived because his numbers were small and his technology limited, and he was unable to do any major harm to his environment. Even so, the only powerful technique that he possessed, the use of fire, was used virtually without discrimination and greatly modified many areas of the Earth. Animals were exterminated by effective, indiscriminately applied hunting techniques.[1]

Dasmann also discusses the impact of agricultural practices of earlier societies. He points out that they could not destroy forests because of their limited technology, but they could affect the fertility of the soil. Nevertheless, they moved on to new sites before they did serious harm. An exception was that of grassland soils and dryer forest areas and "In the Asiatic homelands of Western agriculture, there is widespread evidence of serious soil damage and loss during ancient times."[2]

We now have reached a historical period in which the consequences of human actions cross state and national boundaries and are even worldwide. Examples are nuclear plant disasters, nuclear bomb testing, global warming trends as a consequence of human technology, the decreasing supply of fossil fuels, oil spills, and industrial contamination of water supplies and the soil.

The systems developed to deal with these issues have had several functions. One function centers on the preservation of wild nature for psychological and even esthetic reasons. This concern was a major force behind the creation of national parks. The prevention of the extinction of living species is seen as worthwhile in its own right and not because of a use of the species for human consumption.

Another function is more utilitarian and seeks to prevent the use of a resource in such a way as to damage or destroy it. Examples are measures to prevent soil depletion, water contamination, and air pollution. A related issue is that of the waste or exhaustion of natural resources. Measures that lead to recycling of resources, substituting the use of plentiful resources for scarce ones, and using a resource more sparingly are related to this function.

A third function pertains to preventing major environmental catastrophes. This includes efforts to stop nuclear testing or even the use of nuclear power in any way that is potentially dangerous and to prohibit the creation of products that can destroy the earth's ozone layer.

Housing issues are of a somewhat different order but also represent an environmental component that has a very contemporary aspect. Preindustrial societies, however primitive their housing, tended by contemporary standards to make provision for those considered to be members of the society. The industrial revolution required large concentrations of people. It created crowded populations who lived in inadequate housing but were not homeless. The latter problem has been a consequence of several types of circumstances.

The first is that of unemployment and poverty in which some people cannot pay for housing, even if it is cheap or available. This problem becomes more acute when a society experiences an economic depression. Large numbers of people then lose their incomes and are evicted when they cannot pay their rent or mortgages. The function of housing programs, in these instances, is to either supply low-cost housing or a housing subsidy, or both.

The second circumstance is even more of a contemporary phenomenon than the first. It is a result of deinstitutionalization policies. Many people, such as those suffering from mental illness and the aged, were formerly housed in large institutions but now have been thrust on the community. They suffer from the problems of poverty and the lack of low-cost housing just referred to, but also are handicapped by the unwillingness of many landlords to rent to them and of their families to retain them. In addition, they may have requirements for suitable housing that cannot be met. An example is an elderly person who cannot climb stairs and who needs a bathroom that can accommodate a wheel chair. One function of housing programs in these situations is the creation of suitable housing for these special populations. Another has been to intervene with the individuals themselves to help them adapt to the available housing.

The third set of circumstances is the general lack of affordable housing in our society.

The cost of housing is staggering, and the consequences are profound for social workers' most vulnerable clients. During the past 15 years, housing costs have accelerated almost three times faster than incomes. From 1981 to 1987, rents increased 16 percent more than commodity prices in general and now are at their highest level in more than 2 decades. More than 6 million American households pay half or more of their income for rent. Of these, 4.7 million pay 60 percent or more, far beyond the widely accepted standard of 30 percent. Of homeowners with mortgages, 2 million pay half or more of their income for housing. In 1949, the average 30-year-old could buy a home using 14 percent of his or her income. This figure now has risen to 44 percent of income.[3]

The function of housing programs with reference to this third issue has primarily been to create affordable housing. This has involved preservation of housing as well as expanding the supply.

The Function of Social Work in Enhancing the Environment and Housing

We believe that social workers have many functions with respect to the environment and housing despite our earlier assertion that these are not typically social work domains. This is because many problems that social workers deal with are caused or exacerbated by the conditions of the environment and housing: it is inappropriate and even impossible to deal with interpersonal and emotional issues when people are struggling to secure wholesome food or adequate housing.

In addition, some problems that social workers focus on result from environmental conditions. Examples are the sick child whose illness results from lead poisoning, the family struggling to survive because the wage earners in the family have malignancies caused by exposure to asbestos in the workplace, and the mother whose earning capacity is limited due to obesity resulting from an inability to afford the right foods. Admittedly, the required immediate response to these conditions is medical. Nevertheless, social workers do focus on prevention, and this involves them with others who are struggling with these conditions.

Social workers help empower people to change the circumstances that oppress them. Thus, social workers engaged in community organization activities often target some aspect of the environment. Early settlement workers were engaged in this activity. Jane Addams of Hull House in Chicago was appointed to a neighborhood sanitation position; other settlement workers, such as Lilian Wald of Henry Street Settlement (originally Nurses Settlement) in New York, came from the nursing profession, which provided a good basis for their understanding of unhealthy environments.

Social workers deal with environmental and housing issues at every level of their activity. When working with individuals and families, they often see the consequences of environmental problems. Examples are physical illnesses and the stress and fatigue caused by environmental conditions. The tasks of the social worker in these situations include helping the individuals to cope with their circumstances, as well as to escape from or change their environments. Governmental agencies may be utilized to enforce environmental standards. Although we do not believe the major solution for housing problems is modifying tenants' behavior, we agree that at times this is necessary.

It is also appropriate for social workers to help people become conscious of environmental threats and to affiliate with groups established to fight them. The same is true of tenants' and other groups that assist individuals to demand their rights from landlords. To help such groups to deal with environmental concerns, social workers will need substantive knowledge regarding the environment and housing. Social work curricula seldom include environmental content. Such curricula include housing information a little more frequently. With a greater realization of the implications of an ecological approach, these kinds of data should find a place in schools of social work. Social workers should be able to learn enough to interact with other professionals in joint efforts to ensure a more healthy environment.

Social workers also have a role to play in their agencies with regard to these issues. Agencies should make resources available to their staff and clients to help them deal with environmental concerns. An example is the Franklin-Wright Settlement in Detroit, which worked with community residents to establish a corporation to create more housing in the area.

At the community level, social workers must help residents to prioritize their community concerns and to have sufficient awareness of environmental and housing issues to seriously consider them. The workers must be able to draw on expertise from other professions to ensure that these concerns are effectively met.

Whether at the agency, community, or societal levels social workers should be involved in influencing environmental policy. They are not likely to have expertise on many environmental issues, but they should be aware of the problems the environment can cause for people. Their role should be able to point out these problems and should advocate for the right of people to live in healthy environments. With respect to housing, many social workers have developed high levels of knowledge regarding the housing needs of people and how to meet these needs.

Social work education must do a better job of educating social workers regarding these matters. Thus social workers must have more knowledge regarding human biology and the natural environment. The Council on Social Work Education now insists that biology should be a prerequisite for a social work educational program. The profession has always recognized that social workers need specialized knowledge related to their chosen fields of service yet have often failed to see the importance of the kind of proficiency we refer to here.

Values and Ideologies for Services to Enhance the Environment and Housing

The oppressed and disadvantaged populations suffer most from environmental and housing problems. An important social work value, therefore, in relationship to the environment and housing is to point out the human consequences of any plan that focuses on these problems. Social work shares many values in this area with environmentalists and conservationists. As Dasmann states:

> By the 1970's achievement of the highest sustainable quality of living for mankind by the rational utilization of the environment had become the definition of conserva-

tion that was most widely accepted by such organizations as the International Union for the Conservation of Nature and Natural Resources. The emphasis was on man [sic]; by stressing the quality of living rather than the sustained production of commodities, however, the scope of the definition was broadened so that conservation now includes, in addition to the protection of wild nature to enrich the life of man, the control or elimination of environmental pollution in its many manifestations.[4]

This stance, however, presents a number of dilemmas for all concerned with these issues. First, there can be conflicts between two sets of values: the protection of wild nature and the use of natural resources to meet the needs of humans for food and housing. For example, should an area be preserved as a park or used as a location for low-cost housing? Another example is whether farmland should be used for housing. In addition, what appears to be a conflict between meeting one need, such as food, and another need, housing, is actually due to more complex economic considerations. Thus, much farmland is being destroyed by a combination of economic forces. These include the plight of the small farmer and the market for large and expensive houses in the continuously growing suburban areas around some cities. The values placed on environmental preservation must be informed by a good understanding of the economic, sociological, and political circumstances surrounding all environmental planning efforts.

An Overview of Services for Enhancing the Environment and Housing

HISTORY OF ENVIRONMENTAL SERVICES

From earliest times, humans engaged in practices that were harmful to the environment as well as practices intended to preserve it. There are many ancient instances of species that became extinct because humans destroyed them and of land whose fertility was similarly ruined.[5] However, some animal species were protected by religious taboos and vegetation areas were guarded by being designated as sacred.

Early civilizations such as the Phoenicians and the Incas created systems of terracing to inhibit soil erosion.[6] And other early societies, such as the Romans, Japanese, and Chinese, developed an understanding of what to do to maintain soil fertility. Nevertheless, the scope of these matters was controlled by the comparatively small number of humans and the limitations of their energy and machinery in inflicting widespread destruction on the environment.

As the capacity of humans to harm their environment grew, this affected all continents. This was most severe in North America; according to Dasmann,

> The great herds of wildlife that inhabited the plains and prairies vanished as hunters reduced the numbers of bison, elk, antelope, and deer. Even the larger predatory animals were nearly exterminated, and some of them—varieties of grizzly bear, cougar, and wolf—subsequently became extinct. Many types of birds that once had occurred in great abundance—e.g., the passenger pigeon, Carolina paroquet, and heath hen—were wiped out. Logging and fires combined to menace the once luxurious forests of New England, the states surrounding the Great Lakes, and the South. The

grasslands were overgrazed, and in some areas such as California native vegetation was eliminated over most of its range and replaced by species of European and Asian origin.[7]

Because of this, the conservation movement got its start in North America. Some pioneers were George Catlin, a painter and writer, who proposed a national park system in the 1830s, and William Bartram, a botanist, and John James Audubon, an ornithologist, who about the same time suggested preserving wildlife. Shortly afterward, the writers Ralph Waldo Emerson and Henry David Thoreau argued that the survival of nature was linked to the psychological well-being of people. The first text on conservation, *Man and Nature,* was published in the 1860s.[8]

Developments related to the preservation of nature continued throughout the nineteenth century almost everywhere in the world. A comprehensive and integrated approach did not develop to any significant degree, however, until after World War II. At that time, the quality of the air and water became a matter of serious concern, as did the danger posed by radioactive fallout from atomic and hydrogen bomb testing. Many countries, consequently, developed government agencies focused on the environment. The United States, for example, passed the National Environmental Policy Act in 1969 to coordinate environmental efforts.

Despite these national efforts, environmental problems became more severe. These included pollution of the oceans, the spread of water and air damage from pesticides, contamination from radioactive materials, and oil spills at sea.[9] A number of international conferences were held, and the World Health Organization and the World Meteorological Organization began to monitor pollution levels.

An international research effort, the International Biological Programme, has identified many of the natural biological communities in need of protection. Additional organizations involved in this type of effort are the International Union for the Conservation of Nature and such United Nations units as the Food and Agricultural Organization and the UN Educational, Scientific, and Cultural Organization. Nevertheless, such international organizations have often lacked the power to do much more than inform national and international organizations of the problems.

The following are a few examples of the kinds of problems that exist today:

(1) "[A]ir pollution has driven many forms of agriculture from the Los Angeles basin, has had a serious effect upon the pine forests in nearby mountains, and has caused respiratory distress, particularly in children. elderly people, and those suffering from respiratory diseases."[10]

(2) "Tokyo has such a serious air-pollution problem that oxygen is supplied to policemen who direct traffic at busy intersections."[11]

(3) "Thus, as a result of the growing worldwide consumption of fossil fuels, atmospheric carbon dioxide levels have increased steadily since 1900, and the rate of increase is accelerating. Now the output of carbon dioxide is believed by some to have reached a point such that it may exceed both the capacity of plant life to remove it from the atmosphere and the rate at which it goes into solution in the oceans. In the atmosphere carbon dioxide creates a 'greenhouse effect.' Like glass in a greenhouse, it allows light rays from the sun to pass through, but it does not allow the heat rays generated when sunlight is absorbed by the surface of the ground to escape."[12]

The air we breathe. (United Nations photo/FAO/F. Botts.)

(4) "Mining for coal has created widespread devastation in the Appalachian mountains, in Bohemia (Czechoslovakia), and, in the past, in England and Germany because deposits in these regions are found near the surface."[13]

(5) Plant and animal species have been exploited for their commercial value. Examples are the removal of mahogany trees in the Caribbean, the extensive hunting of whales, and the use of crocodile, tiger, and leopard skins for high-fashion products.[14] It is estimated that an original population of 200,000 blue whales in the Antarctic was reduced by 1965 to about 2,000.[15] The same kind of reduction in numbers occurred for other species of whales. The International Whaling Convention in 1946 made an effort to avoid total extinction through a system of scientific controls. This did not work well for several decades, but recent actions have been taken that may better serve this purpose. Steps to limit the destruction of animals used for fashion products have often been ineffective because the money people in wealthy nations are willing to pay for such products is very hard for poor people to resist in the nations where such animals live.

(6) All the above problems stem from people's demands for various kinds of resources. Thus, an important variable is the number of people on the planet. July 11, 1987, was designated as the Day of Five Billion by the United Nations Fund for Population Activities to mark the likely day on which the world's population reached this number. According to one authority, the following population increases are projected:

The latest UN medium (most probable) estimates projected that world population would reach six billion in 1999, seven billion in 2010, eight billion in 2022, and stabilize at around ten billion late in the 21st century. Well over 90% of future growth would take place in the less developed countries of Africa, Asia (minus Japan), and Latin America, which accounted for about 73% of world population in 1987.[16]

It is likely that this degree of population growth will be associated with famines and other disasters in precisely those areas of the world that can least handle them. This makes it incumbent on all relevant professions, which certainly includes social work, to strive in ethical ways to slow the increase in the population. Our main point is that preserving the quality of the environment cannot be separated from this issue.

Many organizations engaged in dealing with population issues employ social workers. One example is Planned Parenthood; social workers in that setting have helped people determine the size of the families they desire. Another is agencies that work with adolescent parents. In those settings, social workers have helped teenagers to plan their education and careers while learning to be responsible with regard to sexuality. Social workers, together with others, have devised educational programs on family planning for use in both industrialized and nonindustrialized societies.

HISTORY OF HOUSING SERVICES

The quality of housing for poor people has been a concern to urban reformers throughout the history of the United States. Nevertheless, until comparatively recently, studies of the adequacy of housing were few. It is also hard to compare studies conducted at different time as standards have changed regarding what is adequate housing and, as one authority points out, early surveys of housing adequacy were seldom based on expert inspection of premises.[17] The same author indicates, however, that studies of housing since World War II have made use of similar standards, which allowed for a "reasonable approximation of housing quality," and census surveys included data relevant to this.[18]

Substandard housing is defined to include major shortcomings in the foundations, walls, and roofs, as well as substantial external damage. Poor original construction such as "shacks with makeshift walls or roofs or dirt floors is also included,"[19] as well as houses that do not have a toilet or bathing facilities.

The picture with regard to such substandard dwellings has changed somewhat in the last few decades. The 1960 census showed, for example, that 8.5 million families or 16% of all U.S. families were living in substandard housing.[20] By the 1980s, however, the overall quality of housing had improved and the issue became much more whether it was affordable. From 1940 to 1990, there was a steady decrease in the crowded housing and a gradual elimination of the worst housing.[21] Nevertheless, many people either had to spend a larger proportion of their income on housing or accept less adequate housing than previously.[22]

Before the depression the social philosophy of the United States was primarily oriented toward depending on free enterprise to meet housing needs. A major shift took place in 1937 with the passage of a Housing Act that supported the creation of public housing projects. This direction continued after World War II because of the backup of housing needs developed during the Depression and war years.

Another housing act, passed in 1949, provided for a public housing program of

135,000 units each year for six years and for slum clearance and urban redevelopment. The latter provisions were intended to provide locations on which housing could be constructed by private enterprise. This act had as its aim "a decent home and a suitable living environment for every American family."[23]

Another shift took place in 1950 when Congress reduced the appropriation for housing with the assumption that private enterprise would do the job if interest rates were low. The alternative that was created was the Federal National Mortgage Association (Fanny May). Even this alternative was handicapped when Congress eliminated the program that had liberalized Federal Housing Authority (FHA) mortgage terms.

In January 1966, the Nixon administration began an experiment through which private builders built houses that were subsequently purchased by various levels of government and rented to families who met eligibility requirements. These types of programs for subsidizing housing were seen as a desirable alternative to the large, low-income projects that were the thrust of housing programs during the previous decade. The projects were now seen as undesirable because of the unattractiveness of many of them, combined with their tendency to become islands of poverty within which many social problems, such as vandalism, drug use, and crime, could flourish.

The Housing and Urban Development Act of 1968 provided government financial assistance to help low-income families to acquire individual or cooperative home ownership, mainly through substantially reducing interest rates. Another section of this act subsidized mortgage holders so they could charge low rentals and still make a profit.

As a result of these types of programs and the state of the economy, in the early 1970s housing production significantly increased, but this has to be matched against increases in the number of new households. As Frieden states,

> Measured against household formations, even this production record marked a slippage from the recent past. From 1950 to 1960 and again from 1960 to 1970, the number of new housing units averaged 1.6 times the number of new households. In these two decades the production surplus made possible steady and widespread improvements in the quality of American housing for people of all income levels. From 1970 to 1974, however, new production averaged only 1.4 times the number of new households. With this relative decline in the production of surplus housing the trend toward improvement undoubtedly slowed in pace.[24]

To add to the problem of maintaining momentum in the creation of housing, in January 1973, President Nixon placed a moratorium on many federal programs, including housing, and impounded congressional appropriations for this purpose. This contributed to a housing recession and widespread unemployment in the housing industry.

President Ford signed the Housing and Community Development Act in August 1974. Part of this act consolidated community development programs by providing for block grants for urban renewal. The federal agency responsible for administering this was the Department of Housing and Urban Development (HUD). State housing and development agencies were also eligible to borrow funds for slum rehabilitation, and the federal government guaranteed this money. In addition, federal subsidies for rehabilitation of 400,000 units of old housing and the creation of new housing were provided.

All these programs provided some support to a housing industry that had just experienced a very difficult period. The national economic picture was still quite bleak, however, and this had very negative effects on efforts to attain better and less expensive housing.

Throughout the rest of the 1970s and 1980s, the approaches just described for increasing housing availability for low-income families continued. To summarize, these included programs that (1) help communities preserve and upgrade neighborhoods, (2) provide direct loan and loan guarantees to underwrite the private sector's risk for lending mortgage money, and (3) support nonprofit housing groups. A major part of federal housing policy continues to be the deductions allowed homeowners on their income taxes related to housing. Commenting on this, Dluhy states,

> Ironically, federal tax policy, by default, has become the dominant strand of national housing policy. Without other initiatives, it appears that the Reagan administration hopes that macro-economic policy, which fosters economic growth and lower interest rates, will eventually pay off in a more privatized housing market in which credit is more readily available for middle- and upper-class home owners. The lower class, given this view, will benefit primarily from filtering and, when necessary, housing assistance in the form of vouchers.[25]

A 1990 *New York Times* article summarized the current situation with regard to public housing.[26] The largest proportion of tenants continue to be people of low income, including those who have many needs for social services. This latter problem has occurred because of preference given in some authorities to people least able to care for themselves, such as those who are mentally or physically ill or who suffer from disabilities. In Chicago, for example, more than 80% of the city's 200,000 housing tenants were on welfare. The same article further summarizes the situation as follows:

> The debate has sharpened as the Federal Government has reduced its role in providing new housing and the nation's stock of privately owned low-income housing has declined because of gentrification, the demolition of many single-room-occupancy hotels and the conversion of many apartments to condominiums. Meanwhile the number of low-income households has grown.
>
> This has put more pressure on the nation's existing stock of 1.4 million public housing units as housing of last resort, as more and more people crowd waiting lists for the few vacancies that open each year.
>
> Although the demand for public housing units varies greatly from city to city, a survey in 1986 counted 247,500 families on lists waiting for vacancies among 374,150 units in 64 cities. It also counted 32,555 elderly people on lists for 103,203 units for the elderly.

Selected Components in Detail

HOUSING AND HOMELESSNESS

Social workers have three types of roles with relationship to housing issues.[27] The first, based on their knowledge of the needs of people, is to promote public policies that enhance the amount and adequacy of housing. This is especially true with regard to that available to low-income people, as well as to the elderly, handicapped, mentally ill, and minorities. This task will fall most heavily on workers in agencies that serve these groups, such as public welfare, mental health, and older adult organizations. These workers must keep informed about the adequacy of housing available to their constituencies and must advocate with respect to housing in the relevant legislative bodies. In addition, social workers may be employed in agencies engaged in social planning, such as federal, state, and local housing organizations.

Many members of the groups just referred to require special housing facilities, such as halfway houses and group homes, partly because of the policy of deinstitutionalization. Even when resources are made available for these facilities, community pressures of the "not in my backyard" variety can prevent their creation. Social workers in these situations must develop the kinds of community organization skills needed to diminish local opposition. Such skills involve engaging in community education, mobilizing support from allies, and, when necessary, using tactics to negate those used by the opposition.

Social workers who have acquired housing knowledge may also manage public housing projects, as well as provide a variety of services to residents of such housing. At various times, appropriations for public housing and the operating budgets of such housing have included support for social welfare functions, including the allocation of space for a variety of community services.

A major step in this regard occurred in 1971 when the Departments of Health, Education, and Welfare and Housing and Urban Development authorized agreements between state welfare departments and housing authorities. These local agencies could contribute 25% to match the federal 75% contribution. The services developed in this and other ways include daycare, family counseling, support for tenant organization, home management, protective services, and information and referral. The major emphasis, however, was on locating and developing community resources.

The actions taken by the New York City Housing Authority in the 1960s and 1970s are illustrative of what can be done. The authority built an array of facilities during that period, including health clinics, community centers, old age centers, mental health clinics, daycare centers, libraries, and school annexes. A number of the divisions of the authority were involved in these efforts, for example, the Community Services Division, the Social Services Division, and the Tenant Organization Division.

One of the authors of this book was employed in the late 1950s as a social worker in a community center located in a housing project in Chicago that had just been built (Henry Booth House in Ickes Homes). The center was erected by the Chicago Housing Authority and in addition some operating funds were awarded the agency. The center performed a variety of services for all ages of people who had recently moved to the project and who were seeking to adapt to their new surroundings. The same author revisited the center over 30 years later (both the author and the center somewhat the worse for wear) and saw that the center had continued to find ways of meeting the old as well as emerging needs of the residents.

Another role for social workers is to help individuals find housing. This can be done through housing assistance bureaus and the creation of new organizations that "counsel and place the homeless, those in emergency situations, the displaced, those interested in home sharing, and elderly people who need barrier-free housing with congregate facilities."[28]

A specialized aspect of this role is relocation, in which large numbers of individuals must be simultaneously helped to find new housing because their existing housing is being destroyed, usually for urban development. The stress of relocation can be great, and a number of services can be performed by social workers to allay this stress. These include making early contact with residents and forming relationships with them; coordinating the services of a variety of systems, such as churches, schools, employment agencies, legal assistance, and welfare organizations; carefully assessing the needs of residents; and using this assessment to make sound plans. Many social work skills are called into play as people cope with their feelings of loss and develop the ability to insist that their needs be met.

One of the most important services social workers perform relates to homelessness. The people in this category include the following:[29]

1. Homeless men who are relatively young with limited skills and without social networks. "About one-third have histories of psychiatric hospitalization and about one-half are substance abusers."[30]
2. Homeless women, many from minorities, who are also relatively young.
3. Homeless families, typically in severe economic circumstances. This is one of the fastest growing segments of the homeless population.
4. Youths who are not classified as runaways who may return home. Instead, homeless youths in this category are prevented from doing so by highly untenable situations, such as those in which they have been severely abused (it is estimated that 84% have been physically abused).
5. Mentally ill individuals who also are predominantly young and male. A New York study of men who use shelters found 22% of them to be in need of mental health services and 3% of hospitalization.[31]

Social workers have fulfilled a number of roles in relationship to the problem of homelessness. With regard to young people, they have sought to identify those who are likely to become homeless because of family problems and to work to either prevent the family breakdown or to plan as early as possible for alternative arrangements.

They have worked with seriously mentally ill people to determine the type of living situation that will meet the person's need and to locate that type of accommodation. They have also sought to create an appropriate array of housing possibilities for this purpose, such as adult foster care homes, group homes, and other supported arrangements. They have also advocated for psychiatric, medical, and other services to be integrated with housing programs to meet the needs of such special populations and to stabilize their housing arrangements.

NEIGHBORHOOD ORGANIZATION AND ENVIRONMENTAL CONCERNS

Social workers engaged in social planning have had concerns about the environment since the turn of the century. As Mayer states:

> The origin of interest in the environment as the focus for social planning can be traced within the field of social welfare to the tradition of social reform prevalent in the early

1900s. In that period, individuals and organizations worked to improve the lives and living conditions of the poor and the destitute, not on the basis of some scientific theory or professionally defined field of practice, but out of personal conviction or from experience in working with the poor. . . . The reformers were not content with the nineteenth-century philosophy of social Darwinism—expressed so brashly in the words of Andrew Carnegie: "Those worthy of assistance, except in rare cases, seldom require assistance. The really valuable men of the race never do." They believed that exploitation of labor, slum housing, overcrowding, and a polluted environment were themselves causes of poverty.[32]

Nevertheless, the early social workers concerned themselves more with ways of enhancing the functioning of individuals and groups than with seeking to create a better physical environment. According to Mayer, however, a change took place with the passage of the 1954 Housing Act in which "public responsibility for upgrading the physical environment of cities was extended to the broader program of urban renewal."[33] As Mayer states, "Under this new program, the association between social work and physical planning blossomed."[34] Social workers, typically employed by settlements, welfare councils, and local community organizations, acted to develop citizen participation in planning and to help citizens to relocate.

Despite the fact that social workers were involved in these exciting activities, the profession of social work as such lacked a conceptual framework for "what makes a desirable neighborhood."[35] Again quoting from Mayer;

> Social workers tended to rely on what had in the past been the basis of their profession's claim to competence: a psychiatric model of behavior and a model of intervention resting on individual, family, and small group change. Therefore, most planning in which social workers were involved consisted of analyzing social process in relation to the need for social welfare, health, and recreational services. Plans consisted of projecting the resources necessasry for the provisions of such services in the community. Even experimental programs such as those launched by the President's Committee on Juvenile Delinquency, the War on Poverty, and the Model Cities program tended to define their social thrust in terms of the concentration of services to help the poor, the delinquent, and the ill-housed to break out of their defective environment. There was a lack of focus on the environment itself as the object of change.

In an effort to develop a conceptual scheme for social planning with relationship to the environment, Mayer drew on a variety of works, such as those of Jacobs and Gans, in which social problems were studied in relationship to how the environment structured social interactions.[36] Jacobs, for example, saw crime as related to lack of visibility of street activity to people in the neighborhood. Gans saw the use of social services as related to the need-meeting functions of the social system.

The implications of this type of analysis for social planning are that planners should focus on social problems in relation to the system of social relationships within which they occur, and these relationships are substantially affected by the environment. Some aspects of the environment that can be modified for this purpose are land use, housing policies, and the physical location of social service agencies. An example of planning for the latter is the work of Shannon and Dever.[37]

Mayer concludes that the environmental movement "has given new impetus to social planning."[38] Social workers who wish to pursue this type of work are increasingly likely to link their social work studies with courses in urban planning departments and in environmental psychology. The School of Social Work at the University of Michigan is not unique in recently approving a joint degree program in social work and urban planning. This coincides with Mayer's statement that[39] "Such planning has a unitary focus on the man–environment [sic] relationship and breaks down the domain structure of the traditional service professions."

Many changes are occurring in how the field of social welfare is defined, and the incorporation into social work of planning with respect to the environment is one of the most important of such changes.

Energy Usage and Conservation

Social workers have become more and more appreciative of how they must view the problems of people as occurring within a large, systemic configuration that includes both physical and social elements. As an example of this view, we have chosen interactions that incorporate that part of the physical environment that supplies *energy*, which heats our homes, operates our appliances, transports us from one place to another, and so forth.

Charping and Slaughter have presented a good example of this type of thinking.[40] (Before we proceed to discuss their work, it is interesting to note that Slaughter, a social worker, has the job title of Social Service Counselor for the Nashville Gas Company in Tennessee.) These authors point out that the gap between income and the cost of gas and electrical services for low-income people has become serious. To support this assertion, they cite evidence that unpaid gas and electric bills in the United States are estimated to be $500 million annually. Despite the severity of this problem, social service programs have not adequately addressed it.

To respond to this problem, the Nashville community created a self-help program called Project HELP staffed by volunteers and funded by contributions that were earmarked for this purpose. These consist of those individuals who are willing to donate $1.00 at the time they make their monthly payments. This type of program is now available in over 100 communities.

The program serves elderly and disabled persons who need help in paying utility bills. Need is determined in Project HELP through a budget interview. The amount of assistance may be greater than $350 with managerial approval and may only be requested once a season. The money can be used for repairs to heating equipment as well as for fuel.

This project is a good example of cooperation between a social agency and a business and may serve as a prototype of other similar endeavors. Such programs are necessary as long as public arrangements do not exist for this purpose. Some people have recommended that these be created and that energy should be seen as an entitlement; a few states have taken this stand by enacting laws prohibiting energy from being cut off in the winter for nonpayment. An example is the Michigan Energy Assurance Program that provides for direct payment of utilities.

Issues and Directions

Social workers and the institutions that educate them must strengthen the ways in which practitioners include attention to the environment with their service to people. This is an integral part of the ecological approach that we have stressed throughout this book. Social workers are in a unique position to demonstrate the harm done to people by deleterious environments, and they should develop their expertise in collecting such information and working with and on behalf of people to ameliorate these conditions.

One of the most important environmental aspects is the serious housing problem we have described throughout this chapter. Many problems workers face in helping people are made worse by lack of adequate housing. Consequently, social welfare agencies should seek to make attention to housing a major aspect of their services.

This attention can include having staff members who are experienced in locating existing housing, but matters should not rest there. Many agencies have used resources such as those provided through the McKinney Act to create forms of housing that are absent in their communities. Community organization workers should help their constituencies to pressure agencies to offer these services when they are reluctant to do so.

Social workers should learn how to form coalitions with conservationist and environmentalist organizations. These organizations are working to create the kinds of environments the clients of social workers need; consequently, social workers should see that they have common cause with these movements.

Social workers and their clients should examine ways in which contemporary life-styles create environmental problems. The emphasis on acquiring goods and then carelessly disposing of them should be changed. A greater respect for the environment will be associated with a better environment and may, as well, give us more respect for ourselves.

Conclusion

This chapter began with a discussion of the interests of social workers in environmental and housing issues, which are more typically thought of as being in the domain of engineers, public health experts, and city planners. We argued that these issues affect many of the needs and problems that clients bring to social agencies. Social workers, consequently, must be aware of such issues when they assess situations and when they consider solutions to problems.

The next topic dealt with was the nature of the systems that focus on the environment and housing. Such systems seek to protect nature for esthetic and utilitarian reasons, prevent the destruction of living species, and preserve the natural resources required by humans. In addition, they seek to prevent environmental conditions that are unhealthy for life. Meeting housing needs is a somewhat different but related topic.

We described the role of social work with reference to helping individuals to locate the environments they need and helping people to work together to preserve or change their current environments. This involves work with individuals, groups, communities, and organizations of many types. Many values are relevant to this work, and include the idea that environments should be primarily evaluated in terms of their impact on the health and welfare of people. Other values held by social workers are similar to those of the conservation and environmentalist movements.

We described the history of society's attention to environmental and housing issues and noted that these have existed throughout written history, and probably earlier. To survive, humans have engaged in acts that affect the environment, often negatively; such acts, however, had less serious impact on the environment when the size of the population and the power of human technology were less than they are today. The problem of providing housing is also related to population growth. It is further affected by current social policies, ideologies, and economic circumstances. An example is the change that has taken place in government policies in the United States related to the role of government in the provision of housing.

A major current issue is homelessness. Social workers have had a major interest in working with the homeless and creating policies to house them. This is a very important issue for those populations that suffer most strongly from homelessness, such as the seriously mentally ill and runaway youth.

Social work curricula have been paying more attention to these issues, especially housing, but should also educate social workers with regard to broader environmental issues and how to use community organization and other techniques to address them.

Notes

1. R. F. Dasmann, "Conservation of Natural Resources," *Encyclopedia Britannica* (1975), 5, p. 42.
2. Ibid.
3. Frederic G. Reamer, "The Affordable Housing Crisis and Social Work," *Social Work,* 34 (1) (January 1989), p. 5.
4. "Conservation of Natural Resources," p. 39.
5. See Dasmann, "Conservation of Natural Resources," for a description of the destructive practices of ancient societies.
6. Ibid., p. 42.
7. Ibid.
8. George Perkins Marsh, *Man and Nature* (New York: Charles Scribner, 1864).
9. Dasmann, "Conservation of Natural Resources," p. 43.
10. Ibid., p. 49.
11. Ibid.
12. Ibid., p. 50.
13. Ibid., p. 51.
14. Ibid., p. 52.
15. Ibid., p. 57.
16. Jean Van Der Tak, "Populations and Population Movements," *1988 Britannica Book of the Year* (Chicago: Encyclopedia Britannica, Inc., 1988), p. 282.
17. Bernard J. Frieden, R. Morris, ed., "Housing," *Encyclopedia of Social Work,* Vol. I, 16th ed. (New York: National Association of Social Workers, 1971), p. 589.
18. Ibid.
19. Ibid., p. 589.
20. Ibid., p. 590.
21. Milan J. Dluhy, "Housing," in A. Minahan, ed., *Encyclopedia of Social Work,* Vol. I, 18th ed. (Silver Spring, Md.: National Association of Social Workers, 1987), p. 822.
22. Ibid.

23. Julian Hess, "Housing: Federal and State Programs," in Morris, ed., *Encyclopedia of Social Work,* Vol. I, 16th ed., p. 607.
24. Frieden, "Housing", p. 642.
25. Dluhy, "Housing," p. 831.
26. *New York Times,* April 17, 1990, sec. 1, p. 1.
27. These roles have been adapted from Dluhy, "Housing," p. 833.
28. Ibid.
29. This listing draws from Sarah Connell, "Homelessness," in Minahan, ed., *Encyclopedia of Social Work,* Vol. I, 18th ed., pp. 791–792.
30. S. Hoffman and others, "Who are the Homeless?" Study prepared by New York State Office of Mental Health, New York City, May 1982.
31. Ibid.
32. Robert R. Mayer, "Environment and Social Planning," in J. B. Turner, ed., *Encyclopedia of Social Work,* Vol. I, 17th ed., (New York: National Association of Social Workers, 1977), p. 336.
33. Ibid., p. 336.
34. Ibid.
35. Ibid., p. 337.
36. Jane Jacobs, *The Death and Life of Great American Cities* (New York: Random House, 1961); Herbert J. Gans, *People and Plans* (New York: Basic Books, 1968).
37. See Gary W. Shannon and G. E. Alan Dever, *Health Care Delivery, Spatial Perspectives* (New York: McGraw-Hill Book Co., 1974).
38. Mayer, "Environment and Social Planning," p. 340.
39. Ibid., p. 340.
40. John W. Charping and Miriam M. Slaughter, "Voluntary Energy Assistance Programs: Community Self-Help in Action," *Social Work,* 33 (2) (March–April 1988), pp. 161–163.

CHAPTER 17
Knowledge Development, Data Collection, and Research

The Relationship Between Social Work and Research

It has long been debated whether social work practice is an art or a science. In the best sense, it is both. The art relates to the fact that social work is carried out by human beings with other human beings. Practitioners are confronted with the uniqueness of each human situation and seek to adapt to this uniqueness, even though they draw on principles and apply procedures that have been developed for various situations.

On many occasions, no approach appears to be specifically applicable to the immediate situation and the practitioner must improvise. As one wise teacher who believes strongly in the idea that social workers should primarily use interventions that have been tested through research (or could be so tested) put it, "If I only used what has been tested, there are many situations in which I could do nothing!"

In addition to what we have defined as the artistic, social workers also seek to be scientific. Before we can explain what we mean by this, we must discuss the term "science." We join with Borowski in recognizing that despite the everyday use of this word it is not so easy to define it. In dealing with this question, Borowski chooses to state the relevant characteristics of science.[1] The first of these is that it contains an *empirical* component. This is defined as follows:

> Empirical data are data which are based on factual information, observation, or direct sensory experience. Put simply, seeing is believing. A key assumption of empiricism, then, is that reality can only be known as a result of direct experience processed through the human intelligence.[2]

The second characteristic of science noted by Borowski is that it is *provisional.* By this he means that no matter how much information we collect in support of some idea we have about reality, a subsequent piece of information may not conform to that idea. He puts it well when he states that "there can be no valid knowledge in an absolute sense since all knowledge is potentially fallible and, thus, always provisional."[3]

The third characteristic is that science is *a public way of knowing.* This is only partially an ethical issue in that scientists have a responsibility to inform others of the knowledge they have obtained so that the latter may, in turn, build on this knowledge so as to create even more knowledge. Equally important is the requirement that scientists present to the scrutiny of others the sources of their information, the way it was collected, the way it was analyzed, and how conclusions were drawn. This helps the scientific community to identify sources of error and to repeat the investigation (a process called *replication*) to see if similar results will be obtained. Only through this repetitive process can scientists have confidence in scientific findings.

Now that we have explained the concept of science, let us explain our statement that social workers seek to be scientific. One way is that each act of a social worker produces information that can support or undermine an idea we have about what works, with whom, and under what circumstances. Thus, each act is, in a sense, a small *experiment* that tests a *hypothesis.* These two terms are so important that we shall take a moment to define them.

A *hypothesis* is an assertion about what is true in a given instance or a statement about a relationship among two or more events. An example of the former is the hypothesis that a majority of the children in a specified community do not receive an adequate diet. An example of the latter is that children who do not receive an adequate diet are not as likely to do well in school as children who do receive an adequate diet.

One subtype of a hypothesis, regarding the relationship among several events, is of particular importance to social workers. This is the *causal hypothesis* in which one event is viewed as causing another. (The many technical issues regarding how to test a causal hypothesis are well beyond the scope of this chapter.[4]) Since social workers are interested in *changing* things, this makes such causal ideas of central importance for at least two reasons.

First, if one event causes another and the latter is undesirable, the social worker may seek to eliminate the cause. In the example cited, if malnutrition leads to poor school performance, that might be one reason for making more resources available to poor children. The complications here are that some causes cannot easily be removed *and* some consequences can be changed by other means than removing their causes.

Another type of causal hypothesis of importance to social workers is that an action of a social worker is likely to cause a result that is beneficial to the social worker's client. In the example cited, such a hypothesis is that social-work-led groups in which students support each other in doing school assignments are more likely to lead to school success than social-work-led groups in which students only discuss their feelings about school success.

The reader should note that in our examples of hypotheses the word *likely* is frequently used. This is again because we deal with human situations in which no two are identical and, consequently, some of the differences among situations create different outcomes, even though the social worker acted in a similar manner each time. Any prediction of an outcome is a probability statement very much like the daily weather forecast, which informs us that there is a 50 percent chance of rain today.

Knowing from research what the chances are, the worker has to think about the risks of being helpful or not and may even share these thoughts with the client. Workers and clients would prefer if possible, for example, to take fewer risks in an approach to preventing suicide than in ensuring that a student will earn high grades. But even then, the careful worker will add the phrase "other things being equal," because earning high grades is sometimes very much linked to other, more serious, consequences.

It should now be evident what we mean by each social work act being an experiment. Social workers should know about research projects, if they have been conducted, that test the causal hypothesis that a particular intervention is likely to lead to a specified outcome. Each time a social worker uses that intervention, however, the hypothesis is tested again. And if there is no research, the hypothesis is being tested for the first time. Thus, all social workers are acting in a scientific manner if, each time they help a person, family, group, or larger system, they collect information in a careful manner and relate this information to hypotheses about what works.

This also means that social workers should keep abreast of the research that has been done in areas that relate to those in which they are working. This requires them to know how to gain access to research knowledge and how to assess whether the research has been done in such a way that the conclusions can be trusted.

In these ways, social workers operate scientifically as described by Borowski. Their work is empirical in that they seek to collect factual information about what they are doing and what happens consequently. Their work is provisional in that each new intervention is a way of reexamining the question of what works. And they should operate publicly, not by publicizing confidential information about clients, but by communicating the results of their actions to their clients, agencies, sources of support, and larger professional community.

These ideas about the relationship of the social worker to research are clearly stated by the Code of Ethics of the National Association of Social Workers, which states:

> *Development of Knowledge.*   The social worker should take responsibility for iden-
> tifying, developing, and fully utilizing knowledge for professional practice.
> (1) The social worker should base practice upon recognized knowledge relevant to
> social work.
> (2) The social worker should critically examine, and keep current with emerging
> knowledge relevant to social work.
> (3) The social worker should contribute to the knowledge base of social work and
> share research knowledge and practice wisdom with colleagues.[5]

Thus, the responsibilities of social workers include three research related roles: (1) consumers of research, (2) disseminators of knowledge, and (3) contributing partners in efforts to broaden the knowledge base of the social work profession.[6] We shall examine each of these roles in turn.

THE SOCIAL WORKER AS CONSUMER OF RESEARCH

A consumer of research must know how to look for relevant studies and publications, determine whether they apply to the situation in question, decide whether they are valid, and use the study to guide his or her subsequent actions.

Looking for relevant studies means that the worker should know how to use the catalog of a library as well as the publications that briefly summarize the contents and findings of books and articles. For social work purposes, the most important of these is *Social Work Research and Abstracts,* which appears quarterly and provides abstracts of all the social-work-related articles that have become available since the last issue. Many other abstract publications may be useful, such as *Psychological Abstracts* and *Socio-logical Abstracts.* Sometimes, also, the work has already been done, as in journals such as *Social Work,* which frequently publish review articles in which the author examines all the literature on a topic and describes the state of knowledge on that topic.

Because of the great amount of publications being produced at a constantly increasing rate, social workers are now also likely to use the library's computers (or even their own) to draw upon computerized files of abstracts. The way this works is that the social worker selects key words that define her or his area of interest. Thus a worker who wants to know about group approaches to helping the seriously mentally ill will select such words as "schizophrenia," "group work," and "chronically mentally ill." These are fed into the computerized file and the worker receives a printed list of abstracts of all publications that deal with the selected terms. If the worker anticipates that the list will be too long (and this is important as the user is sometimes charged by the length of the list), there are ways of shortening it, such as by adding key words or by asking only for articles published after a given date.

After social workers have located appropriate pieces of research, they must evaluate whether the research applies to their own situation and whether the conclusions of the research are warranted. Most research reports, in fact, make a statement to the effect that the investigator is only seeking to generalize to situations like those that were investigated. The applicability of the research, therefore, depends on answers to the following questions:

1. Were the subjects in the research similar to those whom the worker will be serving? Some research is conducted on all white or all male samples or there is no information on whether people of different sexes or cultural backgrounds responded differently.
2. Were the subjects' problems similar to the problems experienced by those the worker will be serving?
3. Were the interventions similar to those the worker intends to employ? Many research reports do not give details on how the intervention was employed or whether the researchers knew whether the model was actually employed in each instance in the way it is described.
4. Were the situations (type of agency, community) similar to the ones in which the worker operates? Using an intervention such as behavior modification, for example, is very different when imposed on a prisoner in a jail compared to being voluntarily accepted by an individual in a community setting.

Often the social worker will find a research-based article that offers information that fits his or her situation on some but not all the bases listed above. This may be the best than can be found. The worker is then in the unique situation of adding to what is known by applying a finding to people, situations, and problems in ways that have not been previously tested. The worker will then have to be more skeptical as to whether his or her results are similar to those described in the report, but, on the other hand, it is an excellent opportunity to make a contribution to knowledge.

Even when the report does seem applicable, the worker must examine how carefully the research was done. We will describe later how to evaluate research.

THE SOCIAL WORKER AS DISSEMINATOR OF RESEARCH

There are many ways in which social workers can and should communicate the knowledge they have gained through their work. These include staff conferences, workshop presentations, and professional publications. The latter can include carefully prepared practice descriptions, statements of problems encountered, and actual reports of research efforts. Increasingly, social workers as part of their training at the master's level learn to use empirical techniques such as *single-case design* in their day-to-day work.

Social workers are also likely to receive education regarding how to set up or use already established information systems in their agencies. These are likely to be computer based and to include information about each client, the services offered, the problems that brought the clients to the agency, and the outcomes of the service. These systems have a rich potential for adding to the knowledge base of practice; once graduate-level social workers are more universally educated in ways of handling data, a major issue will be to convince agencies to provide their workers with the time (and often consultation) that is required to make use of these data.

THE SOCIAL WORKER AS CONTRIBUTING PARTNER

Operating alone, the social worker usually does not have the time and resources to secure comprehensive data on more than a few clients at best. Thus, we would like to propose that workers see themselves as part of a larger team and that they seek to link up with others, even if they work a long distance apart. As we have stated elsewhere:

> [W]e believe that the most effective innovations in technology are likely to be achieved when many persons are involved at one stage or another. This is why the third role is described as contributing partner in the process of knowledge development. There are many subroles the social work practitioner/researcher can fill. Some workers are skillful at identifying and giving priority to important problem areas. Others are creative in seeking possibilities for new social work practices from obvious as well as unlikely sources. Still others are excellent as promoters of new, yet tested, ideas. The central idea is to reduce the randomness that has typified technical development in social work.[7]

Types of Research

Before we present more details on the research process, it is important to clarify some of the distinctions among various types of research endeavors. A distinction is often made between *pure* (often called *basic*) and *applied* research. In the social sciences, pure research concerns human phenomena so as to better understand them as an end in itself. Applied research is conducted so as to do something better or more efficiently.[8] Selltiz and her colleagues in a classic discussion of this matter state:

> Historically the scientific enterprise has been concerned both with knowledge for its own sake and with knowledge for what it can contribute to practical concerns. This double emphasis is perhaps especially appropriate in the case of social science. On the one hand, its responsibility as a science is to develop a body of principles that make possible the understanding and prediction of the whole range of human interactions. On the other hand, because of its social orientation, it is increasingly being looked to for practical guidance in solving immediate problems of human relations. . . . [I]n the long run, neither goal can be fully realized without the other. Only as general principles are developed can social science offer sound guidance for immediate action, and only to the extent that it can make predictions about the results of action in specific situations does it justify its claim of providing an adequate systematic body of knowledge about social interactions. Moreover, the starting point of a study does not necessarily determine what the nature of its contribution will be. Both in the social sciences and in the physical sciences, research on practical problems may lead to the discovery of basic principles, and "basic" research often yields knowledge that has immediate practical usefulness.[9]

Social workers make considerable use of pure research. This includes the results of studies of human development and emotions, behaviors, and thought processes; group dynamics; family processes; and organizational, community, and societal conditions. The charge can be made, however, that social workers may understand many phenomena but do not know how to *change* them. The statement cannot be made too often that understanding something does not necessarily lead to changing it. We do not belittle such understanding because it sometimes leads to ideas about change, but that step still must be taken.

Applied research specifically related to social work does not have a very long history. According to Reid, it began in the late 1940s through several efforts.[10] One was a study of client change through a content analysis of process records; another was the development of scales to monitor client progress. A third was a classification of casework methods. These projects led to a number of controlled experiments to test the effectiveness of one or another social work modality. Unfortunately, these early studies failed to provide strong evidence for the effectiveness of social work methods, although the picture has been gradually changing.[11] In examining this history, Reid comments:

> Thus the 100-year effort to construct a base of scientific knowledge for the profession has fallen far short of the enthusiastic hopes of the pioneers. There is now a greater appreciation of the reality that research-based knowledge can be only a part—albeit an important one—of the vast network of information that informs practice. Newer research strategies, such as developmental research . . . offer hope of forging more direct and solid links between research and practice.[12]

One weakness of social work applied research strategies has been the wide gap between those who developed new approaches to practice and those who did research on the effectiveness of such practice. A major step forward was taken through the creation of what has come to be known as *developmental research.*[13] The purpose of such research is not to generate knowledge but to build intervention technology.

Developmental research begins with an examination of existing research regarding the methods that have been employed to deal with the problem of interest. Ideas about interventions may also be gained from an examination of existing practices, even if research has not been done. This stage helps the investigators to design the interventions that they wish to test. They then gather data on the implementation of the interventions as well as their outcomes. These data help the investigators to improve the interventions and to design subsequent experiments in order to move closer to the desired outcomes. As Thomas states, "Developmental research may be the single most appropriate model of research for social work because it consists of methods directed explicitly toward the analysis, development, and evaluation of the very technical means by which social work objectives are achieved."[14]

Stages of the Research Process

The stages of the research process are the components that researchers have agreed on as the scientific method. Social workers must understand these stages for two reasons: the major one is that to determine the credibility of a piece of research the worker must know how to evaluate each stage. The way each stage was accomplished may either make the study irrelevant to the concerns of the worker or, if relevant, untrustworthy. The other reason workers should understand these stages is to be able to make their own contributions to the research process.

PROBLEM FORMULATION

The first stage is problem formulation. This begins with a determination of the problem that the research should help to solve. The problem may be a concern as to whether a particular social work approach to a situation is effective. It may also be a question about the causes of a situation or even whether some conditions are present or absent in the situation. The following are examples of these concerns:

1. Is social skills training effective in helping severely mentally ill people to function independently in the community?
2. What conditions are more likely to be found in an agency that has poor morale than one that has good morale?
3. If a program of support for victims of acquired immune deficiency syndrome (AIDS) is developed in the community, how many individuals might be potential clients?

The problem statement is important because it tells the worker whether the study will be relevant or not to her or his interests. The study may be very well conducted, but still be irrelevant to the specific problems of interest to the worker.

The next aspect of problem formulation is a definition of concepts. In the first research problem cited, we use the terms "social skills training" and "severely mentally ill." The worker may have an interest in these phenomena but mean something so different by them that the study becomes irrelevant. Even worse is that sometimes, some concepts are so poorly defined that the reader does not know what to make of the study.

For example, the study may define severely mentally ill people as "those who have been diagnosed as schizophrenic; have exhibited this condition for more than six months; and have not been able to work or attend an educational program during this period because of the severity of the disability created by this illness." The worker may be interested in social skills training (assuming that the researchers define it the same way the worker does), but this research will not tell the worker how the approach works with people diagnosed as "affective disorder: bipolar type," which is this worker's main concern.

Another aspect of problem formulation is the specification of *hypotheses,* which are statements framed in such a way that information can be collected to support or refute them. They therefore guide the collection of data and also open to public scrutiny the biases of the investigators. By this latter statement, we mean that, if an investigator has a hunch about what is true, there may be a tendency to only see what supports the hunch; the hypothesis alerts the reader to this possibility.

A hypothesis may be fairly general if little is known about the phenomena that are to be studied. Thus, a worker may wish to learn more about the needs of a community of new Asian immigrants. This worker may plan a survey that asks about health, housing, financial, employment, and educational needs. The hypothesis (often implicit in this type of study) is that these needs will be identified by people contacted through the survey.

On the other hand, in the community we have just referred to, more may be known than we have implied (often because such a survey was accomplished). The issue may be more one of how to help people to make use of resources. For the latter purposes, a hypothesis such as the following might be constructed: "A resident of this Asian-American community will be more likely to use a health resource if this use is proposed by another Asian-American than if it is proposed by a person who is not of this ethnic origin."

Another important aspect of problem formulation is a statement of assumptions. These are conditions that are thought to be present in the situation to be investigated, but the researcher believes they will not affect the results of the research in unpredictable ways. The researcher does not typically gather data to test the assumptions (if he or she does so, they then can be considered as hypotheses). Nevertheless, assumptions should be identified and a rationale given for accepting them. In the example we have been using, the researcher may ask the reader to accept the assumption that people are aware of their needs and will state them to an interviewer.

Researchers should seek to relate their problem formulation to a theory. *Theory* is essentially a statement that links a number of hypotheses (that have received empirical support) with an explanation of why these findings occur as they do. A theory can then guide us in developing and testing new hypotheses that support, modify, or negate it.

RESEARCH MEASUREMENT AND DESIGN

After the researchers have formulated the research problem, the next steps are as follows:

1. They decide how the data will be collected. This includes whether they will interview the subjects, ask them to fill out questionnaires, or observe them. In each case, some instrument must be used to record the information that is secured through the interview, the observation, or the subjects direct response.
2. They decide how often and under what circumstances each instrument will be administered.
3. They decide how the data that are secured will be coded and analyzed. The former refers to how the information will be converted into a form that can be easily scrutinized; the latter to what the nature of that scrutiny will be.
4. Finally, the researcher must relate the data to the original problem formulation so as to answer the questions posed at that point and determine whether the hypotheses have been supported or not.

We shall now discuss each of these steps in turn.

The first issue in deciding how to collect data is to assure its *validity* and *reliability*. Validity means that the instrument does what the researcher says it will do. Reliability refers to how accurate the instrument is. At times the validity of an instrument is fairly obvious, particularly when what is asked is a direct question that means exactly what it says; this is referred to as content validity. If we wish to know, for example, whether clients believe a certain service will be useful in their community and we ask the question in precisely that way, it will have content validity.

There are a number of other ways that validity is determined when the measurement is not so clearly related to the research question. One of these is concurrent validity, which is determined when a measure of unknown validity produces similar results to one whose validity is known. Still another is predictive validity, which is demonstrated when the instrument predicts future events at a high level of frequency.

A final approach to validity is construct validity. This is more difficult for the newcomer to research to understand because it relies on a theoretical formulation as a justification of the chosen approach to measurement. This type of validity must be established when we seek to study phenomena such as people's feelings, the emotional climate of a group, the morale of an organization, and so forth, that cannot be directly observed, but must be inferred from other measures. These measures are chosen because a theoretical framework describes them as signs that the thing we wish to study is actually present or absent.

Reliability, which we have related to accuracy, is usually determined by seeing if individuals respond the same way each time they complete an instrument (assuming they have not changed in the meantime) or whether they respond in the same way to similar items.

A major issue in social work research is the relationship of *quantitative* to *qualitative* research. The former is a type of research in which the person who supplies the data does so in numerical form or in which the data are converted into numerical form by the investigator. Examples of quantitative data are the following:

☐ What is your religion? (circle one)
   1. Catholic 2. Protestant 3. Jewish 4. Moslem 5. Other
☐ How frequently to you feel sad?
   5. Always 4. Frequently 3. Sometimes 2. Seldom 1. Never
☐ How many cigarettes do you smoke a day? ____

The first of these questions is not related to an *amount,* but rather to a category; but nevertheless numbers are used in connection with each category; the second is related to an amount, but one that is ranked in terms of frequency; and the third is related to a precise quantity. These three types of questions represent what researchers call types of scales. (A discussion of scaling would take us beyond the scope of this chapter.[15])

Qualitative research, on the other hand, seeks to be descriptive of actual events as they occur. Sometimes the researcher also wants to know how these events are perceived by the actual participants and how they feel about them. Rather than using questionnaires, qualitative researchers are more likely to rely on observations and/or interviews with people in which they are encouraged to tell their stories in their own way. Qualitative research, therefore, is more likely to present things as they occur in much of their complexity, whereas quantitative research singles out specific aspects of reality.

A major challenge to qualitative researchers is to follow the basic tenets of science such as those of reliability and validity. When this is done, we believe that all phenomena of interest to social workers can and should be studied through both methods. The qualitative offers us a more total view of complex reality and how various events interact than the quantitative. The quantitative, in a sense, provides a microscope in which we can focus on specific types of information while recognizing that much has been excluded.

The next issue is how often and to whom each instrument will be administered. These are design questions. Again, a full discussion of this topic is well beyond the scope of this chapter, but we will present some of the major alternatives.[16]

Two major types of designs are *single-case* and *group* designs. The former is a fairly recent innovation in research, having come into its own in the last 25 years. It has the advantage of being usable by the individual practitioner while making use of the scientific methods outlined earlier. The basic components of a single-case design are a careful specification of the intervention and of the goal to be achieved, the use of an instrument to measure states of goal attainment, a determination of the state of the problem related to the goal before the intervention is applied, and regular observations (that is, securing measurements) throughout the course of the change effort to see if and how the problem condition changes.

Many specific single-case designs can be used according to the circumstances. These designs differ depending on how many different interventions are to be used, whether it is possible to see the effect of the intervention by withdrawing it and then reintroducing it, and how the base line (the state of the problem before an intervention) is to be secured. It is also possible to use statistical tests to determine the likelihood that the changes that occur after intervention might have occurred by chance, as compared to being the result of the intervention.[17]

Group designs, in contrast, are those in which the researcher studies a number of people (or groups or families or larger systems), usually because they have experienced a similar event, such as having lived in the same community or having had the same type of treatment. An example is an investigator who wished to help a number of groups to have more positive feelings among the members. He selected the groups and gave the members a questionnaire to determine how they felt about each other. He then helped each group to plan a party, after which he again administered the questionnaire to see how the members felt about each other. His hypothesis was that they would feel better in this way after the party than before.

In this example, the party is referred to as an *independent variable* and the feelings members have about each other as a *dependent variable*. A *variable* is simply something that varies, and the dependent variable is called that because it depends on the independent variable in the way that the researcher has conceived of in this study.

There are several different kinds of group designs. The first is called an *exploratory* design and is used when very little is known about the subject being studied. A hypothetical example is of a researcher who wishes to know more about a community that has never been studied before. This researcher may visit the community to secure basic facts about the type of people who live there and where they came from. Thus, this type of group design primarily is one whose intent is to gather facts.

When this kind of information has been obtained, the researcher may wish to conduct a *descriptive* study in which she seeks to learn more specifically what proportions of the members of the community are from each ethnic background, how many are men and women, and what their ages are. To do this, she might seek to accurately count the community members. In this case, however, since it was a large community, she selected a *random* sample of community members. In a random sample, each member has an equal likelihood of being chosen for the sample. There are statistical principles that indicate that random sampling makes it very likely (within a known range of probability) that the proportion of people of different characteristics in the sample will be a reasonable estimate of the proportion in the larger population.

The researcher may then choose to move on to a type of design referred to as an *explanatory* design. This frequently takes the form of an experiment that must have the following characteristics. Researchers must be careful to specify the independent variable, which is often some form of intervention. They must also make sure that other variables that may have an effect on the outcomes are either measured so that their effects can be accounted for or that such variables are the same for all subjects in the study. This is referred to as *experimental control.* They must also be sure to select the subjects randomly so that they are representative of the population from which they have been chosen.[18]

There are many different kinds of experimental designs, which vary according to how many different groups are studied, how often the variables are measured, how many different types of variables are examined, what interactions among variables are hypothesized to occur, and so on. The task of the researcher is to select a design that is appropriate for the hypotheses that have been proposed and that ensures that the results occur as a result of the experimental manipulation, rather than as a result of other events. This is a technical subject, but one that social workers must understand in order to assess the research that is pertinent to their work.[19]

DATA ANALYSIS

After the researcher has collected the data as prescribed by the measurement and design procedure, it must be organized into a form that allows it to be analyzed. Typically, in quantitative research, this involves transforming the data into numerical form and placing the data into a computer so that various statistical procedures can be utilized to test the hypotheses. This work must be carefully supervised, for if it is done in a sloppy manner, very little trust can be placed in the findings. The researchers seldom report on these procedures, so trust must be placed in them that they understand and have followed through on this computer work in a careful manner.

Various *statistical tests* are used to analyze the data. Some of these are called *descriptive* statistics because they help the researcher to portray information in a manner that is easier to digest than flooding the reader with many small items of information. The most common of these statistics is known to the nonresearcher as an *average.* This term actually refers to a number of possible ways of describing a sample. For example, the mean is a statistic computed by totaling all the values of a variable and dividing the result by the number of subjects. (An example is that the mean age of three people whose ages are 10, 11, and 12 is 11; 10 + 11 + 12 = 33; 33 divided by 3 = 11.)

The researcher is then likely to use statistics referred to as *inferential* statistics. These are used to determine what the relationship is likely to be among several variables;

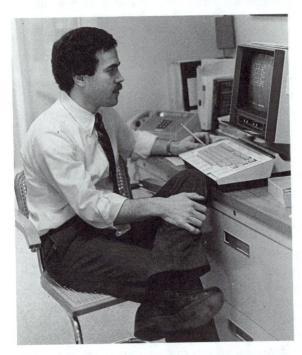

Crunching the numbers. (Photo by Laimute E. Druskis.)

the statistical result also informs the researcher what the *probability* is that this relationship could be due to chance, rather than to the interaction that was hypothesized to exist.[20]

RESEARCH REPORTING

The final stage of the research activity occurs when the researcher reports her or his findings to a professional audience or even the wider public. A good research report will inform the reader as to how the researcher conducted all the preceding phases. It includes, then, the following:

1. The research problem
2. The hypotheses
3. Definitions of relevant concepts
4. Assumptions
5. What the variables were and how they were measured
6. How the sample was chosen
7. What the design of the research was
8. How the data were analyzed
9. Specific ways in which the data answered the research question that was posed and tested the hypotheses that had been specified
10. How this piece of research adds to existing theory

Research Issues and Social Work Methods

Now that we have described the research process, we can discuss some of the issues related to studying and evaluating different kinds of social work interventions. We will deal with this topic by discussing the interventions according to the level of the system in which intervention takes place: the individual, group, family, organization, community, and the larger society.

THE INDIVIDUAL

The traditional way in which individually oriented practitioners examined their practice was through the use of process records. In these records, they recorded in detail the kinds of comments and responses made by the client and the practitioner. The record was sometimes made somewhat more objective when workers indicated their goals for the session and how they anticipated achieving these goals. Such workers were likely to indicate how well the goals were achieved at the end of the record.

Workers who engaged in this type of recording could refer to these records periodically in order to describe changes in the client, as well as changes in the kinds of interventions utilized. Researchers have sometimes examined such records and through such approaches as content analysis[21] used a systematic means to derive reliable data from them. Nevertheless, this is a laborious job and often rendered impossible because of the movement in the field away from process recording. This may not be a big loss, because such records had dubious reliability in that different people observing the same session may record it very differently.

For research purposes, a more reliable way of obtaining information regarding what occurred during a session is through some form of electronic recording, such as on audiovisual tape. There will be no doubt that what occurred during the session is recorded, but the task still remains to find some way to analyze the events that were recorded. In these circumstances, researchers utilize rating scales and content analyses or may even count the number of times an event happens during the interview.

Still another approach to capturing important details of what transpires during a session is *critical incident recording* in which the worker or other observer records specific incidents in detail. These incidents are likely to be those chosen because of the topic under investigation. For example, one practitioner was interested in how she handled client anger, and so she recorded all instances of client anger including what led up to the expression, how she responded, and what the result was.

A more current approach to identifying the events that occur during a session is to use *coded recording forms*. In these instruments, workers use codes to categorize the content of the session, the kind of interventions, and the goals and outcomes of each intervention.

Probably the greatest developments have occurred in the tools that are now used to measure outcomes. Hudson and Thyer classify these into three types:[22]

1. Paper-and-pencil self-report scales or indexes designed to measure a variety of problems

2. Single-item, self-anchored scales
3. Behavioral measures

We shall now illustrate some of these types. An example of a self-anchored scale is provided by Hudson and Thyer as follows:

> [A] client . . . experiences severe facial pain. In such cases it is often difficult for this client to describe accurately the severity of the pain, which may lead to difficulties in its management. To address this problem, one client was asked to assign a score of 0 whenever she felt no facial pain and to assign a score of 10 when she experienced pain so severe that she would have to go to the hospital emergency room to find relief. In this manner the client could easily monitor the severity of her pain on an hourly basis.[23]

A behavioral measure is *behavioral counts* in which the client, or some significant other, counts the number of times a behavior that has been targeted for change occurs. Examples are the number of school assignments completed, the number of times one initiates a conversation, or the number of times one starts an argument.

A good example of a paper-and-pencil measure is the series of scales developed by Hudson.[24] This includes scales to measure marital satisfaction, generalized contentment, self-concept, sexual satisfaction, parental attitudes, and the child's attitude toward each parent. Hudson has also devised a computer program that allows the client to respond to the items directly on the computer. The program scores the instruments and even performs a single-subject design analysis when the instrument is administered on a regular basis over time.

Yet another approach to assessing client change is *goal attainment scales,*[25] which measure a client's goal achievement. The procedure requires the worker to utilize a form in which each column on the form is used to record a client goal. The rows on the chart provide cells in which the worker, usually with the participation of the client, specifies five levels of goal achievement. These are "most unfavorable outcome thought likely," "less than expected success," "expected level of success," "more than expected success," and "most favorable outcome thought likely." These levels are idiosyncratic to the client's specific situation.

Kiresuk and Garwick have devised statistical approaches through which each client is assigned a goal attainment score. This allows scores to be compared for any number of clients. Criticisms have been leveled at the statistical approach taken with this instrument. Nevertheless, it is one of the few ways in which workers can measure client changes uniquely related to that client's idiosyncratic problems and goals.

Until now, social work investigators did not have readily available the kinds of more complex instruments required to assess individual work. Corcoran and Fischer have performed an important service through their publication of a comprehensive sourcebook of instruments that may be appropriately used by social workers.[26] These instruments include a wide array that covers many of the most frequently treated problem areas for children, as well as for adults, couples, and families.

THE GROUP

When workers work with groups to help individual members enhance their functioning, they typically use some of the same measures to evaluate client change that they use on a one-to-one basis. Another set of procedures, however, is necessary when they examine how the group is functioning.[27] An examination of group conditions, such as group processes, is done for several reasons. One may be that the worker wishes to establish some type of group condition, such as participation by all the members, and wants to carefully assess whether this is occurring. Another is that the worker may wish to examine group conditions as variables that affect outcomes and needs to measure such conditions for this purpose.

To assess group conditions, some workers write process records that are similar to those prepared by individual workers, but in which the interactions among members and how the worker focused on these are highlighted. The strengths and limitations of this method are the same as with individual process records. For this reason, critical incident recordings have been utilized as well as summaries of group sessions.

In an analgous manner to individual situations, workers are increasingly turning toward coded recording forms. Garvin presents an example of this in which codes have been devised to identify the types of content covered in the meeting, the way the worker intervened with reference to such content, the kinds of processes that occurred, the goals for the session, and how well the goals were attained.[28]

Group workers can also utilize behavioral counts to identify group conditions. For example, workers may wish to increase certain classes of behavior for all group members, such as expression of feelings, self-disclosure statements, requests for help from others, and promptness in coming to meetings. Counts of these behaviors can be made by the worker, by an outside observer, or even by a member.

A dimension of a group that accounts for many outcomes is group structure, which is the pattern of relationships among members. Several communication patterns are of interest to workers, such as who speaks to whom. If the concern is over whether members speak to each other or the worker, a simple tally can be kept in which "M" means a member spoke and "W" means the worker spoke. A brief segment of a meeting might look like this: M M M W M W M W M M M M). The worker can then tally the number of times members spoke to the worker by counting the number of M's followed by a W and the number of times members spoke to each other by the M's followed by an M. The percentage of time members spoke to the worker can be found by dividing the first number by the second (and multiplying by 100).

Some ways of measuring group conditions may also have treatment effects (probably the same thing can be said of any measurement). For example, Rose developed a procedure to help a group become aware of the frequency with which reinforcing remarks were made. Members placed poker chips in a can, using one color to show they felt reinforced and another to show feelings of being criticized.[29] While this mechanism was immediately used by the members to change their behavior, it also provided an easily countable piece of information.

Rose also developed a way to assess the content of communications among members. He generated the following content categories: suggestion–opinion giving response; questions; responses to questions; self-suggestions; negative affect; positive affect; and information giving.[30] An observer coded each remark according to who said it, who it was directed to, and the category into which it fit. The worker could then calculate who spoke or was spoken to the most frequently and the frequency of different kinds of comments.

Another dimension of groups is the degree to which members are attracted to the group because there will be no group if members do not show up. Yalom has developed a tool to measure this variable, which is usually referred to as group cohesiveness. He asks the members to complete a questionnaire that asks them such things as how well they like the group, how hard they would work to convince others not to disband the group, and whether they think the group is helping them to attain their goals.[31]

Rose has developed another measurement that provides information on several group processes. This is in the form of a questionnaire given to members at the end of each session. This instrument includes questions such as the following: How useful was today's session for you? Describe your involvement in today's session. Rate the extent of your self-disclosure of relevant information about yourself or your problem. How important to you were the problems or situations you discussed (others discussed) in the group today? Circle the number on the scale that best describes the interrelationships among group members and leaders in the group. Circle all the words that best describe you at today's session. How satisfied were you with today's session?[32]

THE FAMILY

A number of efforts have been undertaken in recent years to study both the processes and the outcomes of family interventions. These are difficult tasks because of a lack of agreement among practitioners as to what the important categories of intervention and the desired outcomes are.

In a survey of the literature on this subject, Pinsof concludes that all the research in this area should be regarded as exploratory, and he is dubious about much of the quality.[33] One, however, that he has been involved with himself, the Family Therapist Coding System, is described as showing promise, although much work remains to be done to attest to its validity and reliability. This system develops an interrelated set of ratings of the worker's interventions in terms of topic, type of intervention, temporal orientation, to whom directed, interpersonal structure, system membership, grammatical form, and event relationship.[34] If this system proves useful, it would be one of the most comprehensive ways developed to measure a worker's intervention in a multiperson situation.

Researchers have also been working on ways of coding family members' behavior during sessions. The problem is not too different from coding group members' behavior except that family member codes must incorporate some of the intimate ways that family members interact that are not as likely to occur in a group. One example of such approaches is that of Sheflen.[35] His codes included such categories as explaining, passive protesting, listening, questioning, contending, accusing, defending, and tactile contacting.

The issue of evaluating family therapy outcomes is complicated by the lack of agreement as to what the outcomes of family therapy should be. If family therapy is intended to improve the functioning of a single member, then we could utilize the same measures for family treatment that we use for individual treatment.

Another approach is to declare each family therapy situation to be unique, in which case the worker would use some equivalent to goal attainment scaling, but define the scale points in terms of systemic conditions rather than individual ones. The challenge here would be to do so in a reliable manner. For example, it would be clear whether all family members do or do not sit down together to eat supper, but not so clear whether or not the mother is overinvolved with her son unless this were stated in more behavioral terms.

An alternative also would be to use a questionnaire that has items that deal with issues of autonomy and control. Gurman and Kniskern, two noted authorities on the evaluation of family therapy, believe it is just a matter of time until we have available a series of core instruments, each of which is "centered on a specific clinical problem or on logical classes of problems."[36] Corcoran and Fischer, in a reference book for social workers, offer a number of instruments that they believe would be appropriate for measuring the effects of social work interventions with families.[37] Examples of these instruments are measurement of parent behavior with adolescents, marital discord, family competence, spouse abuse, and marital communication.

Gurman and Kniskern believe that in any case change in three entities should be evaluated in any family treatment situation or in research on such situations: the "identified patient" whose problems prompted the family treatment, the marital dyad, and the entire family. This recommendation is based on their proposition that "a higher level of positive change has occurred when improvement is evidenced in systematic (total family) or relationship (dyadic) interactions than when it is evidenced in individuals alone (note that we make the assumption . . . that individual change can occur without system change)."[38]

Finally, in their authoritative discussion of research on family therapy, Gurman and Kniskern indicate that there is a close association in family therapy between the outcome variable to be studied and the source of the data.[39] They assert that simple behavioral counts as well as perceived family interactional patterns during sessions can be made by trained observers; and self-reports of one's behavior as well as of interactions with other family members can be supplied by the family members.

On the other hand, despite the charges of bias that other researchers are likely to make, they believe that the therapist or a professional judge is in the best position to make judgments about family psychodynamics (by which we assume that they mean the emotional significance of interactional patterns) and family system properties such as enmeshment. In this latter respect, however, we believe that structural diagrams, such as those developed by Minuchin, provide at least a framework for several observers to compare judgments and to report on the reliability of this judgment.[40]

THE AGENCY

There are many different kinds of research with regard to social agencies in which social workers engage. However, we shall confine our discussion to the topic of *program evaluation*, which means an examination of the effectiveness and efficiency of the agency. A more comprehensive definition is offered by Hornick and Burrows as "a collection of methods, skills, and sensitivities necessary to determine whether a human service is needed and likely to be used, whether it is conducted as planned, and whether the human service actually does help people in need."[41]

As indicated by this definition, one aspect is needs assessment. This is an important topic because the presumed reason the agency exists is to meet at least some of the needs of a defined set of people. There are several ways an investigator can undertake a needs assessment. One is to examine the records of the agency itself (or of other agencies in the community) to find out how many individuals have identified a particular need and how often they have done so. Another approach is to choose a specified time period and to monitor the number of times requests are made for a service.

A third approach is to conduct a community survey (usually based on a carefully selected sample) in which individuals are asked about their needs. These individuals may represent all the people in a community or a subset, such as those already using the agency or those with some characteristic in common, such as age, sex, race, or handicap.

When an agency wishes to evaluate the program it has in place to meet needs, several conditions must be in place, which parallel those for evaluations of individuals, groups, and families. One is that the agency's objectives be stated specifically enough to be evaluated. Another is that the agency's program be sufficiently standardized so that the results of the evaluation can be attributed to identifiable programs.

One way of determining the degree to which the program has been standardized is to look for the times when decisions must be made as the clients enter the agency, secure one or more services, and then terminate. A somewhat abbreviated example of this is provided by an agency that provides job training for handicapped individuals. A first stage is how the agency receives referrals; another is how such referrals are screened and a decision made to accept the referral; another, how the individual is evaluated to determine a specific training plan; another, the selection of the training plan; another, job placement; and still another is when to close the case.

When these key decision points have been identified, program evaluators examine the degree to which each set of procedures has been standardized. Hornick and Burrows indicate several ways that this can be done:

> There are three methods for monitoring an agency: (1) direct observation by the program evaluator; (2) examination of service records; and (3) analysis of data collected from the social workers themselves. . . . In terms of analysis of the data gathered, it is suggested that the agency's director and/or evaluator be primarily concerned with (1) describing the actual treatment interventions being delivered and (2) comparing what is occurring with what was proposed, that is, checking for agency conformity.[42]

Some agencies will have installed computer-based client information systems. While the number of such agencies is increasing, many still do not have such systems or have not installed them in such a way as to fit most easily into a program evaluation.

The next stage in program evaluation is to assess outcomes. Ideally, this should be based on an experimental design in which individuals who receive a specified set of agency services are compared to those who did not and clients are randomly assigned to these two groups. Tripodi, Fellin, and Epstein recognize that this may not always be possible and they suggest instead that the evaluator may have to use the following alternatives:

1. A group similar to the experimental group on many relevant variables, selected after the experimental group has received program intervention.

2. A group similar to the experimental group that receives less frequent program efforts rather than no program intervention.
3. A group similar to the experimental group that receives a routine, traditional intervention in contrast to the experimental group, which also receives the routine, traditional intervention, as well as an additional innovative intervention.
4. The experimental group used as its own control, with comparisons made on criterion measures before and after program intervention.[43]

After the program evaluation design has been determined, the evaluators will choose appropriate measurement instruments. They will often use several outcome instruments so as to better establish the validity of the results. They will also try, whenever possible, to select instruments that have already been developed and standardized so as to facilitate comparisons among programs.

A final type of program evaluation is cost–benefit analysis. This analysis consists in part of an effort to determine agency costs per unit of service when this unit is either the case (which may consist of several clients), the client, or the number of hours spent on each case or client. Other examples of outputs that can be measured are "number of children placed in adoption, number of therapy interviews, number of health examinations, and so forth."[44]

The benefit aspect is much more difficult to assess in social work than in industry because we are not talking about how much income is generated from a product but how much better off people are after services. And as we have shown throughout this chapter, there are many different ways (none fully agreed on) to measure this.[45]

THE COMMUNITY

Social workers conduct many different kinds of research at the community level, but probably the most important is the community needs assessment. This is done to help the social planner to determine the kinds of services that ought to be developed and to help the grass roots organizer to determine the issues that might be used to mobilize people.

One way of approaching a needs assessment is through the use of existing demographic data such as the U.S. Census and reports generated from it. A disadvantage of this approach for the grass roots organizer is that the lack of involvement of people in collecting the data misses a mobilization opportunity. For this reason, the community organizer will often use observations of events in the community, interviews with community residents, and group meetings.

In group meetings, an approach to data collection that is often used is the nominal group technique.[46] This technique starts with a generation of responses regarding needs from the participants in which every person has an opportunity to add to the list. Procedures are then used to clarify the items. Participants then vote for the items that they see as high priority. Care is taken not to associate the item with specific individuals so that it can be considered on its own merits, rather than on the status of a person.

Community investigators also approach individuals. These might be key informants, such as community leaders, service providers, or individuals chosen in some random manner. Marti-Costa and Serrano-Garcia describe an interesting model that joins together the process of community needs assessment and community development.[47] There are four phases to this process. In the first the organizer becomes familiar with the community by reviewing demographic material, history, and structures and processes. In the second, the organizer composes a core group that engages in planning, coordination, and evaluation activities throughout, including the needs assessment. In the third, task groups are formed to identify goals based on the assessment; these groups are often generated out of a community meeting. The last phase, which occurs after projects are underway to meet needs, involves linking with other groups so that new goals and activities can be generated.

THE SOCIETY

At a societal level, social workers are likely to be involved in what has been termed *policy research*. Policy research is the generation and analysis of data in order to shape policy decisions. In a more technical sense, Austin offers the following definitions:

> Policymaking can thus be understood as the social process through which multiple actors, aided by technical data, interact to formulate policy. Policy research is intended to facilitate this process by providing the technical data needed to determine the most effective and efficient means to achieve the desired objective.[48]

Austin draws on the work of Mayer and Greenwood to describe the steps of policy making.[49] The following is a brief summary of these steps along with some of the roles researchers fulfill at many of the stages.

1. *Determining goals.* This is similar to the way any research process is initiated. The researcher helps the policy maker to state goals in ways that will lead to operationalization and measurement. The researcher might also conduct exploratory studies to suggest dimensions along which goals can be selected.
2. *Determining a needs assessment.* This is done to determine the amount of change to be sought through the policy objective. The research design that is often used here is the exploratory study.
3. *Specifying objectives.* This step involves further specification of the goals, usually in quantitative terms, and of the time frame in which these are to occur. The researcher will interpret the data used to make the decisions around objectives.
4. *Designing alternative courses of action.* This is the creative phase and depends on inputs from knowledgeable people who have expertise in the area.
5. *Estimating the consequences of alternative courses of action.* This involves a projection of effects. Increasingly, policy makers are able to make use of the researcher's knowledge of computer technologies that project such effects as costs and outcomes under a variety of assumptions. The researcher might also help the policy maker to gain access to the results of small-scale studies related to the projected policies.
6. *Selecting a course of action.* This phase draws on the previous one, but also uses such devices as public hearings. The researcher must be aware of the fact that policy makers consider political factors that are not associated with the immediate consequences of the projected policy.
7. *Implementing the course of action.* Implementation involves many smaller decisions that require their own data bases. All the roles of researchers noted above will be repeated here.

8. *Evaluating the outcomes.* The actual results achieved should ultimately be measured. The researcher will often utilize explanatory and experimental designs that lead to such evaluations.
9. *Feedback.* The results of the evaluation should be fed back into another cycle of policy making. The researcher will be called on to create written reports and to interpret them at public and legislative gatherings to facilitate the next cycle.

Conclusion

We began this chapter with a discussion of the role of research in social work. We described the research process that informs any research in which social workers engage. We also stressed that the social worker, as a consumer of research, should use this understanding to evaluate the research that should guide their work. The research process was seen as beginning with problem formulation and proceeding through phases of deciding on measurement, design, data collection, data analysis, and presentation of results.

We then discussed some research issues, particularly those of measurement, that relate more specifically to practice at various levels. These levels are the individual, group, family, organization, community, and the society.

We believe that research is likely to play a larger and larger role in social work practice. This is not only because of the demand on social workers for accountability, but because we believe more practitioners are seeing the value that research can have in improving services to clients. This is associated with more attention being paid in schools of social work as to how their graduates can be prepared better to work on an empirical basis.

However, there are many barriers to this process. Many students are more interested in doing than in learning to evaluate what they do. Agencies are also frequently more interested in processing clients than in ensuring quality of service. This problem is not helped at all by the lack of funding for research and the way that insurance companies compensate agencies for services—ways that do not provide resources for research.

Nevertheless, the possibilities for the use of research to improve practice are increasing. Social workers are becoming knowledgeable about computers and computer programs that simplify the evaluation process. For example, expert systems are now being created by social workers. These computer programs apply "the formal knowledge and reasoning of a narrowly defined problem area to the facts of a specific case in order to arrive at an acceptable solution to a problem."[50] Expert systems require the practitioner to supply information to the program, and the decisional rules built into the program to generate its output can and should be based on empirical findings.

The conclusion of this chapter, therefore, is that we now have the means to enhance the scientific basis of social work and for practitioners to draw on it. It remains to the institutions that train social workers and the agencies that employ them to ensure that the practitioners of this profession utilize these tools to offer the best possible services to people and to add to the knowledge that all can draw on for this purpose.

Notes

1. Allan Borowski, "Social Dimensions of Research," in Richard M. Grinnell, Jr., ed., *Social Work Research and Evaluation,* 3rd ed. (Itaska, Ill.: F. E. Peacock, 1988), p. 45.
2. Ibid.
3. Ibid., p. 46.
4. See a discussion of this issue in Deborah H. Siegel and Frederick G. Reamer, "Integrating Research Findings, Concepts, and Logic into Practice," in Grinnell, ed., *Social Work Research,* pp. 496–497.
5. National Association of Social Workers, NASW Code of Ethics. *NASW News,* 25 (1980) pp. 24–25.
6. Charles D. Garvin, "Research-related Roles for Social Workers," in Richard D. Grinnell, Jr., ed., *Social Work Research and Evaluation* (Itaska, Ill.: Peacock, 1981), pp. 547–552.
7. Ibid., p. 551.
8. Claire Selltiz and others, *Research Methods in Social Relations* (New York: Holt, Rinehart and Winston, 1959), p. 4.
9. Ibid., pp. 4–5.
10. William J. Reid, "Research in Social Work," in A. Minahan, ed., *Encyclopedia of Social Work, Vol. II,* 18th ed. (Silver Springs, Md.: National Association of Social Workers, 1987), p. 475.
11. W. J. Reid and P. Hanrahan, "Recent Evaluations of Social Work: Grounds for Optimism," *Social Work,* 27 (2), pp. 328–340.
12. William J. Reid, "Research in Social Work," p. 476.
13. For a comprehensive discussion of developmental research, see Edwin J. Thomas, *Designing Interventions for the Helping Professions* (Beverly Hills, Calif.: Sage Publications, 1984).
14. E. J. Thomas, "Mousetraps, Developmental Research, and Social Work Education," *Social Service Review,* 52 (3) (1978), p. 470.
15. See Gerald J. Bostwick, Jr., and Nancy S. Kyte, "Measurement," in Grinnell, ed., *Social Work Research and Evaluation,* pp. 93–129, for more details on different types of scales and how they are used.
16. For more details, see Richard M. Grinnell, Jr., and Margaret Stothers, "Utilizing Research Designs," in Grinnell, ed., *Social Work Research and Evaluation,* pp. 199–239.
17. For a classic treatment of this subject, see M. Hersen and D. H. Barlow, *Single Case Experimental Designs: Strategies for Studying Behavior Change,* 2nd ed. (Elmsford, N.Y.: Pergamon Press, 1984).
18. The subject of sampling is technical. The interested reader can consult James R. Seaberg, "Utilizing Sampling Procedures," in Grinnell, *Social Work Research and Evaluation,* pp. 240–257, for a good discussion of this topic.
19. For a good discussion of this topic, see Grinnell and Stothers, "Utilizing Research Designs," pp. 199–239.
20. Again this is a very technical subject. The interested reader can consult John L. Craft, *Statistics and Data Analysis for Social Workers* (Itaska, Ill: F. E. Peacock, 1985), for an introduction to this topic.
21. Selltiz and others, *Research Methods in Social Relations,* pp. 335–342.
22. Walter W. Hudson and Bruce A. Thyer, "Research Measures and Indices in Direct Practice," in Minahan, ed., *Encyclopedia of Social Work,* Vol. II, 18th ed., pp. 487–498.
23. Ibid., p. 492.
24. W. W. Hudson, *The Clinical Measurement Package. A Field Manual* (Homewood, Ill.: Dorsey Press, 1982.
25. Thomas Kiresuk and Geoffrey Garwick, "Basic Goal Attainment Procedures," in Beulah Roberts Compton and Burt Galaway, eds., *Social Work Processes,* 2nd ed. (Homewood, Ill.: Dorsey Press, 1979), pp. 412–421.

26. Kevin Corcoran and Joel Fischer, *Measures for Clinical Practice: A Sourcebook* (New York: The Fress Press, 1987).

27. This section of the chapter draws heavily from Charles Garvin, *Contemporary Group Work* (Englewood Cliffs, N.J.: Prentice Hall, 1987, pp. 202–203), and this work may be consulted for more detail on research approaches to group work practice.

28. Ibid., pp. 202–203.

29. Sheldon Rose, *Group Therapy: A Behavioral Approach* (Englewood Cliffs, N.J.: Prentice Hall, 1977), p. 142.

30. Ibid., pp. 50–51.

31. Irvin D. Yalom, *Theory and Practice of Group Psychotherapy,* 2nd ed. (New York: Basic Books, 1975), p. 51.

32. Sheldon D. Rose, "Use of Data in Identifying and Resolving Group Problems in Goal Oriented Treatment Groups," *Social Work with Groups* 7 (2) (Summer 1984), pp. 23–36.

33. William M. Pinsof, "Family Therapy Process Research," in Alan S. Gurman and David P. Kniskern, eds., *Handbook of Family Therapy* (New York: Brunner/Mazel, 1981), pp. 699–741.

34. Ibid., p. 710.

35. A. E. Scheflen, *Communicational Structure: Analysis of a Psychotherapy Transaction* (Bloomington: Indiana University Press, 1973).

36. Alan S. Gurman and David P. Kniskern, "Family Therapy Outcome Research: Knowns and Unknowns," in Alan S. Gurman and David P. Kniskern, eds., *Handbook of Family Therapy* (New York: Brunner/Mazel, 1981), pp. 742–775.

37. Corcoran and Fischer, *Measures for Clinical Practice,* pp. 416–466.

38. Gurman and Kniskern, "Family Therapy," p. 765.

39. Ibid., p. 770.

40. S. Minuchin, *Families and Family Therapy* (Cambridge, Mass.: Harvard University Press, 1974.)

41. Joseph P. Hornick and Barbara Burrows, "Program Evaluation," in Grinnell, *Social Work Research and Evaluation,* 3rd ed., p. 402.

42. Ibid., p. 412.

43. Tony Tripodi, Phillip Fellin, and Irwin Epstein, *Differential Social Program Evaluation* (Itaska, Ill.: F. E. Peacock, 1978), p. 75.

44. Ibid., p. 93.

45. For a more comprehensive and yet simplified discussion of cost–benefit analysis in social work, see Tripodi, Fellin, and Epstein, *Differential Social Program Evaluation,* pp. 89–104.

46. A. Delbecq, A. Van de Ven, and D. Gustoffsen, *Group Techniques for Program Planning: A Guide to Nominal Group and Delphi Processes* (Chicago: Scott, Foresman, & Co., 1976).

47. The authors attribute the model to A. Irizarry and I. Serrano-Garcia,"*I.* Intervencion en la investigacion: Su aplicacion al Barrio Buen Consejo. *Boletin AVEPSO,*" (1979), pp. 6–21. See Sylvia Marti-Costa and Irma Serrano-Garcia, "Needs Assessment and Community Development: An Ideological Perspective," in Fred M. Cox and others, *Strategies of Community Organization,* 4th ed. (Itaska, Ill.: F. E. Peacock, 1987), pp. 362–373.

48. David M. Austin, "Policy Research," in Grinnell, ed., *Social Work Research and Evaluation,* p. 292.

49. Robert R. Mayer and Ernest Greenwood, *The Nature of Social Policy Research* (Englewood Cliffs, N.J.: Prentice Hall, 1980), as quoted in Austin, "Policy Research."

50. Dick Schoech and others, "Expert Systems: Artificial Intelligence for Professional Decisions," *Computers in Human Services* 1, (1) (Spring 1985), pp. 81–115.

CHAPTER 18
Social Work and the Elimination of Social Exploitation

Basic Principles

Throughout this book we have indicated how such sources of exploitation and oppression as racism and sexism compound every social problem. As a consequence, the service delivery systems that have been established to solve social problems must deal with racism and sexism as important contributors to the problems. For example, in discussing health services we pointed out the unmet health needs of members of minority groups, and in discussing child welfare services we indicated the disproportion of minority children who do not receive necessary services. We also underscored how interventions such as casework, group work, and agency management must take cultural and status issues into consideration.

Integration of this information into all aspects of the book was necessary because social work and social welfare topics cannot be adequately discussed without indicating how human diversity must be considered in working with or on behalf of people. Some of the most important aspects of diversity relate to people's gender and cultural heritage. There are, of course, other human variations, such as age, presence or absence of handicap, education, and income. But we believe that race and gender have been the occasions for a major share of the denial of human rights found in our society.

This denial of human rights is also often referred to as *social oppression*. In our discussion of this topic elsewhere, we stated:

> We define oppression as the destructive effects of social institutions on people when such institutions damage their identities, denigrate their life styles, and deny them access to opportunities. This oppression becomes social oppression when it is based on attributes people share. The most apparant examples of this are the sexism directed at women and the racism directed at members of ethnic groups such as African Americans, Hispanics, Native Americans, and Asian Americans. Others who experience such oppression are members of sexual minorities such as gay men and lesbians, age groups such as the elderly, handicapped people, those who are stigmatized by a label such as "mental patient" and "offender," individuals from nontraditional families, and the working and nonworking poor.[1]

The issues of exploitation and oppression must be understood by social welfare practitioners and this understanding must be utilized in practice. Social work has a commitment to enhancing the opportunity for all citizens to fulfill their potential; that is, to learn what they are capable of learning and do what they are capable of doing, and to freely make those choices that promote self-fulfillment. A major reason why many individuals develop psychological problems, engage in conflict with others, and fail to contribute to society is that opportunities are denied them at crucial times in their lives because of their sex or their ethnic group.

This is a complex matter that goes beyond refusing to hire a person, for example, because of his or her sex or race. Members of groups that are dominant either because they control major sources of power in the society or because they represent a numerical majority often require that those whom they hire or educate or grant other benefits to think like, speak like, and act like themselves.

This leads us to several principles that we believe almost always apply when working with people who are exploited. One is the principle of *empowerment*. Solomon defines empowerment as:

> a process whereby persons who belong to a stigmatized social category throughout their lives can be assisted to develop and increase skills in the exercise of interpersonal influence and the performance of valued social roles. Power is an interpersonal phenomena: if it is not interpersonal it should probably be defined as "strength." However, the two concepts—power and strength—are so tightly interrelated that they often are used interchangeably. In any event, the transformation of the abstraction of power into an observable reality will be the dominant theme of the chapters that follow.[2]

The goal of enhancing the empowerment of people with whom social workers come into contact can be pursued at any system level. Social workers can help to empower individuals when they interact with them on a one to one basis by indicating to them that their rights will be respected by the worker. The worker can also help individual clients to find ways to change situations that exploit or oppress them.

When workers serve families or groups, they can directly help individuals in these situations to learn how to be *assertive* with one another, which is defined as acting in ways that secure a person his or her rights without denying the rights of others. In addition, in the group situation, members can be helped to understand that the group is *their* group and they are responsible for its direction. Family and group members can also be helped to plan ways to attain changes in environments (whether within the agency or the community) that oppress or exploit the family or the group.

Social workers can also have an empowerment perspective when they function as administrators of social agencies. For example, they can create agencies in which the consumers have the power to affect its policies such as when the people who use the services of the agency are represented on its board of directors and on advisory committees to specific programs. Many governmental agencies have policy boards and advisory groups where this can also happen.

When social workers act as community organizers, they can utilize many mechanisms to enable community residents to participate in creating the kinds of neighborhoods in which they want to live. And when social workers operate in organizations that mold public policy they can also ensure that the voices of the people most affected by the policies are heard.

Another major principle relevant to work with exploited people is that of enhancing their *critical consciousness*. Many people who are oppressed, while they are aware of their suffering, do not comprehend its social basis and may blame themselves for their situations. A Brazilian educator, Paulo Freire, has added a great deal to our understanding of this phenomenon.[3] In his efforts to overcome illiteracy in his country, he utilized the idea that people will be motivated to become literate if they connect literacy to the concept that culture is created by human beings and can be altered in the same way. This association occurs through the development of critical consciousness, which is people's understanding of the forces that maintain their exploitation. The highest form of critical consciousness Freire refers to as *critical transitive consciousness.*

> The critically transitive consciousness is characterized by: depth in the interpretation of problems, by the substitution of causal principles for magical explanations; by the testing of one's "findings" and by openness to revision; by the attempt to avoid distortion when perceiving problems and to avoid preconceived notions when analyzing them; by refusing to transfer responsibility; by rejecting passive positions; by soundness of argumentation; by the practice of dialogue rather than polemics; by receptivity to the new for reasons beyond mere novelty and by the good sense not to reject the old just because it is old—by accepting what is valid in both old and new.[4]

The value of a critical consciousness is not only to promote literacy but also to help people understand the social sources of their exploitation, to find ways to minimize these sources, and to become more hopeful that their suffering will come to an end. The message of the song that was the anthem of the civil rights struggle of the 1960s, "We Shall Overcome," is highly pertinent to this point.

Consciousness raising experiences have been utilized by social workers to help exploited people develop their critical consciousness. One example occurred in a group of African-American teenagers in a school setting who were failing in school. While not minimizing the obligation of these young people to do school work, the worker helped them to see that when teachers disparaged their work on racist grounds this discouraged their efforts; their doubts whether they will find employment also contributed to their lack of motivation.

In a group of depressed women, the worker helped the members over time to see that they had often been blamed for the problems of men, had been denied access to employment and educational opportunities, and had been expected to behave aggressively in order to succeed in the workplace. Their despair was often a consequence of their unwillingness to play by men's rules. Alternative ways of coping with situations and securing support from other women were explored.

Another principle is that workers should seek to become as nonracist and nonsexist as possible, given that our culture has many racist and sexist elements. Solomon describes the characteristics of practitioners with African Americans, and we believe these apply to the avoidance of sexism as well.[5] One is to eschew, as Solomon states, "stereotypic explanations for behavior and stereotypic choices of helping strategies."[6] Examples of stereotypic explanations are seeing all African Americans as "nonverbal, nonpsychological-minded and therefore not given to introspection or amenable to psychotherapeutic intervention" or all women as more prone to emotional than rational responses, more invested in relationships than outcomes, or envious of men's attributes.

Solomon indicates that the practitioner can avoid stereotyping in several ways. One is to be able to generate alternative explanations for any behavior of members of a culture through an understanding of their experiences in the society. An example of this from our experience was a worker who was helping Mr. M, an African-American young adult who had just taken a new job. Mr. M. complained that he was given the least desirable tasks, was watched closely, and was avoided by the other employees who were white during work breaks. Using a framework suggested by Solomon, the worker considered two hypotheses: (1) Mr. M. was experiencing discrimination, and (2) Mr. M. was prone to blame others, view situations in a suspicious way, and to isolate himself.

The second way to avoid stereotyping is to be able to use all the verbal and nonverbal cues at one's disposal to single out the alternative that is most probable for *a given client*. Mr. M.'s worker in the example just cited, using a technique described by Solomon, assigned a probability of .70 to hypothesis 1 and .30 to hypothesis 2.[7] This was based on the worker's knowledge of Mr. M's ways of approaching new situations and his emotions in describing this one, as well as the worker's information about this workplace based on previous clients who had worked there.

In view of this evaluation, the worker decided to focus with Mr. M. on helping him to specify how and by whom he was experiencing discrimination as a means of helping him decide what he could do about it. Two ideas that emerged early in this process were that Mr. M. would seek to discuss his situation with the union steward, who appeared sympathetic, and that he would contact an African-American employee he knew in another unit so that they could support one another in further actions that each might take.

Solomon further asserts that nonracist practitioners should strive to remove barriers to experiencing warmth, genuine concern, and empathy for people of backgrounds that differ from their own. She believes that an awareness of these barriers, even when the difficulty resides in the practitioner, is a first step.

Solomon provides an extensive written account by a student to make this point. The student in question worked with a client who was a poor African-American woman who was struggling to deal with all the problems of having a critically ill husband who was in a hospital some distance from her home and whom she visited regularly. The hospital team, despite the student's recommendation and the client's wishes, determined to place the husband in a nursing home. The student, who had low status also by virtue of both being a social worker and a student, nevertheless supported the woman in her insistance on bringing her husband home. She succeeded in this, although shortly afterward he had a medical emergency and died. Later, the client expressed to the student how much her understanding and support had meant and how she thought this would help her in the future.[8]

A final skill of a nonracist practitioner, according to Solomon, is to be able to confront the client "when true feelings of warmth, genuine concern, and empathy have been expressed but have been misinterpreted or distorted."[9] She gives an example of a social worker's interactions with an African-American pregnant teenager who was making a mobile for a baby's crib in a crafts class. The worker praised this work, which was offensive to the teenager, who took it to mean that the white worker would want a "new" one for her baby but a handmade one was good enough for a black person.

The worker used this incident to discuss differences in values and the feelings of the client about this. She also included some consciousness raising by noting the kind of consumerism in the society that makes people value purchased over handmade objects.

These ideas about the nonracist practitioner refer to the actions of a worker who is not a member of the minority group in question. The comparable issue with regard to sexism is how a man might adopt a profeminist attitude. Before we discuss this issue, however, we should note the distinction that is made between a *nonsexist* and a *feminist* perspective. By the former, we mean an outlook in which gender stereotypes are rejected and men and women are not judged in ways that are based on whether or not they conform to such stereotypes. A definition of *sexism* is "any action or institutional structure that subordinates individuals or groups because of their sex."[10] Feminism takes the issue of being nonsexist and places it in a political perspective. As Van Den Bergh and Cooper state:

> Feminism is a transformational politics, a political perspective concerned with changing extant economic, social, and political structures. Basically, feminism is concerned with ending domination and resisting oppression. . . . As a politics of transformation, feminism is relevant to more than a constituency of women. It is a vision born of women, but it addresses the future of the planet with implications accruing for males as well as for females, for all ethnic groups, for the impoverished, the disadvantaged, the handicapped, the aged, and so on.[11]

Tolman and co-authors present a detailed discussion of the development of a profeminist commitment among men in social work. They argue that "Men in social work, by virtue of their professional status, training, and contact with the survivors and perpetrators of oppression, must take a leadership position locally, regionally, and nationally in supporting the feminist struggle to end the oppression of women."[12] They argue that this posture is consistent with social work values and that it will also benefit men, who will be enabled "to move beyond the destructive confines of the traditional male role into a healthier nonhierarchical, noncompetitive system of relationships."[13]

The ways that Tolman and his colleagues see men developing a profeminist commitment are the following:[14]

(1) Men should develop "a historical, contextual understanding of women's experience." One way that this can be done is by keeping up with feminist writing. Particularly relevant are feminist critiques of social science and social work literature, as well as research conducted by feminists and profeminists. Men should seek to understand the historical basis of such events as feminist-oriented discussions from which men are excluded. As these authors state, "A profeminist commitment includes an awareness that men will not be responded to in an 'ahistorical' manner simply because they have begun examining their own psyches and privileges with a feminist lens."

(2) "Men should be responsible for themselves and other men." Thus, men should raise feminist issues on their own and in the company of other men and not only when the issues are raised by women.

(3) Men should redefine masculinity. Men must examine what they gain from masculine privilege. Furthermore, they should examine the process of male bonding by which men reinforce each other's attitudes. We would go further and recommend that men examine and redefine much of their behavior. Of particular importance are such issues as competition, expressions of aggression, values regarding achievement, and the way they interact with women alone as well as in the presence of other men.

(4) Men should "accept women's scrutiny without making women responsible." Even when men get together to become less sexist or more profeminist, they may still do this in ways that reinforce masculine privilege. One approach to struggling with this is to accept feedback from women.

(5) Men should "support the efforts of women without interfering." This principle sees the work of helping women as victims as having priority over helping men as perpetrators. We should work with men who batter, for example, but not at the expense of programs for women who have been abused.

(6) Men should "struggle against racism and classism." This principle is based on the proposition that various forms of exploitation in the society are linked together. For example, African-American mens' exploitation as blacks cancels their advantage as men to a degree.[15]

(7) Men should "overcome homophobia and heterosexism." This principle is based on the idea that men are prevented from forming close relationships with other men because of their fears of the societal stigma against those who deviate from definitions of masculinity.

(8) Men should "work against male violence in all its forms." Male violence is not only a physical phenomenon but also includes psychological and social forms. As they state, "Men who want to work against rape, for example, must be aware of the less obvious oppressions of pornography, sexual harassment, and the sexual objectification of women."

(9) Men should "not set up a false dichotomy and should take responsibility for sexism." We must oppose the tendency of men who profess a profeminist orientation to proclaim their separateness from and superiority over men who do not. This makes such men as individuals the enemy rather than a larger system that supports masculine privilege.

(10) Men should "act at the individual, interpersonal, and organizational levels." This principle is related to the ecological and systemic orientation of this book, which sees all social problems as being manifested at all levels from individual behavior to broad social policies.

(11) Men should "attend to process and product." Many times men who gather together to support feminist principles perpetuate patterns of hierarchy and competition in their groups. This leads to a split in which the men operate on one set of principles ideologically and another behaviorally. This is hardly a platform from which to examine the patterns of domination in our society.[16]

Exploitation and Social Problems

Racism and sexism are linked to social problems in the following ways:

(1) *Most social problems are aggravated by the status of particular groups in the society.* The discrimination leveled at some ethnic groups as well as women increases the likelihood that they will succumb to difficulties related to a variety of social problems. One way for this to happen is through the greater prevalence of poverty in such groups. As Danziger states with reference to the effects of cash transfers, such as through income maintenance programs, upon various groups: "Adjusted poverty rates in 1982 for blacks, Hispanics, and female household heads remained above the official rates for whites in 1966, when in-kind transfers had little impact."[17]

Poverty increases the probability that a person will resort to illegal means to attain necessary goods. It also means that some people will despair that they can have the benefits that others have because channels of employment and education are not as open to them as they are to others. This is referred to by sociologists as limitations in their *opportunity structures.*[18]

Poverty also produces great stress as people worry about securing necessities, paying bills, and providing for their families. Stress can lead to physical and mental illness, family breakdown, inability to work, and many other problems as well.[19]

Another way that racism and sexism aggravate social problems is through the deficits in social power of women, as well as members of minority groups. Solomon describes ways in which the power of members of racial groups is diminished both indirectly and directly. Indirect blocks are "incorporated into the developmental experiences of the individual as mediated by significant others."[20] This happens at three levels:

> At the primary level, negative valuations or stigmas attached to racial identification become incorporated into family processes and prevent optimum development of personal resources . . . i.e., positive self-concepts, cognitive skills, etc. At the secondary level, power blocks occur when personal resources that have been limited by primary blocks in turn act to limit the development of interpersonal and technical skills. At the tertiary level, power blocks occur when limited personal resources and interpersonal and technical skills reduce effectiveness in performing valued social roles.[21]

Direct blocks are those that are not "incorporated into the developmental experiences of the individual but are applied directly by some agent of society's major institutions." Solomon describes these as also occurring at three levels. One level occurs when inadequate health services impair the health of individuals and the community. Another level is when limitations are placed on opportunities for members of minority groups to attain interpersonal or technical skills. The third level is when valued social roles are denied.[22]

Such power deficits add to the effects of poverty in making social problems more severe. Examples are the depression experienced by members of oppressed groups when they are powerless to improve their circumstances, the lack of motivation to improve their circumstances that some members of exploited groups may develop over time, and even that some members of oppressed groups may turn to alcohol and drugs to overcome feelings of impotence.

(2) *Problems may be aggravated by the lack of appropriate services available to members of minority groups and women.* One way this can occur is when minority communities do not have the necessary range of services. For example, a minority community may not have a hospital located in an accessible place or the hospital to which it has access may not offer needed specializations. Other services such as mental health centers, family counseling agencies, or specialized educational facilities may also be absent.

Because of the poverty level of many minority communities, when services are present they are typically government supported. But we are in a period in the United States (as well as many other countries) in which government services are being diminished for both economic and political reasons. This has been true for many family and children's services, school social work services, mental health services, and rehabilitation services in correctional settings. When members of more affluent groups in the society need these services, they can often pay for them individually, through insurance coverage, or through their ethnic associations. Thus, many factors conspire to deny needed services to members of oppressed groups.

Even when the services are available, they may be supplied in ways that are insensitive to the needs of members of minority groups or of women. One way this occurs is through the use of interventions that are unacceptable to or inappropriate for members of the groups. An example is offering a group service that requires a good deal of self-disclosure in an Asian American community that frowns on disclosing intimate matters to people who are not members of one's family. Another way this occurs is through offering a service in a manner that hinders some group from using it, such as a program for poor women that does not provide for child care.

There are many other ways in which agencies may discourage use by members of such groups. This may result from a lack of affirmative action in hiring so that potential clients do not observe people with whom they can identify in the agency or, if they are there, they are only in nonprofessional roles such as janitorial positions. The agency decor may also discourage its use, such as when the pictures on the walls in an agency in an African-American community are only of white people.

One reason these situations occur is through the phenomenon that Blauner calls *internal colonialism.*[23] This term means a circumstance in which the institutions of a community are governed from outside the community by representatives of the dominant groups in the society. One example in social welfare is when a welfare service is governed by a city, state, or other government in which the members of the minority group are not adequately represented. Another is when a nongovernmental service is offered by an organization whose governing structure (such as its board of directors) does not adequately include members of the minority group.

We also believe that analogous situations occur in services for women. This is not because women do not see other women employed in professional social service positions; a recent count showed that 73% of the NASW members are women, and women are overrepresented in direct practice and underrepresented in administrative positions.[24] Rather, policies and procedures have often been designed by men without an understanding of and identification with the needs of women. As Jones states:

> Just as men have been the norm against which women have been seen as deficient or abnormal, white middle-class women no longer can be the norm against which all other women are compared. Women obviously differ in terms of race, ethnicity, class, age, sexual preference, lifestyles, and abilities. Any effective role that social work plays in contributing to changing the position of women in this society will be grounded in the profession's ability to understand and validate the unique, as well as the universal, among women.

One way to assess the deficiencies in the programs and services for women of the traditional social agencies is to compare such programs to those of the many alternative agencies that have been founded in the past 10 to 15 years. Typically guided by feminist values, principles, and methods in their structure and operation, organizations such as rape crisis centers, shelters, and programs for battered women and their children, nontraditional employment, training and educational programs, and women's counseling and health centers have provided services to individuals in addition to advocating for institutional and policy changes. Social workers should examine the work of these agencies to learn about the gaps in traditional services and successful methods for effecting positive changes in women's lives.[25]

(3) *Problems may be aggravated when the solutions offered by social institutions do not take into consideration the ways that minority groups and women define and cope with these problems.* An important fact for social workers to remember is that members of different cultures have different ways of viewing themselves, their problems, and the world around them. As Green states:

> Problem recognition occurs in a cultural, social, and economic context, and there may be instances where what is perceived by clients as normality or as the working out of some inevitable sequence of events is to the professional an instance of pathology, requiring intervention and corrective action.[26]

Green gives as an example of this issue of cultural definitions of problems the issue of "Native American drinking." He points out that there are many stereotypes regarding American Indians and alcohol to the effect that there is a "whole continent of uncivilized tribes incapable of resisting the white man's 'fire-water' and reduced by it, along with warfare and the reservation system, to near-total loss of their lands, livelihood and dignity."[27]

Green first points out the mythology associated with this view. First, the evidence is that drinking is primarily associated in the Indian community with social disorganization brought about by poverty and the destruction of tribal organization. Second, drinking should be seen as "an extension of cultural traditions deriving from precontact as well as postcontact times and, secondly, as a category of learned behavior specific to differing tribal and cultural groups."[28]

Flowing from these propositions, Green explains that behavior associated with drinking varies from one cultural context to another, and the image of a non-Indian drinking is not the same as the Indian reality. There is a large range of Indian drinking behaviors. An example that Green gives of this is the following:

> Among some groups such as the Menomini, religious ceremonies focused on the attainment of visions and dreams, and alcohol was used, often generously, within carefully controlled ritual settings to advance that aim.[29]

Green also cites evidence of other and different cultural responses to drinking found in the Northwest coast groups, the Hopi, the Navajo, the Apache, and the Cree. He presents arguments, consequently, that drinking behavior occurs "within limits" that are culturally defined and that individuals observe even when inebriated. These limits are also part of "time out from normal" behavior found in one form or another in all societies.

This leads to Green's conclusion that there are positive and negative consequences of Native American drinking and internal and external controls on it. He notes that heavy drinking among Indians tends to be a "young man's pastime" that declines rapidly after age 40. It is handled in the dominant society by the police and the courts as well as through such helping mechanisms as Alcoholics Anonymous (AA). AA, however, is seen by many Indians as a white model because it defines alcoholism as a disease and requires abstinence and public confession.

While Green does not chart out a response to the issue of Native American drinking, he does indicate that this response would have to take the above cultural factors into consideration. As he states, "One cannot know a priori that a 'drinking problem' exists unless one knows the values of 'time out' and 'within limits' associated with it."[30]

Another example of social issues in problem definition is that of how women are diagnosed in psychiatric situations as compared to how men are diagnosed. A now classic presentation of this topic is the work of Broverman and co-authors.[31] They found that mental health professionals categorized the typical healthy woman as gentle, quiet, and tactful with a strong need for security and sensitivity for the feelings of others. Healthy males were described as aggressive, dominant, adventurous, and competitive. When asked to describe a mentally healthy *adult,* the professionals used the same terms they chose for the male. Thus, in the judgments of the clinicians the terms *healthy woman* and *healthy adult* were almost mutually exclusive.

There are many implications of the above findings for how problems are seen in mental health settings. Many women do not conform to the stereotype of feminine attitudes and behavior and yet lead happy and productive lives, and the same is true of men in relationship to masculine stereotypes. Nevertheless, these people may well encounter criticisms of their behavior that are stressful for them, and this may elicit in them a variety of ways of coping with stress. It would be a serious mistake, however, for a clinician to regard nonconformity to stereotypes as the problem, rather than societal responses to nonconforming people.

Our remarks regarding gender issues in problem definition just touch the surface of a complex issue. Nevertheless, it should serve to remind the reader of a major point; how problems are defined has major implications for how they will be solved, and cultural values play an important role in this regard.

Ways of Understanding Diversity

When working with members of oppressed and exploited groups, it is important to have a framework for understanding the group as such. We first present our framework for examining the effects of ethnicity and conclude with a discussion of the effects of gender.

UNDERSTANDING ETHNICITY

Literature on ethnicity is pertinent to understanding groups that experience racism.[32] We utilize Gordon's definition of an ethnic group as "any group which is defined or set off by race, religion, or national origin, or some combination of these categories."[33] The importance of understanding ethnicity is emphasized by Gordon:

[W]ithin the ethnic group there develops a network of organizations and informal social relationships which permits and encourages the members of the ethnic group to remain within the confines of the group for all of their primary relationships and some of their secondary relationships throughout all of the stages of the life cycle.[34]

The effects of ethnicity in a society such as ours are not easy to understand, however. One reason is that the ethnic group and its relationship to the larger society are constantly changing. These changes can be understood ecologically as both the group and the larger society evolve and changes in one affect the other.

Another reason why ethnic factors are hard to assess is that a great deal of diversity exists *within* the ethnic group. Not to recognize this places us in the position of stereotyping rather than individualizing members of the ethnic group. In a sense, all we can claim is that members of an ethnic group share a common history and are often treated the same by social institutions. Nevertheless, certain patterns of beliefs and behaviors may be more prevalent in some groups than others, even if everyone does not conform. The individuals who deviate, however, may pay a price.

A further complexity is that variations within the group may be found in different geographical regions. Within the group, also, are social class and other divisions that affect behavior.

Therefore, social workers should seek information to help them understand the relevant ethnic situation. This can be done in part by acquiring general information about the group, and a number of texts are now available that present this in ways that are useful to social workers.[35]

However, the situation is constantly changing, and ethnic communities differ from one another. The worker, consequently, must seek to gain information from people in the local community as well as from the service recipients themselves. The community people who are likely to be helpful are professionals in the community who are members of the ethnic group, such as teachers, ministers, and political leaders. In some cases, professionals who have worked in the community for a long time but who come from other ethnic backgrounds may be helpful if they have seriously sought to overcome their own biases and have sought reliable information.

The use of a framework for collecting such information is something that we have found very useful in reminding us of the kinds of things we should seek to understand. Our framework is based on one created by Valentine.[36] It consists of six dimensions: (1) communications, (2) habitat, (3) social structure, (4) socialization, (5) economics, and (6) beliefs and sentiments. This list does not include history, although knowledge of ethnic history should help workers to understand the experiences and memories that have molded both the attitudes of the larger society and members of the ethnic group. These variables, therefore, should be looked at in both historical and contemporary light.

COMMUNICATIONS. There are two issues that should be examined by practitioners. One is the language used by consumers of their services and the other is the rules as to who communicates with whom and about what in that culture. In relationship to the language issue, we are usually referring to people whose primary language is other than English, such as members of various Hispanic cultures. It is equally important to acknowledge that members of some ethnic groups may speak what the linguists refer to as "nonstandard English," and a major example of this is black English.

It is important for practitioners to consider how they will communicate with service recipients. This may require workers who speak languages other than English, but the use of interpreters is also possible. A different issue surfaces with regard to nonstandard English. This does not require workers to learn a new language, but they must become familiar with specific meanings of words that differ from customary usage. Even more important is the principle that people should not be evaluated negatively for their use of nonstandard English. Social workers, for this reason, have worked with other professionals to increase their awareness of this issue.

Our second point with regard to communications is that cultures vary in their communication rules. For example, in some Hispanic communities when workers contact a family they are expected to speak first with the father before speaking with other family members. In other cultures, members of one sex do not speak about certain topics with members of the other sex. Still other rules relate to communications between members of different generations. At times, workers may deliberately violate one of these rules, perhaps because of an ethical consideration. Nevertheless, workers should always seek to understand communications rules and the costs of violating them.

HABITAT. Workers should also seek to understand how service consumers use physical space, as this is often determined by cultural factors. This dimension relates to different levels of space, including the community and the residence. This should help the practitioner to decide where to make contact with people.

In some cultures, a first contact with a person who is not a family member typically occurs outside the household, while in other cultures the opposite is true. Variations also occur, if contact is made in the home, with regard to which room in the home should be used and where the visitor should sit. In some cultures the visitor is immediately escorted into the kitchen, in others into a sitting room.

The worker who seeks to understand peoples' social interactions will benefit from knowing about community spatial rules. An example of this comes from the activities of a worker with youth gangs. He learned that there were spatial rules regarding each gang's territory. When the gang planned an excursion into the territory of another gang, he correctly inferred that a fight was imminent and he was able to prevent it.

Another ethnic aspect of the community habitat is the nature of community facilities and how they are used. Which are meeting places and which are used for resolving social conflicts? Which are primarily used by one age or sex? Which are prohibited for some or all members of the culture?

It is also important to know how the ethnic community experiences the space of the larger community. Some areas may be utilized and some avoided, and at times these rules exist because of racist experiences. Other reasons for these rules have to do with ethnic values and identity. Nevertheless, the practitioner may not understand an individual's choice of employment resources, transportation, recreation, places to shop, and schools without this information about habitat.

SOCIAL STRUCTURE. Ethnic communities have social structures that determine the patterns of relationships among their members. These structures include those found in families, religious organizations, between generations, and in the many other institutions that exist in each ethnic community.

In many ways different, in many ways the same. (Photo by Eugene Gordon.)

Family patterns are particularly important for practitioners to assess because so many services either affect the family or are offered to families as units. In some ethnic groups the extended family influences members' lives more that in others. The intricate family patterns found in many Native American communities and how families relate to their tribe must be understood in working with members of that group. Families in the African-American community tend to be strong sources of support, and this resource should not be neglected.

Beyond the family are many other sources of social structure. For example, in many Chinese American communities in large cities, economic associations create opportunities for members of that ethnic group, but impose restrictions as well. In Hispanic communities, social structures associated with religious institutions influence relationship patterns and affect beliefs, spiritual and otherwise.

A conflict sometimes arises between the demands of ethnic structures and those embedded in the larger society. An example is that of youths who are accepted as adults in their own culture but not in the larger society; other individuals may occupy prestigious and influential positions in their ethnic community, but are given no recognition for this outside that community.

SOCIALIZATION. This refers to the ways provided by the ethnic group for members to enter into social roles that exist in the culture and to learn how to act in these roles. Workers, particularly when they are also members of the ethnic group, can be enlisted to help with the socialization process.

Workers can be helped to understand ethnic socialization processes by employing the following list of variables developed by Henry, an anthropologist:

1. On what does the socialization process focus? Included here are the nonhuman environment, the world view of the culture, values, social skills, and cultural fictions.
2. How is the information communicated? This consists of opportunities for imitation, formal instruction, problem solving, and gradation of tasks.
3. Who socializes? The choices of these persons are based on sex differences, peer influences, and the status of the educator (for example, parent, expert).
4. How does the person being socialized participate? Henry identifies variations related to emotional responses, social distance, and interactions among individuals in the cohort of people to be socialized.
5. How does the socializer participate? This is affected by the willingness of the socializer to assume that role and his or her attitudes toward the learner's degree of spontaneity and creativity, ways of manipulating the cohort of learners, and use of sanctions.
6. Are some things taught to some and not to others? That is, among a cohort of people socialized at the same time within a culture, further differentiation may occur in view of the sex, social class, or other statuses of the culture.
7. Are there discontinuities in the educational process? This question considers the fact that some stages of the socialization process may require the individual to unlearn things they were taught at other stages.
8. Are there limits to the quantity and quality of what is taught to the socialized person related to the availability of resources? To institutional biases?
9. How is the behavior of the person being socialized controlled?
10. What is the relationship between the intent of the socialization process and its outcomes? In some ethnic groups, the intents of the socialization activity are not realized.
11. What forms of discipline are used?
12. How long does the socialization process last? The actual process, as it affects an individual, may take varying amounts of time, but whether an individual's experience is slower or more rapid than the norm will have implications for the individual.[37]

Examples of socialization processes within ethnic communities of interest to social workers are how children learn family roles, how and when young adults attain independence, how work habits and skills are acquired, how religious obligations are instilled, and how people prepare for death. Again, issues arise when the ethnic group has ways of handling these transitions that differ from those employed in the larger society.

ECONOMY. We consider two types of questions under this heading. An important one is how the economic system of the society affects the ethnic community. Another is the internal economy of the ethnic community itself. The first question can be answered for exploited groups through the use of the concept of internal colonialism. Blauner, in his analysis, states that

> Colonization begins with a forced, involuntary entry. . . . [T]here is an impact on the culture and social organization of the colonized people which is more than just a result of such "natural" processes as contact and acculturation. The colonizing power carries

out a policy which constrains, transforms, or destroys indigenous values, orientations and ways of life. . . . [C]olonization involves a relationship by which members of the colonized group tend to be administered by representatives of the dominant power. Here is an experience of being managed and manipulated by outsiders in terms of ethnic status. A final fundamental of colonization is racism. Racism is a principle of social domination by which a group seen as inferior or different in terms of alleged biological characteristics is exploited, controlled, and oppressed socially and physically by a superordinate group.[38]

The phenomenon of internal colonialism is seen in social work in several ways. One is that social welfare institutions that serve oppressed ethnic groups are likely to be controlled by what Blauner calls the dominant power. Second, much of the power in the community is often held by economic interests, such as businesses, that come from the outside. When they perceive these things, members of the community may avoid such institutions or their use of them may be hesitant and suspicious.

Many economic forces within the community also affect the lives of people. These include the presence of some businesses that are owned by members of the ethnic group and that uniquely respond to its needs for ethnically relevant goods and services. In addition, the values of the ethnic community and the constraints from outside it may determine the occupations individuals do or do not select. Some occupations, also, may exist uniquely to serve the needs of members of the ethnic group, such as the indigenous healers in Puerto Rican, Chicano, and Native American communities.

BELIEFS AND SENTIMENTS. Finally, we find belief systems that differ among ethnic communities and that maintain structures and institutions. These are also perpetuated through socialization processes. They are expressed through religion, folklore, and ritual. They affect who one marries, how children are raised, how one responds to illness (mental and otherwise), and how people interact in countless other ways.

Papajohn and Spiegel, utilizing a model created by Kluckhohn, identify a series of variables that can be used to describe the dominant beliefs of an ethnic group.[39] The first dimension is *activity,* which refers to attitudes toward action. Cultures may favor acting spontaneously, acting so as to bring about self-fulfillment, or acting so as to achieve desired external ends.

The second dimension focuses on *relations among people.* These may emphasize heritage, group membership, or the attributes of individuals. The third describes the culture's posture toward *time,* which may be past, present, or future oriented.

The fourth dimension establishes *how humans are expected to relate to the natural world.* Some cultures see humans as subjected to nature, some as in harmony with it, and others as mastering nature. The last dimension presents the culture's *view of human nature.* Some see humans as essentially good, others as evil, and others as a mixture of good and evil.

This typology has sometimes been criticized as tending to treat cultures too stereotypically. We believe, however, that used with caution and due regard for the fact that almost all people in our society are heavily influenced by the values of the larger society, it can be useful in illuminating issues that arise between social welfare professionals and ethnic community members. In another context, we summarized this issue as follows:

The worker should seek, therefore, to understand the dominant profile of beliefs within a culture, how the individual relates to it, and how it may be changing. The degree to which the individual client perceives and attempts to follow or resist the cultural influences of his group should be assessed. Resistance to cultural influences and subsequent conflicts is often a result of the client's efforts to identify with the larger culture. Such clients experience a social status that social scientists term "marginality" in which individuals identify with aspects of two cultures yet are not fully accepted in either. This is a stressful social position and the interpersonal practitioner should recognize when a client suffers from his or her marginality and help such clients to develop suitable coping strategies.[40]

UNDERSTANDING GENDER

In the strictest sense, men and women do not form different cultures, but, in many ways, how members of one sex view the world is substantially different from the other. It is also true that men and women differ in a variety of other ways, but the issue is complicated because many of these ways are matters of differences in socialization rather than biology. Unfortunately, also, many studies of human behavior have either suffered from the biases of the men who conducted them or have not distinguished between men and women but have described all individuals as if they were members of the same, usually masculine, sex.

Social workers should be familiar with studies of male and female behavior and attitudes, particularly those that have been conducted with the most conscientious attention to the concerns we have just stated. The following are some conclusions that can be drawn from such studies.[41]

(1) Much current research challenges traditional assumptions about biologically based female traits. Rather, it is apparent that "girls are socialized toward dependence, submissiveness, and achievement through others by way of marriage and child rearing."[42]

(2) The women's movement has had a major impact on women's socialization and on expectations of women.

(3) Because of the continued presence of pressure on women, however, to conform to more traditional roles, some women who do not succumb to this pressure experience ambivalence and anxiety about their choice. This is because "achieving women are judged more harshly than men, are considered unfeminine, and are perceived and treated as deviants."[43]

(4) There are only four areas in which consistent sex differences are shown. Studies have indicated superiority for females in the areas of verbal ability, superiority for males on measures of visual-spatial and mathematical ability, and greater physical aggressiveness by males. Nevertheless, feminist psychologists place these differences within a sociocultural rather than biological framework, as these differences conform to cultural conceptions; in addition these findings place men and women in overlapping distributions so that many men and women have similar capacities.[44]

(5) Many studies of sex differences have focused on white, middle-class females. Less is known about women from exploited ethnic groups, lesbians, and those from the working class. Nevertheless, expectations of men and women are different in every

cultural group "with women in each group having problems related to gender inequality in their own culture and in the dominant culture."[45]

(6) Studies of African-American women have shown, however, that they "are less tied to stereotypical female roles and behaviors, view work as compatible with family roles, and have more egalitarian marital relationships."[46]

(7) Hispanic women are particularly affected by patriarchal family, community, and religious systems, which, together with the *machismo* norm, promote "female passivity and frequent childbearing and discourages education and employment for women."[47]

(8) Formerly, Asian American women held unassertive roles, but more recently "have assumed more authority in their families, are increasingly questioning the traditional roles of Asian women in their ethnic communities, and are becoming more assertive. . . ."[48]

(9) The status of Native American women appears to be more a product of their poverty and the fact that federal policies have placed power in the hands of Native American men than a result of strong patriarchal norms in their own communities.[49]

(10) Many of the stereotypes of lesbian women have been disproved, and these women vary as much as heterosexual women "in personality, family constellation, and developmental experiences." In addition, "lesbians are more inner directed, assertive, and self-sufficient and have greater job satisfaction" than heterosexual women.[50]

Conclusion

Reducing the amount of exploitation and oppression in our society is a central concern for social workers and an important part of the profession's mission, and we have highlighted this topic in this chapter.

We began the chapter with a presentation of basic principles. Among these is an understanding of the concepts of oppression and empowerment, one leading us into a comprehension of societal forces and the other of ways of enhancing the ability of people to cope with and change these forces. We see empowerment as beginning with the development of a *critical consciousness.* The operation of these concepts at different levels of social intervention was also illustrated. This section of the chapter concluded with a discussion of how a profeminist vision can contribute to dealing with exploitation and oppression, particularly as these stem from sexism.

We then described how exploitation affects the various kinds of social problems that social work addresses. We focused on three topics. The first was how the status of oppressed groups in the society affects their exposure to sets of social problems and handicaps their ability to solve these problems. The second dealt with the ways that services are established that limit their effective use by members of exploited groups. The third topic analyzed the effects of various ways of defining problems that are not attuned to cultural differences, thus resulting in inappropriate and ineffective services.

Finally, we offered ways of adding to our understanding of the impact of gender and culture on all of us. Such understanding should lead to an increase in the ability of social workers to work more effectively with people through a better awareness of the nature and value of human diversity.

Notes

1. Charles Garvin, *Contemporary Group Work,* 2nd ed. (Englewood Cliffs, N.J.: Prentice Hall, 1987), p. 285

2. Barbara Solomon, *Black Empowerment* (New York: Columbia University Press, 1976), p. 6.

3. Paulo Freire, *Education for Critical Consciousness* (New York: Seabury Press, 1973).

4. Ibid., p. 18.

5. Solomon, *Black Empowerment,* pp. 300–313.

6. Ibid., p. 300.

7. Ibid., pp. 301–308.

8. Ibid., pp. 309–311.

9. Ibid., p. 311.

10. Diane Goldstein Wicker, "Combatting Racism in Practice and in the Classroom," in Nan Van Den Bergh and Lynn B. Cooper, eds., *Feminist Visions for Social Work* (Silver Spring, Md.: National Association of Social Workers, 1986), p. 33.

11. Nan Van Den Bergh and Lynn B. Cooper, eds., *Feminist Visions for Social Work* (Silver Spring, Md.: National Association of Social Workers, 1986), pp. 1–2.

12. Richard M. Tolman and others, "Developing Profeminist Commitment among Men in Social Work," in Van Den Bergh and Cooper, eds., *Feminist Visions for Social Work,* p. 62.

13. Ibid.

14. These ways are summarized from Tolman and others, "Developing Profeminist Commitment," pp. 66–72.

15. Robert Staples, "Masculinity and Race: The Dual Dillemma of Black Men," *Journal of Social Issues,* 34 (1) (1978), pp. 169–183.

16. All quotes in this list are from Tolman and others, "Developing Profeminist Commitment," except as noted.

17. Sheldon Danziger, "Poverty," in A. Minahan, ed., *Encyclopedia of Social Work,* Vol. II, 18th ed. (Silver Springs, Md.: National Association of Social Workers, 1987), p. 299.

18. A now classic presentation of this subject may be found in Richard A. Cloward and Lloyd E. Ohlin, *Delinquency and Opportunity* (New York: The Free Press, 1969).

19. B. S. Dohrenwend and B. P. Dohrenwend, eds., *Stressful Life Events: Their Nature and Effects.* (New York: Wiley-Interscience, 1974).

20. Solomon, *Black Empowerment,* p. 17.

21. Ibid., pp. 17–18.

22. Ibid., p. 18.

23. Robert Blauner, "Internal Colonialism and Ghetto Revolt," *Social Problems* 16 (Spring 1969), pp. 393–408.

24. June Gary Hopps and Elaine B. Pinderhughes, "Profession of Social Work: Contemporary Characteristics," in *Encyclopedia of Social Work,* Vol. II, 18th ed., p. 357.

25. Linda E. Jones, "Women," in *Encyclopedia of Social Work,* Vol. II, 18th ed., pp. 879–880.

26. James W. Green, *Cultural Awareness in the Human Services* (Englewood Cliffs, N.J.: Prentice Hall, 1982), p. 33.

27. Ibid.

28. Ibid., p. 34.

29. Ibid.

30. Ibid., p. 36.

31. I. H. Broverman and others, "Sex Role Stereotypes and Clinical Judgments of Mental Health," *Journal of Consulting and Clinical Psychology,* 34 (1970), pp. 1–7.

32. The material in this section draws on Charles Garvin and Brett Seabury, *Interpersonal Practice in Social Work* (Englewood Cliffs, N.J.: Prentice Hall, 1984), pp. 321–331.

33. Milton Gordon, *Assimilation in American Life* (New York: Oxford University Press, 1964), p. 27.

34. Ibid., p. 34.

35. For example see chapters on each ethnic group in Green, *Cultural Awareness in the Human Services;* D. W. Sue, *Counseling the Culturally Different: Theory and Practice* (New York: John Wiley & Sons, 1981); Richard H. Dana, ed. *Human Services for Cultural Minorities* (Baltimore: University Park Press, 1981).

36. Charles Valentine, *Culture and Poverty: Critique and Counter Proposals* (Chicago: University of Chicago Press, 1968), pp. 178–180.

37. This list was developed by Jules Henry in *Essays on Education* (Baltimore: Penguin Books, 1971), pp. 72–183, and adapted for social work settings in Garvin and Seabury, *Interpersonal Practice in Social Work,* p. 326.

38. Blauner, "Internal Colonialism," pp. 393–408.

39. John Papajohn and John Spiegel, *Transactions in Families* (San Francisco: Jossey-Bass, 1975), p. 21.

40. Garvin and Seabury, *Interpersonal Practice in Social Work,* p. 329.

41. This discussion draws heavily from Diane Kravetz, "Women and Mental Health," in Van Den Bergh and Cooper, eds., *Feminist Visions for Social Work,* pp. 101–127.

42. Kravetz, in "Women and Health," cites the following for this conclusion: Jean Baker Miller, *Toward a New Psychology of Women* (Boston: Beacon Press, 1976); Virginia E. O'Leary, ed., *Toward Understanding Women* (Monterey, Calif.: Brooks/Cole Publishing Co., 1977); and Juanita H. Williams, *Psychology of Women: Behavior in a Biosocial Context* (New York: W.W. Norton, 1977).

43. Kravetz, "Women and Mental Health," p. 103.

44. Ibid., pp. 103–104.

45. Ibid., p. 105.

46. Ibid.

47. Ibid., p. 106.

48. Ibid.

49. Ibid.

50. Ibid., pp. 106–107.

CHAPTER 19
The Profession of Social Work

Introduction

The profession of social work is relatively new as professions go, starting mainly in the twentieth century. In contrast, the classical professions, law, medicine, and theology, are hundreds of years old. Social work is not unique in its newness; many other occupational groups (nursing, dentistry, for example) are aspiring to professional status, and for them, as well as for the profession of social work, full social acceptance of professional status remains elusive.

Social work has made great strides in moving toward achieving professional status. Nonetheless, substantial questions remain about social work itself and its claims to professionalism, on the one hand, and about the question "What is a profession, anyway?" on the other. The purpose of this chapter is to outline the entire issue of professionalism in its relationship to social work and to make an argument for qualified acceptance of social work as a profession.[1]

THE DEFINITION OF A PROFESSION

Professions have been defined variously. These definitions contain a range of components. What is needed is to first identify the most common components. Second, it is important to look at the difference between the profession, on the one hand, and the professional, on the other. It will then be possible to assess the extent to which social work meets the criteria that would most commonly be used in describing a profession.

KEY POINTS IN THE DEFINITION

Our overall review suggests seven common themes or criteria that are used when talking about a profession: (1) body of knowledge, (2) theoretical basis, (3) university training, (4) produces income, (5) professional control of practitioners, (6) internal moral or ethical control of professional activities, and (7) measurable or observable results. Let us consider each briefly in turn.

BODY OF KNOWLEDGE. Professions have a common body of knowledge that practitioners use to carry out their work. The body of knowledge is codified in the sense that it is not simply lore passed on from person to person, but rather is accessible to novices through review of the professional literature. There is also an art to the implementation of a professional skill, which one needs to develop. An important component in most professional education is some kind of internship or training for the novice in which the application of knowledge can be attempted and observed and additional points and tips can be suggested. In other words, the art of practice is explored and honed. This practice, however, needs to derive from a codified body of knowledge if an occupation is to qualify for professional status.

THEORETICAL BASIS. An additional demand on the codified body of knowledge is that it have some theoretical basis in scientific fact, as in the case of medicine, or in closely reasoned logic, as in the case of law. Theory is an interconnected set of propositions, each of which supports and extends the others. Theory explains the conditions under which particular procedures are valuable and helpful or not. Theory allows practitioners to do more than have an unintegrated list of helpful hints or guides. Professions usually have theoreticians who spend some time developing this theory base. It is not necessarily required that all professionals be acquainted in depth with all the theoretical underpinnings, but they need to be acquainted with those relative to their particular part of the enterprise. Hence, social workers using behavior modification need to know that theoretical area, community organization workers need to know community theory, and so on.

UNIVERSITY TRAINING. To achieve professional status, training must be provided within a university or college context. This education usually deals with the scientific bases for professional work, contains courses that promote the integration of knowledge and practice, and may contain courses that look at the profession in a societal context. Frequently, an integral component of the training is clinical or experiential aspects under college or university instruction and supervision. Such experiential training is characteristic of medicine, dentistry and social work, where important clinical activities are carried on within the university umbrella. Law on the other hand has a more modest clinical aspect.

INCOME-PRODUCING. Professions allow one to make an income or derive a living from the practice of the profession. While not all professionally trained individuals use their skills as their source of income, they nonetheless could do so.[2]

CONTROL OF PRACTITIONERS. An important requisite of professional status is that the profession as such controls those who practice it. This control is usually achieved through legislative influence. Laws restrict and limit who may use the title of the profession in question and may also stipulate legal requisites for training and continued qualification. Individuals who misrepresent themselves as professionals are open to legal sanctions.

MORAL AND ETHICAL CONTROLS.[3] While legal controls often limit who may enter the profession, they do not assure that the professional practice in any given instance is appropriate. That job is left to the profession itself and involves internal or moral and ethical controls with respect to the practice of professional activities. Problems of appropriateness are, in the initial instances at least, policed by the profession. Hence, the physician is not supposed to recommend that you have your appendix removed just because the physician may need a few more dollars. Complaints of unnecessary surgery are reviewed first by professional boards. (Actually, all surgical procedures are reviewed by hospital committees.) But legal authorities may become involved as well.[4]

Similarly, social workers are constrained by the National Association of Social Workers' Code of Ethics to keep the client interests, rather than the professional's interests, at the forefront. In general, there is a social exchange here. There is an implied contract between the client or patient on one hand and the professional practitioner on the other. In exchange for a guild or monopoly status with respect to practicing the particular skill, the professional agrees not to take advantage of the client's vulnerabilities. (The client or patient may be in great physical and emotional pain, frightened, ignorant of what needs to be done, which allows the professional the possibility of recommending complex and costly procedures that the client or patient does not need and which the client or patient cannot properly evaluate.) In short, the professional agrees to be competent, to put the client's interest first, and not to take advantage of the client.

MEASURABLE, OBSERVABLE RESULTS. An important criterion for professional status is that the professional perform a task, activity, or service that can in some way be publicly verified, observed, or seen. Other professionals are available to check the work. The client or patient is also a reporter on what has happened. Still others, although amateurs (as opposed to professionals), are able to provide some kind of overall judgment on professional competence. All professions have products that can be evaluated in these ways. In the case of the law, it is the provision of legal service and the accomplishment of legally desired ends. The goal can be a will drawn up, a contract executed, or legal representation provided in court. In the case of medicine, it is a return to healthy status. In the case of dentistry, improved dental condition is the goal.

PROFESSION VERSUS PROFESSIONAL

Before assessing the extent to which social work meets or does not meet the preceding criteria, it is important to consider the issue of the difference between the profession and the professional. The profession is an institutional form into which professionals fit. However, not all the individuals we consider professionals are actually in a profession. This confusion of language requires attention.

A *professional* at a job (a "pro") is an individual who can perform a given task at a high level of competence and do so repeatedly under a wide range of conditions. One can think of professional musicians, professional baseball players, professional chess players, and so on. In this usage, these individuals are extremely skilled at a relatively narrow range of tasks. The problem is that simply being extremely skilled does not necessarily mean one has professional status, as defined here. Being an excellent, extremely skilled, plumber, for example, does not by itself qualify one for professional status. There is a lack of university training in plumbing. There is a lack of theoretic knowledge (however, the mathematics, hydraulics, metallurgy, and so on, on which plumbing is ultimately based are available by training and education; these aspects, however, have not been integrated into the typical apprentice plumber's curriculum).

A professional musician, however, may occupy a sort of intermediate professional status; on the one hand, there are journeymen musicians who have learned to play an instrument themselves and do so with unbelievable skill; on the other hand, there are musicians who have graduated from university music schools, have studied music theory, history, and commentaries on that history, and perform on an instrument. Music, then, may as a field have professionals who have been conventionally qualified, through actual playing, but do not have professional status. Social work is something like this itself, with university qualified and conventionally qualified people in it.

Thus, one more criterion must be added to the list already given—a high level of skill. Professionals must have and professions must affirm a high level of skill.[5] Embodied in the phrase "she's a real pro" is the idea of high-quality performance repeated over and over again. The only caveat is that being able to do something well over and over again may make one a professional at the task but does not qualify the task for professional status as an occupational group. Similarly and conversely, being a professional in the sense of meeting the definitions required by professional associations and bodies does not mean one is any good at what one does.

One more issue about professionals and professions needs to be mentioned here. The problem for music, at least in the performance end, is that it has customers rather than clients or patients. The individual musical appreciator listening to a performance is not considered as vulnerable as the person who needs a plumber or a surgeon.[6] Apart from the issue of skill, most professions have clients in a vulnerable position. They need the services of the doctor or social worker. High skill and protection of the vulnerable are two final requisites of the professional.

Is Social Work a Profession?

The question can now be addressed: Is social work a profession? Criteria are available to assess our field and against which we can measure our particular position. The overall answer is a bit equivocal at this point: Yes and no. We are definitely moving toward full professional status, yet in some areas we do not meet the criteria and are thus open to challenge and criticism. From one point of view, whether society considers social work a full-fledged profession or not is more of an internal concern related to the social worker's own feelings of self-esteem and status security than anything else. The key point that will emerge in this discussion is that we have plenty of knowledge and training. We do a job that is needed and valued in the society and perform that job competently. Whether we meet technical professional definitions or not is useful to think about, indeed an important question, but not the only question.[7] Let us look at each criterion and assess the extent to which social work meets, somewhat meets, or does not meet this particular measure or assessment.

COMMON BODY OF KNOWLEDGE.   Social work does have to a large degree a common body of knowledge developed historically over time, one that comes from both practice wisdom and social science. However, there are certain limitations to the application of this body of knowledge. The knowledge remains highly general, and as yet the profession of social work has no accepted taxonomy of problems and conditions that would bond together social workers from different backgrounds and trainings. This makes understanding difficult for the lay person who may not know exactly what is meant by a service called, for example, "daycare." Unfortunately, even social workers may not all understand and agree on what is meant by the concept. Hence, we have the need to make some progress in this particular area.

THEORY BASED. A number of social work theories are used as the underpinnings of intervention. These theories include behavioral modification, ego psychology, and various social-psychological community and organizational theories, as well as theories of the state. However, two problems remain at this time.

First, there are often ideological arguments over the theories. They seem to compete rather than complement each other. Those who follow ego psychological theories may dispute the validity of behavioral modification theories, and conversely, so that we are in a stage of theoretical competition rather than amalgamation and consolidation. These theoretical conflicts exist within the same level of intervention as well as across levels. Some social workers believe that the individual level is where causes for problems should be sought and repaired. Others believe that it is in the larger system of social structure that the problem lies. Thus, in treating a woman client with low self-esteem, some workers might look at the family background and relationships with parents, while others would look at her status as a women in a male-dominated social system. Obviously, both play a part, and the ratio will differ depending on the individual case; the profession must avoid wasting time fighting about one being *always right.*

Second, there is disagreement over which theory applies to what problem. Or it may be that the same symptom, depending on the individual, has different causes among which we are unable as yet to discriminate. The overweight individual, for example, may be treated with counseling and ego psychological techniques, or behavioral modifications, or both. There is no completely clear way as yet to distinguish which kind of treatment is most appropriate in which kinds of settings and for which kinds of syndromes.

UNIVERSITY TRAINING. In this area, social work can answer with a resounding yes. Our profession has had university training, the Master of Social Work Degree, since 1907 when the School of Civics and Philanthropy became a part of the University of Chicago. Other schools have developed since then, and now close to 90 professional schools of social work offer the M.S.W. degree. There are also B.S.W. degrees. Being new, the exact professional position of the B.S.W. is still under development. The National Association of Social Workers recognizes B.S.W. degrees for membership, and it has become the requirement for many jobs (more than once in replacement of an M.S.W. degree).

INCOME-PRODUCING. Training and education in social work do lead to livelihoods and as such we qualify for professional status on this dimension. However, there is an important caveat: generally, there is an ambivalence about money making that runs throughout our field and that is not fully resolved. Partly this ambivalence stems from the fact that we have, as well, an important volunteer tradition in our field. This tradition springs out of altruistic feelings of concern for others and implies that help should be given freely. It also implies that one earns money, then, elsewhere. Furthermore, social work's association with the disadvantaged has not put the profession in an area where access to support (money, community support, and so on) is easy. And some social workers may feel guilty about "making money off the poor." But there is a further complexity as well. The man who founded Alcoholics Anonymous, Bill W., commented at one point, "There are some things that can be done with money and some things which can't be done with money." This comment suggests that some kinds of help must be given freely; they cannot be paid for. Hence, a tension exists here about where, when, and how treatment and intervention are to be paid for. So, in some sense, the answer to the question, "Can you make a living in social work?" is "Yes, but certainly not a posh one."

CONTROL OF PRACTICE. Once again the answer with respect to the field of social work on this question must be somewhat equivocal. A number of individuals with a variety of training and backgrounds use the term social worker. State licensing for the use of the term is now developing in many states. But the licensing requirements are various, and the presence of an M.S.W. or other social work degree is not necessarily required to have an official "social work" license.

INTERNAL MORAL AND ETHICAL CONTROL. Social work can score a resounding yes on this criterion. There is a code of ethics developed in considerable detail by the National Association of Social Workers. Sanctions have been taken against individual social workers under this code of ethics. Ethical considerations are among the most important guides that a profession has. One reason for this importance lies in the vulnerability of the client. This vulnerability provides opportunities for exploitation, and ethical norms control these situations. (However, laws do so as well.)

OBSERVABLE, MEASURABLE RESULTS. In this area, social work must once again give an equivocal response. At the interpersonal level our product is the same that other mental health and counseling professionals espouse—individuals and families with smoother, less troubled and less self-destructive patterns of behavior toward self and others. All the behavior change occupations and professions will have difficulty on this criteria. What is the end state that is desired and is that to be considered the product? Or is the product, in the case of clinical workers, counseling hours or sessions?[8] Social work, like the other behavior change professions, needs to more systematically and definitively define what its products and services are. Such definition will make assessment easier (though more painful perhaps, in some instances, because lack of progress and improvement will be revealed) and allow for greater focus and targeting in the training enterprise.

All social workers need to define goals for their practice. Social workers at the individual level define goals for their clients and often set benchmark periods for accomplishment. Social workers who work at the organizational, community, and policy levels set goals as well. In fact, these social workers are usually requested to define certain goals for their intervention. The results are changed community conditions, enhanced organizational performance, and legislation passed or legislative rules changed. While there is some resistance to these kinds of measures within the field of social work, we are overall moving toward a recognition that in every instance of social work intervention goal setting is appropriate. And goal setting is the first step toward client assessment. Without a goal, assessment is difficult. Assessment is appropriate, but we do not imply that the assessment is a complete measure of all that went on or that it should be taken completely at face value. Just as student evaluations of professors' teaching are understood thoughtfully, criticism of any sort should be understood thoughtfully. However, without assessment, public confidence in professional practice is undermined.

PROFESSIONAL COMPETENCE. Competence is doing something extremely well. Unfortunately, here, too, social work is not as strong as we would like. Behavior change occupations do much of their work apart from public view; hence, unlike the performing musician, the performing social worker cannot often be observed in action. But the issue of competence hangs, finally, on a prior issue: What is it you are to be competent *at?* The lack of clear outcome measures creates a problem here as well. Thus, social work needs to define more specifically the goals, in general, that it claims itself competent to achieve. Surgery, legal representation, and repair of teeth are examples from other professions. Once general goals are set, individual versions of them can be set for specific clients.

Overall, then, social work is moving toward professional status but has areas where more work needs to be done. The development of a taxonomy and a more unified body of theory are areas where much improvement is needed. Greater precision in product and service specification and measurement of outcomes is another, along with development of assessments for professional competence. And the development of more precise legal controls on who may use the professional title is another area. Progress is being made in each of these, and in other criteria social work scores "very well." It is for this reason we conclude that social work is in the emergent phase of professional development.

CRITICISMS OF SOCIAL WORK'S PROFESSIONAL STATUS

A number of thinkers both within the profession and closely allied to it have raised questions about social work's professional status. In 1915, Abraham Flexener in a powerful paper asked the question, "Is social work a profession"?[9] Flexener had just completed an impressive study of the medical field and made suggestions that fundamentally revised medical education. He did not have such a big influence on social work, however, and, as implied by his question, the answer was "probably not" at that particular time. Questions continue to be raised in a variety of contexts about social work's professional status. Saunders talked about the semiprofession, an occupation "on the way" to professional status.[10] The semiprofession tag was reiterated by Etizioni in his review of the semiprofessions.[11] Semiprofession issues were discussed again by Toren.[12] In each case the (semi) profession of social work was a focus of the discussion. These authors reached, in a variety of ways, a conclusion similar to our own; that is, social work meets some but not all the criteria that we might employ to assess professional status.

Still others, notably Willard Richan and Allan Mendelsohn, talk about the social status of the profession in their book *Social Work—The Unloved Profession.*[13] They talk about the climate of negativity and, in some cases, hostility that surround the field of social work and the tensions and troubles that such a constant sense of beleagerment engenders. Why should there be hostility and negativity toward this helping profession? The reasons are complex and manifold. Among the important factors is that social work seeks to help the poor, and U.S. society is hostile toward the poor. Some of that hostility rubs off. Perhaps a second reason has to do with gender. The women's professions tend to come under more attack than others. Then there is the issue of societal expectation. Somehow, social workers are seen as being there to solve social problems. When the hoped for results do not appear, negativism can result. Social workers are often called "bleeding hearts." Thus, social workers are perceived of as excusing individuals from taking responsibility for their actions. In a responsibility-oriented society, such a charge can generate negativism. Finally, social workers are often in the forefront of pointing out social problems in society, such as racism, classism, agism, and sexism, that cause further social problems. The messenger of bad news is often not appreciated.

The clinical part of social work has its own difficult problems to contend with. Janet Malcolm has written a book on the profession of psychoanalysis called *Psychoanalysis:The Impossible Profession,* and such a title might well apply to aspects of social work's counseling mission.[14] Counseling is done in private, assessment is very difficult, results are often equivocal, and professional activity is often sustained more by commitment than by external reinforcement.

Within the field, therefore, as well as in the minds of citizens at large, questions are raised about social work's professional status. We would like to reiterate again that these questions are legitimate and should not be threatening or require any kind of overcompensating response. Social work is seeking to develop professional status and is following a trajectory that is appropriate and useful to itself in an area of great difficulty and with many external constraints. As a professional field, we should be able to interpret these constraints to others in a positive rather than a defensive way. After all, we understand them better than they do. We should also understand that our explanations and interpretations may not always be convincing to our critics. That, too, is acceptable. We cannot convince everyone. In many important respects, and in the helping professions certainly, the journey toward improvement is as important as the destination.

KEY PROFESSIONAL TOUCHPOINTS FOR SOCIAL WORK

In assessing the professional status of social work and the supports and attacks that have evolved over the years, some key touchpoints have emerged that deserve special comment. The three stressed here are the gender ratio of the profession, the focus on the poor, and the emphasis on criticism of the establishment.

A WOMEN'S PROFESSION. The gender ratio in social work is very heavily female. According to the National Association of Social Workers, 74% of its membership (around 100,000 in 1987) was female.[15] In this respect, social work shares a similar position with education (71% female in elementary and secondary education, 1980 Census), and nursing (95% of general nurses, 1980 Census).[16] These women's professions share certain common characteristics. One is lower pay. The 1986–1987 salary average for teachers was $26,704 and for all general nurses, $24,200. The overall National Association of Social Workers salary for the same time period was $27,800.[17]

A second characteristic has to do with the lower level of seriousness with which a male-dominated society takes the wisdom of the female professions. A gender balance in these professions would be as desirable as in business, law, and medicine—occupational professional areas previously closed to women. These areas are now open to women, and one sees important fractions of female students in law schools, medical schools, and business schools.[18] These fractions seem to be greater than the proportion of male students found in many social work schools. Thus, U.S. society seems to be in a position of gender redistribution among the occupations, and social work might wish to take a more competitive posture with respect to the male minority; but it is not clear how social work can overcome the problem of needing more males. Problems that are diverse require a diversity of staff to help with them.

A FOCUS ON THE POOR. Historically, social work has emphasized the needs and problems of the disadvantaged population, those at the bottom of the economic and social ladder. This identification is still very much with members of the profession today. It is a source of considerable concern to social workers as to how new areas for social work can be explored without losing the historical professional focus on those who are disadvantaged. To further complicate the problem, most professionals offer their services to the entire range of citizenry. Doctors, dentists, attorneys, and others, do not restrict their services to any one group (although they sometimes avoid the poor). In many ways, the problems with which social work deals, problems of malperforming personal and family systems, organizations, and communities, are similarly stretched across the board. Hence, a very good argument could be made that social work should focus on the problem, not on the population. The reply, however, is that when we focus on the *problem,* we may often neglect the *population* that is most in need of help, especially if that population is poor.[19] The difficulty is that the poor cannot pay for help, and if we wish to make a living at our professional activities, then we needs to be paid.

However, the poor's *own* resources may be only part of the issue. Third-party payments are available in some instances, and Department of Welfare and Social Services workers help in others; or the departments may contract out services on a fee for service basis. It may also be the case that the disadvantaged, or the poor (never a clear category), may be a difficult client group. Social workers may have avoided them in part because it is tough to work, day in and day out, with those who have multiple problems and a poverty of solutions.

Such tensions are likely to beset the field for awhile and will be worked out only over time. Our own view is that the shape of an ultimate solution will involve social work offering its services to the full range of the population, while developing a combination of professional norms and assessments so that special attention can be given to those who are so important to our historical formulation and who are in need of services. Perhaps the eventual shape of the social work profession will involve two kinds of differentiation. One kind will involve workers going into different kinds of practices, such that the *profession* will provide services to the full range of population groups, while individual *professionals* might have specialized practices, either with special groups (by race, sexual preference, type of problem, or poverty–nonpoverty status. At the same time *some individual professionals may* introduce diversity into their own practice, either at a single point in time (seeing diverse patients or clients within a single day/week/month) or may, over the course of a year or several years, seek to maintain a heterogeneous practice. Special attention will need to be given to the poor, the multiproblem cases, the difficult situations, which, in all likelihood, all professions might feel pressure to ignore. Perhaps professional norms will develop that encourage that a certain fraction of everyone's workload be devoted to these cases. And funding, perhaps through social service vouchers, may make provision of service more possible.[20]

CRITICISM OF THE ESTABLISHMENT. Partly because of its focus on the disadvantaged, social work has been more acutely aware than most professions of those aspects of our social system that operate unjustly, cruelly, and without regard for the essential humanity of individuals. This perception has often led social work, as an institution and as individual members, to criticize the community and societal elites. Big government, big business, and community elites all come in for their share of attack. And, indeed, there is very little question that these institutions have been and continue to be responsible for portions of the plight of the disadvantaged. The difficulty is that it is from the dominant institutions that much of the support for social work ultimately comes, since the disadvantaged, by definition, cannot do it. Social work is thus in the position of biting the hand that feeds it, and this tension lies deep within the organizational framework of our field. How to make appropriate criticism in a way that highlights discrepancies, unfairness, exploitation, racism and sexism, but to do so in a way that does not completely alienate needed support is a very difficult organizational and professional question.[21]

Targets of the criticism often respond by demeaning the professional status of social work, thus undermining the credibility of the charge, rather than fixing what is wrong. Perhaps this response is to be expected. No one likes to be criticized, especially if the criticism is valid. However, it may also be true that social work, because of a sense of moral superiority, may make its charges more sweeping and less documented than focused and factual. It is likely that tensions among these dimensions will exist for some time.

Overall, then, the fact that social work is dominated by female professionals, that it has a historical and contemporaneous focus on the disadvantaged, and that it tends to criticize the members of the establishment operate to generate criticism of its professional status. When social work achieves gender balance, focuses more on problems rather than on populations, and seeks to make targeted rather than ideological charges, it is likely that acceptance of its professional status will increase.

Might the direction of these changes involve selling out and constitute a denial of historical foci? We think not; indeed without transformation, improvement, and enhancement, social work may have trouble sustaining itself as a profession over the years to come. The trick in transformational change is to retain the best of the past with the best of the new.

A Brief History of the Social Work Profession

The history of social work and social welfare, as well as its professional aspects, has been considered in detail in a number of texts.[22] What is important here is to consider the historical development of the profession as including its organizations and institutions, because so much of the profession of social work can be understood through these.

Social work began before the profession with individual ministers and friendly visitors undertaking important tasks of interpersonal and communal helping. It began in the work of Dorothea Dix, in the Charity Organization Societies, and in the imperatives of scientific philanthropy. A key step was the establishment of university education at the University of Chicago for training in social work.[23]

In terms of professional associations, the National Conference of Charities and Corrections, an annual meeting held to bring a variety of interested persons together, served as a sort of nascent professional organization until 1921, when the American Association of Social Workers was established. In addition to the AASW, six other associations were formed around the same time to reflect a variety of specific social work interests and professional concerns. On July 7, 1955, the organizations combined into the National Association of Social Workers (NASW).[24] The National Association of Social Workers has served since that time as the central social work organization for the profession and has undertaken activities that have served to strengthen and broaden its social work base.

In 1952, three years prior to the formation of NASW, however, the Council on Social Work Education (CSWE) was organized. The council is an affiliation of schools of social work that sets standards for the teaching of social work in university settings. Its journal, *Education for Social Work,* along with the National Association of Social Workers' journal, *Social Work,* are among the key professional publications. From the educational point of view, the journal established in the early 1920s at the University of Chicago, *The Social Service Review,* remains the premier scholarly journal in the field and is read by teachers and researchers, as well as professionals.[25]

Recently, the National Association of Social Workers has taken leadership in developing the Academy of Certified Social Workers (ACSW). Being a member of the ACSW entitles the individual to use this set of initials after her or his name, which has come to signify the achievement of professional competence in the practice of social work. Entrance into the academy is by exam and experience supervised by another ACSW, and membership in NASW is a prerequisite. Continuing membership in NASW is required to retain ACSW status.

The ACSW is part of the professional development process that is moving the profession in the direction of increased professional status.

Competing and Complementary Trends in the Profession of Social Work

The developments toward professionalization that we have outlined have not come without conflict. Some specific conflicts deserve attention here.

IN SCHOOLS OF SOCIAL WORK

Within schools of social work there is conflict over the configuration of programs and training. Originally, the Master of Social Work was the only degree offered. Later Ph.D.'s in social work and in social welfare began to appear, as well as Doctors of Social Work, the D.S.W. (98 programs as of 1990). Recently, the Bachelor of Social Work, B.S.W., has begun to appear. Differences of view within the professional training community exist with respect to the criteria required for these various degrees. It should be stated from the outset that the M.S.W. degree remains the highest professional degree in the field of social work. While it is true there are D.S.W. and Ph.D. degrees, these are, in almost every instance, degrees of research and scholarship, rather than certificates of advanced practice of any kind. Indeed, the absence of an advanced practice degree at the doctoral level equivalent to the Medical Doctor (M.D.) or Juris Doctor (J.D.) has raised questions in some quarters and has generated a set of advocates for such advanced training. Others reply that the Master of Public Health and the Master of Business Administration are sufficient, and a Master of Social Work should be sufficient as well.

These conflicts have led to some dilution of the scientific emphasis in some D.S.W. and social work Ph.D. programs, where an accommodation to the desire for advanced practice qualifications, even if offered under a research guise, has been made.

Similarly, tensions between the B.S.W. program and M.S.W. program are now emerging. These tensions involve several dimensions. For many years there was an undergraduate major in social work at many colleges and universities, often housed in the Department of Sociology. As a major, however, the social work emphasis had no specific professional status. In recent years the Council on Social Work Education has begun to accredit (set standards for compliance and provide certification for) Bachelor of Social Work programs. Hence, the B.S.W. programs have now emerged as the first step on the professional ladder, a step that ends, at the moment, with the M.S.W. M.S.W. programs have responded in many instances by giving advanced standing to those students who have completed Bachelor of Social Work programs. However, students often criticize M.S.W. programs as being repetitive of Bachelors of Social Work curricula (B.S.W.), rather than, as the M.S.W. programs claim, providing greater depth and sophistication of content.

Some professionals have criticized the accreditation of the BSW programs on the grounds that it has allowed agencies to decredentialize their job descriptions; whereas previously the M.S.W. as the only professional degree, was required in some places, there is now an option for the less expensive B.S.W. For example, a Department of Social Services could now hire B.S.W.s to do some of the basic social work. As is often the case in situations of social change, it is not exactly clear which trend preceded which, and it is very difficult to predict what the results of these conflicts will be.

BETWEEN SCHOOLS OF SOCIAL WORK
AND THE COUNCIL ON SOCIAL WORK EDUCATION

Another type of conflict is emerging between schools of social work on the one hand and the Council on Social Work Education on the other. As the accrediting body, the

Council on Social Work Education sets standards and provides the review process for accrediting schools of social work. Because of the wide range and number of programs that require accreditation, both M.S.W. and B.S.W., fairly rigid guidelines have been set up with respect to the nature of content, course, emphasis, and the like. On the one hand, some individuals claim that these kinds of restrictions are necessary and helpful, particularly for assisting weaker schools of social work or schools of social work in weaker universities to secure resources that would otherwise be denied them to develop programs to the level of compliance. On the other hand, opponents argue that this rule specification process is one of bureaucratization and rigidification that is now becoming institutionalized, and that now and in the future fails to recognize and support innovation and appropriate new approaches.

There is also a tension between schools and professional associations as to who controls the various credentials—and the fees attached to credentials—that will be required for the profession of social work. As already mentioned, the NASW has sponsored and maintains the Academy of Certified Social Worker process. Since individuals must be a member of the NASW to enjoy academy status (they must also pass an exam and have supervision by an ACSW), questions are raised about the independence of NASW as a professional organization from its own certification process. Is it appropriate to force membership in the professional association only to retain a professional credential if, in the eyes of the individual social worker, the national association is not providing the kinds of services that would warrant an expensive membership independently of its association with accreditation?

Further conflicts are arising about the role of continuing education and advanced certification. NASW and other organizations are now in conflict over issuing diplomate certificates that are supposed to indicate levels of competence (and membership) over and above that which has been achieved by the ACSW level.

CONFLICT AMONG PROFESSIONAL ASSOCIATIONS

The conflict between different kinds of professional associations emerges also with professional areas. In social work, for example, we have already mentioned the NASW and its certificate, the ACSW. But many social workers who work in specialized fields feel the need for additional substantive certification. For example, a marriage counselor certification program provides specific endorsement in that area. In the alcohol field, certificates provide endorsements for special competencies, training, and legitimacy for working in that particular area.

And apart from individual professional accreditation and review, there are similar instrumentalities at the agency level. Hospitals have long been accredited by hospital accrediting organizations. In the child welfare area, the Child Welfare League of America, apart from having individual members, also has organizational members and provides an accrediting service that sets standards and thereby provides assurance to the public.

We will not, of course, resolve the issues raised here, but we can alert professionals to the potential conflict of who controls professional and allied status and how these decisions in the final event are to be made.

LEGAL PROTECTIONS AND LICENSING

A conflict exists also within the field of social work over legal protections and licensing. Some states have begun the process of licensing social workers. Karger and Stoesz report that "By the end of 1987, 45 states had licensed social workers, with the majority requiring a master's degree in social work."[26] However, because of the heterogeneous number of individuals who already have been in the field and call themselves social workers, it is unlikely that, at least in the near term, widespread legal protections will restrict the use of the term "social worker" to those who have M.S.W. degrees. Even within the field, there is some question about what the legal status of licensing should be. Some feel that licensing is an important protection for the public and is a minimal assurance that the profession can give to a potentially vulnerable public that appropriate training has been received. Others, however, feel that this kind of licensing violates the ability of clients to choose the professional they wish and restricts access of potential workers to the helping profession, especially to individuals who may have been denied opportunity or access to the higher education required for professional status.

INTEREST GROUPS IN THE SOCIAL WORK AREA

Social workers have a variety of interests that transcend a specific focus on social work alone and embrace such fields as alcohol abuse, gerontology, and public health. Many are members of several associations, such as the American Public Health Association, the Gerontological Society of America, the American Gerontological Society, the Policy Studies Association, the American Orthopsychiatric Association, and the Child Welfare League of America. These associations are quasi-professional in the sense that they are associations of professionals, but do not necessarily pretend to provide any kind of affirmative credential with respect to the practitioner. Nonetheless, there continues to be a push in all these fields for credentialing. For example, there is no specific credential for the aging field at this particular time; rather there are university degrees, continuing education certificates, and the like, which people can secure and whose weight largely depends on the overall prestige of the institution. We can expect additional conflict among interest groups as they vie for professional memberships in the future. This conflict is likely to be exacerbated as fees for organization memberships rise sharply. It is difficult to maintain a plurality of professional association memberships when each membership costs $150 to $200.

Professional Demographics

In the late 1980s, there were about 100,000 members of NASW. This membership was 90% white.[27] Some basic information on the field has already been mentioned: the gender ratio (75% women) and the average salary ($27,800 in 1986–1987). The median salary for NASW members was $300 lower ($27,500) and is the same as the median salary (in 1987) for M.S.W.s, who comprised more than 90% of the sample surveyed. The median annual salary for B.S.W.s, however, was substantially lower, $18,750. And the median salary for members of NASW who had obtained their Ph.D./D.S.W. degree was somewhat higher, at $32,000 at the time of the survey.[28]

Education and Training for Our Profession of Social Work

Training for social work involves university attendance. First-step training is available at many universities, where the individual begins a major in social work and receives the degree of Bachelor of Social Work. Some individuals with a B.S.W. degree then seek positions in professional practice. Others go on to seek the Master of Social Work degree. In addition, a number of individuals who had social science majors or humanities majors (and in a few instances natural science majors) seek additional professional training as candidates for the M.S.W. degree. Frequently, these individuals need to supplement some of their undergraduate work with specific courses in the social science area.

There are some 367 Bachelor of Social Work programs in the United States today and about 102 Schools of Social Work granting the MSW degree. (According to the Council of Social Work Education, there are 327 candidate B.S.W., and 14 candidate M.S.W. programs, as of 1990.) They don't accredit D.S.W. or Ph.D.'s. Almost all schools of social work accept individuals from all educational levels, from those right out of college to those returning after many years of professional or life experience. Typically, though, schools of social work prefer individuals who apply after they have worked a bit; the average age for students in the School of Social Work is likely to be in the upper twenties and sometimes even in the early thirties. In part, this pattern results from the fact that financial support for higher education beyond the undergraduate degree is increasingly difficult to come by, and individuals need the opportunity to spend some time and garner resources for the next step in their professional ladder. Too, lore in social work supports the idea that experience is good to have before additional training is pursued.

Many schools of social work not only offer the M.S.W. degree but a variety of potentially combined degrees as well. We have already mentioned the combined degree with schools of business that is offered at some schools of social work; combined degrees with law or schools of public health are also among the most common. Many schools are also flexible with respect to developing unique joint degrees if an individual has a special interest and competence and can persuade the relevant schools to join together around her or his particular need. And there are Doctors of Social Work Degrees (D.S.W.) and Ph.D.'s in Social Work that represent scholarly degrees aimed at providing teachers and researchers for the field, rather than advanced practitioners (although there has been some attrition of scholarship in some instances with respect to the advanced degree, as the needs and demands for opportunities for advanced practice training and credentials make themselves felt.)

Two key interrelated issues need urgent attention now with respect to the education and training of professional social workers. One is the issue of advanced certification. At the moment the field is rather open. There are even some private independent organizations offering doctors' degrees for individuals interested in advanced clinical training and certification, completely independent of university affiliation. (This trend violates one of the criteria for professionalism, university-based training.) While unusual, this kind of approach is not unknown. Some law schools, for example, are of this type. There are also some independent, freestanding schools of psychology that do the same thing and have no university affiliation whatsoever. The reason for this development partly lies in the absence of leadership by schools of social work in offering strong, advanced clinical doctorate programs. Whether any school with requisite stature and expertise will undertake this venture remains to be seen.

A parallel but independent question has to do with continuing education in social work. The issue of continuing education is important, whether or not a particular continuing education leads to some advanced competence or advanced practice status. The obsolescence of professional training in most fields is well known. To this issue in social work we might add the constant burden of human problems and the generally uphill fight toward individual and systematic improvement. These kinds of tensions and stresses can lead to burnout. While postdegree training is not necessarily the antidote to burnout, it does provide a fresh perspective, as well as new techniques and approaches. Some fields, such as medicine, require continuing education as an ongoing part of viable professional status. A certain number of courses, for example, must be completed each year in the specialty of the individual. Social work has not yet achieved this level of sophistication. A variety of schools of social work offer episodic summer institutes in which social work professionals and others provide specific kinds of training on a fee-for-training basis. They tend, however, not to be programmatically integrated. Independent trainers also offer courses, weekends, sessions, and retreats on a variety of psychology-related topics on an almost constant basis. Nothing is necessarily wrong with these offerings; however, they tend to be commercial in nature, unevaluated, and often of questionable professional quality. Most professionals are besieged with junk mail about these offerings. An important next step, therefore, in the development of the profession of social work is to erect a rigorous and sensible set of requirements for continuing education in our field. When that is done, we might then look at the implications such requirements have for the development of advanced practice certificates, degrees, and the like.

Employment in the Social Work Profession

Any assessment of the social work profession must comment on two questions: where do social workers work and what do social workers do.

WHERE DO SOCIAL WORKERS WORK?

Almost 41% of the respondents work in the public sector and 20% in the proprietary (for profit) sector; the remaining 39% were employed in the nonprofit sector.[29] The largest concentration of practice is in a social service agency, about a quarter of the members. Another 21% practice in a hospital, while almost 18% work in an outpatient facility. Over 15% of the membership indicated employment in private practice.[30] Barker reports that about 30,000 social workers have some form of private practice.[31]

The rich array of social work employment is hardly reflected in these statistics, however. Social workers are found in almost every occupational realm. State and federal officials have a number of M.S.W.s within their ranks. As noted, the private practice of social work represents a developing area. The environmental and community change and planning areas have their share of social workers as well. In short, there is almost no area that is exempt from social work representation, although it is really the dominant force within the social agency.

Social workers also work in what is called, for lack of a better term, secondary settings. A secondary setting is one in which there is a department or area specifically identified for social work personnel, who performs a service function for the organization through assisting the organization to achieve its purposes. Medical social workers working in hospitals perform such a function. So do school social workers working in schools. Both hospital and school social workers perform social work functions, but they are not an end in themselves; rather, they are subordinate ends and thus become a means to the accomplishment of the overall organizational goal of educating the child or making the patient healthy.

WHAT DO SOCIAL WORKERS DO?

Social workers perform numerous roles in the places in which they work. These range from the direct practice of social work in clinical intervention with individual clients, to managerial and executive roles, or legislative and policy roles. In terms of the nature of the actual job, 67% of the respondents practiced in direct service; another 19% worked in management and administration. Much smaller proportions of the respondents function in other areas. For example, policy, planning, and research account for only 1.2% of the employment distribution.[32]

Some social workers have become elected public officials or occupy high government positions; they are involved in both issues of social policy and national policy, such as welfare reform and health policy.

Basically, social work skills involve, as Helen Harris Perlman said, "the disciplined use of self in relationship." In most professions, there are specific and more general applications of professional skills. The specific applications involve using social work skills in a narrow way, the way in which most social workers were specifically trained. Hence, if the individual is trained as a clinical social worker, she or he uses the discipline of self in a clinical relationship with troubled individuals. If the individual is trained as a community social worker, she or he uses the disciplined self in relationship with community members to increase community confidence, coordination, and cohesion. On the other hand, an individual may be promoted to roles such as manager, executive, policy maker or to other kinds of professional activities that do not specifically involve the development of a professional social work relationship. The interpersonal and organizational skills learned as a social worker may lead to success as a general manager of a commercial business or a state legislator, or as a journalist, stockbroker, or owner of a McDonald's franchise. As with legal training, it is possible to identify yourself as a social worker and yet do nonsocial work jobs.

Issues in the Profession of Social Work

All professions are beset with a range of issues and conflicts. A number of them have already been mentioned in the course of discussing professionalization itself. It is important, however, to identify four that are a continuing source of vital debate within the field today. These are questions of cause versus function, public versus private auspice, fee versus free service, and achievement versus equality. Because of its historical precedence, let us begin by talking about the issue of cause versus function.

CAUSE VERSUS FUNCTION

In 1929, Porter R. Lee wrote an influential paper entitled "Social Work—Cause or Function."[33] The issue that Lee raised is unsettled as of today. Basically, he identified the ideological and cause-related impetus that stimulated much of the initiation of social work. But he argued then, more than 60 years ago, that the cause orientation should pass, that social work should assume a more functional role by providing services to those in need across the board, as part of the ongoing network of services that society has established to help people get needs met. *Cause* motivation involves wanting to change the world, to right wrongs, and often at the same time involves the subordination of the self to such motivations. Individuals who are extraordinary altruists fall into this category. *Functional* motivation involves a deep desire to help people and find ways to assist them in meeting their needs. It has, perhaps, a little less zeal than the cause motivation and more of a cooperative spirit.

Social work, as a profession, provides both ideological (cause) and occupational (functional) rewards to its members. There is a tension between these conflicting values, and they form the different bases on which people entered the profession. These commitments are capable of eliciting strong feeling. Some social workers are accused, especially those in private practice, of fleeing the poor. The assumption behind such a charge is that we belong with the poor, and there is an impressive history of social work's attention to that particular disadvantaged group. Others reply that the pain of alcohol abuse and the like is not limited to those who are financially disadvantaged. The social work profession should take its rightful place in the professional firmament, offering, as professions do, its services to all who have need of its services, not just to special populations. It is unlikely that this issue will be solved quickly.

FEE VERSUS FREE

A second conflict in social work has to do with whether and how much to charge for services provided to clients. If clients are poor, then charging them doesn't make a lot of sense. On the other hand, if clients are well to do, then charging them is the obvious thing to do. Should we then seek well-to-do clients in order to overcharge them to provide funds to subsidize those who cannot pay? It sounds like a sensible practice; but if that were the practice, individual clients who can pay may find more attractive pricing elsewhere from other social work sources or nonsocial work sources. A further complication lies in the fact that unless fees from or on behalf of clients are increased in some way, it is very difficult to provide salary increases for social workers. Although social workers do not necessarily wish to make lots of money, they wish to make some money. They may indeed hope the amount they make can be increased marginally or modestly over the years. But they may be made to feel that these increases, since they must come from "squeezing" clients, are illegitimate or unfair. The issue is again one that will not be resolved easily.

PUBLIC VERSUS PRIVATE

The public versus private controversy essentially involves the auspices of social work service, that is, under what kind of organizational umbrella should social work service be offered. The concept is made more complex because of the different and historically changing meanings of the concept of "private." Services today are offered through governmental (public) and voluntary (an older meaning of private, as in private agency), and corporate agencies (commercial organizations, today called private to distinguish them from government and voluntary/social agency auspices). There are several dimensions to the debate. One reflects the history of social work. Social work began in the voluntary/private agency, and one argument suggests that this place is still where much of social work should go on. Another argument suggests that, because of the scope and complexity of social problems, only public agencies have the resources to accept that responsibility, and the government should accept it.

Still another argument is that the government should be a safety net, with needs being met first through voluntary agencies and corporate social welfare (with corporate social welfare being the new private agency). The issue is especially complex because of different meanings of public and private in the public's mind and in the mind of the professional social work community. The issue of auspices has ideological weight for many. But, beyond the auspice itself, the issue of public versus private involves who is or should be served by social work. Because public agencies in the social welfare field, like departments of social services, tend to serve the disadvantaged, a strong link between public service and service to the disadvantaged became established. Hence, when we hear today about conflicts between public and private, we hear the strains of hidden debates between public agencies and commercial agencies, on the one hand, and between services to the poor (thought of as characteristic of public agencies) and services to the well to do (thought of as characteristic of private–commercial organizations) on the other. But, to some extent, because public agencies do not often charge for their services, it is a repetition, of the free (public) versus fee (private) debate. Voluntary, not-for-profit agencies fall into the middle in many of these debates, sometimes charging fees, sometimes not, sometimes spending government money, and sometimes their own. Aspects of these conflicts exist within most social workers as well.

Again, there is no easy solution but the generally permissive posture that social workers should have the broadest range of employment opportunities, as is characteristic of other professions. Furthermore, within the social work profession, full-scale professional experience should include exposure to a variety of settings and auspices, some of which should be public, but others, private.

ACHIEVEMENT VERSUS EQUALITY

Social workers come into the field with a strong commitment to equality. Yet that commitment does not necessarily mean that a commitment to achievement simply goes away.[34] Everyone is interested in getting ahead, in improving their financial occupational situation. The choice of social work as a professional career involves a tempering, but not a canceling, of achievement motivations. Yet the professional norms remain unclear as to how much is OK.

Simultaneously, the issues of achievement and equality arise with clients as well. Should we spread our social work talents equally, or should we work with those who may be able to better use the skills that a particular worker has? If the latter course is chosen, does that mean that the worker is guilty of choosing only the desirable clients? And how can we achieve a successful balance between emphasis on those clients who are hard to reach and less likely to be productive in terms of worker time invested versus those who are easy and likely to make maximum use of workers' skills and insights?

Conclusion

The profession of social work is in a developing stage, moving from its historically voluntaristic origins, with a heavy dose of on the job training and episodic theoretical formulations, to a well-recognized, well-orchestrated and powerful group of individuals who are beginning to codify and agree on knowledge, who have an impressive record of university training, but who have several steps to go to achieve full professional status. Because the movement toward professionalization is a process, we should attend to that process, rather than to the end result. As long as we are moving in the right direction and at an appropriate pace, and we are, then that part of our job is completed. Professional development takes time; codification of knowledge is a lengthy process; the testing and retesting of practice precepts are also lengthy. We may not have reached optimum professional status, but we have certainly reached a satisfactory one.

Nonetheless, a number of areas continue to trouble the social work profession. Our perspective, which is itself controversial, is that social work needs to move to the modern posture in which its services are offered to everyone who is in trouble. Special attention should be paid, however, to honoring our historical origins by being sensitive to the fact that all social workers need to spend some of their time with the truly disadvantaged. This effort may be as part of a caseload, it may be in a volunteer capacity, or it may occur in a variety of ways that, on the basis of a yearly self-assessment, should satisfy the individual worker that her or his professional mandate has been achieved.

Simultaneously, it should be recognized that it is OK to make money from the profession of social work; that is what a profession is partly for, to provide a career path for individuals. It should also be emphasized that a variety of practice roles is acceptable. Indeed, the wider the range of practice roles enjoyed by social workers is, the wider the likelihood of acceptance of social work by the community at large, as the community sees the ability of social workers to perform in a variety of contexts. It is an exciting time and a positive time. Conflicts and problems are a fact of life. As challenges are met and mastered, those solutions will generate yet other problems not mentioned here or only dimly perceived at the moment. Professionalization is a constant challenge and is implied by the word; it is, as we have said, a process, not a goal.

Notes

1. The word "qualified" is used because there are questions and issues that we are not fully able to be deal with satisfactorily now, such as the scientific basis of the profession, and the empirical testing of the results of intervention, but that in due time will be answered satisfactorily for members of the profession, as well as for critics of the profession.
2. Most social workers practice their profession. The social worker who takes a job doing something else could always return after appropriate refresher courses to the practice of social work. The same is true for physicians, attorneys, dentists, and others.
3. Moral and ethical controls refer to the normative bases of right and wrong that guide some of our behavior. The Code of Ethics of the National Association of Social Workers represents a written version of such controls.
4. Ethical issues do not necessarily involve competence. The surgeon may remove your appendix competently or brilliantly. But, if it did not need to come out, issues of ethics are involved.
5. It is technically possible to be a professional while meeting a range of professionally specified criteria and yet having a very low level of skill.
6. Vulnerability is what differentiates clients from customers. Clients are not considered in full control of their fortunes.
7. It is important to add that professionalism is not *only* a matter of internal concern. Society as well has claims here for competence and certification as well.
8. Sometimes the word "session" is used because the hour shrinks to 40 or 45 minutes. For a wonderful set of stories about the clinical experience, see Robert Lindner, *The Fifty-Minute Hour.* (New York: Holt, Rinehart and Winston, 1954).
9. Abraham Flexner, "Is Social Work a Profession?" in *Proceedings of the National Conference of Charities and Corrections, 1915* (New York: The Conference, 1915, pp. 576–590.
10. A. M. Carr-Saunders, "Metropolitan Condition and Traditional Professional Relationships," in M. R. Fisher, ed., *The Metropolis in Modern Life* (Garden City, N.Y.: Doubleday, 1965), pp. 279–287.
11. A. Etizioni, *The Semi-Professions and Their Organization* (New York: The Free Press, 1969).
12. N. Toren, *Social Work: The Case of the Semi-Profession* (Beverly Hills, Calif.: Sage Publications, 1972).
13. Willard Richan and Allan R. Mendlesohn, *Social Work—The Unloved Profession* (New York: New Viewpoints, 1973).
14. Janet Malcolm, *Psychoanalysis: The Impossible Profession* (New York: Alfred A. Knopf, 1981).
15. National Association of Social Workers, *Salaries in Social Work: A Summary Report of NASW Members, July 1986–June 1987* (Silver Spring, Md.: The Association, 1987), p. 4.
16. According to the 1980 census, 95% of registered nurses are women, and about 71% of elementary and secondary schoolteachers are women. U.S. Department of Commerce, Bureau of the Census, *1980 Census of Population, Occupation by Industry* (Washington, D.C.: U.S. Government Printing Office, 1984), p. 1, Table 1.
17. National Association of Social Workers, *Salaries in Social Work,* p. 10, Table 12.
18. Note that it is the previously all male professions that are becoming more gender integrated.
19. R. Cloward and I. Epstein, "Private Social Welfare's Disengagement from the Poor," in G. Brager and F. P. Purcell, eds., *Community Action against Poverty* (New Haven, Conn.: College & University Press, 1967).
20. Vouchers are a system where a client or consumer is given a check that can be used for service at a place of her or his choosing. Some states are experimenting with educational

vouchers. Perhaps the public school would get them, but perhaps not; it would be the student's choice.

21. Part of the answer has come from developing a morally superior attitude toward others. After all, if social workers are working with the poor and doing so for low wages, then the field is entitled to feel "just a little bit superior." Superiority is, however, a two-edged sword. It may allow criticism while retaining claims of support (religion has done this for years), but it also creates social distance between the profession and the victim/supporter, which further isolates the profession.

22. For a comprehensive overview, see Ann Minahan, ed., *Encyclopedia of Social Work,* 18th ed. (Silver Spring, Md.: National Association of Social Workers, 1987).

23. June G. Hopps and Elaine Pinderhughes, "Profession of Social Work: Contemporary Characteristics," in A. Minahan, ed., *Encyclopedia of Social Work,* Vol. II, 18th ed., pp. 351–366; Walter Freedlander and Robert Z. Apte, *Introduction to Social Work,* 5th ed. (Englewood Cliffs, N.J.: Prentice Hall, 1980).

24. Rex Skidmore and Milton G. Thackeray, *Introduction to Social Work,* 3rd ed. (Englewood Cliffs, N.J.: Prentice Hall, 1982), p. 377.

25. Other associations also formed. Two are Family Service America (FSA) and the Child Welfare League of America (CWLA). Public welfare organizations have an association, the American Public Welfare Association (APWA), and religious organizations have banded together. Catholic Charities—USA is the national organization of Catholic social service organizations, and the Jewish organizations have a similar national body. Each of these organizations also has a journal.

26. H. J. Karger, and D. Stoesz, *American Social Welfare Policy* (New York: Longman, 1990), p. 157. They cite the *NASW NEWS,* 32(8) (September 1987), p. 10.

27. NASW, *Salaries in Social Work,* p. 5.

28. Ibid., p. 3, Tables 2 and 3. The median figure, the middle number in a distribution, is often used to reflect salary because it is not influenced by outlying values. (For example, if five social workers made, respectively, $1, $2, $3, $4, and $5 per hour, the median salary would be $3; the mean would be $3. If however, the distribution was $1, $2, $3, $4, and $20, the median would still be $3, but the mean would be $6!)

29. Ibid., p. 8, Table 9.

30. Ibid., p. 7, Table 8.

31. R. Barker, "Private and Proprietary Services," in A. Minahan, ed., *Encyclopedia of Social Work,* 18th ed., p. 326.

32. NASW, *Salaries in Social Work,* p. 8, Table 10.

33. Porter R. Lee, "Social Work: Cause or Function," in *Procedures of the National Conference of Social Welfare, 1929* (Chicago: University of Chicago Press, 1930), pp. 3–20.

34. See John E. Tropman, *American Values and Social Welfare* (Englewood Cliffs, N.J.: Prentice Hall, 1989).

Code of Ethics of the National Association of Social Workers

Preamble

This code is intended to serve as a guide to the everyday conduct of members of the social work profession and as a basis for the adjudication of issues in ethics when the conduct of social workers is alleged to deviate from the standards expressed or implied in this code. It represents standards of ethical behavior for social workers in professional relationships with those served, with colleagues, with employers, with other individuals and professions, and with the community and society as a whole. It also embodies standards of ethical behavior governing individual conduct to the extent that such conduct is associated with an individual's status and identity as a social worker.

This code is based on the fundamental values of the social work profession that include the worth, dignity, and uniqueness of all persons as well as their rights and opportunities. It is also based on the nature of social work, which fosters conditions that promote these values.

In subscribing to and abiding by this code, the social worker is expected to view ethical responsibility in as inclusive a context as each situation demands and within which ethical judgement is required. The social worker is expected to take into consideration all the principles in this code that have a bearing upon any situation in which ethical judge-ment is to be exercised and professional intervention or conduct is planned. The course of action that the social worker chooses is expected to be consistent with the spirit as well as the letter of this code.

In itself, this code does not represent a set of rules that will prescribe all the behaviors of social workers in all the complexities of professional life. Rather, it offers general principles to guide conduct, and the judicious appraisal of conduct, in situations that have ethical implications. It provides the basis for making judgements about ethical actions before and after they occur. Frequently, the particular situation determines the ethical principles that apply and the manner of their application. In such cases, not only the particular ethical principles are taken into immediate consideration, but also the entire code and its spirit. Specific applications of ethical principles must be judged within the context in which they are being considered. Ethical behavior in a given situation must satisfy not only the judgement of the individual social worker, but also the judgement of an unbiased jury of professional peers.

This code should not be used as an instrument to deprive any social worker of the opportunity or freedom to practice with complete professional integrity; nor should any disciplinary action be taken on the basis of this code without maximum provision for safeguarding the rights of the social worker affected.

NASW Code of Ethics, as adopted by the 1979 NASW Delegate Assembly and revised by the 1990 NASW Delegate Assembly. Copyright 1990, National Association of Social Workers, Inc.

The ethical behavior of social workers results not from edict, but from a personal commitment of the individual. This code is offered to affirm the will and zeal of all social workers to be ethical and to act ethically in all that they do as social workers.

The following codified ethical principles should guide social workers in the various roles and relationships and at the various levels of responsibility in which they function professionally. These principles also serve as a basis for the adjudication by the National Association of Social Workers of issues in ethics.

In subscribing to this code, social workers are required to cooperate in its implementation and abide by any disciplinary rulings based on it. They should also take adequate measures to discourage, prevent, expose, and correct the unethical conduct of colleagues. Finally, social workers should be equally ready to defend and assist colleagues unjustly charged with unethical conduct.

The NASW Code of Ethics

I. The Social Worker's Conduct and Comportment as a Social Worker
  A. *Propriety.* The social worker should maintain high standards of personal conduct in the capacity or identity as social worker.
     1. The private conduct of the social worker is a personal matter to the same degree as is any other person's, except when such conduct compromises the fulfillment of professional responsibilities.
     2. The social worker should not participate in, condone, or be associated with dishonesty, fraud, deceit, or misrepresentation.
     3. The social worker should distinguish clearly between statements and actions made as a private individual and as a representative of the social work profession or an organization or group.
  B. *Competence and Professional Development.* The social worker should strive to become and remain proficient in professional practice and the performance of professional functions.
     1. The social worker should accept responsibility or employment only on the basis of existing competence or the in-

tention to acquire the necessary competence.
     2. The social worker should not misrepresent professional qualifications, education, experience, or affiliations.
  C. *Service.* The social worker should regard as primary the service obligation of the social work profession.
     1. The social worker should retain ultimate responsibility for the quality and extent of the service that individual assumes, assigns, or performs.
     2. The social worker should act to prevent practices that are inhumane or discriminatory against any person or group of persons.
  D. *Integrity.* The social worker should act in accordance with the highest standards of professional integrity and impartiality.
     1. The social worker should be alert to and resist the influences and pressures that interfere with the exercise of professional discretion and impartial judgement required for the performance of professional functions.
     2. The social worker should not exploit professional relationships for personal gain.
  E. *Scholarship and Research.* The social worker engaged in study and research should be guided by the conventions of scholarly inquiry.
     1. The social worker engaged in research should consider carefully its possible consequences for human beings.
     2. The social worker engaged in research should ascertain that the consent of participants in the research is voluntary and informed, without any implied deprivation or penalty for refusal to participate, and with due regard for participants privacy and dignity.
     3. The social worker engaged in research should protect participants from unwarranted physical or mental discomfort, distress, harm, danger, or deprivation.
     4. The social worker who engages in the evaluation of services or cases should discuss them only for the professional purposes and only with persons directly

and professionally concerned with them.

5. Information obtained about participants in research should be treated as confidential.

6. The social worker should take credit only for work actually done in connection with scholarly and research endeavors and credit contributions made by others.

II. The Social Worker's Ethical Responsibility to Clients

F. *Primacy of Clients' Interests.* The social worker's primary responsibility is to clients.

1. The social worker should serve clients with devotion, loyalty, determination, and the maximum application of professional skill and competence.

2. The social worker should not exploit relationships with clients for personal advantage.

3. The social worker should not practice, condone, facilitate or collaborate with any form of discrimination on the basis of race, color, sex, sexual orientation, age, religion, national origin, marital status, political belief, mental or physical handicap, or any other preference or personal characteristic, condition, or status.

4. The social worker should avoid relationships or commitments that conflict with the interests of clients.

5. The social worker should under no circumstances engage in sexual activities with clients.

6. The social worker should provide clients with accurate and complete information regarding the extent and nature of the services available to them.

7. The social worker should apprise clients of their risks, rights, opportunities, and obligations associated with social service to them.

8. The social worker should seek advice and counsel of colleagues and supervisors whenever such consultation is in the best interest of clients.

9. The social worker should terminate ser-

vice to clients, and professional relationships with them, when such service and relationships are no longer required or no longer serve the clients' needs or interests.

10. The social worker should withdraw services precipitously only under unusual circumstances, giving careful consideration to all factors in the situation and taking care to minimize possible adverse effects.

11. The social worker who anticipates the termination or interruption of service to clients should notify clients promptly and seek the transfer, referral, or continuation of service in relation to the clients' needs and preferences.

G. *Rights and Prerogatives of Clients.* The social worker should make every effort to foster maximum self-determination on the part of clients.

1. When the social worker must act on behalf of a client who has been adjudged legally incompetent, the social worker should safeguard the interests and rights of that client.

2. When another individual has been legally authorized to act in behalf of a client, the social worker should deal with that person always with the client's best interest in mind.

3. The social worker should not engage in any action that violates or diminishes the civil or legal rights of clients.

H. *Confidentiality and Privacy.* The social worker should respect the privacy of clients and hold in confidence all information obtained in the course of professional service.

1. The social worker should share with others confidences revealed by clients, without their consent, only for compelling professional reasons.

2. The social worker should inform clients fully about the limits of confidentiality in a given situation, the purposes for which information is obtained, and how it may be used.

3. The social worker should afford clients reasonable access to any official social work records concerning them.

4. When providing clients with access to records, the social worker should take due care to protect the confidences of others contained in those records.

5. The social worker should obtain informed consent of clients before taping, recording, or permitting third party observation of their activities.

I. *Fees.* When setting fees, the social worker should ensure that they are fair, reasonable, considerate, and commensurate with the service performed and with due regard for the clients' ability to pay.

1. The social worker should not accept anything of value for making a referral.

III. The Social Worker's Ethical Responsibility to Colleagues

J. *Respect, Fairness, and Courtesy.* The social worker should treat colleagues with respect, courtesy, fairness, and good faith.

1. The social worker should cooperate with colleagues to promote professional interests and concerns.

2. The social worker should respect confidences shared by colleagues in the course of their professional relationships and transactions.

3. The social worker should create and maintain conditions of practice that facilitate ethical and competent professional performance by colleagues.

4. The social worker should treat with respect, and represent accurately and fairly, the qualifications, views, and findings of colleagues and use appropriate channels to express judgements on these matters.

5. The social worker who replaces or is replaced by a colleague in professional practice should act with consideration for the interest, character, and reputation of that colleague.

6. The social worker should not exploit a dispute between a colleague and employers to obtain a position or otherwise advance the social worker's interest.

7. The social worker should seek arbitration or mediation when conflicts with colleagues require resolution for compelling professional reasons.

8. The social worker should extend to colleagues of other professions the same respect and cooperation that is extended to social work colleagues.

9. The social worker who serves as an employer, supervisor, or mentor to colleagues should make orderly and explicit arrangements regarding the conditions of their continuing professional relationship.

10. The social worker who has the responsibility for employing and evaluating the performance of other staff members, should fulfill such responsibility in a fair, considerate, and equitable manner, on the basis of clearly enunciated criteria.

11. The social worker who has the responsibility for evaluating the performance of employees, supervisees, or students should share evaluations with them.

K. *Dealing with Colleagues' Clients.* The social worker has the responsibility to relate to the clients of colleagues with full professional consideration.

1. The social worker should not assume professional responsibility for the clients of another agency or a colleague without appropriate communication with that agency or colleague.

2. The social worker who serves the clients of colleagues, during a temporary absence or emergency, should serve those clients with the same consideration as that afforded any client.

IV. The Social Worker's Ethical Responsibility to Employers and Employing Organizations

L. *Commitments to Employing Organization.* The social worker should adhere to commitments made to the employing organization.

1. The social worker should work to improve the employing agency's policies and procedures, and the efficiency and effectiveness of its services.

2. The social worker should not accept employment or arrange student field placements in an organization which is currently under public sanction by NASW for violating personnel stan-

dards, or imposing limitations on or penalties for professional actions on behalf of clients.

3. The social worker should act to prevent and eliminate discrimination in the employing organization's work assignments and in its employment policies and practices.

4. The social worker should use with scrupulous regard, and only for the purpose for which they are intended, the resources of the employing organization.

V. The Social Worker's Ethical Responsibility to the Social Work Profession

M. *Maintaining the Integrity of the Profession.* The social worker should uphold and advance the values, ethics, knowledge, and mission of the profession.

1. The social worker should protect and enhance the dignity and integrity of the profession and should be responsible and vigorous in discussion and criticism of the profession.

2 The social worker should take action through appropriate channels against unethical conduct by any other member of the profession.

3. The social worker should act to prevent the unauthorized and unqualified practice of social work.

4. The social worker should make no misrepresentation in advertising as to qualifications, competence, service, or results to be achieved.

N. *Community Service.* The social worker should assist the profession in making social services available to the general public.

1. The social worker should contribute time and professional expertise to activities that promote respect for the utility, the integrity, and the competence of the social work profession.

2. The social worker should support the formulation, development, enactment and implementation of social policies of concern to the profession.

O. *Development of Knowledge.* The social worker should take responsibility for identifying, developing, and fully utilizing knowledge for professional practice.

1. The social worker should base practice upon recognized knowledge relevant to social work.

2. The social worker should critically examine, and keep current with emerging knowledge relevant to social work.

3. The social worker should contribute to the knowledge base of social work and share research knowledge and practice wisdom with colleagues.

VI. The Social Worker's Ethical Responsibility to Society

P. *Promoting the General Welfare.* The social worker should promote the general welfare of society.

1. The social worker should act to prevent and eliminate discrimination against any person or group on the basis of race, color, sex, sexual orientation, age, religion, national origin, marital status, political belief, mental or physical handicap, or any other preference or personal characteristic, condition, or status.

2. The social worker should act to ensure that all persons have access to the resources, services, and opportunities which they require.

3. The social worker should act to expand choice and opportunity for all persons, with special regard for disadvantaged or oppressed groups and persons.

4. The social worker should promote conditions that encourage respect for the diversity of cultures which constitute American society.

5. The social worker should provide appropriate professional services in public emergencies.

6. The social worker should advocate changes in policy and legislation to improve social conditions and to promote social justice.

7. The social worker should encourage informed participation by the public in shaping social policies and institutions.

Bibliography

Alderson, John, "Models of School Social Work Practice," in *The School in the Community,* Rosemary Sarri and Frank Maple, eds., pp. 57–74. Washington, D.C.: National Association of Social Workers, 1972.

Alexander, C., and D. N. Weber, "Social Welfare: Historical Dates," in *Encyclopedia of Social Work,* Vol. 2 17th ed., J. Turner, ed., pp. 1497–1503. Washington, D.C.: National Association of Social Workers, 1977.

Alinsky, Saul, *Reveille for Radicals.* Chicago: University of Chicago Press, 1946.

———, *Rules for Radicals.* New York: Random House, 1971.

———, "Of Means and Ends," in *Strategies of Community Organization,* F. M. Cox and others, eds., pp. 426–437. Itaska, Ill.: Peacock, 1979.

Allen, Jo Ann, "Understanding the Family," in *A Handbook of Child Welfare: Context, Knowledge, and Practice,* Ann Hartman and Joan Laird, eds., pp. 149–177. New York: The Free Press, 1985.

Allen-Meares, Paula, "Analysis of Tasks in School Social Work," *Social Work* 22 (3) (May 1977), 196–201.

———, "An In-school Program for Adolescent Parents: Implications for Social Work Practice and Multidisciplinary Teaming," *School Social Work* 3 (2) (1979), 66–77.

———, and Bruce A. Lane, "Grounding Social Work Practice in Theory: Ecosystems," *Social Casework* 68 (1987), 515–521.

———, Robert O. Washington, and Betty Welsh, *Social Work Services in the Schools.* Englewood Cliffs, N.J.: Prentice Hall, 1986.

Alston, Jon, *American Samurai.* New York: deGruyter, 1986.

Altemeier, William, and others, "Prediction of Child Abuse: A Prospective Study of Feasibility," *Child Abuse and Neglect* 8 (1984), 393–400.

American Humane Association, *Highlights of Official Aggregate Child Abuse and Neglect Reporting 1987.* Denver, Col.: The Association, 1989.

Anderson, N., *The Hobo.* Chicago: University of Chicago Press, 1923.

Anderson, Ralph E., and Irl Carter, *Human Behavior in the Social Environment.* Chicago: Aldine, 1974.

Angell, Robert C., *The Family Encounters Depression.* New York: Scribner's, 1936.

———, "The Moral Integration of American Cities," in *Cities and Society,* P. K. Hatt and H. J. Reiss, Jr., eds., New York: The Free Press, 1957.

Ashford, Douglas E., *The Emergence of the Welfare States.* New York: Blackwell, 1987.

Austin, David M., "Policy Research," in *Social Work Research and Evaluation,* Richard M. Grinnell, ed., pp. 291–315. Itaska, Ill.: Peacock, 1981.

Axin, J., and H. Levin, *Social Welfare.* New York: Dodd, Mead, 1975.

Bahr, Howard, *All Faithful People: Change and Continuity in Middletown's Region.* Minneapolis: University of Minnesota Press, 1983.

Bailey, Ronald H., "Can Delinquents Be Saved by the Sea?" *Corrections Magazine* 8 (February 1982), 22–32.

Banta, H. David, "What Is Health Care?" in *Health Care Delivery in the United States,* 3rd ed. Steven Jonas, ed., pp. 12–34. New York: Springer, 1986.

Baran, Annette, Reuben Pannor, and Arthur D. Sorosky, "Open Adoption," *Social Work* 21 (2) (March 1976), 97–100.

Barker, Robert L., "Private and Proprietary Services,"

in *Encyclopedia of Social Work,* Vol. 2, 18th ed., A. Minahan, ed., pp. 324–329. Silver Spring, Md.: National Association of Social Workers, 1987.

Barker, Roger, *Ecological Psychology: Concepts and Methods for Studying the Environment of Human Behavior.* Stanford, Calif.: Stanford University Press, 1968.

Bartollas, Clemens *Correctional Treatment: Theory and Practice.* Englewood Cliffs, N.J.: Prentice Hall, 1985.

———, *Juvenile Delinquency,* 2nd ed. New York: Macmillan, 1990.

———, Stuart J. Miller, and Simon Dinitz, *Juvenile Victimization: The Institutional Paradox.* New York: Halsted Press, 1976.

Bass, Bernard M., *Bass and Stodgill's Handbook of Leadership: Theory, Research, and Managerial Applications,* 3rd ed. New York: The Free Press, 1990.

Beaubien, A., "Library Resources for the Community Organizer," in *Tactics and Techniques of Community Practice,* F. M. Cox and others, eds., pp. 56–66. Itaska, Ill.: Peacock, 1977.

Becker, Dorothy G., "Grace Longwell Coyle," in *Encyclopedia of Social Work,* Vol. 1, 17th ed., John B. Turner, ed., pp. 197–198. New York: National Association of Social Workers, 1977.

———, "Mary Ellen Richmond," in *Encyclopedia of Social Work,* Vol. 2, 17th ed., John B. Turner, ed., pp. 1224–1225. New York: National Association of Social Workers, 1977.

Bellah, R., and others, *Habits of the Heart.* New York: Harper & Row, 1986.

Benedict, Ruth, *Patterns of Culture.* Boston: Houghton-Mifflin, 1934.

Bennis, W., and B. Nanus, *Leaders.* New York: Harper & Row, 1985.

Bernard, J., "Community Disorganization", in *International Encyclopedia of the Social Sciences,* Vol. 3, D. L. Sills. ed., pp. 163–169. New York: The Free Press, 1968.

Bernstein, Douglas A., and Thomas D. Borkovec, *Progressive Relaxation Training.* Champaign, Ill.: Research Press, 1973.

Bettelheim, Bruno, *A Home for the Heart.* New York: Knopf, 1974.

Birdsall, William, "Does the Generosity of Welfare Encourage Participation." Ann Arbor: University of Michigan, 1987 (unpublished manuscript).

Black, C., *It Will Never Happen to Me.* New York: Ballantine Books, 1981.

Blau, Joel, "Theories of the Welfare State," *Social Service Review* 63 (March 1989), 27–38.

Blaug, Marc, "The Myth of the Old Poor Law and the Making of the New," *Journal of Economic History* 23 (2) (June 1963), 151–184.

Blauner, Robert, "Internal Colonialism and Ghetto Revolt, *Social Problems* 16 (Spring 1969), 393–408.

Bloom, M., *Life Span Development,* 3rd ed. New York: Macmillan, 1985.

Blum, D. J. Scrivner, *Group Counseling for Secondary Schools.* Springfield: Charles C. Thomas, 1990.

Bolton, R., *People Skills.* Englewood Cliffs, N.J.: Prentice Hall, 1979.

Booher, D., *Send Me a Memo.* New York: Facts on File, 1984.

Booth, Charles, *Life and Labor of the People of London.* London: Macmillan, 1891–1897.

Borowski, Allan, "Social Dimensions of Research," in *Social Work Research and Evaluation,* 3rd ed., Richard M. Grinnell, ed., pp. 42–64. Itaska, Ill.: Peacock, 1988.

Bostwick, Gerald J., Jr., and Nancy S. Kyte, "Measurement," in *Social Work Research and Evaluation,* 3rd ed., Richard M. Grinnell, ed., pp. 93–129. Itaska, Ill.: Peacock, 1988.

Bowlby, John, *Maternal Care and Child Health.* Geneva: World Health Organization, 1951.

Bracht, Neil, "The Scope and Historical Development of Social Work," in *Social Work in Health Care,* Neil Bracht, ed., pp. 3–18. New York: Haworth, 1978.

Breckinridge, Sophonisba P., "Some Aspects of the Public School from a Social Worker's Point of View," *Journal of the Proceedings and Addresses of the National Education Association,* July 4–11, 1914. Ann Arbor, Mich.: National Education Association, 1914.

Bremner, Robert H., *American Philanthropy.* Chicago: University of Chicago Press, 1960.

———, ed., *Children and Youth in America—A Documentary History,* Vol 1. Cambridge, Mass.: Harvard University Press, 1970.

Broverman, I. H., and others, "Sex Role Stereotypes and Clinical Judgments in Mental Health," *Journal of Consulting and Clinical Psychology* 34 (1970), 1–7.

Brown, Lanette, Irvan Corbett, and Linda Paricio, "Desegregating Public School System: A Community Human Relations Approach," in *Federal Legislation and the School Social Worker,* pp. 29–37. Washington, D.C.: National Association of Social Workers, 1978.

Buckley, Walter, *Sociology in Modern Systems Theory.* Englewood Cliffs, N.J.: Prentice Hall, 1967.

Buell, Bradley, and others, *Community Planning for Human Services.* New York: Columbia University Press, 1952.

Burghardt, S., "Community Based Social Action," in *Encyclopedia of Social Work,* Vol. 1, 18th ed., A. Minahan, ed., pp. 292–299. Silver Spring, Md.: National Association of Social Workers, 1987.

Burke, E., "The Search for Authority in Planning," *Social Service Review* 39 (4) (September 1965), 261–270.

Butrym, Z., and J. Horder, *Health, Doctors, and Social Work.* London: Routledge and Kegan Paul, 1983.

Callahan, Daniel, "Health and Societies: Some Ethical Imperatives," in *Doing Better and Feeling Worse: Health in the United States,* John H. Knowles, ed., pp. 23–34. New York: Norton, 1977.

Carbino, Rosemarie, *Foster Parenting: An Updated Review of the Literature.* New York: Child Welfare League of America, 1980.

Carr-Saunders, A. M., "Metropolitan Condition and Traditional Professional Relationships," in *The Metropolis in Modern Life,* M. R. Fisher, ed., pp. 279–87. Garden City, N.Y.: Doubleday, 1965.

Charping, John W., and Miriam M. Slaugter, "Voluntary Energy Assistance Programs: Community Self-help in Action," *Social Work* 33 (2) (March–April 1988), 161–163.

Checkoway, B., ed., *Strategic Perspectives on Planning Practice.* Lexington, Mass.: Lexington Books, 1986.

Child Welfare League of America, *Standards for Foster Family Care.* New York: Child Welfare League of America, 1959.

———, *Standards for Group Home Services for Children.* New York: Child Welfare League of America, 1978.

Cloward, R., and I. Epstein, "Private Social Welfare's Disengagement from the Poor," in *Community Action against Poverty,* G. Brager and F. P. Purcell, eds., pp. 40–63. New Haven: College and University Press, 1967.

———, and L. Ohlin, *Delinquency and Opportunity.* New York: The Free Press, 1960.

Cohen, Wilbur, James Morgan, and Martin David, *Income and Welfare in the United States.* New York: McGraw-Hill, 1962.

Coll, Blanche D., "Social Welfare History," in *Encyclopedia of Social Work,* Vol. 2, 17th ed., pp. 1503–1512. Washington, D.C.: National Association of Social Workers, 1977.

Comte, A., *The Positive Philosophy of Auguste Comte.* London: G. Bell, 1896.

———, *System of Positive Philosophy,* R. Fletcher, ed. London: Heinemann, 1974.

Connell, Sarah, "Homelessness," in *Encyclopedia of Social Work,* Vol. 1, 18th ed., A. Minahan, ed., pp. 789–794. Silver Spring, Md.: National Association of Social Workers, 1987.

Constable, Robert T., and John P. Flynn, *School Social Work: Practice and Research Perspectives.* Homewood, Ill.: Dorsey, 1982.

Cooley, Charles H., *Social Organization: A Study of the Larger Mind.* New York: Scribner's, 1909.

Corcoran, Kevin, and Joel Fischer, *Measures for Clinical Practice: A Sourcebook.* New York: The Free Press, 1987.

Costin, Lela B., "Social Work Contribution to Education in Transition," in *The School in the Community,* Rosemary Sarri and Frank Maple, eds., pp. 30–43. Washington, D.C.: National Association of Social Workers, 1972.

———, "The Historical Context of Child Welfare," in *A Handbook of Child Welfare: Context, Knowledge, and Practice,* Ann Hartman and Joan Laird, eds., pp., 34–60. New York: The Free Press, 1985.

———, "School Social Work," in *Encyclopedia of Social Work,* Vol. 2, 18th ed., A. Minahan, ed., pp. 538–545. Silver Spring, Md.: National Association of Social Workers, 1987.

Cottrell, Leonard, *Interpersonal Competence and Divorce.* Chicago: University of Chicago Press, 1955.

———, and Nelson Foote, *Identity and Interpersonal Competence.* Chicago: University of Chicago Press, 1955.

Coulton, Claudia, "Person–Environment Fit as the Focus in Health Care," *Social Work* 26 (1) (1981), 26–35.

———, and N. Butler, "Measuring Social Work Productivity in Health Care," *Health and Social Work* 6 (3) (1981), 4–12.

Cox, F. M., and others, eds, *Tactics and Techniques of Community Practice,* 2nd ed. Itaska, Ill.: Peacock, 1984.

Craft, John L., *Statistics and Data Analysis for Social Workers.* Itaska, Ill.: Peacock, 1985.

Crumm, D., and W. K. Knecht, "Parishes Go on the Line: Catholics Await Fate of Churches," *Detroit Free Press,* Sept. 25, 1988, p. 10.

Cullen, Francis T., and Karen E. Gilbert, *Reaffirming Rehabilitation.* Cincinnati: Anderson, 1982.

Dana, Richard H., ed., *Human Services for Cultural Minorities.* Baltimore: University Park Press, 1981.

Danziger, Sheldon, "Poverty," in *Encyclopedia of Social Work,* Vol. 2, 18th ed., A. Minahan, ed., pp. 294–302. Silver Spring, Md.: National Association of Social Workers, 1987.

———, and R. Plotnick, "Poverty and Policy: The Lessons of Two Decades," *Social Service Review* 60, 1 (March 1986), 34–51.

Daro, Deborah, and Leslie Mitchel, *Child Abuse Fatalities Continue to Rise: The Result of the 1988 Annual Fifty State Survey,* Working Paper 808. Chicago: National Committee for Prevention of Child Abuse, 1989.

Dasmann, R. F., "Conservation of Natural Resources," *Encyclopedia Britannica* , 5 (1975), 39–62.

David, S. M., *Managing Corporate Culture.* Cambridge, Mass.: Ballinger, 1984.

Davis-Sacks, M. L., and Y. Hasenfeld, "Organizations: Impact on Employees and Community," in *Encyclopedia of Social Work,* Vol. 2, 18th ed., A. Minahan, ed., pp. 217–228. Silver Spring, Md.: National Association of Social Workers, 1987.

Deegan, Mary Jo, *Jane Addams and the Men of the Chicago School: 1892–1918.* New Brunswick, N.J.: Transaction Books, 1988.

Delbecq, A., A. Van de Ven, and D. Gustoffsen, *Group Techniques for Program Planning: A Guide to Nominal Group and Delphi Processes.* Chicago: Scott, Foresman, 1976.

DeSchweinitz, Karl, *England's Road to Social Security.* New York: Barnes, 1961.

Deshler, Betty, and John L. Erlich, "Changing School–Community Relations," in *The School in the Community,* Rosemary Sarri and Frank Maple, eds., pp. 233–244. Washington, D.C.: National Association of Social Workers, 1972.

Dluhy, Milan, "Developing Coalitions in the Face of Power: Lessons from the Human Services," in *Strategic Perspectives on Planning Practice,* B. Checkoway, ed., pp. 153–164. Lexington, Mass.: Lexington Books, 1986.

———, "Housing," in *Encyclopedia of Social Work,* Vol. 1, 18th ed., A. Minahan, ed., pp. 821–835. Silver Spring, Md.: National Association of Social Workers, 1987.

Dohrenwend, B. S., and B. P. Dohrenwend, eds., *Stressful Life Events: Their Nature and Effects.* New York: Wiley-Interscience, 1974.

Douglass, R., "How to Use and Present Community Data," in *Tactics and Techniques of Community Practice,* 2nd ed., F. E. Cox and others, eds., pp. 383–395. Itaska, Ill.: Peacock, 1984.

Downs, Anthony, *Urban Problems and Prospects.* Chicago: Markham Publishing, 1970.

DuBois, W. E. B., *The Suppression of the African Slave-Trade to the United States of America: 1638–1870.* New York: Longmans, 1904.

———, *Black Reconstruction: An Essay toward A History of the Part Which Black Folk Played in the Attempt to Reconstruct Democracy in America, 1860–1880.* New York: Harcourt Brace & Company, 1935.

———, *Dusk at Dawn: An Essay toward an Autobiography of a Race Concept.* New York: Harcourt Brace, 1940.

———, *The Souls of Black Folk.* Chicago: A. C. McClora, 1953.

Durkheim, Emile, *Suicide: A Study in Sociology.* New York: The Free Press, 1951.

Edelman, Murray, *Political Language: Words That Succeed and Policies That Fail.* New York: Academic Press, 1977.

Ehrenreich, B., *The Hearts of Men.* Garden City: Doubleday, 1983.

Ellis, A., and R. A. Harper, *A New Guide to Rational Living.* North Hollywood, Calif.: Wilshire, 1975.

Emlen, Arthur C., "Child Care Services," in *Encyclopedia of Social Work,* Vol. 1, 18th ed., A. Minahan, ed., pp. 232–242. Silver Spring, Md.: National Association of Social Workers, 1987.

Empey, LaMar T., and Stephen Lubeck, *The Silverlake Experiment: Testing Delinquency Theory and Community Intervention.* Chicago: Aldine, 1971.

Engels, F., *Origin of the Family, Private Property, and the State,* in *Collected Works: Karl Marx and Frederick Engels,* R. Dixon, tr. London: Lawrence and Wishart, 1975.

Erickson, A. Gerald, "Family Services," in *Encyclopedia of Social Work,* Vol. 1, 18th ed., A. Minahan, ed., pp. 589–593. Silver Spring, Md.: National Association of Social Workers, 1987.

Erikson, Erik, *Childhood and Society.* New York: Norton, 1950.

Etzioni, A., *The Semi-professions and Their Organization.* New York: The Free Press, 1969.

———, *Societal Guidance.* New York: Crowell, 1969.

Fairbairn, Gavin, and Susan Fairbairn, *Ethical Issues in Caring.* Aldershot, Hampshire, U.K., and Brookfield, Vt.: Avebury, 1988.

Family Service America, *Family Service Profiles: Agency Staffing and Coverage.* New York: Family Service America, 1984.

———, *The State of Families: 1984–85.* New York: Family Service America, 1985.

Federal Bureau of Investigation, *Uniform Crime Reports for 1984.* Washington, D.C.: U.S. Department of Justice, 1985.

Fegin, Joe, *Subordinating the Poor.* Englewood Cliffs, N.J.: Prentice Hall, 1975.

Feigelman, William, and Arnold R. Silverman, *Chosen Children: New Patterns of Adoptive Relationships.* New York: Praeger, 1983.

Fellin, Philip, *The Community and the Social Worker.* Itaska, Ill.: Peacock, 1987.

Fischer, D., *Growing Old in America.* New York: Oxford University Press, 1977.

Fischer, R., and W. Ury, *Getting to Yes.* New York: Penguin, 1983.

Fisher, Joel, "Is Casework Effective: A Review?" *Social Work* 18 (1973), 5–20.

———, and Harvey Gochros, *Planned Behavior*

Change: Behavior Modification in Social Work. New York: The Free Press, 1975.

Flamholtz, Eric, *How to Make the Transition from an Entrepreneurship to a Professionally Managed Firm.* San Francisco: Jossey-Bass, 1986.

Flexner, Abraham, "Is Social Work a Profession?" in *Proceedings of the National Conference on Charities and Corrections, 1915,* pp. 576–590. New York: National Conference on Charities and Corrections, 1915.

Follett, Mary Parker, *The New State.* New York: Longmans, Green, 1926.

——, *Dynamic Administration: Collected Papers of M. P. Follett,* V. Metcalf and V. Wick, eds. New York: Harper & Row, 1957.

Francek, J., "Foreword," in *National Survey of Occupational Social Workers,* R. Teare, ed., pp. vi–vii. Silver Spring, Md.: National Association of Social Workers, 1987.

Freire, Paulo, *Education for Critical Consciousness.* New York: Seabury Press, 1973.

Freud, Sigmund. *A General Selection of the Works of Sigmund Freud,* John Rickman, ed. New York: Hogarth Press and the Institute of Psychoanalysis, 1937.

Frieden, Bernard J., "Housing," in *Encyclopedia of Social Work,* Vol. 1, 16th ed., R. Morris, ed., pp. 587–606. New York: National Association of Social Workers, 1971.

——, "Housing," in *Encyclopedia of Social Work,* Vol. 1, 17th ed., J. B. Turner, ed., pp. 639–652. New York: National Association of Social Workers, 1977.

Friedlander, Walter A., and Robert Z. Apte, *Introduction to Social Welfare,* 5th ed. Englewood Cliffs, N.J.: Prentice Hall, 1980.

Fromm, Eric, *Escape from Freedom.* New York: Holt, Rinehart, and Winston, 1941.

Galbraith, John Kenneth, *The Affluent Society.* New York: New American Library, 1958.

Gans, Herbert J., *People and Plans.* New York: Basic Books, 1968.

Gardner, Howard, *Frames of the Mind.* New York: Basic Books, 1983.

Garvin, Charles D., "Research Related Roles for Social Workers," in *Social Work Research and Evaluation,* Richard M. Grinnell, ed., pp. 547–552. Itaska, Ill.: Peacock, 1981.

——, "Resocialization: Group Work in Social Control and Correctional Settings," in *The Group Worker's Handbook: Varieties of Group Experience,* Robert Conyne, ed., pp. 113–134. Springfield: Charles C Thomas, 1985.

——, *Contemporary Group Work,* 2nd ed. Englewood Cliffs, N.J.: Prentice Hall, 1981, 1987.

——, and F. M. Cox, "A History of Community Organizing Since the Civil War with Special Reference to Oppressed Communities," in *Strategies of Community Organization.* 4th ed., F. M. Cox and others, eds., pp. 26–63. Itaska: Peacock, 1987.

——, and Brett Seabury, *Interpersonal Practice in Social Work.* Englewood Cliffs, N.J.: Prentice Hall, 1984.

Gerard, R. W., "Units and Concepts of Biology," in *Modern Systems Research for the Behavioral Scientist,* Walter Buckley, ed., pp. 51–58. Chicago: Aldine, 1968.

Germain, Carel B., "The Place of Community Work within an Ecological Approach to Social Work Practice," in *Theories and Practice of Community Social Work,* S. H. Taylor and R. W. Roberts, eds., pp. 20–35. New York: Columbia Univ. Press, 1985.

——, "Understanding and Changing Communities and Organizations in the Practice of Child Welfare," in *A Handbook of Child Welfare: Context, Knowledge, and Practice,* Ann Hartman and Joan Laird, eds., pp. 122–148. New York: The Free Press, 1985.

——, and Alex Gitterman, "Ecological Perspective," in *Encyclopedia of Social Work,* Vol. 1., 18th ed., pp. 488–499. Silver Spring, Md.: National Association of Social Workers, 1987.

Gerth, H., and C. W. Mills, *From Max Weber.* New York: Oxford University Press, 1958.

Gil, David, "The Ideological Context of Child Welfare," in *A Handbook of Child Welfare: Context, Knowledge, and Practice,* Ann Hartman and Joan Laird, eds., pp. 11–33. New York: Free Press, 1985.

Gilbert, Neil, *Capitalism and the Welfare State.* New Haven, Conn.: Yale University Press, 1983.

——, Henry Miller, and Harry Specht, *An Introduction to Social Work Practice.* Englewood Cliffs, N.J.: Prentice Hall, 1980.

Gilder, G., *Wealth and Poverty.* New York: Basic Books, 1981.

Giovannoni, Jeanne M., and Rosina M. Becerra, *Defining Child Abuse.* New York: The Free Press, 1979.

Girivitz, H., "Social Welfare," in *International Encyclopedia of the Social Sciences,* Vol. 16, D. Sills, ed., pp. 512–521. New York: The Free Press, 1968.

Glaser, Barney G., and Anselm Strauss, *The Discovery of Grounded Theory.* Chicago: Aldine, 1967.

Glasser, Paul, Rosemary Sarri, and Robert Vinter, *Individual Change through Small Groups.* New York: The Free Press, 1974.

Goffman, Erving, *The Presentation of Self in Everyday Life.* Garden City, N.Y.: Doubleday, 1959.

——, *Asylums.* Chicago: Aldine, 1961.

——, *Stigma.* Englewood Cliffs, N.J.: Prentice Hall, 1963.

Golan, Naomi, *Treatment in Crisis Situations.* New York: The Free Press, 1978.

Goldman, Howard H., "Epidemiology," in *The Chronic Mental Patient: Five Years Later,* John A. Talbott, ed., pp. 15–32. Orlando, Fla.: Grune and Stratton, 1984.

Goleman, Daniel, "Social Workers Vault into a Leading Role in Psychotherapy," *New York Times,* April 30, 1985, 17 and 20.

Gordon, Milton, *Assimilation in American Life.* New York: Oxford University Press, 1964.

Gottman, J., and R. Clason, "Troubleshooting Guide for Research and Evaluation," in *Tactics and Techniques of Community Practice,* F. M. Cox and others, eds., pp. 396–407. Itaska, Ill.: Peacock, 1984.

Green, James E., *Cultural Awareness in the Human Services.* Englewood Cliffs, N.J.: Prentice Hall, 1982.

Greene, Roberta R., "The Ecological Perspective: An Eclectic Theoretical Framework for Social Work Practice," in *Bridging the Gap between Human Behavior Theory and Social Work Practice,* Roberta Greene and Paul Ephross, eds., Chicago: Aldine de Gruyter, in press.

Grinnell, Richard M., Jr., and Margaret Stothers, "Utilizing Research Designs," in *Social Work Research and Evaluation,* 3rd ed., Richard M. Grinnell, ed., pp. 199–239. Itaska, Ill.: Peacock, 1988.

Grow, Lucille, and Deborah Shapiro, *Black Children–White Parents: A Study of Transracial Adoption.* New York: Child Welfare League of America, 1974.

Gummer, Burton, *The Politics of Social Administration.* Englewood Cliffs, N.J.: Prentice Hall, 1990.

Gurman, Alan S., and David P. Kniskern, "Family Therapy Outcome Research: Knowns and Unknowns," in *Handbook of Family Therapy,* Alan S. Gurman and David P. Kniskern, eds., pp. 742–775. New York: Brunner/Mazel, 1981.

Gusfield, J., *Symbolic Crusade.* Urbana: University of Illinois Press, 1963.

Haber, D., *Health Care for an Aging Society: Cost Conscious Community Care and Self-care Approaches.* New York: Hemisphere, 1989.

Hancock, Betsy L., *School Social Work.* Englewood Cliffs, N.J.: Prentice Hall, 1982.

Harrigan, B., *Games Mother Never Taught You.* New York: Warner Books, 1977.

Hartford, Margaret, *Groups in Social Work.* New York: Columbia University Press, 1972.

Hartman, Ann, and Joan Laird, *Family-centered Social Work Practice.* New York: Macmillan, 1983.

Harvey, J., "The Abilene Paradox: The Management of Agreement," *Organizational Dynamics* (Summer 1974), 64–79.

Hasenfeld, Y., *Human Service Organizations.* Englewood Cliffs, N.J.: Prentice Hall, 1983.

———, *Administrative Leadership in the Social Services.* New York: Haworth, 1989.

Hearn, Gordon, ed., *The General Systems Approach: Contributions toward an Holistic Conception of Social Work.* New York: Council on Social Work Education, 1969.

Helfgot, Joseph H., *Professional Reforming: Mobilization for Youth and the Failure of Social Science.* Lexington, Mass.: Lexington Books, 1981.

Hellenbrand, Shirley, "Gordon Hamilton," in *Encyclopedia of Social Work,* Vol. 1, 17th ed., John B. Turner, ed., pp. 517–519. New York: National Association of Social Workers, 1977.

Henry, Jules, *Essays on Education.* Baltimore: Penguin, 1971.

Hersen, M., and D. H. Barlow, *Single Case Experimental Designs: Strategies for Studying Behavior Change,* 2nd ed. Elmsford, N.Y.: Pergamon, 1984.

Hess, Julian, "Housing: Federal and State Programs," in *Encyclopedia of Social Work,* Vol. 1, 16th ed., R. Morris, ed., pp. 606–617. New York: National Association of Social Workers, 1971.

Hirshman, A. O., *Shifting Involvements.* Princeton, N.J.: Princeton University Press, 1982.

Hoffman, S., and others, *Who Are the Homeless,* study prepared by New York State Office of Mental Health, New York City, May 1982.

Hogan, Patricia Turner, and Sau-Fong Siu, "Minority Children and the Child Welfare System: An Historical Perspective," *Social Work* 33 (6) (November–December 1988), 493–498.

Holcomb, M., and J. Stein, *Writing for Decision Makers.* Belmont, Calif.: Lifetime Learning, 1981.

Homans, George C., *The Human Group.* New York: Wiley, 1950.

Hookey, P., "Social Work in Primary Health Care Settings," in *Social Work in Health Care,* Neil Bracht, ed., pp. 211–226. New York: Haworth, 1978.

Hopps, June Gary, "Deja Vu or New View," *Social Work* 33 (4) (July–August 1988), 292.

———, and Elaine B. Pinderhughes, "Profession of Social Work: Contemporary Characteristics," in *Encyclopedia of Social Work,* Vol. 2, 18th ed., A. Minahan, ed., pp. 351–366. Silver Spring, Md.: National Association of Social Workers, 1987.

Hornick, Joseph P., and Barbara Burrows, "Program Evaluation," in *Social Work Research and Evaluation,* 3rd ed., Richard M. Grinnell, ed., pp. 400–424. Itaska, Ill.: Peacock, 1988.

Howard, M., and L. Eddinger, *School Age Parents.* Syracuse, N.Y.: National Alliance Concerned with School-Age Parents, 1973.

Hudson, R. B., and J. Strate, "Aging and Political Systems," in *Handbook of Aging and Social Sciences,* 2nd ed., R. H. Binstock and E. Shanas, eds., pp. 554–585. New York: Van Nostrand-Reinhold, 1985.

Hudson, Walter W., *The Clinical Measurement Package: A Field Manual.* Homewood, Ill.: Dorsey, 1982.

———, and Bruce A. Thyer, "Research Measures and Indices in Direct Practice," in *Encyclopedia of Social Work,* Vol. 2, 18th ed., A. Minahan, ed., pp. 487–498. Silver Spring, Md.: National Association of Social Workers, 1987.

Hunter, Floyd, *Community Power Structure.* Chapel Hill, N.C.: University of North Carolina Press, 1953.

Hunter, S., and M. Sundel, *Mid Life Myths.* Newbury Park, Calif.: Sage, 1989.

Huttman, Elizabeth D., *Social Services for the Elderly.* New York: The Free Press, 1985.

Jacobs, Jane, *The Death and Life of Great American Cities.* New York: Random House, 1961.

Jansson, B., *Social Welfare Policy.* Belmont, Calif.: Wadsworth, 1984.

Jenks, Christopher, "Who Should Control Education?" *Dissent* (March–April 1966) 145–163.

Jesness, Carl F., and others, *The Youth Center Research Project.* Sacramento, Calif.: American Justice Institute, 1972.

Johnson, A. S., "Preliminary Conclusions of the Family Impact Seminar," in *New Strategic Perspectives on Social Policy,* J. E. Tropman and others, eds., pp. 410–421. Elmsford, N.Y.: Pergamon Press, 1981.

Johnson, H. R., and J. E. Tropman, "The Settings of Community Organization Practice," in *Strategies of Community Organization,* F. M. Cox and others, eds., pp. 213–223. Itaska, Ill.: Peacock, 1979.

Johnson, Julie, "Child Care: No Shortage of Proposals," *New York Times,* March 26, 1989, Sect. 4, p. 5.

Jonas, Steven, "Planning for Health Services," in *Health Care Delivery in the United States* 3rd ed., Steven Jonas, ed., pp. 383–415. New York: Springer, 1986.

———, "Population Data for Health and Health Care," in *Health Care Delivery in the United States* 3rd ed., Steven Jonas, ed., pp. 35–53. New York: Springer, 1986.

———, and Stephen N. Rosenberg, "Ambulatory Care," in *Health Care Delivery in the United States,* 3rd ed., Steven Jonas, ed., pp. 125–164, New York: Springer, 1986.

———, and others, "Monitoring Utilization of a Municipal Hospital Emergency Department," *Hospital Topics* 54 (1) (1976), 43–48.

Jones, E. D., "On Transracial Adoption of Black Children," *Child Welfare* 51 (March 1972), 156–164.

Jones, Linda E., "Women," in *Encyclopedia of Social Work,* Vol. 2, 18th ed., A. Minahan, ed., pp 872–881. Silver Spring, Md.: National Association of Social Workers, 1987.

Kadushin, Alfred, "Child Welfare Services," in *Encyclopedia of Social Work,* Vol. 1, 18th ed., A. Minahan, ed., pp. 265–275. Silver Spring, Md.: National Association of Social Workers, 1987.

———, and Judith Martin, *Child Welfare Services,* 4th ed. New York: Macmillan, 1988.

Kahn, A. J., "Social Problems and Issues," in *Encyclopedia of Social Work,* Vol. 2, 18th ed., A. Minahan, ed., pp. 632–644. Silver Spring, Md.: National Association of Social Workers, 1987.

Kane, R. L., and R. A. Kane, *Values and Long Term Care.* Lexington, Mass.: Lexington Books, 1982.

Kane, Rosalie A., "Long Term Care," in *Encyclopedia of Social Work,* Vol. 2, 18th ed., A. Minahan, ed., pp. 59–72. Silver Spring, Md.: National Association of Social Workers, 1987.

Kanter, Rosabeth, *Men and Women of the Corporation.* New York: Basic Books, 1977.

———, *The Change Masters.* New York: Simon and Schuster, 1983.

Karger, H. J., and D. Stoesz, *American Social Welfare Policy.* New York: Longman, 1990.

Kasius, Cora, ed., *A Comparison of Diagnostic and Functional Casework Concepts.* New York: Family Service Association of America, 1950.

Keith-Lucas, Alan, "The Political Theory Implicit in Social Casework Theory," *American Political Science Review* 57 (1953), 1076–1091.

Kellogg, P., *The Pittsburgh Survey.* New York: Charity Organization Society, 1909.

Kemmer, Elizabeth, *Violence in the Family—An Annotated Bibliography.* New York: Garland Publishing Co., 1984.

Kempe, C. Henry, and others, "The Battered Child Syndrome," *Journal of the American Medical Association* 181 (1) (1962), 17–24.

Kiesler, Charles, and Amy E. Sibulkin, *Mental Hospitalization: Myths and Facts about a National Crisis.* Newbury Park, Calif.: Sage, 1987.

Kimmich, Madeleine H., *America's Children Who Cares?: Growing Needs and Declining Assistance in the Reagan Era.* Washington, D.C.: Urban Institute Press, 1985.

Kiresuk, Thomas, and Geoffrey Garwick, "Basic Goal Attainment Procedures," in *Social Work Processes,* 2nd ed., Beulah R. Compton and Burt Galaway, eds., pp. 412–421. Homewood, Ill.: Dorsey, 1979.

Kobrin, Solomon, and Malcolm W. Klein, *Community*

Treatment of Juvenile Offenders: The DSO Experiments. Beverly Hills, Calif.: Sage, 1983.

Kotter, John, Leonard Schlesinger, and Vijay Sathe, *Organization.* Homewood, Ill.: R. D. Irwin, 1986.

Kovner, Anthony R., "Hospitals," in *Health Care Delivery in the United States,* 3rd ed., Steven Jonas, ed., pp. 183–213. New York: Springer, 1986.

Kozaitis, K., "Culture and Social Work: An Anthropological Perspective," unpublished manuscript. Ann Arbor: University of Michigan, 1990.

Kravetz, Diane, "Women and Mental Health," in *Feminist Visions for Social Work,* Nan Van Den Bergh and Lynn Cooper, eds., pp. 101–127. Silver Spring, Md.: National Association of Social Workers, 1986.

Krisberg, B., and others, "The Watershed of Juvenile Justice Reform," *Crime and Delinquency* 32 (1) (1986), 5–38.

Kropotkin, Peter, *Mutual Aid: A Factor of Evolution.* New York: Knopf, 1925.

Kurtz, E., *AA: The Story.* New York: Harper & Row 1988.

Kurtzman, P., "Industrial Social Work (Occupational Social Work)," in *Encyclopedia of Social Work,* Vol. 1, 18th ed., A. Minahan, ed., pp. 899–910. Silver Spring, Md.: National Association of Social Workers, 1987.

Laird, Joan, "Women and Stories: Restoring Women's Self-constructions," in *Women in Families: A Framework for Family Therapy,* Monica McGoldrick, Carol M. Anderson, and Froma Walsh, eds., pp. 427–450. New York: Norton, 1989.

Lamb, Sir Michael, *The Role of the Father in Child Development.* New York: Wiley, 1976.

Lammers, W., *Public Policy and the Aging.* Washington, D.C.: CQ Press, 1983.

Lane, Robert P., "The Field of Community Organization," in *Proceedings of the National Conference of Social Work, 1939.* New York: Columbia University Press, 1939.

Lang, Judith, "Book Review of *Family-centered Social Work Practice,*" *Social Work,* 30 (1985), 278.

Lardner, Joyce, *Mixed Families: Adoption across Racial Boundaries.* Garden City, N.Y.: Doubleday, 1978.

Lasswell, Harold, *Psychopathology and Politics.* Chicago: University of Chicago Press, 1930.

Lauffer, A., *Social Planning at the Community Level.* Englewood Cliffs, N.J.: Prentice Hall, 1977.

Leavitt, J., "Feminist Advocacy Planning in the 1980's," in *Strategic Perspectives in Planning Practice,* B. Checkoway, ed. pp. 181–194. Lexington, Mass.: D. C. Heath, 1986.

LeBon, G., *The Crowd.* London: T. F. Urwin, 1910.

Lee, Porter R., "Social Work: Cause or Function," *Proceedings of the National Conference of Social Work, 1929.* Chicago: University of Chicago Press, 1930, 3–20.

Leiby, J., "Social Welfare: History of Basic Ideas," in *Encyclopedia of Social Work,* Vol. 2, 17th ed., J. Turner, ed., pp. 1512–1529. Washington, D.C.: National Association of Social Workers, 1977.

Levinson, Daniel, *The Seasons of a Man's Life.* New York: Knopf, 1978.

Lewin, Kurt, *Principles of Topological Psychology.* New York: McGraw-Hill, 1936.

———, *Twentieth Century Psychology.* New York: Philosophical Library, 1946.

Lewis, M., "Social Policy Research: A Guide to Legal and Government Documents," in *New Strategic Perspectives on Social Policy,* J. E. Tropman and others, eds., pp. 577–584. Elmsford, N.Y.: Pergamon, 1981.

Lewis, Oscar, *Children of Sanchez.* New York: Random House, 1961.

———, *La Vida: A Puerto-Rican Family in the Culture of Poverty.* New York: Random House, 1966.

Liebow, Eliot, *Tally's Corner.* Boston: Little Brown, 1967.

Lillienthal, David, *T.V.A. Democracy on the March.* New York: Harper & Row, 1953.

Lindeman, Eduard C., *The Community.* New York: Association Press, 1921.

Lindner, Robert, *The Fifty-minute Hour.* New York: Holt, Rinehart and Winston, 1954.

Lindsay, Jean Warren, *Open Adoption: A Caring Adoption.* Buena Park, Calif.: Morning Glory Press, 1987.

Lippitt, R., H. J. Watson, and B. Westley, *The Dynamics of Planned Change.* New York: Harcourt Brace Jovanovich, 1958.

Lipset, S. M., *The First New Nation.* New York: Basic Books, 1963.

———, and W. Schneider, *The Confidence Gap.* New York: The Free Press, 1983.

Lipton, Douglas, Robert Martinson, and Judith Wilks, *The Effectiveness of Correctional Treatment: A Survey of Treatment Evaluation Studies.* New York: Praeger, 1975.

Lum, Doman, "Health Service System," in *Encyclopedia of Social Work,* Vol. 1, 18th ed., A. Minahan, ed., pp. 720–732. Silver Spring, Md.: National Association of Social Workers, 1987.

Lynd, Robert, and Helen Lynd, *Middletown.* New York: Harcourt Brace Jovanovich, 1959.

Maas, Henry, *Social Service Research.* Washington, D.C.: National Association of Social Workers, 1978.

MacGregor, Douglas, *The Human Side of Enterprise.* New York: McGraw-Hill, 1960.

Maier, Henry, *Developmental Group Care of Children and Youth: Concepts and Practice.* New York: Haworth, 1987.

Malcolm, Janet, *Psychoanalysis: The Impossible Profession.* New York: Knopf, 1981.

Malinowski, Bronislaw, *Magic, Science, and Religion.* New York: Ill.: The Free Press, 1948.

Manser, Ellen P., *Family Advocacy—A Manual for Action.* New York: Family Service Association of America, 1973.

Marcus, Leonard J., "Health Care Financing," in *Encyclopedia of Social Work,* Vol. 1, 18th ed., A. Minahan, ed., pp. 697–709. Silver Spring, Md.: National Association of Social Workers, 1987.

Margenaw, E., and others, *Encyclopedia of Private Practice.* New York: Gardner Press, 1990.

Marsh, George Perkins, *Man and Nature.* New York: Charles Scribner, 1864.

Marti-Costa, Sylvia, and Irma Serrano-Garcia, "Needs Assessment and Community Development: An Ideological Perspective," in *Strategies of Community Organization,* 4th ed., F. M. Cox and others, eds., pp. 362–373. Itaska, Ill.: Peacock, 1987.

Martinson, Robert, "What Works?—Questions and Answers about Prison Reform," *Public Interest* 35 (Spring 1974), 22–54.

Marx, Karl, *Das Kapital.* New York: Penguin Books, 1976.

Mayer, Robert R., "Environment and Social Planning," in *Encyclopedia of Social Work,* Vol. 1, 17th ed., J. B. Turner, ed., pp. 335–341. New York: National Association of Social Workers, 1977.

———, and Ernest Greenwood, *The Nature of Social Policy Research.* Englewood Cliffs, N.J.: Prentice Hall, 1980.

Mayhew, Henry, *London Labor and the London Poor.* New York: Dover, 1968.

McCarthy, Carol M., and Kenneth E. Thorpe, "Financing for Health Care," in *Health Care Delivery in the United States,* 3rd ed., Steven Jonas, ed., pp. 303–332, New York: Springer, 1986.

McDonald, James E., and George Shepherd, "School Phobia: An Overview," *Journal of School Psychology* 14 (4) (Winter 1976),

McGowan, Brenda, and William Meezan, *Child Welfare: Current Dilemmas. Future Directions.* Itaska, Ill.: Peacock, 1983.

———, and Elaine Walsh, "Social Policy and Legislative Change," in *A Handbook of Child Welfare: Context, Knowledge, and Practice,* Ann Hartman and Joan Laird, eds., pp. 241–268. New York: The Free Press, 1985.

McKeown, T., "A Historical Appraisal of the Medical Task," in *Medical History and Medical Care,* G. McLaughlin and T. McKeown, eds. New York: Oxford University Press, 1971.

McKinney, Edward A., "Health Planning," in *Encyclopedia of Social Work,* Vol. 1, 18th ed., A. Minahan, ed., pp. 718–719. Silver Spring Md.: National Association of Social Workers, 1987.

Mead, Margaret, *Coming of Age in Samoa.* New York: Blue Ribbon, 1928.

———, *Culture and Commitment.* New York: Columbia University Press, 1978.

———, *Growing up in New Guinea.* London: Routledge, 1931.

———, *Male and Female.* New York: Sparrow, 1949.

———, *Sex and Temperament in Three Primitive Societies.* London: Routledge, 1935.

Mechanic, David, *Medical Sociology,* 2nd ed. New York: The Free Press, 1978.

Mehr, Joseph, *Human Services: Concepts and Intervention Strategies.* Boston: Allyn and Bacon, 1980.

Merton, Robert K., "The Bureaucratic Personality," in *Social Theory and Social Structure,* R. K. Merton, ed. New York: The Free Press, 1957.

Meyer, Carol H., "The Institutional Context of Child Welfare," in *A Handbook of Child Welfare: Context, Knowledge, and Practice,* Ann Hartman and Joan Laird, eds., pp. 100–116. New York: The Free Press, 1985.

Meyer, H., E. Borgatta, and W. Jones, *Girls at Vocational High.* New York: Sage Foundation, 1965.

Meyer, Henry, and others, "Social Work and Social Welfare," in *The Uses of Sociology,* Paul F. Lazarsfeld, William H. Sewell, and Harold L. Wilensky, eds., pp. 156–192. New York: Basic Books, 1967.

Middleman, R., and G. Goldberg, *Social Service Delivery: A Structural Approach.* New York: Columbia University Press, 1974.

Miller, C. A., "An Agenda for Public Health Departments," *Journal of Public Health Policy* 6 (2) (1985), 158–172.

Miller, James G., *Living Systems.* New York: McGraw-Hill, 1978.

Miller, Rosalind S., "Legislation and Health Policies," in *Social Work Issues in Health Care,* Rosalind S. Miller and Helen Rehr, eds., pp. 74–120. Englewood Cliffs: Prentice Hall, 1983.

———, "Primary Health Care," in *Encyclopedia of Social Work,* Vol. 2, 18th ed., A. Minahan, ed., pp. 321–324. Silver Spring, Md.: National Association of Social Workers, 1987.

———, and Helen Rehr, "Health Settings and Health Providers," in *Social Work Issues in Health Care,* Rosalind S. Miller and Helen Rehr, eds., pp. 1–19. Englewood Cliffs: Prentice Hall, 1983.

Mills, C. Wright, *The Power Elite*. New York: Oxford University Press, 1956.

———, "The Professional Ideology of Social Pathologists," in *Power, Politics, and People: The Collected Essays of C. Wright Mills*. Irving L. Horowitz, ed., pp. 525–552. New York: Ballantine Books, 1963.

Minahan, Ann, ed., *Encyclopedia of Social Work*, 18th ed. Silver Spring, Md.: National Association of Social Workers, 1987.

Minuchin, Salvador, *Families and Family Therapy*. Cambridge, Mass.: Harvard University Press, 1974.

———, and H. Charles Fishman, *Family Therapy Techniques*. Cambridge, Mass.: Harvard , 1981.

Moroney, Robert M., *The Family and the State: Considerations for Social Policy*. New York: Longman, 1976.

———, "Social Planning and Community Organization," in *Encyclopedia of Social Work*, Vol. 2, 18th ed., A. Minahan, ed., pp. 602–619. Silver Spring, Md.: National Association of Social Workers, 1987.

Morris, I., *The Nobility of Failure*. New York: Holt, Rinehart, and Winston, 1975.

Morris, Wayne, "The Attorney General's Survey of Release Procedures," in *Penology: The Evolution of Corrections in America*, George C. Killinger and Paul F. Cromwell, Jr., eds., pp. 20–30. St. Paul, Minn.: West, 1973.

Moss, F. E., and V. J. Halamandaris, *Too Old, Too Sick, Too Bad: Nursing Homes in America*. Germantown, Md.: Aspen Systems Corp., 1977.

Murray, Charles, *Losing Ground—American Social Policy, 1950—1980*. New York: Basic Books, 1984.

Myer, John, "An Exploratory Nationwide Survey of Child Care Workers," *Child Care Quarterly* 9 (1) (Spring 1980), 17–25.

Myers, Robert J., and Peter Ufford, *On-site Analysis: A Practical Approach to Organizational Change*. Etibicoke, Ontario: On-Site Change Associates, 1989.

Naisbett, John, *Megatrends*. New York: Warner Books, 1982.

National Association of Social Workers, "NASW Code of Ethics," *NASW News* 25 (1980), 24–25.

———, *NASW Standards for Social Work Services in Schools*. Washington, D.C.: The Association, 1978.

———, *Register of Clinical Social Workers*, 6th ed. Silver Spring, Md.: The Association, 1991.

———, *Salaries in Social Work: A Summary Report of NASW Members, July 1986–June, 1987*. Silver Spring, Md.: The Association, 1987.

National Committee for Adoption, *Adoption Fact Book: United States Data Issues, Regulations, and Resources*. Washington, D.C.: The Committee, 1985.

Netherland, Warren, "Correction Systems: Adult," in *Encyclopedia of Social Work*, Vol. 1, 18th ed., A. Minahan, ed., pp. 351–360. Silver Spring, Md.: National Association of Social Workers, 1987.

Nicols-Casebolt, A., "Black Families Headed by Single Mothers: Growing Numbers and Increasing Poverty," *Social Work* 33 (4) (July–August 1988), 306–314.

Ogden, Evelyn Hunt, and Vito Germinario, *The At-risk Student*. Lancaster, Pa.: Technomic Publishing, 1988.

Olsen, Marvin, *The Process of Social Organization*. New York: Holt, Rinehart and Winston, 1968.

Orloff, A., and T. Skocpol, "Explaining the Politics of Public Spending," *American Sociological Review* 49 (6) (December 1984), 726–750.

Palmer, Ted, *Correctional Intervention and Research: Current Issues and Future Prospects*. Lexington, Mass.: D.C. Heath, 1978.

Papajohn, John, and John Spiegel, *Transactions in Families*. San Francisco: Jossey-Bass, 1975.

Perlman, Helen H., "Intake and Some Role Considerations," *Social Casework*, 41 (1960), 171–177.

———, "Putting the 'Social' Back in Social Casework," in *Perspectives on Social Casework*, Helen H. Perlman, ed., pp. 29–34. Philadelphia: Temple University Press, 1971.

Piaget, J. *The Language and Thought of the Child*. New York: Harcourt, Brace, and Co., 1926.

———, *Child's Conception of the World*. New York: Harcourt, Brace, and Co., 1929.

———, *The Construction of Reality in the Child*. New York: Basic Books, 1954.

Pinsof, William M., "Family Therapy Process Research," in *Handbook of Family Therapy*, Alan S. Gurman and David P. Kniskern, eds., pp. 699–741. New York: Brunner/Mazel, 1981.

Piven, F. F., and R. Cloward, *Regulating the Poor*. New York: Pantheon, 1971.

Polansky, Norman, *Social Work Research*. Chicago: University of Chicago Press, 1960.

Polanyi, Karl, *The Great Transformation*. Boston: Beacon Press, 1957.

Polsky, Howard, *Cottage Six—The Social System of Delinquent Boys in Residential Treatment*. New York: Russell Sage Foundation, 1962.

Portnoy, R., *What Every Leader Should Know About People*. Englewood Cliffs, N.J.: Prentice Hall, 1986.

President's Research Committee, *Recent Social Trends*. New York: McGraw-Hill, 1933.

Pumphrey, R., and M. Pumphrey, eds., *The Heritage of American Social Work*. New York: Columbia University Press, 1961.

Quadango, Jill, "Race, Class, and Gender in the U.S. Welfare State," *American Sociological Review* 55 (February 1990), 11–28.

Quattrociocchi, S., "Fringe Benefits as Private Social Policy," in *New Strategic Perspectives on Social Policy,* John E. Tropman, Milan Dluhy, and Roger Lind, eds., pp. 422–433. Elmsford, N.Y.: Pergamon, 1981.

Radin, Norma, "Alternatives to Suspension and Corporal Punishment," *Urban Education* 22 (4) (January 1988), 476–495.

Rainwater, Lee, and Karol Kane Weinstein, *And the Poor Get Children.* Chicago: Quadrangle Books, 1960.

Rapoport, Anatole, "Foreword," in *Modern Systems Research for the Behavioral Scientist,* Walter Buckley, ed., pp. xii–xxii. Chicago: Aldine, 1968.

———, "General Systems Theory," in *International Encyclopedia of the Social Sciences,* Vol. 15, ed. D. Sills, pp. 452–58. New York: Free Press, 1968.

Reamer, Frederic G., "The Affordable Housing Crisis and Social Work," *Social Work* 34 (1) (January 1989), 5–11.

Redick, Richard, and Michael Witkin, "Residential Treatment Centers for Emotionally Disturbed Children, United States, 1977–1978 and 1979–1980," *Mental Health Statistical Note No. 162.* Washington, D.C.: Department of Health and Human Services, 1983.

Rehr, Helen, *Ethical Dilemmas in Health Care: The Professional Search for Solutions.* New York: Prodist, 1978.

Reid, William J., "Sectarian Agencies," in *Encyclopedia of Social Work,* Vol. 2, 17th ed., J. B. Turner, ed., pp. 1244–1254. Washington, D.C.: National Association of Social Workers, 1977.

———, "Research in Social Work," in *Encyclopedia of Social Work,* Vol. 2, 18th ed., A. Minahan, ed., pp. 474–487. Silver Spring, Md.: National Association of Social Workers, 1987.

———, and P. Hanrahan, "Recent Evaluations of Social Work: Grounds for Optimism," *Social Work* 27 (2) (1982), 328–340.

Reitz, H. J., *Behavior in Organizations.* Homewood, Ill.: Irwin, 1987.

Report of the National Advisory Committee on Civil Disorders. New York: Bantam Books, 1968.

Resnick, H., and R. Patti, *Change from Within.* Philadelphia: Temple University Press, 1980.

Reynolds, Bertha C., "Social Casework: What Is It? What Is Its Place in the World Today?" *The Family* (December 1935). Reprinted in *Readings in Social Casework: 1920–1938,* Fern Lowry, ed., pp. 136–147. New York: Columbia University Press, 1939.

———, *Learning and Teaching in the Practice of Social Work.* New York: Farrar and Richart, Inc., 1942.

Reynolds, C. H., and R. V. Norman, eds., *Community*

in America. Berkeley: University of California Press, 1987.

Ricci, James, "The Autoworkers and the Dumpster," *Detroit Free Press,* November 15, 1989, p. 11a.

Rice, Robert M., *American Family Policy—Content and Context.* New York: Family Service Association of America, 1977.

———, "The Well-being of Families and Children: A Context for Child Welfare," in *A Handbook of Child Welfare: Context, Knowledge, and Practice,* Ann Hartman and Joan Laird, eds., pp. 61–76. New York: The Free Press, 1985.

Richan, W., and Allan E. Mendlesohn, *Social Work—The Unloved Profession.* New York: New Viewpoints, 1973.

Richmond, Mary, *Family Visiting among the Poor: A Handbook for Charity Workers.* New York: Macmillan, 1899.

———, *Social Diagnosis.* New York: Russell Sage, 1917.

———, "Some Next Steps in Social Treatment," *Proceedings of the National Conference of Social Work, 1920,* pp. 254–258. New York: Columbia University Press, 1939.

Riley, Patrick V., "Family Services," in *Handbook of the Social Services,* Neil Gilbert and Harry Specht, eds., pp. 82–101. Englewood Cliffs, N.J.: Prentice Hall, 1981.

Roberts, Albert R., "An Introduction and Overview of Juvenile Justice," in *Juvenile Justice Policies, Programs, and Services,* Albert R. Roberts, ed., pp. 3–15. Chicago: Dorsey, 1989.

———, *Juvenile Justice: Policies, Programs, and Services.* Chicago: Dorsey, 1989.

———, "Wilderness Experiences: Camps and Outdoor Programs," in *Juvenile Justice Programs, Policies, and Services,* Albert R. Roberts, ed., pp. 194–218. Chicago: Dorsey, 1989.

Robinson, Nancy Day, "Supplemental Services for Families and Children," in *A Handbook of Child Welfare: Context, Knowledge, and Practice,* Ann Hartman and Joan Laird, eds., pp. 397–416. New York: The Free Press, 1985.

Robinson, Virginia, *A Changing Psychology of Social Casework.* Chapel Hill: University of North Carolina Press, 1934.

Rogers, Joseph W., and G. Larry Mays, *Juvenile Delinquency and Juvenile Justice.* Englewood Cliffs, N.J.: Prentice Hall, 1987.

Rokeach, Milton, *Understanding Human Values.* New York: The Free Press, 1979.

Rooney, Ronald, "Adolescent Groups in Public Schools," in William J. Reid and Laura Epstein, eds., *Task-Centered Practice,* pp. 168–182. New York: Columbia University Press, 1977.

Root, Larry, "Employee Benefits and Income Security," in *New Strategic Perspectives on Social Policy,* J. E. Tropman, M. Dluhy, and R. Lind, eds., pp. 97–109. Elmsford, N.Y.: Pergamon, 1981.

———, *Fringe Benefits: Social Insurance in the Steel Industry.* Beverly Hills, Calif.: Sage, 1982.

———, Lawrence, and John E. Tropman "Income Sources of the Elderly," *Social Service Review* 58 (3) (September 1984), 383–404.

Rorabaugh, W. J., *The Alcoholic Republic: An American Tradition.* New York: Oxford, 1979.

Rose, Sheldon, *Group Therapy: A Behavioral Approach.* Englewood Cliffs, N.J.: Prentice Hall, 1977.

———, "Use of Data in Identifying and Resolving Group Problems in Goal Oriented Treatment Groups," *Social Work with Groups* 7 (2) (Summer 1984), 23–36.

Rosen, Sumner M., David Fanshel, and Mary E. Lutz, eds., *Face of the Nation 1987: Statistical Supplement to the 18th Edition of the Encyclopedia of Social Worker.* Silver Spring, Md.: National Association of Social Workers, 1987.

Rosenberg, Gary, "Concepts in the Financial Management of Hospital Social Work Departments," *Social Work in Health Care* 5 (3) (1980), 287–296.

———, "Practice Roles and Functions of the Health Social Worker," in *Social Work Issues in Health Care,* Rosalind S. Miller and Helen Rehr, eds., pp. 121–180. Englewood Cliffs, N.J.: Prentice Hall, 1983.

Ross, M. G., *Community Organization.* New York: Harper, 1955.

———, *Case Histories in Community Organization.* New York: Harper, 1958.

Rossen, Salie, "Hospital Social Work," in *Encyclopedia of Social Work,* Vol. 1, 18th ed., A. Minahan, ed., pp. 816–821. Silver Spring, Md.: National Association of Social Workers, 1987.

Rothman, Jack, *Social R & D.* Englewood Cliffs, N.J.: Prentice Hall, 1980.

———, "Community Theory and Research," *Encyclopedia of Social Work,* Vol. 1, 18th ed., A. Minahan, ed., pp. 308–315. Silver Spring, Md.: National Association of Social Workers, 1987.

———, with J. E. Tropman, "Models of Community Organization and Macro Perspectives: Their Mixing and Phasing," in *Strategies of Community Organization,* 4th ed., pp. 3–26. Itaska, Ill.: Peacock, 1987.

Russell, Alene B., and Cynthia M. Trainor, *Trends in Child Abuse and Neglect: A National Perspective.* Denver, Colo.: American Humane Association, Children Division, 1984.

Russell, Bertrand, *A History of Western Philosophy.* New York: Simon and Schuster, 1945.

Ryan, William, *Blaming the Victim.* New York: Random House, 1971.

———, *Equality.* New York: Pantheon, 1981.

Santamour, Miles B., and Bernadette West, "The Mentally Retarded Offender: Presentation of the Facts and a Discussion of the Issues," in *The Retarded Offender,* Miles B. Santamour and Bernadette West, eds., pp. 7–37. New York: Praeger, 1982.

Sargent, Alice, *The Androgynous Manager.* New York: American Management Association, 1983.

Sarri, Rosemary, and Robert D. Vinter, "Justice for Whom? Varieties of Juvenile Correctional Approaches," in *The Juvenile Justice System,* Malcolm W. Klein, ed., pp. 161–200. Beverly Hills, Calif.: Sage, 1976.

Schein, Edgar, *Organizational Culture and Leadership.* San Francisco: Jossey-Bass, 1985.

Schlesinger, A., Jr., *The Crisis of the Old Order.* Boston: Houghton-Mifflin, 1957.

Schlesinger, Elfriede G., *Health Care Social Work Practice: Concepts and Strategies.* St. Louis: Times Mirror/Mosby, 1985.

Schoech, Dick, and others, "Expert Systems: Artificial Intelligence for Professional Decisions," *Computers in Human Services* 1 (1) (Spring, 1985), 81–115.

Schwartz, M., "Community Organization," in *Encyclopedia of Social Work,* 15th issue Vol.1, 17th ed., H. L. Lurie, ed., pp. 177–189. New York: National Association of Social Workers, 1965.

Schwartz, William, "The Social Worker in the Group," in *New Perspectives on Service to Groups,* pp. 7–29. New York: Columbia University Press, 1961.

Scope and Methods of the Family Service Agency, Report of the Committee on Methods and Scope. New York: Family Service Association of America, 1953.

Seaberg, James R., "Utilizing Sampling Procedures," in *Social Work Research and Evaluation,* 3rd ed., Richard M. Grinnell, ed., pp. 240–257. Itaska, Ill.: Peacock, 1988.

Seaver, Judith W., and Carol A. Cartwright, *Child Care Administration.* Belmont, Calif.: Wadsworth, 1986.

Segal, Steven P., "Deinstitutionalization," in *Encyclopedia of Social Work,* Vol. 1, 18th ed., A. Minahan, ed., pp. 376–382. Silver Spring, Md.: National Association of Social Workers, 1987.

Segalman, Ralph, *Poverty in America.* Westport, Conn.: Greenwood Press, 1981.

Selltiz, Claire, and others, *Research Methods in Social Relations.* New York: Holt, Rinehart and Winston, 1959.

Selznick, Philip, *Leadership in Administration.* New York: Harper & Row, 1957.

Shannon, Gary W., and G. E. Alan Dever, *Health Care Delivery, Spatial Perspectives.* New York: McGraw-Hill, 1974.

Shaw, C., *The Jack-Rollers.* Chicago: University of Chicago Press, 1938.

Shaw, Marvin E., *Group Dynamics: The Psychology of Small Group Behavior,* 3rd ed. New York: McGraw-Hill, 1981.

Sheflen, A. E., *Communicational Structure: Analysis of a Psychotherapy Transaction.* Bloomington: Indiana University Press, 1973.

Shyne, Ann, and Anita Schroeder, *National Study of Social Services to Children and Their Families.* Washington, D.C.: Department of Health, Education, and Welfare, 1978.

Siegel, Deborah, and Frederick G. Reamer, "Integrating Research Findings, Concepts, and Logic into Practice," in *Social Work Research and Evaluation,* 3rd ed., Richard M. Grinnell, ed., pp. 483–502. Itaska, Ill.: Peacock, 1988.

Simmel, G., *The Functions of Social Conflict.* New York: The Free Press, 1955.

———, *The Web of Group Affiliations.* New York: The Free Press, 1955.

Simon, Paul, "Social Group Work in the Schools," *Bulletin of the National Association of School Social Workers* 31 (1) (September 1955), 3–12.

Simon, Sydney, Leland W. Howe, and Howard Kirschenbaum, *Values Clarification: A Handbook of Practical Strategies for Students and Teachers.* New York: Hart, 1972.

Sinclair, Upton, *The Jungle.* New York: Doubleday, Page & Co., 1906.

Skidmore, Rex, and Milton G. Thackeray, *Introduction to Social Work.* Englewood Cliffs, N.J.: Prentice Hall, 1982.

Skinner, B. F., *About Behaviorism.* New York: Knopf, 1974.

Slater, Philip, *The Pursuit of Loneliness.* New York: Beacon Press, 1970.

Smith, Adam, *The Wealth of Nations.* Chicago: Encyclopedia Britannica, 1952.

Smith, B. C., *Community Health: An Epidemiological Approach.* New York: Macmillan, 1979.

Solomon, Barbara, *Black Empowerment.* New York: Columbia University Press, 1976.

Speck, R. V., and C. Attneave, *Family Networks.* New York: Random House, 1973.

Spergel, I. A., "Community Development," in *Encyclopedia of Social Work,* Vol. 1, 18th ed., A. Minahan, ed., pp. 299–308. Silver Spring, Md.: National Association of Social Workers, 1987.

Stack, C., *All Our Kin.* New York: Harper & Row, 1974.

Staples, Robert, "Masculinity and Race: The Dual Dilemma of Black Men," *Journal of Social Issues* 34 (1) (1978), 169–183.

Steffens, Lincoln, *The Shame of the Cities.* New York: P. Smith, 1948.

Stein, M., *The Eclipse of Community.* Princeton, N.J.: Princeton University Press, 1960.

Stein, Theodore J., Eileen Gambrill, and Kermit T. Wiltse, *Children in Foster Homes: Achieving Continuity of Care.* New York: Praeger, 1978.

Straussner, S., *Occupational Social Work Today.* Binghampton, N.Y.: Haworth, 1990.

Studt, Elliot, "Crime and Delinquency: Institutions," in *Encyclopedia of Social Work,* Vol. 1, 17th ed., J. B. Turner, ed., pp. 208–213. Washington, D.C.: National Association of Social Workers, 1977.

———, Sheldon L. Messinger, and Thomas P. Wilson, *C-Unit: Search for Community in Prison.* New York: Russell Sage Foundation, 1968.

Sue, D. W., *Counseling the Culturally Different: Theory and Practice.* New York: Wiley, 1981.

Tax, S., and L. Krucoff, "Social Darwinism," in *International Encyclopedia of the Social Sciences,* Vol. 14, D. Sills, ed., pp. 403–405. New York: The Free Press, 1968.

Taylor, R., and J. Ford, *Research Highlights in Social Work: Social Work and Health Care.* London: Kingsley Publishers, 1989.

Terris, M., "Approaches to an Epidemiology of Health," *American Journal of Public Health* 65 (10) (1965), 1038.

Thomas, Edwin J., *Utilization and Appraisal of Sociobehavioral Techniques on Social Welfare.* Ann Arbor: University of Michigan, 1969.

———, "Mousetraps, Developmental Research, and Social Work Education," *Social Service Review* 52 (3) (1978), 468–483.

———, *Designing Interventions for the Helping Professions.* Beverly Hills, Calif.: Sage, 1984.

Thurston, Henry, *The Dependent Child.* New York: Columbia University Press, 1930.

Titmuss, Richard, *The Gift Relationship.* New York: Pantheon, 1971.

Toch, Hans, ed., *Therapeutic Communities in Corrections.* New York: Praeger, 1980.

Tolman, Richard M., and others, "Developing Profeminist Commitment among Men in Social Work," in *Feminist Visions for Social Work,* Nan Van Den Bergh and Lynn B. Cooper, eds., pp. 61–79. Silver Spring, Md.: National Association of Social Workers, 1986.

Toren, N., *Social Work: The Case of the Semi-Profession.* Beverly Hills, Calif.: Sage, 1972.

Trieschman, Albert, James Whittaker, and Lawrence Brendtro, *The Other Twenty-three Hours.* Chicago: Aldine, 1969.

Tripodi, Tony, P. Fellin, and H. Meyer, *The Assessment of Social Research,* 2nd ed. Itaska, Ill.: Peacock, 1983.

Tropman, E. J., "Staffing Committees and Studies," in

Tactics of Community Organization, F. M. Cox and others, eds., pp. 105–111. Itaska, Ill.: Peacock, 1971.

———, and J. Tropman, "Voluntary Agencies," in *Encyclopedia of Social Work,* Vol. 2, 18th ed., A. Minahan, ed., pp. 825–839. Silver Spring, Md.: National Association of Social Workers, 1987.

Tropman, John E., "Public Welfare," *Sociology and Social Welfare* 3 (3) (January 1976), 264–296.

———, "The Constant Crisis," *California Sociologist* 1 (1) (Winter 1978), 68–87.

———, and others, eds., *New Strategic Perspectives on Social Policy.* Elmsford, N.Y.: Pergamon, 1981.

———, "The Relationship between the Staffer and Policy Committees," in *New Strategic Perspectives on Social Policy,* J. E. Tropman and others, eds., pp. 185–201. Elmsford, N.Y.: Pergamon Press, 1981.

———, *Meetings: How to Make Them Work for You.* New York: Van Nostrand-Reinhold, 1985.

———, *Policy Management in the Human Services.* New York: Columbia University Press, 1984.

———, "Value Conflicts and Decision Making: Analysis and Resolution," in *Tactics of Community Organization,* 2nd ed., Fred M. Cox and others, eds., pp. 89–98. Itaska, Ill; Peacock, 1984.

———, "Value Conflicts and Policy Decision Making," *Human Systems Management* 4 (1984), 214–219.

———, "The Catholic Ethic v. the Protestant Ethic," *Social Thought* 12 (1) (Winter 1986), 13-22.

———, "Policy Analysis: Methods and Techniques," in *Encyclopedia of Social Work,* Vol. 2, 18th ed., A. Minahan, ed., pp. 268–283. Silver Spring, Md.: National Association of Social Workers, 1987.

———, *Public Policy Opinion and the Elderly.* Westport, Conn.: Greenwood Press, 1987.

———, "Quality of Long Term Care," *Danish Medical Bulletin,* Special Supplement Series 5 (1987), 2–6.

———, "A Taxonomy of Social Services," in *Social Work: A Knowledge Driven Approach,* John E. Tropman and Harold R. Johnson, eds., pp. 88–98. Ann Arbor: University of Michigan School of Social Work, 1987.

———, *American Values and Social Welfare.* Englewood Cliffs, N.J.: Prentice Hall, 1989.

———, "Social Exploitation and Social Amelioration," unpublished manuscript. Ann Arbor: University of Michigan, 1990.

———, and Ann Alvarez, "Writing for Effect," in *Tactics and Techniques of Community Practice,* F. M. Cox and others, eds., pp. 377–391. Itaska, Ill.: Peacock, 1977.

———, and Fred M. Cox, "Society: American Values as a Context for Community Organization and Macro Practice," in *Strategies of Community Organization,* 4th ed., Fred M. Cox and others, eds., pp. 213–231. Itaska, Ill.: Peacock, 1987.

———, and John L. Erlich, "Strategies," in *Strategies of Community Organization,* 4th ed., F. M. Cox and others, eds., pp. 257–269. Itaska, Ill.: Peacock, 1987.

———, and Harold Johnson, "Settings of Community Practice," in *Strategies of Community Organization,* 3rd ed., Fred M. Cox, and others, eds., pp. 213–223. Itaska, Ill.: Peacock, 1979.

———, and Carol Kinny, "Fringe Benefits," unpublished paper. Ann Arbor: University of Michigan, n.d.

———, John L. Erlich, and Fred M. Cox, "Introduction," in *Tactics and Techniques of Community Practice,* Fred M. Cox and others, eds., pp. 1–14. Itaska, Ill.: Peacock, 1977.

———, Harold Johnson, and Elmer J. Tropman, *The Essentials of Committee Management.* Chicago: Nelson-Hall, 1979.

U.S. Bureau of the Census, *Statistical Abstract of the United States,* 1990 110th ed. Washington, D.C.: U.S. Government Printing Office, 1990.

U.S. Department of Commerce, Bureau of the Census, *1980 Census of Population, Occupation by Industry.* Washington, D.C.: U.S. Government Printing Office, 1984.

U.S. Department of Health and Human Services, Children's Bureau, National Center on Child Abuse and Neglect. *National Study of the Incidence and Severity of Child Abuse and Neglect.* Washington, D.C.: U.S. Government Printing Office, 1981.

U.S. Department of Health, Education and Welfare, *Health Resources Statistics: Health Manpower and Health Facilities, 1966–67 Edition.* Hyattsville, Md.: U.S. Department of Health, Education, and Welfare, Public Health Service, Office of Health Research, Statistics, and Technology, National Center for Health Statistics, 1979.

U.S. Department of Justice, *Sourcebook of Criminal Justice Statistics, 1983.* Washington, D.C.: The Department, 1985.

United Way of America, *Environmental Scan.* Alexandria, Va.: United Way of America, 1985.

———, *What Lies Ahead.* Alexandria, Va.: United Way of America, 1989.

Valentine, Charles, *Culture and Poverty Critique and Counter Proposals.* Chicago: University of Chicago Press, 1968.

Van Den Bergh, Nan, and Lynn B. Cooper, *Feminist Visions for Social Work.* Silver Spring, Md.: National Association of Social Workers, 1986.

Van Der Tak, Jean, "Populations and Population Movements," *1988 Britannica Book of the Year.* Chicago: Encyclopedia Britannica, 1988, pp. 282–285.

Vinter, Robert D., "The Essential Components of Social Group Work Practice," in *Individual Change through Small Groups,* Paul Glasser, Rosemary Sarri, and Robert D. Vinter, eds., pp. 9–33. New York: The Free Press, 1974.

———, David Street, and Charles Perrow, *Organization for Treatment.* New York: The Free Press, 1966.

———, ed., *Time Out: A National Study of Juvenile Correctional Programs,* Ann Arbor: University of Michigan, 1976.

———, and Rosemary Sarri, "Exemplar Schools Project: A School of Social Work, Agency, and Community Collaboration," in *The Future of Social Work and Social Work Education: Final Report of the Interdisciplinary Seminar,* Rosemary Sarri, ed., with Robert Vinter and Martha Steketee. Ann Arbor: School of Social Work of the University of Michigan, 1988.

———, and J. E. Tropman, "The Causes and Consequences of Community Studies," in *Strategies of Community Organization,* F. M. Cox and others, eds., pp. 315–322. Itaska, Ill.: Peacock, 1971.

Vondra, Joan, "Sociological and Etiological Factors," in *Children at Risk: An Evaluation of Factors Contributing to Child Abuse and Neglect,* Robert T. Ammerman and Michael Herson, eds., pp. 151–170. New York: Plenum, 1990.

Vorrath, Harry, and Larry Brendtro, *Positive Peer Culture.* Chicago: Aldine, 1974.

Wald, Lillian D., *The House on Henry Street.* New York: Henry Holt and Co., 1915.

Weber, Max, *The Protestant Ethic and the Spirit of Capitalism,* Talcott Parsons, tr. New York: Scribner's, 1958.

Weinbach, Robert, *The Social Worker as Manager.* New York: Longman, 1990.

Weiner, M., *Human Services Management,* 2nd ed. Belmont, Calif.: Wadsworth, 1990.

Weitzman, Lenore J., *The Divorce Revolution.* New York: The Free Press, 1985.

Westinghouse Learning Corp., *The Impact of Headstart: An Evaluation of the Effects of Headstart Experience on Children's Cognitive and Affective Development.* Executive Summary. Athens: Ohio State University, 1969.

Wetle, Terrie T., and David A. Pearson, "Long Term Care," in *Health Care Delivery in the United States* 3rd ed., Steven Jonas, ed., pp. 214–236. New York: Springer, 1986.

Wheeler, Etta Angell, *The Story of Mary Ellen Which Started the Child Saving Crusade throughout the World.* Albany, N.Y.: American Humane Association, Publication No. 280, circa 1910.

Whittaker, James K., "Group and Institutional Care," in *A Handbook of Child Welfare: Context, Knowledge, and Practice,* Ann Hartman and Joan Laird, eds., pp. 617–637. New York: The Free Press, 1985.

Whyte, W. F., *Street Corner Society.* Chicago: University of Chicago Press, 1943.

Wicker, Diane Goldstein, "Combatting Racism in Practice and in the Classroom," in *Feminist Visions for Social Work,* Nan Van Den Bergh and Lynn B. Cooper, eds., pp. 29–44. Silver Spring, Md.: National Association of Social Workers, 1986.

Wilensky, Harold, *The Welfare State and Equality.* Berkeley: University of California Press, 1975.

———, "Leftism, Catholicism, and Democratic Corporatism," in *The Developments of Welfare States in Europe and America,* P. Flora and A. J. Heidenheimer, eds., pp. 345–382. New Brunswick, N.J.: Transaction Books, 1981.

———, and C. Lebeaux, *Industrial Society and Social Welfare.* New York: Russell Sage, 1958.

Winters, Wendy Glasgow, and Freda Easton, *The Practice of Social Work in Schools: An Ecological Perspective.* New York: The Free Press, 1983.

Wissow, Lawrence C., *Child Advocacy for the Clinician: An Approach to Child Abuse and Neglect.* Baltimore: Williams and Wilkins, 1990.

Witmer, H., *Social Work: An Analysis of a Social Institution.* New York: Holt, Rinehart and Winston, 1942.

Wohlwill, Joachem F., "The Emerging Discipline of Environmental Psychology," *American Psychologist* 25 (April 1970), 303–312.

Wolff, K., "Cultural Lag," in *A Dictionary of the Social Sciences,* J. Gould and W. Kolb, eds., pp. 158–159. New York: The Free Press, 1964.

Yalom, Irvin D., *Theory and Practice of Group Psychotherapy,* 2nd ed. New York: Basic Books, 1975.

Yankelovich, D., *New Rules.* New York: Random House, 1981.

Zald, Mayer, *Organizational Change: The Political Economy of the Y.M.C.A.* Chicago: University of Chicago Press, 1970.

———, "Trends in Policy Making and Implementation in the Welfare State," in *New Strategic Perspectives on Social Policy,* J. E. Tropman and others, eds., pp. 167–180. Elmsford, N.Y.: Pergamon, 1981.

———, and G. Martin, eds., *Social Welfare in Society.* New York: Columbia University Press, 1981.

———, and Gary Wamsley, *The Political Economy of Public Organizations.* Lexington, Ky.: Lexington Books, 1973.

Zander, A., *Making Groups Effective.* San Francisco: Jossey-Bass, 1982.

Zorbaugh, H., *The Gold Coast and the Slum,* Chicago: University of Chicago Press, 1929.

Name Index

Abbott, Edith, 19
Abbott, Grace, 19, 341
Ackerman, Nathan, 116
Addams, Jane, 17, 18, 49, 85, 203, 205, 212, 276, 282, 397
Alexander, C., 34*n*34
Alinsky, Saul David, 46, 61*n*24, 186, 200*n*14
Allen, Jo Ann, 330, 370*n*2
Allen-Meares, Paula, 309–10, 312, 313, 317, 321, 322, 323, 325*n*3, 326*n*16, 327*n*63
Alston, Jon, 180*n*14
Altemeier, William, 374*n*113
Alvarez, Ann, 223*n*22
Anderson, 348
Anderson, Mary, 19
Anderson, Nels, 62*n*35
Anderson, Ralph E., 85, 86, 87, 104*n*1
Angell, Robert Cooley, 48–49, 62*n*36
Aponte, Harry, 116
Apte, Robert Z., 85, 104*n*4, 279, 301*n*33
Aristotle, 41–42
Arsdale, Martin Van Buren, 357
Ashford, Douglas, 68, 79, 81*n*8
Attneave, C., 327*n*45
Audubon, John James, 400
Austin, David M., 432, 435*n*48
Axin, Joan, 34*n*34

Bahr, Howard, 55, 63*n*60
Bailey, Ronald H., 267*n*39
Banta, H. David, 269, 300*n*2
Baran, Annette, 356–57, 373*n*92
Barker, R., 473, 478*n*30
Barlow, D.H., 64*n*78, 434*n*17
Bartollas, Clemens, 246, 249, 251, 258, 260, 261, 266*n*10, 267*n*46
Bartram, William, 400
Bass, Bernard M., 223*n*23
Bateson, Gregory, 116
Battle, J., 267*n*33

Beaubien, A., 222*n*15
Becerra, Rosina M., 373*n*105
Becker, Dorothy G., 128*n*2, 129*n*10
Bell, John, 116
Bellah, R., 81*n*13
Benedict, Ruth, 51, 62*n*46
Bennis, W., 201*n*22
Bergh, Henry, 340
Bernard, J., 200*n*3
Bernstein, Douglas A., 129*n*19
Bernstein, Leonard, 35*n*53
Bettelheim, Bruno, 368, 374*n*127
Birdsall, W.C., 32*n*12
Birtwell, Charles, 357
Black, C., 200*n*10
Blau, Joel, 67–68, 79, 81*n*7
Blaug, Marc, 32*n*10
Blauner, Robert, 444, 450–51, 454*n*23
Bloom, M., 240*n*12
Blum, D.J. Scrivner, 326*n*18
Bolton, R., 180*n*6
Booher, D., 223*n*22
Booth, Charles, 54, 63*n*56
Borgatta, E., 57, 63*n*67
Borkovec, Thomas D., 129*n*19
Borowski, Allan, 413, 415, 434*n*1
Bostwick, Gerald J., 434*n*15
Boszormeny-Nagy, Ivan, 116
Bowen, Murray, 116
Bowlby, John, 365, 374*n*120
Brace, Charles Loring, 15, 339–40, 357
Bracht, Neil, 302*n*67
Breckinridge, Sophonisba P., 314, 326*n*31
Bremner, Robert H., 60*n*1, 371*n*19
Brendtro, Lawrence, 267*n*44, 367, 374*n*128
Broverman, I.H., 446, 454*n*31
Brown, Lanette, 326*n*15
Buckley, Walter, 86, 104*n*9
Buell, Bradley, 58, 64*n*73

499

Subject Index